ROOTS AND WINGS

Senior Authors
Carl B. Smith
Virginia A. Arnold

Linguistics Consultant
Ronald Wardhaugh

Macmillan Publishing Co., Inc.
New York

Collier Macmillan Publishers
London

ACKNOWLEDGMENTS

The publisher gratefully acknowledges permission to reprint the following copyrighted material:

"About Finding Yourself" from pages 94–97 of *What Every Kid Should Know* by Jonah Kalb and David Viscott, M.D. Copyright © 1974, 1976 by Sensitivity Games, Inc. Reprinted by permission of Houghton Mifflin Company.

"Abunuwas the Trickster" is from *The Tiger's Whisker,* © 1959, by Harold Courlander. Reprinted by permission of Harcourt Brace Jovanovich, Inc.

"The Acceptance" is from the Nobel Prize Acceptance speech by Martin Luther King, Jr. Copyright © 1964 by The Nobel Foundation. Reprinted by permission of Joan Daves.

"Actions Speak Louder Than Words" from *Body Talk* by Kathlyn Gay. Copyright © 1974 Kathlyn Gay. Reprinted by permission of Charles Scribner's Sons.

"Addie" is adapted by permission of Alfred A. Knopf, Inc. from *Addie and the King of Hearts* by Gail Rock. Copyright © 1976 by Gail Rock.

"Armindo Miranda Beats 38,000 in Poster Contest." Reprinted by permission of the New York Post. © 1978, New York Post Corporation.

"Arthur Makes a Friend" is adapted from *Arthur Ashe, Tennis Champion* by Louie Robinson, Jr. Copyright © 1967, 1969 by Doubleday & Company, Inc. Reprinted by permission of the publisher.

"Atalanta's Race" is reprinted with permission of Macmillan Publishing Co., Inc. from *The Golden Fleece, and Other Heroes Who Lived Before Achilles* by Padraic Colum. Copyright 1921 by Macmillan Publishing Co., Inc. Renewed 1949 by Padraic Colum.

"Be Yourself" by Marina Chow. Reprinted from *Sojourner III.* Copyright © 1973 Linda Wing and the Berkeley High Asian Student Union. Reprinted by permission of the Asian American Bilingual Center, Linda Wing, Director.

"Boris" is adapted from *Boris* by Jaap ter Haar, translated from the Dutch by Martha Mearns. Copyright © 1969 by Blackie and Son Limited. Reprinted by permission of Delacorte Press/Seymour Lawrence. Permission also by Blackie & Son Limited.

"Bravo Baryshnikov!" is adapted from *Bravo Baryshnikov!* by Alan LeMond. Copyright © 1978 by Alan LeMond. Published by Grosset & Dunlap, Inc. (A Filmways Company), New York and reprinted with their permission.

"Calculator" by Cecily Nabors from *Child Life Mystery and Science-Fiction Magazine,* copyright © 1977 by The Saturday Evening Post Company, Indianapolis, Indiana. Reprinted by permission of the publisher.

"Carry On, Mr. Bowditch" is adapted from *Carry On, Mr. Bowditch* by Jean L. Latham. Copyright © 1955, by Jean Lee Latham and John O'Hara Cosgrave III. Reprinted by permission of Houghton Mifflin Company and the author.

"Close Encounters of the Third Kind" adapted from the book *Close Encounters of the Third Kind* by Steven Spielberg. Copyright © 1977 by Columbia Pictures, a division of Columbia Pictures Industries, Inc. Reprinted by permission of Delacorte Press.

"A Colorful Symphony" from *The Phantom Tollbooth* by Norton Juster. Copyright © 1961 by Norton Juster. Reprinted by permission of Random House, Inc. and Collins Publishers, London.

This work is also published in individual volumes under the titles: *Awareness, Exchanges, Pathways, Observations, Reflections,* and *Storytelling,* © copyright 1983 Macmillan Publishing Co., Inc. Parts of this work were published in earlier editions of SERIES r.

Continued on page 607.

Contents

AWARENESS

One of the challenges of growing up is learning to deal with the changes that occur in yourself and the world around you. As you grow, you learn more and you become more aware. You become more aware of your feelings and abilities, of your responsibilities, and of your family and the heritage that helps make you who you are.

The selections in "Awareness" are about the changes in awareness that occur as people grow. A thirteen-year-old girl develops a strong and special friendship with her teacher. A young tennis player begins to turn his talents into winning skills. A girl on the American frontier learns that being part of a family means sharing the family's work as well as its fun. Another girl learns from her grandmother what it is like to be old. An adult writer looks back on his childhood and recognizes the gifts of love that his home and family have given him. In Africa, a newborn boy is named according to the ancient rituals of his people.

As you read, think how people grow and how their awareness of their families and themselves changes. It is from your family that you get your roots, and it is through learning about yourself that you acquire wings. What kinds of experiences make you see yourself and others in new ways?

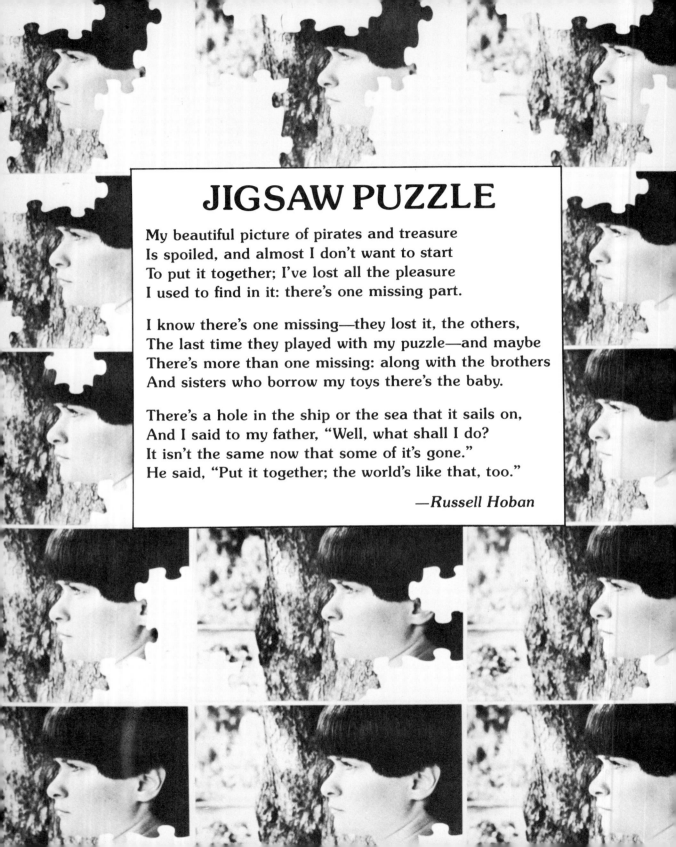

JIGSAW PUZZLE

My beautiful picture of pirates and treasure
Is spoiled, and almost I don't want to start
To put it together; I've lost all the pleasure
I used to find in it: there's one missing part.

I know there's one missing—they lost it, the others,
The last time they played with my puzzle—and maybe
There's more than one missing: along with the brothers
And sisters who borrow my toys there's the baby.

There's a hole in the ship or the sea that it sails on,
And I said to my father, "Well, what shall I do?
It isn't the same now that some of it's gone."
He said, "Put it together; the world's like that, too."

—*Russell Hoban*

A Dog on Barkham Street

Mary Stolz

**Learning to be responsible is a part of growing up. But what
does the word *responsible* mean? Edward Frost wants a dog,
but his parents don't think he is ready to take on the responsibility of caring for a pet. Edward disagrees. As you read this
story, think about what it means to be responsible for the care
of another. What does this responsibility involve?**

Edward Frost stood at the window and watched the rain, tossing
in sudden gusts along the street when the wind caught it, then falling straight again. Once in a while, a car went by, its tires hissing;
and once, a wet, ruffled robin bounded across the grass and then
took to its wings and flew, apparently, over the roof.

Now a dog came running along, its nose to the ground, its back
quite sleek with water. Edward watched it, hopefully. There were so
many stories in which the boy wanted a dog but didn't get one until
a wonderful dog came along and selected *him*. In the stories, these
dogs were either stray ones, or the people who owned them saw
how the boy and the dog loved each other and gave the dog up.

In the stories, the parents agreed to keep the dog, even if
they'd been very much against the idea earlier.

Edward was always looking around for some dog that would
follow him home from school and refuse to leave. In a case like
that, he didn't see how his mother could refuse. He had even, a
couple of times, tried to lure a dog to follow him—whistling at it,
snapping his fingers, and running in a tempting way. But he must
have picked dogs that already had homes and liked them. Now if
this dog, this wet dog running along by itself in the rain, should
suddenly stop at his house, and come up to the door, and cry to be
let in . . . wouldn't his mother be *sure* to let Edward have it? You
couldn't leave a dog out in the rain, could you? The dog ran across
the street, ran back, dashed halfway over the lawn, stopped to
shove its nose in a puddling flowerpot, backed off sneezing, sat
down, and scratched its chin.

Edward held his breath, waiting. After a moment, he tapped lightly on the windowpane. The dog cocked its head in an asking gesture, got to its feet, then wheeled around and continued down the street. Edward sighed. He was not at all surprised—the dog had a collar with at least four license tags dangling from it—but still he sighed. He was pretty sure he'd forgotten to make his bed and suspected that a hammer he'd been using yesterday was now lying in the backyard getting pretty wet. Mr. Frost was particular about his tools, and Edward felt that dogs, if they weren't getting further away from him, they certainly weren't coming any nearer. He decided to go up and make his bed. He didn't see what there was to do about the hammer just now, since his mother would notice if he went out in the rain to get it.

The letter carrier turned the corner, and Edward lingered to watch him. Mr. Dudley had his mail sack and a tremendous black umbrella to juggle. He wore a black slicker that glistened in the rain and shining mud-splashed rubbers and a plastic cover on his hat. He was late already, but he moved slowly, as if he were tired.

"Mr. Dudley's coming," Edward said, as his mother came in the room.

Mrs. Frost came over to the window. "Poor man," she said. "Stay and ask him if he'd like to come in for a cup of coffee."

Edward waited, and when Mr. Dudley turned up their walk, he ran to the front door and opened it. "Mother says do you want some coffee, Mr. Dudley," he asked, as he took the mail.

"Well now, that's a handsome offer," Mr. Dudley said, frowning down at his rubbers, "but does your mother know I'm just this side of drowned?"

"Oh, that's all right," Edward said, cheerfully. "You take off your rubbers and raincoat here on the porch."

Mr. Dudley laid down the mail sack and his huge black umbrella. "Can't say a cup of coffee won't be welcome," he observed, as he and Edward made for the kitchen.

Mrs. Frost gave the letter carrier a sweet bun with his coffee, and she gave Edward a cup of cocoa. They sat in the breakfast nook, and the rain beat against the window, making things quite snug. Edward glanced out in the backyard. There was the hammer, all right, in perfectly plain view. He guessed his mother hadn't noticed it yet, so he decided that rain or no rain he was going to have to go after it. It was too good a hammer to leave there until his father got home and saw it.

Mr. Dudley licked the sugar daintily from his fingers, and Edward watched with admiring envy. He wondered if Mr. Dudley's mother had told him when he was a little boy, "Don't lick your fingers, dear. Use the napkin." He decided she probably had, and now Mr. Dudley, all grown-up, was doing as he pleased. It was satisfying to watch and to look forward to the time when he was all grown-up. Edward was really looking forward to growing up.

After the letter carrier had gone, Mrs. Frost asked Edward if he'd made his bed, and he said maybe he ought to go up and see. He climbed the stairs to his room and found that, sure enough, everything was rumpled and tossed around just as he had left it.

Suddenly, because that possible dog was on his mind and because there was nothing else to do, Edward decided to make a tremendous gesture. He would clean his entire room. He would stack the books that lay around so carelessly. He would straighten his games and his clothes. He'd get out the vacuum cleaner and do the rug. Maybe he'd even clean the closet. Yes, that was a great idea. He'd never cleaned the closet in his life. His mother would be so bowled over she'd probably offer him a St. Bernard on the spot.

5

He plunged in at once, dragging out clothes, books, fishing equipment, old forgotten trucks, and games. He put the clothes on the still-unmade bed and shoved everything else out on the floor. It seemed to take an awfully long time to get the closet emptied, and then when he thought he was done, he looked up, saw the shelves, and wished he'd never started.

They were absolutely jammed with junk. Well, maybe it wasn't all junk, but it looked like junk. Soon his room was filled to brimming with things that would have to be put away again. He sat on his heels and stared around, thinking that the whole idea of cleaning up was pretty silly. Everything was just going to have to be put back in the closet, so what was the point of taking it out in the first place?

"My word, Edward," said his mother at the door, "what are you doing?"

"Cleaning my room," he said, glumly.

"That's a good idea," she said, coming in. "Did all that come out of the closet?"

Edward nodded. "And it all has to go back," he said. "So I was just thinking, what's the point? I mean, where do you get *ahead*? I don't think I'll clean it after all."

"You can't leave it this way," said Mrs. Frost.

She picked up a battered green dump truck. "Do you ever use this?" When Edward said he didn't suppose so, at least he hadn't in a long time, she said, "Why don't you get a box from the cellar and put the things you don't really want in it, and we'll give it to the Salvation Army? They're marvelous at fixing things. It seems to me there must be a lot of things you've outgrown. When you get all that sorted out, you won't have so much to put back, and you'll be neater *and* ahead. Sweep the closet out before you put your things away, of course, and put them away tidily. I see you hadn't made your bed after all."

There was no reasonable answer to this, so Edward stumped down to the basement for a box, wondering if dogs appreciated what people had to go through to get them. He paused at the cellar door, looking out. The rain hadn't slackened any—or had it? He leaned forward, pressing his nose to the glass. He wasn't fifteen feet from that hammer, and his mother was busy upstairs, so if he just dashed out . . .

Pulling his sweater up so that it partly covered his head, he opened the door and dashed. The grass was sopping; the earth beneath it marshy; and, though he got the hammer all right, his shoulders and feet were drenched even in so short a run. Back in the cellar, he dried the hammer thoughtfully and stared at his shoes. Finally, he removed them. The socks were dry enough. He took a towel from the hamper and rubbed his head and the sweater. Picking up the box, he went upstairs in his stocking feet, hoping his mother wouldn't notice anything.

"Here's the box," he said in a loud, cheerful voice. "Think it's big enough?"

His mother had her back to him. She was on a chair, getting things down from the shelves. "I thought," she said, not turning around yet, "that I'd help you out a little. This is really quite a big job. Here, you take these things, and I'll hand you down some more—" She glanced around and stopped talking. Her eyes went from his head to his feet.

"I suppose," she said, "you had some reason for going out in the pouring rain—aside from its nuisance value, that is?"

Edward wiggled his shoulders. He disliked that kind of remark. He would have preferred to have her come right out and ask what he thought he was doing. But just saying something right out was a thing grown-ups rarely did. In this, as in so many matters concerning adults, Edward failed to see the reason but accepted the fact.

"Somebody had left the hammer out in the rain," he mumbled. "It might've rusted."

"Somebody?" said Mrs. Frost, lifting one eyebrow.

Edward debated, and then said with inspiration, "Well, *I'm* somebody, don't you think?"

Mrs. Frost began to scowl, looked at the ceiling, half-smiled, turned back to the closet, and said, "How about all these jigsaw puzzles?"

"They're a bit on the simple side," said Edward. He almost added that they could get him some harder ones, but decided this wasn't the best time for requests of any sort. His mother was being very nice about the rain and the hammer, so there was no point in annoying her.

It was a funny thing, he mused, piling things in the box for the Salvation Army, that lots of times he asked for things not really much wanting them at all—for instance, jigsaw puzzles. He didn't actually want any. He didn't even like doing them very much when he got them. But the habit of *asking* was just one he sort of had. He asked for ice cream if the ice cream vendor happened to be around, for clothes if he happened to be in a store where they were sold, and games if he happened to see them in an advertisement or a shop window. He guessed that one way and another he asked for something or other every single day, whether he wanted it or not. Sometimes he got the thing and sometimes he didn't, but anyone could see that the asking annoyed his parents. Once Mr. Frost had said, "Edward, don't you ever bore yourself with these constant requests?" Edward had said he didn't think so.

Still, thinking it over now, he wondered if it wouldn't be wiser to limit all the asking to a dog. If he concentrated on that, one of several things might happen. Either he'd wear them down so that at last they'd give in; or he'd impress them so much with how he wanted a dog and nothing else that they'd give in; or they'd get to be so sorry for him that they'd give in. But—he had to admit—they might also get so irritated that he'd never see a dog until he was grown-up himself. He piled a fleet of little trucks in the box and sat back on his heels to think.

"Problems?" said his mother, coming away from the closet to inspect the box. Edward nodded. "Could I help?" Mrs. Frost asked.

"Probably not," he said sadly. Then he looked up and met his mother's blue, friendly eyes. "*How* responsible do I have to be before I can have a dog?"

"Quite a bit, I'm afraid. Now, Edward . . . look at today: bed unmade again; hammer out in the rain; *you* out in the rain—"

"But I'm cleaning my whole room," he protested.

"You started to," his mother reminded him. "If you recall, you got everything out and then changed your mind."

"When I grow up," Edward said, "my boy will have a dog as soon as he asks for it. In fact, I bet having the dog will *teach* him to be responsible," he added, hopefully.

"But suppose it doesn't? Suppose you get him the dog, and he doesn't take care of it at all?"

"I wouldn't mind taking care of it myself."

"Well, that's where you and I differ," said Mrs. Frost. "I would mind."

Edward, realizing that he hadn't handled his end of the argument well at all, gave up for the time being.

So now he could either get on with the room because he'd started and ought to finish, or he could get on with it because his mother was perfectly sure to make him. He decided on the former, and, in as responsible a voice as he could manage, he said, "Guess I might as well finish up here, eh?"

"I guess you might as well," said Mrs. Frost with a smile. "I'll have to leave you. I'm making a lemon meringue pie."

"You are?" said Edward with pleasure. There were few things he preferred to lemon meringue pie. "Gee, that's great!" He went and fetched the vacuum cleaner and set to work in a good humor, the matter of dogs dwindling to the back of his mind.

Even people who wanted something badly couldn't think about it every single minute.

1. Why did Edward, as he watched Mr. Dudley eat, look forward to growing up?

2. Edward decided to clean out his closet, and he thought that "His mother would be so bowled over she'd probably offer him a St. Bernard on the spot." Do you think this statement is true? Why or why not?

3. Do you think Edward was ready to take on the responsibility of having a dog? Why or why not?

4. Put yourself in Edward's place. How would you go about getting a dog?

ABOUT FINDING YOURSELF

Jonah Kalb and
David Viscott, M.D.

One of the most difficult parts of growing up is learning about yourself—your feelings, your ideas, and your talents. Deciding on your goals, selecting the kind of work you will do, working to become the kind of person you want to be—all these things involve making choices. This essay offers you some help in learning to make wise choices. Read to understand the meaning of the two important suggestions which the authors make. These suggestions will help you make decisions about your life.

TRY IT: YOU MAY LIKE IT

It is impossible to decide whether or not you like something until you have tried it. This sounds obvious, but many people do not think trying something new is necessary. It is.

Give each idea a *fair* trial—not a brief brush. If you have decided to try out something new, also decide how long you will stick with it before you can make a fair judgment. For example, if you decide that you would like to play the violin, you need to take more than one lesson before you can know anything about your potential skill or interest.

Then, the best thing to judge is not the goal but the process of reaching the goal. Almost everybody would like to be highly skilled. But becoming highly skilled at anything requires a great deal of time and work. You must decide if you enjoy working toward the goal.

It's not enough to want to be a great violinist. You also have to like the process of becoming a great violinist. Do you enjoy the lessons? Do you enjoy practicing? If you would enjoy being a great violinist but hate the work, forget it. Being a great violinist means loving the work involved in becoming one.

It's a good plan to try as many ideas as possible when you are still young. That's the time for self-discovery. Don't restrict yourself to the few goals and standards that other people think you should try. Expand your views as far as you can.

BE PREPARED TO FAIL

Finding yourself means not only that you find out what you're good at and what you like, it also means discovering what you're *not* good at and what you *don't* like. Knowing what isn't right for you is almost as valuable as knowing what is. Both help to steer you in the right direction.

Everyone gets upset when he or she fails at something, but failing can be valuable. Although most kids would be upset if they found that they had failed an advanced math course, they have actually learned a great deal about themselves. They know they should not become engineers or physical scientists and that they would not be good at accounting work or work that involves statistics. So failing can help a kid to lead a much happier life if he or she draws the right conclusion from the failing: that he or she isn't so much a failure as unsuited to the particular subject.

1. What two important suggestions did the authors make to help you make choices about your life?
2. What reasons did the authors give for trying new things and for facing failure?
3. What did the authors mean when they said: "The best thing to judge is not the goal but the process of reaching the goal"?
4. Describe a new idea or activity that you have tried. Did you succeed at first or did you have trouble? What did your success or failure teach you about yourself?
5. Make a list of some of the careers you might choose. Now think about what you would have to do—what kind of training and experience you would need—to enter these careers. Would you still choose to do all the things on your list? Explain why or why not.

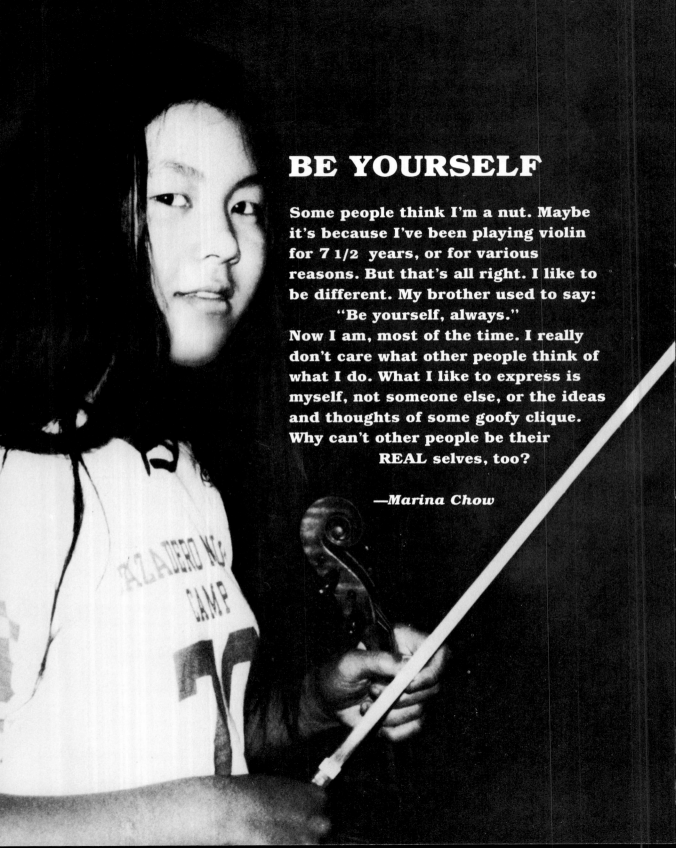

BE YOURSELF

Some people think I'm a nut. Maybe it's because I've been playing violin for 7 1/2 years, or for various reasons. But that's all right. I like to be different. My brother used to say:
"Be yourself, always."
Now I am, most of the time. I really don't care what other people think of what I do. What I like to express is myself, not someone else, or the ideas and thoughts of some goofy clique. Why can't other people be their
REAL selves, too?

—*Marina Chow*

How Beautiful with Mud

Hildegarde Dolson

An autobiography is a story that a person writes about his or her own life. Sometimes a life experience is unpleasant when it happens, but when you look back on it years later, you often forget the pain and see the humor instead. In this autobiographical sketch, Hildegarde Dolson describes how, during her first year in high school, she spent hours and hours trying to make herself look like the people in advertisements in magazines for teenagers. The ads for one product, "Beauty Clay," prompted Hildegarde to save her money for weeks so she could order some of the "miraculous substance." As you will find from reading this selection, the experience had some unexpected results. As you read, notice the humorous way in which Hildegarde describes this experience.

A whole week passed before I could achieve the needed privacy for my quick-change act. Mother was taking Jimmy and Sally downtown to get new shoes; Bobby was going skiing; and my father, as usual, would be at the office. I got home to the empty house at twenty minutes of four and made a beeline for the "Beauty Clay." According to the directions, I then washed off all make-up, which in my own case was a faint dash of powder on my nose, and wrapped myself in a sheet "to protect that pretty frock," or, more accurately, my blue-serge middy blouse. Then I took a small wooden spatula, which the manufacturer had thoughtfully provided, and dug into the jar.

The "Beauty Clay" was a rather peculiar shade of grayish-green, and I spread this all over my face and neck—"even to the hairline where telltale wrinkles hide." The directions also urged me not to talk or smile during the twenty minutes it would take the clay to dry. The last thing in the world I wanted to do was talk or smile. That could come later. For now, a reverent silence would suffice. In fact, as the thick green clay dried firmly in place, it had to suffice. Even though my face and neck felt as if they'd been cast in cement, the very sensation reassured me. Obviously, something was happening. I sat bolt upright in a chair and let it happen.

After fifteen minutes of sitting, the doorbell rang. I decided to ignore it. The doorbell rang again and again, jangling at my conscience. Nobody at our house ever ignored doorbells, and I was relieved when it stopped. In my eagerness to see who had been calling on us, I ran to my window, opened it, and leaned out. The departing guest was only the man who brought us country butter each week, I was glad to note.

Hearing the sound of the window opening above him, he looked up. When he saw me leaning out, his mouth dropped open and he let out a hoarse, awful sound. Then he turned and ran down the steep hill at incredible speed. I couldn't imagine what had struck him to make him act so foolishly.

It wasn't until I'd remembered the clay and went to look in a mirror that I understood. Swathed in a sheet and with every visible millimeter of skin a sickly gray-green, I scared even myself.

According to the clock, the "Beauty Clay" had been on the required twenty minutes and was now ready to be washed off. It occurred to me that if twenty minutes was enough to make me beautiful, thirty minutes or even forty minutes would make me twice as beautiful. Besides, it would give me more lovely moments of anticipation, and Mother wouldn't be home until after five.

By the time my face was so rigid that even my eyeballs felt yanked from their sockets, I knew I must be done—on both sides. As I started back to the bathroom, I heard Bobby's voice downstairs yelling "Mom!" With the haste born of horror, I ran back and just managed to bolt myself inside the bathroom as Bobby leaped up the stairs and came down the hall toward his room. Then I turned on the faucet and set to work. The directions had particularly warned: "Use only gentle splashes to remove the mask.

No rubbing with washcloth." It took several minutes of gentle splashing to make me realize it was getting me nowhere fast. Indeed, it was like splashing playfully at the Rock of Gibraltar. I decided that maybe it wouldn't hurt if I rubbed the beauty mask just a little—with a nailbrush. This hurt only the nailbrush. I myself remained embedded in "Beauty Clay."

By this time, I was getting worried. Mother would be home very soon, and I needed a face—even my old face. Suddenly, it occurred to me that a silver knife would be a big help, although I wasn't sure just how. When I heard Bobby moving around in his room, I yelled at him to bring me a knife from the dining-room sideboard. Rather, that's what I intended to yell, but my facial muscles were still cast in stone, and the most I could do was grunt. In desperation, I ran down to the sideboard, tripping over my sheet as I went, and got the knife. Unfortunately, just as I was coming back through the dusky upstairs hall, Bobby walked out of his room and met me, face to face. The mental impact on Bobby was terrific. To do him justice, he realized almost instantly that this was his own sister, and not, as he at first imagined, a sea monster. But even this realization was not too reassuring.

I had often imagined how my family would look at me after the "Beauty Clay" had taken effect. Now it had taken effect—or even permanent possession of me—and Bobby was certainly reacting, but not quite as I'd pictured it.

"What—what?" he finally managed to croak, pointing at my face.

His concern was so obvious and even comforting that I tried to explain what had happened. The sounds that came out alarmed him even more.

Not having the time or the necessary freedom of speech to explain any further, I dashed into the bathroom and began hitting the handle of the knife against my rocky visage. To my heavenly relief, it began to crack. After repeated blows, which made me a little groggy, the stuff had broken up enough to allow me to wriggle my jaw. Meanwhile, Bobby stood at the door watching, completely bemused.

Taking advantage of the cracks in my surface, I scraped, gouged, dug, and pried until I got part of my face clear. As soon as I could talk, I turned on Bobby. "If you tell anybody about this, I'll kill you," I said fiercely.

Whether it was the intensity of my threat or a sense of compassion aroused by seeing a person tortured before his very eyes, I still don't know, but Bobby said, "Cross my heart and hope to die."

He then pointed out that spots of the gray-green stuff were still very much with me. As I grabbed up the nailbrush again to tackle these remnants, he asked in a hushed voice, "But what is it?"

"'Beauty Clay,'" I said. "I sent away for it."

Bobby looked as though he couldn't understand why anyone would deliberately send away for such punishment when there was already enough trouble in the world. However, for the first time in a long, hideous half-hour, I remembered why I'd gone through this ordeal. Now I looked into the mirror expecting to see results that would wipe out all memory of suffering. The reflection that met my eyes was certainly changed all right, varying as it did from an angry scarlet where the skin had been rubbed off to the greenish splotches still clinging.

"Maybe if I got it all off . . . " I thought. When it was all off, except those portions wedded to my hair, I gazed at myself wearily, all hope abandoned. My face was my

STEP 1 Wash off all make-up.

STEP 2 Wrap self in sheet to protect that pretty frock.

own—but raw. Instead of the *Body Beautiful* I looked like the *Body Boiled*. Even worse, my illusions had been cracked wide open—and not by a silver knife.

"You look awfully red," Bobby said. I did indeed. To add to my troubles, we could now hear the family assembling downstairs, and Mother's voice came up, "Hildegarde, will you come set the table right away, dear?"

I moved numbly.

"You'd better take off the sheet," Bobby said.

I took off the sheet.

When Mother saw my scarlet, splotched face, she exclaimed in concern. "Why, Hildegarde, are you feverish?" She made a move as if to feel my forehead, but I backed away. I was burning up, but not with fever.

"I'm all right," I said, applying myself to the table. With my face half in the china cupboard, I mumbled that I'd been frostbitten and had rubbed myself with snow.

"Oh, Cliff," Mother called, "Hildegarde has been frostbitten."

My father immediately came out to the kitchen. "How could she be

STEP 3
Apply with small wooden spatula over face and neck, even to the hairline where telltale wrinkles hide.

STEP 4
Let clay dry. Do not talk or smile.

17

frostbitten?" he asked, reasonably. "It's thirty-four above zero."

"But her ears still look white," Mother said.

They probably did, too, compared to the rest of my face. By some oversight, I had neglected to put "Beauty Clay" on my ears. "I'm all right," I insisted again. "I rubbed hard to get the circulation going."

This at least was true. Anyone could tell at a glance that my circulation was going full blast— from the neck up.

Bobby had followed me out to the kitchen. As Mother kept exclaiming over my condition he now said staunchly, "Sure she's all right. Let her alone."

My father and mother both stared at him in this role of "Big Brother Galahad." Against this new setup of "Brother Loves Sister," they were suspicious, but inclined to do nothing.

In a way I *had* been frostbitten —to the quick. Lying in bed that night, still smarting, I tried to think up ways to get even. It wasn't clear to me exactly with whom or what I had to get even. All I knew was that I was sore and unbeautiful and mulcted of five dollars. I suddenly conceived my plan for revenge. It was so simple and logical and yet brilliant that my mind relaxed at last. Someday, I, too, would write advertisements.

---

1. How long did Hildegarde leave on the "Beauty Clay"? Why?
2. How did Bobby prove to be very helpful?
3. How do you think Hildegarde's experience with "Beauty Clay" affected her feelings about advertisements? Will she send away for other products? Why or why not?
4. Hildegarde described her situation and her frantic, frightened efforts to solve her problem in a calm, simple way. The *contrast* between the two feelings—frenzy and calm—creates much of the humor in the story. Choose a section of the story that seems humorous to you and show how contrast makes it funny.
5. Hildegarde blamed the "Beauty Clay" for what happened to her. Was she correct? Are consumers always correct in blaming products that don't work properly? Why or why not?

Using Decoding Skills

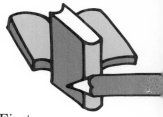

There are many ways to understand words in your reading. First you should be able to pronounce the words correctly. There are different rules regarding the pronunciation of words in English. Here are three rules about long and short vowels:

1. When a one-syllable word contains two vowels separated by a consonant, and one of the vowels is the final *e*, the two vowels usually stand for the long sound of the first vowel.

    space   scheme   prime   home   mute

2. When a one-syllable word contains only one vowel and that vowel does not come at the end of the word, the vowel is usually short.

    span   speck   prim   flock   plug

3. When two vowels come together in a one-syllable word, the two vowels usually stand for the long sound of the first vowel.

    main   least   die   groan   soul

After pronouncing the word, see if you recognize its meaning. You will be already familiar with many words just by looking at them.

If you do not recognize an entire word, perhaps you notice a familiar prefix, root, or suffix within the word. Here are a few common word parts and their meanings:

Prefixes	Roots	Suffixes
ex- out	ject throw	-less without
com- with,	spect look	-ize make
together	tract draw	-ist one who is
pre- before		expert in

Another way to determine the meaning of a word is by studying its context in a sentence. For example,

"That woman is only a visitor here, not a *resident*."

The way *resident* is used in the sentence tells you it means "a person who lives in a place."

Each sentence below contains an underlined word. After the sentence are questions about the word. Write the answer to each question on your paper.

1. John is strong enough to box, but Fred is too <u>frail</u>.
   a. Is the *a* in *frail* a long *a* or a short *a*?
   b. Based on its context in the sentence, what does the word *frail* mean?

2. The doctor <u>extracted</u> the bullet during the operation.
   a. What does the prefix *ex* mean?
   b. What does the root *tract* mean?
   c. What does the word *extracted* mean?

3. I rarely get hurt, but my sister is <u>prone</u> to accidents.
   a. Is the *o* in *prone* a long *o* or a short *o*?
   b. Based on its context in the sentence, what does the word *prone* mean?

4. We use a special sauce to <u>tenderize</u> our hamburgers.
   a. What does the suffix *ize* mean?
   b. What does the word *tenderize* mean?

5. I no longer play baseball but am still a loyal <u>spectator</u>.
   a. What does the root *spect* mean?
   b. Based on its context in the sentence, what does the word *spectator* mean?

6. The <u>drab</u> walls were made colorful with bright paints.
   a. Is the *a* in *drab* a long *a* or a short *a*?
   b. Based on its context in the sentence, what does the word *drab* mean?

7. The <u>biologist</u> won a prize for her study of the rare plants of Asia.
   a. What does the suffix *ist* mean?
   b. What root do you recognize in the word *biologist*?
   c. What does the word *biologist* mean?

8. Sheila talked in the morning but remained <u>mute</u> for the rest of the day.
   a. Is the *u* in *mute* a long *u* or a short *u*?
   b. Based on its context in the sentence, what does the word *mute* mean?

Using the Dictionary

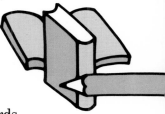

A dictionary is a book containing an alphabetical list of words. Each word in the list is called an *entry word*. The word may be divided by dots or spaces into *syllables*. The dots or spaces indicate where you may divide the word when it must be broken at the end of a line. A word with no dots or spaces has only one syllable and cannot be divided. Look at the following entry from a dictionary:

> **re·cep·ta·cle** (ri sep′ tə kəl) *n*. **1.** an object or place which receives and holds something, as a box or bag: *Linda put the flowers in a receptacle*. **2.** a swollen tip of the stem of a flower, which bears the sepals, the petals, the stamens, and the carpels. [Latin *receptāculum*, place to receive things.]

The entry word above is *receptacle*. The dots show you that the word has four syllables.

The *pronunciation* tells you how to say the word and appears in parentheses after the entry word. The pronunciation is indicated with special symbols. A *pronunciation key* explains these symbols. The key might look like this:

> a bad, ā cake, ä father; e pet, ē me; i it, ī ice; o hot, ō open, ô off; oo wood, ōō food, oi oil, ou out; th thin, th that; u cup, ur turn, yōō music; zh treasure; ə ago, taken, pencil, lemon, helpful

Using the key, you find the vowels in *receptacle* are pronounced: *i* as in *it*; *e* as in *pet*; *ə* as the *a* in *ago*. The *accent mark* (′) tells you that the second syllable is stressed.

Following the pronunciation is an abbreviation for the *part of speech*. The part of speech indicates how the word is used in a sentence. These are the major parts of speech and their abbreviations:

n.	noun	*v*.	verb	*adv*.	adverb
pron.	pronoun	*adj*.	adjective	*prep*.	preposition

The dictionary entry tells you that *receptacle* is a noun.

The *definition*, or meaning, of the word follows the part of speech. When a word has two or more definitions, the dictionary lists them by number. There are two definitions for *receptacle*. A *sample sentence* sometimes follows the definition. This sentence helps show how the word is used.

Sometimes the dictionary gives the *derivation*, or history, of the word. The dictionary entry tells you that the word *receptacle* comes from Latin.

Two *guide words* appear at the top of each page of the dictionary. They show the first and last entry words on that page of the dictionary. Use the guide words to help find a particular entry word. If the guide words were *radar/river*, for example, you would be able to find *receptacle* listed on that page. If the guide words were *radar/reader*, however, you would not find *receptacle* on that page.

Some dictionaries provide other features besides those already mentioned. For example, a dictionary may give synonyms and antonyms for the entry word. It might show other forms of the entry word, such as the plural form of a noun or the past tense form of a verb. Often illustrations are provided for certain words, such as pictures of animals or diagrams of machines.

The last section of a dictionary may contain extra features, such as a pronunciation guide for place names and proper names. Some dictionaries have lists of rhyming words, or they may list commonly used foreign phrases.

ACTIVITY A   Use the dictionary entries below to answer the questions that follow. Write the answers on your paper.

---

curb (kurb) *n*. **1.** a border of concrete or stone along the edge of a street or sidewalk: *The car is parked too far from the curb.* **2.** something which restrains or controls: *The committee recommended a curb on national spending.* **3.** the chain or strap fastened to a horse's bit, used to check the horse when the reins are pulled. [Old French *courber*, to bend, from Latin *curvāre*.]

cu·ri·ous (kyoor'ē əs) *adj*. **1.** eager to know or learn. **2.** arousing attention because of rarity or strangeness; odd; unusual: *We found a curious Greek coin in our backyard.* [Latin *cūriōsus*, careful, inquisitive, from *cūra*, care.]

---

1. What is the first entry word shown?
2. How many syllables are in the word *curb*?
3. According to the pronunciation key, how is the *ur* in *curb* pronounced?
4. What part of speech is *curb*?
5. How many definitions are given for *curb*?
6. From what languages does *curb* come?
7. Write the number of the definition that applies to each sentence below:
   a. The curb snapped, leaving the rider helpless on his horse.
   b. She stepped off the curb and crossed the street.
   c. My parents put a curb on the number of hours I may watch TV.
8. What is the second entry word shown?
9. How many syllables are in the word *curious*?
10. Which syllable is stressed when you say *curious*?
11. What part of speech is *curious*?
12. How many definitions are given for *curious*?
13. From what language does *curious* come?
14. Write the number of the definition that applies to each sentence below:
    a. The boomerang is a curious instrument.
    b. Jody is curious to know why it grows cold in winter.

ACTIVITY B Suppose the guide words on a dictionary page were *pencil/plaza*. Which of the following entry words would appear on that page? Write those words on your paper.

1. piano	2. photograph	3. pinpoint
4. pointer	5. private	6. plush
7. please	8. Peking	9. planter
10. phantom	11. pepper	12. polyglot
13. pedal	14. pizza	15. porcelain

ADDIE

Gail Rock

In this novel excerpt, you will meet thirteen-year-old Addie Mills, who finds that her life is very different after a new teacher comes to her class. Her feelings about herself and her friends change, and she finds new meaning in the idea of friendship. The author carefully describes Addie's feelings and how they change. As you read, look for the phrases that describe these feelings and their changes.

We were milling around the seventh-grade classroom that morning, laughing and talking. For once, almost all of us had been early. It was the first day back in school after the winter recess, and there was a lot of talk about what we all got for Christmas and Chanukah and about the fantastic blizzards that had been smothering Nebraska that winter.

The main topic of conversation, however, was speculation about the new teacher we would meet that morning. Miss Collins, who had started teaching our class that fall, had decided to get married over the holidays. All the other kids thought that was very romantic, but I thought it was stupid. The whole idea made me laugh. I planned to grow up and be an artist and never get married.

I was sitting on top of my desk talking to my best friend, Carla Mae Carter. Carla Mae and her big family lived next door to my dad, my grandmother, and me, and we had been friends for years. My worst friend, Tanya Smithers, came hurrying through the door. Tanya had been my worst friend ever since I could remember. We annoyed each other a lot, but we continued to be a part of the same group. There were only 1,500 people in the town of Clear River, so sometimes you didn't have a big choice of friends. Tanya planned to be a famous ballet dancer when she grew up, and she was always twirling around on her toes or striking some dramatic pose to remind us all of how talented she was.

"Here comes Pavlova," said Carla Mae when she saw Tanya coming toward us.

"If she tells me one more time that she got new ballet shoes for Christmas, I'll scream!" I said.

"Addie! Carla Mae!" Tanya said to us breathlessly. "Guess what I just heard when I went by the principal's office?"

"The principal got new ballet shoes?" I asked sarcastically.

Carla Mae snickered.

"No!" said Tanya. "Listen to me! We're getting a *man* teacher to replace Miss Collins!"

"What?" said Carla Mae. "You've got to be kidding!"

"A man!" I said. "Yuck! That's awful!"

"We've never had a man teacher," said Carla Mae. "There aren't any in the whole school!"

"I don't believe it!" I said.

"I'm telling you it's true!" said Tanya, annoyed. "The principal says he's going to be here in a few minutes."

The rumor spread around the room as others overheard our conversation.

"Oh, ugh!" I said. "He'll probably be a grouch."

"Tanya, what does he look like?" Carla Mae asked.

"I don't know," Tanya answered. "I didn't see him. But I heard his name. It's Davenport."

"Like the sofa?" asked Carla Mae.

Suddenly, Jimmy Walsh shot a paper airplane across the room at us. I grabbed it in midflight, making a spectacular catch. I was good at that sort of thing.

"That's Billy Wild's New Year's resolution!" Jimmy shouted to me.

"It is not!" shouted Billy from across the room. "He made it up! It's his!"

Everybody was always teasing me about liking Billy Wild, and I always insisted I didn't. I had to admit he was tall and handsome —with dark curly hair and blue eyes—and that he was one of the smartest boys in the class and was good at sports, too. But that didn't mean I liked him any more than anyone else. He was forever strutting around in his cowboy boots, showing off. We had known each other for years, but we always seemed to be arguing about something; so I didn't see how anyone could say I liked him.

I unfolded the paper airplane and read it to myself, then burst out laughing.

"Okay, attention, everybody!" I shouted, running to the front of the classroom. "Here's Billy Wild's New Year's resolution!"

"It is not!" he shouted again.

Everyone was laughing, and I just had to read it aloud.

"It's dated January 1," I read. "I, Billy Wild, resolve for this year to kiss every girl in the seventh-grade class."

Everyone screamed with laughter, and Billy's face got bright red.

"It's not mine!" he shouted.

"That's one resolution you'll never keep!" I shouted, as I folded the airplane and shot it back in his direction.

Suddenly, everyone stopped laughing, and the room fell quiet. I couldn't imagine what was happening; and then, I realized that they were all looking at something behind me. I turned.

There, standing just inside the door, was a tall, handsome, young man. For a moment I thought I must have seen him in the movies. Of course, he had to be the new teacher—and he had found me flying paper airplanes!

I stood there frozen. Miss Collins would have dragged me to the principal's office. He just smiled. He had a wonderful smile and crinkly blue eyes. I thought he was the most handsome man I had ever seen. He was so attractive that I felt I should look away.

"Won't you have a seat?" he said, and I sheepishly went back to my desk. I knew I should say something to him, but I was tongue-tied. That was not at all like me.

"My name is Douglas Davenport," he said to the class, "and I'm your new teacher." He turned to the chalkboard and wrote his name there.

Carla Mae, who sat behind me, leaned forward and whispered to me.

"Isn't he gorgeous? I don't believe it!"

I didn't say anything. I was still speechless.

Tanya leaned over, from her desk across the aisle, to join in the conversation.

"He is an absolute doll!" she said.

Mr. Davenport turned back to the class and noticed a watercolor hanging on the wall near his desk.

"Did someone in the class do this painting?" he asked.

I opened my mouth, but no sound came out.

Carla Mae spoke up behind me.

"Addie Mills did it," she said, pointing to me. "She's the best artist in the class."

"Oh, the paper-airplane pilot," Mr. Davenport said, smiling at me again.

Everyone laughed, and my face burned.

He was still smiling at me.

"Well, Addie," he said, "I can tell you're very talented. Studying art is one of my hobbies. I'll have to talk more with you about that."

Carla Mae swooned behind me and whispered, "You lucky dog!"

I just sat there staring at Mr. Davenport and feeling strange.

In the next few weeks, we all got to know Mr. Davenport better, and it was soon clear that he was to be one of the most popular teachers our class had ever had.

All the girls agreed that he was an absolute dish, and though the boys thought we were ridiculous for gushing about him, they liked him a lot, too. We discovered that he was only twenty-four years old, that he drove a tan car with white sidewall tires and that he wore neat, tweedy suits and incredible argyle socks. We spent hours discussing these little details about him, and I collected this information more avidly than anyone, though I never let on.

The strange feeling that had stricken me when I first saw Mr. Davenport still lingered whenever I would talk with him. I talked with him often, too. I felt I had much more in common with him than did the other kids in the class. Somehow I was more grown-up than they were, and I was able to talk to him about all kinds of things that didn't interest the others.

I knew that I understood Mr. Davenport better than anyone in the class, because I was going to be an artist when I grew up and he was particularly interested in art. He had been in Paris and had brought back some French art books that he loaned me now and then. I couldn't read the texts because they were in French, but I poured over the paintings for hours and tried to copy some of the artists' styles with my own paints at home. Then I would discuss the paintings with Mr. Davenport, and he always seemed very pleased that he had somebody to talk to who understood art as well as he did. He encouraged me to continue my studies in art, and I knew there was a special bond between us, even if he was eleven years older than I.

By the end of January, I realized that I was spending a lot of my time either talking to Mr. Davenport or thinking of a reason to talk to him—or just thinking of him for no reason at all.

I studied art more feverishly than ever, so we would have something to discuss. I learned that he liked poetry, so I dug up a copy of Robert Browning that someone had once given me. I had looked at it scornfully when I first got it and had never opened it. I had thought love poems were disgusting. Now I studied them carefully, trying to find an appropriate verse to discuss with Mr. Davenport.

My grandmother wondered why I was sitting around the house all the time, reading and "mooning about," as she called it, rather than going out with the girls. I couldn't explain it, but I just wanted to be alone. I stopped wearing jeans all the time and, for the first time in my life, worried about how my clothes looked. I stood in front of the mirror, wondering how I could look older.

My father threatened to take my favorite record and grind it up for fertilizer if I didn't stop playing it over and over. I told him he had no romance in his soul.

Addie was caught up in a whirl of confused thoughts about Mr. Davenport, about her friends, and about the meaning of friendship. How did she resolve her confusion? Eventually, she realized that "feeling something for other people was the important thing, even if it didn't always work out the way you thought it would."

1. What impression did Mr. Davenport make on Addie and her classmates? What did he and Addie have in common?

2. What did Addie want to be when she grew up? What do you learn from the story that suggests her wish might be a "realistic goal" for her?

3. What do you think Addie meant when she called Tanya Smithers her "worst friend"? In what ways were Tanya and Addie alike?

4. In what ways did Addie's behavior change after Mr. Davenport became her teacher? What caused this change?

5. Think about an adult who impresses you. Why does this person impress you? What qualities do you admire in him or her? In what ways are the two of you alike?

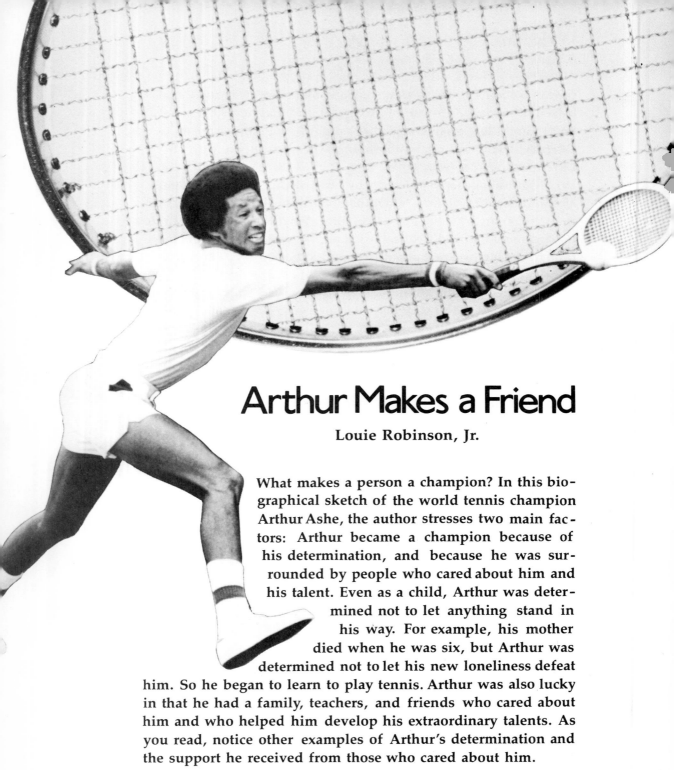

Arthur Makes a Friend

Louie Robinson, Jr.

What makes a person a champion? In this biographical sketch of the world tennis champion Arthur Ashe, the author stresses two main factors: Arthur became a champion because of his determination, and because he was surrounded by people who cared about him and his talent. Even as a child, Arthur was determined not to let anything stand in his way. For example, his mother died when he was six, but Arthur was determined not to let his new loneliness defeat him. So he began to learn to play tennis. Arthur was also lucky in that he had a family, teachers, and friends who cared about him and who helped him develop his extraordinary talents. As you read, notice other examples of Arthur's determination and the support he received from those who cared about him.

Ronald Charity stopped working on the practice board long enough to wipe the sweat out of his eyes and sneak a closer look at the small boy who had been watching him for so long. He had seen the child before—many times—running around the playground, usually playing baseball.

More than once, Ronald had stopped by the baseball diamond to watch in amusement as the boy swung at the air with a bat almost as big as himself. Many times, too, he had seen the boy studying him as he practiced his tennis.

Arthur Ashe, Junior, looked small for his age. "Sixty pounds of bare bone," Ronald said to himself with a smile. Today Arthur was carrying a tennis racket.

"That racket is about as big as you are, young fellow," Ronald called to Arthur as he walked over to him.

"It's my daddy's,"Arthur replied.

"What's your name?" Ronald asked.

"Arthur Ashe, Junior," the boy spoke out with pride. "What's yours?"

"Mr. Charity, Ronald Charity."

Ronald Charity had been employed by the Richmond Recreation Department to teach tennis at Brookfield Park during the summer. He was working his way through Virginia Union University and had taken the job because he loved to play tennis and because he needed all the money he could earn for the coming year.

"It would be impossible to teach tennis to anyone that young," Ronald thought to himself as he talked to the boy. But then, Ronald Charity had been doing the impossible for years. Ronald hadn't been very much older than Arthur when he had taught himself to play tennis with the help of nothing more than a "how-to" book. He had read in the newspaper that one of his schoolmates had won a local tennis tournament—a contest in which many players are matched against each other. He had decided then and there that "if that kid can win a tennis tournament, so can I." He had saved up, bought the book, borrowed a racket, and begun. It took him some time to learn the game, but he taught himself well enough to win some of those tournaments he read about in the newspaper. So, if a little voice inside Ronald Charity said "impossible," Ronald knew better.

"Do you want me to show you how to hit the ball?" he asked.

"Yes, sir!" Arthur answered.

"Okay, come on out on the court and give it a try. The first thing you have to learn is how to hold the racket properly."

"Yes, sir!" Arthur said again, eagerly, and he followed his new friend onto the court.

"There's a trick to making sure your hand is in the proper place on the racket," Ronald explained. "You just stand your racket on its rim, like so, and then take the handle in your hand, like this, and you can't go wrong."

Arthur watched his teacher closely, trying to do exactly what Ronald told him.

"Now," Ronald was saying, "push your hand as far down on the handle as you can without changing the position of your hand or making your grip uncomfortable. It's best if you can get your palm behind it." Ronald held out his hand so that Arthur could see exactly how the end of the racket should rest in his palm.

"Okay," Ronald went on, "now that you've got the grip right, try swinging the racket straight back, then straight forward, about hip high."

Arthur swung the racket back and forth just as Mr. Charity told him.

"Good." Ronald put a hand on Arthur's shoulder. "When you hit the ball that way, it's called a *forehand drive*."

"Now," Ronald continued, "you see how to hit a forehand. That stroke is okay if the ball bounces in front of you or to your right, but what are you going to do if the ball bounces on your left side?"

Arthur looked at him and shook his head.

"Simple: You just turn your body around like this." Ronald turned

on his left foot so that his right hip, rather than his left, now faced the net. "You switch your grip on the racket so that your thumb is behind the handle. This stroke is called a *backhand drive*. Okay, you try it."

Arthur copied Ronald's motion perfectly. It surprised the young man to see such a small boy do so well.

"Can we play now?" Arthur asked. He was in a hurry to begin hitting the ball the way Ronald Charity did.

"Soon," Ronald promised.

So they went on, the young man explaining the proper way to hit the ball, the little boy watching closely and following the instructions carefully.

The first time Arthur had ever tried to hit a tennis ball, he had taken the racket in both hands like a baseball bat and had swung at the ball with all his might. He had thrown himself at the ball so wildly that, although he had managed to hit it, he had fallen down on the court. Now, with Ronald Charity guiding him, Arthur quickly learned that you didn't hit a tennis ball like a baseball, you *stroked* it.

"Hey!" Ronald yelled to Arthur, as the boy once again took a full swing at the ball and sent it flying over the fence. "There aren't any home runs in tennis, you know."

Arthur listened while his teacher explained that "you have to learn how to stroke the ball properly in a kind of slow motion before you can hope to hit it hard."

His next try was much better, and the one after that was even better. Each time Arthur hit the ball, Ronald would tell him what he had done wrong, and the next time Arthur would dig in and try harder. In the beginning, Arthur often hit the ball out of the court, sending his teacher into fits of laughter.

"How can a little boy like you hit that ball so far and so hard?" Ronald would ask.

But slowly, Arthur learned how to keep his shots in the court, and soon he was driving the ball very well.

"That kid's size and age don't seem to matter at all," he heard Ronald tell another man.

Arthur liked learning how to play tennis, but most of all, he liked Ronald Charity. So every after-noon he made his way to the tennis courts to practice hitting the ball against the practice board by himself.

Arthur soon became the most familiar figure at the Brookfield Park tennis courts, but he was far from the most popular one.

"Ronald Charity may find him amusing, but we don't," the older people would say. "He always keeps us waiting for a court."

"Pest" was the favorite word for Arthur among the teenage set, par-ticularly when Arthur would an-swer their demands to give up his court with "first come, first served." The only way to get Arthur away from the courts and the practice board, they decided, was to chase him.

One afternoon, Arthur got to the tennis courts early. No one had come back from lunch yet, but Arthur knew it wouldn't be long before the whole park would be alive with noise, and people would be waiting to use the courts. He wished Ronald were there, so that they could play before anyone else came.

Arthur began hitting the ball against the practice board. When-ever he hit it too high and sent it flying over the fence, he had to run outside and around the courts to get it back.

Then, while he was off looking for the ball, an older boy and girl arrived at the courts and began to use the practice board.

"Hey, I'm using that!" Arthur yelled to them, as he ran back to the practice area.

"Yeah? Well, we are using it now," the big boy answered.

"That's not fair. You two can play on the court. I have to prac-tice here until Mr. Charity comes."

"Beat it!" the older boy growled.

Arthur wanted to fight for his rights, but how could a seven-year-old fight such a big boy? He decided, instead, to pay no atten-tion to the boy and girl. He would just go right on with what he had been doing.

Arthur Ashe shown winning the National Interscholastic Tennis championship in Charlottesville, Virginia on June 22, 1961.

Arthur shows his concern for kids by participating in a tennis clinic. Here he shows his form to a group of youngsters in Washington, D.C.

Arthur holds up his trophy after defeating his gallant opponent, Tom Okker, on September 9, 1968. He had won the men's singles title in the U.S. Open Tennis Championship at Forest Hills Stadium, New York.

The supreme moment for father and champion!
Arthur Ashe, Sr., gives way to tears as he
embraces his victorious son. It had been a
long road from the tennis courts in a
Richmond, Virginia, park to the acclaim
at Forest Hills, New York.

Arthur reaches low to make
a return during his match
against Jan Kodas in the
French
Tournament on
June 3, 1978.

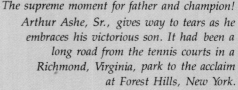

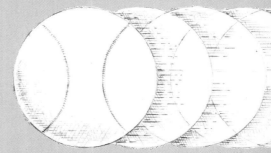

Acting as though there were no one else around, Arthur approached the narrow board and began practicing. Soon, both balls were bounding back toward the bigger boy at once, making it impossible for him to hit either one.

"Get out of here!" the boy yelled at Arthur, taking a swing at the youngster.

But Arthur, experienced in such matters, had already jumped back out of reach, and he began to laugh at the older boy's fury. That laughter was just enough to drive the older boy and girl to more serious action.

"Why don't we take his racket away from him?" the girl suggested. "He's nothing but a pest."

The chase was on. Almost before the girl spoke, Arthur guessed what was coming. He picked up his tennis ball and began to run. Around the tennis court the three went, seven-year-old Arthur in the lead, but only a step or two ahead. Finally, Arthur ran around the net and over to the door. Before the other two could grab him, he was free and away.

He darted off between the two great maple trees near the fence and over to the vast lawns beyond. The boy and girl stayed close behind for a while, but they soon gave up. Arthur ran on until, with a final burst of speed, he fell exhausted on the cool grass, his body and clothes wet with sweat.

He lay there for a few minutes, looking up at the sky and thinking about what he might be when he grew up, and about Mr. Charity, and finally, about his mother.

Then he rolled over and closed his eyes. He thought about the sanitation workers, whom he often watched in the morning while they picked up the heavy trash cans and tossed them into the truck. Some-day—he thought—when he grew up, he'd be a sanitation worker. Sanitation workers were big and strong. No one would ever bother him then.

"What on earth are you doing, son?" It was the sharp voice of his father.

"Just thinking," Arthur answered.

"Thinking about what?" his father asked.

"Nothing," came the answer.

"Get up here, son," Mr. Ashe said. "Come on. I want to talk to you."

Arthur couldn't remember anything that he had done wrong recently. Still, he knew his father wanted to talk about something important. He could tell from the way his father looked and spoke, and even from the way he walked toward the benches near the baseball diamond. He walked *ahead* of Arthur instead of *with* him.

"Arthur," his father said, sternly, "how many times have I told you not to bother the older people over at the tennis courts and not to talk back to anybody? I told you to come to me if you had any trouble over there."

"I didn't talk back to anyone," Arthur protested. "I was there first. They came after I did and chased me away from the practice board."

"There's a boy and girl over there who say that you yelled some bad things at them and that you bothered them while they were trying to play," Arthur's father replied.

Arthur shook his head. "It's not true," he told his father. Then he explained all that had happened.

"Arthur," the boy's father said softly but seriously, "if I have told you once, I have told you a hundred times: I don't want you giving anyone sass. If someone tells you to leave the courts, you just come to me and let me handle it."

"But I don't sass anyone, Daddy," Arthur answered.

"Well, just you see that you don't." His father got up to leave. "I want you to grow up to be a fine young man and a gentleman first. *Then* you can be a tennis player, or anything else you want to be."

Arthur nodded and watched his father walk off toward the pool. He didn't follow. He decided to stay where he was for a while before going back to the courts to look for Ronald Charity.

Ronald had come along just when he had most needed a friend —someone who could be like an older brother to him. As Arthur waited, he tried to think what it would be like if his father told him he couldn't spend his afternoons with Ronald at the courts. He remembered the lonely times, and he thought about his mother. She had been on his mind all day.

"Hey?" Ronald Charity's voice brought a sudden end to Arthur's thoughts. "Where have you been?"

"Aw, some kids chased me again," Arthur said, walking toward the fence where Ronald was standing.

"Who?" Ronald asked.

"It doesn't matter," Arthur answered.

"Well, then, why are you looking so sad?"

"I'm not sad. I was just thinking," Arthur explained.

"Come on out here on the courts and think a little about tennis." Ronald smiled as he spoke.

"Okay," Arthur said, and the day's lesson began.

The rest of the summer was a happy time for Arthur. He had learned a new sport, found a new friend, and though he was often chased from the courts, he was no longer lonely.

"One of these days," he told his father, "I'm going to be as good a tennis player as Mr. Charity."

"Well, Arthur," his father replied, "I guess people can do just about anything they want, as long as they make up their minds to do it and work hard enough at it. If you want to play tennis, I will help you all I can. Just don't ever let it get in the way of your education. There's more to life than baseball and tennis, you know."

Arthur wasn't sure that he agreed, but if his father said so, it was good enough for him.

That fall and winter Arthur worked hard in school, and he did well. He wanted his father to be proud of him. He wanted Mr. Charity to be proud of him, too. And they were.

Two years later, at the age of nine, Arthur Ashe won his first tournament. But he still had many years of practice and hard work ahead of him. Finally, he started winning other tournaments with his cannonball serve, split-second timing, and quick thinking on the courts. Arthur's goal was to reach the top in tennis—and he did! He became the first American man to win the United States Open Championships, and he was a member of the victorious team which, after many years, brought the Davis Cup back to the United States in 1968. In 1975, he won one of the world's most famous tournaments, the men's singles championship at Wimbledon, England. Arthur Ashe has also received the Johnston Sportsmanship Award, one of this country's highest tennis honors. It is given to the U.S. player who best exhibits courtesy, a spirit of cooperation on the court, and is most willing to help younger players develop their skills.

1. Why did Ronald Charity decide to teach Arthur to play tennis?

2. How did Arthur feel about his father? Support your answer with evidence from the story.

3. Because Arthur was younger and smaller than the other players at Brookfield Park, he chose another way to stand up for his rights. What did he do? Did his father approve of what he did? Why or why not?

4. Why did the teenagers at Brookfield Park call Arthur a pest? Knowing what you know about Arthur, do you think he acted like a "pest"? Why or why not?

5. Arthur heard Ronald Charity tell someone: "That kid's size and age don't seem to matter at all." What effect do you think that remark had on Arthur? What effect would a comment like that have on you?

THE SECRET

David Moncibaiz Herrera

As you grow up, you learn to think about other people's needs as well as your own. The characters in this short story needed the special confidence that Don Terco, the *curandero* (folk doctor), offered them. Don Terco's confidence-giving power was based on a secret that he alone knew. Juan, the narrator of the story, inherited the secret and, as a result, learned an important lesson about people and their needs. What was the secret? Why did it have special power?

Pénjamo, the name of my *barrio* (neighborhood), was an area filled with strange occurrences.

I remember the time when the gossip reached a fervent peak, and the whole *barrio* trembled with fear. The rumors and gossip echoed throughout the *barrio*, for it seemed that our *barrio* had been cursed by an evil eye.

Stories about balls of fire rolling down dark alleys and people with the feet of chickens and the legs of lambs circulated from house to house, and doors and windows were barred and locked. Few people dared step out of their homes after dark.

One person who did dare the unknown was a *viejito* (old man) called Don Terco. Don Terco was the oldest person in our *barrio* and the most respected, for he was widely known throughout the state of Texas as the best *curandero* in the whole state. Wherever he went, doors were always open to him, for he had the secret which he carried with him in a little tin box.

Rumor had it that this little tin box had been in his family since time unknown; and now, as Don Terco quickly approached his last days, he had no family to whom he could leave his little tin box.

Matters started getting worse when Doña Petra fell off a chair while fixing her curtains. Ten minutes after the accident occurred, everyone in the *barrio* knew about it. Everybody was placing the blame on everybody else for Dōna Petra's dreadful accident

(actually she only bruised her left hip a little but the gossips made it sound as if Dōna Petra were at her deathbed).

At this time, Don Terco started visiting all the homes in the *barrio*. He would stay with a family for a day or two, then move on to another home; for, you see, Don Terco had no house, but the whole *barrio* was his home. Those who could afford to usually had him stay in their homes when he wasn't needed somewhere else to cure somebody. Don Terco would enter the home and assure the family that they had nothing to worry about because, in his little tin box, he had a secret that would protect the family from the dangers of the evil eye.

I still remember that eventful day when he arrived at our home—our home being the last one in our *barrio* in which he was to lift the dreadful curse of the evil eye. After assuring our family that we had nothing to worry about, he asked us if he could stay there with us, for his job was done. My father then reminded Don Terco that our home was always his home and that what little we had was his to share with us.

Don Terco then picked my grandmother's old rocking chair and slowly rested his bones on the unsteady chair. He then called me and my parents to his side. I can still recall his very words as he spoke to my father: "Jorge, the time for me to join the rest of my family has come. As you know, I have no close family to leave my secrets with; so if it is all right with you, I would like to leave this little tin box with your son. You see, I still remember the time you risked your life to save mine. I need someone who is young to take my place, so that when I leave here, I will leave happy, knowing the secret will be here for many years to come."

My father then assured Don Terco that I would be the only one to know the secret that the little tin box contained and that he and my mother would not try to find out what the little tin box contained.

At that time, Don Terco called me closer and said to me: "Juan, I leave my secret with you, and someday you will pass it on to your son. But always remember that the secret in this box must stay with you until you are ready to join those in your family who have gone away. Reveal this secret to no one, for if someone else learns about it, the power this secret has will disappear forever."

With these last words, Don Terco closed his heavy eyes and left to join the rest of his family. He had a smile on his face. My father then took me to the bedroom where I could be alone and start studying the secrets Don Terco had left me.

As I sat there alone in my parents' small bedroom, I could hear my mother crying and my father consoling her. My hands trembled as I opened the little tin box. My tear-filled eyes looked inside to find absolutely nothing—and I understood.

1. Why did Don Terco decide to leave his secret with Juan?
2. Don Terco told Juan: "Reveal this secret to no one, for if someone else learns about it, the power this secret has will disappear forever." Do you think Don Terco was correct? Why or why not?
3. Juan told us that when he saw the empty box, he understood. What did he understand? What did he learn about Don Terco and about the needs of the people in his *barrio*?
4. If Don Terco gave his secret to you, would you reveal it or keep it secret? Why?

I Belong

All that I see around me
I am a part of.

I am the mountain, to stand
    with pride, strength, and faith.
I am the tree, to stand tall and straight,
    above all to be honest with myself,
    and to my brothers and my sisters.

I am the grass, to show kindness and love
    to all who surround me and
    above all
    to love myself as well as others,
    to be more considerate of my
    brothers and my sisters.
To understand more clearly.

I am the fire, which is shared among my
    brothers and my sisters
    for survival.
    Sharing also comes from my four-legged
    relations who eat only enough
    to survive
    and save some for us.

We use the fire to light our Sacred Pipe
    but only to share
    with our Grandfather.
    No matter how small the flame,
    it is still our life
    and we must care for and protect it.

We are the keepers of the fire
    We share this together.

      —A. Whiterock
      A Paiute Sister

Classifying

Imagine a supermarket where the food was put on the shelves in no special order. It might take a long time to find a single item. The food in most stores is arranged according to type. All the vegetables are in one section, all the meats are in another section, and so on. Having the food organized makes shopping much easier. To help the customers, grocers classify their products. *Classifying* is grouping things according to type. Each group is called a *category*. One category in a supermarket would be vegetables.

Items are the things in each category. Items in the category of vegetables would include beans, corn, and carrots. Here is another example of a category and its items:

> **Category:** meats
> **Items:** ground beef, steak, lamb chops

ACTIVITY A Read each group of items. Then read the categories that follow. Choose the correct category for each group of items. Write the category on your paper.

1. **Items:** poodle, collie, terrier, beagle, dalmatian
   Category: monkeys, dogs, horses

2. **Items:** Iowa, Wisconsin, Michigan, California, Louisiana
   Category: countries, cities, states

3. **Items:** green, blue, red, purple, black
   Category: colors, numbers, letters

ACTIVITY B Read each group of words. One word in the group names the category. The other words are the items in the category. Write the word that names the category.

1. school, museum, library, buildings, post office, courthouse
2. baker, jobs, teacher, bus driver, secretary, doctor
3. oxygen, hydrogen, neon, helium, gases, argon
4. soccer, tennis, baseball, sports, hockey, swimming

Sometimes a group of items may be named by more than one category. In such cases, label the items with the most specific category. For example, ground beef, steak, and lamb chops all belong in the category *food*. But a more specific category is *meats*.

ACTIVITY C   Read each group of items. Then read the categories that follow. Write the more specific category for each group of items.

1. **Items:** woodpecker, parrot, robin, eagle, sparrow
   Categories: animals, birds

2. **Items:** grape, apple, pear, peach, orange
   Category: fruit, food

3. **Items:** Thomas Jefferson, Abraham Lincoln, George Washington
   Category: names of people, names of Presidents

ACTIVITY D   Read each group of items. Think of the most specific category for the items. Write the category on your paper.

1. **Items:** Venus, Jupiter, Mars, Saturn, Pluto
2. **Items:** triangle, rectangle, square, circle, octagon
3. **Items:** water, milk, soda, juice

ACTIVITY E   Read each group of items. One item in each group does not belong. Write the item that does not belong on your paper. Then write a sentence explaining why the item you chose did not belong.

1. **Items:** violin, guitar, piano, musician, drum
2. **Items:** hammer, garage, pliers, saw, wrench
3. **Items:** roar, rattle, squeak, hum, ear

ACTIVITY F   Read each group of items. Some of the items belong in one category. The other items belong in a second category. Write each category and the items that belong in it.

1. **Items:** spring, oak, elm, fall, winter, maple
2. **Items:** house, pen, chalk, apartment, hotel, pencil
3. **Items:** rain, book, snow, magazine, newspaper, hail

ACTIVITY G   Read each category. Think of four items that belong in each category. Write the items on your paper.

1. **Category:** holidays
2. **Category:** cities
3. **Category:** types of transportation

Sentence Structure
(Subjects and Predicates)

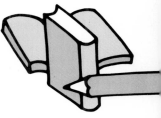

A *sentence* is a group of words that expresses a complete thought. When you read, you should be able to understand the thought expressed in each sentence. In other words, the meaning of the sentence should be clear to you. Look at the following groups of words:

David Herrera   David Herrera wrote a story.

is "The Secret "   The name of the story is
                                 "The Secret."

The words on the left do not express complete thoughts. They are not complete sentences. The words on the right, however, do express complete thoughts. They are complete sentences.

A group of words is a complete sentence if it has a subject and a predicate. The *subject* of a sentence names whom or what the sentence is about. The *predicate* of a sentence tells what action the subject does. Sometimes it tells what the subject is or is like.

<u>Don Terco</u> <u>visited many people in the community.</u>
   subject   predicate

<u>This man from Pénjamo</u> <u>was a folk doctor.</u>
        subject   predicate

ACTIVITY A   On your paper, write *S* if the group of words is a sentence. Write *NS* if it is not a sentence.

1. People had faith in Don Terco.
2. Don Terco owned a little tin box.
3. The helpful doctor.
4. Rumors in the town.
5. Went from house to house.
6. The box was magic.

ACTIVITY B   Write each sentence on your paper. Draw one line under the subject. Draw two lines under the predicate.

1. The folk doctor arrived at the house of Jorge.
2. The poor man had no relatives in the community.
3. Don Terco gave his little tin box to a young boy.
4. The child opened the box in his parents' bedroom.
5. The little tin box from the folk doctor was empty.

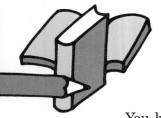

Paragraph Structure (Main Ideas and Details)

You know that items which are alike can be put into a group. The group is called a category. Sentences that are alike may also be put into a group. The group is called a paragraph.

A *paragraph* is a group of sentences that tell about the same subject. Usually one sentence in the paragraph states the *main idea* of the paragraph. The other sentences in the paragraph give *details* to support the main idea. Read this paragraph about Arthur Ashe, the tennis player:

> Arthur Ashe is a tennis champion. He won his first tournament at age nine. Later he became the first American to win the United States Open Championship. Ashe also won the men's singles championship at Wimbleton, England. He received the Johnston Sportsmanship Award, this country's highest tennis honor.

In the above paragraph, the first sentence states the main idea. The other sentences provide details to support the main idea.

In a paragraph, all the details should support the main idea. If a detail does not tell about the main idea, it does not belong in the paragraph. Read the following paragraph about newspapers:

> Newspapers provide us with a variety of information. We can learn about national and international events. Papers also report local happenings. Television broadcasts report important news as well. Many newspapers give the latest developments in sports, weather, and entertainment.

In the above paragraph, the main idea is that newspapers provide a variety of information. The first sentence states the main idea. The second, third, and fifth sentences support the main idea with details. The fourth sentence, however, does not support the main idea. Instead, it talks about a different idea—television broadcasts. Although the information may be true, this sentence does not belong in the paragraph.

ACTIVITY A   Read each group of details. Then read the three choices for a main idea. On your paper, write the choice that correctly states the main idea.

1. One type of stringed instrument is rubbed with a bow to produce sounds. A second kind is plucked. The player hammers a third kind to produce a tone. In a fourth type, the strings vibrate in the wind.
   a. Stringed instruments are hammered and plucked.
   b. There are four basic types of stringed instruments.
   c. Stringed instruments can be difficult to play.

2. The clock may be an old grandfather clock they remember from childhood. It might be the clock by which they learned to tell time. The clock could be a cuckoo clock from a nursery or a tower clock seen on a special trip.
   a. Clocks today are different from those of the past.
   b. Grandfather clocks are the oldest kind of clocks.
   c. Many people remember a special clock from the past.

ACTIVITY B   Read each group of details. Write a sentence that states the main idea that the details support.

1. One problem of large cities is impure air. Some city school buildings are too old to be effective. Many people who live in the city have poor housing. Other problems include poverty and crime.

2. One of Benjamin Franklin's inventions was the lightning rod. Another was bifocal glasses. Franklin also invented a special stove and a device for removing objects from shelves.

ACTIVITY C   Find the sentence that does not belong in each paragraph. Write the sentence on your paper.

1. Spiders travel in different ways. Some jump forty times the length of their bodies. Others move under water. Spiders are often black or brown. Some spiders can even walk on water.

2. The metric system of measurement uses different units from the linear system. Metric units include meters, grams, and liters. Linear units include feet, pounds, and ounces. Sixteen ounces equals one pound.

FAMILY TRADITIONS

David Weitzman

Families, like nations, have histories. These family histories can be fascinating, because they help you find out about you. *One important part of a family's history is its traditions. As you read this essay about family traditions, think about the traditions of your family. What do these traditions tell you about your family and yourself?*

Have you ever wondered about the things you and your family do in a certain way? Why are they always done *that* way? Why are there things like dinner at your grandmother's every Friday night and those plates that come down off the top shelf of the cupboard only on Thanksgiving Day? How about the chores that are passed down to the youngest son or youngest daughter? What about the Fourth of July house-cleaning and yard sale?

These are probably family traditions—things your mother and father did as children, and their mothers and fathers did before them.

Some old traditions are very much alive, but the memory of why they're done in those particular ways has probably been lost somewhere. Other traditions, from earlier days, are lost entirely —except perhaps in the memories of older folks. But you can find out about some of them and maybe even get some of them going again.

Family life, in the days of your grandparents and great-grandparents, was strictly governed by tradition. Tradition actually made things simpler, and it wasn't as much of a burden as it might sound at first.

Raising a family is hard work, and for generations, many parents found raising their kids the way they were raised and doing things the way their own moms and dads did them, just seemed to make good sense. That's tradition.

Traditions like special holiday dishes or Sunday family picnics, repeated year after year, gave each child and each adult a sense of family time.

As the children grew up and moved away to different cities, the Thanksgiving dinner made sure that at least once a year there was a family again. It also made sure that new members of the family knew who their relatives were.

Special chores for kids of different ages gave even the youngest child a role. Jobs like setting the table, going out for the Sunday paper, giving the dog its weekly bath, or helping younger sisters and brothers with homework, gave everyone a part in the family's day-to-day life. Traditions made certain no one was left out.

Traditions gave each family member a sense of place. You learned names for the other members of your family, which helped you understand who they were and what they were to you—names like Grandpa Joe, or Uncle Jim, or Cousin Beth, or Aunt Martha.

And traditions set rules for giving names to new babies.

So try to find out about *your* family traditions.

1. What is tradition?

2. Why are traditions important to a family?

3. What did the author mean when he said that "for generations, many parents found raising their kids the way they were raised and doing things the way their own moms and dads did them, just seemed to make good sense"?

4. How can learning about a family's traditions teach you about your family's past?

5. Ask an older person in your family to tell you about a family tradition that existed during his or her childhood and may or may not exist today. Write a description of this tradition and share it with your classmates.

There are only two lasting bequests we can hope to give our children.
One is roots; the other, wings.
—*Hodding Carter*

ROOTS

Alex Haley

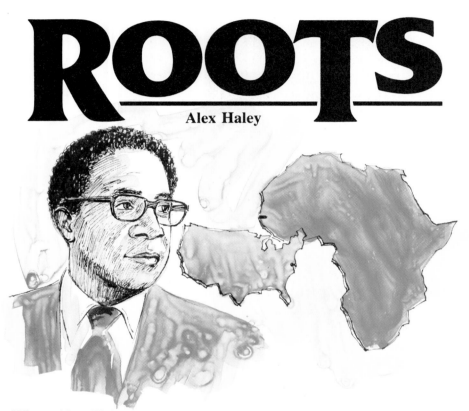

When Alex Haley was very young, his grandmother told him stories about "the African," the first person in his family to come to America. When Haley grew up, he searched until he found the village where his African ancestor, Kunta Kinte, was born. This search, and other searches like it, resulted in Haley's historical novel, *Roots*.

"Roots" is another word for "heritage," or that part of ourselves we inherit from our ancestors. Our heritage is a part of us and, in learning about it, we learn about ourselves. Naming ceremonies, like the one in this excerpt from *Roots*, are one obvious way in which our ancestors affect our lives. As you read, think how your heritage affects you and the lives of your family and friends.

50

Early in the spring of 1750, in the village of Juffure, four days upriver from the coast of The Gambia, West Africa, a manchild was born to Omoro and Binta Kinte. The two wrinkled midwives, old Nyo Boto and the baby's Grandmother Yaisa, saw that it was a boy. They laughed with joy. Their ancestors had told them that a boy firstborn meant Allah would give a special blessing to the parents and to the parents' families. Nyo Boto and Grandma Yaisa were proud. They knew this child would bring greatness to the name of Kinte. Through him, the name of Kinte would live on into the future.

It was the hour before the first crowing of the cocks. Along with Nyo Boto and Grandma Yaisa's chatterings, the first sound the child heard was the muted, rhythmic *bomp-a-bomp-a-bomp* of wooden pestles. The other women of the village were pounding couscous grain in their mortars. They prepared the traditional breakfast of porridge. It was cooked in earthen pots over a fire built among three rocks.

The thin, blue smoke was pungent and pleasant. It went curling up over the small, dusty village of round mud huts. The nasal wailing of Kajali Demba, the village *alimamo,* began. He called men to the first of the five daily prayers. For as long as anyone could remember, they had offered up these prayers to Allah. The men of the village rose quickly from their beds of bamboo cane and cured hides. They put on their rough cotton tunics and filed briskly to the praying place. There the *alimamo* led the worship. *"Allahu Akbar! Ashadu an lailahai-lala!"* ("God is great! I bear witness that there is only one God!") After this, as the men were returning toward their home compounds for breakfast, Omoro rushed among them. He was beaming and excited. He told them of his first-born son. All the men congratulated him. They echoed the omens of good fortune.

Each man went back to his own hut. He accepted a calabash of porridge from his wife. The wives then returned to their kitchens in the rear of the compound. They fed next their children and finally themselves. When they had finished eating, the men took up their short, bent-handled hoes and set off for their day's work. These hoes had wooden blades which the village blacksmith had covered with metal. The men used them to prepare

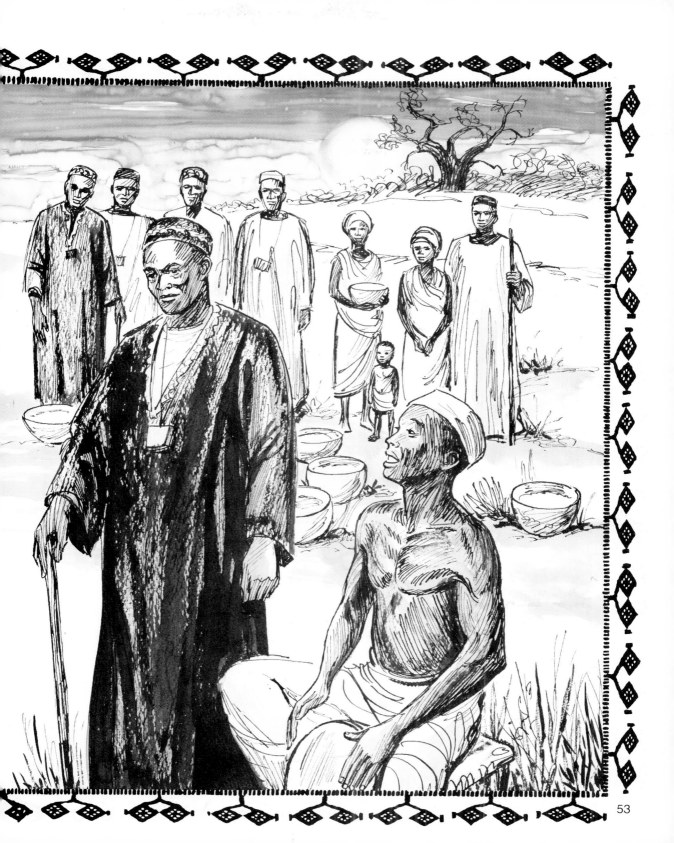

the land for farming. In this hot, lush, savanna country of The Gambia, the men farmed groundnuts, couscous, and cotton. The women farmed rice.

For the next seven days, however, Omoro would occupy himself with but one task. He, and only he, would select a name for his firstborn son. This was an ancient Mandinkan custom. The name Omoro chose would have to be rich with history and with promise. The Mandinkan people believed that the children of their tribe would develop seven of the characteristics of whomever or whatever they were named for.

The naming ceremony of newborn children took place traditionally on the eighth day of their lives. The entire village took part in this ceremony. It was in this way that all children and their parents and grandparents before them had become members of the Mandinkan tribe. During his week of thinking, Omoro visited every household in Juffure. On behalf of himself and Binta, Omoro invited each family to the naming ceremony.

In the early morning of the eighth day, the villagers gathered before the hut of Omoro and Binta. On their heads, the women of both families brought calabash containers. In these containers were ceremonial sour milk and sweet munko cakes of pounded rice and honey. Karamo Silla, the *jaliba* of the village, was there with his tan-tang drums. The *alimamo* was there. The *arafang*, Brima Cesay, was

there. He would someday be the child's teacher. Omoro's two brothers, Janneh and Saloum, had come, too. The drum-talk news of their nephew's birth had reached them days before. They had journeyed from far away to attend the ceremony.

Binta proudly held her new infant. A small patch of his first hair was shaved off. This custom was always part of the ceremony. All the women spoke of how well formed the baby was. Everyone quieted as the *jaliba* began to beat his drums. The *alimamo* said a prayer over the calabashes of sour milk and munko cakes. During the prayer each guest touched a calabash brim with his or her right hand. In this way, they showed their respect for the food. Next, the *alimamo* turned to pray over the infant. He asked Allah to give the child long life. He asked that the child have success—that he bring credit and pride and many children to his family, to his village, and to his tribe. Finally, the *alimamo* asked Allah to give the child strength and spirit. These the child would need to be worthy of the name he was about to receive. The child would need strength and spirit to bring honor to his name, too.

Omoro then walked out before all the assembled people of the village. He moved to his wife's side and lifted up the infant. Everyone watched. Omoro then whispered three times into his son's ear the name he had chosen for him. It was the first time the name had ever been spoken as this child's name. Omoro's people felt that each human being should be the first to know who he or she was.

The tan-tang drum resounded again. Now Omoro whispered the name into the ear of Binta. Binta smiled with pride and pleasure. Then Omoro whispered the name to the *arafang*, who stood before the villagers.

"The first child of Omoro and Binta Kinte is named *Kunta*!" cried Brima Cesay.

Everyone knew the name Kunta. It was the name of the child's late grandfather, Kairaba Kunta Kinte. Kairaba Kunta Kinte had come from his native Mauritania into The Gambia. He had saved the people of Juffure from a famine. He had married Grandma Yaisa. Then, till his death, he had served Juffure honorably as the village's holy man.

Old Kairaba Kinte had often told of the Mauritanian ancestors. Now, one by one, the *arafang* recited their names. The names were great and many. They went back more than two hundred rains. Then the *jaliba* pounded on his tan-tang. All the people called out their admiration and respect for such a superb line of ancestors.

Omoro carried little Kunta in his strong arms and walked to the edge of the village. There—out under the moon and the stars, alone with his son that eighth night—Omoro completed the naming ritual. Omoro lifted Kunta up and turned his face to the heavens. Omoro spoke softly to Kunta:

*"Fend kiling dorong
leh warrata ka iteh tee."*

("Behold—the only thing greater than yourself.")

1. Why was a child's name so important to the Mandinkan people?

2. Define in your own words the terms *alimamo, jaliba,* and *arafang*. What did each of these people do?

3. Do you think that the Mandinkan people were proud of themselves and of their history? Why or why not?

4. Why were you given the name you have? Ask your parents how they chose your name and share the information with the class.

5. Most names have a meaning and a history. Select five first names that you like. Look up the origin and meaning of each name. Make a class list of names, their origins, and their meanings.

Grandma's Secret

John Daniel Stahl

How does it feel to grow old? This question concerns us all, because all of us grow old. During a day spent with her grandmother, Joyce begins to ask herself what it is like to grow old. The more she learns about her grandmother, the more surprised she is, until finally, she is able to answer this vital question for herself. As you read, think of the ways in which Joyce's answer applies to your own life or to the life of an older person you know.

Jakey came running out of the pump house into the yard where Grandma sat husking corn. He held his hand out as if it were on fire and screeched like a stuck pig.

"Yelling won't help," Grandma said calmly. "What happened, Jakey?"

"A bee—" Jakey gasped. "I caught it, but it bit me." Then he began to scream again. Betty stuffed her fingers in her ears to shut out his yells.

Grandma laid aside her towel full of corn and took Jakey's hand. She examined the small red spot on his palm. "Here's the stinger," she said, pulling it out and showing it to Jakey. "That bee will die. A bee can't live without its stinger." She tweaked his nose. "But you'll live. Run inside and put ice on it. Soon it won't hurt, and then you can help us finish up here." She lifted the corn onto her lap again.

"How much do we have to do yet?" Joyce asked.

"Just three baskets and cleaning up—that's all," Grandma said, pointing at the scattered corn husks and the piles of fresh, beady corn. She wiped her forehead with the back of her hand.

"I'm going to dream about corncobs tonight," Joyce thought. "I'll be tearing open corn in my sleep." She gripped the fuzzy silk

and forced the husk open, hearing the rubbery squeak of leaves against moist corn.

She looked at Grandma's hands. How old they look, she thought. Grandma's hands were wrinkled and crossed with veins, but they were strong and gripped the corn firmly. Joyce stared at her own hands in amazement. "What's it like to have old hands?" she wondered.

A shimmer of haze rose above the fields at the horizon; the sun had beaten down from a cloudless sky all day.

"It's awfully hot," Betty said. "I can't wait to swim."

With the cool pond in mind, it didn't take long to husk the remaining ears and clean up the yard. The children changed into their bathing suits and tramped downstairs into the kitchen.

"Will you come along, Grandma?" Joyce asked.

"You can bring a rope and be our lifeguard," Betty said, laughing, "a lifeguard who can't swim."

Grandma only smiled in reply.

Joyce and Betty skipped through the field toward the pond, and Jakey ran to keep up. But Grandma walked leisurely and noticed that the sun had advanced far enough to lose its midday heat. She heard the distant drone of an airplane, then splashes and laughter from the pond. Joyce and Betty swam a race across the pond and back, while Jakey stood, bent over, looking between his legs at the reflection of the farm on the hill—right side up because it was twice upside down.

"The water's wonderful," Joyce called to Grandma. "You should at least get your ankles wet."

"Come swim," Jakey said, making motions as if he were swimming in air.

"Try it, Grandma!" Betty shouted. "Maybe you can learn to swim. Watch!" she yelled, and disappeared under the water. Just when Jakey began to wonder whether she had drowned, she came up with a big splash ten feet from where she had been. She snorted and pushed her streaming hair back out of her eyes. "We dare you to come in, Grandma," she said.

Grandma stood on the bank, looking at them. She did not answer. She smiled a little. Then she turned back toward the house. The children stood in the water, wondering.

"Where are you going, Grandma?" Betty shouted. Grandma merely turned and waved briefly, then went on—a frail figure in the sun-parched field.

"Do you think we hurt her feelings?" Joyce asked Betty, letting herself fall backwards into the water.

"I don't think so," Betty replied. "She's not that way."

"Then why did she leave?"

"Maybe to make supper. Hey, Jakey, that water's no good to drink!"

"Jakey!"

Jakey left off drinking pond water and began practicing his strokes. Betty and Joyce swam lazily, enjoying the cool water.

Suddenly, Joyce stopped swimming and stood up. "Hey, look," she said, staring up the hill as if she were seeing an apparition.

Betty shaded her eyes to see better. It was Grandma, wearing what looked like pajamas. Betty and Joyce doubled up with laughter. Grandma paid no attention. Very calmly, she walked down to the edge of the water, tested the temperature with her big toe, and stepped in. Before the children had time to catch their breath, Grandma was swimming a slow but skillful crawl across the pond.

Seeing the gray head moving across the rippling surface of the pond filled Joyce with a strange exultation, as if she were watching something as amazing as cows flying. She swam over to Grandma and laughed. "That swimsuit must be an antique! Where did you get it? Where did you learn to swim?" she asked. She felt as if she were about to burst. Grandma could swim!

Grandma looked at her with amusement. "I learned to swim as a girl, in my father's farm pond," she said.

"But you never told us!" Betty said, joining her sister.

Grandma only smiled and swam around them.

"Hurrah for Gram!" Jakey shouted.

Later, they rested on the bank of the pond, feeling clean and comfortably tired. They smelled the rich pond and field smells and listened to the crickets.

Joyce looked at Grandma. "There must be so much more about her I don't know," she thought. Despite the floppy green-and-white striped swimsuit, Grandma looked dignified and serene.

"What's it like to be old, Grandma?" she asked.

Betty sat up on her towel and frowned at Joyce. "You shouldn't ask questions like that," she said angrily. "It's not nice."

Grandma looked at Joyce thoughtfully, as if she were reading something in Joyce's face, but she did not answer.

After supper was over and the dishes were washed, Grandma and the children sat out on the porch with glasses of iced lemonade. At the horizon, the sun lit a thin strip of clouds with flame colors. They listened to the squeak of Grandma's rocker on the porch floor and watched the first fireflies spark their signal lights across the lawn.

Joyce's tired muscles ached pleasantly, and she remembered with satisfaction the work she had done that day: the eggs she had gathered in the morning; the floors she had swept; and the long rows of corn she had "picked down." "Evening is the best time of all," she thought.

"Evening is a remember-time," she said aloud.

"That's what being old is, too, Joyce," Grandma said quietly, "a remember-time."

Joyce looked out across the lawn, past the huge shadowy trees that sheltered the porch, and imagined what Grandma was seeing: people—invisible to Joyce—moving across the grass, talking and laughing; horse-drawn carts rattling up the lane in summer sunshine; a sudden thunderstorm fifty years ago, perhaps; or a calm evening just like this one.

"The past becomes a part of you," Grandma said.

"Do you think of Grandpa a lot?" Joyce asked. She saw Betty's disapproving frown, but decided to pretend she hadn't.

Grandma was silent. Her husband had been dead for two years now. "Grandpa is a part of me," she said after a little while. "I think of him as if he just went upstairs or around the corner. I'm remembering all the time," the old woman continued. "It's better than dreaming."

Joyce understood. She walked over to her grandmother and hugged her. "I want to be old some day," she said, her young arms across her grandmother's aged shoulders, "like you."

---

1. What did Joyce think when she looked at Grandma's hands?

2. Why do you think the children assumed that Grandma couldn't swim?

3. What did Grandma mean when she said: "The past becomes a part of you"?

4. In your own words, describe how Grandma felt about being old.

5. Joyce thought: "There must be so much more about her [Grandma] I don't know." What made Joyce feel this way? Have you ever wondered the same thing about older members of your own family? Why do you think it is difficult to imagine an older person being young?

6. Why did Grandma think remembering was better than dreaming? What is the difference between remembering and dreaming? About what parts of your own life do you dream? What parts do you like to remember?

GOING HOME

Wyatt Cooper

Growing up involves change. You gain much as you grow older, but you also lose some things that become treasured memories. In this essay, the author describes the holiday traditions of his childhood—traditions that made his house a home—and shows how those traditions changed. He uses the experiences of his past to explore the meaning of the word *home*. As you read, look for the conclusion he comes to about the meaning of *home*. Does his description of the traditions of childhood and the changes they underwent support his conclusion?

Back in the thirties, when I was growing up on a farm near Quitman, Mississippi, we used to recite a poem around Thanksgiving and Christmas that went, "Across the river and through the woods to Grandmother's house we go." These words described pretty accurately what, in those days, we did for the holidays. To get to my Grandmother Andersen's place, we children simply walked a couple of miles through our own woods, crossing Tallybough Creek by way of a fallen log, while Mama and Papa, the baby, and several containers of food rode the slightly longer route by road.

Those gatherings at Grandma's were joyous occasions for me. I loved to see everyone together in a holiday mood, with their jokes and laughter and their familiarity with each other. They were my kin. We were of the same blood and bone. They belonged to me, and we had claims on one another. There were lots of cousins, many of them my age. We could run all over the farm, matching skills and heights and strengths, testing each other, sharing opinions, comparing accounts of our various teachers, and watching the parading of uncles and aunts with their adult and

different ways, their secret lives, and their mysterious conversations.

Those reunions were of major importance to us. They registered the changes that took place in our lives: the marriages, the births, the moves, the prosperings, and the failures to prosper. We watched each other growing up or growing old. We felt ourselves to be a part of some timeless process, which applied equally to us all.

Gifts were exchanged—small gifts, inexpensive, often made by loving hands—but gifts, nevertheless, that had magic in them. Christmas trees, then, were cedars or hollies from the farm, cut down by Grandpa and my uncle. Set up in the parlor, they were hung with strings of popcorn, walnuts dipped in gold paint, and chains of colored paper, while a silver star glistened at the top. The smells of freshly baked cookies, mince pies, fruitcake, ambrosia, apples, raisins, oranges, and peppermint mixed

with the scent of evergreen in the house. The holiday belonged to us in those days. We made it for ourselves. It was our doing, not something plastic and sold to us in prefabricated form.

The time comes, of course, in the history of families, when we no longer go back for the holidays. We grow up and go out on our own. Some of us become parents, and all of us form ties and alliances beyond the original family circle.

Thomas Wolfe wrote a book called *You Can't Go Home Again.* The truth is that we do not have to go to a physical place to go home, for we are already there. We have never left it. We carry it around with us. It is a part of our dreaming and our waking; it is part of our very breathing. I doubt that there is a day in my life in which some fleeting image of that treasured country does not cross my inner eye. I will suddenly become aware that I have been standing beside the path that led down to the pump beside the schoolhouse. I remember the smell of new overalls on the first day of school or the lighting of kerosene lamps.

I remember what it felt like to be driving the cows home from the pasture in the late afternoons under the red sky of sunset. I moved slowly and lazily, dreaming hazy dreams of glory, watching out for snakes and stinging nettles, avoiding the cow droppings. I can close my eyes and know once more the lurking sense of terror as twilight faded, and darkness gathered in clumps at the edge of the woods. I can hear the wail of the congregation singing at night in the church nearby. The collective sound of it floated mournfully through the still mystery of a starlit world, riding on the air with the scent of honeysuckle or crab apple bloom. It mingled in my ear with the cries of crickets, of frogs, of whippoorwills, and the rhythmic creaking of the porch swing I sat in.

I remember the sights and sounds and smells of home because the memory of home, the pain of it and the passion of it, is the thing that never leaves us. Whatever your country has been, it is forever part of what you are.

We sometimes say, "Home is where the heart is." Home means more than where you came from; home, really, is wherever love resides; it is in all we hold dear, and we go home whenever we reach out in tenderness, one toward another.

1. Describe the objects and activities of a traditional holiday in the author's childhood.

2. What did the author mean when he said of his cousins, "They belonged to me, and we had claims on one another"?

3. Why did the author say that the gifts his family exchange had "magic in them"? How do you think people put "magic" into gifts?

4. Explain the meaning of the author's statements about home: "We do not have to go to a physical place to go home, for we are already there. We have never left it. We carry it around with us."

5. What details do you think you will remember about your own home when you are older?

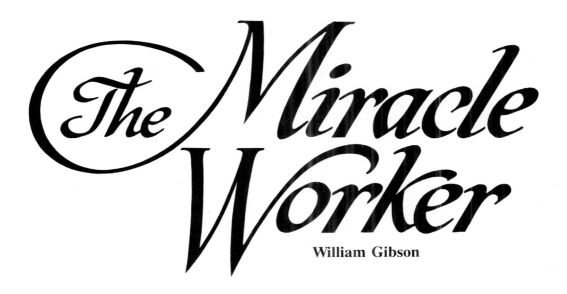

The Miracle Worker

William Gibson

When Helen Keller was nineteen months old, she developed a fever that left her blind and deaf. Very few people in the 1880's knew how to help disabled people overcome their disabilities. Her family did their best to help her; but until she was nearly seven, Helen was ignorant, wild, and almost uncontrollable. Finally, her father wrote to the Perkins Institution for the Blind in Boston, Massachusetts. In response, the Institution sent twenty-year-old Annie Sullivan, a newly graduated student who, until the age of fourteen, had been blind herself. As you read this excerpt from a play, think about Annie's personality, and her method of teaching. Do you think she will be able to help Helen?

Characters: **HELEN KELLER**
JAMES KELLER, *her half-brother*
KATE KELLER, *her mother*
CAPTAIN KELLER, *her father; a former officer in the Confederate Army, now a newspaper publisher*
ANNIE SULLIVAN, *her governess*
VINEY, *a servant in the Keller family*

Time: The 1880's.
Place: In and around the Keller homestead in Tuscumbia, Alabama.

JAMES. (*Coolly.*) Miss Sullivan?

ANNIE. (*Cheerily.*) Here! At last, I've been on trains so many days I thought they must be backing up every time I dozed off—

JAMES. I'm James Keller.

ANNIE. James? (*The name stops her.*) I had a brother Jimmie. Are you Helen's?

JAMES. I'm only half a brother. You're to be her governess?

ANNIE. (*Lightly.*) Well. Try!

JAMES. (*Eying her.*) You look like half a governess.

(KATE *enters.* ANNIE *stands moveless, while* JAMES *takes her suitcase.* KATE'S *gaze on her is doubtful, troubled.*) Mrs. Keller, Miss Sullivan. (KATE *takes her hand.*)

KATE. (*Simply.*) We've met every train for two days.

ANNIE. (*She looks at* KATE'S *face and her good humor comes back.*) I changed trains every time they stopped, the man who sold me that ticket ought to be tied to the tracks—

JAMES. You have a trunk, Miss Sullivan?

ANNIE. Yes. (*She passes* JAMES *a claim check, and he bears the suitcase out behind them.* ANNIE *holds the battered book.* KATE *is studying her face, and* ANNIE *returns the gaze; this is a mutual appraisal, southern gentlewoman and working-class Irish girl, and* ANNIE *is not quite comfortable under it.*) You didn't bring Helen, I was hoping you would.

KATE. No, she's home.

(*A pause.* ANNIE *tries to make ladylike small talk, though her energy now and then erupts; she catches herself up whenever she hears it.*)

ANNIE. You—live far from town, Mrs. Keller?

KATE. Only a mile.

ANNIE. Well, I suppose I can wait one more mile. But don't be surprised if I get out to push the horse!

KATE. Helen's waiting for you, too. There's been such a bustle in the house, she expects something, heaven knows what. (*Now she voices part of her doubt, not as such, but* ANNIE *understands it.*) You're very young.

ANNIE. (*Resolutely.*) Oh, you should have seen me when I left Boston. I got much older on this trip.

KATE. I mean, to teach anyone as difficult as Helen.

ANNIE. *I* mean to try. They can't put you in jail for trying!

KATE. Is it possible, even? To teach a deaf-blind child *half* of what an ordinary child learns—has that ever been done?

ANNIE. Half?

KATE. A tenth.

ANNIE. (*Reluctantly.*) No. (KATE'S *face loses its remaining hope, still appraising her youth.*) Dr. Howe did wonders, but—an ordinary child? No, never. But then I thought when I was going over his reports—(*She indicates the one in her hand.*)—he never treated them like ordinary children. More like—eggs everyone was afraid would break.

KATE. (*A pause.*) May I ask how old you are?

ANNIE. Well, I'm not in my teens, you know! I'm twenty.

KATE. All of twenty.

ANNIE. (*She takes the bull by the horns, valiantly.*) Mrs. Keller, don't lose heart just because I'm not on my last legs. I have three big advantages over Dr. Howe that money couldn't buy for you. One is his work behind me, I've read every word he wrote about it and he wasn't exactly what you'd call a man of few words. Another is to *be* young, why, I've got energy to do anything. The third is, I've been blind. (*But it costs her something to say this.*)

KATE. (*Quietly.*) Advantages.

ANNIE. (*Wry.*) Well, some have the luck of the Irish, some do not.

KATE. (*She smiles; she likes her.*) What will you try to teach her first?

ANNIE. First, last, and—in between, language.

KATE. Language.

ANNIE. Language is to the mind more than light is to the eye. Dr. Howe said that.

KATE. Language. (*She shakes her head.*) *We* can't get through to teach her to sit still. You *are* young, despite your years, to have such confidence. Do you, inside?

ANNIE. (*She studies her face; she likes her, too.*) No, to tell you the truth I'm as shaky inside as a baby's rattle!

(*They smile at each other, and* KATE *pats her hand.*)

KATE. Don't be. (JAMES *returns to usher them off.*) We'll do all we can to help, and to make you feel at home. Don't think of us as strangers, Miss Annie.

ANNIE. (*Cheerily.*) Oh, strangers aren't so strange to me. I've known them all my life!

KATE *smiles again,* ANNIE *smiles back, and they precede* JAMES *Offstage. The* LIGHTS *dim on them, having simultaneously risen* FULL *on the house;* VINEY *has already entered the family room, taken a water pitcher, and come out and down to the pump. She pumps real water. As she looks Offstage, we hear the clop of hoofs, a carriage stopping, and voices.*)

VINEY. Cap'n Keller! Cap'n Keller, they comin'! (*She goes back into the house, as* Keller *comes out on the porch to gaze.*)

KELLER. (*He descends, and crosses toward the carriage; this conversation begins Offstage and moves On. Very courtly.*) Welcome to Ivy Green, Miss Sullivan. I take it you are Miss Sullivan—

KATE. My husband, Miss Annie, Captain Keller.

ANNIE. (*Her best behavior.*) Captain, how do you do.

KELLER. A pleasure to see you, at last. I trust you had an agreeable journey?

ANNIE. Oh, I had several! When did this country get so big?

JAMES. Where would you like the trunk, Father?

KELLER. Where Miss Sullivan can get at it, I imagine.

ANNIE. Yes, please. Where's Helen?

KELLER. In the hall, Jimmie—

KATE. We've put you in the upstairs corner room, Miss Annie, if there's any breeze at all this summer, you'll feel it—

(*In the house the setter,* BELLE, *flees into the family room, pursued by* HELEN *with groping hands; the dog doubles back out the same door, and* HELEN *still groping for her makes her way out to the porch; she is messy, her hair tumbled, her pinafore now ripped, her shoelaces untied.* KELLER *acquires the suitcase, and* ANNIE *gets her hands on it too, though still endeavoring to live up to the general air of propertied manners.*)

KELLER. *And* the suitcase—

ANNIE. (*Pleasantly.*) I'll take the suitcase, thanks.

KELLER. Not at all, I have it, Miss Sullivan.

ANNIE. I'd like it.

KELLER. (*Gallantly.*) I couldn't think of it, Miss Sullivan. You'll find in the south we—

ANNIE. Let me.

KELLER.—view women as the flowers of civiliza—

ANNIE. (*Impatiently.*) I've got something in it for Helen! (*She tugs it free;* KELLER *stares.*) Thank you. When do I see her?

KATE. There. There is Helen.

(ANNIE *turns, and sees* HELEN *on the porch. A moment of silence. Then* ANNIE *begins across the yard to her, lugging her suitcase.*)

KELLER. (*Sotto voce.*) Katie—

(KATE *silences him with a hand on his arm. When* ANNIE *finally reaches the porch steps she stops, contemplating* HELEN *for a last moment before entering her world. Then she drops the suitcase on the porch with intentional heaviness,* HELEN *starts with the jar, and comes to grope over it.* ANNIE *puts forth her hand, and touches* HELEN'S. HELEN *at once grasps it, and commences to explore it, like reading a face. She moves her hand on to* ANNIE'S *forearm, and dress; and* ANNIE *brings her face within reach of* HELEN'S *fingers, which travel over it, quite without timidity, until they encounter and push aside the smoked glasses.* ANNIE'S *gaze is grave, unpitying, very attentive. She puts her hands on* HELEN'S *arms, but* HELEN *at once pulls away, and they comfort each other with a distance between. Then* HELEN *returns to the suitcase, tries to open it, cannot.* ANNIE *points* HELEN'S *hand overhead.* HELEN *pulls away, tries to open the suitcase again;* ANNIE *points her hand overhead again.* HELEN *points overhead, a question, and* ANNIE, *drawing* HELEN'S *hand to her own face, nods.* HELEN *now begins tugging the suitcase toward the door; when* ANNIE *tries to take it from her, she fights her off and backs through the doorway with it* ANNIE *stands a moment, then follows her in, and together they get the suitcase up the steps into* ANNIE'S *room.*)

KATE. Well?

KELLER. She's very rough, Katie.

KATE. I like her, Captain.

KELLER. Certainly rear a peculiar kind of young woman in the north. How old is she?

KATE. (*Vaguely.*) Ohh—Well, she's not in her teens, you know.

KELLER. She's only a child. What's her family like, shipping her off alone this far?

KATE. I couldn't learn. She's very closemouthed about some things.

KELLER. Why does she wear those glasses? I like to see a person's eyes when I talk to—

KATE. For the sun. She was blind.

KELLER. Blind.

KATE. She's had nine operations on her eyes. One just before she left.

KELLER. Blind, good heavens, do they expect one blind child to teach another? Has she experience at least, how long did she teach there?

KATE. She was a pupil.

KELLER. (*Heavily.*) Katie, Katie. This is her first position?

KATE. (*Bright voice.*) She was valedictorian—

KELLER. Here's a houseful of grown-ups can't cope with the child, how can an inexperienced half-blind Yankee schoolgirl manage her?

(JAMES *moves in with the trunk on his shoulder.*)

JAMES. (*Easily.*) Great improvement. Now we have two of them to look after.

KELLER. You look after those strawberry plants!

(JAMES *stops with the trunk.* KELLER *turns from him without another word, and marches off.*)

JAMES. Nothing I say is right.

KATE. Why say anything? (*She calls.*) Don't be long, Captain, we'll have supper right away—

(*She goes into the house, and through the rear door of the family room.* JAMES *trudges in with the trunk, takes it up the steps to* ANNIE'S *room, and sets it down outside the door. The* LIGHTS *elsewhere dim somewhat.*)

(*Meanwhile, inside,* ANNIE *has given* HELEN *a key; while* ANNIE *removes her bonnet,* HELEN *unlocks and opens the suitcase. The first thing she pulls out is a voluminous shawl. She fingers it until she perceives what it is; then she wraps it around her, and acquiring* ANNIE'S *bonnet and smoked glasses as well, dons the lot: the shawl swamps her, and the bonnet settles down upon the glasses, but she stands before a mirror cocking her head to one side, then to the other, in a mockery of adult action.* ANNIE *is amused, and talks to her as one might to a kitten, with no trace of company manners.*)

ANNIE. All the trouble I went to and that's how I look? (HELEN *then comes back to the suitcase, gropes for more, lifts out a pair of female drawers.*) Oh, no. Not the drawers! (*But* HELEN, *discarding them, comes to the elegant doll. Her fingers explore its features, and when she* raises it and finds its eyes open and close, she is at first startled, then delighted. She picks it up, taps its head vigorously, taps her own chest, and nods questioningly. ANNIE takes her finger, points it to the doll, points it to HELEN, and touching it to her own face, also nods. HELEN sits back on her heels, clasps the doll to herself, and rocks it. ANNIE studies her, still in bonnet and smoked glasses like a caricature of herself, and addresses her humorously.) All right, Miss O'Sullivan. Let's begin with doll. (She takes HELEN'S hand; in her palm ANNIE'S forefinger points, thumb holding her other fingers clenched.) **D.** (Her thumb next holds all her fingers clenched, touching HELEN'S palm.) **O.** (Her thumb and forefinger extend.) **L.** (Same contact repeated.) **L.** (She puts HELEN'S hand to the doll.) **Doll.**

JAMES. You spell pretty well. (ANNIE in one hurried move gets the drawers swiftly back into the suitcase, the lid banged shut, and her head turned, to see JAMES leaning in the doorway.) Finding out if she's ticklish? She is. (ANNIE regards him stonily, but HELEN after a scowling moment tugs at her hand again, imperious. ANNIE repeats the letters, and HELEN interrupts her fingers in the middle, feeling each of them, puzzled. ANNIE touches HELEN'S hand to the doll, and begins spelling into it again.) What is it, a game?

ANNIE. (Curtly.) An alphabet.

JAMES. Alphabet?

ANNIE. For the deaf. (HELEN now repeats the finger movements in air,

exactly, her head cocked to her own hand, and ANNIE'S eyes suddenly gleam.) Ho. How *bright* she is!

JAMES. You think she knows what she's doing? (He takes HELEN'S hand, to throw a meaningless gesture into it; she repeats this one too.) She imitates everything, she's a monkey.

ANNIE. (Very pleased.) Yes, she's a bright little monkey, all right.

(She takes the doll from HELEN, and reaches for her hand; HELEN instantly grabs the doll back. ANNIE takes it again, and HELEN'S hand next, but HELEN is incensed now; when ANNIE draws her hand to her face to shake her head no, then tries to spell to her, HELEN slaps at ANNIE'S face. ANNIE grasps HELEN by both arms, and swings her into a chair, holding her pinned there, kicking, while glasses, doll, bonnet fly in various directions. JAMES laughs.)

JAMES. She wants her doll back.

ANNIE. When she spells it.

JAMES. Spell, she doesn't know the thing has a name, even.

ANNIE. Of course not, who expects her to, now? All I want is her fingers to learn the letters.

JAMES. Won't mean anything to her. (ANNIE gives him a look. She then tries to form HELEN'S fingers into the letters, but HELEN swings a haymaker instead, which ANNIE barely ducks, at once pinning her down again.) Doesn't like that alphabet, Miss Sullivan. You invent it yourself?

(HELEN *is now in a rage, fighting tooth and nail to get out of the chair, and* ANNIE *answers while struggling and dodging her kicks*.)

ANNIE. Spanish monks under a—vow of silence. Which I wish *you'd* take! (*And suddenly releasing* HELEN'S *hand, she comes and shuts the door in* JAMES' *face.* HELEN *drops to the floor, groping around for the doll.* ANNIE *looks around desperately, sees her purse on the bed, rummages in it, and comes up with a battered piece of cake wrapped in newspaper; with her foot she moves the doll deftly out of the way of* HELEN'S *groping, and going on her knee she lets* HELEN *smell the cake. When* HELEN *grabs for it,* ANNIE *removes the cake and spells quickly into the reaching hand.*) **Cake**. From Washington up north, it's the best I can do. (HELEN'S *hand waits, baffled.* ANNIE *repeats it.*) **C, a, k, e**. Do what my fingers do, never mind what it means. (*She touches the cake briefly to* HELEN'S *nose, pats her hand, presents her own hand.* HELEN *spells the letters rapidly back.* ANNIE *pats her hand enthusiastically, and gives her the cake;* HELEN *crams it into her mouth with both hands.* ANNIE *watches her, with humor*). Get it down fast, maybe I'll steal that back too. Now. (*She takes the doll, touches it to* HELEN'S *nose, and spells again into her hand.*) **D, o, l, l**. Think it over. (HELEN *thinks it over, while* ANNIE *presents her own hand. Then* HELEN *spells three letters.*

ANNIE *waits a second, then completes the word for* HELEN *in her palm.*) **L**. (*She hands over the doll, and* HELEN *gets a good grip on its leg.*) Imitate now, understand later. End of the first les—(*She never finishes, because* HELEN *swings the doll with a furious energy, it hits* ANNIE *squarely in the face, and she falls back with a cry of pain, her knuckles up to her mouth.* HELEN *waits, tensed for further combat. When* ANNIE *lowers her knuckles she looks at blood on them; she works her lips, gets to her feet, finds the mirror, and bares her teeth at herself. Now she is furious herself.*) You little wretch, no one's taught you *any* manners? I'll—(*But rounding from the mirror she sees the door slam,* HELEN *and the doll are on the outside, and* HELEN *is turning the key in the lock.* ANNIE *darts over, to pull the knob; the door is locked fast. She yanks it again.*) Helen! Helen, let me out of—

(*She bats her brow at the folly of speaking, but* JAMES, *now downstairs, hears her and turns to see* HELEN *with the key and doll groping her way down the steps;* JAMES *takes in the whole situation, makes a move to intercept* HELEN, *but then changes his mind, lets her pass, and amusedly follows her out onto the porch. Upstairs* ANNIE *meanwhile rattles the knob, kneels, peers through the keyhole, gets up. She goes to the window, looks down, frowns.* JAMES *from the yard sings gaily up to her:*)

JAMES. *Buffalo girl, are you coming out tonight,*
      Coming out tonight,
      Coming out—

(He drifts back into the house. ANNIE *takes a handkerchief, nurses her mouth, stands in the middle of the room, staring at door and window in turn, and so catches sight of herself in the mirror, her cheek scratched, her hair dishevelled, her handkerchief bloody, her face disgusted with herself. She addresses the mirror, with some irony.)*

ANNIE. Don't worry. They'll find you, you're not lost. Only out of place.

     Helen was intelligent—intelligent enough to lock Annie in her room so that Captain Keller had to use a ladder to rescue her. But could anyone rescue Helen by unlocking her intelligence? Annie was determined to try, but the Keller family only made her job harder because they were frightened and angered by her methods. Annie exhausted herself in resisting them and in trying to break the wall of silence and darkness around Helen's mind. Finally, her efforts were rewarded: the breakthrough occurred and Helen understood what language was. Through language, Helen learned about the people and the world around her. She also learned that the ability to use language was a miraculous gift which her teacher had given her.

1. Describe the reactions of Captain Keller, Kate, and James to Annie Sullivan.
2. Annie claimed that her own experience with blindness would make her a good teacher for Helen. Do you agree or disagree? Why?
3. Explain Annie's plans for teaching language to Helen.
4. Briefly describe Annie Sullivan's personality.
5. Close your eyes and sit very still for a moment. Concentrate on your senses of smell, taste, and touch. Then explore your nearby surroundings using only these senses. Describe what you were able to learn and experience.

News from China

Christopher T. McMillan

Not all families live together in the same place. Sometimes, parents have to be separated from one another and from their children. The short story you are about to read shows how the feelings that hold a family together can endure over thousands of miles and for many years. As you read, picture Mai Ling's mother in your mind. What kind of person do you think she was?

Mai Ling told the story in Chinese if she could. She preferred the sounds her own language made when she got to the sad parts. Besides, in Chinese, there were more words that got to the bottom of how her heart felt when she remembered that day.

But she didn't mind telling the story in English. Sometimes her nieces and nephews would want to hear the story, and most of them spoke very little Chinese. So, even though she knew some of the children were only pretending they had never heard the story before, she would tell it each time they asked.

"My mother was a strong woman," Mai Ling always began. "She was small, even smaller than I am, and very fragile looking. But she was strong in her will and strong in her spirit. She knew from an early age that she wanted to write poetry. But she also knew that in those days, Chinese women were not supposed to be active in things like writing poetry. Women were supposed to stay home and make a home for a man; and that was all.

"But my mother wanted to write poetry more than anything else in the world. So she decided to write her poems under a man's name. She chose the name Ai Nanze, which means 'The Little Gentleman.' Then she began to send her poems to the newspapers and

magazines, until one day, after many failures, one of her poems was bought by a newspaper.

"My mother was overjoyed, and she laughed with delight when she saw that the letter from the newspaper began: 'Dear Sir.' She was glad she had given herself a man's name, for she was sure the poem would not have been bought if she had used her real name.

"Soon my mother sold another poem, and then another. Before long, many newspapers and magazines wanted poems by Ai Nanze, never knowing that the writer was a woman.

"But in those days, there was a great deal of trouble in China. Different groups struggled for power in the country, and there were three groups that were especially strong. My mother, like most people in China at the time, belonged to one of the three. But because of her beliefs and because the group she believed in was the weakest of the three, my mother was often put in jail. She was very brave, as I have said. She never cried in jail, and she never gave up her beliefs. Instead, she wrote more poems. I am told that I was almost born in jail. My mother had been released two days before I was born.

"Eventually, as the two strongest groups fought to rule China, my mother grew afraid. She was not afraid for herself, but for her children. So when I was thirteen years old and my little brother was ten, we were sent to America with an aunt.

"Oh, how we cried when we left my mother at the dock in Tsingtao. We knew the chances were very good that we would never see her again. My brother and I waved our white handkerchiefs until my mother was a small dot standing on the pier.

"Many years passed. My mother stayed on in China, but she wrote us long letters with clippings of her poems. They were printed in all the newspapers, no matter who was in power in the country.

"Meanwhile, I and my brother made our life here in the United States. We learned to speak English, and we came to love this country as much as our homeland. Both my brother and I made many

friends in this country who were also Chinese. That is natural, I think. But we never stopped hoping that our mother would leave China. We never stopped missing her, even for a day.

"Then came a time when we did not hear from my mother for many months. We sent letters to China, asking after her, but we got no answers. We were worried, because by then, my mother was quite old. We did not know what to do. Then came the day I will never forget.

"I had gone for a walk in the park, because it was early spring and the sun was trying for the first time to be hot. The trees had not blossomed, but I could see tiny dots of color where the buds were getting ready to escape. I saw a friend across the park, a Chinese gentleman who had lived in the United States many years, but missed China very much. He always bought the latest newspapers and books from China. I sometimes thought he liked to pretend he was still in China, when he read things from the homeland.

"This day he looked very sad, which was unusual for him. His face was drooping, and he did not seem to notice the sun.

"'Why do you look so sad?' I asked him. 'The day is so beautiful.'

"'I did not notice,' he said. 'I have lost a friend.'

"'I am sorry,' I said. 'Is it someone I know?'

"'No,' he said. 'It is a man in China I have admired for years. I do not know him personally, but for many years, I have read his writing. For many years, I have felt this man talking to me. For many years, he has entered my heart through my newspaper. Today, I opened the newspaper to look for him in his usual place, but he was not there. Instead, there was an announcement—a very sad announcement that my friend had died the month before. I know it must seem silly to you, since I have never met the man. But believe me, I will miss him as much as if we shared the same father.'

"My heart at this moment began to beat faster. I was not sure why. When I spoke to my friend, I was almost afraid to ask the question that came into my mind.

"'I understand your sadness,' I said. 'But tell me: what sort of writing did this man do?'

"'Poetry,' my friend said. 'He wrote beautiful poems about China.'

"My heart felt as if it were beating too fast to ever slow down.

"'Please, what was the name of this man?' I asked in a whisper.

"He spoke the name and said: 'Don't tell me you know him!'

"The tears had already begun to stream down my cheeks.

"'My friend,' I said, 'if you are sad for the death of this poet, imagine how I must feel. This person whose poems touched your heart gave me mine, for the man you admired so much was my mother.'"

1. What did Mai Ling's mother want to do more than anything else? How did her strength of will help her to do it?

2. Why do you think Mai Ling's nieces and nephews wanted to hear the story again and again?

3. In "Going Home," the author said: "Whatever your country has been, it is forever part of what you are." How does this statement apply to Mai Ling, to her mother, and to the Chinese gentleman?

4. Why did Mai Ling's mother send her children to America? Why didn't she go with them? Would you have done the same thing in her place? Why or why not?

5. Do you think Mai Ling's mother's poems would have been published in so many papers for such a long time if they had known her true identity? Why or why not? Can you think of some other reasons why writers sometimes use "pen names"?

My Roots

my roots
do i live by my roots?
do i work in my roots?

but what are my roots?
a place?
a time?
a person

am i my roots?
i don't think my father could tell me,
nor my mother . . .
if i could communicate with my grandmother maybe
i could catch just half of my
roots.

—*Bobby Fone*

THE LEGEND

Robert Douglas Livingston

You learn about life in many different ways. You learn from your own experiences, and you also learn from other people. In this short story, Sarah learns the importance of responsibility in both these ways. She learns a lesson from her own experience, but it is the legend told by her friend, Singing Squirrel, that drives the lesson home. Through the legend, Sarah learns that, like herself, all the creatures in the world have responsibilities which they must fulfill. As you read, notice how the legend—a story within the story—mirrors the actions and feelings of the characters.

The sun danced across the wrinkled water. Sarah threw out her arms as if to gather up the sunlight. The warm wind whipped her long skirt out behind her. She turned to look at the whitewashed buildings which made three sides of the fort's parade grounds. Slowly, she turned back to the blue inland lake which stretched along the fourth side of the level drilling lawn.

How she loved the north country —to be out in the sun with the roaring winds sweeping over Lake Superior, which beat on the rocky shore. Even though the huge lake was hidden beyond the great pines that towered above the fort's stockade, she could hear it pounding.

Her brother John appeared on the long porch which ran the length of the quarters where the Carters lived. Seeing Sarah, he sauntered across the green parade grounds toward her. "It's beautiful, isn't it? We're lucky Father was sent here."

"John," Sarah whispered, "it's so lovely that sometimes it hurts. I want to take it inside of me somehow. When the wind is rocking the pines and the sun is bright, I feel so free."

"Mama wants you to take Peter and pick thimbleberries. They'll soon be gone, and she still has plenty of sugar for more preserves."

"Oh, John! I did that yesterday, and the day before, and all last week. I want to go to the lake shore today. After last night's storm, there's bound to be some new agates. Can't Peter go with you?"

"Sorry, Sarah, but I'm going all the way to Lake Nora to fish. It's too far for Peter. He'd never make it."

"Why do I always get stuck with him? You never have to play nurse-maid. It's not fair!"

"Look, Sis, we each have to do our part. Mine is bringing home some fish."

"Well, I don't see why you can't do it somewhere that Peter can go, too. I'm sick of dragging him everywhere with me."

John didn't answer. He just looked at Sarah in disgust and set off for the road.

"Sarah!" It was Mrs. Carter. "Sarah!" her mother called again.

Angrily, Sarah turned from the glittering water. She was bored with working. Thimbleberry jam! Who needed it? But if it weren't thimbleberries, it would be something else—and always Peter. Well, not always . . . and he really was a good baby most of the time. But today he was a nuisance. If she didn't hunt agates today, everyone else would get them all. It just wasn't fair.

She reached the door. There sat Peter, waiting expectantly.

"Go, Sarah. Timberry."

Rebellion welled up in her. "Mama, I hate picking those dumb things. We have all we need. I'm tired of working all the time. John gets to go fishing, and I have to watch that little brat. It's not fair! I want to hunt agates today. I never get to do what I want."

She gave Peter a mean look. Though he couldn't understand her, he could tell by her tone and her frown that she was not happy with him. His smile died from his eyes and lips.

"But, Sarah, next winter you'll want jam for your bread." Her mother's voice was slightly reproving.

"No, I won't. I'll eat it dry. I just won't pick another berry. Why can't you watch Peter? He's your baby."

As soon as she said it, Sarah wanted to call back the words. The look of pain and sadness in her mother's face almost made her cry. After a silence that seemed to go on forever, broken only by the sound of Peter's breathing, Mrs. Carter said in a very quiet voice, "All right, Sarah, go look for agates."

She turned back to the stove. "Come here, Peter. You aren't going berry picking with Sarah. You can help Mama with the washing."

The words cut Sarah deeper than her mother's hurt look. She turned and left the porch. She was still angry at the unfair way she was always treated, but she felt awful, too. Peter would be in Mama's way. He'd want to get too close to the fire, or pull the clothes off the line. But she wouldn't give in now.

The beach was empty. The sun beat hotly on the rocks. Birds floated on warm currents over the shimmering water. But the big lump in Sarah's stomach wouldn't go away. After some searching, she discovered a banded agate, more beautiful than any she had ever seen. Even that didn't help. Glumly, she decided to visit Singing Squirrel.

Singing Squirrel was an old American Indian woman who lived on the opposite side of town from the army fort. She had become like a grandmother to Sarah. When things were going wrong, talking them over with Singing Squirrel usually straightened everything out.

Arriving at the tiny log house, Sarah found Singing Squirrel bent over a large boiling pot, making soap.

"Hello, Singing Squirrel."

"Ah, Sarah, my little daughter. Come. You are in time to help me stir the soap." Looking closely at Sarah, the old woman noticed two tears slide down her cheeks. "Something is wrong."

"Oh, Singing Squirrel, I feel awful."

"Come. Sit and tell me."

So Sarah told her about her lovely feeling that morning, about not wanting to pick thimbleberries with Peter, about hunting agates all alone, and about how terrible she felt.

Singing Squirrel listened quietly until Sarah was finished. They were both silent for several minutes. The gulls could be heard over the harbor. The wind rustled the trees overhead. A chipmunk ran across the yard and under the cabin. It was very peaceful.

Finally, Singing Squirrel said, "There is a legend about the daisy. My grandmother told it to me one hot summer day when I ran away to keep from sewing winter shirts. The daisy was created to be the most beautiful of all flowering bushes. The royal hummingbird would only build her nest in a daisy. No berries were sweeter than hers. So sweet were they that the bees borrowed her secret, and today their honey is the reminder of that fruit."

"But daisies don't grow on bushes and have berries."

"But when the Great Spirit first made them, they did," said Singing Squirrel.

"How did they become just flowers?"

The old woman settled herself beside Sarah. "When the Great Spirit filled the world with the plants and animals, the waters with fish, and the air with birds, He gave everyone three gifts. First, He bestowed on each creature its own beauty so as to teach all His children their own worth to Himself. Next, he gave each one the gift of need for some other kind of creature. This was to teach humility by realizing that nothing can live by itself. Lastly, every fish, bird, flower, tree, and animal received a service to perform for one of its fellows. In fulfilling a duty to another, He knew they would learn to love; for the path of service is the pathway of love.

"He made the pine tree tall and thick. Within its branches, He taught the winter birds to build their nests. Then when the snows and winds of winter came, there was safe shelter for all who hid there.

"He made the maple tree broadleafed and spreading. Beneath her, He planted the woodland flowers—the trillium, the mayapple, the violet— shaded from the hot summer sun.

"He made the daisy a beautiful bush. Her flower was like a tiny sun. The jeweled hummingbird alone built her nest in the daisy's arching arms. She was crowned with golden berries, sweet and meaty, to feed birds and beasts who passed by.

"When the Great Spirit was finished, He commanded, 'Fill this land with life. Be kind to one another, for you are all brothers and sisters. Prosper. Be faithful to your duties.' Then He went away.

"The pine tree grew tall and straight. Deep into the earth, he drove his roots to grasp the rocky ground. He filled his boughs with food cones and spread his branches to shelter all who would come. He dropped his needles to make a warm blanket around his feet for those who could not climb into his arms.

"The maple lifted wide her branches to hold back the sun and make sweet shade for her neighbors. When the flowers around her fell asleep for the winter, she shook herself to cover them with leaves against the cold. Silently through the long winter she stood waiting to greet the spring flowers when they awakened.

"The daisy bush bloomed, catching the golden sunlight in her flowers. She was a beautiful sight. But it was such an effort to arch her branches for the hummingbirds. 'Go away and live in the brambles,' she told them. 'I'm too busy gathering sunlight to bother with you.' When it came to making berries, she did try at first, but it took too much energy to create the sweet fruit. When the Queen Bee asked to borrow her sweet taste, she was more than happy to oblige her. 'Take it. It will save me considerable trouble,' was her reply. And as for putting roots deep into the earth for food and water, she would not admit that she needed to anchor herself in another's strength.

"One day, the Great Spirit returned. He stood before the pine tree.

" 'Mighty pine, how have you obeyed My command?'

" 'I have held the birds close to my breast through the cold winter. I have spread a blanket of needles to cover the small beasts from the snow.'

" 'You have done well. For your care of my children, you shall remain green throughout the year. The winter shall be beautiful because of your faithfulness.'

"The Great Spirit came to the maple tree. 'My daughter, tell Me of your care for those around you.'

" 'I have spread my arms far out over the flowers, holding the sun in my hands and letting only a few rays slip through my fingers to warm the ground. Many birds have found shelter in my branches; and in the autumn, I covered my little sisters with leaves.'

" 'Well done. For this, I shall clothe you in scarlet and gold in the autumn before you shake bare your branches.'

" 'Lastly, the Great Spirit came to the daisy. 'My daughter,' he cried in amazement. 'You are no larger than when I left!'

" 'I was too busy catching sunlight and scattering it to the winds to think of growing.'

" 'Where are my tiny hummingbirds?'

" 'In the brambles. I did not have the patience to arch my branches and help them weave their homes in my hair. I have to gather sunbeams.'

" 'And where are your golden berries?'

" 'The Queen of Bees asked for their sweetness, so I gave it to her. I now have more time to bathe in the sun's warm caresses.'

"The Great Spirit was very angry because the daisy had wasted her time on vanity and had given no thought to others. 'For this, you shall no longer be a blooming bush. I shall scatter you across the fields to stand alone; and with the end of summer, you, too, shall cease to be. Selfishness and vanity pass quickly away. Those who live only for the whims of a day shall perish with that day.'

"The daisy bowed her yellow head and wept great white tears.

"The Great Spirit continued, 'But I will show mercy, for I love every child I have made. Though you be scattered to the sea, you shall keep your beauty, catching the summer sun in your circle of tears.'

"And so today, the daisy stands straight and alone, a tiny sun in a ring of tears."

Sarah sat silently, watching a cloud pass overhead. At last she said, "I guess I really would have had time to hunt agates after Peter and I had picked thimbleberries."

Singing Squirrel stood up. "The sun is still high. I have a secret patch of berries on the shore down beyond those trees."

Sarah got up. "Well," she said with a determined twist of her lips, "I won't have taken Peter to make Mama's job of washing easier, but at least I can bring her some fresh berries. Do you have a pail I can borrow, Singing Squirrel?"

"There is a birch basket by the door."

Sarah lifted the basket from its peg. "Thank you, Singing Squirrel."

Singing Squirrel had already returned to her soap kettle. She seemed not to have heard. Just as Sarah reached the trees, the old woman called to her, "And why not carry a bouquet of daisies to your mother?"

1. According to the legend that Singing Squirrel told, what were the three gifts that each plant and animal received?

2. At the beginning of the story, how did Sarah feel before her brother John appeared? Why did she feel that way?

3. For what reasons did Sarah think she was being treated unfairly? Do you think she was? Why or why not?

4. Sarah got her way, yet she was almost immediately disappointed. Why?

5. What lesson did Sarah learn? How did her experience and Singing Squirrel's legend teach her this lesson? Do you think she would have understood the meaning of the legend if she had not had the experience first? Why or why not?

I'm Me

People used to
Ask me

Why are you so quiet?

And
I'd answer

I don't know.

People still
Ask me

Why are you so quiet?
But
Now I answer

Because I'm me.

They
Reply
With

Oh.

—Shirley Lai

Analogies

An analogy is a way of reasoning used to show relationships. Often analogies show relationships between pairs of words.

Example 1   Collie is to dog as robin is to bird.
Example 2   hot:cold :: high:low

In Example 1, *collie* is a type of *dog* and *robin* is a type of *bird*. The relationship is the same for both pairs of words. The first word is an item in a category; the second word names the category.

In Example 2, the analogy is written in a shorter way. The relationship shown is also different. *Hot* and *cold* are opposites, so are *high* and *low*. Analogies show many different relationships.

Often you must complete an analogy by supplying one of the words. For example,

   racket:tennis :: _____:hockey
   a. goal   **b.** defense   **c.** stick   **d.** ice

The correct answer is *stick* because a *racket* is used to hit the ball in *tennis* and a *stick* is used to hit the puck in *hockey*.

To supply a missing word in an analogy, you should analyze the relationship between the words in the given pair. Then you should look for a word in the answer list that relates in the same way to the remaining word in the analogy. You must eliminate answer choices until you find the best answer. For example,

   planet:sun :: _____:earth
   a. star   **b.** rocket   **c.** moon   **d.** distant

Planet, *sun*, and *earth* are all nouns, so you need a noun to complete the analogy. This eliminates *distant* since *distant* is an adjective. *Planet, sun* and *earth* are all heavenly bodies. *Star* and *moon* are also heavenly bodies. But *rocket* is not, so you can eliminate it. To decide whether *star* or *moon* is correct, look again at the relationship between *planet* and *sun*. A *planet* orbits the *sun*. Since the *moon*, not a *star*, orbits the *earth*, the correct answer is *moon*.

ACTIVITY A   Write the word which completes each analogy.

1. fresh:stale :: _____ :dark
   a. bread   **b.** light   **c.** night   **d.** damp

2. chickens:poultry :: turnips: _____
   a. parsnips   **b.** protein   **c.** bread   **d.** vegetable

3. airplane:hanger :: _____ :dock
   a. anchor   **b.** flies   **c.** boat   **d.** coat

4. needles:sew :: scissors: _____
   a. cut   **b.** knife   **c.** thread   **d.** shears

5. friend:pal :: foe: _____
   a. war   **b.** cousin   **c.** enemy   **d.** foal

6. mechanics:garage :: _____ :court
   a. criminals   **b.** judges   **c.** customers   **d.** defendants

7. mathematics:numbers :: English: _____
   a. difficult   **b.** French   **c.** words   **d.** science

8. milk:cow :: _____ :sheep
   a. shepherd   **b.** lamb   **c.** farm   **d.** wool

9. fish:water :: birds: _____
   a. fly   **b.** wings   **c.** air   **d.** robin

10. spider:web :: caterpillar: _____
    a. moth   **b.** cocoon   **c.** butterfly   **d.** silkworm

ACTIVITY B   Each of the following relationships was used in Activity A. On your paper, write each relationship and then write the number of the exercise in Activity A that used the relationship.

1. means about the same as
2. are opposites
3. are used to
4. comes from
5. move in
6. are a kind of
7. is kept at
8. deals with
9. work in
10. makes

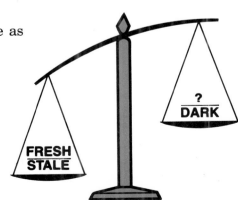

Using the Library

A library has many books containing different kinds of information. The *card catalogue* will help you find the specific books that you need. The card catalogue is a case of drawers containing cards arranged in alphabetical order. Each book in the library is generally listed on three separate cards: a title card, an author card, and a subject card.

The *title card* is headed with the title of the book. If the title starts with *A*, *An*, or *The*, the book will be filed under the second word in the title. Use this card if you know the name of the book you need.

The *author card* is headed with the author's name, last name first. Use this card if you know the name of the author of the book you want.

The *subject card* is headed with the subject of the book. Use this card if you are looking for a book on a particular subject but don't know a book title or author.

918.4 RO	Life with the Cherokees. Rodrigues, E. M. Life with the Cherokees.

Title Card

918.4 RO	Rodrigues, E. M. Life with the Cherokees.

Author Card

918.4 RO	INDIAN TRIBES Rodrigues, E. M. Life with the Cherokees.

Subject Card

Notice that each card has a number on the left side of the card. This is the *call number*. It is a code that indicates where the book is located in the library.

ACTIVITY A   On your paper, write whether you would use a *title card*, an *author card*, or a *subject card* to find each of the following books:

1. a book about World War I
2. a book entitled *The Great Inventors of Europe*
3. a book with information about ecology
4. a book written by Jackson Reynolds
5. a book with the title *Three Days to Burma*
6. a book that tells about modern architecture
7. a book with information about United States Presidents
8. a book called *Ready for the Northwest*
9. a book entitled *The History of the Earth*
10. a book written by Marie Doonesbury

Libraries usually have a separate section for reference books. These are special books with important information on different subjects. There are many types of reference books.

An *encyclopedia* is a set of reference books that contains articles on a variety of subjects. The articles are arranged alphabetically. An encyclopedia tells about important people and events in history. It also has information on general subjects such as music, religion, and art. Many encyclopedias also print a *yearbook* that contains articles about events which happened during a given year.

An *almanac* is a single book that lists current facts and figures on events and records. Almanacs are usually printed each year.

An *atlas* is a book of maps. The most complete atlas is the *world atlas*. It has maps of locations around the world. These maps may give information about the population, natural resources, or land surfaces of an area. An *historical atlas* has maps which show how an area looked in earlier times.

To find specific information about people, you could use a special *biographical dictionary*. *Who's Who in America* and *Current Biography* give information about people who are living. *Dictionary of American Biography* and *Who Was Who in America* tell about Americans who are no longer alive.

ACTIVITY B   Write whether you would use an *encyclopedia*, a *yearbook*, an *almanac*, an *atlas*, an *historical atlas*, or a *biographical dictionary* to find the following information. In some cases more than one reference source may be appropriate.

1. information about the inventor of the frozen-food process
2. information about the current governor of New York
3. the winners of last year's Pulitzer Prize for Journalism
4. an article about the history of politics in America
5. a map showing the mountain ranges of Asia
6. information about the major religions of the world
7. a list of the winners in the latest World Olympics
8. information about General Robert E. Lee
9. a map of Europe as it appeared in the 1600's
10. the winner of the World Series in 1958

ACTIVITY C   Use the reference books in your school or local library to answer each question below. Write each answer in a complete sentence. Then write the name of the reference book in which you found the information.

1. What position in the United States government did Cordell Hull hold?
2. Who won the Nobel Prize for Peace in 1960?
3. When was the typewriter invented, and by whom?
4. Where was James Earl Carter born?
5. What is the capital of Switzerland?
6. Through which states does the Mississippi River pass?
7. What occupation did Edward R. Murrow pursue?
8. What three continents have the largest population?
9. What baseball records does Ty Cobb hold today?
10. When and where was the first flight in an air balloon?

ACTIVITY D   Use the card catalogue in your school or local library to answer each question below. Write each answer in a complete sentence.

1. What is the title of one book by John Steinbeck?
2. What is the title of a book about Mexico?
3. What is the title of a play by William Shakespeare?
4. Who wrote a book called *Roots*?
5. Who is the author of *Charlie and the Chocolate Factory*?
6. What was O. Henry's real name?
7. What is the title of one book by Shirley Jackson?
8. What is the title of one American drama?
9. What is the title of a book about the Civil War?
10. Who is the author of *The Wizard of Oz*?

Job Applications

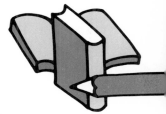

Sometime in the future you may apply for a job. Many companies require you to fill out a job application. The application asks for information about you. The employer usually keeps the application on file as a record. Here is a sample of a job application:

Application For Employment (*please print*)

1. _____   2. _____
   last name   first name   middle initial   today's date

3. _____   4. _____
   street address   city   state   zip code   date of birth

5. _____   6. _____
   telephone number   Social Security number

7. _____
   name and address of school most recently attended

8. _____
   last grade completed

9. _____   10. _____
   name and address of previous employer   date begun—ended

11. _____
    brief description of physical condition

12. _____   13. _____
    position desired   salary expected

14. _____   15. _____
    hobbies or special interests   languages spoken

Follow the directions carefully as you fill out each item on a job application. Be sure you are both accurate and honest. Always write neatly.

Number your paper from one to fifteen. Write the information you would give for each line of the above job application. If any of the items do not apply to you, write *none* in those spaces on your paper.

AWARENESS

The selections in "Awareness" dealt with people who learned about their feelings, their talents, their responsibilities, and their heritage. The learning that took place helped them grow upward and outward from the firm roots of their heritage. Like the characters in these selections, you will become, as you grow, more aware of yourself and of the world around you.

Thinking About "Awareness"

1. Did both Edward in "A Dog on Barkham Street" and Sara in "The Legend" learn to be responsible? Use examples from the stories to support your answer.

2. Compare Addie's feeling for Mr. Davenport in "Addie" with Arthur's feeling for Mr. Charity in "Arthur Makes a Friend." How are their feelings for their adult friends alike? How do their feelings differ?

3. What discoveries did Juan in "The Secret" and Joyce in "Grandma's Secret" make that changed their awareness?

4. Annie Sullivan in "The Miracle Worker" and Singing Squirrel in "The Legend" are both teachers. Compare their approaches to teaching their young friends important lessons.

5. Think about the things that make up your heritage: your life at home, your family traditions, your family's past, your ethnic background, the town or city in which you live. Describe briefly how these things have helped make you the person you are now.

EXCHANGES

An exchange is a way of sharing with others. We communicate when we exchange our thoughts, feelings, and experiences with other people. We communicate through words and through nonverbal signals, such as gestures and facial expressions. Yet, though we continually strive to communicate, we do not always communicate well. Sometimes we do not express ourselves clearly; at other times, we misunderstand what others are trying to express.

In "Exchanges," you will read about some people who try to communicate. Sometimes, they are successful; but sometimes, they are not. You will see how a young woman copes with someone who uses words to mean anything he wants them to mean. In a play set in a television station, you will see how misunderstanding words creates a humorous situation. You will read about the "body language" we all use—often without being aware of it. Sign language is a special way of communicating without words, and you will read about ancient and modern sign systems. You will learn about the language barriers that separate nations and how people overcome these barriers. You will also meet a father and son from China, who strive to overcome the barriers of adjusting to a new way of life.

As you read, think about the different kinds of exchanges that take place between people. What can you do to communicate more clearly with others?

VOICES

There are songs and sounds in stillness
In the quiet after dark,
Sounds within sounds,
Songs within songs.
There are rhythms in the quiet
And pulses in the night,
Beats within beats,
Drums within drums.

Something calling in the embers,
Something crying in the rocks,
And out beyond the darkness
There are voices in the stars.

—Felice Holman

Harold & Burt & Sue & Amy, Etc.

Casey West

Some people love to talk. They enjoy talking so much that when they can't talk to people, they talk to animals—and even, to plants. Sometimes, it seems that the animals and plants understand what is being said, and in their own ways, respond. As you read this short story, notice how Mark treats his plant and how the plant responds.

This girl walked up to me in the hall and said, "Do you like plants?"

"No."

"Good," she said. "Take this one home."

I said, "I don't want it."

"Go on," she said, holding the pot out to me. "It's an *Aralia spinosa*. That's Latin. Just keep it for me, for a science experiment."

Larry, beside me, laughed. "He wouldn't know what to do with a plant. Actually, that's rather a nice specimen of *spinosa*. Why are you entrusting it to Mark?" (That's the way Larry talks.)

"It's a secret experiment."

"Mark'll fail, whatever it is."

I put out my hand. "I'll take it," I said.

"What are you going to do?" Larry asked. "Eat it for lunch?"

"Just water it twice a week and put it in an east window," she said.

"Yeah, yeah," I said. "Okay." I took the damp-feeling clay pot. The few little leaves were shiny, and there were thorns on the stems.

So I took the *Aralia spinosa* home with me, walking hunched over so that every Tom, Dick, and George wouldn't see me with this plant and start asking funny questions.

I put it on my window sill and started my records and put on my earphones. I like my sound kinda loud, but my mother has other ideas. She got into such a habit of saying, "Turn that thing down, Mark," that pretty soon she was saying it before I even turned it on. So she gave me the 'phones. Now it's in one ear and *in* the other, too; and the guitars meet in the middle right over the percussion; and that is where I *live*.

One day, I found this article about plants, and it had a picture of my own *Aralia spinosa* in it, so I read on. It also said some plants like to be talked to, as long as you talk nicely.

This was when I decided to do my reading aloud. It wouldn't bother me—I would be inside the groovy sound from my 'phones, and Old Spiny would be out there taking advantage of all this knowledge. If I came to any bad parts, like wars or famines or—especially—forest fires, I wouldn't read them aloud.

So every night, I plugged myself in and read to Old Spiny, and I watered him on Mondays and Thursdays. I noticed that he grew a couple of new leaves with a third one ready to uncurl, and his stems were growing very, very tall.

Sometimes Jill asked me, "How's the *Aralia*? Still alive?"

"Sure."

"I bet," she said.

Well, he was not only alive, he was thriving; but I wasn't going to argue with her. Besides, Larry was there.

Old Spiny and I really communicated. Naturally, he didn't talk back, or even groan and sigh like a dog, but it was nice to have company. Even when I didn't have anything to read, I still talked aloud to him. He just sat there and grew.

Leaves, sprouts, and stems seemed to pop out from him. He must love geometry was all I could say, and history and—very probably—science. I was also taking this poetry course. I needed something for third period, and it was that or dressmaking.

The first few days, I sat in the class with my chin in my hands and stared out the window. I was not going to like poetry, and no one could make me like it. But then, some of the sounds started to creep into my ears, and my brain opened up and let them in, and they were cool.

We had to memorize poems and dissect them like frogs in biology. We even had to write some of our own. So at home, I had to read poetry aloud to hear the rhythms. Old Spiny loved it. He grew to Whitman and Poe all right, but I could almost see him expanding to the rhymes and rhythms of Longfellow.

"You're getting to be a long fellow yourself," I told him one Thursday when I was watering him.

His branches had shot upward and outward, and so many new leaves had appeared that I could hardly keep up with the names. The first three that came were named Harold, Nancy, and Stephanie. But then, after Burt appeared, and Louise and Sue and Amy and James and Virginia and Matthew, I couldn't keep track, so I talked to them collectively.

"Leaves," I said, and then I told them what the history assignment or poem was for that night; and they listened and they grew.

I had to move the pot to the bookcase—it was too tall for the window sill—then, finally, to the floor.

Near the end of the year, Jill said to me, "Can you bring the plant to school tomorrow? First period?"

My heart thumped. I hadn't thought about giving Old Spiny back. "I don't know," I said.

"Listen, I need it. It's mine, you know."

"Okay," I said. "Don't get excited."

"Just wait in the hall until I call you," she said.

My mom and I wrapped a sheet of plastic around him, and I sat with the pot between my knees and the long stems bent over at the top.

I waited with Old Spiny outside the science room. Then the door whooshed open, and Jill came out.

"Okay," she said. "You can bring it in now." Then she stopped and threw up her hands. "Good grief!" she hollered. "What have you done?"

"Me?" I said. "What?" I looked around.

"Look at that plant!"

I did. There stood Old Spiny, tall as I was, leafy and green, holding out Nancy and James and Virginia and the others, and just

unrolling Albert and Frank. I didn't see anything wrong with him.

"You've ruined my experiment."

"Look, I don't understand your problem, but I'm going to find out." I picked up Old Spiny and carried him, swaying over my head, into the room.

The whole class started to laugh. Some even clapped. What was happening? Then they told me.

Jill had given Old Spiny to me to neglect. She had given another to Larry to care for, and she had taken one home to care for herself. (Those were the two scrawny, undersized plants on the table.) She and Larry, since they were conscientious types, would take such good care of their plants that they would thrive; while Old Brown Thumb (me) would ignore mine, and the poor thing would wither.

So I told them about the reading, the earphones, and the poetry, and about how sometimes I had even put the 'phones on Old Spiny and let him listen directly to the sounds.

"Actually," I said, "I think I proved your experiment. You will probably get an *A*. If you talk to plants and play them some music, then they grow—especially if you love them. I love this plant."

Jill did get an *A*, and she told me I could keep Old Spiny.

I told him on the way home: "Not so much poetry next semester, Spiny, or you'll grow too much and I'll have to send you to a greenhouse." But then I told him I didn't mean it.

"In fact," I said, "I'll get you a nice fern to keep you company. That's a *Filicales*, you know."

He knew.

---

1. Why did Jill give Mark the *Aralia spinosa?*
2. At first, Mark refused to take the plant. Why did he change his mind?
3. Do you agree with Mark's statement that he and Old Spiny "really communicated"? Why or why not?
4. Do you think that plants respond to words and music? Give reasons for your answer.
5. If you have a pet or a favorite plant, describe how you take care of it. If you don't have a pet or a plant, think of one that you would like to have and describe how you might care for it.

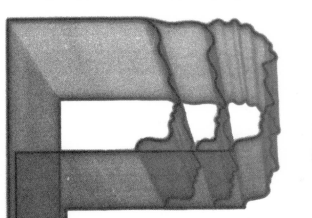
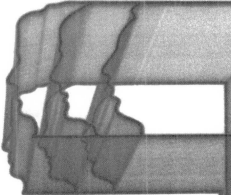

PERSON~TO~PERSON

Kathleen Galvin and Cassandra Book

When you talk, people listen. After they respond to what you have just said, it is your turn to listen. Then you respond to what they have said . . . and so on. This is an exchange. If each one has talked, listened, and understood, communication has taken place. But is this the only way that people communicate? In this essay, you will explore some of the other ways in which people communicate. As you read, notice how the diagrams clarify the ideas presented in the essay.

What must people do for communication to take place?

Usually, the answer is "speak and listen," and the people communicating are called the speaker and the listener. Although this is not a wrong answer, it is incomplete. What other terms could we use instead?

Consider the following:

IT WAS ABOUT 2 A.M., AND MY STOMACH WAS ACTING AS IF IT WERE MORNING. IT SEEMED ONLY REASONABLE TO FILL IT. AS I QUIETLY REACHED THE BOTTOM OF THE STAIRS, I SAW A LIGHT IN THE KITCHEN. I SILENTLY APPROACHED AND SAW MY BROTHER JOE, A LAW STUDENT, SLUMPED OVER A PILE OF BOOKS WITH HIS HEAD IN HIS HANDS. HE MUST HAVE HEARD SOMETHING, FOR HE TURNED, SAW ME, AND GROANED.

"YOU STARTLED ME," HE SAID. "I'M SO TIRED I CAN'T EVEN SEE THE PRINT ANY MORE."

In the preceding example, the hungry younger brother can understand certain things Joe is communicating without hearing him talk. If Joe is communicating through ways other than words, how is he communicating?

Joe is doing more than speaking. Instead of calling him a speaker, we can refer to him as a *sender* of communication. Joe's brother is doing more than just listening to Joe's words to know how he feels. He sees as well as hears Joe express tiredness. In this case, he would not be called a listener, but would be referred to as a *receiver* of communication. In any communication situation, we can refer to the persons involved as the

Sender(s) and Receiver(s)

Human senders and receivers use words and physical expressions to communicate. The words can be called *verbal* (word) communication. Physical expressions can be called *nonverbal* (wordless) communication.

A sender may communicate both verbally and nonverbally in the communication process. But what is being communicated between the sender and the receiver? Ideas? Words? Thoughts?

Any of the above could be correct. But because these terms sometimes refer only to verbal communication, we usually say that a *message* is being communicated. A message may be both verbal and nonverbal. For example, as a sender, you may communicate that you are warm by

—mopping your forehead and taking off your sweater (nonverbal);

—saying, "It's very warm in here" (verbal);

—mopping your forehead and taking off your sweater while saying, "It's very warm in here" (verbal and nonverbal).

If we were to diagram the process of communication, it would look like this:

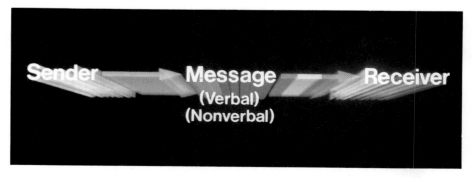

Do you think the diagram at the bottom of page 104 really represents a complete communication situation? What part of the communication process might be missing? Do receivers only receive the message? How can the sender tell if the receiver actually got the message?

Think about the following problems:

—How can you tell if your parents believe your excuse for being late?

—How do you know if your teacher agrees with your answers?

—How do you know if your friend likes the joke you just told?

Probably, you can tell how well you got your message across by listening to the receiver's words and voice inflections and by watching his or her movements. Receivers usually tell you in some way how accurately they are receiving your message. This reaction of the receiver is called *feedback*. Very simply, feedback is the way the receiver responds to the sender about the message that was sent. Once senders get the feedback, they can decide what the next message they send should contain.

Depending on the feedback to the three problems noted above, you might react in these ways:

—If your parents look annoyed and say that they have "heard that one before," you might guess that they do not believe your excuse.

—If your teacher looks puzzled and asks you to repeat the answer, you might conclude that he or she did not hear it or is confused by it.

—If you get a lot of laughs telling a joke about something, you will probably tell a few more. If no one responds to your joke, you will probably switch to joking about something else.

Feedback (verbal and nonverbal) tells the sender how he or she is doing. If we add feedback to the communication-process diagram, it looks like this:

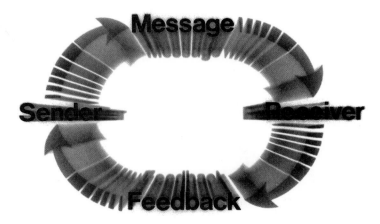

This diagram shows that communication is a two-way process. Communication is not complete when the sender's message reaches the receiver. The receiver's feedback must reach the sender to finish the communication process.

1. What four things make up the communication process?

2. People often prefer to talk about important matters face-to-face, rather than on the telephone. How can you explain this preference in terms of the communication process?

3. Communication is not always successful. If, for example, the receiver is not paying attention to the sender, communication cannot take place. Describe three other situations that might interfere with communication.

4. Do you think that understanding the ways in which we communicate will help people avoid problems in communication? Why or why not?

THE TISBURY TOADS

Russell Hoban

*Communicating with words can be fun, funny, and even a bit
dangerous. The danger lies, as the characters in this short story learn,
in using words without knowing what they mean. As you read, think
about the toads' unsuccessful experiment with words.*

"Ten miles to Tisbury," said the first toad. He was a toad of few
warts.

The second toad wasn't very warty either. "What's Tisbury?" he
said.

"I don't know," said the first toad.

"What's a mile?" said the second toad.

"I don't know," said the first toad.

"You don't know much," said the second toad. "If you're so
ignorant, how come you can read?"

"I don't know," said the first toad. "I just looked at the stone, and
it said ten miles to Tisbury."

"Maybe a mile's something good to eat," said the second toad.
"Maybe if we say we're Tisbury, somebody'll give us ten of them."

"Righty ho," said the first toad. "Let's have a go. I am hopful of
results."

They hopped into the mazy misty distance until they came to a
farmhouse.

They knocked at the door.

The farmer's wife opened the door, and when she saw the toads
she said, "Bad luck. Somebody's ill-wishing me."

"No such thing," said the first toad. "We're Tisbury."

"That's a new one," said the farmer's wife. "And I thought I'd heard everything. How can you be Tisbury when it's seven miles to Tisbury?"

"They were offering ten just a little while back," said the second toad. "I knew no good would come of this."

"You're right," said the first toad. "Let's hop to it before the price drops again."

They hopped back to the milestone and waited for somebody to give them ten miles.

"Maybe nobody knows we're here," said the second toad. "Let's sing out."

Both of them opened their mouths and bellowed, "We're Tisbury! Tisbury here!"

A crow was flying overhead, at the time, with a silver spoon he'd stolen in Tisbury. When he heard the shouts he thought, That's it. The whole town's after me just for one teeny-weeny silver spoon. Crime doesn't pay. He dropped the spoon and flew off cawing, "I didn't do it! I'm innocent!"

Both toads still had their mouths open shouting, and the silver spoon dropped right into toad number one. It happened so fast he never had time to swallow until it was in his stomach.

"They do a very hard, cold, smooth mile here," he said. "And still nine more to come. I don't know if I want to go ahead with this."

"It's all very well for you to talk," said the second toad. "I haven't even had a sniff of one." He opened his mouth and started shouting, "What about the other nine?"

"Corblimey!" said the crow in his crow's nest in the distance. "What a wide lot they are in Tisbury! I'd have sworn nobody saw me nick the other spoons."

He grabbed nine more spoons from his hoard and flew back over the two toads. "I'm innocent!" he yelled. "I didn't do it!" And he dropped the nine spoons one after the other like a bombardier.

Blip, blip, clink, clink, clink went the nine spoons as they rapidly shot into the open mouth of toad number two.

"They do a heavy mile here," he said. "And I have gotten so many of them in me, I am rooted to this spot. There is no hop in me any more. Why did we say we were Tisbury?"

"It seemed a good idea at the time," said the first toad. "How were we to know what a mile was? And even after I'd learned my lesson, you would not be convinced until you were laden well above your Plimsoll line."

"What's a Plimsoll line?" said the second toad.

"Let's not start one of those things again," said the first toad. "Our first consideration should be how to get you out of this predicament."

"You're a troublemaker, but you're loyal," said the second toad. "I'll give you that."

"The farmer's wife down the road was offering seven to Tisbury," said the first toad. "Miles must be pretty tight there. If we can get you that far, maybe we can make a deal."

"Not only have I no hop," said the second toad, "but I can't even bend, I am that stiff with the miles in me."

"Never say die," said the first toad. "I will push you there end over end." Which he did, loyal fellow that he was.

The first toad heaved the second toad up against the farmhouse door where he clinked heavily.

The farmer's wife opened the door. "You lot again," she said. "Best get out of here before I call the police."

"Listen, madam," said the second toad. "I have a lot of mileage in me. I am silverful and heavy laden. Do you happen to have a mile extractor handy?"

"Will you take away my warts if I do?" she said.

"How far do we have to take them?" said the first toad. "I'm pretty tired already."

"I don't care how far you take them," said the farmer's wife. "Just take them."

"Done," said the second toad. "Now unmile me."

The farmer's wife turned toad number two upside down and rapped his bottom smartly. There was a good deal of clinking on the floor. She unspooned the first toad as well.

"Well done," said both toads.

"You're lucky I was here to do it," she said. "Take my warts for it."

"It's your warts against ours, isn't it," said the first toad. "Maybe we're already as unsmooth as we want to be. Maybe we don't want to bandy warts with you."

"Take them," said the farmer's wife, "or I'll ring up Tisbury and tell about the spoons, and you'll be in jail before you can say a wart."

"All right," said both toads. "We've had too much of Tisbury already. Give us your warts and let us be gone."

She did and off they went. They were so wartbegone that they never did any more work. They became known as the slothful two toads.

1. What guess about a word's meaning did the toads make that got them into trouble?

2. Why did the crow drop silver spoons into the toads' mouths?

3. At the beginning of the story, you learned that the toads were toads "of few warts." Why did the author include this detail at the beginning of the story?

4. Most people constantly hear and see words they don't understand. So they make guesses about the words' meanings. Give an example of a word you have seen or heard, but that you don't understand. Make a guess about its meaning, and then compare your guess with a dictionary definition.

What Can a Poem Do?

Eve Merriam

Eve Merriam is a poet and writer. In this essay, she discusses the power of words in a poem to make music and paint pictures. As you read, think of poems you have read and compare your own experience with Eve Merriam's descriptions.

There is no rhyme for silver, but a poem can do just about anything else you want it to. It can be solemn or bouncy, gay or sad—as you yourself change your own moods. A poem, in fact, is very much like you, and that is quite natural, since there is a rhythm in your own body: in your pulse, in your heart beat, in the way you breathe, laugh, or cry; in the very way you speak. When you run or tap your feet—even when you sit still and dance only with your feelings—there is the rhythm of a poem. Many kinds of rhythms surround us every day of our lives, although we go on our way unaware of them until a poem comes along to bring the hidden music out into the open. There is the majestic rhythm of the changing seasons. The daily journey of daylight and darkness. The man-made rhythms of motors. The tides; the cycle of a seed growing; the great human experience of life, death, and new generations arising.

It is this built-in rhythm or meter, as it is called when it is very measured, that sets poetry apart from prose. A poem has its own portable music, like a transistor radio that you can carry with you. Just turn it on, tune in, and listen to the music flow: a poem will give you high tones, low tones, fast tones, slow tones.

How does it create these effects? In addition to rhythm or meter, very often, through rhyme endings. *A rhyme is a chime that rings in time*—like the little typewriter bell that pings out at the end of each row. It can be serious, like rhyming *breath* with *death*: it can be joyful, like matching *spring, wing,* and *sing*: it can also be funny. Thomas Bailey Aldrich, in *The Story of a Bad Boy,* claimed that his favorite rhyming poem was *Root beer/Sold here*. One of the shortest rhymes in the world is one that you probably see every day on your way to and from school. At the traffic intersection, when the green light turns red: *Go/Slow*. Not all poems have rhymes; blank verse and free verse are without it. But a rhyme at the end of a line is like a bow tying up a package—it keeps everything neat and tidy and at the same time gives it a festive air.

Another way that poetry expresses itself in musical terms is through alliteration. When the same consonant or vowel sound reappears, that is **alliteration**. It can be *l*ean, *l*ong, and *l*ovely; *s*weet, *s*nappy, *s*picy; *b*old, *b*rave. Or it can show up in the middle of a word, or near the end; and sometimes you have to hunt to find it, f*ar* off in a g*ar*den of *or*anges. But the musical effect is there. When you read a poem, you can go treasure-seeking and *l*ook for a*ll*iteration *l*etters a*ll* a*l*ong the *l*ines.

Still a third way that poetry's built-in music makes itself heard is through the use of **repetition**—of words, or entire phrases. They are used over and over (and sometimes over and over and over!) like a melody that returns so that you can recognize it as a familiar friend. The repetition may serve to lull you to rest: "hushaby, hushaby, sleep, my baby, sleep." Or it can startle you awake: "clang, clang, clang went the cymbal; bang, bang, bang went the drums."

You can make whatever kind of music you like with a poem. You can also paint pictures. In a poem, the pictures are called word-images. All of us, every day, use word-images when we talk. We say "it's hot as blazes," "she's slow as molasses," "he's a poke or a stick." We say "my heart was in my mouth" or "I felt all gooseflesh." Some of these word-images have become so worn out through usage that we call them **clichés**. A poem tries to create new word-pictures. Instead of saying hot as blazes, cold as ice, or slow as molasses, a poem seeks out new images for hot and cold and slow.

As you read more poems, and perhaps write some yourself, you will find that some word-pictures, or images, paint things exactly the way they look, and some paint them in terms of something quite the opposite—somewhat like the Roman god Janus, whose name we associate with the first month of the year, and who looked back to the old and forward to the new at the same time. An image in a poem may suit what you are describing so that it feels at home and fits like the old comfortable hat on your head; more often, it may seem strange and unexpected at first—as when the wind suddenly snatches the hat off your head.

You can make music with a poem. You can paint pictures. You can also be a sculptor and carve words into all kinds of shapes. You can make the words in a poem sputter like a fountain, as "the musty fust of a dusty road." You can turn words into tongue-twisters. You can play a game of tag with the words in a poem—use rhymes like a ball to toss back and forth. In fact, all kinds of games are possible.

A poem makes you aware of language so that even in prose you can enjoy using words more because you know what tricks they can do and what they can *not* do. Also, because a poem is condensed and makes every word count—like a telegram instead of a longer message—it can help you do setting-up exercises to stretch all five of your senses. When you read a poem, you also savor the texture of the words. You should be able to see, smell, hear, touch, and even taste in a richer, deeper way.

You can write a poem or read a poem about many things. About everything in the world in fact; about "a rolling leaf or a standstill wheel; laughter and grief, whatever you feel." It can express your mood or take you out of it. For, although it may seem surprising at first, even if you feel sad or lonely, when you read a poem that speaks of loneliness or sadness, you feel that emotion more intensely, but you also feel happier for sharing the poem's experience and for knowing that you are not isolated in your mood. In a way, it is like the relief of a rainstorm after sullen, glowering clouds; and after the rainstorm, a clearing of the sky.

You may not "get" all of a poem the first time you read it, because the words and the built-in music are so concentrated. Don't let it worry you; just go on to the end and then go back and read it again. You will find that the meaning begins to shine through. For a poem, with its rhythmic effects and use of word-pictures, has more than one level to explore. It becomes like a stone that you skim onto a lake; the ripples widen. New meanings unfold, and you have the pleasure of discovering more and more each time.

To come back to our original question, what can a poem do? Just about everything—even though there is no rhyme for silver.

[Or orange.
Any others?]

ALICE
THROUGH
THE
LOOKING-
GLASS

Lewis Carroll

In the fantasy, *Alice Through the Looking-Glass,* Lewis Carroll *makes* us ask these questions: Why does he write about such strange and ridiculous things? Is his writing nonsense, or does it mean something? If it means something, what *is* that something? There are no simple answers to these questions, but keep them in mind as you read about Alice's adventures.

She has stepped through a looking-glass, or mirror, in her home and found an exciting but strange world on the other side. In the Looking-Glass Room, she has found a book that, at first glance, seems to be written in a peculiar language. But when she holds the book up to the mirror, she discovers that she can read its reflection. What she reads is the poem, "Jabberwocky."

JABBERWOCKY

'Twas brillig, and the slithy toves
  Did gyre and gimble in the wabe;
All mimsy were the borogoves,
  And the mome raths outgrabe.

'Beware the Jabberwock, my son!
  The jaws that bite, the claws that catch!
Beware the Jubjub bird, and shun
  The frumious Bandersnatch!'

He took his vorpal sword in hand:
  Long time the manxome foe he sought—
So rested he by the Tumtum tree,
  And stood awhile in thought.

And as in uffish thought he stood,
  The Jabberwock, with eyes of flame,
Came whiffling through the tulgey wood,
  And burbled as it came!

One, two! One, two! And through and through
  The vorpal blade went snicker-snack!
He left it dead, and with its head
  He went galumphing back.

'And hast thou slain the Jabberwock?
  Come to my arms, my beamish boy!
O frabjous day! Callooh! Callay!'
  He chortled in his joy.

'Twas brillig, and the slithy toves
  Did gyre and gimble in the wabe;
All mimsy were the borogoves,
  And the mome raths outgrabe.

" 'It seems very pretty,' Alice said when she finished it, 'but it's
rather hard to understand!' (You see, she didn't like to confess, even
to herself, that she couldn't make it out at all.) 'Somehow, it seems
to fill my head with ideas—only I don't exactly know what they are!
However, *somebody* killed *something*. That's clear, at any rate—' "

Alice leaves the Looking-Glass Room in order to explore more of the world behind the mirror. In her travels, she meets a famous character.

HUMPTY DUMPTY

However, the egg only got larger and larger, and more and more human. When she had come within a few yards of it, she saw that it had eyes and a nose and mouth; and when she had come close to it, she saw clearly that it was **HUMPTY DUMPTY** himself. 'It can't be anybody else!' she said to herself. 'I'm as certain of it, as if his name were written all over his face!'

It might have been written a hundred times, easily, on that enormous face. Humpty Dumpty was sitting with his legs crossed on the top of a high wall—such a narrow one that Alice quite wondered how he could keep his balance—and, as his eyes were steadily fixed in the opposite direction and he didn't take the least notice of her, she thought he must be a stuffed figure.

'And how exactly like an egg he is!' she said aloud, standing with her hands ready to catch him, for she was every moment expecting him to fall.

'It's *very* provoking,' Humpty Dumpty said after a long silence, looking away from Alice as he spoke, 'to be called an egg—*very!*'

'I said you *looked* like an egg, Sir,' Alice gently explained. 'And some eggs are very pretty, you know,' she added, hoping to turn her remark into a sort of compliment.

'Some people,' said Humpty Dumpty, looking away from her as usual, 'have no more sense than a baby!'

Alice didn't know what to say to this. 'It wasn't at all like conversation,' she thought, as he never said anything to *her*; in fact, his last remark was evidently addressed to a tree—so she stood and softly repeated to herself:

> 'Humpty Dumpty sat on a wall;
> Humpty Dumpty had a great fall.
> All the King's horses and all the King's men
> Couldn't put Humpty Dumpty in his place again.'

'That last line is much too long for the poetry,' she added, almost out loud, forgetting that Humpty Dumpty would hear her.

'Don't stand chattering to yourself like that,' Humpty Dumpty said, looking at her for the first time, 'but tell me your name and your business.'

'My *name* is Alice, but—'

'It's a stupid enough name!' Humpty Dumpty interrupted impatiently. 'What does it mean?'

'*Must* a name mean something?' Alice asked doubtfully.

'Of course it must,' Humpty Dumpty said with a short laugh. '*My* name means the shape I am—and a good handsome shape it is, too. With a name like yours, you might be any shape, almost.'

'Why do you sit out here all alone?' said Alice, not wishing to begin an argument.

'Why, because there's nobody with me!' cried Humpty Dumpty. 'Did you think I didn't know the answer to *that*? Ask another.'

'Don't you think you'd be safer down on the ground?' Alice went on, not with any idea of making another riddle, but simply in her good-natured anxiety for the queer creature. 'That wall is so *very* narrow!'

'What tremendously easy riddles you ask!' Humpty Dumpty growled out. 'Of course I don't think so! Why, if ever I *did* fall off—which there's no chance of—but *if* I did,—Here he pursed his lips and looked so solemn and grand that Alice could hardly help laughing. '*If* I did fall,' he went on, '*the King has promised me*—ah, you may turn pale, if you like! You didn't think I was going to say that, did you? *The King has promised me—with his own mouth*—to—to—'

'To send all his horses and all his men,' Alice interrupted, rather unwisely.

'Now I declare that's too bad!' Humpty Dumpty cried, breaking into a sudden passion. 'You've been listening at doors—and behind trees—and down chimneys—or you couldn't have known it!'

'I haven't indeed!' Alice said very gently. 'It's in a book.'

'Ah, well! They may write such things in a *book*,' Humpty Dumpty said in a calmer tone. 'That's what you call a History of England, that is. Now take a good look at me! I'm one that has spoken to a King, *I* am. Mayhap you'll never see such another, and to show you I'm not proud, you may shake hands with me!' He grinned almost from ear to ear, as he leant forwards (and as nearly as possible fell off the wall in doing so) and offered Alice his hand. She watched him a little

anxiously as she took it. 'If he smiled much more, the ends of his mouth might meet behind,' she thought, 'and then I don't know *what* would happen to his head! I'm afraid it would come off!'

'Yes, all his horses and all his men,' Humpty Dumpty went on. 'They'd pick me up again in a minute, *they* would! However, this conversation is going on a little too fast. Let's go back to the last remark but one.'

'I'm afraid I can't quite remember it,' Alice said very politely.

'In that case, we may start fresh,' said Humpty Dumpty, 'and it's my turn to choose a subject—('He talks about it just as if it were a game!' thought Alice.) 'So here's a question for you. How old did you say you were?'

Alice made a short calculation and said, 'Seven years and six months.'

'Wrong!' Humpty Dumpty exclaimed triumphantly. 'You never said a word like it.'

'I thought you meant "How old *are* you?"' Alice explained.

'If I'd meant that, I'd have said it.' said Humpty Dumpty.

Alice didn't want to begin another argument, so she said nothing.

'Seven years and six months!' Humpty Dumpty repeated thoughtfully. 'An uncomfortable sort of age! Now if you'd asked *my* advice, I'd have said "Leave off at seven"—but it's too late now.'

'I never ask advice about growing,' Alice said indignantly.

'Too proud?' the other inquired.

Alice felt even more indignant at this suggestion. 'I mean,' she said, 'that one can't help growing older.'

'*One* can't, perhaps,' said Humpty Dumpty, 'but *two* can. With proper assistance, you might have left off at seven.'

'What a beautiful belt you've got on!' Alice suddenly remarked. (They had had quite enough of the subject of age, she thought; and if they were really to take turns in choosing subjects, it was her turn now.) 'At least,' she corrected herself on second thoughts, 'a beautiful cravat, I should have said—no, a belt, I mean—oh, I *beg* your pardon!' she added in dismay, for Humpty Dumpty looked thoroughly offended, and she began to wish she hadn't chosen that subject. 'If only I knew,' she thought to herself, 'which was neck and which was waist!'

Evidently, Humpty Dumpty was very angry, though he said nothing for a minute or two. When he *did* speak again, it was in a deep growl.

'It is a—*most*—*provoking*—thing,' he said at last, 'when a person doesn't know a cravat from a belt!'

'I know it's very ignorant of me,' Alice replied, in so humble a tone that Humpty Dumpty relented.

'It's a cravat, child, and a beautiful one, as you say. It's a present from the White King and Queen. There now!'

'Is it really?' said Alice, quite pleased to find she *had* chosen a good subject, after all.

'They gave it to me,' Humpty Dumpty continued thoughtfully, as he crossed one knee over the other and clasped his hands round it,—'for an un-birthday present.'

'I beg your pardon?' Alice said with a puzzled air.

'I'm not offended,' said Humpty Dumpty.

'I mean, what *is* an un-birthday present?'

'A present given when it isn't your birthday, of course.'

Alice considered a little. 'I like birthday presents best,' she said at last.

'You don't know what you're talking about!' said Humpty Dumpty. 'How many days are there in a year?'

'Three hundred and sixty-five,' said Alice.

'And how many birthdays have you?'

'One.'

'And if you take one from three hundred and sixty-five, what remains?'

'Three hundred and sixty-four, of course.'

Humpty Dumpty looked doubtful. 'I'd rather see that done on paper,' he said.

Alice couldn't help smiling as she took out her memorandum-book and worked the sum for him:

$$\begin{array}{r} 365 \\ \underline{1} \\ \underline{364} \end{array}$$

Humpty Dumpty took the book and looked at it very carefully. 'That *seems* to be done right—'he began.

'You're holding it upside down!' Alice interrupted.

'To be sure I was!' Humpty Dumpty said gaily, as she turned it around for him. 'I thought it looked a little queer. As I was saying, that *seems* to be done right—though I haven't time to look it over thoroughly just now—and that shows that there are three hundred and sixty-four days when you might get un-birthday presents—'

'Certainly,' said Alice.

'And only *one* for birthday presents, you know! There's glory for you!'

'I don't know what you mean by "glory," ' Alice said.

Humpty Dumpty smiled contemptuously. 'Of course you don't—till I tell you. I meant "there's a nice knock-down argument for you!" '

'But "glory" doesn't mean "a nice knock-down argument," 'Alice objected.

'When *I* use a word,' Humpty Dumpty said in rather a scornful tone, 'it means just what I choose it to mean—neither more nor less.'

'The question is,' said Alice, 'whether you *can* make words mean different things.'

'The question is,' said Humpty Dumpty, 'which is to be master—that's all.'

Alice was too much puzzled to say anything, so after a minute, Humpty Dumpty began again. 'They've a temper, some of them—particularly verbs, they're the proudest—adjectives you can do anything with, but not verbs—however, *I* can manage the whole lot! Impenetrability! That's what I say!'

'Would you tell me, please,' said Alice, 'what that means?'

'Now you talk like a reasonable child,' said Humpty Dumpty, looking very much pleased. 'I meant by "impenetrability" that we've had enough of that subject, and it would be just as well if you'd mention what you mean to do next, as I suppose you don't intend to stop here all the rest of your life.'

'That's a great deal to make one word mean,' Alice said in a thoughtful tone.

'When I make a word do a lot of work like that,' said Humpty Dumpty, 'I always pay it extra.'

'Oh!' said Alice. She was too much puzzled to make any other remark.

'Ah, you should see 'em come round me of a Saturday night,' Humpty Dumpty went on, wagging his head gravely from side to side, 'for to get their wages, you know.'

(Alice didn't venture to ask what he paid them with; and so, you see, I can't tell *you*.)

'You seem very clever at explaining words, Sir,' said Alice. 'Would you kindly tell me the meaning of the poem "Jabberwocky"?'

'Let's hear it,' said Humpty Dumpty. 'I can explain all the poems that ever were invented—and a good many that haven't been invented just yet.'

This sounded very hopeful, so Alice repeated the first verse:

> *'Twas brillig, and the slithy toves*
> *Did gyre and gimble in the wabe;*
> *All mimsy were the borogoves,*
> *And the mome raths outgrabe.*

'That's enough to begin with,' Humpty Dumpty interrupted: 'there are plenty of hard words there. "*Brillig*" means four o'clock in the afternoon—the time when you begin *broiling* things for dinner.'

'That'll do very well,' said Alice: 'and "*slithy*"?'

'Well, "*slithy*" means "lithe and slimy." "Lithe" is the same as "active." You see, it's like a portmanteau—there are two meanings packed up into one word.'

'I see it now,' Alice remarked thoughtfully: 'and what are "*toves*"?'

'Well, "*toves*" are something like badgers—they're something like lizards—and they're something like corkscrews.'

'They must be very curious creatures.'

'They are that,' said Humpty Dumpty: 'also they make their nests under sun-dials—also they live on cheese.'

'And what's to "*gyre*" and to "*gimble*"?'

'To "*gyre*" is to go round and round like a gyroscope. To "*gimble*" is to make holes like a gimlet.'

'And "*the wabe*" is the grass plot around a sun-dial, I suppose?' said Alice, surprised at her own ingenuity.

'Of course it is. It's called "*wabe*," you know, because it goes a long way before it, and a long way behind it—'

'And a long way beyond it on each side,' Alice added.

'Exactly so. Well then, "*mimsy*" is "flimsy and miserable" (there's another portmanteau for you), and a "*borogove*" is a thin shabby-looking bird with its feathers sticking out all around—something like a live mop.'

'And then "*mome raths*"?' said Alice. 'If I'm not giving you too much trouble?'

'Well, a "*rath*" is a sort of green pig; but "*mome*" I'm not certain about. I think it's short for "from home"—meaning that they'd lost their way, you know.'

'And what does "*outgrabe*" mean?'

'Well, "*outgribing*" is something between bellowing and whistling with a kind of sneeze in the middle; however, you'll hear it done, maybe—down in the wood yonder—and when you've once heard it, you'll be quite content. Who's been repeating all that hard stuff to you?'

'I read it in a book,' said Alice. 'But I had some poetry repeated to me, much easier than that, by—Tweedledee, I think.'

'As to poetry, you know,' said Humpty Dumpty, stretching out one of his great hands, '*I* can repeat poetry as well as other folk if it comes to that—'

'Oh, it needn't come to that!' Alice hastily said, hoping to keep him from beginning.

'The piece I'm going to repeat,' he went on without noticing her remark, 'was written entirely for your amusement.'

Alice felt that in that case she really *ought* to listen to it; so she sat down, and said 'Thank you' rather sadly.

> '*In winter, when the fields are white,*
> *I sing this song for your delight—*'

only I don't sing it,' he explained.

'I see you don't,' said Alice.

'If you can *see* whether I'm singing or not, you've sharper eyes than most,' Humpty Dumpty remarked severely. Alice was silent.

> '*In spring, when woods are getting green,*
> *I'll try and tell you what I mean.*'

'Thank you very much,' said Alice.

> '*In summer, when the days are long,*
> *Perhaps you'll understand my song:*
>
> *In autumn, when the leaves are brown,*
> *Take pen and ink and write it down.*'

'I will, if I can remember it so long,' said Alice.

'You needn't go on making remarks like that,' Humpty Dumpty said: 'they're not sensible, and they put me out.'

> '*I sent a message to the fish:*
> *I told them "This is what I wish."*
>
> *The little fishes of the sea,*
> *They sent an answer back to me.*
>
> *The little fishes' answer was*
> *"We cannot do it, Sir, because—"*'

'I'm afraid I don't quite understand,' said Alice.

'It gets easier further on,' Humpty Dumpty replied.

> '*I sent to them again to say*
> *"It will be better to obey."*
>
> *The fishes answered with a grin,*
> *"Why, what a temper you are in!"*
>
> *I told them once, I told them twice:*
> *They would not listen to advice.*
>
> *I took a kettle large and new,*
> *Fit for the deed I had to do.*

My heart went hop, my heart went thump;
I filled the kettle at the pump.

Then someone came to me and said
"The little fishes are in bed."

I said to him, I said it plain,
"Then you must wake them up again."

I said it very loud and clear;
I went and shouted in his ear.'

Humpty Dumpty raised his voice almost to a scream as he repeated this verse, and Alice thought with a shudder, 'I wouldn't have been the messenger for *anything!*'

'But he was very stiff and proud;
He said "You needn't shout so loud!"

And he was very proud and stiff;
He said "I'd go and wake them, if—"

I took a corkscrew from the shelf:
I went to wake them up myself.

And when I found the door was locked,
I pulled and pushed and kicked and knocked.

And when I found the door was shut,
I tried to turn the handle, but—'

There was a long pause.
'Is that all?' Alice timidly asked.
'That's all,' said Humpty Dumpty. 'Good-bye.'

'This was rather sudden,' Alice thought: but, after such a *very* strong hint that she ought to be going, she felt that it would hardly be civil to stay. So she held out her hand. 'Good-bye till we meet again!' she said as cheerfully as she could.

'I shouldn't know you again if we *did* meet,' Humpty Dumpty replied in a discontented tone, giving her one of his fingers to shake; 'you're so exactly like other people.'

'The *face* is what one goes by, generally,' Alice remarked in a thoughtful tone.

'That's just what I complain of,' said Humpty Dumpty. 'Your face is the same as everybody has—the two eyes, so—' (marking their places in the air with his thumb), 'nose in the middle, mouth under. It's always the same. Now if you had the two eyes on the same side of the nose, for instance—or the mouth at the top—that would be *some* help.'

'It wouldn't look nice,' Alice objected. But Humpty Dumpty only shut his eyes and said, 'Wait till you've tried.'

Alice waited a minute to see if he would speak again, but as he never opened his eyes or took any further notice of her, she said 'Good-bye!' once more; and, on getting no answer to this, she quietly walked away. But she couldn't help saying to herself as she went, 'Of all the unsatisfactory—' (she repeated this aloud, as it was a great comfort to have such a long word to say) 'of all the unsatisfactory people I *ever* met—' She never finished the sentence, for at this moment a heavy crash shook the forest from end to end.

---

1. Why was Humpty Dumpty not worried about falling off the wall?

2. Why did Alice say: "Of all the unsatisfactory people I *ever* met—"?

3. What kind of person do you think Humpty Dumpty was? Explain your answer.

4. Do you think Alice and Humpty Dumpty communicated well? Support your answer with examples from the story.

5. Humpty Dumpty said: "When *I* use a word . . . it means just what I choose it to mean—neither more nor less." What do you think would happen to communication if everyone used words this way? Why do you think so?

What's Behind the Word?

Harold Longman

Language is changing all the time. Words enter our language; they change in spelling and in meaning over time; and sometimes, they disappear because they are no longer useful. This history of a word is called its *etymology*. The etymologies of words have a great deal to do with the history of people and places. In these essays, you will read about two words that have long and unusual histories—and that are *still* a part of our language today.

TRUE LOVE—WITH A TOUCH OF SALT

> **pret • zel**   *n.*   A glazed, salted biscuit, usually baked in the form of a loose knot.

The Pennsylvania Dutch, who know as much about pretzels as anybody, say that pretzels are twisted as they are to represent angels with arms crossed in supplication.

This may or may not be; but in saying so, they have come extremely close to the original meaning of the word, which has as twisted a history as the pretzel itself.

In a long, involved sort of way, it comes from a medieval Latin word meaning "arm." What do arms have to do with pretzels? Quite a bit when the arms are entwined, if you want to believe the old legend.

Centuries ago, a young German woman was in love with a young man in her village. The young man, however, was either too shy to speak, or not interested. It was unthinkable, then, for a woman to approach a man; but with a little ingenuity, any bright woman could let her feelings be known.

It happened that the young man was to see her father on business. It was an opportunity not to be missed. What did she do? She baked some cookies.

When the young man came to the house, the young woman served a tray of cookies.

"What an interesting shape!" said the shy young man, looking at the cookies. "What do you call them?"

"*Brezitella*" (the Old German word for "little arms"), said the young woman. "They are entwined into a true love's knot." She gave the young man a long look.

It is hoped that he got the message.

Brezitella, in Old German, comes from the medieval Latin *braciola*, "little arms." In later German, *brezitella* became, more simply, *bretzel*, and then *pretzel*.

There are some who say it comes from the medieval Latin *bracellus*, "bracelet," perhaps because the sellers of pretzels stack them on a stick, like bracelets on an arm.

Whatever the truth of the matter, pretzels—thick, thin, curved, straight, crisp, or soft—have come a long way from the little German village. A popular snack, the chances are that you would never think of a pretzel as a message of love.

THE MUDDY SOLDIERS OF THE QUEEN

> **khak • i** *n.* 1. A color ranging from light sand to medium brown. 2. A stout cotton cloth of this color used for uniforms.

"More tea, Mr. Leeman?"

"Thank you, no, Colonel. Now about the matter we were discussing . . . "

"Ah, yes, the uniform fabric." The colonel looked out over the dusty Indian plain. A platoon of soldiers, their uniforms covered with mud, were moving toward them back to the compound. It was the year 1883—only seven years after Queen Victoria had been proclaimed Empress of India.

Mr. Leeman, turning to see what the colonel was watching, smiled. "They could do with a good wash," he said.

"Wash, sir? Nonsense! All our soldiers roll their uniforms in the dirt. *Khaki*, the natives call it—the Hindustani word for dirt, you know."

"And you permit this?" Mr. Leeman raised an eyebrow. It had seemed to him that discipline was lax in India, but for Her Majesty's soldiers to appear like dirty ragamuffins? Shocking!

"Permit it, sir? We have made it a rule. It is quite necessary. If our soldiers wore those whites you send from Manchester, they'd be picked off like birds in a grouse shoot. Only trouble is, the mud washes off in the rain." The colonel looked at the salesperson from the cotton firm. "You know," he said, "your firm could make quite a good thing of it, if you would only send us fabric of this *khaki* color that wouldn't fade in the sun."

"Interesting," said Mr. Leeman, "very interesting." He was suddenly overcome with a vision of supplying all the fabric for Her Majesty's army in India. Why, he could become a millionaire!

When he returned to England, he set to work at once. Together with a Lancashire dyer, he prepared sample after sample of dye. These, together with pieces of cotton twill, he brought home to Mrs. Leeman, who boiled them in a copper pan in her kitchen. It was not too hard to get the right color, but when dried in the sun, the cloth invariably faded.

Mr. Leeman, not about to give up, brought home still more samples for patient Mrs. Leeman to boil. One evening, when the copper pan was being used to cook dinner, Mrs. Leeman threw the fabric and dye into an old rusty pan, feeling that it wouldn't make much difference. She let it boil away on the back of the stove.

By accident, she had discovered the trick. This time, the fabric held its color. The chromium oxide dye was made fadeproof by the iron oxide from the rusty pot.

Leeman's vision of becoming a millionaire proved true enough. He and a friend formed a private company, and for more than half a century, they provided uniforms for the troops of the entire British Empire.

The Hindustani word was adopted; the fabric became known simply as *khaki*. So widely was it used that the uniforms came to be called *khakis* as well. For many a civilian, putting on khakis was merely another way of saying, "You're in the army now."

Whether khaki turned out to be the life-saving camouflage it was meant to be, no one knows—but at least Her Majesty's troops no longer had to roll in the mud.

1. Why did the young German woman bake cookies?
2. Why was Mr. Leeman's new cloth called *khaki*?
3. There is an old saying to the effect that great discoveries are often made by accident. Explain how the story of the invention of khaki cloth supports this idea.
4. In "True Love—With a Touch of Salt," the young woman invented a name for her cookies: "brezitella." People invent words or give old words new meanings all the time. One example is the word "rubberneck," which describes exactly the action of someone trying to get a look at something. Think of an event, object, or action. Then make up your own new word to describe it.

ON CAMERA, NOAH WEBSTER!

Claire Boiko

Claire Boiko has written a play about words. While writing about words, Ms. Boiko also has fun with words. She also has fun with television programs and commercials. She parodies—or pokes fun at by imitating—these programs and commercials. See if you can recognize the author's use of parody.

Characters

LEX LEXICON, *an announcer*	MARY MISNOMER	LARRY'S FATHER
PAULA PALABRA, *a newscaster*	MOTHER TONGUE	MR. LINGO
HAUNTED MAN	SINGING GROUP	PENELOPE PATOIS
THREE SPELLING DEMONS	CHORUS	VIRGINIA VERBAL
WHICH DOCTOR	LARRY	CAMERA OPERATOR

Setting: *A television studio. A large sign on rear wall reads:*

CHANNEL 26—ENTERTAINMENT AND EDUCATION FROM A TO Z.

A desk and chair are down left; a washing machine is at center; and down right are a table and chair; a small cart holding cooking utensils is nearby.

At Rise: LEX LEXICON, *carrying a dictionary, enters down right, followed by* CAMERA OPERATOR *pushing a TV camera. As* CAMERA OPERATOR *positions camera near desk,* LEX *speaks to audience.*

LEX: Have you ever noticed what a neglected book the dictionary has come to be? Oh, people open it now and then, but there are literally thousands of words gathering dust on their hyphens, never to be uttered by a single human voice. For instance—when was the last time you mentioned the muntjac, or barking deer? Why, I'll bet you didn't even know there was a barking deer. *(Points to dictionary)* It's right there—in the dictionary. Now, some of us feel that there should be equal time for the dictionary. We have come to the conclusion that the dictionary should have its own television channel and sponsors. So here, without further ado, is Channel 26—your doorway to a better vocabulary. *(He smiles and adjusts his tie.* CAMERA OPERATOR *moves in for a close-up of* LEX.) Good morning, Word Watchers of the World. This is Lex Lexicon, your staff announcer, welcoming you to Channel 26, operating on 50,000 megasyllables. Now we switch you to Paula Palabra with her summary of the news. Take it away, Paula . . .

(PAULA PALABRA *enters on the run, down left, a bulletin in her hand, and sits at desk. Sound of teletype clicking is heard.* CAMERA OPERATOR *directs camera toward* PAULA.

NOTE: CAMERA OPERATOR *follows each act with camera as it appears.)*

PAULA: Morning, Word Watchers. This is Paula Palabra, your anchorperson on the news front. Flash! An important bulletin has just come over the wires. Flash! Explorers report that they have found an area containing peace, harmony, friendship, health, wealth, and happiness. Don't everybody rush to buy a ticket, however. These items exist together only in one place—the dictionary! Take it away, Lex Lexicon. *(She runs off left.)*

LEX: And now . . . a message from our sponsor.

HAUNTED MAN *(Running in down right and falling to his knees in supplication):* Help me! Somebody help me! They're haunting me! The Spelling Demons! Here they come! (THREE SPELLING DEMONS *enter and dance around* HAUNTED MAN, *jabbing at him with their tridents.)*

DEMONS *(Ad lib):* A spell. A spell. We have you under a spell.

1ST DEMON: Spell "there." Is it *(spelling)* t-h-e-r-e?

2ND DEMON: Or is it *(spelling)* t-h-e-i-r?

HAUNTED MAN: I don't know! I don't know!

3RD DEMON: Maybe it's *(spelling)* t-h-e-y-apostrophe-r-e.

HAUNTED MAN: Apostrophes are catastrophes! Please, somebody . . . help me! (WHICH DOCTOR *dances on, waving a dictionary at* DEMONS, *who shriek and cover their eyes.)*

DEMONS: No, no! Take it away! You'll break our spell! *(They retreat fearfully.)*

WHICH DOCTOR: Be gone, Spelling Demons. I have the antidote for you. I am the Which Doctor and I bring this magical book. (WHICH DOCTOR *waves the dictionary at them. They exit right.)*

HAUNTED MAN: You have saved me. But why are you called the Which Doctor, and what is this wonderful book of magic?

WHICH DOCTOR: I am called the Which Doctor because I tell you *which* way to spell words correctly by using *this* dictionary.

HAUNTED MAN: Dictionary!

WHICH DOCTOR: Pick a word—any word at all. This book will show you how to spell it in one easy glance.

HAUNTED MAN: Oh, where has this dictionary been all my life?

WHICH DOCTOR: You will find it in your local bookcase. Remember— the dictionary is the all-time best

speller. Now, I must be off to rescue more unfortunates. You'd be surprised how many poor souls are caught between double *r*'s and double *t*'s. Farewell! That's *(spelling)* f-a-r-e-w-e-l-l. *(Exits)*

HAUNTED MAN: I will run right down to my local bookcase and find a dictionary. Those Spelling Demons haven't seen the last of me! *(He runs off down right.)*

LEX: And now . . . Channel 26 presents the moving story of the girl-next-door's fight for truth, happiness, and the presidency of her class. Let's look in at the language laundromat where Mary Misnomer is trying to brighten her campaign speech . . . **MARY MISNOMER** *enters up left, a laundry basket full of crumpled papers under her arm. She takes out a paper and tries to smooth it out.)*

MARY: Just look at that dull, lifeless speech. "Whatchamacallits, please vote for me for class thingamajig because . . . and also . . . and in conclusion . . ." I can't give a speech like this. Oh dear, why is my prattle always tattle-tale gray? *(MOTHER TONGUE enters down left, a dictionary in her hand.)*

MOTHER TONGUE *(Crossing to MARY)*: Did I hear you say your speeches were dull and lifeless, dearie? Let Mother Tongue, the linguist, help you. Let me introduce you to the dictionary. *(MARY puts crumpled papers into washing machine. Sound of a noisy washing machine is heard. MOTHER TONGUE drops dictionary into machine.)* Now let's add a few words to the wash. You know, the

dictionary contains five active ingredients to clarify your thoughts:
synonyms for sparkle, antonyms for
action, homonyms for humor, and
metonyms for magnificence. Now,
dearie, your speech is ready. Try it
on for size. (**MARY** *takes fresh piece
of paper from machine and reads it*.)

MARY: "Students: As your candidate
for president of this class, I request
the honor of your vote. If I am
elected, as your faithful president, I
will guarantee you all a two-hour
lunch period, a reduction in the
homework load, and a field trip to
Disneyland." (*Looks up*) My good-
ness, what a difference a dictionary
makes!

MOTHER TONGUE: All the difference in
the word! Don't forget, dearie—

If your speech needs a bleach,
Help for you is right in reach.
Do not fume and do not rage.
Let your fingering do the lingering
On the dictionary page!
Get the giant, unabridged size—
today!

(**MARY** *and* **MOTHER TONGUE** *exit
down left*.)

LEX: And now, a few words from
our sponsor . . . (**SINGING GROUP**
enters up right and strikes a pose.)

SINGING GROUP (*Singing to the tune of
"All God's Chillun Got Shoes"*):

I love soup,
You love soup,
Everybody's children love soup.
(*Humming*) Hm-m-m-m.

(**LARRY** *runs in down right*. **LARRY's**
FATHER *follows, holding out bowl
and spoon*.)

LARRY: I hate soup!

FATHER: But, Larry, soup is good for
you. Now take a spoonful for Father.
(**LARRY** *sits at table, arms folded
stubbornly*.)

LARRY: I wouldn't take a spoonful
even for Wonder Woman. (**MR. LINGO**
*zooms across stage from up right. He
crosses to* **LARRY**.)

MR. LINGO: Man-from-Word!
Man-from-Word! What seems to be
the problem here?

FATHER: Why, it's Mr. Lingo, the
Man-from-Word. Oh, Mr. Lingo,
Larry won't eat his nice soup.

LARRY: Aw, it tastes like dishwater.

MR. LINGO (*Sipping soup*): Hm-m-m.
So it does. (*He takes a bowl from
his briefcase*.) Here Larry—try a
bowl of "Adjective Soup."

FATHER *and* **LARRY**: Adjective Soup? (**LARRY** *tastes it doubtfully, then downs it with gusto.*)

LARRY: Oh, boy! Savory . . . delectable . . . toothsome . . . gusty . . . scrumptious . . . yummy . . .

MR. LINGO (*Patting his head*): That's enough, Larry. See—he's getting the benefit of all those healthful adjectives already.

LARRY: Flavorful—mouthwatering—piquant. . .

MR. LINGO: Enough, Larry. (*To audience*) When you feel that life is one long bowl of dishwater, spice up your soup and soup up your spice with adjectives like—

LARRY: Peppery . . . nippy . . . snappy . . . gingery. . .

MR. LINGO (*Putting hand over* **LARRY'S** *mouth*): And others too numerous to mention. All these adjectives come to you prepackaged, alphabetized, and ready to use in this handy, easy-to-open package—the dictionary! (*He zooms off up right, with* **LARRY** *and* **FATHER** *following.*)

SINGING GROUP (*Singing*):

I love words,
You love words,
Everyone's children love words.
(*Humming*) Hm-m-m.
(*They exit down right.*)

LEX: And now . . . for you lovers of gourmet glossaries, here is your favorite queen of the cuisine, Ms. Penelope Patois. What's cooking, Penelope? (**PENELOPE PATOIS** *enters up right with large bowl. She goes to table.*)

PENELOPE: Hello there, food-for-thought fans. Today we're going to make a really exciting international dish: "Polyglot Pie!" All ready? All righty! Take your chopping boards and half a cup of assorted Greek epithets. Now, mince your words well. (*She pours out wooden letters and pretends to chop them. Then she returns them to bowl and tosses them as she speaks.*) Then take several finely parsed Chinese sentences and combine with some well-aged Sanskrit roots. Stir rapidly. Add a little French phrase here, and a little Spanish phrase there, turning the phrases well. There's nothing like a well-turned French phrase, is there? Now toss in several salty Siamese sayings and a couple of Norwegian notions. Garnish it all prettily with asterisks and a dash of a dash. All ready? All righty! Now bake it in a moderate oven for at least forty minutes. We don't want any half-baked notions, do we? Now, take your pie out of the oven. (*From the cart, she takes a pie decorated with flags of all nations.*) If you have followed instructions, your "Polyglot Pie" should look just like this one. (*She sniffs it, then vigorously shakes a pepper shaker over it.*) It needs just a little more Italian accent. There, isn't that heavenly? You can eat your words in twenty-seven languages. Now, if you want my recipe, all you have to do is print the word *dictionary* on a large piece of paper and present it to your neighborhood librarian. Tune in next week, won't you? We're going to learn to make "Swedish Idioms on the Half-Shell." Toodle-oo! (*She shakes pepper shaker at audience, and exits down right.*)

LEX: It's time now for Channel 26 to sign off. But before we do, here is our "Thought for the Day," brought to you by the pensive Virginia Verbal. (**VIRGINIA VERBAL** *enters with dictionary,* **CHORUS** *enters, forms a semi-circle behind her, and hums "Home, Sweet Home," as she speaks.*)

VIRGINIA (*Crossing down center*):

Feeling kind of sad and low?
Feeling mighty blue?
Somewhere in this great big world,
A good word waits for you.

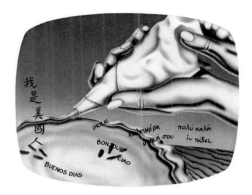

(*She points to the open dictionary.*)

CHORUS (*In unison*):

Open up your dictionary,
Look upon each page.
Happy words await your glance,
From every clime and age.

VIRGINIA (*As* **CHORUS** *hums*):

So take a word that's cheery;
If they are small, take two.
For somewhere in this great big world,
A good word waits—for you.

LEX: Yes, there's no substitute for words. Why, I can't even imagine a world without words—because I even *imagine* with words. Words are the indispensable building blocks of our minds. We ought to take care of them.

1ST SOLO: How do you take care of words?

LEX: Why, Channel 26 gave us a clue. We take care of words by using them effectively and by spelling them correctly. Don't use the same tired old words all the time.

6TH SOLO: I know a tired word—*interesting*. That word should be retired!

5TH SOLO: But if you take away *interesting*, what will I use in my composition when I want to talk about people and places and things?

LARRY (*Running in, followed by* **MR. LINGO**): I know! I know! Try stimulating . . . inspiring . . . rousing . . . electrifying . . . (**MR. LINGO** *leads him offstage*.)

LEX: Yes, folks, take care of your words, and your words will take care of you. Keep them polished and ready, and they'll trip off the tip of your tongue.

CHORUS: You said a mouthful!

LEX: Now, Channel 26 bids you *adieu*, *adios*, and so long. We sign off with our last word of the day: the motto of Noah Webster himself. . .

ALL (*slowly*): A word to the wise—is sufficient. (*Curtain*)

---

1. For what reason was Channel 26 founded?
2. How did Mr. Lingo get Larry to eat his soup?
3. In this play *about* words, the author had fun *with* words. Give two examples of the tricks she played with words.
4. This play parodied a number of things you see on television. Describe the kinds of programs and commercials which the play parodied.
5. Why, according to the play, should we use the dictionary?

A History of the English Language

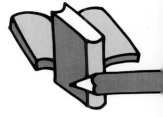

No one knows exactly how language began. People called *linguists* have tried to trace the origins of language. Linguists generally believe that one important early language was called *Indo-European*. The people who spoke it lived between India and Europe.

The Indo-Europeans eventually broke into smaller groups. As these groups moved to different areas, their language slowly changed. New words came into their vocabulary. The pronunciations and spellings of words also changed. Eventually no one spoke Indo-European. Instead each group had its own language. Some languages that grew from Indo-European are Spanish, French, Russian, Italian, German, and English.

ACTIVITY A   Many words in English come from other languages. Look up each word below in a dictionary. Write the word and the language from which it comes on your paper.

1. kimono	**2.** fiesta	**3.** tomahawk
4. typhoon	**5.** piano	**6.** balalaika
7. igloo	**8.** bazaar	**9.** kangaroo
10. sauerkraut	**11.** pretzel	**12.** boutique

English is one of the languages that grew from Indo-European. However, the way English is spoken today is not the way it has always been spoken. English has gone through three major periods. The earliest English is called *Old English*. It was spoken by people called Jutes, Angles, and Saxons. They moved to England in 449 A.D.

Later, in 1066 A.D., a French duke named William conquered England. Many French people moved to England. Consequently, many French words replaced Old-English words. This was the start of *Middle English*.

The period of Middle English lasted until around 1450 A.D. At that time, the language began to change to *Modern English*. Modern English is the English that we speak today.

ACTIVITY B Pronounce each of the following Middle English words just as it is spelled. Write each word with its correct Modern English spelling.

1. Aprille
2. poyson
3. nyght
4. syde
5. depe
6. erly
7. hoom
8. streem
9. melodye

You know that spellings and pronunciations of words in English have changed over a period of time. In addition, the meanings of words have changed. For example, the word *naughty* used to mean "having nothing, poor." Today, *naughty* means "not behaving properly."

ACTIVITY C Below is a list of words and their former meanings. After each word is a sentence using the word in its old context. Write the modern-day meaning of each word. Then write a sentence using the word in its modern context. Use a dictionary if necessary.

1. **nice:** ignorant, foolish
   The <u>nice</u> person gambled away all his money.

2. **villain:** a rude person from the country
   The <u>villain</u> offended many people he met in the city.

3. **bully:** a fine fellow
   Everyone who knew the <u>bully</u> admired him.

4. **tremendous:** terrifying, frightening
   We had a <u>tremendous</u> trip through the bad storm

Today the English language continues to change and grow. Because of progress in science and technology, words like *astronaut* and *bionics* have entered our vocabulary in recent years.

ACTIVITY D Use a dictionary to find the meaning of each word below. Write the meaning of each word on your paper.

1. astronaut
2. sputnik
3. cassette
4. bionics
5. aerospace
6. quadraphonic
7. laser
8. retrorocket
9. Cinerama

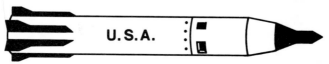

Prefixes

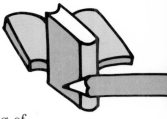

A *prefix* is a letter or group of letters added to the beginning of a base or root. Adding a prefix usually changes the meaning of the word. Here are some common prefixes and their meanings:

Prefix	Meaning	Example
equi-	equal	equiangular (having equal angles)
mis-	wrong, poorly	misjudge (judge poorly)
anti-	against	antisocial (against being social)
inter-	between, among	interchange (change between)
sub-	under, below	substandard (below standard)
trans-	across, through	transship (ship across)
ex-	former, out	ex-student (former student)
		expand (spread out)

ACTIVITY A   Write a word which begins with a prefix to replace the underlined words in each sentence.

1. The library and school are <u>equally distant</u> from my house.
2. The temperature is <u>below normal</u> for this time of year.
3. We made an <u>across the Atlantic</u> flight last month.
4. The <u>former president</u> visited the White House in May.
5. Our country has many <u>against aircraft</u> missiles in stock.
6. They <u>behave poorly</u> every chance they get.
7. The <u>between nations</u> agreement went into effect.
8. The official <u>used in a wrong way</u> the funds given to him.

ACTIVITY B   Write each sentence and supply the missing word.

1. The word *extend* means "to stretch _____ ."
2. The word *equilateral* means "having _____ sides."
3. The word *submarine* means "_____ water."
4. The word *misread* means "to read _____ ."
5. The word *antifreeze* means "a substance to protect _____ freezing."
6. The word *transcend* means "to pass _____ ."
7. The word *interracial* means "_____ races."
8. The word *ex-friend* means "_____ friend."

Synonyms and Antonyms

A *synonym* is a word that has the same or nearly the same meaning as another word. For example, *pretend* is a synonym for *imagine*. *Large* is a synonym for *big*.

An *antonym* is a word that has the opposite meaning of another word. For example, *small* is an antonym for *large*. *Lose* is an antonym for *find*.

ACTIVITY A   Write the word that is a synonym for the first word in each line. Use a dictionary if necessary.

1. **yield:** pray   surrender   hide   attempt   turn
2. **ban:** forbid   wrap   protect   pass   crawl
3. **remark:** verse   plan   surprise   story   comment
4. **desire:** event   curse   wish   agreement   total
5. **companion:** enemy   president   soldier   leader   friend
6. **mature:** ripe   shrunken   bossy   regular   tardy
7. **maximum:** closest   truest   farthest   most   worst

ACTIVITY B   Write the word that is an antonym for the first word in each line. Use a dictionary if necessary.

1. **create:** build   destroy   dig   estimate   multiply
2. **depart:** explore   prepare   return   mend   request
3. **lenient:** happy   loose   mean   silly   strict
4. **wealthy:** poor   friendly   perfect   clumsy   tired
5. **polite:** thoughtful   nervous   calm   rude   mournful
6. **truthful:** angry   concerned   dishonest   ignorant   merry
7. **taut:** tight   grand   sorry   loose   intelligent

ACTIVITY C   Choose the word in each group that is either a synonym or an antonym for the first word. Write the word on your paper. Then write whether it is a *synonym* or an *antonym*.

1. **remember:** pronounce   forget   promote   envy   depend
2. **promptly:** carefully   normally   fully   immediately   nearly
3. **gigantic:** pleasant   boring   dangerous   tiny   noisy
4. **silent:** breezy   quiet   busy   modern   tough
5. **stretch:** lift   fold   dirty   break   expand
6. **request:** discover   ask   conclude   confuse   terrify
7. **separate:** accept   join   wash   relieve   prove

Using the Thesaurus

You know that a *synonym* is a word with the same or nearly the same meaning as another word. There are many synonyms in the English language. One place to find them is in a thesaurus.

A *thesaurus* is a book that lists synonyms for many words. Some thesauruses list their words and synonyms alphabetically. Here is what a thesaurus entry might look like:

laugh	cackle, chuckle, crow, giggle, guffaw, roar, shriek, snicker

This entry lists several synonyms for the word *laugh*. Each word names a different kind of laugh. When you choose a synonym in your writing, use the most specific word to express your idea.

ACTIVITY A   Read the thesaurus entry for the word *talk*. Then write each sentence on your paper using the best possible synonym.

talk	argue, confess, divulge, exclaim, express, gossip, speak

1. The neighbors met each morning to _____ about other people.
2. Both lawyers _____ loudly before the judge warned them to stop.
3. The suspect _____ to a detective that he was guilty.
4. Our teacher _____ about William Shakespeare this morning.
5. "I can't believe it!" she _____ in surprise.
6. _____ yourself clearly so others will understand you.
7. The scientist would not _____ the secret of the experiment.

ACTIVITY B   Each sentence below uses the same word several times. Replace each underlined word with a different, more specific synonym. Write the complete sentence on your paper. Use a thesaurus if necessary.

1. The <u>nice</u> children played in a <u>nice</u> park on a <u>nice</u> day.
2. A <u>big</u> elephant escaped from a <u>big</u> truck at the <u>big</u> zoo.
3. Two <u>bad</u> dogs stole some <u>bad</u> apples from a <u>bad</u> store owner.
4. The <u>small</u> ant crawled to its <u>small</u> home on a <u>small</u> hill.

ACTIONS SPEAK LOUDER THAN WORDS

Kathlyn Gay

People communicate with words, but they also use a silent language of gestures and other body signals. Body language, though we seldom think about it, plays an important role in our daily lives. In this essay on body language, the author discusses some of the ways we communicate without using words. As you read, think about the body language you use and the messages people send you by using body language.

Thump down the stairs and shuffle across the family room in your house. Plop onto a chair, then slide yourself down until the end of your spine is balanced on the edge of the seat. Slouch that way, with your arms crossed and your lips pressed tightly together. Lower your eyes and stare at your crossed arms. Pay no attention to anyone else in your household. Do not speak during the few minutes it takes to perform these actions.

If members of your family watch this silent performance, your father might growl: "Hey, shape up! You have to get ready for school whether you like it or not!"

Your mother might ask: "What's wrong? Don't you feel well?"

A younger sister or brother might tease: "You are mad and I am glad . . ."

Even though you did not speak a single word, each member of your family received some kind of message. Your father decided you didn't want to go to school. Your mother thought you were sick, and to a sister or brother it seemed you were angry about something.

So who was right?

Maybe none of your family or maybe each of them picked up one small part of your message.

With your silent actions, you could have been saying you didn't want to talk to anyone that morning. Possibly you woke up with a headache. You got out of bed and couldn't find the right clothes to wear. Then you really were upset and angry. Whatever the case, you would hardly have to explain how you felt because your actions had "spoken" for you. You had shown that something was definitely wrong, or at least not quite in balance.

The point is, without ever uttering a sound, a person can say all kinds of things with body positions (or postures) and movements (or gestures). A person "speaks" with facial expressions—the variety of ways the eyes and mouth move or the forehead wrinkles. A person "talks" by using certain hand and arm gestures. The way a person holds his or her head and the way he or she walks, sits, or stands—various parts of the body moving separately or together—send messages to an observer.

Often words and actions are used at the same time to put across messages. Suppose your famly moves into a new neighborhood. The first time you meet other young people on the block, you would want to get acquainted. If you asked to join a game or walk with the other kids to a neighborhood store, you might smile a lot (without ever realizing it). You could share part of a candy bar as you talk to a stranger. Your words and gestures say, "I'm friendly." Possibly you'd toss a ball out to one of the neighborhood kids. You would hold your hands up to catch the ball on a return throw. Not only your words, but your actions also would say: "I'd like you to throw the ball and let me be part of your fun."

Scientists who study human behavior point out that the gesture—which can be almost any motion of the body—was probably the first form of human speech. The experts also tell us that the hands and face are the most natural parts of the body to use for gestures. Almost everyone begins very early in life to communicate with some kind of body movement.

In fact, without realizing it, all of us learn a body language as well as a language that is verbalized, or spoken. Young children, for example, copy various kinds of behavior and learn the meaning of a gesture by seeing it over and over again in a particular situation. The up-and-down or the back-and-forth movements of the head are gestures taught even to babies. They soon realize that the nod of a head means "yes" and the shake of the head means "no."

Then, too, you've seen grown-ups teach youngsters how to wave or point. These actions are repeated and explained with directives like "Say bye-bye" or "Show us the kitty." Toddlers often mimic older brothers or sisters in a family. Did you ever see a little guy stand with his feet spread apart, his hands clenched in fists on his hips, his chin jutting out—an exact miniature of a big brother who is arguing or defending someone? Many young children also copy actions by modeling themselves after older children on the school playground, in the halls, or at assemblies.

Most of us are not aware of all the body movements, gestures, facial expressions, and postures we learn through modeling or copying the behavior of others. Young children, for example, often mimic the actions of older brothers or sisters. They learn not only useful skills, such as how to dress and groom themselves, but also how to sit, stand, walk, and perform other actions for specific situations.

Some types of gestures, like the handshake, may have originated centuries ago. One story that tells how the handshake began describes a knight in armor traveling by horseback through a deserted wood. He sees another knight in the distance coming toward him. Quickly, the first knight shifts his sword from his right hand to his left and raises his right hand high to show the approaching knight that his weapon hand is empty. That gesture, saying, "Look, I'm unarmed and friendly," has finally come to be the greeting we know—reaching out an arm to another person, grasping that person's hand and shaking it.

Other types of body language may be instinctive. That is, people seem to do "what comes naturally." The smile is an action that is basic to almost all peoples. Often it means that the person who is smiling is feeling some kind of pleasure. But some smiles say "I'm embarrassed" or "I'm shy" or "Get away from me because I'm feeling uptight!" A fake smile says, "I don't think that's so funny!"

People reinforce or support the words they use with many kinds of body language. Gestures dramatize what a person actually says. For example, a hug from a grown-up, who at the same time is telling you, "I'm sorry you were hurt," can really make you feel the grown-up's sincerity. The words express sympathy, but combined with the gesture, you are bound to feel comforted.

In the same way, a frown on a person's face, along with harsh words, make it quite clear that anger, annoyance, or irritation is being expressed. Or how about seeing people with clenched fists and tight lips waiting to get a flu shot from a nurse? If those people say they're worried or scared, there's no doubt about it. You believe them. Their gestures and actions support what they say.

You may not be aware of all the many kinds of gestures that accompany verbal forms of communication. But just about everyone has had the experience of trying to give someone else directions on how to get to a certain place. It's difficult to give directions without the use of one's hands and arms. Suppose you want to describe a monster movie. Could you do it without gestures? What happens when you want to let someone know you have a stomachache? Usually, you clutch your middle as you give a verbal explanation about where you hurt. Try describing some exciting event like a great football play or the thrill of a carnival ride. During the recital,

dozens of different gestures may be used to show, as well as tell.

In recent years, a few behavior experts have begun to study body language in a scientific manner. This study, called *kinesics*, involves many procedures such as observing people, filming their behavior, and recording their actions. Everything from a blink of the eye to a wiggle of a foot is analyzed and categorized. These body movements are part of a special kind of language that can—with or without verbal speech—indicate fear, sadness, joy, anger, confusion, worry, and other emotions.

Almost everyone can discover how to read or use silent messages. To develop the ability, you can observe the actions of people around you—your friends, relatives, members of your immediate family, classmates, and so on. You can also become aware of what you do with your body—what gestures and movements you use and how these communicate with others.

1. How do people communicate without words?
2. How, according to legend, did the handshake develop?
3. Describe the body language you might use to communicate silently the following messages: "I'm hungry"; "I'm happy"; "Hello"; "I don't know."
4. Make a point of observing people's nonverbal communication during the next few days. Choose three examples. Describe the body signals and what the signals communicated.

Charades

Have you ever played "Charades"? In this game, one player must use body language alone to send a message to other players who then try to guess what he or she is "saying." As you can see in this cartoon, it is not always easy to "say" with gestures only, exactly what you mean. What does this cartoon tell you about the problems of communicating without words?

Drawing by C.E.M.; © 1961
The New Yorker Magazine, Inc.

TALKING HANDS

Indian Sign Language

Sign language is a way of using gestures to communicate. Long before Europeans came to America, American Indian tribes shared a system of hand signs. Using these hand signs, people from two tribes that spoke different languages could understand one another. Nearly all the American Indian tribes used and understood sign language. It is still used today.

As you read this excerpt from the book, *Indian Sign Language*, by Robert Hofsinde (Gray-Wolf), try out the signs for yourself and think about how they developed.

MAN Hold right hand in front of chest, index finger pointing up, and raise it in front of face. Also MALE.

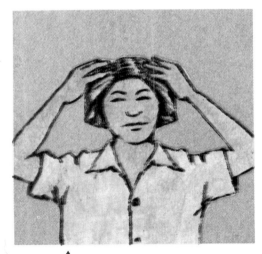

WOMAN With fingers of both hands slightly curved, make downward motions from top of head to shoulders, as if combing long hair. Also FEMALE.

FATHER Touch right side of chest with closed right hand several times.

MOTHER Touch left side of chest in same way as for FATHER.

BROTHER Touch lips with index and second fingers, and move hand straight out from mouth. Then sign MAN. Also PARTNER.

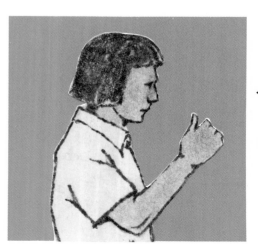

SISTER Sign WOMAN. Then touch lips and move hand as for BROTHER.

BOY Sign MAN, and indicate boy's height with flat right hand.

GIRL Sign WOMAN, and indicate height, as above.

ALL Move flat right hand in a horizontal circle, clockwise, in front of chest.

I (ME) Point to self with right thumb.

YOU Point to person with right thumb.

HE (HIM)
SHE (HER) { If person is present, point to him or her; if person is not present, sign MAN or WOMAN.

THEY (THEM)
WE (US) { Point to persons, and sign ALL.

MY (MINE)
HIS or HERS
YOURS
OURS
THEIRS { Hold right hand in front of neck, thumb up, and move it two or three inches forward, turning the wrist so the thumb points to the person or persons you wish to indicate. Also OWN, GET, HAVE.

FRIEND Hold hand as shown, then raise it to the side of the face. Meaning: Growing up together. Some American Indian tribes make the sign for friend by shaking their own hands.

NEAR (CLOSE) Hold left arm as shown, fingers curved slightly. Then bring hand in until tips of fingers touch shoulder.

FAR (DISTANT) Reverse of NEAR. Start at shoulder and bring hand out to curved position. If showing great distance, extend arm to full length.

Handtalk

American Indians are not the only ones to have developed and used a sign language. Deaf people also use sign language to communicate with each other and with people who can hear. In these pages from *Handtalk*, a book by Remy Charlip, Mary Beth, and George Ancona, you will learn about two sign-systems that deaf people often use: **finger spelling**—forming words letter-by-letter with the fingers of one hand; and **signing**—making a picture or sign with one or two hands for each word or idea.

Hands are not the only tools of sign language. You can make the single sign for *big* also mean *large, huge,* or *gigantic* by changing the feeling of the gesture. You can use your eyes, face, and body to show exactly what, or how much, you mean.

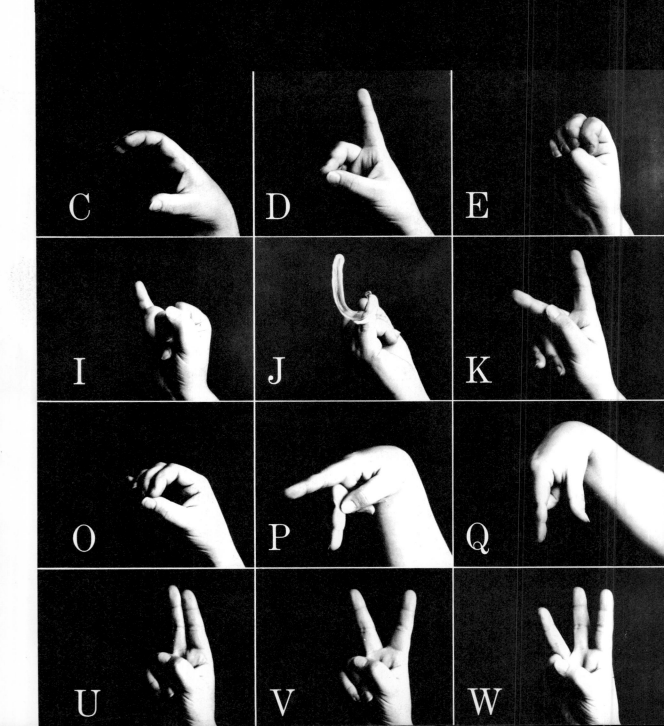

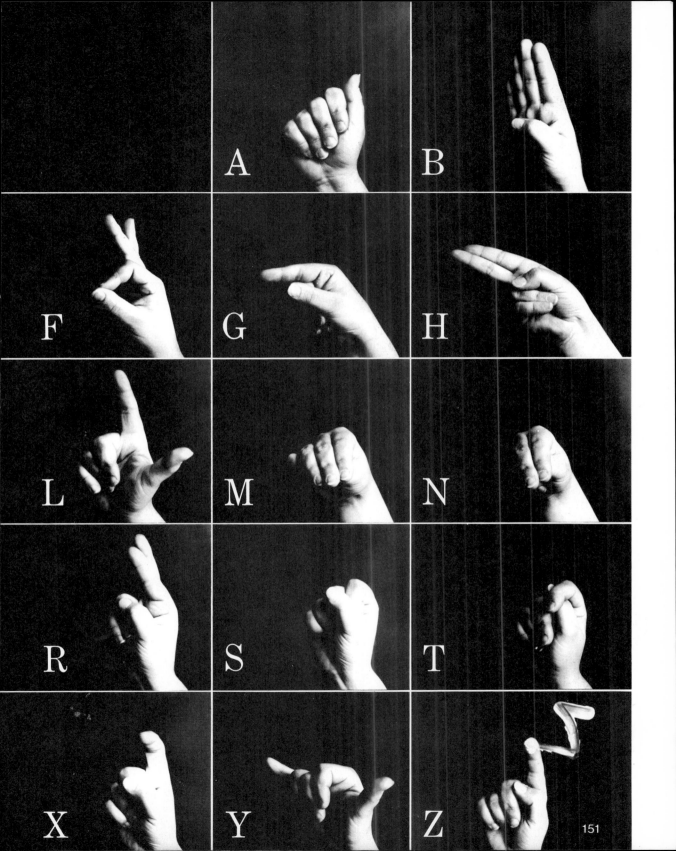

A B

F G H

L M N

R S T

X Y Z

SIGNING: WITH ONE OR TWO HANDS MAKE A SIGN OR PICTURE FOR EACH WORD OR IDEA.

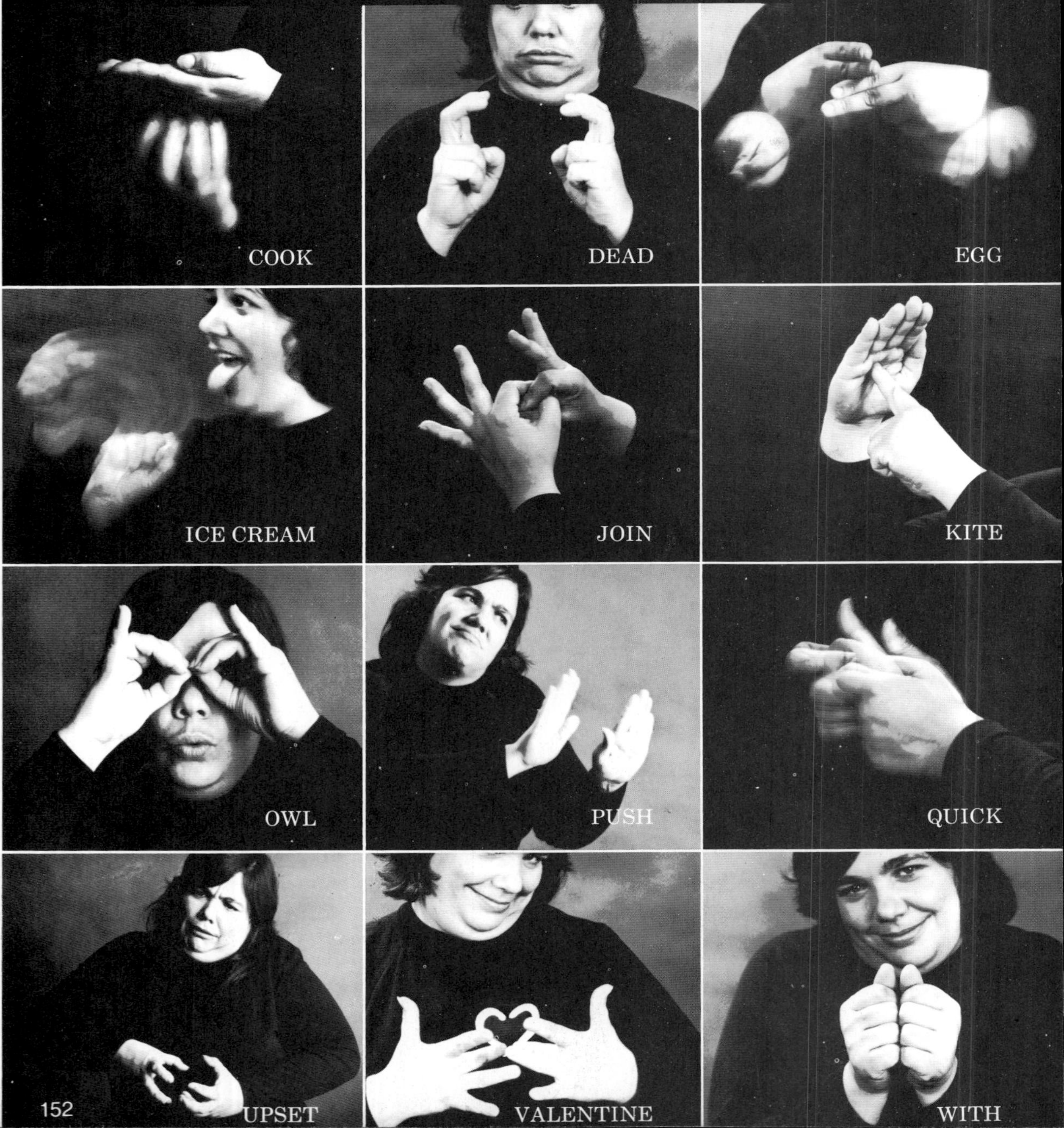
COOK
DEAD
EGG
ICE CREAM
JOIN
KITE
OWL
PUSH
QUICK
UPSET
VALENTINE
WITH

ALLIGATOR

BIG

FUNNY

GROW

HELLO

LAUGH

MY

NAME

READ

SAD

TELEPHONE

XYLOPHONE

YELL

ZERO

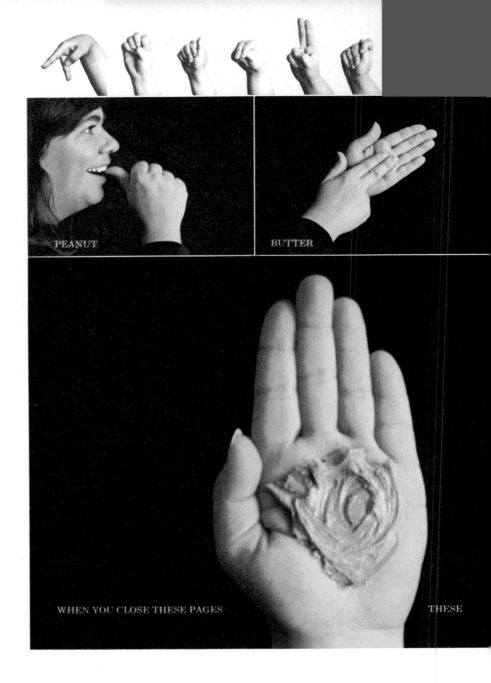

PEANUT

BUTTER

WHEN YOU CLOSE THESE PAGES

THESE

1. How do you think signing and finger spelling might help you communicate with others?

2. Think about two or three activities that you do daily. Explain how these activities would be different if you were deaf.

AND

JELLY

HANDS

MAKE THE SIGN FOR SANDWICH

3. Choose a partner. Each of you should prepare a brief story. Then, using sign and body language, each should tell his or her story. See how well you can make yourself understood. Refer to the text for signs you can't remember.

Main Ideas and Topics

A *paragraph* is a group of sentences that tell about the same subject. A paragraph consists of a *main idea* and *details* that support the main idea. Often the main idea of a paragraph is stated in one sentence. The sentence may come at the beginning, middle, or end of the paragraph. Read the following paragraphs:

A dictionary gives a variety of information about words. It tells the correct spelling and pronunciation of words. It also lists definitions of words. Often, a dictionary gives the history of words, too.

The ancient Greeks and Romans had dictionaries to explain rare and difficult words. Scholars in the Middle Ages used dictionaries to understand hard Latin words. In 1604, the first English dictionary defined 3,000 hard words. The dictionary has been used by many people in history.

In the first paragraph, the main idea is stated in the first sentence. In the second paragraph, the main idea is stated in the last sentence.

ACTIVITY A   Read each paragraph. On your paper, write the sentence that states the main idea of the paragraph.

1. In early times, hunters killed animals daily to have fresh meat. Later, people learned that salting and drying meat preserved it. The American pioneers cooked fruit and then canned it in jars. Finally, people discovered that a cool cellar kept food fresh. Over the years, people have learned many ways of preserving food.

2. Food is best preserved in refrigerators. The reason is that bacteria do not grow at low temperatures. A refrigerator maintains a coolness so the bacteria in the food cannot spread.

3. Food is not the only thing stored in refrigerators. Actually, refrigerators preserve a variety of items. Some store serums and blood for hospitals. Cleaners refrigerate furs to protect them from moths. Flowers are refrigerated to help maintain their freshness.

Sometimes the main idea of a paragraph is not stated directly in one sentence. Instead, the main idea is contained in two or more sentences. Read the following paragraph:

The Earth is one planet that travels around the sun. Eight other planets also orbit the sun. They are Pluto, Saturn, Neptune, Uranus, Venus, Jupiter, Mars, and Mercury. The sun and these nine planets have a special name. They are called the solar system.

In this paragraph, the main idea is contained in the last two sentences. The main idea is: *The solar system consists of the sun and nine planets.*

ACTIVITY B   Read each paragraph. The main idea is not stated directly in one sentence. On your paper, write the main idea of each paragraph.

1. Today we live in an exciting, new era. It is called the Space Age. We can send rockets to distant planets in the solar system. People can land on the moon and explore it. Pictures from outer space can tell us more about the universe.

2. Recently, scientists have discovered extremely bright objects in space. These objects are called quasars. Quasars should prove useful here on earth. They are powerful sources of radio energy. They are about seven billion light-years away but are still very bright.

3. Many people wonder if we could live on Mars. The answer is yes, provided we were protected from Mars' atmosphere. Special suits and heating equipment would be needed. Protection from radiation would also be necessary. People would also need to shelter themselves from solar-flare particles.

So far, you have found the main idea in a single paragraph. Sometimes you read a selection that has many paragraphs. Each paragraph has a main idea. The *topic* of the selection is a statement that summarizes all the important ideas in the paragraphs.

The topic of a selection is not usually stated directly in the selection. You must write this sentence yourself. First, find all the important ideas in the selection. Pay special attention to the first and last paragraphs. Then write a sentence that sums up the important ideas in your own words.

For example, the selection called "Actions Speak Louder Than Words" contains many paragraphs with important ideas. Some paragraphs tell about the different body positions that indicate a person's mood. Other paragraphs discuss gestures which telegraph messages to others. Other paragraphs tell of facial expressions that convey feelings. One way to state the topic of the entire selection is: *People communicate in many ways without using words.*

ACTIVITY C Look again at the selection entitled "Person-to-Person." Find all the important ideas in the selection. Then write a sentence that states the topic of the selection.

ACTIVITY D Read each selection below. Find all the main ideas. Then write a sentence that states the topic of each selection.

1. Henry Ford was interested in mechanical things all his life. As a child, he examined the machinery on his father's farm. He repaired clocks and watches. Later he became an engineer.

    Ford used his mechanical knowledge to produce cars in large numbers. He designed parts that could be made quickly. He also used a moving belt to increase the speed of production. His cars were reasonably priced because they were produced in large quantities.

2. When the Constitution was adopted in 1789, it made no mention of freedom of communication, since leaders took that right for granted. Other Americans insisted on a written law, however. Later, the Bill of Rights was added to the Constitution. This bill guarantees freedom of speech and freedom of the press.

    Although the Bill of Rights guarantees these freedoms of communication, the Supreme Court has held that these rights have limits. For example, freedom of speech does not give someone the right to shout "Fire!" in a crowded theater. The Court has said that freedom may be limited when it creates a "clear and present danger to society."

Note Taking, Paraphrasing, and Outlining

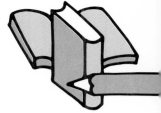

When you prepare a report, you may use many sources of information. You might read an encyclopedia article, a magazine article, and several books. As you find information, you should take notes. These notes will help you to remember and to organize the facts you read.

You do not need to write entire sentences when you take notes. You may write only a few words, called *phrase notes*. You should not copy information word for word. Instead, write the information in your own words. This process is called *paraphrasing*. When you paraphrase, you do not change the meaning of the original material; you merely restate it in your own words.

After taking notes on the information, you should arrange the notes in an *outline*. Outlining helps you to organize the information before you write your report. Each main idea in an outline is placed next to a Roman numeral such as *I* or *II*. Each supporting detail for a main idea is placed next to a capital letter such as *A* or *B* and is placed below the Roman numeral. Read the following article about body language:

Kinesics

Kinesics is the study of body language. Scientists study people's body movements and positions. These movements and positions can tell others how a person feels, even when that person does not speak.

Body positions, or *postures*, tell much about a person. If you slump in your chair, this may mean you are tired or upset. Sitting with your arms crossed may mean, "I am not interested in what is being told to me." Sitting with the body turned slightly away from the speaker may also indicate disinterest.

Body movements, or *gestures*, also tell much about a person. You are already familiar with gestures such as a nod for "yes". Raising your eyebrows shows surprise or doubt in a speaker's words. A simple hug can express affection or sympathy.

The following notes and outline were made from the article about kinesics. Notice that the notes are in phrases, not in complete sentences. The phrase notes do not copy the original source material word for word, yet the meaning of the information has not been changed.

Also notice that the outline does not match the phrase notes word for word. Sometimes only one word in an outline is enough to show what information is being represented.

Phrase Notes	Outline

study of body language called kinesics
movements and positions studied
revealing about people
posture refers to body positions
slumping says tired or upset
arms crossed says disinterested
body away says disinterested
gestures refer to body movements
nodding for yes
eyebrow is doubt or surprise
hug is sympathy or affection
	I. Kinesics
	  A. Study of body language
	  B. Showing of feelings
	
	II. Postures
	  A. Slumping
	  B. Crossing arms
	  C. Turning body
	
	III. Gestures
	  A. Nodding
	  B. Raising eyebrows
	  C. Hugging

ACTIVITY A   Read the following paragraph. Take phrase notes on the information. Write the notes in your own words.

Noah Webster wrote the *American Dictionary of the English Language*. It was published in 1828. Webster felt that Americans must read American books, not British books, to be truly independent. He spent twenty years compiling this dictionary. He also wrote the *American Spelling Book*, and he was responsible for American copyright laws.

ACTIVITY B The following phrase notes were taken from the article about the history of the English language. Organize the phrase notes into an outline. Write the outline on your paper.

Old English first phase
began in 449 A.D.
spoken by Jutes, Angles, and Saxons
Middle English second phase
began in 1066 A.D.
William the Conquerer invaded England
spoken after French came with William
Modern English third phase
began in 1450 A.D.
still spoken today
includes new words invented today

ACTIVITY C Read the following article about dictionaries. Take phrase notes on the information. Write the notes in your own words. Then organize your notes into an outline.

The dictionary is a valuable reference work containing much information about words. It serves as a record of how language is used today. It also indicates how some words were used differently in the past.

Today's dictionary editors constantly search for new words and new uses of old words. They read hundreds of current publications and newspapers. They gather catalogues, advertising brochures, and even menus. Editors can also learn new words and phrases just by hearing others speak.

Each new word, spelling, pronunciation, or usage found by an editor is recorded on an index card. The card is called a *citation*. If a new word has many citations, it will usually be included in the next edition of the dictionary.

LANGUAGE
The Bridge or the Barrier

Robert Bell

It is often hard to communicate clearly, even with people we know well—our family and friends. It is sometimes harder still to discuss issues and ideas with strangers. Can you imagine how difficult it would be to communicate with someone from another country who has learned to think and speak in another language?

This essay explores the problems of communicating with people who don't speak as you do. As you read, notice the small numbers printed within the text. These numbers are used to identify the footnotes which are listed at the bottom of each page. These footnotes show the sources of information which were used for the essay.

Our world is united by communication and travel. The television, radio, and telephone link people who live half a world apart. Jets cross the globe. Sooner or later, many people in this country will come face-to-face and voice-to-voice with people who live in other countries and speak different languages.

Language is the bridge between people, whether they live in the same town or in different nations. Language, however, can also be a barrier. When you deal with people from other countries, it is helpful to know not only their language, but also *the meaning of their gestures*, as well as *their customs and rules of politeness*; otherwise, you will probably misunderstand them or, even worse, insult them without meaning to do so. You will find it easier to deal with foreign people if you know something about *the way they think*, too.

You may be wondering why anyone would need to learn all this—the meaning of gestures, customs and rules of politeness, and ways of thought—just to *talk* with people. Are these things really different in different countries? Aren't all people pretty much the same?

Are they?

Let's say that you are in Mexico, and you make an appointment with a Mexican friend to meet at two o'clock at the town plaza. You are there at two, but your friend does not arrive until a quarter to three. You are naturally annoyed, and you mention to your friend that she has kept you waiting. Your friend looks surprised and then shrugs.

How would you feel in this situation? Would you be insulted? Your friend did not mean to insult you by being late. She didn't mean anything at all by it. The pace of life in Mexico is different from ours. In fact, our way of life, especially the way we try to squeeze as much activity as we can into one day, seems very odd to most Mexicans. They say that we are *agitado*—always in a rush.[1]

This conflict of habits has added two new phrases to the Spanish spoken in Mexico. When you make an appointment in Mexico, you should specify *hora mexicana* (Mexican time) or *hora americana* (American time).[2]

---

[1]Fred West, *Breaking the Language Barrier* (New York: Coward-McCann, Inc., 1961) pp. 54-56.

[2]*Ibid.*

The meaning of words, gestures, and actions *is* different in different countries. In dealing with people from other cultures, we must be on the lookout for these differences and keep them from getting in the way of useful communication.

The Language of Gestures

It is hard to imagine that people in other countries use different gestures. Our gestures are so natural to us that we seem to have been born with them. Two of our most basic gestures, for instance, are the gestures for "yes" and "no." We nod our heads to say "yes," and shake our heads to say "no." What could be more natural?

Arabs do not find these gestures at all natural. When Arabs shake their heads from side to side, they mean "yes." To say "no," Arabs move their heads upward and make a slight clicking sound with their tongues.[3]

Few gestures or body movements are really natural. Each culture has its own body language and attaches its own meanings to various gestures. We learn these gestures and their meanings very early in life, and as we grow older, we forget that we once did not know them. One set of things we learn about is called *space needs*—how close to other people we should stand or sit. Americans who don't know each other, generally like to stand about two or three feet apart when they are talking. If a stranger comes closer than that, thereby invading one's "territory," Americans feel uncomfortable. Between friends, the distance is usually smaller.[4]

[3]Elizabeth McGough, *Your Silent Language* (New York: William Morrow, 1974) p. 111.
[4]*Ibid.*, p. 109.

Space needs differ from country to country. Germans tend to want more space—as much as seven feet between strangers—around themselves than we do.[5] Most Latin Americans, on the other hand, stand much closer together than we do. Strangers in most Latin American countries are perfectly comfortable at the distance we reserve for close friends. An American diplomat stationed in Bolivia reported how these different space needs affected Bolivian-American meetings. During a party at the American Consulate, he watched a pair of officials—one, an American, and the other, a Bolivian—stand together and talk. The Bolivian kept trying to get closer to the American. This was *too* close for the American, who soon stepped back. The Bolivian moved forward. The American moved back. This happened over and over again, like a slow-motion dance, until the pair had drifted all the way across the room.

Space needs are a dramatic difference among people. Other gesture and body-language differences are less great, but can still be important. For example, American men tend to cross their legs by resting one ankle on the opposite knee. The English, however, frequently cross their legs at the knee.[6] Most of us would not notice this difference. But because of it, an American Secretary of State once nearly ruined an important meeting with Arab leaders. During the discussion, he crossed his legs in the American fashion. What he didn't know, or had forgotten, was that in this Arab country it was considered a grave insult to show another

[5]*Ibid.*, p. 115.
[6]*Ibid.*, p. 114.

IN JAPAN, THIS GESTURE MEANS "MONEY." ... ERICA, IT MEANS ...OK."

165

person the bottom of your foot. When he crossed his legs, exposing the sole of his shoe, the Arabs were outraged. But the problem would not even have come up if, instead of the American, the British Secretary of State had attended the meeting.

Customs and Politeness

One day, while driving through the Greek countryside, an American traveler passed several shepherds tending their flock of sheep. As he drove by, he shouted a greeting in English and waved. He was shocked when one of the shepherds picked up a rock and threw it at him. He ducked and stamped on the accelerator, while more rocks flew past him and the shepherds shouted angrily. That evening, an English-speaking Greek told him the reason for the strange reaction. Greeks always wave with their palms facing toward themselves. According to an ancient tradition, you put a curse on someone when you wave at him or her with your palm outward.[7]

People's notions of what is polite vary enormously. People who have grown up with different rules of politeness run the risk of insulting each other when they try to communicate.

In America, when people show you their homes or possessions, it is polite to admire them out loud: "Your room is really fantastic!" or "That's a nice-looking shirt." Don't do this in Mexico! In Mexico, if you say that you like or admire something, the owner will think you want it. He or she will probably insist on giving it to you. You will only make matters worse if you refuse to take it. Your refusal will insult the owner, because it means that you do not think the gift is good enough. But if you accept it, the owner will expect some kind of present in return. Americans in Mexico often create bad feelings because they do not understand this custom.[8]

An American woman learned the hard way about politeness in Thailand, when she invited dozens of Thai women and their husbands to a party. All the couples

---

[7]Fred West, *op. cit.*, p. 58.

[8]John A. Crow, *Mexico Today* (New York: Harper and Row, 1972) p. 53.

promised to be there, but on the afternoon of the party, less than half the people came. The woman was surprised and disappointed. A few days later, one of the women who had not come to the party visited the American. After tea was served and they had talked for a while, the American politely asked her why she had not been at the party. The Thai smiled and explained that she and her husband had planned to take a trip that day, and so they couldn't come to the party.

The American was shocked. "You mean," she said, "you knew when you accepted my invitation that you wouldn't come? I think that's very impolite." Then it was the Thai's turn to be surprised. She explained that in Thailand, it was considered impolite to refuse an invitation. "It might cause you displeasure."

When the American woman later helped brief Thai students who were going to the United States, she was told to stress that Americans feel more displeasure when engagements are broken without notice than when they are refused. She understood the problem very well.[9]

[9]Fred West, *op cit.,* pp. 56-57.

Different customs can make the same idea mean different things. In America, very few women would like being called an "old woman." But in China and other Asian countries, where age is honored, "old woman" is a term of respect.[10]

Different customs can also make simple matters very confusing. Suppose you are in Zuni, New Mexico, and are looking for a friend named John Tewka. You know his address, and when you get to the house, you ask: "Is this John Tewka's house?" You are told, to your surprise, that his house is on the other side of town. You go to the other side of town to the house described and ask again: "Is this John Tewka's house?" You are told, "Yes, this is his mother's house. But he's not here. He lives on the other side of town." In fact, he lives in the house you just left.

Now you are really confused. The problem is that you don't understand the customs of the Zuni people. In Zuni culture, women are considered the heads of the household. Children receive their mother's name. John Tewka lives at his wife's house, but his "real" home, where he keeps his most important possessions, is at his mother's house.[11]

Different Ways of Thought

Language experts tell us that language shapes the way we think. We think, for the most part, in words. Could you think about something for which you had no word? Language even shapes the way we see the world. Studies have shown that people tend to notice only those things around them that they can name. For example, Eskimos have a number of words that all seem to mean the same thing in English: snow. These different words describe different kinds of snow—soft, feathery snow; crunchy, granular snow; wet snow; dry snow; and so on. On the other hand, the Aztecs of Mexico used only one word to describe what, in English, are three different things: cold, ice, and snow.

This different word usage is the result of different climates. The arctic world of the Eskimos is dominated by snow. For most of the year, Eskimos live in close daily touch with snow.

[10]*Ibid.*, p. 54.

[11]David P. McAllester, "The Secret of Anthropology" in *Anthropology in Today's World*, eds. Charles Cutler, *et al* (Middletown, Connecticut: American Education Publications, 1970) pp. 3-4.

Different kinds of snow determine what type of clothing they must wear and what tools they will need for hunting, fishing, and so forth. In winter's terrible cold, noticing the different kinds of snow can even keep a person alive. It is not surprising that Eskimos have so many words for something that is so important to them.

England has a much warmer climate than Alaska or northwestern Canada. The winter brings snow and cold, but they do not make nearly so much difference in the people's way of life. So English has fewer words to describe winter weather.

The Aztec civilization grew up on the warm central plain of Mexico. Snow, ice, and cold were in the mountains far away and were not a daily part of Aztec life. The Aztecs had no need for many words to describe such rare things. It is quite likely that an Aztec traveling through the mountains would not even have noticed that snow and ice were different. In the same way, Eskimos probably see much more variety in a winter landscape than do the English or Americans not born in the far north.

Individually, these differences in words and ways of thought may not seem important. But they add to our knowledge of other people and help us to understand their ways of life. Communication is seldom as simple as it seems. The better we can learn to communicate, the easier it will be to make—and keep—friends, both at home and abroad.

1. What three things that the author discussed would be helpful to know if you are going to deal with people from a foreign country?
2. What are space needs?
3. Why can language be both a bridge and a barrier among people?
4. Explain why an Eskimo and an Aztec would probably see a winter landscape differently.
5. The last sentence says: "The better we can learn to communicate, the easier it will be to make—and keep—friends, both at home and abroad." Explain this statement.

DRAGONWINGS

Laurence Yep

The Wright brothers became famous when, in 1903, they built and flew the world's first airplane. In 1909, near Oakland, California, a Chinese immigrant named Fung Joe Guey flew his own handbuilt airplane. The plane crashed because of a broken propeller. But its design was an improvement on the work of the Wrights and represented a step forward in flight science.

The novel Dragonwings, part of which you will read, was inspired by the story of this little-known air pioneer. Dragonwings is a work of historical fiction. Laurence Yep writes from the point of view of a boy, Moon Shadow. Moon Shadow comes from the Middle Kingdom (China)—the land of the Tang people (the name the Chinese gave themselves)—to join his father, Windrider, in America. Like many Chinese at this time, Windrider comes to America to earn badly-needed money for his family at home. He works as a handyman in buildings owned by Mr. Alger, and he fixes machines in his spare time. Windrider and his son live in a rebuilt stable behind a rooming house run by Miss Whitlaw and her niece, Robin.

The beliefs of the Tang people play an important part in the story. They believed that dragons—wise, powerful, and usually kind beings—controlled the natural world. Dragons could appear in any shape and size they wished. Windrider once dreamed of flying with the Dragon King and this dream fuels his interest in airplanes.

To the Tang people, demons were spirits that could also change shape and size. They were tricky, hard-to-please, powerful spirits that were as likely to do good as evil. Since Americans were strange and new to them, the Tang people naturally thought of them as the legendary demons. The Tang people, in referring to Americans as "demons," did not use the word as an insult, but rather as a means of expressing the unknown. With time and the growth of friendship, strangeness faded and the word "demon" no longer was needed.

In this novel, the English words and sentences are printed in italics; the rest of the text represents the words and thoughts of its Chinese narrator, Moon Shadow. As you read, notice the problems that confront Moon Shadow and Windrider in trying to communicate with the Americans—people who speak another language and have different beliefs and attitudes.

Part I

The next day was much like every day for me during our stay among the demons. I got up just before dawn and got the fire going in the stove and put water on to boil and cooked our morning rice. I would help Father with his handyman chores in certain of *Mr. Alger's* buildings that were in safe areas. Father said it ought to be all right to do my shopping anytime from the morning to the early afternoon, because there were mostly harmless shoppers on the streets then. But I had to be back at the stable before the demon children got out of school. I was also to avoid any demons or demonesses standing about in large groups talking idly. I followed Father's order faithfully. I had no desire to get beaten up. In the evening, after I had cooked dinner and washed up, there would be lessons in reading and writing the Tang people's words and in the use of the abacus for arithmetic. I lived my life like that every day except for the demons' seventh day, *Sunday.*

As you can see, this did not leave me much time to follow my original program of reeducating the demoness, *Miss Whitlaw,* about dragons. But despite everything, Father made it a point to let me have half an hour free each day. I could do anything I wanted during that time. I think Father was secretly pleased when, a few days after we moved in, I decided to use the time to pay another visit to the demoness.

I don't mean to make myself sound like a goody-goody. She was a demoness to me at that time, who lived in a magical kind of lair. It was an adventure. It was a challenge. And if I could remind her of some of the true things about dragons that people ought to know but that she seemed to have forgotten, well, that was to the good. I went up to the demoness' house in my clean tunic and pants, my boots shined and my face scrubbed. She smiled quietly and prettily as she had that first day.

"Why, come in, Moon Shadow." Miss Whitlaw stood away from the door. "Would you like some cookies and milk?"

"Maybe cookies and tea?" I asked. I held up the small package I had brought. It was a jasmine-type tea that is sweet and light and fragrant. On the cover was a dragon.

"Oh, how nice," the demoness said, "but really, we don't need it. I have tea."

Father had warned me that demons sometimes do not have a feeling for the proprieties. It's always good on the first visit to bring a little something to drink or eat. If Father hadn't explained that to me carefully, I might have been offended by the demoness' refusal, because I might have mistaken her statement as saying that my gift was too cheap for her to use. I fumbled around for some excuse. "Please, I drink a lot. Too much. You take tea." I thrust it out at her again.

With a soft laugh, the demoness took it and lifted the lid. "Why, there are flowers inside."

She put water on to boil and then sat down across from me and picked at the tea until she could hold up one of the small white, delicate blossoms. "Isn't that a lovely idea. Flowers in your tea."

She got up and returned with a small white thingamabob that had thickened cow's milk in it. Thickened, yet! And it had an oily kind of smell that nearly made me sick. She also set down a sugar bowl.

"Cream and sugar, Moon Shadow?"

"Oh, but you never put that into it!"

She stood with the sugar bowl in her hand. "You don't?"

"No. No. It ruin tea."

I will say this for the demoness. She was much more open to suggestion than I was. She put the sugar bowl and the—ugh—cream jar away, despite her misgivings. But after we had brewed the tea in the teapot, she sniffed at the spout appreciatively. "Hmmm. But this does smell nice."

And she poured out two cups of the amber liquid. She sipped it tentatively. I watched her face as she broke into a smile and drank more. At least I had broken her of putting cream and sugar into everything. We drank our tea in a friendly kind of silence, and then

Miss Whitlaw picked up the box again. Her fingers traced the long sinuous curves of the golden dragon. *"Oh, my, isn't it a—*it sounded like—*"bu-dee-fu dragon?"*

"Please?"

"Beautiful," she repeated, and explained the word to me.

Once I understood her, I shook my head vehemently. *"No, no. It a. . ."* I fumbled for the right word in the demon language, but all I could come up with was, *"a dragonee dragon."*

Another thing to say for the demoness was her genuine interest in learning about people as people. Where some idiot like myself would have been smug and patronizing, the demoness really wanted to learn. And like Father, she was not afraid to talk to me like an equal. *"I don't think I understand."*

"Dragon do terrible thing, yes," I said, struggling for the right words. *"But dragon, they do good thing too. Bring rain for crops. They king among all . . . all reptile. They emperor of all animal."*

And so on. I went on to tell the demoness everything my Father had told me about dragons.

"Why, how marvelous," the demoness exclaimed when I was finished. *"I never knew dragons did so much."*

"Maybe only bad kind go live here. You know, outlaw, that respectable dragon no want."

"Why yes." The demoness nodded. *"That would make sense. All the dragons I've read about haven't been very pleasant creatures."*

"No dragon pleasant. A dragon dragonee."

At that moment, someone knocked on the door. I looked up at the clock on the demoness' cabinet. I had spent over an hour here. *"That my father,"* I said, frightened. *"He look for me."*

"It was my fault, so don't worry." She added something that sounded like *tee ah.*

"Please?"

The demoness looked embarrassed. *"I said 'dear'—it means a friend, or someone, who is close to you."* She smoothed out a wrinkle in the tablecloth. *"Perhaps I was too forward."*

"No, no. It all right," I said.

"Why, thank you," she said. The knock came again, more insistently this time. Miss Whitlaw opened the door.

"Hello, Mr. Lee. Moon Shadow and I were just talking."

"That boy, him talk too much," Father said sternly.

"No, no, it was my fault, I'm afraid. I kept your boy here listening to the wanderings of an old woman."

"You too kind," Father said.

"On the contrary, you're too kind for loaning your son to me for all this time." Miss Whitlaw laughed pleasantly. "When you get old, you get very selfish. Here I've kept Moon Shadow for so long and it's nearly three. I didn't even give a thought to getting dinner for my boarders either."

Miss Whitlaw had five *boarders* in her house. Each slept in his or her own room, but all of them ate at the dinner table with Miss Whitlaw. Father and I excused ourselves then and left.

I had begun to think that the demons were not really so bad, but that very evening I found out that there can be some bad demons too. I was taking the trash out to the trash barrels when I saw a demon boy lounging against the wall of our alley. I was to find out later that he lived in the tenement house next door. He was about two or three years older than I was, and he was dressed in a gray shirt without a collar. The shirt was of a good, if rough, material. His hair was brown and his face was covered with brown spots—*freckles*, Robin told me later.

As I passed by him, he tripped me. I fell on my back, the breath driven out of me. Our garbage pail spilled out all over the alley. The boy leered down at me. And above me, on the back landing of the tenement house next door, I saw a half dozen boys begin to shout.

> Ching Chong Chinaman,
> Sitting in a tree,
> Wanted to pick a berry
> But sat on a bee.

I jumped to my feet and made the mistake of trying to express my anger in the demon tongue. All I could come up with was, "I no like you."

The boys fell over one another laughing.

"You no likee me?" the boy asked mockingly. "I no likee you."

In my frustration, I began to yell at him in the Tang people's language. But the boy shinnied over the fence while the boys above him began to make mock Tang-people sounds—sounds like "Wing-Duck-So-Long" and "Wun-Long-Hop" in rising and falling voices. I could have bitten off my tongue. But I stood there, staring at them, not wanting to let them chase me away. I felt something soft and wet hit my leg. It was an old tomato. They began to throw bits and pieces of garbage at me. Still I stood there. Finally stones began falling around me. I suppose they had collected the garbage and the stones before they tried to get me. I felt a vague feeling of triumph at having made them use their biggest weapons.

I turned slowly, as if I were not afraid of them but only bored. A stone caught me in the small of the back. I grunted, but I took my time despite the pain. I did not want to give them the satisfaction of seeing me cry.

I did not tell Father about the demon boys. He might have become worried.

The next day I tried to go with Father, but he said he was going into a rougher area that day, so I spent the whole time inside the stable. The demon boys must have played hooky that day. Every now and then I would hear them chant something, and sometimes rocks would thud against the walls. I did my best to go on with my chores and lessons, but it was hard.

It did not help my state of mind when Father came home that evening with a black eye and his right sleeve torn. He set down his tool box and pointed a finger at me. "Before you ask any questions, I'll just say that I got the best of a fight with two demons. They ambushed me inside one of *Mr. Alger's* buildings. I suppose they thought they could rob me."

I went out and got some water for Father to wash up. "Did they?" I asked.

Father grinned. "What do you think?"

During the next demon week, the nighttime was especially bad for me. I could imagine that every sound was made by demons or ghosts gathering in the dark to whisper by the door while they waited to pounce on me. It got so that I was afraid at night to go outside to the pump in the back yard, because I was afraid the demons might be attracted by the sound of splashing water. But I had to wash the dishes, so I would dash out to the pump. With my heart beating fast, I would prime the handle frantically and then run back to the shed as fast as I could, spilling half the water on the way.

It was the demon girl who started to wash her dishes outside for the "fresh air" instead of inside the kitchen at the indoor pump. Though I trusted Miss Whitlaw, I was not so sure about the demon girl. With her flaming red hair, she seemed like a true fox demoness who would delight in tricking humans.

Maybe she was just curious about why I rushed back and forth to the pump. But I still was not too sure about the demon girl. I stayed inside. Finally, the demon girl filled a bucket of water and pointed in my direction, meaning it was for me. I suppose she knew I was watching her from inside the stable.

But the next day, the demon girl was on the back porch peeling potatoes. And after that she peeled some apples. And after that she peeled some onions. She was laying siege to me. She stayed out there for most of the day, until I just had to make a trip to the outhouse. When I came out, I tried to walk quickly back to our stable, but she dashed down the steps and got in front of me. *"Why are you scared of the pump?"* she demanded. I shrugged silently. I trusted Miss Whitlaw not to make fun of my demon talk, but not anyone else.

"But it's stupid," the demon girl persisted. *"You lose half the water your way."* The demon girl pulled one of her pigtails over her shoulder in front of her so she could study its tip. *"Are all Chinamen crazy like you?"*

The kitchen door opened suddenly. *"You, Robin,"* Miss Whitlaw said sternly. *"I told you to leave Moon Shadow alone."*

"But I'm just trying to be friendly with him, but he won't talk to me," protested Robin.

Miss Whitlaw leaned over and spoke gently. *"How would you feel if you were plunked right down in China in a small village with almost no hope of going back? Wouldn't you be scared?"*

"Well, yes," the demon girl admitted reluctantly. Then she looked at me. *"But I'd listen to some Chinaman who told me there wasn't anything in the village pump or anything near it that could hurt me."*

She walked back to the steps and picked up her bucket of potatoes and went inside. Miss Whitlaw stood helplessly by the door. *"I'm sorry, Moon Shadow."*

"It all right," I said. My cheeks were red with embarrassment.

That night I made myself join the demon girl by the pump to do the dishes. I had to prove to her I was not scared. But I still would not speak to her—and I wore the charm against demons. No sense in taking an extra risk.

Part II

It was about two demon weeks after the water-pump incident. The city had steady spring rains every day, but I didn't mind. The demon boys stayed inside, if they were around at all. Though Father was not at home, I had company enough, for the rains here were lively, friendly things. The strong winds would blow in from the sea and catch the rain, so that you never knew from what direction it would hit. Sometimes it would drum suddenly on the roof. The next moment the roof would be silent, as the rain rattled against the glass on one wall. Then the rain would jump and tap at the window on the opposite side.

During this time, Father lined up extra repair jobs—clocks and things to fix in his spare time—until his table was cluttered. Still, he spared a half hour every evening to read to me from his *aeronautical* books. I don't think he ever stopped to consider that the *Wrights* were about the only demons to whom I could have talked for any long period of time. And after the half-hour lesson would come the reward, when we would work at a model of a glider, imitating the pictures and schematics in the books. Father would set the problem of ratios to me, in which I would have to convert the figure for a full-length original to a scaled-down model. Between my head and the abacus, I managed. Then Father and I would cut the bamboo strips and the rice paper and slowly construct the model. But we never got a chance to fly it, because whenever Father was free, it was raining.

So, came his first free day when the skies, though still cloudy, did not look like rain, Father announced we were flying it even though we had to wear boots and heavy coats. In those days *San Francisco* had not been built up as much, and if we walked about a mile to the west, we'd find plenty of open sand dunes for several miles until we hit the ocean. I might have known the demon girl would tag along.

She walked behind us, pretending to be interested in various houses and gardens that just happened to lie along the way we were taking. Finally after this had gone on for three blocks, Father turned. *"You want help us fly it?"* He held up the model glider. It was a good three feet in wingspan.

The demon girl shrugged. *"I guess so."*

I said nothing to her. I felt betrayed by Father, and I was hurt, too, that Father spent most of the time talking to the demon girl. He was only being polite, but I did not see it that way. I kept waiting for her to make fun of the way he talked, but she never did.

"I've never seen a kite like that," she said finally.

"This model of glider take person into sky," Father said.

"Oh, go on." The demon girl shook her head. *"I wasn't born yesterday."*

"No, you born maybe ten years ago," Father said matter-of-factly, and was puzzled when the demon girl sniffed and her back stiffened—she was awfully touchy about people being smart with her, and she thought Father was being smart right then. He was only stating a fact, though, as he understood it. But the demon girl warmed up when we began to fly the glider. Father had me run with it while he jotted down notes with a well-worn stub of a pencil on some of our old bills. The glider behaved erratically, dipping and then soaring and then dipping again. Then Father waved me back to him. When I got there, we pulled in the glider. It came down too quickly, but Father ran and caught it.

Then he turned the glider model over in his hand. I took some more scraps of paper with clean backs out of his pocket. It was my turn to take notes (and also get some writing practice in demonic). *"It need more wing surface,"* Father mused. And he went into a lot of jargon about *center of gravity* and *wing configuration.*

"Wing what?" the demon girl asked.

Father glanced at me. It was my turn to show off. *"Wing config-uration. You know, shape of wing."* I traced the shape of the wing with my pencil. I waited for her to make fun of me.

"Oh," was all the demon girl said. She crossed her arms. *"For someone who doesn't know English too well, you know an awful lot of four-bit words."*

"They in the books," I said cautiously.

"Books?" the demon girl asked. She picked up interest.

"We show," Father said politely.

When we returned to our stable, we gave the demon girl our one good chair—an old stool that Father had found in a vacated apartment and which we had stripped of paint and repainted. She sat down before our bookcase—several fruit crates turned on their sides. She paged through the books, looking more and more puzzled. *"You understand this?"* she asked.

"Yes, some," I said. Father nudged me and I stood beside her, explaining what I could in my broken demonic. In the meantime, Father left to buy some vegetables from a nearby greengrocer for our dinner.

The demon girl closed the book when I finished explaining the paragraphs, and she leaned forward, her body following the line of books. *"But where's the dragon book?"*

"What dragon book?"

"The one that you get all those stories about dragons from. Or did you just make up those things you told to my aunt?"

"I say true things."

"About dragons bringing rain to people? And about their being able to change their size and shape?" The demon girl looked skeptical.

"They true," I insisted.

The demon girl pursed her lips. *"In China?"*

"In whole world. You 'Mericans not know everything."

The demon girl considered that for a moment as she picked at the lint on her coat. *"I suppose,"* she said grudgingly. *"But then, you don't know everything either."*

That was true, but I did not much like admitting it. Instead I shrugged. *"But I know lots about dragons. You like dragons?"*

"I don't know. I never met one." She said that almost as a dare to me, but I did not back down.

"How you know? They can be tiny, tiny as flea. Maybe you hear voice speak to you from nowhere. That them as tiny, tiny as ant, only you no see. Or maybe take shape of people."

The demon girl crossed her arms over her chest and leaned forward on her knees. "Humph!" She still looked doubtful. I couldn't understand her stubbornness in refusing to believe in dragons. I suppose for her part, she could not understand why I believed in them. She added, "I'm from"—it sounded like—"Me-syu-ee."

"Please?"

She spoke very slowly. "Missouri. It's a state."

"Is that like province?"

"I guess. What I mean is that I'm as stubborn as a Missouri mule."

"Please?"

"As my aunt says, it's a creature that pound for pound can out-ornery any other creature on God's earth."

"How you know true? I never see one."

"Sure, you have. There are lots of mules."

"But you know if any come from Missouri?"

"I guess so."

"How you know?" I asked triumphantly.

The demon girl made a small exasperated sound. She mulled that over for a while, chewing at her underlip. "You're a clever, slippery creature, Moon Shadow," she grudged finally. "I'll give you that much. You turned the tables around nice and neat." She glanced at me sideways and smiled again. "And as for telling whoppers, there probably never was your like. You tell some mean stories about dragons."

"Whoppers? Mean stories?"

"Oh, never mind." The demon girl slid the book back into the shelf. "But I'd swear you have an imagination almost as good as E. Nesbit."

"Who that?"

"A new writer." And she made me wait until she got some books from her room. They looked very interesting, but to my embarrassment I found that I had spent so much time learning aeronautical jargon, I had not picked up on the everyday talk. Still, I could look at the pictures while the demon girl outlined the story about flying carpets and phoenixes and magical amulets and cranky old sand elves who lived on beaches. She explained that a cousin of her father's lived now in *England* and shipped them here.

"*I've got some of these, too,*" the demon girl pretended to say casually. She slipped some *dime novels* from behind her back. They were printed on cheap tan-colored paper with the most lurid paper covers, and they ranged across a wide variety of subjects. There were *Ned Buntline* specials about the adventures of *Buffalo Bill* in the wild, wild West (to me it was east, though, since I judged things geographically in relation to the Middle Kingdom). There were others about *Jesse James* and his robberies. But her pride and joy were the *Nick Carter* detective stories.

"*Your cousin send these?*"

She laughed. "*Oh, no. I got these from Maisie, next door. She's a girl in my class in school. She got them from her brother, Jack. We trade back and forth, but*"—she leaned forward conspiratorially—"*you can't tell Auntie. She'd have kittens if she found out.*"

"*She would?*" I said with interest.

"*No, no. It was only a figure of speech. I'd get in trouble if she knew I was reading these,*" she said. I realized then that the demon girl, Robin, was testing me. Well, she was not all that bad to talk to, and she, at least, had never thrown a rock at me.

"*I no tell,*" I said.

She sat back, satisfied. "*You can read them if you like.*"

"*I like to, but I not think I can. Too many words I not know,*" I confessed.

"*I'll teach you,*" Robin said loftily. She put her hand on the stack of E. Nesbit books. "*We'll start with these and then when you know English better, you can read these.*" She touched her precious pile of *dime novels*.

That was how my lessons started. Father gave me permission to go over to Miss Whitlaw for an hour to read with Robin and write. Miss Whitlaw sat in the parlor and helped me too. My vocabulary and grammar picked up enough so that I could stumble through the *E. Nesbit* books. I found that the *dime novels* were easier stuff because they had simple words and ideas. Robin was right. They were great. "*Awash with gore,*" she liked to say.

And even after I had finished the *Nesbit* books, we continued my lessons. We would talk about any number of things, and Miss Whitlaw encouraged me to write short paragraphs about dragons, which she and Robin then corrected. Robin, of course, said she did not believe one word of what I wrote or said about dragons. She would simply sniff or roll her eyes or shake her head at another *whopper*. But she was always there in the parlor, every night, munching away at cookies and listening to what I said or reading what I wrote about dragons, for I went on to tell them of the adventures of the dragons near my village.

In the weeks that followed, I found out that while I had set out to reeducate the demoness about dragons, she was educating me in the demonic language. After a while, we wandered away from dragons, for to explain about the dragons, I had to describe my home—I mean, our home.

In very halting demonic, I told them about the waters of the Pearl River: thick and milky and colored a reddish yellow like the color of sunset distilled from the air. On the river, you might see a stately junk, tottering its way upstream, slatted sails raising to meet the wind. And skittering all around them would be the small, two-person fishing boats—like little water bugs skimming over the surface. Sometimes they sailed in pairs before the wind with a net between them, scooping up the fish. Their square sails danced before the wind like sheets of paper. All this Miss Whitlaw listened to, and more.

But if things were going great for me, I could not say the same for my father. There was so much to learn about the *aeroplanes*. There were tables and charts he needed for various things, like the ratio between the curvature of the *propeller* blades and the revolutions they produced. It was then that I got an idea. I waited until Robin was in school and Father was away on an errand before I went to see Miss Whitlaw.

"*You help me write letter, maybe?*" I asked her.

"Why, of course, Moon Shadow. *To whom are you writing?*"

"*To the Wrights,*" I announced proudly. "The aeronauts."

Miss Whitlaw seemed impressed. "*Oh, yes. I've read all about their exploits, and if half of what they say is true, why it must be marvelous. But why do you ever want to write to them?*"

"*My father,*" I began cautiously, "*he want fly like Wrights.*"

Miss Whitlaw put a hand to her mouth. "*Oh, my. Isn't that rather dangerous?*"

I shrugged. "*Not if he know how.*"

"Does he?"

"Yes and no," I said. I did not think Miss Whitlaw could be told about the dream. *"But he need facts, numbers, to build aeroplane."*

"Robin told me he made such marvelous glider models, but I had no idea it was only a preliminary. To have such ambition!" Miss Whitlaw shook her head in admiration — and I think also a little anxiously.

"You help me write to them?"

"Yes. Do you have their address?" When she saw my puzzled look, she explained the demons' postal system.

"I know village . . . no . . . the town they live in, and . . . and province . . . no, state."

"Well," she said, *"it might get through with just that."*

With her help, I finally wrote something like this:

To the honorable Wrights:

This is to inform you that I am a boy of eleven. I have greatly admired your feats of daring. My father wants to fly, too. Can you help him? We need to know how to shape the propellers. We need to know how big the wings should be in order to lift my father into the air. Father says that no one else in the whole world knows as much as you do about aeroplanes. Thank you.

And I signed it with the sounds of my name spelled out in demon letters. I wrote several drafts of it and then copied it out in the fine elegant hand Miss Whitlaw had taught me. The next day we went down together and mailed the letter. *"You realize though, Moon Shadow, that even if they were to get this letter, there is no guarantee that they'll answer it. They're busy men, you know."*

But two weeks later, I got a letter from the Wrights' bicycle shop, and in a very neat, strong hand *Orville* answered me:

Dear Mr. Lee:

My brother and I are always happy to meet another flying enthusiast. Our brotherhood is too small to lose any one of us. Enclosed you will find some tables and diagrams that should prove of some service to you. If we can be of any further assistance to you, please let us know.

I waited anxiously that whole afternoon until Father came home. I almost danced around him.

He hung his hat up on a nail and grinned. "What is it you want to tell me? Did someone die and leave us a fortune?"

"Better than that," I said. I held up the letter.

"I can't read that kind of demon script." Father handed the letter back to me. He could only read demon printed letters. He sat down on a crate while I read the letter to him. When I finished, I found him staring at me. I could not tell if he was angry or what.

"They also sent us some tables and diagrams . . ." I tried to show them to Father but he would not look at them. "Did I do wrong?" I asked.

"It's just that . . . that it seems like begging," Father said.

"But Miss Whitlaw—"

"Miss Whitlaw?" Father asked sharply. "Did you ask her to write the letter?"

"She only helped." I set the tables and diagrams down on top of a nearby crate.

"You told her about my dream," Father accused me.

"No," I said quickly. I was scared.

"You talk too much," Father snapped. Father crumpled up the letter and threw it into a corner.

I left Father sitting in the stable. Miss Whitlaw and Robin were in the kitchen baking some things; but Miss Whitlaw took one look at my face and told Robin to leave the room. Then she sat me down at the table and took my hand.

"*What is it*, Moon Shadow?"

I told Miss Whitlaw about Father's being mad, and I hinted a little about how he behaved like a dragon sometimes. But Miss Whitlaw did not laugh.

"Perhaps . . ." Miss Whitlaw tapped a finger against her lips for a moment. "*Perhaps the truth of the dragon lies somewhere in between the American and the Chinese versions. It is neither all-bad nor all-good, neither all-destructive nor all-kind. It is a creature particularly in tune with Nature, and so, like Nature, it can be very, very kind or very, very terrible. If you love it you will accept what it is. Otherwise it will destroy you.*"

For a long time, I listened in silence to the steady ticking of her kitchen clock. "*You wise woman*," I said finally.

"No," she laughed. *"Just a foolish old woman who talks so much that every now and then she gets lucky and says the truth."* She patted me on the shoulder. *"Now go back to him."*

I went back. Rather than shout at me, Father had gone to sleep. The next morning, I found that Father had picked up the letter and smoothed it out on the table as best he could. At that moment, he was leafing through the tables and diagrams. He turned around when he heard me get up. "Still, there's so much to know. And they did call us brothers."

"Yes, they did," I said carefully.

Father shook the tin can into which we put our savings. He pulled out some demon paper *dollars* and coins. "Maybe they'd like a crate of oranges."

"Don't you want to write a letter to them?"

"Yes, I guess that would be best. Can you write while I dictate?"

"I can try."

Father thought for a moment. "Maybe you should get Miss Whitlaw to look at the final version," Father suggested. He wagged a finger at me. "But only for the grammar."

---

1. Describe two of the problems that confronted Moon Shadow and Windrider in trying to communicate with the Americans.

2. When Moon Shadow first visited Miss Whitlaw, they almost had a misunderstanding over his gift of tea. Explain the problem and how Moon Shadow avoided trouble.

3. When Windrider talked to Robin on the kite-flying expedition, Moon Shadow felt hurt. Why do you think he felt this way?

4. Why was Windrider angry when he saw the letter from the Wrights?

5. Most people have been in a situation like Moon Shadow's: having to deal with new people in a new place. It often happens on our first day in a new school, or when we visit other people. Describe an incident like this that has happened to you.

Footnotes

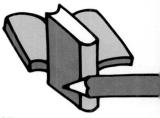

Sometimes authors use quotations or other people's ideas when they write an article. Instead of interrupting the article to cite their source, they use footnotes. A *footnote* is a numbered reference or explanatory note. Usually footnotes appear at the bottom of the page to which they refer. Other times all the footnotes for an article are listed at the end of the entire article.

The selection "Language: The Bridge or the Barrier" lists the footnotes at the bottom of each page. Footnote *1* gives information about a book by Fred West. The author of the selection used material from this book. Footnotes *3, 8,* and *11* give information about other books the author used.

Footnote *2* says *Ibid.* This term refers to the resource cited in the footnote immediately preceding that footnote. The term *Ibid.* is similar to saying "ditto." In this case, *Ibid.* refers to the book by Fred West. Footnotes *4, 5,* and *6* also say *Ibid.* Since they are listed immediately after Elizabeth McGough's book, they refer to her work.

Footnote *7* uses the term *op. cit.* The author of the selection is citing Fred West's book again. But he can't use *Ibid.*, since this would refer to Elizabeth McGough's book. The term *op. cit.*, preceded by West's name, tells you that the footnote refers to West's book.

Use the footnotes following "Language: The Bridge or the Barrier" to answer these questions.

1. Who is the author of *Your Silent Language*?
2. Which page in *Your Silent Language* is referred to in footnote *3*?
3. Which company published the book *Mexico Today*?
4. Which book title is referred to in footnote *9*?
5. What is the publication date of *Breaking the Language Barrier?*
6. Which book title is referred to in footnote *10*?
7. Who is the author of "The Secret of Anthropology"?
8. In which city was *Your Silent Language* published?

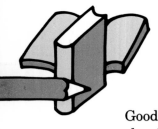

Facts and Opinions

Good communication not only involves expressing yourself clearly to others; it also involves listening carefully to what others say. You should be able to tell if their statements are facts or opinions.

A *fact* is a statement that can be proven true or false. You can prove it by checking a reference source, such as a dictionary or an encyclopedia. You can also prove a statement by personal observation. Here are examples of facts:

The colors red and white, when combined, produce pink.
Franklin D. Roosevelt was born in 1882.

These statements can be proven true or false. You can use personal observation to check the first statement and an encyclopedia to check the second statement.

An *opinion* is a statement that expresses a person's own feelings or beliefs. It is a kind of conclusion drawn from observation. However, an opinion cannot be proven true or false. Here are examples of opinions:

Pink is the prettiest color of all.
Franklin D. Roosevelt was a great president.

These statements cannot be proven true or false. They merely indicate a personal conclusion someone has drawn.

Read each statement. Write *F* if the statement is a fact. Write *O* if the statement is an opinion.

1. Philo Farnsworth and Vladimir Zworykin invented television.
2. Watching television is a waste of time.
3. Today over sixty million Americans own televisions.
4. The best shows are the ones on educational TV.
5. Not one comedy show on television is really funny.
6. People should read books instead of watching television.
7. Each show on television is rated for its popularity.
8. This year twelve new shows were canceled after one season.
9. The best show on television is the news.
10. It's fun to watch television and eat popcorn.

Parts of Speech

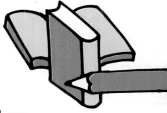

Every word in a sentence performs a specific job. Each word can be placed into one of eight categories called *parts of speech*, depending on the job performed. The parts of speech you will review are noun, pronoun, adjective, verb, and adverb. Understanding the function of each word in a sentence may be helpful to you in your reading.

A *noun* is a word that names a person, place, thing, or idea.
The <u>telephone</u> rang. <u>Jack</u> entered the <u>room</u> in <u>excitement</u>.

The underlined words are nouns. *Telephone* names a thing. *Jack* names a person. *Room* names a place. *Excitement* names an idea.

ACTIVITY A   On your paper, write each noun that appears in the following sentences. After each noun write *person*, *place*, *thing*, or *idea* to show what the noun is naming.

1. Citizens around the world use the telephone each day.
2. These machines are a great convenience.
3. Messages travel long distances in a few seconds.
4. Alexander Graham Bell introduced a brilliant idea.

A *pronoun* is a word that takes the place of a noun.
Marie sent a telegram. <u>She</u> paid two dollars for <u>it</u>.

The underlined words are pronouns. *She* takes the place of *Marie*. *It* takes the place of *telegram*.

ACTIVITY B   Write each pronoun that appears in the following sentences. After each pronoun write the word or words it replaces.

1. The Johnsons sent a telegram to Sheila. She got it from them.
2. Dave and Tina wrote a message. They sent it yesterday.
3. A friend and I fix telegraph wires. We repair them daily.
4. Cables travel beneath the ocean. They cross the continents.

An *adjective* is a word that describes a noun or a pronoun.
A <u>strange</u> voice on the <u>other</u> end spoke. It was <u>loud</u>.

The underlined words are adjectives. *Strange* describes *voice*. *Other* describes *end*. *Loud* describes *it*.

ACTIVITY C   Write each adjective and the noun or pronoun it describes.

1. A secretary sent the broken typewriter to a small shop.
2. A busy worker looked at the old machine. He was kind.
3. Several assistants worked on the typewriter for one hour.

An *action verb* is a word that names an action. A *linking verb* tells what something is or is like.

The caller spoke slowly. The message was important.

The underlined words are verbs. *Spoke* is an action verb. *Was* is a linking verb.

ACTIVITY D   Write each verb that appears in the following sentences. After each verb write *action verb* or *linking verb*.

1. The mail deliverer brought the letters late today.
2. One letter was a note from a friend.
3. I opened that envelope in a hurry.

An *adverb* is a word that describes a verb.
The students wrote quickly. The teacher spoke loudly.

The underlined word are adverbs. *Quickly* describes *wrote*. *Loudly* describes *spoke*.

ACTIVITY E   Write each adverb and the verb it describes.

1. We arrived early for the test. The teacher came later.
2. I read the instructions quickly. Joe read them slowly.
3. A bell rang suddenly. I looked nervously at the clock.

ACTIVITY F   The underlined word is used more than once in each sentence. Write the word and part of speech for each use.

1. Buy a stamp in the stamp machine and stamp the letter.
2. A line of people line up for the movie.
3. The fly and the gnat fly out the window.

ACTIVITY G   Write each underlined word and its part of speech.

1. You know about many means of communication.
2. People use telephones, telegrams, and letters daily.
3. Effective communication is important in this large world.

Resumes

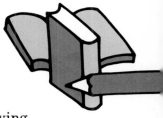

You know that you often fill out a job application when applying for a job. A *resume* is a kind of pre-written job application. It is a statement that summarizes your background and work experience. A resume lets an employer have a quick look at your qualifications, even before you are interviewed.

A resume provides much of the same information supplied on a job application. Here is a sample of a resume:

John Silver
338 South Bend Road
Burbank, California 91501
(704) 764-2335

Education: Burbank Junior High School   1972-present
              Burbank, California 91501   (through 8th grade)

              Selma Elementary School   1965-1971
              Selma, California 93662

Work Record: Hall Newspaper Company   1971-1972
                1103 Haines Drive   paper deliverer
                Burbank, California 91501

                Barris Supermarket   summer 1970
                98 Barris Boulevard   assistant clerk
                Burbank, California 91501

Personal History: I am a member of the Neighborhood Club. We perform helpful services for senior citizens. I also have a special interest in animals. I would like to be a veterinarian someday. My best school subjects are science and English.

Write a resume that indicates your own education, work experience, and personal history. (For work experience, you may include activities such as raking leaves or babysitting.) Follow the form of the above resume.

EXCHANGES

We seldom think about communication. Most of the time, we exchange our thoughts, feelings, and experiences with others so easily that we don't have to think about it. It is not until we fail to communicate clearly—when, for example, we deal with people from other countries—that we realize how complex and difficult communication can be. The selections in "Exchanges" have encouraged you to think about the process of communication, and to consider how well you communicate with others.

Thinking About "Exchanges"

1. Give an example of how Mark and his plant communicated in "Harold and Burt and Sue and Amy, Etc."

2. Would Humpty Dumpty have made a good guest on channel 26 in "On Camera, Noah Webster!"? Why or why not?

3. "Talking Hands" showed you that some body signals have a single, special meaning. "Charades" showed you that other body signals are less clear. Give an example of a body signal that can mean different things to different people.

4. In "Language: the Bridge or the Barrier," the author stated that rules of politeness are different in different countries. Describe one example from *Dragonwings* of the Tang people's rules of politeness and explain how it came into conflict with American rules of politeness.

5. In what ways could you communicate more clearly with others?

PATHWAYS

People throughout history have followed many pathways to learn about themselves and the times in which they live. For example, people have risked their lives to explore and follow pathways to unknown places. People have sought freedom and independence in which to follow their own ideas and beliefs. People have searched for peace as a pathway to understanding others.

In "Pathways," you will read about people who try to learn about the world in which they live. You will read about a young man who, in the 1790's, sails to the South Pacific aboard a merchant ship. You will read about the different pathways people take in search for freedom and independence, from Roger Williams, the founder of Rhode Island, to Belva Lockwood, America's first woman lawyer. You will read about people seeking the pathway to peace. You will meet a boy and girl who find a moment of peace in the middle of war, and a maker of weapons who creates the world's highest award for the makers of peace.

As you read, think about the pathways people take to learn about the world, about themselves, and about others. What events that are happening around you help you to understand the time in which you live?

El Sol

The sun beats down
   on the earth
On the plants and the trees
   on the sea.

The sun smiles
   upon
you and me.

—*Octaviano "Chico" Romano*

Carry On, Mr. Bowditch

Jean Lee Latham

Nathaniel Bowditch began work in 1785 at age twelve as an indentured servant for a ship chandlery, or ship's supply store. Nat had a keen mind that was interested in everything he saw. While working at the chandlery, he learned as much as he could about sailing ships. He had a special talent for mathematics, and he made calculations with great speed and accuracy. One of the things he taught himself was navigation at sea. In this type of navigation, a captain used the position of the sun and moon, information in an almanac called Moore's Navigator, and mathematics to find his ship's position.

When he was twenty-one Nat signed on as second mate aboard a trading ship commanded by Captain Prince. (The captain, first mate, and second mate were the ship's officers. They were usually better educated than the ordinary seamen who lived "before the mast" in the forward part of the ship called the fo'c'sle.) During voyages with Captain Prince, Nat discovered two things. He invented a new and simple method to take sightings of the moon (called lunar sightings or "lunars"). He also found that Moore's almanac, used by sailors who risked their lives on its accuracy, contained errors. Nat became such an expert at navigation that Prince let him handle all of it. On some voyages, Prince even asked Nat to come as a passenger, "supercargo," just so he could make use of Nat's skill. By the time Nat was thirty, he was one of America's most respected mathematicians, navigators, and astronomers.

The story you are about to read is an excerpt from an historical novel about Nathaniel Bowditch. Nat is at sea aboard the merchant ship Astrea with two old friends, Captain Prince and the cabin boy Charlie Waldo. Also aboard are the first mate Mr. Cheevers, the second mate Mr. Towsen, and a sullen and rebellious crew who really did not want to make the trip. The Astrea has set sail "in ballast," carrying lead weights instead of cargo. Captain Prince plans to buy coffee in Batavia, a city on the island of Java. As you read, think about how Nat and the Astrea's crew use navigation as a tool for finding new pathways across the sea, and new pathways in their own lives.

A month later they had weathered the Roaring Forties of the North Atlantic. The crew had begun to be sailors. The last poor lubber had got his sea legs. Fingers that had bled on the halyards were healed, and black with tar. Every man could hand, reef, and steer.

The Astrea was her old self again. Dingy decks were holystoned white, and the rigging was taut, tarred, and dressed in its chafing gear.

But a sullen mood hung over the ship, like an evil mist over a swamp. Even when he was below deck, in his cabin working, Nat could feel hatred staring at the back of his neck, as though an animal stalked him in the night.

Lupe was the worst of the crew, because he smiled. A slim, swarthy young fellow, Lupe moved softly as a cat, and purred when he spoke.

"We can rest easy," Captain Prince had said, "until the Cape."

Nat wondered what Prince would say if he knew how his supercargo felt about Lupe—that it wasn't quite safe to turn your back on him. Was it imagination, Nat wondered, or was Lupe always watching him? For two weeks now, he had had that feeling of someone behind him. Twice, when he'd been standing on deck in the darkness, he'd swung about quickly, as though searching for a star in another direction. But he had seen no one.

Though tonight promised to be a good one for taking a lunar, Nat worked stubbornly at his checking of Moore's tables. Once he thought he heard his door open. He started, wheeled, and broke out in a cold sweat. This had to stop! He slammed Moore's book shut, picked up his sextant and slate, and went topside. Deliberately, he went forward, beyond the waist of the ship, and stood at the larboard rail, facing the water. I'll stand here, he told himself, till I get over being a fool!

He didn't know how long he'd been standing there when he felt, rather than heard, cat-soft movement behind him.

A voice purred, "Señor?"

Nat forced himself to turn slowly. "Yes, Lupe?"

Lupe's teeth flashed white. He held out one brown hand. Across the palm lay a knife. "Do not stop me, what I say, señor. I say it quick, or I lose the nerve. Two weeks—maybe three—I try to get up the nerve."

So Lupe had been following him. Nat said again, "Yes, Lupe?"

"I want to ask you, señor—could we trade the—the—know-how?"

"The know-how?"

"I want to learn the—the—navigation. I teach you to throw the knife—you teach me the navigation, eh?"

Nat began to laugh, then stopped suddenly when he saw the smile stiffen on Lupe's face. "Forgive me, Lupe. But the idea of my learning to throw a knife—it just struck me funny."

"But you could, señor! And it is a good thing to know! Also, I teach you to sing the *serenatas*!"

Nat only smiled this time. "That's funnier still—me singing a serenade."

"No, no! señor! You could do it! Then you win any señorita in the world! You want to get married, don't you, señor?"

"I was married, Lupe. My wife—is dead."

Lupe's smile vanished. His eyes widened. "You win the lady? No *serenata*?"

"No *serenata*."

"Por Díos! How you do it?"

This time Nat didn't even try to stop laughing. "It's all right, Lupe. I'll be glad to teach you navigation. Tell me—how much mathematics do you know?"

"The—the—numbers?" Lupe's smile flashed again. "Very quick! I count on my fingers! Add-up! Take-off! That's good, eh?"

"Well, it's a start," Nat admitted. "Addition and subtraction come first."

"Then you teach me?"

"Er—what else do you know about numbers?"

Lupe's smile faded again. "Just add-up, take-off, señor. There is more? I cannot learn the navigation?"

"Addition and subtraction . . . Let me think, Lupe . . ." Nat took a turn on deck. "If we had logarithmic tables of all the trigonometric functions, you could work any problem in navigation with nothing but addition and subtraction."

"Log tables? I make them," Lupe promised, "with the wood!"

"No, no, Lupe. They aren't that kind of tables. These tables are just lists of numbers. I could figure them out, all right . . ."

"You do that, señor? For Lupe?"

"On one condition," Nat promised.

"Anything, señor! I teach you magnificent *serenatas*! You have the world at your feet! You can't fail!"

"Is that how you won your wife, Lupe? With serenades?"

Lupe sighed. "No, señor. She not marry Lupe. Her brothers—they are first mates. They say she cannot marry Lupe. Cannot marry a man before the mast."

"I'll teach you on one condition, Lupe—that all the fo'c'sle studies with you."

"Por Díos! But why?"

"Because it's easier to teach a dozen men than one man. How about it, Lupe? You think you can persuade them?"

For a moment Lupe frowned. Then his slow smile stretched again. He purred, "Yes, señor. They do it. They do anything for Lupe." He prowled away and disappeared in the shadows.

The next day, Nat began. The men worked hard; Lupe saw to that. But Nat worked harder. The tables he figured now were longer "than main to bowline." And explanations that had worked for other crews were still too hard for these men to grasp. So they worked—across the equator, to the Cape, and into the Indian Ocean they slaved—Nat and the men before the mast.

Mr. Towsen, the petulant second mate, came to Nat's cabin one night. "Mr. Bowditch, just what are you doing with the fo'c'sle?"

"Teaching them navigation."

Mr. Towsen's lip curled. "How much can they learn?"

Nat laid aside Moore, and spread the logarithmic tables he was making. "When these are done, every man of them will be able to work a lunar."

Mr. Towsen flushed, then whitened. "What kind of discipline will you have on this ship? Teaching the hands something your officers can't do?"

"No reason you can't learn it, too," Nat told him. "You're just as bright as Lupe—I think. Now, if you'll excuse me . . ."

Mr. Towsen stamped out. Nat went back to checking Moore's tables. At last he muttered in disgust, slammed the book shut, and went to Prince's cabin. "I'm through with Moore! Do you know how many errors I've found—so far? Eight thousand!"

Prince stared. He said it was impossible.

"I can prove it, point by point! Do you want me to get my figures and—"

Captain Prince said *no*—with trimmings. He'd take Mr. Bowditch's word for it. "So, Mr. Bowditch, what now?"

"I'm going to write a book of my own. And it's going to have three things these books don't have. First, the tables will be correct! Second, every sea term, every maneuver, everything a seaman needs to know, will be explained in words any able seaman can understand. Third, I'll put in tables—so that any seaman can

solve problems in navigation—even if he has to count on his fingers to add!"

Captain Prince thought it was the wildest idea he'd ever heard. He said so—with more trimmings. "Even if you could do it—which I doubt—it would take you the rest of your life—if you lived that long!"

"I can do it," Nat roared. "I'm doing it now! If I can teach Lupe to take a lunar, I can do anything!" He stopped. Silence echoed in the cabin. He'd been yelling again.

Captain Prince stared at him for a count of ten. "Carry on, Mr. Bowditch."

"Aye, aye, sir." Nat went topside. Tonight was going to be a good time to start teaching the fo'c'sle to take lunar observations.

By the time the *Astrea* reached Sunda Strait, Nat had made good his threat to Mr. Towsen. He had taught the crew to take lunars, and Mr. Towsen too. The second mate had fought the idea like a harpooned whale, but he had had to learn, in self-defense.

When they anchored off Batavia, Nat stretched and grinned with relief. They had sailed with a sorry crew and arrived with able seamen—with very able seamen! Smiling, he went ashore with Captain Prince and Mr. Cheevers to bargain for their cargo of coffee.

Two days later the three men stared at each other. There was no coffee to be had.

A British captain gloated over them, and made polite sounds of sympathy. "Too bad—your voyage for nothing. An expensive mistake. If you'd sailed with a cargo, you could sell that. But—you sailed in ballast, didn't you? And now—nothing to buy. Really too bad."

Captain Prince said there was always Manila.

The British captain looked even more pleased and sounded more sympathetic. "The monsoons, my dear fellow. Perhaps you don't know about them? Steady as the trade winds—excepting that they do vary with the seasons. Just now, if you tried to make Manila, you'd be sailing in the teeth of the northeast monsoon all the way. One doesn't sail to Manila this time of year. It just isn't done."

They returned to the *Astrea*, a grim trio. Charlie felt their mood as they sat down to mess. Dishes rattled when he served them.

"Too bad," Mr. Cheevers said, "that our trip has failed."

Nat banged his fist on the table. "It hasn't failed! We can still go to Manila!"

Mr. Cheevers lifted an eyebrow. "Fighting head winds all the way? That, my fine-*figured* friend, would take some navigating!"

Nat snapped, "So we navigate it!"

Prince stiffened. His eyes narrowed. His glance flicked from Mr. Cheevers to Nat and back again. "Mr. Cheevers, how soon can we be ready to sail? To Manila?"

Mr. Cheevers stared at his captain and stuttered, "But—but—sir—the head winds—"

"*Mr. Cheevers!*"

"Aye, aye, sir!" With a wild look in his eyes, Mr. Cheevers went on deck.

On deck that night Charlie approached Nat. "Mr. Bowditch, sir—the monsoon—it's blowing the wrong way now?"

"Yes, Charlie."

"And we'll be—uh—tacking against the wind? Zigzagging back and forth? Like we did for a little while, coming around the Cape?"

"Yes."

"All the way to Manila?"

"All the way."

"We—we'll do it all right, sir?"

"Of course," Nat told him. "It's a simple matter of—We'll do it, all right."

Day after day the *Astrea* moved in a crazy zigzag. Once she'd sailed from Sunda Strait to Manila in fifteen days. No making it in fifteen days this time. December ended; January came and passed; February began. Eight long weeks out of Batavia the *Astrea* anchored in Manila Harbor.

Batavia is now called Djakarta.

The *Phoebe*, from Boston, was anchored nearby. Her master, Captain Hudson, came on board the *Astrea* to ask news of home. "And how was it around the Horn?"

"We came by the Cape," Prince told him. "Stopped in Batavia; no coffee there, so we came on to Manila."

Captain Hudson stared. "Not in the teeth of the monsoon?"

Prince shrugged in an offhand way. "Why not?"

"But—but—no f—I mean, no-body—"

Prince smiled. "*No fool tries to sail in the teeth of the monsoon? Is that what you meant?*"

"Well, yes," Hudson admitted. "I mean—the navigation. You'd have to have somebody who could work lunars—"

Prince shrugged again. "What's so hard about lunars? Every man in my crew can work a lunar."

Hudson's face was blank. Then he laughed, "Come on, tell me. How did you do it? Just sheer blind luck?"

Prince said, "I'm not joking. Ask any man on board."

Charlie, who was nearby, straightened and cleared his throat.

Prince nodded. "Go ahead, Charlie. Tell Captain Hudson how you calculate a lunar."

"Aye, aye, sir!" Charlie stiffened, stared straight ahead and rattled

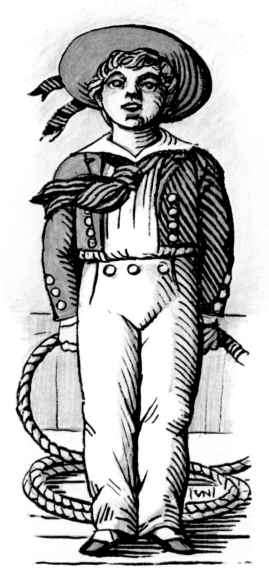

off the formula. "That's the way we do it, sir. It's better than waiting for the moon to oc-cult a star." He looked at the bewildered Captain Hudson. He added helpfully, "*Oc-cult*—that means *cover up*, sir."

Captain Prince had a sudden coughing spell.

A British ship hailed the *Astrea*. Captain Willoughby came aboard. He, too, wanted to know how it was around the Horn.

Captain Hudson began to enjoy himself. "They just arrived from Batavia. Yes, we know it isn't done, but they did it."

Captain Willoughby searched their faces, as though trying to figure out the joke. "You mean you have a man who can work lunars?"

Captain Hudson laughed. "One man? They have a crew that can work lunars! The cabin boy just explained it to me! I tell you, Captain Willoughby, there's more knowledge of navigation on this American ship than there has ever been before in the whole of Manila Bay!"

From across the deck, Lupe lifted his hand in a salute to Nat. His grin flashed white in his swarthy face. A smile danced in his eyes. Nat grinned back at him. A good man, Lupe.

When Nathaniel returned from Manila he began work on his book of navigation. By the time he was thirty, he had published his book, The American Practical Navigator, *and had seen it recognized as the best navigational text of the day. The American Practical Navigator is still used as a standard reference by the United States Navy and is frequently revised by the Secretary of the Navy.*

?

1. For two weeks Nat felt as though he were being watched. Was he right? How do you know?

2. Why did Lupe want to learn navigation?

3. Why did Nat decide to write his own navigational book?

4. Explain why Captain Prince decided to sail to Manila even in the face of the monsoon.

5. Everyone uses simple techniques of navigation. We remember landmarks, names of streets, and so on, and use them to guide us in our chosen direction. Think of a short journey you make often, such as a walk to school, and describe the landmarks that you use to guide you.

The Secrets of
STONE

Robert Bell

The earth has many places to explore. We think immediately of mountains and plains, oceans and rivers—things that lie on the surface of the earth. But what about the parts of the earth that lie beneath the surface? The essay you are about to read examines the Grand Canyon and its neighbors, Zion Canyon and Bryce Canyon. These canyons are pathways into the depths of the earth and its history. As you read, notice the question that begins the essay, and how that question is answered.

What is stone? A stone is something hard and rough that we can hold in our hands. If a stone is big enough, it is something we can climb on. Out of stone we build walls and houses and roads, and when stone stands in the way of a road, it is something we can blast apart with explosives.

But knowing how we *use* stone does not tell us what stone *is,* by itself, when no human being is making use of it. Few of us bother to take the longer, closer look that might reveal the secrets of stone. Stone does have secrets, but all our holding, climbing, building, and blasting will not uncover them.

The Canyons of the Colorado Plateau

If you were to tour Utah and Arizona within one-hundred-fifty miles of the border that separates these states, you might begin to unravel the secrets of stone. In this dry, high country, known as the Colorado Plateau, are three of our country's greatest natural wonders: the Grand Canyon in Arizona, and Zion and Bryce Canyons in Utah.

Millions of visitors are drawn to this area every year. They come to see rugged cliffs and barren mountains of breathtaking size, stone terraces like giants' staircases, rocks that look like temples and royal thrones, like animals, goblins, and melted wax candles. They come to view stone walls the color of roses and lilacs, of pumpkins and sand and rainclouds and golden summer sun.

Any visitor to the canyon country sees these wonders. For those who look closely and who ask questions about what they see, the canyons have more to tell.

The Grand Canyon is 217 miles long, from 4 to 18 miles wide, and about a mile deep. At its bottom, over five thousand feet below the canyon rim, the Colorado River tumbles on its way to the Gulf of California. What could have dug such an incredible chasm?

At Zion Canyon, visitors can wade up a shallow river to a place called The Narrows. Here, the river flows between rock walls less than twenty feet apart and more than a thousand feet high. How did the river end up between such high walls?

The strange, multicolored formations of Bryce Canyon look like the shattered remains of a huge watermelon dropped from the sky. What really occurred there?

Many questions come to mind as you look down from a cliff edge or up at a great, gnarled stone spire. The canyons are mysterious as well as beautiful, and questions about them have teased and troubled people for generations. Today, thanks to the work of geologists, we have begun to find answers to the mysteries of the canyons' birth.

Erosion and Time

The most important answer can be summed up in a single word: *erosion.* Erosion is the process by which water, wind, and other natural forces wear away the land.

Water and wind carving stone? Water is soft and wind is softer—nothing more than moving air. How can water and wind make any mark on rock?

Water soaks into stones and slowly dissolves the mineral "glue" that holds them together, then washes away the freed particles. In winter, rain and snow fill holes and cracks in rock and, since water expands when it freezes, it opens the holes and cracks still further.

Water from the sky eventually finds its way to streams, to rivers, and to the sea. Every drop of water, as it moves, sweeps away a little bit of the land. Rivers and streams carry grains of sand and soil and small pebbles, and roll larger stones along the bottom. The tiny particles strike the riverbed and, like chisels, knock off other chips, and the larger stones scratch along the bottom. As a result, the river digs itself slowly deeper into the earth and exposes more and more of the riverbank to the rain and wind.

The wind, too, carries bits of dust and grit and hurls them against the land. Each piece makes its tiny mark and creates more particles to be washed away by water or be carried onward by the wind.

Erosion is a powerful land-shaper. In the 1920's, the Colorado River (before the Hoover Dam controlled it) raced through the Grand Canyon, and carried an average of 500,000 tons of material away every day. Erosion by wind, rain, and the river itself produced

BRYCE CANYON

all of the river's load. Erosion was so swift because of the region's dry climate. Grasses and other plants that, in other regions, bind the soil together and resist erosion could not grow here. As the river sliced downward, the wind and rain cut into its bare, exposed banks and opened what once must have been a narrow gorge into an enormous canyon.

Still, it's strange to think of water and wind as earth movers more powerful than bulldozers or power shovels or dynamite. If you were to hike into Bryce Canyon, you would see dozens of places where a fat bulb of stone is supported by a slender stone pillar. A geologist would tell you that the rock of the pillar is softer than the rock of the bulb, so it has eroded faster. Someday, it will grow too weak, and the bulb will fall.

You could return twenty years later and find the bulb still in place. If you put off your next visit for fifty years, the pillar would probably still be standing. Generations later, in fact, it might not have broken. Or you might by chance arrive on the day, the minute, when the pillar, worn too thin by erosion, would finally collapse.

This observation would give you a clue to stone's most vital secret. To understand stone, you must learn to think about time in a different way. The lifetime of stone is not measured, like ours, in decades. It is measured not in hundreds, or thousands, or millions, but in *billions* of years.

One speck of dust carried by the wind strikes a cliff face and breaks off a fragment too small to see. So what? But think of all the specks of dust that would strike that stone on all the windy days in a year. In ten years. A thousand years. A billion.

GRAND CANYON   ZION CANYON

It is *time* that makes wind and water so powerful. When dynamite is used to blast away rock at a construction site, it moves tons of earth in less than a second. Erosion does the same thing, but the "explosion" is slow, stretched out through the ages. Instead of a roar, we hear the breeze whisper, the rain hiss, the river murmur to itself among the stones.

Formation of the Canyons

If you toured all three parks, you would probably notice that each one is strikingly different from the others. Bryce is a fantasyland of bizarre shapes like mud castles covered with brightly colored paints. At Zion, instead of mud castles, you find huge slabs of stones like gigantic steps, great winding cliffs, and towering walls. Grand Canyon is deeper and vaster than the other two, and charged with a feeling of immense age. Yet for all this difference, the parks lie within seventy miles from the others.

Again, a question comes to mind: Why are the three canyons so different? The answer to this question has nothing to do with erosion, but has much to do with time and the lifetime of stone.

Stone forms when all of the material of an age, the soil and the once-living things that end up in the soil, are covered over by new material. Perhaps the climate turns hot and dry and a forest is gradually conquered by the sands of a desert. Or, because of shifts in the earth, the area sinks and is flooded by the sea, and sediment covers the bottom.

As this covering-over process continues, the uppermost layers grow heavy and begin to press down on the lower layers. Pressure creates heat, and this combination of intense heat and pressure transforms the dirt, sand, sediment, and once-living matter into stone.

The Colorado Plateau has been all of these things: a mountain range, a marshy lowland, a desert, and a sea. The canyons are made up of layers of different colored stone. Each layer represents the life, geography, and climate of a particular span of time. In cliffs that now are thousands of feet above sea level, we can see the fossils of marine creatures. We also have evidence that, more than once, erosion has worked on the land, leveling high mountains and delving deep into the earth. For billions of years, the entire area shared these cycles of change.

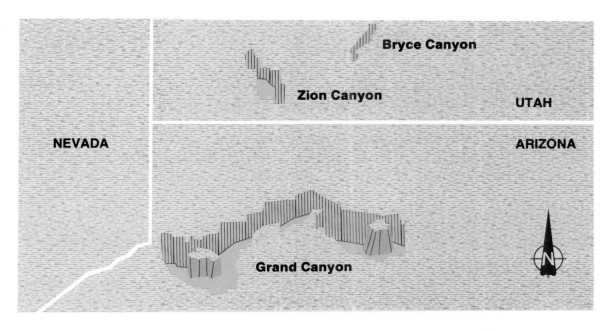

About 180 million years ago, the region was a desert of great rolling pink sand dunes that we now call the Navajo Desert. The Navajo Desert period marked a turning-point in the history of the three canyons-to-be. Between 180 and 130 million years ago, shifting pressures in the earth made the areas that were to be Zion and Bryce Canyons sink until they became the lowest point in the region. Rivers drained into this low point to create an inland sea that we now call the Sundance Sea. The rivers carried mud, silt, and limy sediments and deposited them on the sea floor. While the Grand Canyon area continued to be eroded by wind, rain, and the Colorado River, the Navajo sands of the Zion and Bryce areas were soon covered by new material.

Though the earth is slow to change, change is constant. About seventy million years ago, another revolution in the earth began. Great pressures raised plateaus and mountains at Zion and exposed them to erosion. The Sundance Sea then covered a smaller area—the area that was to be Bryce Canyon. Here, the sea bottom continued to thicken and to exert the pressure that makes stone. When geologic changes finally drained the sea and raised Bryce into a plateau, it was this layer of rock that erosion began to shape.

Since then, shifts in the earth's crust have continued to shape the canyons by opening new faults, new paths for erosion to follow. Rivers have carved further and exposed the ancient layers of stone.

The differences among the canyons result from their differing histories and the different types of rock that erosion has revealed in them.

The Grand Canyon is the oldest of the three. The layers of rock you see there represent many ages; the Colorado River is now revealing stone that last saw daylight 2 billion years ago.

It is Navajo Sandstone, a product of the Navajo Desert, that gives Zion Canyon much of its unique character. In the towering cliffs, you can see wavy patterns called crossbedding. These patterns are the dunes of the Navajo Desert preserved in solid rock.

Bryce Canyon, the youngest of the three, is made of a soft limestone formed in the bottom of the Sundance Sea. Since the stone is soft, it erodes easily and takes on the strange, mud-castle shapes that have made Bryce famous. The limestone is also full of minerals, such as iron and manganese, that tint it orange, red, lavender, and purple. Rain stirs these minerals into a thick mud that, in many cases, drips like paint down the cliffs and walls, leaving streams of bright color.

The secrets of stone lie in its history: a story of pressure and heat, of constant change from mountain peak to lowland to sea bottom, of destruction by wind and water that sometimes yields great beauty, and most of all, of time. To look into these canyons is to run your eyes over the ages, to *see* time. Stone is not simply stone; it is a mark that time makes on the world.

1. Describe the process of erosion.
2. Describe the differences among the three canyons.
3. Explain the following statement: "To look into these canyons is to run your eyes over the ages, to *see* time."
4. The essay stated that "Though the earth is slow to change, change is constant." Find two examples in the essay that support this statement.
5. The essay said that knowing how to *use* stone and knowing what stone *is* are two different kinds of knowledge. Think of an everyday object, such as a bicycle or a can opener. Explain how to use the object, and then try to explain what the object is without discussing its use.

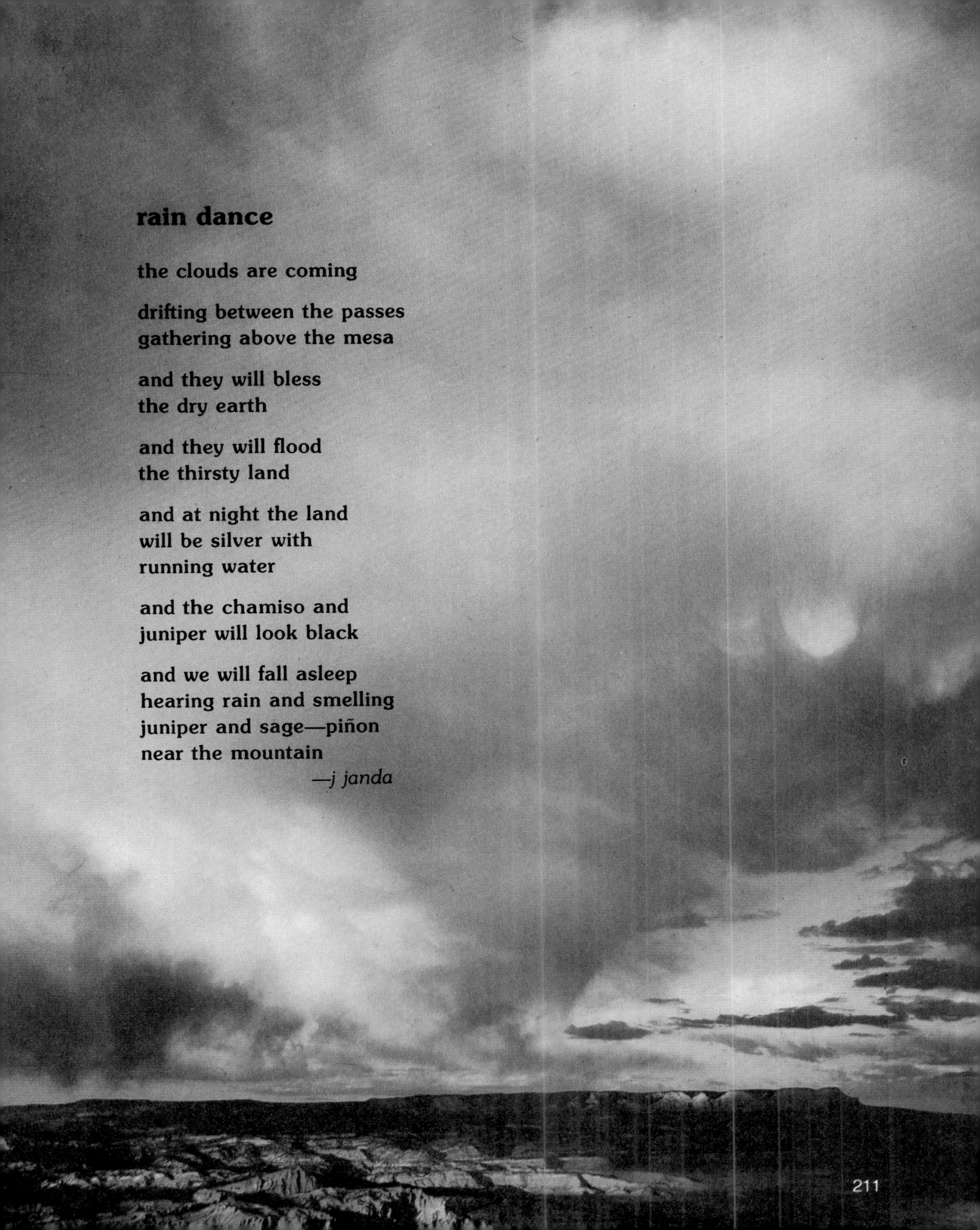

rain dance

the clouds are coming

drifting between the passes
gathering above the mesa

and they will bless
the dry earth

and they will flood
the thirsty land

and at night the land
will be silver with
running water

and the chamiso and
juniper will look black

and we will fall asleep
hearing rain and smelling
juniper and sage—piñon
near the mountain

                —j janda

Reading a Map

A *map* is a drawing that represents an area. Maps can show the location of places and the distances between places. Maps may give other information as well. Special symbols are often used to present this information.

A *color and symbol key* explains what the special colors and symbols on the map stand for. The key might show the symbols for cities, capitals, mountains, highways, or rivers.

A *scale* is a line that shows how distances are represented on the map. For example, one inch (2.54 centimeters) on the map might actually represent ten miles (16 kilometers).

An *index* is an alphabetical list of the cities and physical features represented on the map. A letter and number appear after each city or feature to show where that place is located on the map.

Below is a map of the island of Java. Notice that the color and symbol key indicates the signs for *national capital*, *city or town*, and *rail line*. The scale shows that one-half inch (1.27 centimeters) actually represents 20 miles (32 kilometers).

Index

Now notice the letters running vertically along the left side of the map. Also notice the numbers running horizontally along the bottom of the map. The index indicates that the city of Bogor can be found at point C 4 on the map. By running one finger across from point C and another finger up from point 4, you will locate Bogor on the map.

ACTIVITY A   Use the map, key, and index to answer these questions.

1. Which city on the island of Java is the national capital?
2. Is there a rail line running between Bogor and Cicurug?
3. Is there a rail line running between Jasinga and Cihara?
4. What sea is north of the island of Java?
5. The town of Genteng lies on what ocean?
6. What strait separates Pasangteneng and Ketapang?
7. If Cihara were included in the index, what letter and number would appear after its name?
8. What letter and number indicate the location of Krawang?
9. Name one town that lies on the Pelabuhan Ratu Bay.
10. Name one town that lies on the Lada Bay.

ACTIVITY B   Use the scale and a ruler to answer these questions.

1. What is the approximate distance in miles between:
    a. Jakarta and Bandung?
    b. Indramayu and Sutawangi?
    c. Serang and Cibaliung?

2. What is the approximate distance in kilometers between:
    a. Genteng and Tasikmalaya?
    b. Sukabumi and Mauk?
    c. Sumur and Bayah?

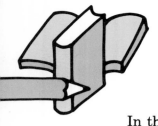

Causes and Effects

In the selection "The Secrets of Stone," you learned that wind and rain cut into the bare, exposed banks of the Colorado River. As a result, a once narrow gorge opened into the enormous Grand Canyon.

A *cause* is the reason something happens. An *effect* is the result. In the formation of the Grand Canyon, the cause was the wind and rain cutting into the riverbanks. The effect, or result, was the enormous canyon.

ACTIVITY A   The paragraph below states the cause for something and the effect. Following the paragraph is a list of causes for the effect. Write the correct cause on your paper.

Christopher Columbus sailed from Spain in 1492 with the intention of finding a short sea route to the Indies. On October 12, he landed on San Salvador Island in the Bahamas. He mistakenly believed that this was an island of the Indies, near Japan or China. Therefore, he called the inhabitants of the land "Indians."

a. Columbus sailed from Spain in 1492.
b. He landed on San Salvador Island.
c. He thought he had landed on an island of the Indies.

ACTIVITY B   Each paragraph below states a cause and an effect. Write your own sentence that states the cause.

1. The most famous ancient maps were made by Claudius Ptolemy, who lived in Egypt around 150 A.D. He produced a map of the world and twenty-six regional maps of Europe, Africa, and Asia. Few people knew of Ptolemy's maps for hundreds of years. Then, in the late 1400's, the maps were printed in an atlas. The result was that the maps became widely known.

2. The first commercial movies were silent films. Sound had not yet been developed to accompany the pictures. The eventual arrival of "talking pictures" proved tragic for some screen stars. Their speech was poor or unappealing. As a result, the careers of these actors and actresses soon ended.

The preceding paragraphs described effects with only one cause. Sometimes there are multiple causes for an effect. In other words, there can be many reasons why something happens.

ACTIVITY C   Each paragraph below states the causes for something and the effect. Following the paragraph is a list of causes for the effect. On your paper, write the causes that are discussed in the paragraph.

1. Today a growing number of cars emit harmful fumes into the air. Large airplanes also contribute to pollution in the sky. In addition, the smoke from the factory chimneys fills the air with dangerous chemicals and pollutants. The effect, or result, is that our air has become less healthy for us to breathe.
   a. Large airplanes create pollution in the sky.
   b. People don't care about the air they breathe.
   c. Factory chimneys give off dangerous chemicals.
   d. Automobiles emit harmful fumes.
   e. Ecology groups cannot get support in Congress.

2. In the early 1800's, Americans in the East were curious to discover what lay west of the Mississippi River. Farmers were anxious to find new land to cultivate. Some people wanted to open businesses and make money in a new location. The effect, or result, was that many pioneers traveled West during the 1800's.
   a. People were forced to travel by the government.
   b. Farmers wanted to cultivate new lands.
   c. Some people were curious about the territory.
   d. The East suffered bad weather conditions.
   e. Business people desired different locations.

ACTIVITY D   The paragraph below states the causes for something and the effect. Write your own sentences that state the causes for the effect that is described in the paragraph.

Computers work faster than human beings. Computers tend to make fewer mistakes than people do. One computer may do the work of ten people and save an employer money. The effect, or result, is that some businesses today are being persuaded to use computers in place of people.

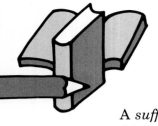

Suffixes

A *suffix* is a letter or group of letters added to a base or root. Adding a suffix changes the meaning of the word. Here are some common suffixes and their meanings.

Suffix	Meaning	Example
-er, -or	one who	driver (one who drives)
-an, -ian	characteristic of	Mexican (characteristic of Mexico)
-ist	one who practices or makes	scientist (one who practices science)
-ward	in the direction of	downward (in the direction of down)
-ize	to make	legalize (to make legal)
-like	resembling	childlike (resembling a child)

Adding a suffix often changes the part of speech of a word. Adding a prefix, however, does not change the part of speech.

ACTIVITY A   Write the meaning of the underlined word in each sentence.

1. An Australian basketball team played at our school.
2. The biologist experimented with the plants.
3. Who was the inventor of the printing press?
4. Sandra realized her dream after many years.
5. The young girl conducted herself in an adultlike fashion.
6. My kite soared in an eastward direction.

ACTIVITY B   Write a word which ends with a suffix that can replace the underlined words in each sentence.

1. The rocket flew in the direction of the sky.
2. The animal had features that were resembling a cat.
3. The one who sails voyaged across the Mediterranean Sea.
4. The teenagers made into an idol the guitar player.
5. That style of costume is characteristic of (Queen) Elizabeth.
6. The one who makes novels completed the final chapter.

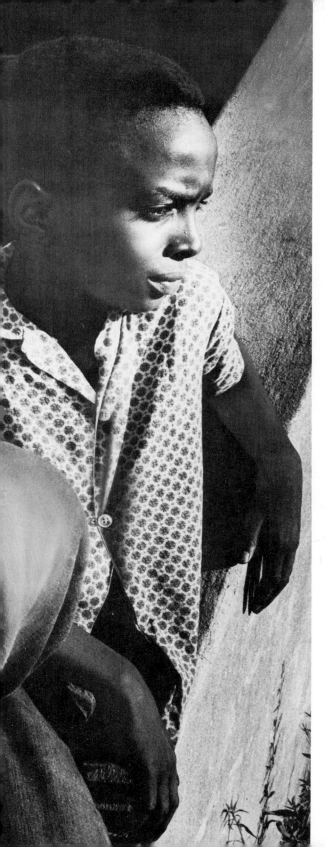

Freedom

Freedom will not come
Today, this year
    Nor ever
Through compromise and fear.

I have as much right
As the other fellow has
    To stand
On my two feet
And own the land.

I tire so of hearing people say,
Let things take their course.
Tomorrow is another day.
I do not need my freedom when I'm dead.
I cannot live on tomorrow's bread.
    Freedom
    Is a strong seed
    Planted
    In a great need.
    I live here, too.
    I want freedom
    Just as you.

–Langston Hughes

An Independent Man

Joan Loykovich

    As Americans, we are free to think, to say, and to believe what we want. These freedoms are rights guaranteed to us by the Constitution of the United States. Our right to freedom exists only because courageous people, today and in the past, have demanded it and, when necessary, fought for it. Roger Williams, the subject of the essay you are about to read, was such a person. As you read, think about how a single, determined person can eventually help change the course of history.

The sea wind blew cold and damp through Newtown, near Boston, that October morning, paving the way for the bitter winter to come. Despite the wind, people thronged outside the church, where the General Court of the Massachusetts Bay Colony was about to begin, their voices rising and falling in excited conversation. The year was 1635.

"He's a bad penny, I tell you," said James Baxter to his neighbor, Charles Taylor. "A troublemaker. A fanatic of the worst kind!"

"Come now, James," said Charles. "You've spoken with him. He's a fair-minded fellow, very pleasant and humble. A learned man as well. He's misguided, perhaps, but—"

"Misguided!" James spluttered. "I have indeed spoken with him. Heard him preach, too, as you have. 'Misguided' is too mild a word for that man's wicked—"

"Good morning, gentlemen." It was Robert Smith, another neighbor. "I see you're talking about the Reverend Williams."

"James was," said Charles with a sad, wry smile.

"Whoever heard of people *choosing* the church they want to attend? Tell me that!" said James. "Claiming that people should be allowed to say anything they please. That he has the *right* to speak whatever treason he likes: to say that the King himself rules only because the people let him rule. You think he should be allowed to defy the law this way?"

"What I object to most," Robert said, more quietly, "is Williams' nonsense about our land claims. The King of England granted us this land. His Royal Charter is all the authority we need. Now comes Williams saying that the King had no right to give the land, that we should pay the natives for it. Imagine, pay the natives!"

"I tell you," said James, "this man is dangerous. His opinions threaten our way of life. More than that. Have you thought, Charles, what the King would think if he heard that we tolerate Williams' ideas? How angry he would be at his ungrateful subjects? Have you thought of that?"

Charles Taylor said nothing. He sighed and shook his head.

The General Court of the Massachusetts Bay Colony was meeting that day to decide what to do about the Reverend Roger Williams. Since he and his wife Mary had arrived in 1631, he had been a source of trouble. Now, four years later, the leaders of the colony were determined to be rid of him.

To understand Williams and the trouble he caused, you must understand how Europeans, and their colonists, felt about government and religion. In the 1600's, kings and queens ruled the nations of Europe. These kings and queens, and the nobles who served them, had absolute power over their subjects. They made laws to govern the people, yet they, for the most part, were above the law. They believed that they had been born to rule, and had a natural right to run things as they saw fit. England, like many countries, had an official church to which everyone had to belong. The English King was head of the English Church, and criticizing that Church was as unthinkable—and as forbidden—as criticizing the King.

Keep in mind that most people thought that this was the way things ought to be. Roger Williams, however, was not one of those people.

"People . . . have fundamentally in themselves the *Root* and *Power* to set up what *Government* and *Governors* they shall agree upon." Rulers, he believed, "have not the least inch of Civil power, but what is measured out to them from the free consent of the [*people*] . . . such *Governments* as are by them erected and established have no more power, nor for a longer time than the . . . people consenting and agreeing shall betrust them with. This is cleere not only in *Reason,* but in the experience of all . . . people . . . [*who*] are not deprived of their *naturall freedom* by the power of *Tyrants*." [1]

Roger Williams believed that governments receive their power from the people they govern, and exist only to serve them. He held that no person is born to rule. He thought that the rulers of a nation should be elected by the people, and that the people should have the right to remove them from office at any time.

The cornerstone of Williams' ideas was a belief in personal liberty—"*naturall freedom.*" (He even named his daughter, Freeborne.) He felt that people should be free to think and speak and, most especially, to worship as they choose.

Do these ideas sound familiar? They should. Another writer more than a century later was to put them this way:

"We hold these truths to be self-evident, that all men are created equal, that they are endowed by their Creator with certain unalienable Rights, that among these are Life, Liberty and the pursuit of

[1]James Ernst, *The Political Thought of Roger Williams* (New York: Kennikat Press, Inc., 1966), p. 64.

Happiness.—That to secure these rights, Governments are instituted among Men, deriving their just powers from the consent of the governed,—That whenever any Form of Government becomes destructive of these ends, it is the Right of the People to alter or abolish it . . ." The document is the Declaration of Independence, drafted by Thomas Jefferson.

Roger Williams did not believe in keeping his opinions to himself. As a minister and a writer in England, he had soon found himself in grave trouble with the King's government. It was to escape the government's anger that he and his wife had sailed for America. But by 1635, Williams was in trouble again.[2]

The General Court heard the accusations against Williams, and his proud defense. There was little doubt of the verdict; some of Williams' angriest accusers were sitting in judgment of him. For his "newe and dangerous opinions," the Court banished him from Massachusetts. He could take six weeks to leave, provided that he stop preaching and speaking of his ideas.

It was not in Roger Williams' nature to be silent about the wrongs he saw. He continued to speak his mind in public. Stung by his defiance, the General Court ordered that Williams be seized and put aboard a ship for England.[3]

But Williams had no intention of being forced back to England. He quickly arranged his affairs, saw to it that his family would have money to live on, and left by night. His goal was the village of Sowans, home of the Wampanoag people and their *sachem*, or chief, Massasoit. Like most colonists, he had dealt with the local American Indians. Unlike most colonists, he had learned their language and their customs, and had dealt with them fairly. He hoped that Massasoit would welcome him.[4]

The fierce winter of New England gripped the land. For four days and nights Williams struggled through snow-filled forests and frozen swamps, carrying what food and clothing he had on his back.

Massasoit did welcome his European friend and gave him a place to live in his own home. Williams was very grateful and did

[2]Clifford Lindsey Alderman, *The Rhode Island Colony* (New York: The Macmillan Company, 1969), pp. 3-7.

[3]*Ibid.*, pp. 9-10.

[4]James Ernst, *Roger Williams: New England Firebrand* (New York: Ams Press, Inc., 1969), pp. 150-156.

his best to make himself useful. When a quarrel broke out between Massasoit and Canonicus, a sachem of the neighboring Narragansett nation, Williams acted as peacemaker. The Wampanoag and the Narragansett had been prepared to go to war, but because both sides trusted Williams, he was able to get the two sachems to sit down and settle the matter peacefully. Massasoit was so impressed and grateful that he made Williams a gift of some land on the Seekonk River, a tributary of the Providence River that feeds into Narragansett Bay.[5]

This gift gave Roger Williams an idea. Why should he not start a colony, far from Massachusetts, where free men and women could live in peace? When spring came, Williams and five other fugitives

---

[5]*Ibid.*, pp. 157-158.

from Massachusetts who had come to Sowans set out by canoe down the river. They soon found the site, built a small settlement, and planted crops.[6]

The Seekonk settlement was not, however, destined to last long. A messenger brought Williams a letter from his friend, Edward Winslow, the governor of the Plymouth colony. The letter said that the Seekonk settlement was on land claimed by Plymouth and, to avoid future trouble, Williams should find a free and unclaimed site.[7]

Williams saw the wisdom of the governor's request. He wanted his new colony to be free of any outside interference. A border fight with Plymouth would bring him to the attention of Massachusetts Bay, and endanger his new colony's early growth. It was hard to give up the months of work they had put into the Seekonk site, but Williams knew they had no choice. He and his people took with them what they could, and found another site a short way up the nearby Mooshassuc River. He tried to buy this land from his friend, Canonicus, but "Canonicus was not to be stirred with money to sell his land to let in foreigners." Instead the Narragansett sachem gave the land to his friend. On Canonicus' generous gift, Williams founded his colony. Because of its beauty, a supply of fresh water, "and many other Providences of the Most High and Only Wise," he said, "I called [it] Providence."[8] Williams' family and many other people joined him at Providence, and the colony grew quickly.

In the beginning, Providence and most of Rhode Island belonged to Roger Williams. He had the power to set up whatever government he wanted. But he, who had such a hatred of tyrants, did nothing without the consent of the other colonists. That consent was symbolized by the "town fellowship," or compact signed by the heads of the families of Providence on June 16, 1636.

The compact called for a government based on four principles. First, all people were equal before the law. There were to be no kings, queens, or nobility in the colony. Second, the government received its power from the consent of the governed. This meant that, unless the government acted in the best interests of the citizens, the citizens had the right to remove the government. Third,

---

[6]Alderman, *op. cit.*, p. 12.

[7]*Ibid.*, p. 13.

[8]Ernst, *Roger Williams: New England Firebrand*, pp. 161-162.

Royal Charter from King Charles II

the government was not to interfere with freedom of conscience. This principle gave people the right to think, speak, and worship as they choose. And fourth, the government's major job was to protect the rights of the citizens, not to increase the power or wealth of the leaders of the government.

Providence was ruled by a town meeting held every two weeks and attended by the heads of Providence families. Anyone at these meetings could speak, to raise issues or suggest answers, and all new laws were made there.[9]

Williams eventually sold or gave away most of his vast lands. And people banished from Massachusetts for the crime of disagreement founded other Rhode Island colonies: Portsmouth, Newport, and Warwick. These new towns were modeled on the example of Providence.[10] To protect the land from the claims of other colonies, Williams went to England and, in 1643, obtained a charter from Parliament. The charter joined the four towns into a single colony and gave that colony legal claim to its land. Later, in 1663, because of political changes in Rhode Island and England, Williams again journeyed to England. This time he got a Royal Charter from King

[9]*Ibid.*, pp. 167-172.

[10]Alderman, *op. cit.*, pp. 32-40.

Charles II. This charter not only made Rhode Island an official colony of England; it recognized Rhode Island's religious freedom and accepted the colony's form of government.

Roger Williams died in 1683. Though he had been the real ruler of Providence in the early years, he never served as the governor of the town or the colony of Rhode Island. He decided to make his contributions as a member of the governor's council, and in other, lesser public offices. Power was less important to him than was the public good.

In 1900, Providence was made the state capital of Rhode Island and the people voted to build a statehouse. On the top of the statehouse, they placed a statue of "The Independent Man." Roger Williams was an inspiration for that statue. To this day, he symbolizes the independent spirit of Rhode Islanders, the spirit on which the United States was built. In the Declaration of Independence, the United States Constitution, and the Bill of Rights, the ideals of government preached and practiced by Roger Williams became the ideals which guide America today.

1. Why did Roger Williams leave the Massachusetts Bay Colony?

2. On what four principles was the government of Providence based?

3. The author said that when the General Court tried Roger Williams for his beliefs, they were sure to decide against him because "some of Williams' angriest accusers were sitting in judgment of him." Explain why having Williams' accusers act as his judges would make sure that the decision went against him.

4. The author quoted a section of the Declaration of Independence and stated that this document reflects Williams' ideas. Do you agree with this statement? State your opinion and explain why you think as you do.

5. Look again at the four principles on which the government of Providence, and later the government of the United States, was based. For each principle, give an example from daily life of how the principle works to protect the freedom of Americans.

A PLAN of the CITY and ENVIRONS of PHILADELPHIA,

with the WORKS and ENCAMPMENTS of His MAJESTY's Forces.

under the Command of Lieutenant General SIR WILLIAM HOWE, K.B

LONDON Engraved and Published as the Act directs by Wm. FADEN, Charing Cross January 6th 1779.

REFERENCES to the PUBLIC BUILDINGS.

Rebecca's War

Ann Finlayson

What can fourteen-year-old Rebecca Ransome do to help the American colonies win their war for independence? Rebecca lives in Philadelphia, a city lately conquered by the British. Her father, Captain William Ransome, and her older brother Will are in France with their trading ship, the Huntress. Her mother is no longer alive, so Rebecca is left in charge of the household and the younger children in a war-torn city that is low on food.

Rebecca is surprised one day when, on a street corner, she meets Will. He tells her that the Huntress is anchored in the Delaware River and is loaded with ingots to be melted down into bullets for Washington's army. He says that Rebecca must hide the lead in the Ransome house until a messenger comes to her bearing one of Will's brass coat buttons. It will match the one that Will puts in Rebecca's hand. Before they part, Will also gives her letters from Benjamin Franklin to Robert Morris, a leading Philadelphia merchant and financial expert. He instructs her to meet him that night at 10 o'clock to receive the secret cargo at the entrance to the old tunnel beneath the Ransome house.

When Rebecca arrives home, she finds a British soldier waiting at her door. He tells her that a British officer is to be quartered in her home and will arrive that afternoon. Rebecca argues in vain. When the soldier leaves, she moves her younger brother and sister into their father's room, and hides the letters from Franklin there in a chest of drawers.

As you read, think about what kind of person Rebecca is and how she handles her difficult situation.

The September sunset came at seven. Rebecca shooed the younger children up the stairs, giggling and excited at the prospect of sleeping in the best bed. With her watching, they washed, donned nightgowns and caps, then scrambled gleefully up the steps to the bed. "Aren't you coming, too, Rebecca? You said you were sleeping here, too. Are you coming to bed with us?"

"In a minute."

She had discovered a new problem. How was she going to know when ten o'clock arrived? The big grandfather clock in the downstairs hall was stopped. The clock maker who came every week to wind it had fled to a cousin's farm in Chester County ten days before, and the timepiece had run down. Besides, with all the excitement of the day, she was more weary than usual, her eyelids already drooping. What if she slept through?

And then she thought, if I go down to the tunnel mouth now, it won't matter whether I doze off or not.

"Go to sleep, you two. I think I'll help Ursula clean up."

"Oh, Rebecca, you said—"

"Be still, Amelia, and go to sleep. I'll be in with you before you know it."

They settled down grumblingly, and she slipped out and closed the door behind her. Then she crept down the stairs and tiptoed into the darkened parlor, where she waited, trying not to breathe, as Ursula made finishing-up noises in the kitchen. At last footsteps scraped on the kitchen stairs, a door closed, and the steps went past the parlor door and up the stairs to the second floor, then up the ladder to the garret. Far at the top of the house, another door closed.

Rebecca gave it five more minutes for good measure, then tiptoed out of the parlor and down the hall. Behind the stairs was the door to the serving pantry, where steps led to the basement. She crept down them, easing her weight with care, and stood with pounding heart in the empty kitchen.

It was pitch black, except for a pink glow from the banked cooking fire. How still the house was—much stiller, it seemed to her, than when she lay listening to it in her cozy bed. Not even street noises penetrated.

She gave herself a shake. First, she told herself briskly, light a candle at the fire. Second, find flint and steel, and put the candle in the lantern. Third, get Ursula's old marketing cloak from the hook, because it's going to be cold down there. Fourth—well, do the first three, and then we'll see.

Her preparations made, she went into the laundry room and lifted the trapdoor that covered the tunnel entrance. Damp air stirred against her face, bringing the faint, fishy smell of brackish water. She held her candle over the hole. It—it certainly was inky black—worse than the kitchen . . .

All Philadelphia knew about the Ransome tunnel nowadays, but it once had been a deep, dark secret, well kept for many years. Her grandfather had dug it himself, with the help of three husky shipmates, and shored up the walls and ceiling with ship's timbers. It ran all the way from the house to the Delaware, emerging under the shelter of what had once been the Willing and Morris wharf. The pier was old and decrepit now, creaking and sagging underfoot as you walked, but it had once been the busiest in the city. It was the easiest thing in the world to offload undutied silks and Dutch tea by night, hustle them straight into the tunnel, and store them there till it was time to have a quiet little sale that the preventive officers knew nothing about.

And now, after years of lying empty or being used as a playroom by the young Ransomes, the tunnel was about to have secrets again.

Rebecca took a deep breath to steady her nerve, clutched her mantle, lantern, and tinderbox tightly, and started down the ladder. Once she was actually in the tunnel proper, it seemed less scary. She set off toward the river, picking her way with care, for the tunnel ran sharply downhill, following the conformation of the surface.

And here, gleaming faintly in the starlight, was the Delaware. Rebecca put out her candle and curled up on the damp floor, leaning her back against the timber shoring. It was a good thing she'd taken precautions, for she fell asleep instantly.

What woke her was the soft thud of a boat snubbing against a piling. "Will?" she whispered and was answered by a faint "Ssssh." There was movement in the darkness beside her, then a faint scraping—they were beaching the ship's boat in the tunnel proper.

"Will, listen," she said. "Something's happened. You can't leave that stuff here now—we're going to have an officer in the house."

Something large loomed up beside her. For one terrified moment, she thought, it *isn't* Will! But then it spoke in her brother's voice: "What are you talking about? No, not here—let's go farther into the tunnel. Did you bring the lantern? Good."

Halfway up the tunnel, Will scratched flint and steel until the candlewick caught—the light could not be seen from here because of the slope of the ground—and then demanded the whole story.

His face changed as she poured out her tale of woe. "So if you just wait here, I'll run up and get the papers, and you can go back downriver and rendezvous with Father and try to deliver it through Charleston."

"Hmmm," he said. He walked to and fro, chewing his lip.

There was a footstep behind him, and another figure loomed up in the lantern light. "Teddy!" Rebecca cried and ran to hug the grinning seaman.

"Hello, Miss Becky. You're looking very pretty for the middle of the night."

He was a tough old Conestoga Indian—"Teddy" was the closest whites could get to his long American-Indian name—who had gone to sea with their grandfather in his youth and for the last thirty years had served as their father's coxswain.

"What do you think, Teddy?" Will said. "Tell him about it, Rebecca."

When she had repeated the story, Teddy immediately shook his head. "No, officers or not, this is still the safest place. That whole coast is crawling with frigates."

"True," Will put in.

"I helped fit those hiding holes myself, and they went a good many years without being discovered. If Miss Becky keeps the secret, there's no reason why the British should find the things."

Easy enough to talk lightly about keeping secrets. It had taken every ounce of willpower Rebecca possessed just to get through this one day. "You mean you won't take the papers back? I have to keep them?"

"Teddy's right," Will said. "Under the circumstances, this is the best arrangement we can make. The officers' being in the house might even be a good thing. Last place they'd look for contraband would be right under their noses."

First the barrackmaster, now Will—everybody trying to convince her that it was for her own good to have officers in the house.

"But, *Will*—"

He patted her arm. "You'll do just fine. Come on, Teddy, let's get these ingots unloaded."

She watched in dismay as the men carried armloads of lead ingots from the boat to the ladder. They made an enormous pile. She wondered how the two of them could have rowed such a heavy load all the way up from the Capes. "It seems silly," she said. "Why didn't you leave these with the rest at Henlopen?"

"Oh, bullets are always needed," Teddy said. "The stairs the best place, do you think, Will?"

"Yes."

Working neatly and fast, like the seamen they were, they rigged block and tackle to a hook in the ceiling of the laundry room, fastened a small cargo net to it, loaded the ingots, and hauled up. Then Teddy with an armful headed for the stairs leading up from the kitchen, where he squatted down before the bottom step.

He took hold of the edge of the tread and pulled on it, and the tread slid off smoothly on well-soaped grooves, revealing a boxlike space a foot deep and two feet long. It just held two ingots. With the tread back in place, it looked as innocent as any staircase in Pennsylvania. As Will brought armloads of ingots from the laundry room, Teddy moved methodically up the staircase, storing two ingots in each step.

"Well, that's it," Teddy said at the top. "We'll have to put the rest in the hall stairs."

"Oh, please, Will—please, don't! You'll wake Ursula!" She caught at his arm, causing him to lose his grip on an ingot, which went crashing to the stone floor and skidded.

"Talk about *me* waking Ursula," he grumbled as he picked it up.

But Rebecca was not listening. The skid had dug a deep groove in the lead, and even in the dim lantern light, she could see that the material at the bottom of the groove was not gray but yellow.

"That isn't lead," she said numbly.

"That's gold."

Teddy and Will exchanged despairing glances. "She'll have to know now," Teddy said.

"Right." But though they both turned to Rebecca, neither of them seemed able to get started.

"It's gold," she repeated incredulously. "You're storing lead-coated *gold* in our house!"

"Three million livres worth," Will acknowledged. "It's a loan from the French king. Nobody knows about it but Father, Teddy, and me, not even the rest of the crew. And now you, of course."

"It's really *gold*!"

"It's got to be kept secret, do you understand, Rebecca? As secret as the grave."

Even in the midst of her shock, Rebecca was aware of something cockeyed. "But—but why bring it here, to this country? Europe is where the supplies are. Why not borrow the money and spend it right in France!"

"It's not for spending. It's for shoring up the currency. Without it our paper money would be worthless. The letter I gave you explains all that—the letter from Franklin to Morris."

"Oh." Gold. Three million livres in gold. It was unimaginable.

"Come on, Teddy, let's get the rest of it put away. Rebecca, you go upstairs, and if Ursula stirs or one of the children, don't let them come out into the hall."

Dutifully, her head still swimming with confusion, Rebecca took her stand in the upper hall, to act as lookout. Will tiptoed back and forth with the ingots, while Teddy knelt and with infinite caution, eased the treads open. Two steps from the top, they stored away the last of the ingots. All three sighed with relief.

Downstairs in the kitchen once more, Will turned to Rebecca. "Now you've got the button?"

"Yes."

"All right, keep it on you. Wear it on a ribbon or something. You can tell people it's a keepsake. We'll try to get word through to General Washington that the gold is here and he's to send an agent. Of course, if the *Huntress* is taken—" He shrugged. "Well, do your best. As long as the British don't discover the gold, it won't matter too much how long it stays there."

It didn't matter to *him* maybe.

A moment later, he and Teddy were climbing down the ladder to the tunnel. "And remember," Will concluded, his top half projecting from the hole, "don't tell *anyone*." Then he vanished, and she eased the trapdoor back in place.

One British officer comes to stay in the Ransome house, and soon another. The second officer presents Rebecca with an unexpected problem. He is a kind-hearted young man, and she soon finds herself making friends with him. But suppose she forgets herself some day and mistakenly reveals the secret to him? Then, as the Americans later fight to recapture Philadelphia and secure the gold, Rebecca's loyalty and courage are tested to the limit. The way in which she meets the test makes an exciting conclusion to Rebecca's War.

1. Why was there a tunnel beneath the Ransome house?
2. Why did Teddy and Will decide to hide the gold in the house even though a British officer would be staying there?
3. At the beginning of the story, Rebecca thinks, "If I go down to the tunnel mouth now, it won't matter whether I doze off or not." Explain why it won't be a problem if she goes to sleep in the tunnel mouth.
4. Was Rebecca a timid person, one who lacked self-confidence or courage? State your opinion and use examples from the story to explain why you think as you do.
5. Rebecca found that keeping an important secret was hard work: "It had taken every ounce of willpower Rebecca possessed just to get through this one day." Why do you think it is sometimes hard to keep an important secret?

Independence and Ink

Marilyn Sachs

The American Revolution was the work of many individuals. Each individual tried in a large or small way to help the cause of independence. In this excerpt from the novel Marv, *you will meet an individual whose mind works in an unusual way. The story is set in the America of 1940. At that time, most people wrote with fountain pens that had to be filled often from inkwells or small bottles set in their desks. As you read, think about Marv and the idea that captures his imagination.*

"We hold these truths to be self-evident that all men are created equal," read Mr. Henderson, Marv's teacher in 8A-2. Marv tried to concentrate deeply on what his teacher was saying.

There was a picture in the book which showed a group of men in wigs and short pants standing around a table. Behind them sat a whole bunch of other men with wigs and short pants who were watching them attentively. The description under the illustration read: *This painting of the signing of the Declaration of Independence was made by the American artist, John Trumbull, 1756-1843.*

". . . Independence Hall in Philadelphia on July 4, 1776, Congress approved the Declaration of Independence," Mr. Henderson was saying, his voice mellow, "and the great experiment in democracy began. Our Declaration of Independence was a source of inspiration to other countries yearning for freedom."

Marv dipped his pen into the inkwell on his desk, and wrote in his notebook *Decklaration of I.—sauce of inspira—*There was not enough ink on the pen to finish the word. He looked into the inkwell, and found it nearly empty. There was possibly enough ink though for him to finish his word.

—tion, he wrote.

Maybe during recess he could ask Mr. Henderson to let him fill his inkwell, and perhaps Mr. Henderson would let him fill the other inkwells too. Marv found it an extremely satisfying job, carrying the bottle with its deep blue contents from desk to desk, and holding the spout over each of the thirsty glass inkwells.

"If these men, who knew they faced imprisonment and even death on the charge of treason, had not had the courage to sign the Declaration of Independence, our country might still be part of England today." Courage, thought Marv, and ink.

He studied the picture in the textbook. There was a quill pen resting in an inkwell, but the picture did not show clearly how much ink there was in the inkwell.

Marv looked at all the people gathered around the table— maybe there were ten on all sides. He studied the number of men seated, who would shortly be on their feet, also prepared to sign— maybe another forty or fifty. He felt a chill run down his spine. Suppose there had not been enough ink in the inkwell. Suppose it had been dry like his own.

Mr. Henderson was smiling. "The first was John Hancock, president of the Continental Congress." The teacher chuckled. "He is supposed to have said that he would sign his name so large that King George wouldn't need his spectacles to see it."

A replica of the Declaration of Independence was shown on the page next to the illustration. Look at the size of John Hancock's signature! Look at all those extra twists and twirls! Marv began to feel panicky. Why, it would take every bit of ink in his inkwell, and maybe more just to supply John Hancock alone, with enough to sign his name.

He felt a mounting irritation with John Hancock. Studying the other signatures on the Declaration showed him that there were some, like Elbridge Gerry and John Morton, not to mention several others whose names he couldn't make out, who had a little more concern for the ink consumption than John Hancock. It seemed to Marv that John Hancock might have been a great patriot, and a brave fighter for freedom and all that, but he certainly didn't understand that this country wouldn't be here today if everybody had the same wasteful attitude toward ink that he did.

Wasn't there that poem they had been studying this term about how a whole war was lost just because of one horseshoe nail that didn't fit right? The horse couldn't run, the rider couldn't deliver his message, the general didn't know where the battle was supposed to be—it was a mess. Same thing though with the ink. If they had run out of ink, and if there had been no ink anywhere else in the building, and if they had to send out for some, and if the British soldiers had seen them and grown suspicious, they might have arrested all of them. The war would never have been fought. This would still be a colony of England, and he, Marv, had no intention of letting that happen.

He squinted at the inkwell in the picture, but it was impossible to see just how much ink there was in that inkwell. All right, then, figure the worst. Figure that there was only enough for John Hancock to sign his name. Then what?

Perhaps some brave person, not an important delegate but someone who was willing to run the risk of danger, might volunteer to go out and find some ink.

A shadowy, muffled figure crept by a British soldier dozing over his rifle. It was night. The muffled figure had something bulky concealed under his cloak. Silently he passed through the shadows and into a house with curtains drawn. Inside, there was a group of men with wigs and short pants, gathered around a table. Behind them sat a whole bunch of other men with wigs and short pants, who were watching them attentively. Into their midst strode the muffled figure. He threw off his cloak. It was Marv, in a wig and short pants, holding a bottle of ink with a spout, just like the one they used in school.

Ridiculous! His face grew warm. How could he be so silly! He dismissed the apparition from the painting, and concentrated on the inkwell. How could it be kept full of ink? How?

His face wrinkled painfully over the painting. The inkwell rested on a table covered by a tablecloth. You couldn't see what was under the table. It was possible to conceal a large bottle of ink, and perhaps to have rubber tubing attached from the bottle of ink up to the inkwell.

Yes, but it was one thing to get fluid to flow down. How did you get it to flow up? Marv pressed his lips together, and sank his head in his hands. How could you get the ink to flow up from the bottle to

the inkwell? Up. That was the key word. But what was the problem? Why did he always make things harder than they really were. If you want something to flow up, you attach a pump. Nothing complicated about that.

Now then, that problem was solved. Or was it? What was to prevent the bottle of ink under the table from running out of ink? Marv hit his head. Shortsighted as usual. No, he needed a greater source of supply. How about in the cellar of Independence Hall? How about a huge vat that could hold enough ink to last for a couple of years? Sure, you could even rig it up so that when the ink dropped below a certain level, a spring-loaded pendulum could begin banging against a couple of pails. You would still have enough ink left for a few days when that happened so that, even if all the signers of the Declaration of Independence heard the banging, they still wouldn't have to worry about going out to find some ink.

Marv leaned his cheek on his hand, and thought with satisfaction how nothing in this world is impossible if you put your mind to it.

Of course, with the vat in the basement of Independence Hall, you could have pipes running into every room in the building. Pipes could connect with every inkwell in the place. No inkwell in Independence Hall need ever run dry again. Marv licked his lips. But wait! Pipes? Were there any pipes in 1776? Maybe not, but there are today. All over the country, important papers have to be signed. John Hancock wasn't the only one who needed ink. How about President Roosevelt? Didn't he need ink? And Governor Lehman? And Mayor La Guardia?

All over the country, people had electricity, didn't they? They had water pumped in and out of their houses. How about ink? Wouldn't people always need ink? Didn't his own father need ink? What would the Bakers Union, Local 27, do if his father didn't have enough ink to write his reports? Nobody should ever be without ink. Every city should have a central supply with pipes that connected to every house. The ink could flow forever, and this country would be safe.

But where was everybody going? Why was everybody getting up? He wasn't finished. He hadn't worked out ink meters for each house. Why was everybody in such a hurry?

"Marvin," said Mr. Henderson, "didn't you even hear the three o'clock bell?"

Marv shook his head, trying to shake himself back into P.S. 63 at three o'clock on a Friday afternoon, April 30, 1940.

1. Describe the final version of Marv's ink supply system.
2. For what reasons did Marv worry about the country's ink supply?
3. Was Marv correct in thinking that ink plays an important role in history? Why or why not?
4. This story is told from Marv's point of view. Describe briefly what the story would be like if it were told from Mr. Henderson's point of view. Be sure to include the details that describe Marv's actions.

WOMAN for the DEFENSE

Mary Virginia Fox

The patriots of 1776 fought for the right of self-government. Other people in other times have fought for different rights. Among them was Belva Lockwood, who demanded the right to pursue the career of her choice. In 1873, she fought for her right to be recognized as a lawyer. Becoming the first woman lawyer in the United States was just the first of the many accomplishments that would make her famous. As you read this biography, try to discover why people in the nineteenth century wanted to deny Belva's right to a career.

On October 23, 1869, Belva Lockwood applied for admission to Columbia College law school. Almost immediately she received a reply from President Samson. "We think the attendance of ladies would be an injurious diversion of the attention to the students."

Belva had expected opposition, but such a flimsy excuse annoyed her. Her husband, Dr. Ezekiel Lockwood, chuckled. "You should be flattered."

Belva was not amused. "I will send my application to every school in the country."

Georgetown University was the next to refuse her request. They gave no other reason than she was a woman and women had never been admitted. She wrote a third letter addressed to Mr. William Wedgewood, Vice Chancellor of the new National University Law School in Washington. Mr. Wedgewood had spoken openly in favor of women's rights. Belva intended to test his sincerity. She took her letter to him personally.

He was surprised but not dismayed at her request. "I don't believe that the university faculty will approve of the publicity that is bound to develop. But I'll speak in your behalf, Mrs. Lockwood."

It was several weeks before he gave her his disappointing answer. "As I thought, the faculty has refused your admission as a student, Mrs. Lockwood. But I am willing to give you private instruction. If other women are interested, I'll conduct classes in my office. However, you must understand this will not entitle you to a university diploma."

Belva was not dismayed. The first stumbling block had been overcome. She'd solve the other problems as they came. She started recruiting other young women for the study program.

Fifteen students enrolled in Mr. Wedgewood's classes. The professor admitted that they far surpassed his male students in determination and concentration. Belva managed to keep up with her lessons by studying late into the night. Frequently she had only four or five hours of sleep, but she seemed to thrive on her exhausting schedule. Extra demands on her time merely seemed to stimulate

her, and even now there were new causes to support.

She took on a new project, fighting for equal pay for female Civil Service employees. Men were often paid two or three times as much as women for an equal workload. Belva questioned many government agencies and came up with some discouraging statistics.

"Ezekiel, did you know that a woman cannot earn more than seventy-five dollars a month as a Civil Service employee? Some of these women are trying to support families on this income!"

"That's a disgrace," Dr. Lockwood agreed. "Those facts ought to be brought to the attention of Congress."

"You're right, Ezekiel. Legislation is the only answer."

Belva took her husband's advice. She drafted a bill that would equalize the salary structure of all Civil Service employees. After much persuasion, the Honorable J. M. Arnell of Tennessee agreed to present it to Congress. He warned her, "Don't expect immediate results. The bill won't be out of committee for voting for several months."

In the meantime, Ezekiel and Belva traveled to New York City. They attended the state and national conventions of the Woman Suffrage Association.

As soon as they returned, she called on Mr. Arnell to learn when her Civil Service bill would be presented for vote. A date had been set. On March 21, 1870, she sat nervously in the balcony of the House of Representatives. She listened to the words she had drafted read before the members of Congress. It was hard to restrain herself from entering the debate. She heard the opposition claim that it was unfair to pay women an equal salary when men had to support families. She wanted to ask: What about widows and unmarried women? Did a woman have to depend on a man for her substance? Shouldn't she have a choice? Shouldn't she have an equal chance to earn an equal living wage?

Belva held her breath when the roll was called. One by one the representatives spoke their yeas and nays. Belva kept her own count. It would be a close decision, but when the last vote was cast, she knew that the bill had passed the House of Representatives. It must still be tested in the Senate, but Mr. Arnell assured her that opinion was favorable. His prediction proved true. The bill became law. Thereafter, men and women in the Civil Service would receive equal pay for equal work. Belva had won her first legal battle in her lifelong fight for women's rights. It was the first women's

rights law ever to be passed by Congress.

"I know it's not very modest of me, Ezekiel, to say that I'm proud of this accomplishment," Belva said, "but it's not conceit I feel. It's only pride that we've shown the public it is possible to correct injustice by legislation."

"You've set an important example," he replied.

By May 1873 Belva had finished her course of study at the National University Law School. Mr. Wedgewood delivered the news he had predicted. "I cannot offer you a diploma, Mrs. Lockwood."

"I failed the examination?" Belva asked.

"No, on the contrary, I would say that you were one of my most outstanding students. I am sure you can guess the reason. The majority of the faculty do not approve of your desire to follow a career in law. It is unfair, Mrs. Lockwood, but there is nothing I can do."

These words again acted as a challenge. "I will not give up," she said firmly. Anyone seeing her mouth set with determination and her shoulders squared for battle could well have predicted the outcome. Her adversary was none other than the President of the United States, Ulysses S. Grant. By

virtue of his office, he was also the honorary head of the National University Law School. He rarely took a hand in any of the school's affairs. He surely must have been more than a little surprised when he received a personal letter on September 3, 1873.

"You are, or you are not, the President of the National University Law School. If you are its President, I wish to say to you that I have passed through the curriculum of study of that school and am entitled to, and demand, my Diploma. If you are not its President, then I ask you to take your name from its papers, and not hold out to the world to be what you are not."

Mrs. Lockwood received no reply to her letter. But within a week she was granted the Degree of L.L.B. signed by the faculty and by President Grant. There was no ceremony, no cap and gown graduation. The diploma was delivered by a letter carrier, but she read and reread it.

"I'm so very proud for you," Ezekiel said. Then he added with a twinkle in his eye, "Do you know this makes me the very first husband of a lawyer, the very first?"

At forty-three years of age Belva Lockwood was about to start on a new career. She was the first woman lawyer in the history of the United States.

Belva opened an office in her home and was soon busy. She did not mean to serve only women in her law practice, but few men were willing to ask for her help.

Though she was a lawyer, she continued to have trouble being accepted in the legal world. Judges often refused to allow her to argue cases in their courtrooms. She had several important victories, but the obstacles angered her.

Instead of giving up, Belva decided to apply for admission to the Supreme Court of the United States, the highest court in the land. If she was accepted there, what other court could refuse her? It would also be an unexpected tactic, and surprise might be in her favor.

She was about to begin this campaign when her husband, Ezekiel, suffered a stroke. Belva canceled all her business appointments and cared for him day and night. Slowly he regained his strength. He spent his time in a bed or in a chair by the window. During the day she sat beside him. She read or, when he felt like talking, chatted about letters she had received. People all over the country asked her legal opinion on how best to fight the local laws of prejudice.

"You are needed in court much more desperately than in the kitchen," Ezekiel remarked.

"Surely we can hire a housekeeper to take care of my wants."

Belva shook her head. "I'm enjoying myself, Ezekiel, selfishly satisfying my own self."

"I thank you for putting it that way," he answered, "but I insist. Soon you will be restless. It is foolish to waste our combined energies in an invalid's room."

Belva reluctantly took his advice. Baking biscuits was not her best talent. Martha Applebe joined the household and relieved Belva of some of her work. Still she took on only the more important cases presented to her. She could handle her correspondence at home. Much of it was directed to her goal of gaining admission to the United States Supreme Court.

Dr. Lockwood made a wise suggestion. "I believe you'll have a better chance if you submit your case to Congress. Only through legislation will the court acknowledge your rights."

Belva reached for her husband's hand. "Ezekiel, you do a great deal to bolster my strength when it is sagging."

"My dear, if it sagged a trifle less, I cringe at the thought of the state of our nation." They both laughed. The day was a happy one.

At once she wrote a petition and submitted it to Congress. The petition asked that Congress pass a law stating that no woman lawyer should be kept from practicing before any United States Court merely because she was a woman.

On May 25, 1874, the petition was submitted to a Senate committee. The unwinding of red tape was just beginning. At times the snarls seemed impossible to unravel.

The years between 1874 and 1879 were eventful ones for Belva. She spoke publicly on many occasions, including the 1877 national convention of the Woman Suffrage Association. "I have been told," she said, "that there is no precedent for admitting a woman to practice in the Supreme Court of the United States. The glory of each generation is to make its own precedents." Her name became familiar to hundreds of people. Her words were quoted, her actions reported.

There were also years of tragedy. On the twenty-third of April in 1877, her husband died in his sleep. Belva was stunned with grief, but she soon turned back to work as a cure for sorrow. Remembering Ezekiel's advice, she drafted a bill that would permit women to appear before the Supreme Court, and convinced a member of the Senate to submit it. In February of 1879, after having passed the House of Representatives the previous year, the bill was approved by the Senate, signed by the President, and became law.

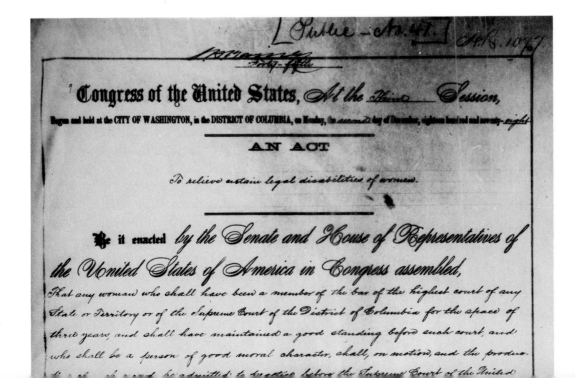

At one o'clock on March 3, 1879, Belva stood between her two sponsors, Judge Samuel Shellabager and the Honorable Jeremiah Wilson, before the judges of the United States Supreme Court. A newspaper reporter in the gallery wrote that Mrs. Belva Lockwood looked frail and nervous. Anyone knowing this indomitable woman would have allowed that she might at this moment be feeling a twinge of nervous excitement. But never would they have described her as frail.

She stood solemnly listening to the order being read that admitted her to the bar of the highest court of the land. Yes, she did feel nervous. So much depended on her own conduct. In the public eye she was a representative of all her sex. If she should falter, those who sought these same privileges of equality would have to fight twice as hard for them. She must remain an example of womanly grace. She must also prove intelligence and capability heretofore attributed only to men. She must combine softness and strength, modesty and aggressiveness, a contradiction not expected of any male lawyer.

The nine judges sat on a raised platform before a gleaming slab of mahogany that served as a common desk for all. Behind the judges, marble columns marched in an impressive line the width of the high, vaulted room. Directly behind the chair of Chief Justice Morrison I. Waite, an arched opening was hung with wine-red velvet. Above the arch a golden eagle hovered on a pedestal.

Chief Justice Waite rose and made his way to the end of the dais. The court clerk came forward from his station. He held in his hand a heavy, leather-bound Bible. Belva placed her small gloved hand on the sacred volume and repeated the oath that she would uphold the justice of the court to the best of her ability. Her voice was strong.

247

When the last word was spoken, Chief Justice Waite and her sponsors warmly offered their congratulations. Many others crowded around to shake her hand. Belva felt proud. But she knew many approached her out of curiosity rather than because they approved. She was now a mature woman of forty-eight, and was about to assume new responsibilities in her life. She wished with all her heart that Ezekiel might have lived to witness this day.

Three days later, on motion of the Honorable Thomas J. Durant, she was admitted to the United States Court of Claims. Her triumph was complete. It was in this court, that Belva was to win some of her most important cases.

A year after she herself was admitted to practice before the Supreme Court, Belva sponsored Samuel Lowry, a black clergyman, to the same position. Thanks to Belva's efforts, he became the first black American to be admitted to the bar of our nation's highest court. While keeping up an active law practice that included other women lawyers, Belva became interested in politics as well. In 1884, the Equal Rights Party nominated her to run for President. Later, the U.S. government sent her as a delegate to the first world peace conference, and she drafted the first legislation proposing a world court to be considered by Congress. At the age of seventy-five, she successfully defended the land rights of the North Carolina Cherokee Indians. It was not until her eighty-third birthday that she finally retired. She died in May of 1917, ending a life of commitment to civil rights and world peace.

1. How did Belva convince the National University Law School to grant her the degree she had earned?
2. Why did Belva decide to apply for admission to the Supreme Court of the United States?
3. Describe two ways in which Ezekiel helped and encouraged Belva in her career.
4. What personal qualities helped Belva obtain her goals?
5. This biography contains a number of clues to nineteenth-century attitudes toward women who, like Belva, wanted a career. Examine the selection closely and explain why, at this time, people wanted to deny Belva's right to a career.

The Party Representative

Ruth Gruber

In 1932, women were allowed to vote for the first time in Puerto Rico. Felisa Rincón Marrero told her father she wanted to register. She had been a dutiful daughter. Since she was twelve, she had acted as a mother to her seven younger brothers and sisters. She had also run her father's farm and looked after the jíbaros, *the peasant workers, for years. But Don Enrique, her father, disapproved of the idea. He had grown up in Puerto Rico's older Spanish traditions, and believed that men alone should run the society. Convincing her father was Felisa's first task on the road to equal rights. Though she did not know it, it was also the first step toward a career. As you read, notice the importance that politics assumes in Felisa's life.*

One Saturday in 1932, Felisa entered the living room, carrying a newspaper. Don Enrique was reading a book.

He looked up. "Yes, Felisa?"

She handed him the paper.

"I've read it," he said.

"Did you read what happened in the legislature?"

"A lot happened. Not all of it very good, either!" He put the book down.

"They've passed the law, Father. Women have the right to vote."

"Why they did it, I'll never know. One of the most stupid laws in Puerto Rican history."

Felisa spoke slowly. "Father, I am going to register."

She was surprised at her own voice. It was the first time she had ever spoken so firmly to her father.

"You are . . . what?"

"I'm going to register to vote." Her voice quavered.

Don Enrique paused. Felisa saw his fingers tremble. He stood up and began to pace the living room. "Why should women want to vote? They will lose their charm, their softness. I know what politics is like. It's a gutter. Women? In the gutter of politics?"

Felisa spoke in a low voice. "Puerto Rican women can vote, Father, and I am going to register to vote with them."

She sat down in her favorite mahogany rocking chair, and clasped her hands tightly.

She did not know how her defiance would affect her father. But she knew that nothing could hold her back. She sensed this decision to vote was the most important in her life thus far.

Don Enrique tried reasoning with her. "Women have so much more to give their husbands and their children than politics.

Men are born to be the ruling class, but women are the heart of the family—the core. What can politics give them to replace what they have? What do you want all this for? You're a lovely woman, Felisa. You're so feminine. Why do you want to change?"

"I can be feminine and still vote, Father." She paused a moment. "Going to vote won't turn me into a man."

"Father," she continued, "can't you see? Everyone in Puerto Rico had the right to vote except criminals, the insane, and women. It took all these years, twelve years after women could vote on the mainland, before our legislature could see that women aren't gangsters or insane."

"Letting women vote is insane." Don Enrique pounded his fist on the top of the sofa.

"You think I'm the equal of a crazy person?"

He was startled. She had never before questioned his judgment. This was a new Felisa. He sat down in his big chair.

Then Felisa watched him as he again rose to his feet. She kept herself under tight control. She was surprised at her own determination, and the sense of power and strength it gave her.

Once again she watched her father stalk up and down. She knew he had tried to live his life in two cultures—Spanish and American. He was an old-fashioned Spaniard within his home; an American liberal outside. Now the two cultures were colliding.

Don Enrique walked to the window. With his back to Felisa, he said in a low, hoarse voice, "Aren't you content? I've tried to give you everything you've asked for . . . money . . . clothes . . ."

Felisa did not answer. She pressed her lips tightly together.

Her father turned toward her. He was pulling at his mustache. "You really want this?" He looked at her as if he were seeing her for the first time.

"I've never wanted anything so much in my life."

He nodded slowly. "All right. I will take you to the polls to register myself."

Felisa jumped up and kissed him.

At five o'clock on Monday morning, she and her father appeared in the Department of Health building at Stop 19. The registration hall had just opened; it was a large, bare room with a few tables and chairs. This registration was for women only, since they had just been given the right to vote.

There were only a handful of people. Felisa recognized the daughter of Doña Ana Roqué, the suffragette leader, standing fourth in line. Felisa was fifth. Somehow it seemed symbolic that she should be standing behind Doña Ana's daughter.

Finally it was her turn. She signed her name in the big registration book, with a little flourish on the *F*. According to Spanish custom, she signed her first name, then her father's surname, and last her mother's surname. She looked at her handiwork as she wrote slowly and gracefully, *Felisa Rincón Marrero*.

She straightened herself to her full height. She had the sense of standing for the first time on equal ground with her father and brothers. She was no longer a non-person in the dynamic

political life of the island. When elections were held, she would cast her vote. The vote was a symbol. From now on, she would be heard.

The large registration room began to fill up. She saw men sitting at the tables. She learned that they represented the Coalition—the Republican party and the Socialist party. But she saw no one who represented the Liberal party. It was the Liberal party that she would join.

At that moment, Don Antonio Barceló, the president of the Liberal party, entered the room. He embraced Felisa with a big hug. "So you have come at dawn to register. It is a good omen for the party."

He slapped Don Enrique on the shoulder. "Its good to see you here with Felisa."

Don Enrique forced himself to smile.

Felisa looked around as more women entered, queuing up to register. "Don Antonio," she said. "I know I don't understand these things. But I see men here helping people to register for the Socialist party and the Republican party. I don't see anyone helping our people register."

Don Antonio nodded. "I asked some men to come, but maybe they had other things to do. Anyway, you're right. Nobody has showed up. It's not good." He looked at her sharply. "What about you, Felisa?"

"Me?" She drew back. "I don't know anything about—about registering people."

A huge smile spread over Don Antonio's face. "Nothing to it. All you have to do is help the women who come here. Afterward, you can go around to your friends and get them to sign up for the Liberal party. They can register for the next two weeks; then they're eligible to vote in the elections next November."

He turned to Don Enrique. "I've decided, Enrique. Felisa will be our party's representative. Don't you agree that she'll be very good at it?"

"I don't know," Don Enrique said hesitantly. "I don't like it . . . truthfully. She can't go out alone at night . . ."

Don Antonio tossed his head and roared with laughter. "Is she a child? Anyway, she doesn't have to go out at night. She can work whenever she likes—morning—afternoons. Don't worry about Felisa. She can take care of herself."

"I'm not happy about it," Don Enrique said.

"Why? She's not running for office. She's not going to be paid. This is a volunteer job. And she has time now; your children are grown. What do you say?"

Don Enrique nodded vaguely.

Without waiting for a further answer, Don Antonio took Felisa by the arm and led her across the room to the area where Judge Carballeira sat overseeing the procedures. The judge swore Felisa in as the official representative of the Liberal party.

As the morning went on, Felisa sat at the table of the Liberal party trying to help newcomers and, at the same time, trying to learn the procedures of registration. The other party representatives looked at her with polite but condescending amusement.

That afternoon when Felisa went home, she thought "By this time next week when I enter that room where they're registering women, those men will notice me. They'll know who I am."

Each morning she went to the Department of Health building to help the women register. At lunchtime, instead of going home, she went out to urge her friends who still had not come to the building to register. In the heat of high noon, she knocked on the doors of their homes.

The women of the household invited her in. "But, Felisa, why should we bother to vote? Politics—that's for men."

Felisa found herself arguing with her friends in the same way she had argued with her father. Even when she succeeded in convincing them that they should register to vote, she still failed to convince most of them to join the Liberal party. They considered themselves aristocrats who did not want to mix with the common people.

Felisa discovered her real success lay with the maids, the cooks, the wives of the gardeners and chauffeurs who worked for her friends. So, each day from noon to one o'clock, she returned to her friends' houses, no longer to talk to them but to get their household workers to register. Some of the people she brought were semiliterate. The law required them to fill out the blanks themselves. But many like Felisa felt that the literacy requirement was an artificial barrier to keep the poor from voting. So she helped them.

She went from person to person. To a maid with a name which began with *O* she said, "The letter *O* is written like this. Make something round. Make a circle. But don't write anything else until I come back."

The maid wrote *O* while Felisa went to the next person and taught her how to write the letter *R* or *S*; then she returned to teach the maid the next letter, until each one had filled the registration blank. When Election Day came in November, they were eligible to vote.

Registration mounted steadily. Leaders of the Liberal party, watching Felisa instruct the people, saw her become a one-woman recruiting team. Two weeks after she herself had registered for the first time, she was appointed a member of the Executive Committee of the Liberal party.

Now when she stood up, the other party representatives noticed her. The men had begun to know who she was.

Felisa's involvement in politics continued to increase. Fourteen years later she became the first woman mayor of San Juan.

As mayor, Dona Felisa never forgot the jíbaros. *She initiated a program called "Operation Bootstrap," which cleaned up San Juan, emptied the city of its beggars, built a chain of nursery schools, improved the hospitals, gave shoes, clothes, and thousands of toys at holiday time, and turned City Hall into a house of the people. During her twenty-two years in office, she won worldwide admiration for her success.*

---

1. Explain how Felisa became the Liberal party's representative.

2. Why was Felisa appointed a member of the Executive Committee of the Liberal party?

3. Why did Don Enrique agree to let Felisa vote?

4. Felisa thought: "By this time next week when I enter that room where they're registering women, those men will notice me." Why did Felisa want the men to notice her?

5. Why do you think politics became so important to Felisa?

Types of Paragraph Organization

A *paragraph* is a group of sentences that tell about the same subject. Usually a paragraph has a main idea and supporting details. The *main idea* states the most important idea of the paragraph. The *supporting details* provide more information about the main idea.

Although most paragraphs have a main idea and supporting details, paragraphs may also be organized in different ways. As you read, remember that writers choose different methods of organizing their ideas depending on their purposes. Here are four types of paragraphs:

1. **Listing of facts**   In this type of paragraph, the details are facts or examples listed after the main idea. The details may be listed in their order of importance. For example,

    > The government in Rhode Island was based on four principles. First, all people were equal. Second, the government received its power from the people. Third, the government was not to interfere with freedom of conscience. Fourth, the government's main job was to protect and insure the rights of the citizens.

In the paragraph above, the main idea is stated in the first sentence. The other sentences list facts that tell more about the main idea.

2. **Sequence**   In this type of paragraph, the details tell about events in a given order. The details may give instructions or describe historical happenings. For example,

    > The struggle for American independence was hard fought. On April 19, 1775, colonists and British soldiers clashed at Lexington and Concord. On June 17, 1775, the British drove the Americans from their position at Bunker Hill. General Washington gained a victory at Princeton on January 3, 1777. On October 19, 1781, the British surrendered in the war's last major battle.

In this paragraph the details tell about events in chronological order. Note the use of dates to tell the sequence of happenings.

3. **Comparison and contrast**   Sometimes the details in a paragraph show similarities and differences between or among two or more things. For example,

In the American War for Independence, a victory for either side was possible. The British were better trained than the colonists. The English fleet outnumbered the American ships. Britain also had cash and credit to support its troops. However, the colonists did not need to send supplies overseas. The colonists were also more familiar with the terrain than the British were.

The paragraph above tells the difference between the British and American armies.

4. **Cause and effect**   In this type of paragraph the cause for an effect, or result, is stated. Sometimes more than one cause or effect is explained. For example,

In 1765, the British parliament passed the Stamp Act. The Stamp Act required colonists to buy stamps and place them on newspapers, diplomas, and legal papers. The angry colonists protested, claiming they were being taxed without being represented. As a result, the Stamp Act was repealed in 1766.

In this paragraph the cause was the protest of the angry colonists. The effect, or result, was the repeal of the Stamp Act.

Read each paragraph. Then read the questions that follow. Write the answers to the questions on your paper.

1. The fight against disease has had significant developments. In 1796, Edward Jenner discovered a vaccine to prevent smallpox. In the late 1800's, Louis Pasteur and Robert Koch found that germs caused many diseases and infections. At the same time, Joseph Lister developed a method of antiseptic surgery. Sulfa drugs and penicillin were developed in the 1930's and 1940's. Jonas Salk introduced the first polio vaccine in the 1950's.
   a. Which type of paragraph is the above paragraph?
   b. What is the main idea of the paragraph?
   c. What dates appear in the paragraph?

2. During the 1880's, United States railroad companies made huge profits. People battled for control of the railroad companies. Dishonest individuals sold worthless railroad stock. Companies fought for freight business. Some joined together to eliminate competition and raise prices. As a result of these unfair practices, Congress passed a law that set up rules for the railroads.
   a. What type of paragraph is the above paragraph?
   b. What is the result mentioned at the end of the paragraph?
   c. List three causes for the result.

3. The shark serves many purposes for people. Shark hide makes a long-lasting leather after the scales have been removed. In some parts of the world, people eat shark flesh. Scientists study the bodies and organs of sharks to understand the human body better.
   a. What type of paragraph is the above paragraph?
   b. What is the main idea of the paragraph?
   c. How many supporting facts appear in the paragraph?

4. The city of Paris has had a long history. In ancient times, a Celtic tribe called the *Parissi* lived in that area of France. Roman invaders established a colony there in 52 B.C. The area became known as Paris about 300 A.D.
   a. What type of paragraph is the above paragraph?
   b. What is the main idea of the paragraph?
   c. What dates appear in the paragraph?

5. The first two political parties in the United States were the Federalist Party and the Democratic-Republican Party. The Federalists, led by Alexander Hamilton, wanted a strong central government. The Democratic-Republicans, led by Thomas Jefferson, supported a weaker central government. Both parties split after the 1816 presidential election.
   a. What type of paragraph is the above paragraph?
   b. What two things are compared in the paragraph?
   c. Write one way in which the things were similar.
   d. Write one way in which the things were different.

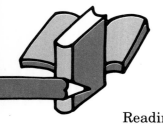

Social Studies Vocabulary

Reading in social studies covers many different areas. You may read articles relating to politics, history, law, geography or maps. Each of these subjects has special vocabulary words that are often used. Here are examples of words you might find in different social studies articles:

Politics: referendum, amendment, liberal, adjournment, lobby
History: reparations, secession, colonial, persecution
Law: injunction, municipal, judicial, martial, extradite
Geography: habitat, continental, glacier, seismograph
Maps: legend, longitude, latitude, hemisphere, peninsula

Sometimes you find an unfamiliar word in your social studies reading. You may look up the word in a dictionary. You might also understand the word by the way it is used in the sentence. The other words and sentences nearby may provide clues to the meaning of the word. Here is an example from the article you read about Roger Williams:

> That he has the right to speak whatever <u>treason</u> he likes: to say that the king himself rules only because the people let him rule. You think he should be allowed to defy the law this way?

Study the usage of the word *treason* in the passage. The first sentence mentions the speaking of treason. The example that follows mentions the king, who rules the people. The last sentence talks about defying the law. From these hints, you may conclude that *treason* means "a betraying of one's country."

Many of the following passages have been taken from this book. Study the usage of each underlined word. Write what you think the word means. Then check your definition in a dictionary.

1. The General Court heard the accusations against Williams and his proud defense. There was little doubt of the <u>verdict</u>: the Court banished him from Massachusetts.

2. It was not in Roger Williams' nature to be silent about the wrongs he saw. He continued to speak his mind in public. The Court was stung by his <u>defiance</u>.

3. He had the power to set up whatever government he wanted. But he, who had such a hatred of <u>tyrants</u>, did nothing without the consent of the other colonists.

4. Perhaps some brave person, not an important <u>delegate</u>, but someone who was willing to run the risk of danger might volunteer to go out and find some ink.

5. It seemed to Mary that John Hancock might have been a great <u>patriot</u>, and a brave fighter for freedom, but he certainly didn't understand that this country wouldn't be here today if everybody had the same wasteful attitude toward ink that he did.

6. Have you thought what the king would think if he heard that we tolerate Williams' ideas? How angry he would be at his ungrateful <u>subjects</u>?

7. Rulers have not the least inch of <u>civil</u> power, except what is measured out to them from the free consent of the people.

8. To protect the land from claims of other colonies, Williams went to England and obtained a <u>charter</u> from parliament. The charter joined the four towns into a single colony and gave that colony legal claim to its land.

9. He's a bad penny, I tell you. A troublemaker. A <u>fanatic</u> of the worst kind.

10. She was very proud of the new law. It showed the public that it was possible to correct injustice by <u>legislation</u>.

11. Many people fought against her. Her main <u>adversary</u> was the head of the law school.

12. She <u>drafted</u> a bill that would permit women to appear before the Supreme Court, and convinced a member of the Senate to submit it.

13. The leaders met to work out an agreement between their countries. The <u>negotiations</u> lasted three months before a settlement was reached.

14. During World War II, France, England, and the United States were <u>allies</u>. They agreed to help each other in the fight against Germany.

Not In Vain

If I can stop one heart from breaking,
I shall not live in vain:
If I can ease one life the aching,
Or cool one pain,
Or help one fainting robin
Unto his nest again,
I shall not live in vain.

—Emily Dickinson

BORIS

Jaap ter Haar

*Translated from the Dutch
by Martha Mearns*

During the second World War, in the winter of 1942, the Russian city of Leningrad was surrounded by German forces. In the hungry, war-torn city live twelve-year-old Boris and his friend Nadia, who is fourteen. One day, Boris and Nadia slip out of the city and into the area between the Russian and German lines called "No-man's-land," to find potatoes. When Nadia, weak from hunger, collapses in the snow, Boris tries to revive her. As you read this excerpt from the novel, ask yourself why the German soldiers behave as they do toward the two young Russians.

"Nadia, oh please, Nadia!" If only he could ask her what he should do. But Nadia lay motionless. Perhaps it would be best to try and find help. He could cover Nadia with his coat. Boris started to get up, then stopped, half-crouched, half-standing. His heart stood still. For a moment he couldn't believe his eyes. He blinked. It was still there—a boot, right next to him in the snow. And above the boot, the rough green of a soldier's uniform. And above that, the edge of a white cape. His heart thumping, Boris let his gaze travel slowly upwards. There was no doubt about it. Over an arm lay a rifle with a hand on the trigger. And above . . .

Numb with fear, Boris stared into the face of a German soldier . . .

His whole body trembled; for a moment he was too shocked to think clearly. He just looked dazedly at the German. What could he do to save Nadia and himself?

The soldier lowered his rifle. Boris crouched closer to the ground. Was he going to be beaten up? Would Nadia and he be flung into a concentration camp? Tears of helpless rage sprang into his eyes. But a German must never think that a young Russian was afraid. With a shaking hand he drew out the revolver in his pocket and pointed it at the soldier. Then he looked timidly up to see if the German was frightened by it. But the soldier showed no fear. He shook his head slowly from side to side; not angrily, not frowning as you would have expected, but only slightly surprised, as if he knew quite well that the gun wasn't loaded. Disappointed, but also relieved, Boris let his hand drop.

"Du kleiner, was machst du hier?"

These were foreign words that Boris didn't understand, but they sounded friendly, almost gentle. Did the soldier want to know what they were doing there?

"We wanted to get potatoes," said Boris and, because the German probably didn't understand Russian, he pointed to the row of trees in the distance and then to his mouth. The soldier would understand then that they hadn't come to fight them, but only to get food.

The soldier threw down his rifle, laid his hand on Boris's head, and knelt down by Nadia. Still confused, Boris looked at the rifle lying so close to his hands. Should he pick it up? If he was quick enough, he could shoot the soldier. That was what he had always wanted to do—to kill Germans. Weren't Germans everyone's hated enemies?

But from the way that the soldier was looking at Nadia, from the way he put his arm around her and tried to make her sit up, Boris realized that he, at least, was no enemy. It was very bewildering.

"Ulli, Karl, Heinz, komm mal hier!" called the soldier over his shoulder. With a start Boris looked round. Only then did he no-tice more Germans; their heads were sticking out from a ditch. Were they a small patrol, out reconnoitering? Or were there thousands of white-caped soldiers in the snow, preparing to launch a huge attack on Leningrad?

The three soldiers crawled out of the ditch and came up. They were carrying rifles and machine-guns.

The soldier who was kneeling tried carefully to revive Nadia. She stirred. "Thank you, Boris!" she murmured. Then her eyes opened. She had no idea where she was. Her great brown eyes were dazed. Slowly she turned her head and looked at the Germans. Boris saw her shrink back, and her eyes grew even bigger with fear.

"Boris!" Nadia tried to get up, but she was too weak.

"They're German soldiers." Boris whispered helplessly.

"Hab keine Angst!" said the kneeling man, softly.

"Oh Boris," said Nadia. She shut her eyes and would have fallen back on the ground if the soldier had not held her tightly.

One of the other men took off his cape and pulled the haversack from his back. When he opened it Boris saw that it held a piece of sausage, and bread, and chocolate. His mouth watered. He watched the soldier break off a piece of chocolate and put it in Nadia's mouth.

Nadia gave a glimmer of a smile. The soldier nodded encouragingly at her. He gave her another piece and then another.

"Hier!" Another of the Germans was holding a piece of sausage right in front of Boris's nose. He looked at it longingly and then looked indecisively at the soldier. Could you accept anything from people who were enemies? How many tales of heroism had he heard about Russians who had refused to accept any such German bribes? He felt his hunger gnaw.

"Ist gut!" said the German.

Sorrowfully, Boris shook his head in refusal. He gulped. He realized just how tired he really was. The soldier seemed to sway before his eyes. Black spots danced among the snow.

"I must put my head down," thought Boris, and he slid slowly on to the snow-covered ground.

He could hear their voices. The words that the Germans spoke sounded hard and sharp. When he really began to listen to them, he could make out that there was some disagreement. He looked up in surprise. Yes, they were quarreling, just like the children in Leningrad when they were playing at being at war, except that, he supposed, none of the Germans had wanted to play in the first place. Boris could not guess what this quarrel was about, but he could understand a few words: "die Kinder . . ." and "sterben . . ."

Nadia tried to sit up. With great frightened eyes she looked towards the Germans, who were still arguing fiercely among themselves.

"What are they saying, Nadia?" whispered Boris.

"They're talking about us," answered Nadia.

Anxiously, Boris looked from one soldier to another. They were beginning to lose their tempers and their voices were getting louder and angrier. It seemed to be three against one.

"Es ist Wahnsinn! Ich geh nicht!" A soldier with a fair beard stamped his foot. The one who had found Boris and Nadia brought the quarrel to an end. He was certainly an officer, decided Boris, because now the others were listening attentively to him. When he had finished speaking, the soldier with the beard shrugged his shoulders. He tapped his finger against his forehead—he obviously thought the officer was out of his mind. Then he picked up his rifle and walked moodily away in the direction of the row of trees. Boris stared after him tensely. What was going to happen? The soldier who had wanted to give him the sausage had pulled his bayonet out. He fixed it into his rifle. Were they going to be tortured? Or were the Germans going to shoot them? Boris held his breath. A shiver of fear ran through his whole body.

But the soldier didn't stab them. He pulled a white handkerchief out of his pocket and tied it to the bayonet.

Then the miracle happened! The officer in charge came over to Nadia and picked her up in his arms. He pulled his cape round her. Next, Boris felt himself lifted up.

"Hab keine Angst!" said the soldier again. His voice sounded gentle and friendly. His kind blue eyes, which looked as if they were used to laughter, were sad now. They began to walk. The man with the handkerchief on the bayonet went ahead. He held his rifle in the air, so that the handkerchief fluttered in the wind.

"Boris . . . Boris . . ." called Nadia. It was a shout of joy. "Boris, they're going to take us back to Leningrad!"

It was almost unbelievable, but they were going in the direction of the city. Again Boris looked at the face of the man who was carrying him. How was it possible that an enemy could have such a kind, friendly face?

Now Boris could smile too. It was quite clear to him that these three Germans were friends, not enemies. He felt even more sorry now that he had refused that lovely piece of sausage. The boots crunched through the snow. Each stride brought them nearer to Leningrad.

After a good hour's marching, they came to a halt at the top of a long slope. Boris and Nadia were put down in the snow. Did the men want to have a rest? Their chests were heaving, and they stood to get their breath back, snorting like horses.

The Germans took off their white capes. They rolled them up neatly and pushed them between the straps of their haversacks. Boris couldn't think why they did that. They stood now in their green-grey uniforms, which looked all the darker and more noticeable against the snowy white background.

"Why did they do that?" Boris asked in a whisper.

Nadia shrugged her shoulders.

"Are they going to fight?" Perhaps it would be easier to fight without the long white capes.

"No," said Nadia. "The handkerchief on the rifle means that they don't intend to fight."

"Are they going to take us any farther?"

"I think so," said Nadia.

She was right. The officer came over to Boris and picked him up. He nodded to the children; for the first time his sad eyes looked slightly happy. One of the soldiers lifted Nadia in his arms.

"Jetzt gehen wir los!"

The soldier who was carrying the rifle with the handkerchief on it muttered. He bit his lip, reluctant to go one step farther.

Once again the heavy boots crunched through the snow. They were walking now straight towards the Russian lines. That must take a lot of courage.

Boris peered anxiously into the distance. Would his fellow countrymen shoot as soon as they saw the three green German uniforms approaching over the snow? He was almost certain they would. In a fight for life or death there was no mercy. Could he warn his new friends about the danger? Or would that be treason against his own country? Boris tugged the officer's arm and pointed towards the Russian lines. "Bang, bang!" he said, hoping the man would know what he meant.

"Danke! Ich weiss!" The officer nodded that he understood and once more smiled ruefully at Boris. He walked steadily on, like the brave soldier he was . . .

One shot rang out and then another. The German soldiers came to an abrupt halt. Tensely, they stared into the distance. Boris held his breath. Was he going to see some action?

"Sie kommen!" grunted the officer in charge. He set Boris on the ground and gestured towards a forward post in the front line. At least fifteen Russian soldiers were to be seen approaching. They moved in close formation over the white ground, rifles at the ready.

"They've come to fetch us," cried Nadia joyfully. Her brown eyes shone.

"Why did they shoot?" asked Boris. He was a bit uneasy.

"They were warning shots," said Nadia. "They didn't want the Germans to come too close to their lines." She grasped Boris's hand and smiled at him. "You needn't be afraid any longer."

But Boris was afraid. With a thumping heart Boris looked at the Russian soldiers as they marched over the snow towards them. He was very happy to see them. But why did they look so stern and forbidding? Why did their grey-coated figures and their rifles look so menacing against the white background? It was impossible to read their thoughts or guess what their next actions would be.

A lieutenant walked on ahead. He was carrying a machine gun, his right hand on the trigger. The earpieces of his fur cap flapped in the wind.

When they came to within about thirty yards, the Russian platoon spread out and formed a half circle. And in this way they came up on three sides, with slow and threatening steps.

When they were close to the Germans, the lieutenant held up his hand. The half circle of his men stood motionless. There was absolute silence.

The officer in charge of the German patrol saluted and nodded a greeting to the Russians. But not one Russian returned his salute. Unmoving, they stared at their enemy. They would sooner kill them than smile at them, thought Boris.

A hopeless feeling of sorrow overwhelmed him. Why did everything have to be so complicated . . .?

"Interpreter!" called the lieutenant.

An older man with glasses stepped forward.

"Ask them what they've come for." His voice sounded grim. The interpreter took another step forward and began to speak. He had some trouble with the harsh German words.

Boris peeped from under his cap at the Russians who stood around him. He saw distrust, hate, bitterness. Could no one begin to understand that these three Germans had shown themselves to be friends? The officer in charge gave his answer to the interpreter's question. Would he deign to tell them how kindly he had treated Nadia?

"They were on patrol in the forward lines," said the interpreter to the Russian lieutenant, "when they came across the children. The little girl had collapsed."

The lieutenant looked sharply at Boris and Nadia. His eyes were hard and his voice abrupt.

"What's your name?"

"I'm Nadia Morozova," Nadia murmured. She looked down at the ground. Everything seemed to be going so differently from what she had expected.

"And you?"

"My name is Boris . . . Boris Makarenko," stammered Boris.

Why did the lieutenant look so stern? Did he regard them as traitors—Russian children carried back in German arms?

"What were you doing so far outside the city?" The lieutenant looked at Nadia again.

"We were looking for food," Nadia said softly.

"Come here!" The lieutenant beckoned.

Nadia and Boris went over to him. They stood beside the Russians, facing the Germans. Two sides, one against the other. Between them lay six feet of No-man's-land, where no one had any identity. Boris couldn't bring himself to look at the German officer; he felt so ashamed of the Russian soldiers' determination to hide any human feelings.

"Ask him why they've brought back the children," said the lieutenant to the interpreter.

Boris scraped the snow with his foot until the ground began to show. A few withered blades of grass still lingered in the frozen soil. Over his head the interpreter and the German officer exchanged questions and answers.

"He says that the children had collapsed in the snow and were completely exhausted," the interpreter translated into Russian. "He says that even in an inhumane war people can show human feelings. Children have no part in the war. He couldn't find it in his heart to leave them lying in the snow. It was impossible to take them to the German lines. So he brought them here."

Boris held his breath and looked anxiously at the lieutenant. Would he understand now that these were good Germans?

Suddenly the sergeant stepped forward. His voice was as cold as steel.

"Lieutenant," he said, "let's take away their guns. Maybe they have done a good deed; but maybe they're spies. Let's take them back and see if we can get any information out of them. After all that's happened, I've lost my faith in good Germans."

Boris was filled with horror. He saw that the lieutenant was hesitating. Nadia pulled at his arm and looked fearfully at the sergeant.

"No, no, you can't do that," she whispered. But no man standing in No-man's-land heard her speak.

"Don't believe a word they say," put in another soldier from behind Nadia. His eyes gleamed with hatred. How much bitterness was bursting out of his heart?

"Shoot them right away, lieutenant! Shoot them right away!" Even as he spoke, the man took a step forward and pointed his rifle at the German officer. Mad with hate, he meant to shoot . . .

Boris sprang forward. He ran to the German and stood with his arm outstretched as if he could thus protect him.

"Don't shoot," he yelled, his voice breaking. "Don't shoot. They saved our lives."

It was deathly silent. No one said a word. No one moved.

"Come here!" commanded the lieutenant. But Boris didn't come. He stood firmly in front of the German. A desperate, helpless wave of passion swept over him; tears of rage against the hatred, terror and madness of war filled his eyes.

"Nadia was lying in the snow." Boris screamed the words at the Russian. "She couldn't even speak to me. I couldn't carry her. I tried to, but I couldn't." He jerked his head at the German behind him. "He carried her. He's my friend." Frantically Boris tried to make them understand. "My friend, do you hear—my friend!" He was crying with rage.

Nadia came over to him.

"Boris, Boris dear," she said gently, but Boris shook with his sobs.

Then Boris felt a firm hand on his shoulder, a friendly hand. He looked up into the German's face. Through his tears he saw the officer smiling at him. At once the terror began to fade from his tearful eyes.

Then Boris looked at the lieutenant. The harshness on his face had given way to astonishment. The soldier who had wanted to shoot had lowered his rifle and was scraping it idly in the snow; some of the other soldiers were gazing into the distance. The sergeant stared at Nadia. Again no one said a word . . .

Then the lieutenant turned to the interpreter. "Tell them they are free to go back, Ivan Petrovitch." He hesitated, as if searching for words. "Say to them that we are grateful; it would be shameful if we, in the brutality of war, should forget all humanity."

The interpreter translated his words.

The German soldiers made to turn on their heels, but the officer remained as he was.

"Ein Augenblick, bitte!" He pulled his haversack from his shoulder and stopped to open it.

"Hier," he said to Boris and Nadia, and handed them each a piece of bread and sausage, and a tin with foreign words on the label.

Once again Boris felt the trustworthy hand on his shoulder. Then the officer stood up straight. Slowly he looked around the watching circle, with that same sad smile that Boris had already seen on his face, clapped his heels together and saluted. He stood as stiff and straight as a candle, the typical German soldier.

The young lieutenant of the Red Army stood smartly to attention. "Platoon," he ordered, "attention!" All the Russians sprang to attention. Slowly the lieutenant brought his hand up to his cap. It was as if he were saluting the Germans for their courage, their help, their humanity.

Boris looked at the officer. He would have liked to thank him again, but the German had turned on his heel. With firm steps he and the others walked away down the slope into the distance: men in No-man's-land.

Nadia waved hesitantly, but the Germans did not look back.

1. Why did the German officer return Boris and Nadia to the Russian lines?

2. Why did Boris refuse the sausage that the German soldier offered him?

3. When Boris threatened the German soldier with his revolver, the soldier was not frightened. Boris put down the gun, feeling "disappointed, but also relieved." Why did Boris feel both of these emotions?

4. The Russian lieutenant said: "Say to them that we are grateful; it would be shameful if we, in the brutality of war, should forget all humanity." What did the lieutenant mean by this remark?

5. We sometimes think of courage as a part of war. "Boris" shows us that courage is a necessary part of peace. Find two examples in the story that support this idea.

I Don't Like Wars

I don't like wars
They end up with monuments;
I don't want battles to roar
Even in neighboring continents.

I like Spring
Flowers producing.
Fields covered with green,
The wind in the hills whistling.

Drops of dew I love
The scent of jasmine as night cools,
Stars in darkness above.
And rain singing in pools.

I don't like wars. They end
In wreaths and monuments
I like Peace come to stay
And it will some day.

—Matti Yosef, Age 9
Bat Yam, Israel

THE DYNAMITE KING

Roberta Strauss Feuerlicht

You have probably heard of the Nobel Prizes, and especially of the Nobel Prize for Peace. The Nobel Peace Prize is given each year to the man or woman who has furthered the cause of peace. But did you know that the Nobel Prizes were created by a man who made and sold weapons for war? As you read this biography of Alfred Nobel, ask yourself why the inventor of dynamite created the world's greatest tribute to the makers of peace.

One day an inventor named Alfred Nobel read in the newspapers that he had died. Nobel knew this was an error for he was very much alive. It was his brother who had died, and the newspapers had got the two men mixed up.

But Nobel was very upset. It was not the story of his death that was so disturbing, but what the newspapers wrote about him. They described him as a rich man who had made his fortune by inventing dynamite and other explosives. They called him "the dynamite king" and a "merchant of death."

This troubled Nobel because he knew it was true. He was a genius who invented arms and explosives. He not only invented deadly weapons but manufactured and sold them. This made him one of the richest people in the world.

Yet there was another side to Alfred Nobel. The inventor of dynamite wrote poetry and loved peace. He once called war "the horror of horrors and the greatest of all crimes." When he really died, he did not want to be remembered for what he had done for destruction and war. He wanted to be remembered for what he had done for humanity and peace.

Alfred Nobel was born on October 21, 1833, in Stockholm, Sweden. When he was nine years old, his family moved to Russia. There his father, Immanuel, was making explosives and weapons for the Tsar, the ruler of the Russian Empire.

Alfred had gone to school in Sweden for just one year and he never went again. In Russia, he and his two older brothers had a tutor. But before Alfred was seventeen, he gave up his studies to join his father's business.

One of the many things he soon learned was that people who make money from war do not like peace. When the Crimean War ended in 1856, Russia stopped ordering weapons from the Nobel family. Immanuel Nobel lost his fortune. He returned to Sweden, where Alfred later joined him.

In Sweden, father and son experimented with explosives. Some years earlier, an Italian chemist had mixed nitric acid and glycerine. The result was nitroglycerine, a highly explosive liquid. It was very powerful but very unstable. Sometimes it blew up when it wasn't supposed to. Other times it didn't blow up at all.

The Nobels tried combining nitroglycerine with gunpowder to make shells for the Swedish army. It was Alfred who figured out the mixture that worked. Then he borrowed money and bought a house next to his parents' home. He turned it into a laboratory to experiment with nitroglycerine and to make explosives for sale.

Sometimes Alfred's younger brother, Oscar Emil, helped in the laboratory. One day in 1864, the building exploded with a roar. Alfred was not there at the time, but Oscar Emil was one of the four persons killed by the blast.

His brother's death did not stop Nobel's experiments. When Stockholm officials said he could no longer work in the city on something so dangerous, he moved his laboratory to a barge anchored in the middle of a lake. Although some people were frightened by Nobel's inventions, others saw how useful nitroglycerine could be for blasting away rock and soil, and building mines, roads, tunnels, and canals. Orders came in from all over the world.

But many of those who used nitroglycerine did not know how dangerous it was. A careless bounce or too much heat could cause a fearful explosion. There were many accidents, and a number of people died.

Nobel said it wasn't his fault if people were careless, but it really was. He was so eager to sell his new product that he hadn't bothered to make it safe first. Even one of his own nitroglycerine factories blew up. People began to call Nobel a murderer and a criminal, and some governments forbade the use of nitroglycerine.

Nobel was forced to find a way to make nitroglycerine safe or lose his business. He mixed it with a certain kind of earth called *kieselguhr*, which absorbed the nitroglycerine and made it stable so it would not explode until it was supposed to. The new product was called dynamite.

Dynamite made Nobel rich and famous, but it did not make him happy. He traveled, read, spoke five or six languages, and wrote poetry and plays, but he had few friends. Like many rich people, he was not sure whether people liked him or his money. He never married. Instead, he lived most of the time in a large house in Paris, France, with his servants and his dreams.

For he did have dreams. He dreamed of a world where scientists would help people and not destroy them. He wanted to be such a scientist, but somehow he always came back to making explosives and weapons. "It is rather fiendish things we are working on," he told one of his assistants. He said that if a weapon was invented that was powerful enough to kill everyone at once, there would be no more

KUNGLIGA SVENSKA
VETENSKAPSAKADEMIEN

CARL DAVID
ANDERSON
FÖR UPPTÄCKTEN AV
POSITRONEN

DE FYSIOLOGISKA OCH MEDICINSKA
VETENSKAPERNA UNDER SENASTE
TIDEN RIKTATS HAR VID SAMMAN-
TRÄDE DEN 17 OKTOBER 1963 BESLU-
TAT ATT TILLERKÄNNA DET ÅR 1963
UTGÅENDE PRISET GEMENSAMT TILL
JOHN CAREW ECCLES
ALAN LLOYD HODGKIN
ANDREW FIELDING HUXLEY
FÖR DER...

GIORGOS
SEFERIS

1963 ÅRS NOBELPRIS I LITTERATUR
FÖR HANS FRAMSTÅENDE
LYRISKA DIKTNING,
INSPIRERAD AV DJUP KÄNSLA
FÖR DEN HELLENSKA KULTURVÄRLDEN

SVENSKA AKADEMIEN
HARVID SAMMANTRÄDE DEN 25 OKTOBER
LÖVER 8 SLAMMELSE MED FÖRESKRIFTERNA
I DET AV
ALFRED NOBEL
DEN 27 NOVEMBER 1895 UPPRÄTTADE TESTAMENTE
BESLUTAT ATT TILLDELA

ALFR. NOBEL

NAT
MDCCC
XXXIII
OB
MDCCC
XCVI

war. But meanwhile, he kept inventing and selling less powerful weapons, and wars continued.

The waste and horror of war upset many people besides Nobel. One of them was his friend Baroness Bertha von Suttner, who was active in an organization that wanted to set up an international court to settle quarrels between nations. Baroness von Suttner asked Nobel to give his fortune to the cause of peace. This was an idea that Nobel had been thinking of ever since the newspapers had printed the story of his death.

In 1893, he made a will which left part of his wealth to science and peace. In 1895, he wrote another will which went much further. A year later, on December 10, 1896, Alfred Nobel died.

Because of his second will, Nobel would be remembered not for what he did when he lived but for what he did when he died. Almost all his huge fortune was to be used to set up five awards. These awards were to be given each year "to those persons who shall contribute most materially to benefitting humanity" in five areas—physics, chemistry, medicine, literature, and peace.

Since 1901, the Nobel Prizes have been awarded annually on December 10, the anniversary of Alfred Nobel's death. The winners receive money, a gold medal, and a diploma. In return, they are required to give a speech or lecture.

The Nobel Prize is one of the highest honors a man or woman can receive. The most important is the one that is given for peace. The man or woman who helps bring peace to the world gives humankind its greatest gift.

---

1. Why did the mistaken newspaper report disturb Nobel?
2. Why did people begin to call Nobel a murderer and a criminal when accidents occurred with nitroglycerine?
3. Why did Nobel create the Nobel Prizes?
4. The author says that, like many rich people, Nobel "was not sure whether people liked him or his money." What does this statement mean?
5. Look up the names of five other winners of the Nobel Peace Prize. Who were they and for what were they awarded the Prize?

THE
ACCEPTANCE

In 1964, civil rights leader, Dr. Martin Luther King, Jr., won the Nobel Prize for Peace for his use of nonviolent protest as an instrument for change. In his acceptance speech before the Nobel Committee and the King of Sweden on December 10th of that year, he stressed that he, alone, did not deserve the Prize. As you read, try to understand why Dr. King felt this way about the award.

" . . . I accept this prize on behalf of all . . . who love peace and [unity], . . . for in the depths of my heart I am aware that this prize is much more than an honor to me personally. Every time I take a flight I am always mindful of the many people who make a successful journey possible—the known pilots and the unknown ground crew. So you honor the dedicated pilots of our struggle who have sat at the controls as the freedom movement soared into orbit. . . .You honor the ground crew without whose labor and sacrifices the jetflights to freedom could never have left the earth. Most of these people will never make the headlines, and their names will not appear in *Who's Who.* Yet when years have rolled past, and when the blazing light of truth is focused on this marvelous age in which we live—men and women will know and children will be taught that we have a finer land, a better people, a more noble civilization—because these humble children of God were willing to suffer for righteousness sake.

I think Alfred Nobel would know what I mean when I say that I accept this award in the spirit of a curator of some precious heirloom which he holds in trust for its true owners—all those to whom beauty is truth and truth beauty—and in whose eyes the beauty of genuine [unity] and peace is more precious than diamonds or silver or gold."

—Martin Luther King, Jr.

1. On whose behalf did Dr. King accept the 1964 Nobel Peace Prize?
2. What point did Dr. King make by comparing the civil rights movement to an airplane flight?
3. Why do you think Dr. King believed that Alfred Nobel would understand the spirit in which he accepted the award?

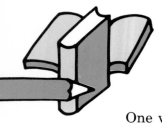

Interviews

One way to gather information is by conducting an *interview*. In an interview, one person asks questions which another person answers. Sometime you may be part of an interview. If you are gathering information for a report, you might interview someone who knows about the topic of your report. A good interviewer remembers the following rules:

1. Prepare the questions for the interview beforehand. Make sure they are clear and to the point. Do not stray from the topic during the interview.

2. Take notes during the interview. They will serve as a written record of the answers that were given.

3. Listen politely as answers are given. Do not interrupt the person during an answer.

ACTIVITY A Suppose you are doing a report on how your town government works. You might arrange an interview with the mayor. Below are ten questions for the interview. Choose the six questions you feel are most appropriate. Write those questions on your paper.

1. What are your main responsibilities as mayor?
2. When does the town council meet?
3. What is your favorite television program?
4. How does the town pay for the services it provides for the people who live in the town?
5. Where do you like to travel on vacation?
6. How does the governor's office assist the town?
7. When are elections held for town representatives?
8. What kind of car do you drive?
9. What requirements must one meet to serve as a town official?
10. How much money do you have in the bank?

ACTIVITY B Suppose you are doing a report on the history of your town. You might arrange an interview with the local librarian, who is an expert on the town's history. Write six questions you would ask during the interview.

Sometime you may not be the person asking the questions during an interview. Instead you might be the one answering them. For example, if you were looking for a job, you might have a job interview. Someone from the company would ask you questions about yourself. Your answers help the employer get to know you better.

Making a good impression at a job interview is important. Dress properly and arrive on time for the interview. Be prepared to answer the questions which the employer may ask you. Answer each question as clearly and intelligently as possible. Also make sure your answers are honest.

The list below includes some of the questions an employer might ask you during a job interview:

1. What are your name, address, and telephone number?
2. What school do you attend? How many grades have you completed?
3. What is the name of your parent or guardian?
4. What jobs, if any, have you held in the past?
5. What are the names and addresses of your previous employers?
6. Why do you want the job you are applying for now?
7. Why do you think you are qualified for the job?
8. What hobbies or special interests do you have?

ACTIVITY C   Imagine you are being interviewed for a job you want. (You may choose the type of job.) Assume the interviewer asks you all of the above questions. Write an answer to each question. Use complete sentences.

What things is this boy doing wrong at his interview?

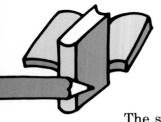

Slanting

The selection "The Dynamite King" told about Alfred Nobel. His experiments with nitroglycerine created a great argument. Some people felt the material was too dangerous and harmful. They called Nobel a "merchant of death." Other people, however, saw how useful nitroglycerine could be for blasting away rock and soil to build mines, roads, tunnels, and canals. Actually, Nobel's experiments had both good and bad points. People who argued for or against Nobel's work may have presented just one side of the story.

The practice of presenting only one side of an issue is called *slanting*. Some people who argue don't want to admit any facts that might hurt their argument. They *slant* the issue by mentioning only the things that support their side. The other facts are left out.

Suppose you were in favor of a superhighway being built through your town. You would present facts to support your view. You would leave out other facts that might hurt your side. Here are arguments you might mention and not mention:

What you say:	The new highway would attract tourists to our town.
What you don't say:	The many cars would create traffic and pollution problems.
What you say:	Building the highway would create jobs for many people in the community.
What you don't say:	Many people's houses would have to be torn down to build the highway.
What you say:	The highway would be close to our shops and businesses.
What you don't say:	The highway would also be near a school and create a danger to children.

As you can see, in a slanted argument you only get part of the picture. Do not judge an issue until you have all the facts.

ACTIVITY A   A student running for class treasurer gave a speech. On the left, are facts the student mentioned in the speech. On the right, are facts the student did not mention. Match each fact on the left with its unspoken fact on the right. Write the matching pairs of numbers on your paper.

1. I have served as class treasurer for two years.

2. I have had experience working at a bank.

3. I have a straight A average in English.

4. The principal has recommended me for treasurer.

5. I only missed two student council meetings last year.

6. Last year every student voted for me for class treasurer.

1. No one ran against me for treasurer last year.

2. Both years I accidentally lost some class money.

3. Only three meetings were held all year.

4. I am failing in math and history.

5. My father is the school principal.

6. My job was collecting trash outside the bank.

ACTIVITY B   Below are slanted arguments telling why students should have school all year round. Write four arguments of your own telling why students should have summer vacation.

1. During summer vacation students forget what they learned during the school year.

2. Many students are bored during summer vacation because they have nothing to do.

3. During the summer students would be able to study in warm, comfortable weather.

4. The long summer days would mean students could return home from school while it was still light.

ACTIVITY C   Imagine you are writing an article for the school newspaper. Choose one of the issues below. Write five arguments to slant the issue in your favor.

1. Why violence on television should (or should not) be shown

2. Why people should (or should not) use solar energy

Charged Words

You have learned that people *slant* an issue by giving arguments for one side only. To be a good judge, you must listen carefully to what is said in an argument. In addition, you must listen to *how* it is said. You need to beware of charged words.

Charged words are words that create a good or bad impression. They stir your emotions and form a pleasant or unpleasant picture in your mind. Charged words can make something sound better or worse than it actually is.

For example, suppose you knew people who saved their money. If you liked the people, you might call them "thrifty." If you disliked the people, you might call them "cheap." The word *thrifty* creates a good impression, while *cheap* creates a bad one. Both words are charged words. Read these two descriptions of a class picnic:

Twenty highly enthusiastic students utilized the park for a class picnic. The students sang and danced energetically before enjoying their meal. The children dined heartily and left evidence of their presence.

Twenty rowdy students invaded the park for a class picnic. The students howled and pranced all over before attacking their food. The kids ate like pigs and left a mess of trash.

Both articles describe the same picnic. The paragraph on the left, however, uses favorably charged words. The paragraph on the right uses unfavorably charged words.

Favorable	Unfavorable
highly enthusiastic	rowdy
utilized	invaded
sang and danced energetically	howled and pranced all over
enjoying their meal	attacking their food
dined heartily	ate like pigs
left evidence of their presence	left a mess of trash

Read the two speeches about a politician. Then read the questions that follow. Write the answers to the questions on your paper.

Favorable	Unfavorable
A. Dewey Chatham is a demanding leader with daring ideas.	**A.** Dewey Chatham is a bossy tyrant with risky ideas.
B. He has invested money in a variety of projects.	**B.** He has gambled money on a bunch of schemes.
C. Chatham has proven himself to be vocal and forceful.	**C.** Chatham has proven himself to be noisy and pushy.
D. He is cautious when faced with challenging decisions.	**D.** He is chicken when faced with really tough decisions.
E. His past errors prove he is only human.	**E.** His past foul-ups prove he is a blundering idiot.
F. Chatham is a concerned man interested in your well-being.	**F.** Chatham is a nosy guy invading your privacy.

1. In sentence *A*, which unfavorable word replaces *demanding*?
2. In sentence *A*, which favorable word replaces *risky*?
3. In sentence *B*, which favorable word replaces *gambled*?
4. In sentence *B*, which unfavorable words replace *variety of projects*?
5. In sentence *C*, which unfavorable word replaces *vocal*?
6. In sentence *C*, which favorable word replaces *pushy*?
7. In sentence *D*, which unfavorable words replace *challenging*?
8. In sentence *D*, which favorable word replaces *chicken*?
9. In sentence *E*, which unfavorable word replaces *errors*?
10. In sentence *E*, which favorable words replace *blundering idiot*?
11. In sentence *F*, which favorable words replace *nosy guy*?
12. In sentence *F*, which unfavorable words replace *interested in your well-being*?

PATHWAYS

By exploring new pathways, we learn about the world in which we live. Americans have followed many paths to attain independence. The road to peace has often been hard to find, but the people of the world have never stopped looking. In "Pathways," you have seen how people have chosen to follow these difficult paths, and how the choices they have made sometimes changed history. Pathways always involve choice. The hardest part of the journey is making your choice, and taking the first step.

Thinking About "Pathways"

1. Nathaniel Bowditch taught navigation to the crew of the *Astrea*. Felisa Rincón Marerro taught the *jíbaros* of Puerto Rico how to register to vote. Compare the situations of the crew and the *jíbaros* and explain why Nathaniel and Felisa wanted to teach them important skills.

2. Roger Williams' struggle for independence helped establish vital American freedoms. For what further freedoms did Belva Lockwood fight?

3. The poem "I Don't Like Wars" declares Matti Yosef's feelings about war. Might the poem also express Boris' feelings about war? State your opinion and explain why you think as you do.

4. The German officer in "Boris" decided to return Boris and Nadia to Leningrad. Alfred Nobel in "The Dynamite King" decided to establish the Nobel Prizes, including the Nobel Peace Prize. Compare the reasons for each of the men's actions. How were their motives alike? How were they different?

5. Choose two events that happened recently in your community or the nation and explain what effect these events may have on your future.

OBSERVATIONS

Observation means "using your senses to gather information." Observation makes us more aware of the world around us. Observation is also the first step in scientific study. In science, the most valuable observations involve logical thinking. Scientific observations, usually made with the help of mathematics, have helped us to understand Earth's environment and to probe the mysteries of outer space.

The selections in "Observations" are about looking at the world around you and at worlds that are far away. You will tour, in words and pictures, a museum that records humanity's conquest of the air and of space. You will read about an encounter with beings from another planet. You will meet a family of environmental scientists and a pair of young people who start a successful toothpaste-making business. You will read about Thomas Jefferson and the metric system, about computers and calculators, and about how public opinion polls are taken.

As you read, think about the importance of careful observation. To learn anything, from mathematics to a new dance step, you must observe closely before you can try for yourself. How can careful observation help you in daily life?

Valentine For Earth

Oh, it will be fine
To rocket through space
And see the reverse
Of the moon's dark face,

To travel to Saturn
Or Venus or Mars,
Or maybe discover
Some uncharted stars.

But do they have anything
Better than we?
Do you think, for instance,
They have a blue sea
For sailing and swimming?
Do planets have hills
With raspberry thickets
Where a song sparrow fills

The summer with music?
And do they have snow
To silver the roads
Where the school buses go?

Oh, I'm all for rockets
And worlds cold or hot,
But I'm wild in love
With the planet we've got!

Frances Frost

THE NATIONAL AIR AND SPACE MUSEUM

A *photo-essay* is a combination of pictures and words that tells a story or gives you information. As you read this essay and study its photographs, think about how the words and pictures work together to introduce you to the National Air and Space Museum.

On July 1, 1976, the National Air and Space Museum in Washington, D.C., first opened its doors to the public. The museum celebrates one of the greatest achievements of our century: human flight.

An unusual building houses the many remarkable exhibits. The museum is six stories high and covers three city blocks. Many of the walls and ceilings have tinted glass, which lets in light and gives the museum some of the open,

free feeling of flight. Three huge galleries—each larger than three basketball courts put together—take up much of the space. Nineteen smaller galleries, a theater, and a planetarium surround the halls. Together, they present visitors with the history of flight—from imaginary attempts in myths and stories, to balloons, gliders, and airplanes, through the *Apollo* space program, to the future of space flight.

Visitors entering the museum come first to the **Milestones of Flight Gallery.** The gallery contains historic flying machines, some of which are shown here. In the center hangs the Wright brothers' *Flyer* (1903). This was the first successful "heavier-than-air" craft operated by a human being. To the right of the *Flyer* is the *Spirit of St. Louis,* in which Charles Lindbergh made the first nonstop, solo flight across the Atlantic Ocean (1927). The bright orange *Bell X-1* was the first airplane to break the sound barrier (1947). The black shape above

the *Flyer* is the *X-15,* the fastest airplane ever to fly (1967). On the floor in the lower right corner, you can see the *Gemini IV* spacecraft from which a space-suited mannequin repeats Edward White's walk in space. Beneath the *Flyer* is the *Apollo II* capsule that carried astronauts to the moon for the first lunar landing.

Most of the museum's exhibits use the original flying machines. Models or back-ups—usually spacecraft that would have flown if the originals had failed—are shown only if the originals are unavailable.

The **Hall of Air Transportation** is a gallery that shows visitors the development of flight as a means of travel.

The Pitcairn Mailwing was a biplane, or double-winged plane, designed to carry mail. The plane you see here began mail service in 1927. The Northrop Alpha was one of the first airplanes to be made entirely of metal instead of wood. It carried three passengers in a cabin, while the pilot sat above and behind them in an open cockpit.

Ford's three-engine passenger plane, the Tri-Motor (1926) was nicknamed "The Tin Goose." The shiny Douglas DC-3 (1935) was known as "The Goony Bird." These two planes carried most of the world's air travelers during the 1930's and 1940's.

In the **Pioneers of Flight Gallery** is another important plane.

Amelia Earhart became the first woman to make a nonstop solo flight across the Atlantic. The aircraft she used was a bright red Lockheed Vega 5B.

Spacecraft past, present, and future are displayed in **Space Hall**, another large gallery. The largest object in the gallery is the *Skylab Orbital Workshop*. Visitors can walk through the space station and see how teams of astronauts lived and worked in space. On the floor to the left of *Skylab* is a *V-2* rocket. Developed in Germany during World War II, it was the first long-range guided missile. Hanging from the ceiling beside the *V-2* are more German missiles, including a *V-1*. To the right of *Skylab*, four huge rockets rise from a deep well in the floor: *Jupiter-C, Vanguard,* and *Scout,* three rockets that launched satellites into orbit; and *Minuteman,* a U.S. guided missile.

Visitors look upward for a spectacular view of giant rockets.

Visitors study a model of the Space Shuttle "Enterprise." Above their heads loom Apollo and Soyuz spacecraft joined like those used in the 1975 joint U.S. and U.S.S.R. space mission.

Skylab, with one of its huge wings—actually solar panels—extended.

The **Apollo to the Moon Gallery** recalls the space missions that took Americans to the moon.

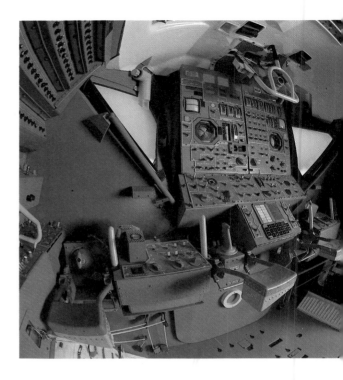

In this exhibit—a full-size replica of the control panel of the Lunar Module—visitors can relive the first moon landing. Films played behind the triangular windows show the moon's surface growing closer, and visitors hear the taped voices of the Apollo astronauts and recall the exciting moments. As Neil Armstrong guided the Lunar Module "Eagle," Edwin Aldrin, Jr., called out the speed and altitude: "Thirty feet. Two and a half down. Faint shadow. Four forward, drifting to the right a little . . . Contact light. Okay, engine stop." Then Armstrong's voice: "Houston, Tranquility Base here. The "Eagle" has landed."

The moon's surface as seen by the astronauts during the landing.

A Lunar Roving Vehicle like this one carried Apollo 15 astronauts more than seventeen miles (twenty-seven kilometers) along the moon's surface.

Astronaut James Irwin salutes the flag during the 1971 Apollo 15 mission. In the center is the Lunar Module. The Lunar Roving Vehicle is on the right.

The twentieth century—our century—can aptly be called the "Century of Flight." It began with the invention of the airplane. Sixty years later, we had taken the first steps into space. By the twenty-first century, the National Air and Space Museum will need space to display new exhibits that record the latest wonders of human flight.

1. What three galleries make up most of the National Air and Space Museum?
2. Why would the *X-15* not be found in the Hall of Air Transportation?
3. Why can the twentieth century be called the "Century of Flight"? What does this phrase mean?
4. Think about the way this photo-essay gives you information. Choose one example of a photograph and its caption, and use this example to answer these questions: What does the photograph add to the information in the caption? How does the caption explain and clarify the photograph?
5. Have you ever flown in an airplane or a helicopter? If so, describe the experience. If not, what do you think it would be like? What would you see and hear and do?
6. Put together a photo-essay that describes something or tells a story. Choose pictures from magazines and newspapers. Then write the descriptive information that combines the pictures into an essay.

Close Encounters of the Third Kind

Steven Spielberg

In a single summer night, life changed drastically for a young widow, Jillian Guiler, and her four-year-old son, Barry. On that night, Barry was awakened by strange noises and bright lights that moved in the sky. He followed them away from the house, and his worried mother chased after him. A man, Roy Neary, was also following the unearthly lights in his truck and nearly ran over Barry. In this way, three people were brought together in time to see the lights descend from the sky—to see that they were spaceships from another world. When the ships disappeared, most people refused to believe in them. But the memory of the ships had a strong hold on the imaginations of Jillian, Roy, and most of all, Barry. Furthermore, the starships were soon to return.

Science fiction is a form of fantasy that is based on scientific facts, or on logical guesses about discoveries and inventions of the future. Space travel, time travel, and contact with aliens are common science-fiction themes. As you read, try to identify what makes this a science-fiction story.

The toy xylophone was poorly tuned. That was why the five notes sounded so strange when little Barry played them. He didn't learn them all at once, Jillian noted from the other room. He had kept working on the tune until he got it . . . well . . . the way he wanted it.

To Jillian's ear, even though the tune was strange, Barry's chuckles were reassuring. He was there. He was happy. The tune's curious sequence of five notes—where do kids get these ideas?—was oddly disturbing, but of course, these toy xylophones were never accurate. It was easy to make them sound . . . well . . . peculiar.

Jillian had spent the day, as she had the day before, making endless charcoal and pastel sketches. She had abandoned a career in art by the simple act of moving this far from big cities. But the habit of it was difficult to shake. She would find herself sketching Barry, a chair, a random arrangement of a catsup bottle, salt shaker, and dirty plate on the kitchen table.

Today she had been drawing landscapes, mountainous ones. In the way they looked—distant uneven rows of teeth, peaks at odd intervals—they somehow reminded her of the tune Barry kept repeating on his xylophone.

Random choice made mountains look as they did, the merest chance crisscross of volcanic thrust and gravity and the beating down of weather over centuries of time.

Only random choice could have brought Barry to pick out those five notes. Yet once he chose them, he remained with them.

The way Barry sounded those notes, it was almost as if in randomness there could be a message.

Jillian threw most of her sketches away in the cleanup process, but she saved one because it reminded her of something. She didn't remember what exactly. This particular mountain she had drawn was terribly tall and thin, needly and distorted. It was like one of those desert spires formed when wind and sand have eaten away the softer stone to lay bare the core spout of harder lava—the ancient throat of a volcano.

Its sides were gashed by harsh grooves as it rose like a misshapen finger thrust accusingly into the eye of the sun.

Thunder rumbled nearby. Jillian shivered and ran outside to see if rain was coming. Clouds had begun gathering in the west, obscuring the weak sun with masses of leaden gray. Behind the clouds, Jillian could see lightning at work. A major electrical storm was coming. But the flashes were strange, as if frozen. Small distant points of light began skipping from cloud to cloud.

The air began to thicken with the sound of swarming bees. The clouds now seemed to be actually moving . . . down.

Yes, down and in toward her. Within them, strange flashes of colored light seemed to jump from one cloud to another.

"No," Jillian said in an undertone.

Across the rolling landscape, a kind of darker mass of cloud seemed to reach from the ground to the sky, a column that grew wider as it rose, almost like a . . . a tornado. Jillian felt defenseless, the way the girl Dorothy had felt in *The Wizard of Oz* as a giant tornado loomed on the Kansas horizon.

"But this isn't Kansas," Jillian told herself. And those bright-colored things dropping from cloud to cloud are not . . . not real? But of course they were real.

"No!" she shouted, suddenly frightened. Jillian eyed the safety of her house and turned slowly, very slowly. She took the first of the long fifteen steps to the back door. She was terrified now and didn't want to make herself panic by running. She continued toward the house in a kind of crazed slow motion. Jillian entered the house, and slowly and deliberately, she shut the back door and locked it. She moved into the living room now and began lowering the blinds. As Jillian moved from room to room, her movements unwillingly became faster. She went from a walk to a trot to a run, jerking the blinds down as panic took control of her hands and made her fumble and miss.

She stood still for a moment, trying to make sense of everything. That *had* been thunder, hadn't it? And lightning? That distant buzz, as of a swarm of bees, that had been something to do with the storm. And the clouds coming down toward her. But she'd never seen clouds do that before.

Barry was laughing. He'd never feared the violence of storms, for which Jillian decided she was probably grateful. But to hear the wholehearted way he laughed now, as the thunder clashed and the lightning flared, was a little too much for Jillian's peace of mind. No child had a right to be that happy.

She hurried into his room. He had stopped playing the xylophone and was standing at the only window in the house whose blind was still up. He was staring intently out at the sky and what he saw filled him with great glee.

He began running through the house, raising the blinds, swinging open doors and windows. "Barry, no!"

Jillian ran after him, shutting, closing, locking. They came upon each other in the living room. The boy had just sent the shade rattling up.

Jillian pushed the boy to one side and yanked the blind shut. As if on cue, an immense roar of thunder shook the house. Behind the blind, a flash of lightning flared with such an orange intensity that it seemed to set the entire wall aflame. The buzzing roared around her.

Jillian cringed from it, but Barry clapped his hands and laughed. Now the house was dark. Only the booming flashes of firelight outside illuminated it from moment to moment. Jillian took Barry's hand and led him to her bedroom, where she picked up the telephone book and began searching for Roy Neary's number.

As she did, another clap of thunder and orange light bashed at the house like a giant fist. The television set went on. So did the stereo. Electric lamps began to switch off and on. She could hear, in her storage closet, the distant sound of her vacuum cleaner starting up.

Barry broke away from her grasp, ran to the window, and sent the blind skyward with one happy swoop. As he did, a strange stillness fell on the place. The television and stereo were quiet. The vacuum cleaner stopped. There was no sound at all, not even of wind or the distant buzz of insects.

Then Jillian heard it. It sounded like . . . claws.

On the roof. Scrambling across the shingles. Claws. Or talons. Long fingernails or toenails. Sharp, scurrying sounds.

She stared at the ceiling above her, eyes moving along in the direction of the scraping, scrambling noises. They stopped for a moment at the chimney.

And now they began to come down the chimney.

Jillian dashed into the living room and raced for the damper handle. At any cost, she had to shut the flue. Barry followed happily.

"Come in!" he shouted. "Come in!"

The clawlike sounds skittered down the inside of the chimney. Jillian dived at the damper, slammed it shut.

Instantly, a harsh roar of noise shook the house. Orange light flooded every corner of the room. All the window shades snapped up.

Jillian dropped to the floor, hands over her ears. The television was blaring away. On the stereo, the turntable was revolving. From the loudspeakers, Johnny Mathis was singing "Chances Are" in a huge voice like the growl of a lion.

Jillian ran for the telephone again, dragging Barry with her.

Eyes wide with fright now, she found Neary's number. As she held the telephone to her ear, instead of a dial tone, it gave forth the same five-note melody that Barry had been playing on his xylophone. Jillian jiggled the hook, got a tone like the angry zzz of bees, and dialed Neary's number. The room lights were doing strange things, dimming to a fitful smoky red, then flaring to a blue-white that hurt her eyes. The telephone was buzzing.

"Hello?" a woman asked.

"Roy?" Jillian's voice was a frightened croak.

"He's not here," Ronnie said matter-of-factly. "I'm his wife. Who's calling, please?"

The overload was so ferocious that even the air in the room seemed to burn orange-hot with a fearful buzzing noise. It was as if some giant high-tension tower, carrying thousands of volts, had toppled down on this house and charged it so thickly with power that—

The vacuum cleaner, like a prisoner being tortured in a cell, screamed in horror. The stereo speakers vibrated and burst apart.

A metal ashtray rose into the air and hovered for an instant, suspended in the terrifying heat of the air. She could hear the clattering on the roof again.

Jillian lost track of what was happening. The phone dropped from her hand. She slid to the floor. Barry was nowh—

"Barry!"

Racing into the room like an auto run amok, the vacuum cleaner began howling across the floor, chasing her as she jumped out of its way. It wheeled, charged again. Jillian ran.

In the horror of crashing, grinding noises and flashing, blinding lights, Jillian lost track of what was happening. Barry was—

"Barry!"

Somewhere in the distance she could hear, over everything, Barry's gleeful laughter. The kitchen. Jill, beyond walking, started the endless crawl across the room to the kitchen.

The refrigerator was vibrating intensely. The door swung open, the light inside blinking on and off spastically.

Then she caught sight of her son. He, too, was crawling on the floor. Toward the dog-door opening. He reached it and started trying to wriggle through the narrow opening.

Jillian lunged forward and grabbed for Barry's foot. She caught it and started to haul him back in. She pulled hard. He slid across the linoleum toward her. The air smelled brassy and dank with electricity.

Then something pulled him away. Some force was tugging him outside the house.

"Let go of him!" she screamed.

Jillian gritted her teeth and pulled back. The boy's body shifted forward and back a few inches.

Jillian held on to her son until she felt, she knew, that if she did not let go, he would be dislocated. Sobbing, Jillian loosened her grip, and Barry slipped away from her hands and out the little door.

In a flash, he was gone.

Jillian heaved herself up off the floor and threw open the kitchen door. Barry was nowhere in sight. She saw the tornado-like formation hovering above the house, as if parked, lit up by the tiny points of flashing lights.

Then the cloud eased away into the gathering darkness. And Jillian, not really knowing what she was doing, not really caring about anything any more, started to chase after it, until an immense shape loomed up, gigantic arms enfolding her. All the breath came out of Jill. She fell to the stubble of a cornfield.

Cringing, she glanced at the giant figure entangling her. A straw-stuffed scarecrow looked down, smiling its idiot grin, arms flapping loosely as she slapped them away. Jill had lost.

Barry was gone.

For a moment, Jillian lay there, sobbing in anger and pain. As she looked up through tears, she saw a lone star overhead change from white to blue to red.

And then disappear.

Barry was later returned safely by the aliens, when they landed to meet human scientists at a spot in the American West. The government kept this landing place a secret, but Jillian Guiler and Roy Neary managed to find it and to take part in humanity's first contact with beings from another planet.

---

1. Several electric appliances in Jillian's home were affected by the presence of the alien ships. Which ones? What happened to them?
2. Why do you think Jillian was frightened by the approach of the "storm"? Did she know what was about to happen?
3. Describe Jillian's and Barry's different reactions to the "storm." How would you explain this difference?
4. Do you think that Steven Spielberg's description of a visit from aliens is realistic? If not, describe what you think would happen during a visit from aliens. Do you think Jillian's reaction to the visit was realistic? How would you have reacted in her place?
5. Imagine that you could get in a time machine and journey fifty years into the future. What would the world be like then? Briefly, describe what you would find.

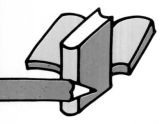

Reading a Floor Plan

You know that maps give information about certain areas. A *floor plan* is one kind of a map. It shows where rooms are located on one floor of a building.

You have read a selection about the National Air and Space Museum in Washington, D.C. The next page shows a floor plan for the first floor of this museum. The plan shows you the name and number of each gallery on the floor.

A key is also provided to explain the symbols used in the floor plan. The symbols indicate the location of the information booth, museum shop, restrooms, elevators, stairs, escalators, and wheelchairs.

Another special symbol appears on the map. The letter *N* with a pointer above it indicates the direction north.

Use the floor plan and the key on the next page to answer the following questions.

1. If you were in the Exhibition Flight Gallery, in which direction would you walk to reach the Hall of Air Transportation?
2. If you were at the Milestones of Flight Gallery, in which direction would you walk to reach Space Hall?
3. Which area would you go to in order to obtain a wheelchair?
4. Between which two galleries is the Museum Shop located?
5. Which gallery number would you go to in order to obtain information?
6. Which three galleries could you reach directly by elevator?
7. If someone directed you to gallery 103, which exhibit would you see there?
8. Where are restrooms located on the first floor?
9. If you were in the South Lobby, which means of transportation would take you to another floor?
10. If you left the Satellites Gallery and walked west, which gallery would you first pass on your left?

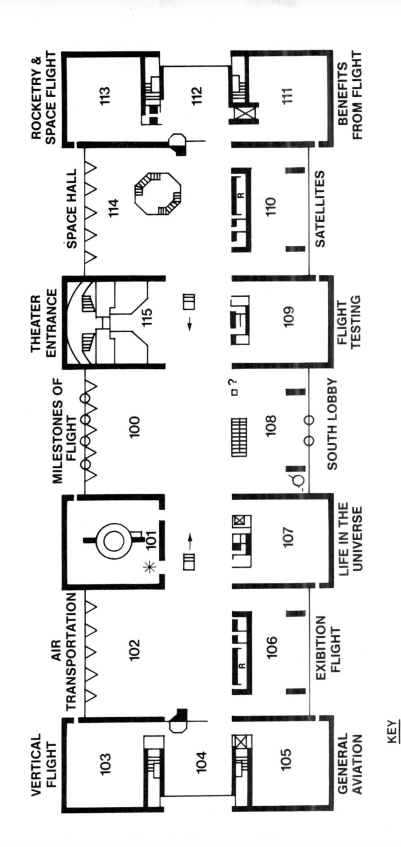

FIRST FLOOR PLAN
NATIONAL AIR AND SPACE MUSEUM

VERTICAL FLIGHT

103

104

105

GENERAL AVIATION

AIR TRANSPORTATION

102

101

106

EXIBITION FLIGHT

107

LIFE IN THE UNIVERSE

MILESTONES OF FLIGHT

100

108

SOUTH LOBBY

THEATER ENTRANCE

115

109

FLIGHT TESTING

SPACE HALL

114

110

SATELLITES

ROCKETRY & SPACE FLIGHT

113

112

111

BENEFITS FROM FLIGHT

N

KEY

? Information

✳ Museum Shop

R Restroom

⊠ Elevator

▦ Stairs/Escalator

⌐○ Wheelchair

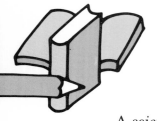

Reading a Scientific Diagram

A *scientific diagram* is a special kind of illustration. It shows the different parts of a machine or other scientific item. The diagram may be accompanied by text that explains how the parts work together.

A scientific diagram has special features. The *title* tells the name of the entire machine. *Labels* indicate the names of the individual parts of the machine. Sometimes the labels are only letters or numbers. A key near the diagram explains what each letter or number stands for.

If the diagram explains how the parts work together, there will be a third feature. The *explanation* is the text that tells how the parts work.

Look ahead to the next selection "Energy Machines." It contains a scientific diagram. The title is "Hydraulic Self Driving Machine." There are nine individual parts to the machine. Each part is labeled with a capital letter. An explanation of the letters accompanies the diagram and tells how the parts work together.

ACTIVITY A   Study the scientific diagram below. Then answer the questions.

An Incandescent Lamp

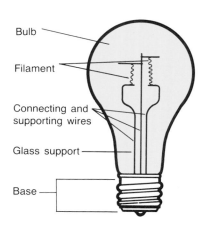

Bulb

Filament

Connecting and
supporting wires

Glass support

Base

1. What is the title of the diagram shown?
2. How many individual parts are labeled in the diagram?
3. What is the bottom part of the lamp called?
4. What are the two wavy coils near the top of the lamp called?
5. How many connecting and supporting wires appear in the diagram?
6. What kind of support is located above the base?

ACTIVITY B Study the diagram below and read the explanation. Then answer the questions that follow.

The Bicycle

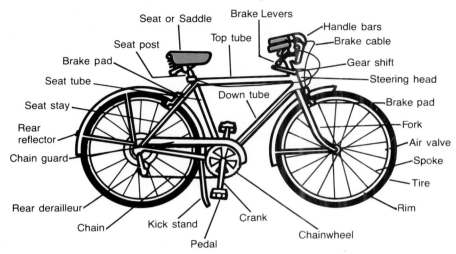

Seat or Saddle

Brake Levers

Seat post

Top tube

Handle bars

Brake cable

Brake pad

Gear shift

Seat tube

Steering head

Down tube

Seat stay

Brake pad

Rear reflector

Fork

Air valve

Chain guard

Spoke

Tire

Rear derailleur

Rim

Chain

Kick stand

Crank

Chainwheel

Pedal

The rider pushes the *pedals* of the bicycle. They turn the *chainwheel*. A *chain* is connected to the chainwheel. As the chainwheel turns, the chain also turns. The chain causes the rear wheel to move.

The rider uses the *handle bars* to guide and balance the bicycle. The handle bars turn the front wheel from side to side. Two *brake levers* on the handle bars are used to stop the bicycle. The levers operate rubber *brake pads* that press against the *wheel rims*. The pressure from the break pads slows down or stops the bicycle.

1. What is the title of the diagram above?
2. How many individual parts are labeled in the diagram?
3. What part of the bicycle causes the chainwheel to turn?
4. What part of the bicycle causes the chain to turn?
5. What part of the bicycle causes the rear wheel to turn?
6. What is the function of the handle bars?
7. What is the function of the brake levers?
8. What is another name for the seat on a bicycle?
9. What is the name of the bar that runs between the steering head and the seat tube?
10. Where is the air valve located?

One Candle Power

Alice Geer Kelsey

Energy
is a vital concern
for us all.
In this short story, Nasr-ed-Din Hodja
and his friends disagree over questions
of energy. How much energy does a person need
to survive during a winter night?
How much energy is needed to cook a meal?
The Hodja answers these questions
in a surprising and humorous way.

Perhaps Nasr-ed-Din Hodja had been sitting too long in the warm coffee house, swapping yarns with his friends. The boasts were growing bigger and bigger. None was bigger than the Hodja's.

"I could stand all night in the snow without any fire to warm me." The Hodja noisily gulped down one more hot cup of sweet black coffee.

"No one could do that!" One of the men shivered as he looked through the window at the falling snow.

"I could!" The Hodja spread his hands over the open pan of burning coals. "I'll do it this very night."

"You can't!"

"I will! If I have so much as a glow of fire to warm myself, I'll—I'll—I'll give a feast for you all at my house tomorrow!"

The wager was on.

The friends of Nasr-ed-Din Hodja went home to their warm beds, while he stood alone in the snow-draped market square. He had never realized how much longer the hours were at night than in the daytime. He had never realized how many hours there were in the night. Once in a while, a prowling dog or an adventuring cat would sniff at him and then slink off to a snugger spot. The cold snow swathing his feet and tickling his neck was hard enough to bear. Harder still was the sleepiness that plagued him. It would never do to fall asleep in the snow. He must keep awake to stamp his cold feet and beat his cold arms. He found

that it was easier to fight off sleep if he fastened his eyes on the flickering candle in Mehmet Ali's house across the market square. There was something cheering about the wavering of that tiny flame, which helped his tired eyes stay open.

Morning came at last. Curious men met the shivering and yawning Hodja on his way home to a cup of hot coffee. They asked about his

night and marveled at what he had done.

"How did you keep awake all night?" they asked.

"I fixed my eyes on a flickering candle in Mehmet Ali's house," he answered.

"A candle?"

"A burning candle?"

"Did you say a candle?"

"Of course!" The Hodja saw no harm in watching a candle.

"A lighted candle gives flame. Flame gives heat. You were warming yourself by the heat of that candle. You have lost your wager."

At first, the Hodja tried to laugh at their joke, but he soon found that they were not joking. For once, the Hodja was too tired to argue successfully. Try as he would, he could not convince his friends that a candle in a distant house could give no warmth to a cold man standing in a snowy market square.

"What time shall we come for the feast at your house tonight?" The

laughing men gathered about the Hodja, insisting that they had won the wager.

"Come at sunset," said the Hodja. He plodded drearily toward home. He was cold and very tired, but he was thinking—and thinking hard.

Just after the muezzin's musical voice sent the sunset call to prayer trilling over Ak Shehir, a group of men knocked at Nasr-ed-Din Hodja's street gate. It creaked open for them. They walked across the courtyard and left their shoes in a row beside the house door. They entered the Hodja's house and sat cross-legged on the floor.

"Dinner is not quite ready." It was the Hodja's voice from the kitchen.

"Oh, that's all right," called the men. "We are in no hurry."

They waited. There was an occasional footstep in the kitchen, but no sound of clattering dishes. They sniffed the air to guess what the feast might be, but they could smell no cooking food. They

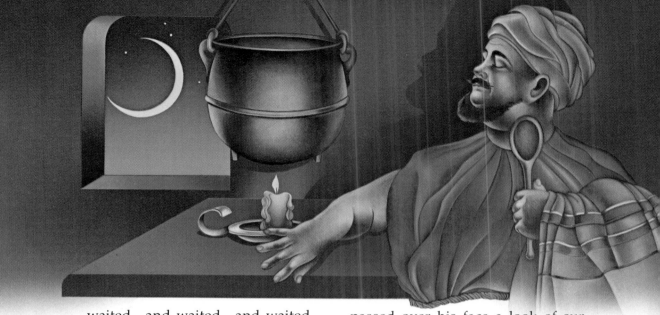

waited—and waited—and waited.

"I hope you are not hungry," called the Hodja from the kitchen. "Dinner is not quite ready yet."

"Perhaps we could help," suggested a hungry guest.

"Fine," called the Hodja. "You might all come out in the kitchen to help."

The men, glad of anything to do, stretched their cramped legs. As each man entered the kitchen, there passed over his face a look of surprise and then a sheepish grin.

There stood the Hodja earnestly stirring the contents of a big copper kettle which was suspended high in the air. Far below it burned one flickering candle.

"Just a few minutes!" The Hodja, standing a-tiptoe, peered into the cold kettle. "It should boil before long. A candle gives so much heat, you know!"

1. Why did the Hodja have to invite his friends to dinner?
2. Why do you think the Hodja found it easier to stay awake when he watched the candle flame?
3. Why didn't the candle make the contents of the kettle boil? Do you think the heat from the candle would have ever been enough to boil the contents of the kettle? Why or why not?
4. Have you ever lost an argument even when you were right? Almost everyone has. Describe the situation. Why do you think this situation sometimes happens?
5. You may want to find out more about the body's need for heat and how the body uses and produces heat. How, for instance, do people who live in very cold climates survive? How about people in very warm climates?

ENERGY MACHINES

Robert Bell

Many people are working to develop new ways of producing and conserving energy. "Energy Machines" explains some of the problems they face.

Before you begin to read, skim through the article. Notice the title, the headings, and the diagrams. Try turning each heading into a question. For example, you can turn the title "Energy Machines" into "What is an energy machine?"

Read the article to find the answers to your questions. In this way, you will be setting purposes for your reading, and it will become easier for you to concentrate on important information and details. Keep in mind that sometimes one thing happens because something else happens. We call this a *cause and effect* relationship. As you read, try to understand *why* certain things happened.

THE MACHINE THAT COULDN'T

What It Should Do You are looking at a diagram of Arthur Sutton's Hydraulic Self Driving Machine (HSDM), patented in 1931. It was conceived as a perpetual-motion machine. Once set in motion, it was supposed to run forever without using any fuel. This was the basic idea:

Water runs out of a water tank *(A)* through a valve *(B)* and onto a water wheel *(C)*. A metal rod *(D)* connects the water wheel to a generator *(E)* and a pulley *(F)*. As water falls onto the wheel, the wheel turns, turning the pulley and spinning the generator to make electricity.

A fan belt *(G)* connects the pulley to a pump *(H)*. After turning the wheel, the water falls into a lower tank *(I)*. The pump lifts the

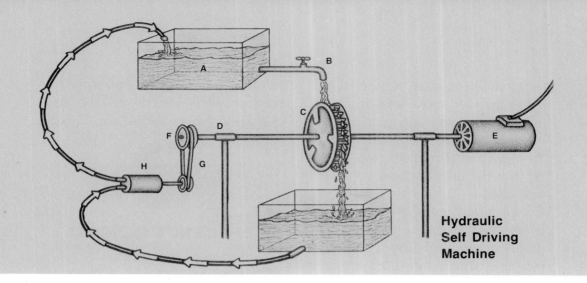

**Hydraulic
Self Driving
Machine**

water from the lower tank *(I)* to the upper tank *(A)*, so the water can be used again and again. The results: perpetual motion and free electricity!

At last, we have solved the energy crisis! Why, you ask yourself, have not hundreds of these wonderful machines already been built? Or have you guessed that there is something wrong with Sutton's machine? The problem is simple. The machine won't work. Perpetual-motion machines cannot work.

Why It Fails Let's take another look at Arthur Sutton's machine to see why it and other perpetual-motion machines don't work.

The HSDM fails for two reasons. In both cases, it ignores basic rules of energy and machines. The first rule is: *You can't get something for nothing.* If you want a machine to do work, you have to feed it energy. Sutton wanted to make his energy source—falling water turning a wheel—do two heavy jobs at once. He wanted the falling water to run the generator *and* pump water back into the upper tank. That would be like dividing four by two and getting four.

The most you could expect from the Self Driving Machine is that it would drive itself. The water would turn the wheel; the pump attached to the wheel would return the water to the upper tank. But, in practice, Sutton's machine can't even do these tasks. The problem has to do with the second rule of energy and machines.

The second rule states: *There is no such thing as a 100% efficient machine. Efficiency* is the amount of energy we get *out* of a machine divided by the amount of energy we put *into* it. On an old, heavy, rusty bicycle, you have to pedal hard to go ten miles (16.09 kilometers) per hour on a level road. On a new,

315

light, well oiled bike, you pedal easily to go ten miles per hour. You have to put more energy into pedaling the old bike than into pedaling the new one. Therefore, we say the old bicycle is less efficient than the new one.

An ideal machine would get every possible bit of work out of a given amount of energy. Such a machine would be 100% efficient. The average car is about 25% efficient; for in machines, a certain amount of energy is always wasted. Surprisingly, a person on a racing bicycle is more efficient than a car.

A force called *friction* is usually the big energy thief. To understand friction, press your hands together, palm to palm. Press hard and slide your palms in opposite directions. Do you feel the resistance and the heat in your palms? Friction is the resistance created between moving parts that touch each other. Friction steals energy by turning it into unwanted heat.

The working parts of a machine rub against each other. The rod in Sutton's machine rubs against its bearings, no matter how well oiled it is. Friction will drain the energy from the HSDM and will make it grind to a halt in a few minutes.

There are no easy answers, like perpetual-motion machines, to the complex problems of efficiency, friction, and energy. Instead, scientists and engineers look for ways to stretch our present energy resources. They also try to find new and better ways to get the energy we need.

EFFICIENCY AND COST

Efficiency Efficiency is a major issue in the design of machines that produce or use energy. If you think of cars and gasoline, you will see why. Compare two cars: Car A can go eighteen miles on a gallon[1] of gas. Car B gets forty miles to the gallon. To go a hundred miles, Car A needs 5.6 gallons of gas; Car B needs only 2.5 gallons. Car B is much more efficient than Car A. It also costs less to run.

Cost Cost is the other major energy issue. When the cost of the sources of energy—oil, coal, and natural gas—goes up, the price of everything we do with that energy—lighting, heating, cooking, driving—goes up, too. The cost of energy can have a great effect on every part of our lives. Efficiency and cost are connected like the two ends of a seesaw. As with the two cars discussed above, when efficiency goes up, cost usually goes down. When efficiency goes down, cost usually goes up.

[1] 1 mile=1.609 kilometers
1 gallon=3.785 liters

USING ENERGY RESOURCES

Limited Resources Oil and coal are expensive because they have to be found and taken from the ground. But there is another reason why they are expensive: When the supply of something people want runs low, the price of that thing rises. The price rises because there is not enough to go around and people are willing to pay high prices to get some of that thing.

Oil and coal are *limited* resources. When we begin to run out of oil and coal, the prices will skyrocket. In other words, the cost of limited resources is tied to the supply. Shrink the supply, and the cost will head for the stars.

Unlimited Resources For this reason, scientists and engineers are trying to find or invent unlimited sources of energy. With unlimited sources, the supply will never run out. The cost of unlimited resources, therefore, is *not* tied to the supply. Instead, the cost is tied to the efficiency with which we use the unlimited energy. The energy is there; we have to figure out how to use it.

Garbage Power: A plant in Lynn, Massachusetts, is using a new kind of fuel to make electricity. The fuel is garbage. The plant takes household garbage from neighboring towns and cities, separates the

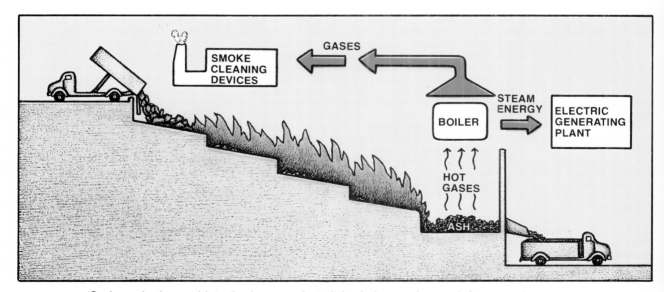

Garbage is dumped into the burner, where it is shaken and moved down a set of steps to make sure there is complete burning. The ash is used for road building and landfill.

metal for recycling, and burns the rest. The hot gases from the burning garbage are used to run a boiler. Steam from the boiler is put through a turbine generator to make electricity. The leftover gases are then cleaned of harmful chemicals and ash and are released to the air.

The plant is highly efficient. Seventy-eight thousand gallons (295 kiloliters) of oil per day would be needed to equal the amount of "garbage power" the plant produces. The supply of garbage is nearly unlimited. An average American throws out about 2,000 pounds (.9 metric tons) of household garbage every year. The plant burns something nobody wants—garbage—to make something everyone needs—energy. The cost of that energy is sure to be low. You can't get something for nothing, but this plant comes as close to that as possible.

Furnace in the Sky: The sun is a mighty energy source. Energy from the sun powers every living thing on Earth. Enough sun power falls on the United States in one minute to run all the homes and industries in the country for a day. Enough solar power reaches the Earth in forty minutes to supply the world's energy needs for a year. That power is free, unlimited, and nonpolluting.

Sunlight is free, but turning it into energy we can use costs money and sacrifices efficiency. One approach to the problem of solar collection is the *solar cell.* Solar cells are gadgets that turn sunlight directly into electricity.

Solar cells work because of something called the "photovoltaic effect" (*photo* means "light"; *voltaic* comes from the name of an Italian physicist who studied electricity, Alessandro Volta). Certain substances, such as silicon (sil′ i kən) and selenium (si lē′ nē əm), give off *electrons* when they are struck by light. What are electrons? Electrons are the particles that make up an electric current.

By tinkering chemically with two pieces of silicon, electrons can be made to "flow" from one silicon piece to the other in a steady stream. If you place the two pieces together and attach wires, you create a kind of battery which is recharged by sunlight. Attach a light bulb to the wires, and the flow of electrons will light the bulb.

At first glance, solar cells would seem to be the perfect answer to our energy problems. But let's not forget cost and efficiency. Solar cells are approximately 12% efficient. That's not very good, but it's not all that bad, either. The big problem is cost. Solar cells take a long time and a lot of money to make. They cost so much that solar electricity is about a thousand times more expensive than the electricity you use at home. But many people are working to make solar cells cheaper and more efficient. Someday soon, perhaps, you may be tapping the sun when you turn on a light.

Another approach to solar power uses *flat-plate collectors* to harness the sun's heat. A flat-plate collector is simply a large, shallow box, painted black inside, with one glass wall.

To understand how this system works, think of sitting in a car with the windows closed on a sunny day. Even in cold weather, the inside of the car is warmer than the air outside. In hot weather, the heat can be stifling. This heat is created by solar energy which enters the glass

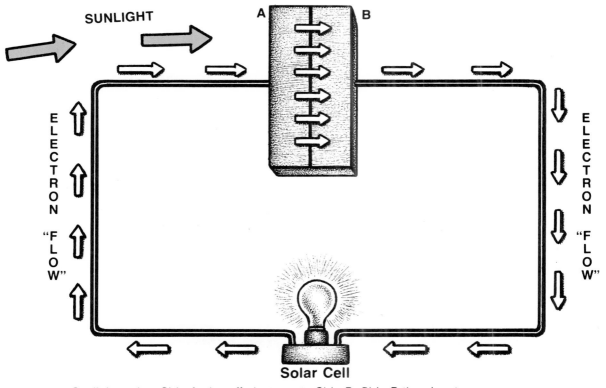

Sunlight makes Side A give off electrons to Side B. Side B then has too many electrons, so the electrons flow through the wire back to Side A, lighting the bulb on the way. Side A passes the electrons to Side B, and the process continues. In this way, the energy of the sun is converted directly into electricity.

windows and is trapped inside. The car acts as a collector of solar heat.

The same thing happens inside a flat-plate collector. It is painted black inside because black traps more of the sun's heat than any other color. Black-painted pipes, filled with water or some other fluid, run through the collector. The water in the pipes gets very hot. It can then be used to heat (or air-condition, believe it or not) a home. It also makes hot water for washing and other household tasks. Flat-plate collectors are no more efficient, but they cost much less than solar cells. They are being used in buildings all over the world.

Weather is another problem for solar collectors. Solar collectors will work on cloudy days, but less sunlight means less power. At present, solar collectors are most useful in places where there is constant sunlight, and in places that have hot, fair weather most of the time.

Wind Power: The solar collector shares its weather problem with another energy machine—the windmill. Winds can be very steady in some places. But, for the most part, winds are always changing speed and direction.

Windmills have been used for centuries to do all kinds of work, from pumping water to grinding grain to making electricity. Like solar

Grandpa's Knob Windmill

power, wind power is basically free and unlimited. But collecting that free power is not easy.

Friction is both the friend and the enemy of the windmill. Windmills use propellers to catch the wind. It is the friction of the wind on the propeller blades that turns the windmill. But the wind also has to overcome the friction of the windmill's machinery before it can do its work. Thus, friction makes the windmill go, but it also eats up much of the wind power.

When windmills were still widely used, many people experimented with them. They wanted to make windmills that were efficient and cheap to build. A few people were also thinking big. They reasoned that a large, expensive windmill might be efficient enough to pay for its high cost. One of these people was Palmer Putman, an engineer. He designed a 110-foot (33.51 meters) windmill with a generator and two eight-ton (7.26 metric tons) propeller blades that each measured over eighty feet (24.37 meters) long. He convinced the S. Morgan Smith Co. and the Central Vermont Public Service Corp. to build the windmill on Grandpa's Knob, a windy 2000-foot (609.33 meters) mountain in Vermont.

On October 19, 1941, the windmill was put to the test. For the next two and a half years, it brought electric power to thousands of Vermont homes. In 1943, it was shut down for repairs. It was not started again until 1945 because metal was hard to get during World War II. When it was finally started again, it ran for only three weeks before a propeller blade sheared off. The project was finally given up because of the continuing shortage of metal.

The Grandpa's Knob project proved that wind power could be an important energy resource. With new and better materials, it should be possible to build stronger and more efficient wind towers. Because of the energy crisis, people all over the country are experimenting again with windmills. Many engineers are busy designing huge wind machines. The tall towers and huge blades may soon be a common sight across America.

New Resources You have probably read about energy research in newspapers and magazines. Perhaps you have your own ideas on producing energy. As you read or develop your ideas, remember those two age-old problems—efficiency and cost.

The search for new energy sources goes on. As you have seen, it is not an easy search, for there are no easy answers. In his poem, "My Invention," Shel Silverstein sums up the promises—and the problems—of energy research.

My Invention

Guess what I have gone and done;
I've invented a light that plugs into the sun.
For the sun is bright enough,
And the bulb is strong enough—
But the cord isn't long enough.

—Shel Silverstein

1. What is the difference between limited and unlimited resources?
2. What are the major problems in using the sun as a source of energy?
3. This article states that "When efficiency goes up, cost usually goes down. When efficiency goes down, cost usually goes up." Can you think of some examples that prove these statements?
4. Though we use many machines, human power still does much of our work. Think about things—jobs, games, transportation—that use human power. Discuss them and try to answer these questions: Where does the human body get its energy? Is human power a limited or an unlimited resource?
5. Keep a running list for one week of all the things you do that use up energy resources (for example, turning on a light or riding in a car). Compare and discuss your list with the members of your class. Do you use more energy than you need to use? Why or why not?

Me and the Ecology Bit

Joan Lexau

A satire often makes fun of human behavior for a specific purpose. "Me and the Ecology Bit" is a satire about a girl who thinks she knows what ecology means. She believes she is doing something to help improve the environment.

As you read, think about whether Maria really understands ecology. Try to identify what makes this story a satire.

Sure is hard to get people to work for ecology. Everybody is in favor of it, but nobody wants to do anything about it. At least I'm doing something, going around telling people what they should do. But all I get is a lot of back talk.

I have this paper route. My father had one when he was a kid, so he made me get one last year. Between it and my homework, I hardly have time for playing ball and stuff. Some days, I only get in a few innings.

But anyhow, on Saturdays when I collect, I put in a good word for ecology. Like last Saturday morning: It was a good collecting day. It had just turned spring, and a lot of people were outside.

I went to Mr. Williams' house. As usual, he tries to pretend he's not home. But I see him burning leaves in the backyard, so he's stuck. He pays me, and I tell him, "You shouldn't burn those leaves. It's bad for the air, bad ecology. You should make a compost pile like we do. Put in the leaves, garbage, and stuff. Good for the garden."

He doesn't agree or hang his head in shame. He says, "That compost pile is your job at home, Maria, isn't it?"

"Yes," I say proudly, which would shock my dad. He somehow has the idea I hate working with compost—which I do.

Mr. Williams says, "Well, why don't you take a little more trouble with it, put enough dirt on top of each layer? And turn it over now and then? Then we wouldn't have this nose pollution."

"Huh?" I say. "You mean noise pollution."

"No," he says. "I mean your compost smells up the whole street."

My feelings are hurt, but that doesn't stop me from trying again. I go to collect from Ms. Greene.

She is putting her garbage out for the weekly pickup on Monday. She goes away weekends, so Saturdays and Sundays we have to look at the big plastic garbage bags on her lawn. But I don't say anything about it; I just look at the garbage.

She says to me, "Go pick up that gum wrapper you threw on my lawn. Put it in one of the plastic bags. Didn't anybody teach you not to litter?"

I hold my temper and go pick up my gum wrapper and put it in a bag.

Then she says, "And there's a law in this town about keeping dogs on a leash. So why is yours always all over the place? That dog digs up my garden and messes up my yard, and last weekend, Mr. Williams saw it tear open one of my garbage bags."

"Well," I say, but I can't think of anything to go with it. Then I see she is piling newspapers next to her garbage bags.

"Listen, Ms. Greene," I say, "save those papers for the school pickup and they can be made into new paper. Save aluminum cans, too."

"Like the last school pickup?" she asks. "When you said you'd come pick them up and you never showed up? It's easier to throw them away a few at a time than have a big mess like that."

I get tired trying to get Ms. Greene to do something about ecology. I go to Mr. Johnson's house. He makes a run for his car, but I can run faster than he can.

"Just trying to get to the post office before it closes," he says, huffing and puffing.

"You have time," I say. "You even have time to walk. It's only two blocks. You shouldn't take your car when you don't need to. The walk would be good exercise and save on gas and not pollute. That's ecology."

"How about trees?" he asks me. "Are trees ecology?"

"They sure are," I say. "We had a lot about trees and ecology in school. They make the air better and stuff like that."

"See that tree over there?" he says, pointing to where there isn't any tree.

"I don't see any tree," I tell him.

"Of course not," he says, "and no grass either, because you made a path there taking a shortcut from Ms. Greene's. There was a little tree just starting to get bigger there, until you killed it by trying to jump over it every day. Remember?"

"Oh," I say.

"And talking about not driving when you can walk: You drive

your motorbike round and round your backyard all summer—and your snowmobile all winter. Isn't that wasting power and making noise pollution, too?"

"But it's fun," I say.

"Well, I enjoy taking the car to the post office," he says. "But now you've made me too late." He goes in the house looking very mad.

Then I remember he hasn't paid me. But I decide to wait until next Saturday. At least I made him not pollute with his car for once.

I don't talk to the rest of my route about ecology. It's very tiring work, this ecology bit.

But when I get home, I see my mother using the electric mixer.

"You should do that with your old egg beater," I point out to her. "Save on electricity. People use too many electric things."

She says in a very cold voice, "So who watches TV twenty-seven hours a day around here? Or is that some other kind of electricity?"

See what I mean? Nobody's willing to do anything about ecology —except me. And nobody listens to me.

1. Mr. Johnson made several points when Maria tried to advise him about ecology. What were these points?

2. Think about the many pieces of advice Maria gave in the story. Was it useful advice? Why?

3. Compare the first and last paragraphs of the story. Do you think Maria learned anything from her conversations with people? Why?

4. A satire often makes fun of human behavior for a specific purpose. What makes this story a satire?

5. Can you think of times when you or someone you know said one thing but did the opposite? Describe the situation.

6. What action can you take to help ecology? (For example, help plan a school or community recycling center and/or help at one that already exists.)

WHOSE GARDEN WAS THIS?

Whose garden was this?
It must have been lovely.
Did it have flowers?
I've seen pictures of flowers,
And I'd love to have smelled one.

Whose river was this?
You say it ran freely.
Blue was its color.
I've seen blue in some pictures,
And I'd love to have been there.

Tell me again, I need to know.
The forests had trees,
The meadows were green,
The oceans were blue,
And birds really flew.
Can you swear that was true?

Whose gray sky was this?
Or was it a blue one?
Nights there were breezes.
I've heard records of breezes,
And you tell me you felt one.

Tell me again, I need to know.
The forests had trees,
The meadows were green,
The oceans were blue,
And birds really flew.
Can you swear that was true?

—TOM PAXTON

327

The Leopolds: A Family for the Environment

As you grow up, you learn about the world from those who have lived longer than you have—your parents, relatives, and adult friends. Often, the examples these adults set—their habits, ways of life, and career paths—strongly influence your own life. As you read this biographical sketch of the Leopold family, notice how the children made their own decisions about life, but were also influenced by their family's way of life and by their father's career. Notice, too, the many different branches of science that contribute to our understanding of the environment.

Starker Leopold is a professor of zoology. He is one of America's leading experts on wildlife. He is also the author of many books on ecology and a member of government committees that plan national park policies.

Estella Leopold is the Director of the Quaternary Research Center at the University of Washington. She is a paleoecologist. She finds and studies fossilized grains of pollen that date back millions of years. From these, she learns about the history of plant life in America. In her spare time, she works to make people and government agencies care about conservation.

During the summer, Estella often goes on camping trips with Luna

and people—are related. They know that we cannot change one part without changing, at least in a small way, the whole. They believe that we must think carefully before we try to change or control any part of nature.

Many Americans share this view. The Leopolds are an unusual family because they are all doing something to help the causes of ecology and conservation. Starker, Estella, Luna, Carl, and Nina are the children of Aldo and Estella Leopold. Aldo Leopold was one of America's pioneers in ecology and conservation.

Aldo Leopold was born in 1887 in Burlington, Iowa. His father was a keen hunter, and Aldo grew up hunting, fishing, and loving the outdoor life. When he grew older, it was natural for him to go to the Yale School of Forestry. He then joined the United States Forest Service. He was not a conservationist when he began work in the Service. Like most people who grew up in his time, he saw the wilderness only as something to be used and made to yield a profit. Forests were for lumbering; wildlife, for hunting.

Then, in 1912, he developed a serious illness. He was bedridden for a year; and, during that time, his ideas began to change. He knew that a wilderness—forest, desert, mountain, or ocean—could be a resource. But he came to believe that when we think of it *just* as a resource, we become blind to its beauty. We fail to see the many things that make the

Leopold. Luna also works for the U.S. Geological Survey. He is a hydrologist, a scientist who studies water and the use of water. He makes it his business to see that large projects, such as dams and canals, are built so that they do the least damage to the environment. He is the author of more than a hundred scientific papers and the coauthor of many books.

Carl Leopold is a biologist. Nina Leopold is active in conservation issues in the area where she lives.

The Leopolds, brothers and sisters, live, study, and work in different parts of the country. They all share a love for the beauty of nature. They know that the many parts of nature—rocks, soil, plants, animals,

wilderness a special and wonderful place. We begin to meddle carelessly with it, and all too often, we upset nature's careful balance. We destroy what we do not understand.

Aldo Leopold was later to write:

"We abuse the land because we regard it as . . . belonging to us. When we see land as a community to which we belong, we may begin to use it with love and respect. There is no other way for land to survive the impact of mechanized man. . . ."

Aldo Leopold

These were new and bold ideas in the first half of the twentieth century. In 1922, Aldo was invited to teach at the University of Wisconsin. He left the Forest Service and became a professor of wildlife management. From that time on, he worked to convince people of the need for conservation. He taught, organized conservation groups, and wrote books and magazine articles. He helped the National Park Service set up wilderness areas. These areas were to be kept in their natural state, without roads or buildings. They exist today and provide ecologists with material for their studies.

Aldo Leopold died on April 21, 1948, while helping neighboring farmers fight a grass fire near his weekend home. He was sixty-two. His lifetime of hard work had important results. He had influenced the growth of ecology as a science, and he had helped make conservation the public concern it is today.

Aldo Leopold influenced his children as well. At first glance, they seem to have followed right in his footsteps. Yet the Leopold children chose their own goals and made their own decisions. It was only later in life that they found they had traveled the same path as their father.

How do parents influence their children? What did Aldo Leopold

teach his children that made them turn to ecology as a way of life?

His daughter, Estella, has one answer: "My father never said, 'You kids ought to be interested in all this.' He just used to get so excited himself that we couldn't help getting interested."

The Leopolds usually spent weekends on their Wisconsin farm. It was 120 acres of wild ground. There, and on camping and canoeing trips, the children were in close touch with nature. They learned to fish and hunt. To Aldo, hunting meant woodcraft—understanding the forest and its life. When he spotted an animal, he stalked it silently,

watching and listening carefully until he was close enough for a clean shot. He taught these skills to his children and showed them how to explore, carefully and silently, the secret worlds of plants and animals. They saw, firsthand, the varieties of life and the ties that joined these varieties together.

These pursuits taught the children a great deal. But what they learned was not always what their father meant to teach. Luna recalls: "All of us, and we are all now very interested in conservation, came to it pretty late. Sure, you learn about woodcraft. You learn outdoor manners. I was interested in hunting, but not in birds as such, when I was growing up. I thought all that was as dull as could be."

Luna's career is a good example of how the Leopold children followed their own career paths. On his way to becoming a hydrologist, he studied engineering, physics, meteorology (the science of weather), and geology (the science of the earth). "I could see that the kind of thing I was most interested in, which happened to be water and water-related problems, was going to require a completely new kind of education. But my father thought I was crazy to study engineering. My professors did, too. But I was convinced that the only way to talk to engineers is to be one yourself."

One of Luna's many projects— one that needed all his many skills—was an attempt to rate in numbers the natural beauty of land. Engineers who designed dams, canals, and other projects had no way to make beauty a part of their calculations. Luna's solution was a system that could compare the beauty, historical value, and wilderness value of many building sites. Engineers could then pick the one that would be least damaged by construction. By translating conservation into engineering language, Luna hoped to save parts of the American wilderness.

Estella also took a roundabout route to her present interest in conservation. She studied botany and plant ecology. Her field of study, fossilized pollen, has nothing to do with conservation. Instead, her work helps to unravel the mysteries of Earth's history. Among many other things, she has discovered that, forty or fifty million years ago, the Rocky-Mountain area had a very different climate from the one it has today. It was hot and humid and covered with a tropical rain forest like those of southeast Asia. She did not become interested

in conservation until the early 1960's. At that time, she helped organize several conservation groups. She has been active in the conservation movement ever since.

Starker answers the question of parental influence in a different way: "I guess my interest in nature and the environment began with the hunting and field trips I went on with my father. My concern with hunting as a sport led me to feel that the study and care of wildlife could be a profession." Like his father, Starker has been interested in animals since his childhood. He has devoted himself to studying the ways in which humans affect wildlife.

In 1951, for example, he was asked to look into the disappearance of the caribou, a type of large deer, in Alaska. Where there once had been millions of caribou, there were only a few hundred thousand left. The Alaskan government placed the blame on wolves and on hunters.

After careful study, Starker unearthed a very different reason. In winter, the caribou lives on plants called lichens, which grow on the ground or on the branches of trees.

During and since the gold rush in Alaska, people have been burning the wilderness to clear it. The lichens burned with the rest of the plant life. Starker found that eighty-five percent of central Alaska had been burned in that fifty-year period. Lichens take a long time to grow back. It can take a century for burned country to be rich in lichens again. Starker concluded that caribou were disappearing because they starved to death during the winter.

Parents influence their children. The children grow up and often become parents themselves. What about the children's children—the grandchildren of Aldo Leopold? Luna reports: "My own son and daughter are not yet concerned about ecology and conservation, though I think they're going to be. That's the way it was with all of us, and maybe it's the most interesting thing about the Leopold family. The attitude was there, because of my father. But each of us has had to develop it through experience. You aren't just made a conservationist from birth. You have to fight for it in your own way."

1. Was Aldo Leopold a conservationist when he started work in the Forest Service? Describe his beliefs at that time. How did they change?

2. List the different branches of science mentioned in this biographical sketch. How do you think each one contributes to the study of our environment?

3. In what ways were the children's paths different from their father's? In what ways were they the same?

4. What do you think is meant by the statement: "The many parts of nature—rocks, soil, plants, animals, and people—are related."

5. Can you think of someone who has influenced you in a special way? It might be someone you know or even someone you have known only through reading. Describe how you have been influenced.

6. Write a brief biographical sketch (a short description) of that special person.

THE FIRST MORNING

Edward Abbey

The science of ecology draws its strength from a very un-scientific feeling: a love of nature. Edward Abbey lived very close to nature and observed it carefully. He recorded his impressions, feelings, and experiences in a journal. As you read the following excerpt from that journal, try to "see" the picture he painted with words. How does it help you appreciate nature?

This is the most beautiful place on earth.

There are many such places. Every man, every woman, carries in heart and mind the image of the ideal place. A houseboat in Kashmir, a view down Atlantic Avenue in Brooklyn, a cabin on the shore of a blue lake in spruce and fir country. Sky pilots and astronauts have even felt the appeal of home, calling to them from up above in the cold black outback of space.

For myself, I'll take Moab, Utah. I don't mean the town itself, but the country which surrounds it—the canyonlands and the slickrock desert. The red dust and the burnt cliffs and the lonely sky—all that which lies beyond the end of the roads.

The choice became apparent to me this morning when I stepped out of a Park Service housetrailer to watch, for the first time in my life, the sun come up over the hoodoo stone of Arches National Monument.

I wasn't able to see much of it last night. After driving all day from Albuquerque—450 miles—I reached Moab after dark in cold, windy, clouded weather. At park headquarters north of town, I met the superintendent and the chief ranger. They are the only permanent employees, except for one maintenance person, in this particular unit of America's national park system. After coffee, they gave me a key to the housetrailer and directions on how to reach it. I am required to live and work, not at headquarters but at this ranger station some twenty miles back in the interior, on my own. The way I wanted it, naturally, or I'd never have asked for the job.

Leaving the headquarters area and the lights of Moab, I drove twelve miles farther north on the highway. I came to a dirt road on the right, where a small wooden sign pointed the way:

ARCHES NATIONAL MONUMENT
EIGHT MILES

I left the pavement and turned east into the howling wilderness. Wind roaring out of the northwest, black clouds across the stars—all I could see were clumps of brush and scattered junipers along the roadside. Then there was another modest signboard:

WARNING: QUICKSAND
DO NOT CROSS WASH
WHEN WATER IS RUNNING

The wash looked perfectly dry in my headlights. I drove down, across, up the other side, and on into the night. I caught glimpses of weird humps of pale rock on either side, like petrified elephants. Now and then, something alive scurried across the road: kangaroo mice, a jackrabbit, an animal that looked like a cross between a raccoon and a squirrel—the ringtail cat. Farther on, a pair of mule deer started from the brush and bounded through the beams of my lights. The road, narrow and rocky, twisted sharply left and right. It dipped in and out of tight ravines, climbing by degrees toward a summit which I would see only in the light of day.

Snow was swirling through the air when I passed the boundary marker of the park. A quarter-mile beyond, I found the ranger station—a wide place in the road, an informational display under a lean-to shelter. Fifty yards away was the little tin housetrailer where I would be living alone for the next six months.

A cold night, a cold wind, the snow falling like confetti . . . . In the lights of the truck I unlocked the housetrailer, got out bedroll and baggage, and moved in. By flashlight I found the bed, unrolled my sleeping bag, pulled off my boots, and crawled in and went to sleep at once. The last I knew was the shaking of the trailer in the wind and the sound, from inside, of hungry mice scampering around. Their long, lean, lonesome winter was over—their friend and provider had finally arrived.

This morning I awake before sunrise and peer through a frosty window at a scene dim and vague with flowing mists, dark fantastic shapes looming beyond. It is an unlikely landscape.

I get up, moving about in long underwear and socks, stooping carefully under the low ceiling and the lower doorways of the housetrailer.

The mice are silent, watching me from their hiding places. The wind is still blowing, and outside the ground is covered with snow. I lie down on the dusty floor and light the pilot on the butane heater. Once this thing gets going, the place warms up fast, in a dense unhealthy way with a layer of heat under the ceiling where my head is and nothing but frigid air from the knees down.

Time to get dressed, get out and have a look at the lay of the land and fix a breakfast. I try to pull on my boots, but they're stiff as iron from the cold. I light a burner on the stove and hold the boots upside down above the flame. Soon they are malleable enough for me to force my feet in. I put on a coat and step outside.

The sun is not yet in sight, but signs of the advent are plain to see. Lavender clouds sail like a fleet of ships across the pale green dawn. Each cloud, planed flat on the wind, has a base of fiery gold. Southeast, twenty miles by line of sight, stand the peaks of the Sierra La Sal. They are twelve to thirteen thousand feet above sea level, all covered with snow and rosy in the morning sunlight. The air is dry and clear, as well as cold. The last fogbanks left over from last night's storm are scudding away like ghosts, fading into nothing before the wind and the sunrise.

The view is open and perfect in all directions, except to the west where the ground rises. Looking toward the mountains, I can see the dark gorge of the Colorado River five or six miles away, carved through the sandstone mesa—though I can see nothing of the river itself down inside the gorge. Southward, on the far side of the river, lies the Moab valley between thousand-foot walls of rock. The town of Moab is somewhere on the valley floor, too small to be seen from here. Beyond the Moab valley are more canyon and tableland stretching away to the Blue Mountains fifty miles south. To the north and northwest, I see the Roan Cliffs and the Book Cliffs. Along the foot of those cliffs, maybe thirty miles off, invisible from where I stand, runs U. S. 6-50, and the main line of the Denver-Rio Grande Railroad. To the east, under the spreading sunrise, are more mesas, more canyons, league on league of red cliffs and arid tablelands—a sea of desert.

In the middle ground and foreground of the picture are the 33,000 acres of Arches National Monument, of which I am now sole inhabitant, observer, and custodian.

What are the arches? From my place in front of the house-trailer, I can see several of the hundred or more which have been discovered in the park. These are natural arches: holes in the rock, windows in stone, no two alike, as varied in form as in dimension. They range in size from holes just big enough to walk through to openings large enough to contain the dome of the Capitol building in Washington, D.C. Some resemble jug-handles or flying buttresses. Others resemble natural bridges, but with this technical distinction: a natural bridge spans a watercourse—a natural arch does not.

The arches were formed through hundreds of thousands of years by the weathering of the huge sandstone walls, or fins, in which they are found. The arches came into being and continue to come into being through the wedging action of rainwater, melting snow, frost, and ice aided by gravity. In color, they shade from off-white through buff, pink, brown, and red—tones which also change with the time of day and the moods of the light, the weather, the sky.

Standing there, gaping at this monstrous and inhuman spectacle of rock and cloud and sky and space, I feel a ridiculous greed come over me. I want to know it all, possess it all, embrace the entire scene, deeply, totally. An insane wish? Perhaps not—at least there's nothing else, no one human, to dispute possession with me.

The snow-covered ground glimmers with a dull blue light, reflecting the sky and the approaching sunrise.

Well—the sun will be up in a few minutes, and I haven't even begun to make coffee. I take more baggage from my pickup, go back in the trailer, and start breakfast. Simply breathing, in a place like this, arouses the appetite. The orange juice is frozen; the milk, slushy with ice. It is still chilly enough

inside the trailer to turn my breath to vapor. When the first rays of the sun strike the cliffs, I fill a mug with steaming coffee and sit in the doorway facing the sunrise, hungry for the warmth.

Suddenly it comes, the flaming globe, blazing on the pinnacles and minarets and balanced rocks, on the canyon walls and through the windows in the sandstone fins. We greet each other, the sun and I, across the black void of ninety-three million miles. The snow glitters between us, acres of diamonds almost painful to look at. Within an hour, all the snow exposed to the sunlight will be gone, and the rock will be damp and steaming. Within minutes, even as I watch, melting snow begins to drip from the branches of a juniper nearby. Drops of water streak slowly down the side of the trailerhouse.

I am not alone after all. Three ravens are wheeling near the balanced rock, squawking at each other and at the dawn. I'm sure they're as delighted by the return of the sun as I am, and I wish I knew their language. I'd sooner exchange ideas with these birds than learn to carry on communications with some race of humanoids on Betelgeuse. The ravens cry out in husky voices, their blue-black wings flapping against the golden sky. Over my shoulder comes the sizzle and smell of frying bacon.

That's the way it was this morning.

1. What are the arches? How are they formed?
2. Speaking of the mice in his trailer, the author says: "Their long, lean, lonesome winter was over—their friend and provider has finally arrived." What does he mean?
3. Explain what you think the author means when, looking at the landscape, he says: "I feel a ridiculous greed come over me. I want to know it all, possess it all, embrace the entire scene, deeply, totally."
4. Do you have a special place? How would you describe your feeling for that place?
5. Keep a journal of your own. Choose a part of nature that you would like to observe. Record your observations in words, sketches, or photos.

Facts and Inferences

In the selection "One Candle Power," the Hodja and his friends had an argument. The Hodja believed the candle in the window did not provide him with warmth. His friends believed otherwise. The Hodja supported his argument by showing that a candle could not boil the contents of the kettle. Therefore it seemed unlikely that the candle could have given warmth to the Hodja while he stood so far away.

When you disagree with someone, you need to give facts to support your argument. A *fact* is a statement that can be proven true or false. You can prove a fact by checking a reference source or by personal observation. The Hodja presented a fact to support his argument: *The candle did not boil the contents of the kettle.* He proved this fact by letting the men observe for themselves.

This fact led to an inference. An *inference* is a conclusion based on facts. The fact led to this conclusion, or inference: *A candle could not have warmed the Hodja from so far away.* Here is another example of an inference drawn from a fact:

Fact: I called a friend on the phone but got a busy signal.
Inference: My friend is talking to someone else.

Remember that an inference is a conclusion. It is a kind of "educated guess" you make from the facts. An inference may not necessarily be true. For example, in the above inference it is possible that the phone is out of order instead.

When you listen to an argument, consider carefully the facts that are mentioned. Do not draw a conclusion, or inference, unless you are sure the facts are true. Also, do not draw a conclusion that does not follow reasonably from the facts. For example,

Fact: I called a friend on the phone but got a busy signal.
Inference: Telephones are an inexpensive way to communicate.

In this example, the fact may be true. However, the inference does not follow reasonably from the fact. The conclusion is not based in any way on the fact.

ACTIVITY A   Read each pair of statements. One statement is a fact. The other statement is an inference drawn from that fact. Write the statement that is the *inference* on your paper.

1a. The house must be on fire.
 b. Smoke is coming from the house.

2a. Kelly has eaten cottage cheese every day this week.
 b. Cottage cheese is Kelly's favorite food.

3a. Four climbers sprained their ankles on that mountain.
 b. That mountain is dangerous to climb.

4a. It will rain this afternoon.
 b. The sky is filled with dark clouds.

5a. The people inside must have gone to bed.
 b. All the lights are out in the house.

6a. John got 100% on his science test today.
 b. John studies hard for science tests.

ACTIVITY B   Read each fact and the inference drawn from it. Decide whether the inference is *reasonable* or *unreasonable* based on the fact.

1. Fact: Seven people have slipped on that patch of ice.
 Inference: It often snows in December.

2. Fact: Trisha speaks Spanish and French.
 Inference: She also speaks Russian and Italian.

3. Fact: George has been yawning all morning.
 Inference: George got little sleep last night.

4. Fact: Our new mayor just appointed a fire chief.
 Inference: The mayor has the hardest job in town.

5. Fact: I switched toothpastes and got fewer cavities.
 Inference: My new toothpaste helps prevent cavities.

6. Fact: The President earns $200,000 a year.
 Inference: The Vice-President has many responsibilities.

7. Fact: My pen is beginning to skip.
 Inference: My pen is running out of ink.

8. Fact: Tom has an expensive watch.
 Inference: Tom is always on time.

Logical Thinking

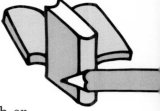

Good readers are careful readers. When you read a paragraph or an advertisement, you must watch for errors in reasoning. A careful reader will not accept statements that are illogical. Here are five examples of errors in reasoning.

1. Jumping to a Conclusion

    George received an *A* on his first science test.
    He also received an *A* on his second science test.
    Therefore George always receives *A*'s on his science tests.

George may or may not receive an *A* on his next science test. Two examples are not enough to "jump to a conclusion."

2. Stereotyping

    All famous scientists did well in school.

Of course, many famous scientists did do well in school, but some famous scientists, including Albert Einstein, did not. The statement ignores differences among scientists.

3. Following Popular Opinion

    Most people think science is very difficult.
    Therefore you should avoid science courses.

Many people find other courses much more difficult than science. Popular opinion only tells what others think. They could be wrong and you could be right. Make up your own mind.

4. Choosing the Wrong Cause

    Some successful scientists do not pay much attention to their clothes.
    If you do not pay much attention to your clothes, you will be a successful scientist.

Certainly people don't believe that to ignore their clothes would make them successful scientists. It is a mistake to choose ignoring clothes as a cause for being a successful scientist.

5. Choosing Either/Or Extremes

    Either scientists are paid excellent salaries by the government, *or* they struggle along on very little.

343

This statement is certainly not true. Many scientists make moderate salaries in industry, education, and government. By looking at only two extremes, the fact that there are many middle possibilities is ignored.

Read each of the following. Decide which kind of faulty reasoning has been used. There is at least one example of each of the five kinds listed above.

1. All Shopgood's butchers offer the best bargains.

2. Either you buy Shopgood's broccoli at $2.00 a bunch, or you eat green beans.

3. Shopgood sells wheat cereal for $1.00 a box. It also sells oat cereal for $1.00 a box. All Shopgood's cereals sell for $1.00 a box.

4. Shopgood's aisles are very wide. If a store has wide aisles, it is very clean.

5. Everyone likes Shopgood. You should shop at Shopgood.

6. All the people employed at Shopgood are very handsome.

7. We bought all our food at Shopgood for $50 last week. We bought all our food at Shopgood for $50 this week. We will always be able to buy all our food at Shopgood for $50.

8. Sarah bought a pair of jeans for $15.00 last year. This year she needed new jeans and also paid $15.00. Next year she plans to buy another pair of jeans for the same price.

9. All people who wear jeans are interested in physical fitness.

10. Either you wear jeans and feel comfortable or wear something else and feel uncomfortable.

11. The store where Sarah buys her jeans is crowded. If a store is crowded, the jeans will be reasonably priced.

12. Steve bought some running shoes at Jogger's Paradise for $12.00. Juan bought a pair of running shoes at the same store for $12.00. All the running shoes at Jogger's Paradise sell for $12.00.

13. Everyone likes the bargains at Jogger's Paradise. It is the right store for you.

What's the Best Buy?

Kathlyn Gay

Both the seller and the buyer of a product must consider price, quantity, and quality. This article provides information you need to help you, the consumer, make the best buy.

As you read, pay attention to the pictures and their captions. They will give you additional information.

A used car sits on a lot with a sign:

**Best Buy.
Beat This Low Price.
$2,100.**

In a discount store, a sign says:

**Best Buys in Town.
Portable TV's. $250.**

In a variety store, a bin with a mixture of such items as packages of notebook paper, felt pens, and boxes of colored pencils is labeled:

Best Buys 69ᶜ.

From signs like these, you could get the idea that any product with a low price is a good buy or the best buy.

However, *quality* (how well a product is made) and *durability* (how long it will last) should be checked, too.

Maybe you want a jigsaw puzzle. You see one for $1.49 and another for $1.29. The higher-priced puzzle is made of heavy cardboard; the other is made of very thin cardboard. Both have the kind of picture you like. Which would be the "best" buy?

If you just wanted to put the puzzle together once, the cheaper one would be the "best" buy. But if you like to work a puzzle over and over again, the heavier, more expensive one would hold up better and therefore be the "best" buy.

You should also check quality and durability when you are buying such products as furniture and clothing. But another factor could enter in, too—**maintenance,** or the care that will be needed. If you have the choice, for example, between two jackets which are the same price, but one can be washed and one must be dry-cleaned, which is the "best" buy? To dry-clean a jacket often costs more than $3.00 each time. But washing it at a laundromat or at home in a washer usually costs about 50¢. So the washable jacket is sometimes the better buy.

When you are comparing food products to find the best buy, you should check the different-sized packages. Candy bars are just one type of product sold in packs. For example, one package containing five bars sells for $1.09; another pack with ten bars sells for $1.99. To find out which pack is the "best" buy, you need to know the **unit price,** or the cost of one candy bar in each of the two different packs. Divide the price of each pack by the number of bars in it. The bars in the $1.09 pack cost almost 22¢ apiece, while the bars in the $1.99 pack cost about 20¢ apiece. So the larger pack is the "best" buy.

You can compare the weights of packaged foods and liquids in the same way. Simply divide the prices of two or more items by their number of ounces, grams, or milliliters. Then compare the resulting unit prices.

To find the best buy in food products, you should check the unit price. For example, the price for a quart of milk might be 55¢. A half gallon of the same brand might sell for 90¢. Since there are two quarts in a half gallon, the unit price for the half gallon is 45¢ a quart. Thus, the best buy is the half gallon of milk.

How a product is made and what material is used might determine whether it's a good buy. Here, a bat made of wood is compared with one made of aluminum. The best buy could depend on which lasts the longest or which hits the best.

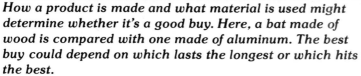

Tags on clothing give instructions for cleaning or washing, and can help you decide whether a garment will be expensive to keep clean.

You do not always get the best buy just because a product is packaged in "Economy Size," "Family Size," "Giant Size," or "Jumbo Size." The words are often used on packages to attract buyers who hope to save money. In some instances, the unit price is less on a smaller package.

One other factor to consider when you're shopping is the **store brand** and how it compares with a **name brand.** Name brands are nationally advertised and known across the country by their trademarks. Store brands, on the other hand, are products sold in certain stores only. They have the store label.

Many store-brand products, such as food, soft drinks, aspirin, soap, plastic bandage strips, and paper tissues are identical to or practically the same as name brands. Yet, because of national advertising, people often think of products by their name brands. Many consumers are convinced that a name brand is a better product, simply because they have heard the name or seen the trademark so often. However, most name brands are higher priced than store brands. Manufacturers add the cost of their advertising to the prices of their products.

Look at vitamins. Maybe your father or mother always buys a name-brand multiple vitamin. Compare that product with a multiple-vitamin product packaged by a discount store, grocery, or drugstore. Make sure you compare packages that are the same size. You will probably find that the store brand sells for half the price of the name brand. Is that because the expensive vitamin is a better product and thus worth more money? Again, compare. The labels will probably show that the various vitamin and mineral units in each tablet are identical or nearly the same for both brands. So, the "best" buy would be the product that costs less.

There is a general formula you can use to measure whether the goods or services you buy are worth the money you pay, or if they are the best buy for your money.

- Determine what you need and want.
- Ask yourself how you are going to use the product.
- Check similar types of products.
- Compare the price and quality.
- Select the best buy.

1. Explain these three terms: *quality, durability,* and *maintenance.*
2. What is the difference between a name-brand product and a store-brand product?
3. If you are choosing among three pairs of sneakers, each at a different price, would the cheapest necessarily be the best buy? Why or why not? What factors should enter into your decision to buy a particular pair?
4. Visit a local supermarket and select one product, such as paper towels. Notice the number of brands the store carries, the various package sizes within each brand, and the price of each package. Make comparisons and decide which package is the best buy.

Jean Merrill

The Toothpaste Millionaire

Jean Merrill's story introduces us to Rufus and Kate. As you read this excerpt from the novel The Toothpaste Millionaire *observe how, through hard work, planning, and a little bit of luck, these two friends turn an idea into a reality. Notice the step-by-step thinking processes they use and the solutions they find to their problems.*

I remember the morning Rufus got the idea for toothpaste. He had to do some shopping, and I went along with him. We were in the drugstore, because toothpaste was one of the things on Rufus's list.

I was looking at a name-brand shampoo that was on sale, when I heard Rufus say, "Seventy-nine cents for a six-inch tube of toothpaste. That's crazy!"

"It's better than eighty-nine cents," I said. I pointed to some 89¢ tubes farther down the shelf.

"That's even crazier," Rufus said. "What can be in those tubes anyway? Just some peppermint flavoring and some paste."

"Maybe the paste is expensive to make," I said.

"Paste!" Rufus said. "You don't need powdered gold to make paste. Paste is just made out of everyday ordinary stuff. Didn't you ever make paste?"

"Toothpaste?" I said.

"I mean just plain paste for pasting things together," Rufus said. "My Grandma Mayflower showed me

how to make paste when I was four years old."

"How do you do it?" I asked.

"Simple," Rufus said. "You just take a little flour and starch and cook them with a little water till the mixture has a nice pasty feel. Then you can use it to paste pictures in a scrapbook or to paste up wallpaper."

"But you couldn't brush your teeth with *that*," I said.

"Well, I don't know," Rufus said. "I never tried. But I bet toothpaste isn't any harder to make. Anyway, I'm not paying any seventy-nine cents for a tube of toothpaste."

Rufus crossed toothpaste off his shopping list.

"But your parents said to get toothpaste," I said. "You can't help it if it's expensive."

"I'll make them some," Rufus said. "I bet I can make a gallon of it for seventy-nine cents. We all need to brush our teeth. If I could make a good cheap toothpaste, that would be worth doing."

"How much do you think it would cost us to make our own toothpaste?" I asked Rufus.

"I don't know," Rufus said. "But

I just thought of something else. You know what I used to brush my teeth with when I stayed at my Grandma Mayflower's? You know what my grandma uses to brush her teeth?"

"What?" I said.

"Bicarbonate of soda," Rufus said, "just plain old baking soda. You just put a little of the soda powder on your toothbrush."

"*Bicarb*?" I said. "That's the stuff my parents try to give me when I feel sick to my stomach— bicarbonate of soda in water. I can't *stand* the taste."

"Really?" Rufus said. "I guess that's why more people don't brush their teeth with bicarb."

The next afternoon when I stopped by Rufus's house to borrow his bike pump, he had about fifty bowls and pans scattered around the kitchen.

"What are you making?" I asked.

"I already made it," Rufus said.

He handed me a spoon and a bowl with some white stuff in it. I took a spoonful.

"Don't eat it," Rufus said. "Just taste it. Rub a little on your teeth."

I tried a little.

"How does it taste?" Rufus said.

"Not bad," I said. "It's better than the kind my parents buy in the pink-and-white-striped tube. How'd you get it to taste so good?"

"A drop of peppermint oil," Rufus said. "But I've got other flavors, too."

He pushed three other pots of paste across the table. The first one had a spicy taste.

"Clove-flavored," Rufus said. "You like it?"

"I don't know," I said. "It's interesting."

"Try this one."

The next sample had a sweet taste. "Vanilla," I guessed.

"Right," Rufus said.

"I like vanilla," I said, "in milkshakes or in ice cream. But it doesn't seem quite right in toothpaste—too sweet."

"This one won't be too sweet," Rufus said, handing me another sample.

"*Eeegh*," I said and ran to the sink to wash out my mouth. "What did you put in *that*?"

"Curry powder," Rufus said. "You don't like it? I thought it tasted like a good shrimp curry."

"Maybe it does," I said, "but I don't like curry."

Rufus looked disappointed.

"What flavor is in that big plastic pan?" I asked. "You've got enough of that kind to frost twenty-seven cakes."

"That's no-kind yet," Rufus said. "That's just seventy-nine cents worth of the stuff that goes in the paste. I didn't want to flavor it till I figured out the best taste."

"What does it taste like plain?" I asked.

"Well," Rufus said, "mostly you taste the bicarb."

"Bicarb!" I said. "You mean all this stuff I've been tasting has got bicarbonate of soda in it?"

Rufus grinned. "Yeah," he said. "It's probably good for your stomach as well as your teeth."

"You must have enough for ten tubes in that plastic bowl," I guessed.

"More, I bet," Rufus said.

We looked at a medium-sized tube of toothpaste.

"Why don't you squeeze the toothpaste in the tube into a measuring cup and then measure the stuff in the bowl," I suggested.

"That would be a waste of toothpaste," Rufus said. "We couldn't get it back in the tube." Rufus hates to waste anything.

I had another idea. "Rufus," I said, "it says on the tube that it contains 3.25 ounces of toothpaste. Why couldn't we just weigh your paste

and divide by 3.25 to see how many tubes it would make?"

"Hey—we could!" Rufus said. "You are *smart*, Kate. I'm always doing things the hard way."

That's what is really so nice about Rufus. It's not just that he gets great ideas like making toothpaste. But if *you* have a good idea, he says so.

Anyway, it turned out Rufus had made about forty tubes of toothpaste for 79¢.

Before I finished breakfast the next morning, there was a knock on the door. It was Rufus. He was very excited.

"Kate!" he said. "Do you know what the population of the United States is?"

"No," I said.

My father looked up from his paper. "According to a recent census—over 200 million," he said to Rufus. My father always knows things like that.

"You're right," Rufus said. "And by now, it must be even bigger."

"Probably," my father said. "The growing population is a very serious matter. Have you thought much about that problem, Rufus?"

"Not yet, Mr. MacKinstrey,"

Rufus said. "At the moment, I was thinking mainly about toothpaste. I was thinking that everybody in the United States probably uses about one tube of toothpaste a month."

"Probably," my father said.

"And if they do," Rufus said, "how many tubes of toothpaste are sold in a year?"

My father thought for a second. "Roughly two-and-a-half billion tubes."

"Right!" Rufus said.

I hate people who can multiply in their heads—except that my father and Rufus are two of the people I like best in the world. How do you explain that?

I really don't like math at all, even when I have a paper and pencil and all the time in the world to figure something out. But at the same time, I look forward every day to Mr. Conti's math class. How do you explain *that*, since that's the class where I'm always getting in trouble?

For example, the same day my father brought up the population explosion, there's Mr. Conti in math class saying: "Kate MacKinstrey, would you please bring me that note."

"Well, it isn't exactly a note, Mr. Conti."

"I see," says Mr. Conti. "I suppose it's a math problem."

"It looks like a math problem, Mr. Conti."

The message from Rufus that Mr. Conti got to read that day said:

If there are two-and-a-half billion tubes of toothpaste sold in the U.S. in one year, and one out of ten people switched to a new brand, how many tubes of the new brand would they be buying?

The right answer is 250 million. It took the class a while to figure that out. Some people have trouble remembering how many zeros there are in a billion.

Then there was a second part to the note:

If the inventors of the new toothpaste made a profit of 1ยข a tube, what would the profit be at the end of the year?

It turns out that the inventors of this new toothpaste would make a two-and-a-half million dollar profit!

Well, that's how Rufus's toothpaste business gets started.

Rufus, Kate, and Mr. Conti's math class turn out to be wrong. Kate and Rufus do not make two-and-a-half million dollars in their first year of business. They only make two million dollars. Their success is the result of hard work, planning—and good luck.

The hard work is needed to get the business started. At first, Rufus and Kate collect used baby food jars, fill them with toothpaste, and sell them door to door for 3¢ a jar. People are willing to try the new low-cost toothpaste, and most of them like it.

Planning is an important part of the business, too. Kate plans a way to increase sales. She writes a letter to a man who interviews people on his daily TV show. In the letter, she tells him about Rufus and the new toothpaste. Rufus is invited onto the show, and hundreds of people hear about him and his toothpaste. In the days after the show, he and Kate are swamped with new orders.

Good luck also helps their business grow. Kate goes to an auction where empty tubes are being sold. She decides to buy a few dozen as a birthday present for Rufus. She ends up buying 7,200 tubes for only $5.00. Later, they are able to buy a machine that fills the tubes automatically.

These are only some of the many things Kate and Rufus do on the road to becoming millionaires.

 1. How did Rufus get the idea for making his own toothpaste?

2. Rufus guessed that everyone in the United States uses about one six-inch tube of toothpaste a month. Do you think that's right? If not, decide how many tubes of toothpaste you might use in a year, and redo Rufus's calculations to find out how much profit he could make in one year.

3. Can you think of any products you or your parents now buy that you could make? If so, why do you think you buy them if they cost more to buy than to make?

4. Do you have an idea that you would like to turn into a reality? Plan the steps you would take.

CONSUMER SAFETY OFFICER

Melvin Berger

We are all consumers. Every time we eat food, wear clothes, ride in a car, listen to a radio, read a book, or have our hair cut, we are being consumers. To be a consumer means that you buy and use products and services.

You, as a consumer, are not alone in the search for a good product—one that meets high standards but is not too high-priced. Cathy King, whom you will read about in this biographical essay, is only one of the many people who protect you as you shop, buy, and use products.

As you accompany Cathy through the macaroni plant, notice the logical steps in her investigation.

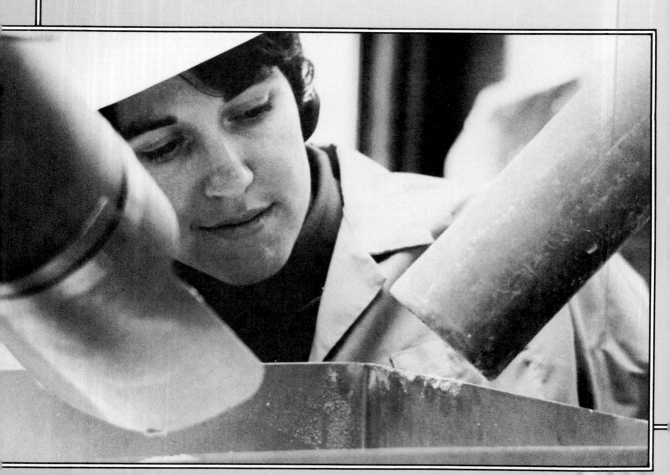

It is still cold and dark outside when the alarm clock wakes Cathy King at her home in Portland, Oregon. She gets out of bed, rushes through breakfast, and sets out in the half-light of dawn.

While the car engine warms up, Cathy checks her equipment—a flashlight, a set of scales, several clean and empty jars, a camera, an ultraviolet "black" light, and a hard hat and coveralls. The patch on her coveralls reads, "Food and Drug Administration."

Cathy is a consumer safety officer of the Food and Drug Administration (FDA). The FDA is a part of the United States Department of Health, Education, and Welfare. It works to protect the consumer by doing scientific research on food, drugs, and cosmetics, by proposing new laws that set standards for making and selling these products, and by enforcing the laws. The job of a consumer safety officer, such as Cathy, is to help enforce the laws.

This morning, Cathy is visiting a macaroni factory. She began to prepare for the visit yesterday. She read the FDA manual that told her what to look for in this type of inspection. She reviewed the rules about the ingredients that must be used for making macaroni, and she reviewed the standards for quality and manufacture. She also checked the regulations on how macaroni products are to be packed and labeled for sale. Finally, she looked through the reports on previous inspections of this plant.

It is just after 6 A.M. when Cathy pulls into the plant's parking lot. She arrives early so that she can check the machines before the workers arrive and start production.

She starts at the place where the raw materials, mostly flour, are received and stored. She checks to see that the flour is kept in a clean, dry area and that the flour bags are all sealed tightly. Using her flashlight, Cathy pokes around the piles of flour bags.

◀ **Cathy King examines the machinery in the macaroni plant very carefully. She wants to be sure it is clean.**

She is looking for any evidence of poor storage. She is also looking for traces of insects or rodents.

At one point, she sees a suspicious stain. To find out if it is rodent urine, she shines the ultraviolet light on it. It does not glow in the black light, so it is probably not from urine. Still, Cathy fills a small jar with flour from the stained bag. She will take it back to the laboratory for further analysis.

Cathy also examines the machines in which the ingredients are mixed. "Conditions are poor," Cathy writes in her notebook. "Flour and dough are encrusted on the machinery. Splintered, dirty wood comes in contact with the macaroni."

At the end of the production line, Cathy inspects the packaging machines. Is any dirt getting into the macaroni as it is put into boxes? Are the grease and glue used in these machines kept near the food? Do the workers observe good sanitary habits?

Cathy takes a few boxes of macaroni to be weighed. Does each one weigh exactly one pound (.453 kilograms)? Is the information on the label correct?

Since this is a small plant, the entire inspection is over in a few hours. But Cathy's job does not end then. She goes back to the FDA offices to write her report. She gives the scientists at the FDA laboratories the jars of flour and encrusted dough. She asks for a complete scientific analysis of the samples. When the tests are done, she will add the scientists' findings to the report on the plant.

The scientists' examination in the lab shows that the flour sample is pure. They do not find any trace of insect or rodent dirt in the flour. The dough, however, shows a high count of bacteria.

As soon as she hears from the scientists, Cathy calls the plant manager. She tells him what they found. He quickly agrees to have the machines cleaned and to replace the old wooden boards.

Cathy and the other consumer safety officers usually get full cooperation in cases where there are violations. No one wants to make or sell anything that might harm others. Also, everyone

The FDA scientist studies the flour sample through her microscope. ▶ She is looking for any sign of insects or rodents.

knows that the FDA can go to court to stop the manufacture and sale of any product. It can also ask for the recall of, or seize and destroy, any item that does not meet the standards set by the government. Anyone who does not cooperate, or who tries to cheat, can be fined thousands of dollars.

Cathy King and the other one thousand consumer safety officers of the FDA are sometimes called the "eyes and ears" of the FDA. They inspect the factories and warehouses where foods, drugs, and cosmetics are manufactured, processed, packed, and stored. They inspect airports, docks, and truck and train freight yards through which these products are shipped. Often, they buy samples right off a store shelf.

All consumer safety officers have college degrees in science. After they are hired, the FDA gives them six months of on-the-job training. They learn how to do inspections. The training covers everything from what to look for to how to handle an angry plant or store owner.

Most consumer safety officers are devoted to their work. They are proud to be helping the consumer. Very few leave the FDA to take other jobs. As Cathy King says, "I feel we're doing something positive for the consumer. The consumer protection role of the FDA is the most important thing about the FDA, in my opinion."

1. What is Cathy King's job? How does it help protect the consumer?
2. What training does a consumer safety officer need?
3. What is the FDA able to do to stop the sale or manufacture of an unsafe product?
4. Cathy prepared for her inspection by reading the FDA manual and the reports of earlier inspections. She did this *before* she visited the plant. Why did she do it beforehand? Would it have made a difference if she had read this material afterward? Why or why not?
5. Would you be interested in a career as a consumer safety officer? Why or why not?

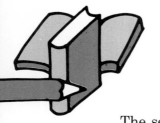

Using a Checking Account

The selection "What's the Best Buy?" gave you advice on how to shop. Suppose you finally decided what to purchase. Now you would need to pay for the merchandise.

You may pay for items with cash, with a credit card, or with a check. In order to write a check, you must have a *checking account* at a bank. You start an account by depositing money at the bank. Each time you deposit money, you fill out a *deposit slip*. This slip indicates how much money you are depositing. Here is a sample of a deposit slip:

CHECKING ACCOUNT DEPOSIT SLIP		CASH	DOLLARS	CENTS	
Jane Sellers			15	00	
328 Oak Drive					
Maintown, California 91000		CHECKS 1	25	00	1-03/210
		2	34	62	
Feb. 13 _____ 19 79		3	10	00	
		4			BE SURE EACH ITEM IS PROPERLY ENDORSED
		5			LIST CHECKS SEPARATELY
DEPOSITED WITH		6			
		7			
IT IMPERIAL TRUST BANKING COMPANY		8			
14 Grove St., Maintown, California 91000		TOTAL	84	62	

SUBJECT TO THE PROVISIONS OF THE CALIFORNIA UNIFORM COMMERCIAL CODE

"-7110140725"-

The name and address of the holder of the account is at the top of the slip. The bottom of the slip shows the special account number for that person. The name of the bank is also on the slip. A space is provided for the date of deposit.

The column on the right of the slip shows how much money is being deposited in the account. The cash you deposit is recorded on the top line. You may also deposit checks made out to you. Write the amount of each check on a separate line. Then indicate the total amount of the deposit at the bottom of the column.

ACTIVITY A   Answer these questions about the deposit slip shown.

1. Who deposited the money in the bank?
2. How much cash was deposited?
3. How many checks were deposited?
4. What was the total amount of cash and checks deposited?

ACTIVITY B   Draw a deposit slip on your own paper. Use your own name and address at the top, but keep the same bank name and account number as shown on the slip. Imagine you wanted to deposit $12 in cash plus checks for the following amounts: $23.00, $9.75, and $5.00. Fill out the deposit slip. Use today's date.

Once you have money in your checking account, you can pay for items by *check*. A check is a written order to your bank to pay someone the stated amount from your account. Here is a sample of a check:

The name and address of the person writing the check are at the top. The special account number appears at the bottom. The date is in the upper right hand corner. After the words *Pay to the order of* is the name of the person or company to receive the money. The amount of the check is recorded both in numbers and in words. The writer signs the check in the lower right hand corner. A space is provided to indicate what was purchased.

ACTIVITY C   Answer these questions about the check shown.

1. Who wrote the check?
2. Who is to receive the money from the check?
3. What is the name of the bank holding the money?
4. When was the check written?

ACTIVITY D   Draw a check on your own paper. Use your own name and address at the top, but keep the same bank name and account number as shown on the check. Imagine you purchased $13.54 worth of clothes from Glad Rags. Write a check for your purchase. Use today's date.

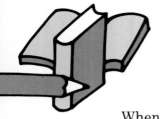

Reading a Mathematics Problem

When you solve a mathematics problem, you use both reading and mathematics skills. Here are some steps to follow.

Steps to Successful Problem Solving
1. Read the problem carefully.
2. Think about the problem.
   a. What do you need to find?
   b. What do you already know?
3. Choose the proper operation. $(+, -, \times, \div)$
4. Think of a sensible answer or estimate the answer.
5. Do the mathematics.
6. Answer each question.
7. Check to see if each answer makes sense.

Here's an example of how to use these steps.

Imagine that Rufus (in "The Toothpaste Millionaire") made 40 tubes of toothpaste. Each tube contained 3¼ ounces of toothpaste. How many ounces of toothpaste did Rufus use in all to fill these tubes?

1. Read the problem carefully.
2. Think about it.
   a. You need to find how many ounces in all.
   b. You know there are 40 tubes, each containing 3¼ ounces.
3. The words *how many in all* often indicate multiplication.
4. Since you know you will multiply 40 by more than 3, your answer should be more than 120.
5. $40 \times 3¼ = 130$
6. Rufus used 130 ounces of toothpaste.
7. That sounds sensible for 40 tubes of toothpaste.

Here are some key words to help you choose the proper operation.

how many (much) in all	addition or multiplication
how many are left	subtraction
how many more are needed	subtraction
how many sets or groups	division
how many in each set or group	division

Some problems may contain extra or unnecessary information. Other problems may not contain enough information. For example,

Unnecessary information

Thomas Jefferson was born on April 13, 1743, and *died on July 4, 1826.* He became President on February 17, 1801. How old was he when he became President?

You do not need to know when Jefferson died in order to do this problem.

Not enough information

Rufus made 575 toothbrushes. He sold them all. How much money did he make?

You need to know *how much* Rufus sold each toothbrush for in order to solve this problem.

Read each of the following problems carefully. Write what you need to find and what you already know. Write whether you will add, subtract, multiply, or divide. Estimate the answer. Do the mathematics. Write the answer to the problem. Check to see if it is a sensible answer. If the problem has any extra information, write it down and label it unnecessary. If the problem does not contain enough information, write down what is missing.

1. Thomas Jefferson was President for 8 years. When he became President, there were 16 states in the United States. Now there are 50. How many more states are in the United States now?

2. The United States paid France $11,250,000 for the Louisiana Territory. The United States also said that France did not have to pay debts of $3,750,000. How much in all did it cost the United States for the Louisiana Territory?

3. A drugstore manager who was 38 years old bought 600 tubes of toothpaste. The tubes came packed in 5 large boxes. How many tubes were in each box (set)?

4. Each tube of toothpaste costs the manager $0.56. How much altogether did 600 tubes cost?

5. One customer bought 7 tubes of toothpaste. Another customer bought 3 toothbrushes and some toothpaste. How many tubes of toothpaste did the manager sell?

Table of Tens

S. Carl Hirsch

*Did you know that it was because of Thomas Jefferson
that the United States began to use a coin system based on
the table of tens? As you read this selection, think about
why it has taken more than two hundred years
for Congress to decide the fate of Jefferson's idea
for a metric system of measurement.*

One morning long ago, Thomas Jefferson climbed into his horse-drawn buggy and left his fine house in Virginia. He was traveling to the nation's capital, Washington, D.C., where he had once served as President of the United States.

The summer morning was quiet, except for the clip-clop of the horse trotting along the country road. But Jefferson frowned. From the sound of the hoofbeats, he could tell something was wrong. His horse was limping slightly.

"Easy, Molly," he called out to the little mare in a soothing voice. "We'll get you a new shoe in the next town."

As the horse moved along, Jefferson could hear the tinkle of a bell that he had attached to the back of the buggy together with a wheel for measuring distance. This wheel was much smaller than the two wheels of the buggy, and every time it turned one hundred times, the bell rang. After ten rings of the bell, the traveler had covered exactly one mile.

Jefferson was not only a great patriot, but also a scientist and inventor who liked to make things with his hands. But his greatest wish was to solve the many puzzling problems that faced the young United States.

For example, there was the troublesome matter of America's coins. The new nation was made up of people from many lands. They had brought with them their many kinds of money. All these were the coins with which people bought and sold goods, received their wages, and paid their debts.

What confusion for the poor storekeeper! He tried to read the words on French, Spanish, and Dutch coins but had little idea about their value. In addition, each of the colonies of America had its own kind of coins, adding to the muddle of America's money.

For this problem, Jefferson gave the nation a simple solution. He held up his hands, explaining to the Congress of the United States that since ancient times people had counted on their fingers. That was why, he pointed out, the world had a system of counting based on the number ten. In planning a new system of coins, suggested Jefferson, America would be wise to use the simple table of tens.

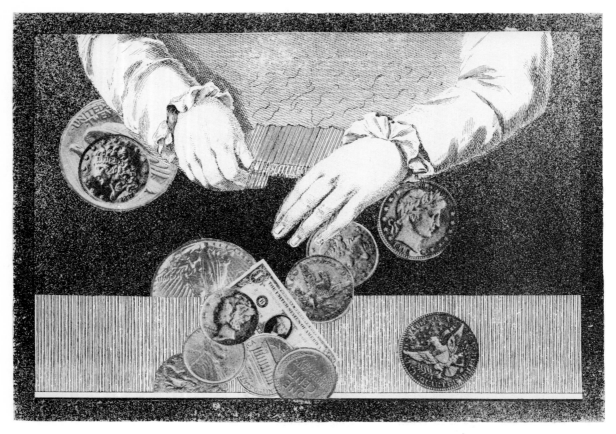

The counting system has ten numbers, and as a schoolboy in Virginia, Jefferson had learned the table of tens. "Count to ten; then start over again," the schoolmaster taught his pupils.

"Most of us are schoolboys throughout life," Jefferson declared, "and we need coins which any child can understand."

Jefferson's plan began with the penny. Ten pennies were a dime, and ten dimes were equal to a dollar. What could be easier than that? All America agreed, and the United States became the first country in the world to have coins based on the table of tens.

Still another problem for America was its weights and measures. Few people knew the exact area of an acre of land. A bushel of apples was one size in North Carolina and another size in New Hampshire.

Silversmiths and grocers worked with unlike systems of weights. Printers and carpenters used different terms of measurement in their work. To this day, America still uses a jumble of odd terms, such as pennyweights and grains, rods and yards, pecks and pints, which have no clear relationship with each other.

Jefferson offered a new plan. But he could not get Congress to adopt it. As he grew old, he returned many times to the capital to plead for a simple system of weights and measures. But the Members of Congress would not listen to him.

On this summer morning, the aged Jefferson was journeying once more to Washington, D.C. In a tiny village along his route, he found a blacksmith who made a new shoe for his limping horse.

"How far did you ride today, sir?" asked the blacksmith.

"I'll answer that question for you in a strange way," Jefferson replied with a twinkle in his eyes. As the blacksmith watched with much curiosity, Jefferson checked the mileage shown on his little third wheel.

"Now, let us say a mile is like a dollar," explained the statesman. "In that case, I have traveled nine dollars, two dimes, and three cents."

The blacksmith was puzzled for a moment. But soon his face lit up. "Yes, I understand you very well," he said, chuckling.

Jefferson's idea was that not only money but also distances could be measured by the table of tens. The same simple method could be used for measuring the size of a field, the contents of a box, the weight of a bale of cotton, and the speed of a horse and buggy as well.

In almost every country in the world, people are now weighing and measuring by the table of tens. The system they use is called the metric system.

The United States is now changing to this simple system. Thomas Jefferson had faith that the day would come when Americans would measure by the table of tens. But he did not realize it would take more than two hundred years!

---

1. Why, according to Jefferson, do people use a system of counting based on the number ten?
2. Why did storekeepers in early America have to deal with so many kinds of coins?
3. Why do you think Congress accepted Jefferson's metric currency but rejected the metric measurement system?
4. Do you think the metric system is easier or harder to use than our current measurement system? Explain why.
5. What are your height and weight—in our current system? In the metric system?

RIDDLES AND MORE RIDDLES

Riddle:
If you went to bed at 8 P.M. and set the alarm for 9 in the morning, how many hours of sleep would you get?

Answer: 1 hour. The alarm would go off at 9.

What does this have to do with mathematics?
Subtraction, of course: 9−8=1.

Riddle:
There are 12 1-cent stamps in a dozen, but how many 2-cent stamps are there in a dozen?

Answer: 12

What does this have to do with mathematics?
A dozen is a dozen is a dozen.

Riddle:
Some months have 30 days; some 31. How many have 28?

Answer: All of them.

What does this have to do with mathematics?
Logical thinking.

Riddle:
If your bedroom were pitch dark and you needed a pair of matching socks, how many socks would you need to take out of the drawer if there are 10 white socks and 10 blue ones?

Answer: 3

What does this have to do with mathematics?
A little probability theory comes in handy here.

Riddle:

How much dirt may be removed from a hole that is 3 feet deep, 2 feet wide, and 10 feet long?

Answer:
You can't take dirt from a hole!

Riddle:

A farmer had 17 sheep. All but 9 died. How many does the farmer have left?

Answer: 9

What does this have to do with mathematics?
Volume is often a useful math concept, but it wasn't very useful here.

What does this have to do with mathematics?
Subtraction isn't always the best way to get the right answer.

Riddle:

Divide 30 by 1/2 and add 10.

What's the answer?

Answer:
70.
$30 \div 1/2 =$
$30 \times 2/1 = 60$
$60 + 10 = 70$

What does this have to do with mathematics?
Good old arithmetic stumps all.

Riddle:

Take 2 apples from 3 apples and what do you have?

Answer:
You have 2 apples!

What does this have to do with mathematics?
This doesn't have much to do with math, but you could have fooled me!

369

DO YOU LIKE
Spinach?

John Weiss

What do you like? What do you dislike? How do you feel about pollution, the mayor, flights to the moon? There are many people who want to know the answers to questions such as these. People who make things, people who run for public office, even people who plan TV programs—all want to know how many people will like what they have to offer. They find the answers to their questions by taking polls.

As you read this magazine article, notice how polls are taken. On what subject would you like to take a poll?

You are sitting at home, watching the evening news on television. During the program, an announcer makes this statement: "A survey indicates that seventy-five percent of all Americans like spinach." Then the announcer comments on how this news is affecting the spinach growers.

But how did they find out how many Americans like spinach when they didn't ask you? You are an American, and you don't like spinach. Everyone you know hates spinach.

They did it by conducting a survey.

To take a survey or a poll is to question a certain group of people about a topic or an issue. This certain group of people is called a *sample*; it was picked from a larger group of people called a *population*. A sample can be taken of the population of a state, a city, or even a neighborhood. In the announcer's statement, the population would be all the people in America, but the sample is only certain Americans.

A sample is normally taken at random; that is, each person in the population is given an equal chance of being picked for the sample. Imagine that you are in a dark room, holding up a bunch of grapes. You cannot see or feel all the grapes at once, but you want to know if the bunch is ripe or rotten. So you pick some from the top of the bunch and some from the bottom and some from the sides, taste them, and you get a pretty good idea of the quality of the whole bunch. You have just taken a random sample. Now you can say, for example, that the bunch is ripe or rotten, or that the grapes on the top are okay but the ones on the bottom are rotten. Yet you haven't seen or eaten the whole bunch of grapes, only certain ones picked at random.

Mathematically, this process of picking certain things at random (certain Americans, certain grapes, etc.) and then making statements about all the things (Americans, a bunch of grapes, etc.) is based on the *laws of probability*. The laws were first explained by a seventeenth-century French scientist, Blaise Pascal. At first, not many people used the laws of probability when they sampled a population. The 1936 American Presidential election is often used to illustrate what happens when people are not surveyed correctly.

In 1936, a magazine called the *Literary Digest* sent out ten million survey forms to all the people on its mailing list to try to find out who would win the Presidential election between Democrat, Franklin D. Roosevelt, and Republican, Alfred Landon. Based on almost two-and-one-half million returns, the *Literary Digest* predicted Alfred Landon would win with fifty-seven percent of the popular vote. But when the votes were counted, Alfred Landon had only received thirty-eight percent of the popular vote. The *Literary Digest* poll was not even close!

If you go back to the example of the grapes, you can see why the poll was so wrong. When you examined the grapes in the dark, you took some from all over the bunch—a random sample. If you had picked only from the top or only from the bottom, you could not have said for sure if the whole bunch were ripe or rotten. When the *Literary Digest* received survey forms back from the people on its mailing list, the people were not a random sample of Democrats and Republicans at all. In fact, the people were mostly Republicans, who would eventually vote for the Republican candidate, Alfred Landon.

Survey researchers or pollsters —those who conduct surveys or polls—have refined the technique of sampling since 1936. The two most famous polls in use today are the Gallup Poll and the Harris Poll—named for the men who pioneered them. On certain questions, these two polls survey the entire United States population— over 210 million people—using a sample of only 1,500 people.

The results of these national surveys are correct to within three percentage points. If, for example seventy-five percent of Americans say they like spinach, that percentage could be as low as seventy-two percent or as high as seventy-eight percent, but it is most likely to be seventy-five percent. This difference one way or the other is the *margin of error*. The survey researchers could decrease the margin of error by increasing the number of people surveyed—just as you could pick more grapes to test the ripeness of the bunch. But the margin of error decreases only slightly as larger and larger numbers of people are surveyed. It would require a survey of 4,000 people, instead of 1,500, to lower the margin of error to two percentage points.

What determines whether or not you will be among those surveyed? Simply, it's where you live. For the Gallup Poll, five people are selected from within three hundred randomly chosen areas of the United States. Thus, the total sample is 1,500.

But don't feel bad if you are never asked to fill out a survey form. It would take the Gallup Poll, which switches survey locations every four months, over four hundred years to interview every adult in America just once.

In the meantime: Do *you* like spinach?

1. What are the two most famous polls in use today?
2. Why was the poll by the *Literary Digest* for the 1936 election so wrong?
3. Why do we need polls? What purpose do they serve? What question would you like answered by a poll?
4. Have two students in your class conduct a survey. Ask one to poll ten people, selected randomly from your school, to see how they feel about rock music. Ask the other to choose ten students who play musical instruments and ask them the same question. Compare the results. Which is a true random sample? Why?

PUSH THE MAGIC BUTTON

Some time ago, there was a man
who had a job to do
to count the money and the goods
the loss and profit too.
He loved to write the numbers
in big and lovely books
his statements were all correct
he kept away the crooks.

His company did prosper
it flourished and it grew
and now his books were very big
he had too much to do.
He hired an assistant
and he another two
and then a full department
containing quite a few.

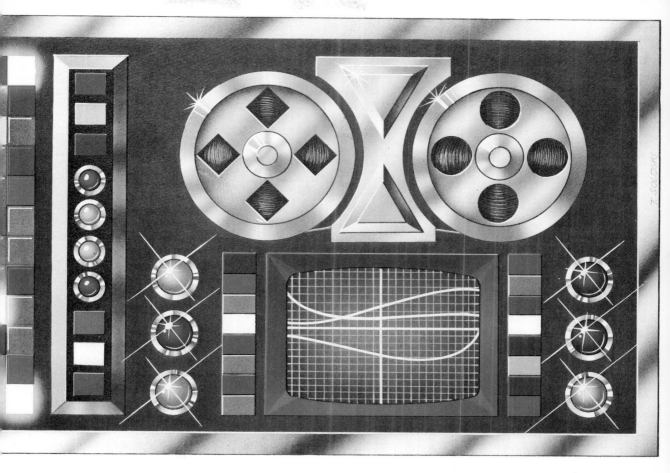

The books became too many
the load too much to bear
his days were full of management
his mind was full of care.
To solve his mammoth problem
an engineer he hired
and she designed a grandiose
computer he admired.

'Cause he could ...

Push the magic buttons
and program the machine
and using Matrix he obtained
hard copy nice and clean
yes, push the magic buttons
and the computer plays
in microseconds it can do
what he could do in days.

The room is air-conditioned
humidity controlled
he doesn't know if outside
is stormy, hot or cold
he works the magic buttons
and thinks of days gone by
of ledger books and pens with quills
and ink that would not dry.

Yes, push the magic buttons
and the computer plays
in microseconds it can do
what he could do in days.

—Renn Zaphiropoulos

375

CALCULATOR

Cecily Nabors

Why do we bother to learn mathematics? That little wonder, the calculator, can do the job faster and easier than we can. As you read this science-fiction story, think about the reasons why we study mathematics.

Lisa flounced onto the back porch swing and shoved her foot against the floor. The swing jerked up and down. Her math book, with its unfinished homework papers, lay in her lap. Dumb homework! What was the point, anyway? "No one needs to know how to do long division any more—what are calculators for?" she thought. She could look through the window and see her mother using a minicalculator to figure out her checkbook. "I have to sit here and do all these long division problems—and with decimals, too. It's not fair."

The swing slowly steadied to a gentle rocking motion as Lisa calmed with it. Resigned, she opened her book and got out her papers. As Lisa became absorbed in her work, the swing stopped moving.

She didn't notice that the air in the backyard suddenly shimmered and glowed. Her ears couldn't hear the ultrahigh-frequency hum that caused all the neighborhood dogs to bark. Lisa kept on working.

Part of the shimmer opened, revealing a space-suited creature. His three yellow eyes set in purple fur studied the girl. Gradually, the creature's appearance changed, as the space suit with its dials and instruments seemed to melt and then congeal into an imitation of Lisa's jeans, plaid shirt, and sneakers. His three eyes and eating opening also changed and began to resemble the features of a human face. Only the hair remained exotic-looking, as if the creature could not eliminate a faint lavender tint.

Adjusting the buttons on his shirt, which focused the plaid a bit better, he stepped away from the shimmer and moved toward Lisa. Swaying a little, as if not used to two legs, he arrived at the edge of the steps and tapped on the handrail.

"Six into forty-four goes seven," said Lisa to herself as she looked up. One of her visitor's buttons hummed a bit, and a yellow square of the plaid shirt glowed slightly brighter. The visitor pushed the button, seemed to read his sleeve, and replied politely, "Nine times eight is seventy-two," in a rather mechanical voice.

"Hi!" said Lisa, somewhat surprised. "Are you selling something, or what?"

"Hi," echoed the visitor, without expression. "I am Wirrinix. Are you the great mathematician of this planet?"

Lisa laughed. "Not me," she said. "It's not even my best subject."

Turning away, Wirrinix twirled one of his shirt buttons, tapped on his belt buckle, and read his other sleeve. His voice was low. "The gravity of this planet is equal to one-point-three dedrons. The surface area is two-seven-eight square nids. That's very suitable. We will use this planet."

Lisa was writing again. She wanted to finish that problem while she still had seven times six in her mind. That was the one she was always forgetting.

Wirrinix leaned over the railing to see what she was writing. "Where is your calculator?" he asked.

That was a sore point with Lisa. She flushed angrily and wrote down another problem without answering.

"What are those numbers?" droned Wirrinix.

"My homework," said Lisa, "long division." She moved the decimal point in the divisor and dividend. "Boring."

"How can you do it without a calculator?" Wirrinix's mechanical voice sounded almost excited. His shoelaces stiffened and twitched until they were pointing at Lisa.

"I do it in my head," said Lisa, beginning to feel almost proud not to be using a calculator.

Two of the visitor's shirt buttons started rotating, and the lavender hair momentarily deepened to purple. "No one can do calculations without a calculator," said Wirrinix. "That is only logical." He tapped his belt buckle and read his sleeve as if for reassurance.

"I never use a calculator," bragged Lisa, seeing the impression she was making. "I just do it myself."

"None of the Wirrinni can . . ." muttered the visitor, his mechanical voice trailing off in alarm. "I do not believe it."

Lisa sighed. She really *did* want to finish her homework before "Star Trek" came on, but still she felt challenged by this unusual stranger. "Give me a problem," she suggested.

"Five eight six point five plus nine six, divided by three point nine." Wirrinix's yellow eyes gleamed as he tapped his buttons and read his shirt cuff.

Lisa wrote down the numbers as she heard them and soon had the answer. "It comes out even," she said approvingly. "One seven five. And I did do it in my head, Mr. Nix," she reminded him, triumphantly rocking the swing.

"No calculators. This civilization does not need calculators." Wirrinix backed away from the porch. "They are too clever to be subdued easily. That's not suitable. This planet is not suitable." Wirrinix turned and swayed back to the shimmer in the yard. The plaid in his shirt seemed to run together.

"Good-bye, Mr. Nix," said Lisa politely. She watched no longer, but bent her head over her paper. "Guess I showed that guy," she thought. "Who needs a calculator, anyway? Now, thirty-five into seventy-four is . . ." The swing once again slowed to a stop.

1. Why was Lisa angry as the story began?
2. Why did Wirrinix come to Earth? Wirrinix decided that: "This planet is not suitable." Why?
3. Do you have a calculator? Do you think you should learn mathematics, or let a machine do all the work? How can both a knowledge of mathematics and a calculator be helpful?
4. If you were to visit beings on another planet, how would you judge their society? Would you judge it by their people? Their machines? Their culture?

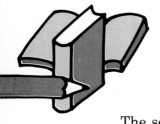

Metric Prefixes

The selection "Tables of Ten" told about Thomas Jefferson's plan for a metric system of measurement. Today many countries use such a system. The United States is slowly changing to the metric system, too. You may notice that road signs often give distances in kilometers as well as in miles. Food packages show grams as well as ounces. Bottles of liquid indicate the number of liters as well as the number of quarts.

The basic units of measurement in the metric system are the *gram, liter,* and *meter.* These units often appear with special prefixes before them. The prefixes are based on multiples of tens. Look at this chart to find the meaning of each prefix:

Metric Prefix	Meaning	Numeral
kilo-	one thousand	1,000
hecto-	one hundred	100
deka- or deca-	ten	10
deci-	one-tenth	1/10
centi-	one-hundredth	1/100
milli-	one-thousandth	1/1,000

Here are examples of how the prefixes work with each unit:

A *kilogram* equals *one thousand* grams.
A *hectoliter* equals *one hundred* liters.
A *decameter* equals *ten* meters.
A *decimeter* equals *one-tenth* of a meter.
A *centigram* equals *one-hundredth* of a gram.
A *milliliter* equals *one-thousandth* of a liter.

ACTIVITY A   Complete each of the following sentences correctly.

1. A decagram equals _____ gram(s).
2. A millimeter equals _____ meter(s).
3. A kilometer equals _____ meter(s).
4. A decigram equals _____ gram(s).
5. A hectoliter equals _____ liter(s).
6. A centimeter equals _____ meter(s).
7. A deciliter equals _____ liter(s).

8. A decaliter equals _____ liter(s).
9. A kilogram equals _____ gram(s).
10. A milligram equals _____ gram(s).

ACTIVITY B Use the metric chart to answer each of the following questions. Write the answers on your paper.

1. How many liters equal one kiloliter?
2. How many centimeters equal one meter?
3. How many decigrams equal one gram?
4. How many grams equal one decagram?
5. How many liters equal one hectoliter?
6. How many meters equal one kilometer?
7. How many milliliters equal one liter?
8. How many decimeters equal one meter?
9. How many liters equal one decaliter?
10. How many grams equal one kilogram?

ACTIVITY C Use the metric chart to answer each of the following questions.

1. If *gon* means *side*, how many sides does a *hectogon* have?
2. How many sides does a *dekagon* have?
3. How many sides does a *kilogon* have?
4. How many years equal a *decade*?
5. In science, the term *milliampere* refers to what part of an ampere?
6. In radio, the term *kilocycle* refers to how many cycles per second of electromagnetic waves?
7. The term *kilocalorie* refers to how many calories?
8. In electricity, the term *kilowatt* means how many watts?
9. The coin that is worth one-hundredth of a dollar is called a penny. What is another name for the coin?
10. In France, a *centime* equals what part of a franc?

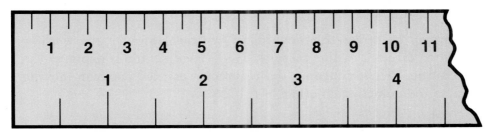

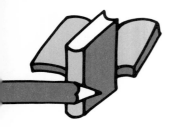

Science and Mathematics Vocabulary

As you read articles about science and mathematics, you may find many unfamiliar words. One way to learn the meaning of each word is to look in a dictionary. However, you might be able to figure out the meaning of the word without a dictionary. The sentence context may provide clues to help you to understand the word.

Sentence context refers to the way a word is used in a sentence. Looking at how a word is used in a sentence will often help you to understand the meaning of the word. Here is a passage from the selection you read about the National Air and Space Museum:

> In this exhibit—a full-size *replica* of the control panel of the Lunar Module—visitors can relive the first moon landing. Films played behind the triangular windows show the moon's surface growing closer . . .

Suppose you did not know the meaning of the word *replica*. The other words in the sentence and the next sentence might help you. The first sentence says the exhibit is a *replica* of the control panel. It also says visitors in the exhibit can relive the moon landing. The next sentence talks about films that show the moon's surface. You may figure out from these sentences that a *replica* is a reproduction or a copy of something.

Sometimes difficult science words are defined for you directly in the sentence. Read this passage from the selection "Energy Machines":

> A force called *friction* is usually the big energy thief . . . . Friction is the resistance created between moving parts that touch each other. Friction steals energy by turning it into unwanted heat.

You may not know the meaning of *friction*. However, the word is defined directly in the passage. The second sentence explains the meaning. *Friction* means "the resistance created between moving parts that touch each other."

Many of the following passages have been taken from this book. Write the definition of the underlined word based on its sentence context. Then check your definition in a dictionary.

1. To take a survey or a poll is to question a certain group of people about a topic or an issue. This certain group of people is called a sample.

2. Visitors can walk through the space station and see how teams of astronauts lived and worked in space.

3. There is no such thing as a 100% efficient machine. Efficiency is the amount of energy we get out of a machine divided by the amount of energy we put into it.

4. To find out which pack is the "best" buy, you need to know the unit price, or the cost of one pencil, in each of the two different packs.

5. However, quality (how well a product is made) and durability (how long it will last) should be checked, too.

6. The cost of producing one tube of toothpaste was thirty cents. The producers sold the tube for seventy-nine cents. Therefore, the producers made a profit of forty-nine cents on the tube.

7. If, for example. seventy-five percent of Americans say they like spinach, that percentage could be as low as seventy-two percent or as high as seventy-eight percent, but it is likely to be seventy-five percent. This difference one way or the other is the margin of error.

8. Lisa did not own a calculator. She preferred working out mathematics problems in her head instead of using a machine.

9. Sidney was greatly interested in the science of making and flying airplanes. Paul, on the other hand, had no special interest in aeronautics.

10. One approach to the problem of solar collection is the solar cell. This special device turns sunlight directly into electricity.

OBSERVATIONS

Through observations, we learn about our environment. *Environment* does not simply mean plants and animals, human beings and the societies they live in, or even the whole earth itself. In "Observations," you have seen that our environment includes all these things, but it also extends outward into space. In science, we try to make our observations as accurately and logically as possible. In this way, we hope to gain a true picture of the processes that make up the universe.

Thinking About "Observations"

1. "Close Encounters of the Third Kind" and "Calculator" are both about visitors from other worlds. How are Jillian's experience and Lisa's experience different?

2. Use the idea of efficiency, as it is discussed in "Energy Machines," to explain why Nasr-ed-Din Hodja's dinner took so long to cook in "One Candle Power."

3. Compare Maria's concern for ecology in "Me and the Ecology Bit" with the Leopold family's concern for ecology in "The Leopolds: A Family for the Environment." Who has done more for ecology? Why do you think so?

4. Think about the selection, "What's the Best Buy?" Do you think the people who bought Rufus' toothpaste in "The Toothpaste Millionaire" were getting the "best" buy? State your opinion and explain why you think as you do.

5. How can careful observation help you in daily life?

REFLECTIONS
REFLECTIONS

Since the beginning of time, art has held a special place in people's lives. People have always been drawn to art both because of its beauty and because of its ability to express human emotions. In turn, art also acts as a mirror. Art reflects the lives of the artists who create it: their heritage and the times in which they live.

In "Reflections," you will read about music, dance, painting, and sculpture, and about modern American artists who are making new and exciting contributions to these arts. A woman struggles for decades to be accepted as an orchestral conductor. A young man tries to find the confidence he needs to audition for a place in a television rock group. A professional choreographer gets her first dance training as a car hop in a snack bar at a drive-in. You will read about an adult collage-maker and about two teenage painters. An elderly artist strives to finish his masterpiece—a matchstick model of a bridge. A sculptor collects oddly-shaped scraps of wood and turns them into beautiful works of art.

As you read, think about art as a reflection of the people who create it. Artists often put themselves into their art. They draw on their family and ethnic heritage, on their past experience, and on their present ways of life to create new works of art. When we enjoy art, it is often because we see how the artists' experiences and feelings reflect our own experiences and feelings. What kind of art do you enjoy?

SOMETHING OF LIFE

Reflection
      is
          music
             and
               each
                  song
                    is
                       something
                           of
                             life.
                         How
                     softly
                 music
              flows
                against
                      the
                       watersides.

—Gordon Parks

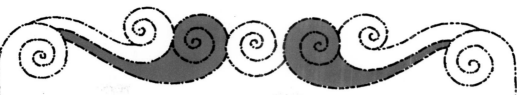

A Colorful Symphony

Norton Juster

You come home, and in your room, you find a big turnpike tollbooth. There are some coins to pay your way through the tollbooth, and a note telling you that the tollbooth is "for use by those who have never traveled in lands beyond." What would you do?

In this excerpt from the novel, The Phantom Tollbooth, *Milo decides to go through the tollbooth into the "lands beyond." In his travels, he meets Tock, a talking dog with a body made out of a loudly ticking alarm clock. Milo also meets Alec, a boy who can walk on air and see through solid objects. Alec takes Milo and Tock to a very unusual musical concert.*

Norton Juster's novel is a work of fantasy, a story full of unreal, make-believe events and characters. As you read, pay attention to the details that make this story a fantasy.

The sun was dropping slowly from sight, and stripes of purple and orange and crimson and gold piled themselves on top of the distant hills. The last shafts of light waited patiently for a flight of wrens to find their way home, and a group of anxious stars had already taken their places.

"Here we are!" cried Alec, and, with a sweep of his arm, he pointed toward an enormous symphony orchestra. "Isn't it a grand sight?"

There were at least a thousand musicians ranged in a great arc before them. To the left and right were the violins and cellos, whose bows moved in great waves, and behind them in numberless profusion the piccolos, flutes, clarinets, oboes, bassoons, horns, trumpets, trombones, and tubas were all playing at once. At the very rear, so far away that they could hardly be seen, were the percussion instruments, and lastly, in a long line up one side of a steep slope, were the solemn bass fiddles.

On a high podium in front stood the conductor, a tall, gaunt man with dark deep-set eyes and a thin mouth placed carelessly between his long pointed nose and his long pointed chin. He used no baton, but conducted with large, sweeping movements which seemed to start at his toes and work slowly up through his body and along his slender arms and end finally at the tips of his graceful fingers.

"I don't hear any music," said Milo.

"That's right," said Alec; "you don't listen to this concert—you watch it. Now, pay attention."

As the conductor waved his arms, he molded the air like handfuls of soft clay, and the musicians carefully followed his every direction.

"What are they playing?" asked Tock, looking up inquisitively at Alec.

"The sunset, of course. They play it every evening, about this time."

"They do?" said Milo quizzically.

"Naturally," answered Alec; "and they also play morning, noon, and night, when, of course, it's morning, noon, or night. Why, there wouldn't be any color in the world unless they played it. Each instrument plays a different one," he explained, "and depending, of course, on what season it is and how the weather's to be, the conductor chooses his score and directs the day. But watch: the sun has almost set, and in a moment you can ask Chroma himself."

The last colors slowly faded from the western sky and, as they did, one by one the instruments stopped, until only the bass fiddles, in their somber slow movement, were left to play the night and a single set of silver bells brightened the constellations. The conductor let his arms fall limply at his sides and stood quite still as darkness claimed the forest.

"That was a very beautiful sunset," said Milo, walking to the podium.

"It should be," was the reply; "we've been practicing since the world began." And, reaching down, the speaker picked Milo off the ground and set him on the music stand. "I am Chroma the Great," he continued, gesturing broadly with his hands, "conductor of color, maestro of pigment, and director of the entire spectrum."

"Do you play all day long?" asked Milo when he had introduced himself.

"Ah yes, all day, every day," Chroma sang out, then pirouetted gracefully around the platform. "I rest only at night, and even then *they* play on."

"What would happen if you stopped?" asked Milo, who didn't quite believe that color happened that way.

"See for yourself, roared Chroma, and he raised both hands high over his head. Immediately the instruments that were playing stopped, and at once all color vanished. The world looked like an enormous coloring book that had never been used. Everything appeared in simple black outlines, and it looked as if someone with a set of paints the size of a house and a brush as wide could stay happily occupied for years. Then Chroma lowered his arms. The instruments began again and the color returned.

"You see what a dull place the world would be without color?" he said, bowing until his chin almost touched the ground. "But what pleasure to lead my violins in a serenade of spring green or hear my trumpets blare out the blue sea and then watch the oboes tint it all in warm yellow sunshine. And rainbows are best of all—and blazing neon signs, and taxicabs with stripes, and the soft, muted tones of a foggy day. We play them all."

As Chroma spoke, Milo sat with his eyes open wide, and Alec and Tock looked on in wonder.

"Now I really must get some sleep," Chroma yawned. "We've had lightning, fireworks, and parades for the last few nights, and I've had to be up to conduct them. But tonight is sure to be quiet." Then, putting his large hand on Milo's shoulder, he said, "Be a good fellow and watch my orchestra till morning, will you? And be sure to wake me at 5:23 for the sunrise. Good night, good night, Good night."

With that he leaped lightly from the podium and, in three long steps, vanished into the forest.

"That's a good idea," said Tock, making himself comfortable in the grass as Alec stretched out in mid-air.

And Milo, full of thoughts and questions, curled up on the pages of tomorrow's music and eagerly awaited the dawn.

One by one, the hours passed, and at exactly 5:22 (by Tock's very accurate clock) Milo carefully opened one eye and, in a moment, the other. Everything was still purple, dark blue, and black, yet scarcely a minute remained to the long, quiet night.

He stretched lazily, rubbed his eyelids, scratched his head, and shivered once as a greeting to the early-morning mist.

"I must wake Chroma for the sunrise," he said softly. Then he suddenly wondered what it would be like to lead the orchestra and to color the whole world himself.

The idea whirled through his thoughts until he quickly decided that since it couldn't be very difficult, and since they probably all knew what to do by themselves anyway, and since it did seem a shame to wake anyone so early, and since it might be his only chance to try, and since the musicians were already poised and ready, he would—but just for a little while.

And so, as everyone slept peacefully on, Milo stood on tiptoes, raised his arms slowly in front of him, and made the slightest movement possible with the index finger of his right hand. It was now 5:23 A.M.

As if understanding his signal perfectly, a single piccolo played a single note and off in the east a solitary shaft of cool lemon light flicked across the sky. Milo smiled happily and then cautiously crooked his finger again. This time two more piccolos and a flute joined in and three more rays of light danced lightly into view. Then with both hands he made a great circular sweep in the air and watched with delight as all the musicians began to play at once.

The cellos made the hills glow red, and the leaves and grass were tipped with a soft pale green as the violins began their song. Only the bass fiddles rested as the entire orchestra washed the forest in color.

Milo was overjoyed because they were all playing for him, and just the way they should.

"Won't Chroma be suprised?" he thought, signaling the musicians to stop. "I'll wake him now."

But, instead of stopping, they continued to play even louder than before, until each color became more brilliant than he thought possible. Milo shielded his eyes with one hand and waved the other desperately, but the colors continued to grow brighter and brighter and brighter, until an even more curious thing began to happen.

As Milo frantically conducted, the sky changed slowly from blue to tan and then to a rich magenta red. Flurries of light-green snow began to fall, and the leaves on the trees and bushes turned a vivid orange.

All the flowers suddenly appeared black, the gray rocks became a lovely soft chartreuse, and even peacefully sleeping Tock changed from brown to a magnificent ultramarine. Nothing was the color it should have been, and yet, the more he tried to straighten things out, the worse they became.

"I wish I hadn't started," he thought unhappily as a pale-blue blackbird flew by. "There doesn't seem to be any way to stop them."

He tried very hard to do everything just the way Chroma had done, but nothing worked. The musicians played on, faster and faster, and the purple sun raced quickly across the sky. In less than a minute it had set once more in the west and then, without any pause, risen again in the east. The sky was now quite yellow and the grass a charming shade of lavender. Seven times the sun rose and almost as quickly disappeared as the colors kept changing. In just a few minutes a whole week had gone by.

At last the exhausted Milo, afraid to call for help and on the verge of tears, dropped his hands to his sides. The orchestra stopped. The colors disappeared, and once again it was night. The time was 5:27 A.M.

"Wake up, everybody! Time for the sunrise!" he shouted with relief, and quickly jumped from the music stand.

"What a marvelous rest," said Chroma, striding to the podium. "I feel as though I'd slept for a week. My, my, I see we're a little late this morning. I'll have to cut my lunch hour short by four minutes."

He tapped for attention, and this time the dawn proceeded perfectly.

"You did a fine job," he said, patting Milo on the head. "Someday I'll let you conduct the orchestra yourself."

Tock wagged his tail proudly, but Milo didn't say a word, and to this day no one knows of the lost week but the few people who happened to be awake at 5:23 on that very strange morning.

1. Certain instruments in this story create the colors of particular times of the day, seasons, or objects. List three instruments and the effects they have.
2. Describe what happened when Milo conducted the orchestra.
3. Why did Milo lose control of the orchestra?
4. Look up the word *chromatic* in the dictionary. Explain why the conductor is named Chroma.
5. Describe two characters or events in the story that make it a fantasy.
6. Many people find that music creates color pictures or patterns in their minds. Other sounds can be paired with colors, as well. Try closing your eyes and listening to the sounds around you. Describe the sounds you choose and the colors they bring to mind.

"*Let's take it again from 'klonk.'*"

NEW YORK WOMEN'S
SYMPHONY ORCHESTRA

ANTONIA BRICO
Conductor

CARNEGIE HALL
57th STREET AND 7th AVENUE

FOURTH
SEASON
1937 - 1938

FOUR TUESDAY E

NOVEMBER 30
MARCH 15

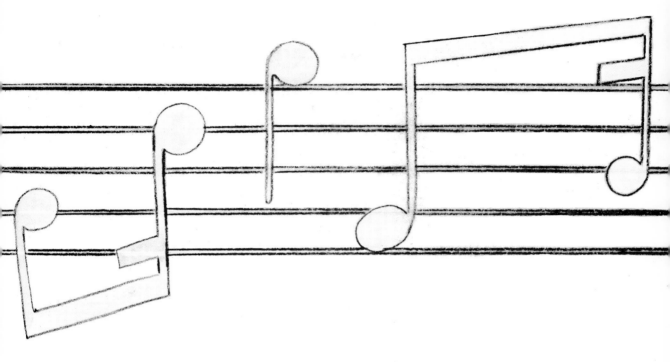

Doing the Impossible

Suppose you have a very special talent. Naturally you want to use this talent. How would you feel if people told you, "You don't have a chance! It's impossible!" Would you give up? In the past, many talented women have faced this problem. Antonia Brico, the orchestral conductor, is such a woman. As you read this biographical sketch and interview, think about how Brico's talent and perseverance helped turn the "impossible" into reality.

"My musical life, I suppose, began when I was ten years old for the simple reason that I used to bite my nails. The doctor said to my stepmother, 'I think if you let her play the piano, I think she'll stop biting her nails.' On such slim beginnings, I became a musician."

This is how Antonia Brico, one of America's leading conductors of symphony orchestras, described her start in music. Antonia was born in Holland, but moved to California when she was five. When she began music lessons at age ten, she said, "I was crazy about the piano . . . right from the start. And my first teacher was the girl across the street who was twelve years old."

At the same time that Antonia began piano lessons, the great dream of her life took root. On Sunday afternoons she would go with her family to hear band concerts conducted by Professor Paul Steindorf. She was fascinated at once by the conductor and his baton: "What a wand, a magic wand could do, a little stick . . ." The piano makes wonderful music, but here Antonia saw the most expressive, powerful, and beautiful instrument of all: the orchestra. The orchestra is the conductor's instrument; it is the conductor who blends the work of dozens of musicians into a single sound. At age ten, Antonia made her decision: she would be a conductor.

She found a chance to talk to Steindorf, and she mentioned her dream to him. "Oh, that's not possible," he said. "You'll never, never have an opportunity. That's not possible. Women can't be conductors!" This was not the last time that Antonia would hear these words. At that time, women musicians were very seldom able to find work in symphony orchestras. And a woman conductor? The idea was unheard of.

"I had a philosophy," Antonia said, "that if you wanted something and you got the first step, the subsequent steps would come. If you were not meant to do it, you wouldn't even get the first steps." She continued her study of the piano, received a degree in music at the University of California, and went to Germany, where she became the first American to graduate from the Master School of Conducting in Berlin. Following this, in 1930 at the age of twenty-eight, she made her first public appearance as a conductor, leading the Berlin Philharmonic Orchestra. She was the first American woman to conduct this world-famous orchestra, and music critics came from all over Germany and from the United States because, as Antonia said, "they were so suspicious that I couldn't do anything."

She was to prove them wrong. Rave reviews of her performance appeared in scores of newspapers, and a picture of Antonia leading the orchestra was published around the world.

She had taken her first step. But the subsequent steps did not follow easily. For the next forty years, she was to struggle in a world, the music world, that refused to believe in her talent. *Women can't be conductors!* Few people, other than Antonia, disputed the idea.

Following her Berlin performance, she returned to the United States and was engaged by Mrs. Olin

Antonia Brico: "It's too bad that it took so long, but it happened. . . ."

Downes to conduct a concert at the Metropolitan Opera Company. This was one of a series of twenty concerts sponsored by a distinguished committee of women to help unemployed musicians. "I was having a lovely time. I was going to conduct . . . and so there we were . . . and it was the most screaming . . . success."

A second successful concert followed, and a third one, featuring a famous singer of the day, was scheduled. But when the singer was told that Antonia Brico would conduct, he said, "No, I am not going to sing under a woman conductor." He was reminded of the terrific publicity that Antonia, as a woman conductor, attracted. "That's just the point," he replied. "That will take all the attention away from me."

"So," Antonia recalled, "he denied me that third concert at the Metropolitan."

Several years later, nine women musicians approached Antonia and asked her to conduct their group. She thought about it: "I made this remark—the remark of all remarks—'if nine can play together, why not ninety?'" An announcement to the newspapers soon followed. "I said, 'I'm going to form a women's symphony.' . . . They said, 'You'll never get enough instruments!' But I did . . . the whole, full . . . one-hundred-person orchestra!

"We had our first concert in Town Hall," Antonia said. The performance was free, "just to interest people and to get press . . . but anyway, it was a great sensation and a great success . . . The New York Women's Symphony was in business for several years."

Antonia formed the Women's Symphony to make a point: that women were the equal of men as musicians. "However, however . . . I want people to mix in orchestras as they do in life. Men and women mix in life and they should mix in orchestras." She brought men into her orchestra and changed its name to the Brico Symphony Orchestra. "And then the Board of Directors said that that was no sensation anymore. The Board of Directors wasn't so interested."

Antonia Brico was occasionally invited to be a guest conductor for symphony orchestras in the United States and Europe. Sometimes she gave a concert or two a year. Some years she gave none at all. For all her proven talent and fame, no symphony offered her what a conductor needs most—a permanent job with an active conducting schedule.

"How would you feel if you had, in the whole year, four performances? . . . I was strong enough to have five performances a month. I was squeezed . . . frustrated because . . . I could not play my instrument which is the orchestra . . .

"If you're a violinist . . . you can play it, play it, play it for yourself, but an orchestra . . . slips through your fingers and it's not anything you can hold. You can't see it. You can't touch it . . . And as I said, the piano you can play and play and play in the privacy of your domain but conducting is a public affair . . . You have to have people to conduct and people to listen."

In 1947, Antonia moved to Denver, Colorado, to accept a conducting position, but the job, with the Denver Symphony Orchestra, fell through. "I don't talk about it every day. I don't let everybody know my heartbreak. The people closest to me don't understand . . . The Denver Symphony—do you know what they said? Do you know there's a club there called the Cactus Club, a very, very fashionable male club? The people said, 'How can we have a woman conductor if we can't invite her to the Cactus Club?'"

Antonia remained in Denver and, for the next twenty-seven years, taught musically gifted children in the Denver area. She also conducted the Denver Businessman's Orchestra, soon to become known as the Brico Symphony. The orchestra gave five performances a year, and was made up of semi-professionals who, like Antonia, were not paid for their work. She conducted concerts in different states and countries including Mexico and Japan.

One of Antonia's students was a ten-year-old girl named Judy Collins. Judy studied piano with Antonia and a very close friendship sprang up between teacher and student. Judy sang and played the guitar as well as the piano and, as an adult, she became a world-famous folksinger.

In 1973, Judy Collins and Jill Godmilow began work on a film tribute to Antonia Brico. They filmed her with the Brico Symphony in rehearsal and in concert. They brought cameras into her home and let them roll while Judy talked with Antonia about her life and career. *Antonia:*

A Portrait of the Woman attracted national attention and won many awards, including an Academy Award nomination. But it had an even more important result.

The film dramatized a vital talent that had been neglected. As important people in the music world were reminded of the almost forgotten Brico, offers to conduct came to her from orchestras all over the world. In order to accept the offers, she had to rearrange the schedules of her music students, but she refused to consider giving up teaching.

By 1977, Antonia Brico, seventy-five years old, had seen her dream come true. Her conducting schedule was so packed that she told a *New York Times* reporter, "I am conducting as many concerts now as I can handle. Am I happy? . . . Now, I'm happy, yes."

1. How did Antonia begin her musical life?
2. Why do you think people believed that a woman couldn't conduct an orchestra?
3. Almost anybody can do the "possible." For those who are determined, "the impossible" just takes a little longer. What impossible thing did Antonia Brico do?
4. What effect did Judy Collins' film have on Antonia's life?
5. Suppose you want to use a very special talent that you have. How would you feel if people told you, "You don't have a chance! It's impossible!" What would you do?

THE TEDDY BEAR HABIT

James Lincoln Collier

Confidence: when you have it, it's easy to do your best. When you lack confidence in yourself, even the things you know how to do become hard.

Confidence is George Stable's problem in this excerpt from James Lincoln Collier's novel—only George calls his problem by another name. According to George, his problem is "a worn out, beat up, patched old teddy bear with one of its glass eyes missing and the threads that made up its mouth mostly rubbed away. It was a little smaller than a football, and I had owned it all my life . . . Pop bought it for me the day I was born . . . The truth is that I don't own it. It owns me. The thing is, I discovered a long time ago that I wasn't so much of a loser when I had the teddy bear around. It's magical . . . I don't understand it. I just feel stronger and more confident when he's around. I can't explain it. He's nothing but some cloth and a lot of old cotton batting. There shouldn't be any magic in that. But there is . . ."

I live on Manhattan Island, which is the most famous part of New York City. Manhattan is where Times Square is, and Radio City Music Hall, and the Empire State Building, and Wall Street, and the stage shows, and all that jazz.

You would think that being an artist and living in Greenwich Village would make Pop very hip, but he isn't. The truth is, he's square, just like everybody else's dad. In fact he's worse, because as he says, "I'm trying to be a mother to you too, Georgie."

He was out when I got home from the Winnie-the-Pooh audition. I was just as glad Pop wasn't home. I was feeling pretty bad about goofing up the audition, and I didn't much feel like answering a lot of questions. It wasn't that I minded not getting a part in the musical. That was always a long shot. I just hated thinking that I'd fallen to pieces again. I hated myself for being a loser.

I went into my room, took the teddy bear out of the bag, flung it up in the air and punched it like a handball. It bounced off the wall and landed on my bed. I felt bad that I'd hit it; so I looked around to see if anyone was looking, which of course they weren't, and then I picked up the teddy and hugged it to make up for hitting it. That made me feel stupid. Finally I shut the teddy in the top drawer of my bureau. Then I took off my good clothes and hung them up, and put on some dungarees and my dirty sneakers.

It was getting late. I made myself a sandwich out of some leftover baked beans and catsup, jammed the dollar Pop had left me into my pocket, and got out of there.

I was already a little bit late. I peeled across Sixth Avenue and down West Fourth. Just a couple of doors down there is a shop called Wiggsy's Wig-Wam.

Wiggsy is a fantastic guitar player, but he really doesn't play very much any more. His main business is running his store. He sells guitars and folk records and sheet music and picks and strings and junk like that. I was taking lessons in how to play rock and roll on the guitar.

Wiggsy said that with my voice I was going to be a big star in a few years. Of course Wiggsy could just be saying that to get my two bucks every week. That was the deal: a buck a week for the lesson, and a buck a week for the second-hand guitar he was selling me.

When I went in, there was another fellow there with Wiggsy. "You're late, babe," Wiggsy said when I came in.

"Gee, I'm sorry," I said, trying to think of an explanation. I leaned back against the music racks in a casual way, and crossed my arms. "I had to audition for a Broadway show this morning and I got held up."

Wiggsy said, "Ummm. You puttin' me on, babe?"

"It's true," I said. The music rack was beginning to dig into my back, but I'd gotten everybody's attention, and I didn't want to spoil my casual pose. "It's a musical comedy about Winnie-the-Pooh, and they need a bunch of kids."

Wiggsy's pal gave me a look. "Exactly what experience have you had, fella?" He leaned back against Wiggsy's glass counter in a pose that had me out-casualed.

"Well, you know, it isn't much. Mostly these recitals Mr. Smythe-Jones puts on for the parents and stuff."

"You take guitar from Wiggsy? And study voice?"

"I'll be honest," I said, which was a nice change. "My Pop wants me to study classical, but what I really like is rock and roll. I study voice with this Mr. Smythe-Jones on Wednesday, and I take guitar from Wiggsy on Saturday."

"Can you read music, fella?" Music Biz asked.

"Sure, some. If it's not too hard."

Music Biz reached into his pocket and flipped out a card. "Listen fella," he said, "maybe I can use you. Have Smythe-Jones give me a horn on Monday." He handed me the card and slapped Wiggsy on the shoulder. "I've got to split."

I stared at the little card in my hand. It said:

Thomas Woodward

AL 5-9210

Woodward and Hayes
Television Productions

I spent the next three days thinking up excuses for not getting Mr. Smythe-Jones to call up Woodward, the television producer. Thinking up excuses is something I've always been pretty good at.

But I was having a lot of trouble getting myself to believe the ones I was making up to get out of asking Mr. Smythe-Jones to call the television producer.

I should have known better than to get started on my excuses so far in advance. By the time I got onto the Sixth Avenue Subway to go up to Mr. Smythe-Jones for my vocal lesson, I'd used up all the good ones.

Mr. Smythe-Jones's studio is on Fifty-sixth Street facing the back of Carnegie Hall. Carnegie Hall is about the most famous concert hall in the United States, I guess, and Mr. Smythe-Jones likes to give everybody the idea that he used to sing there a lot. He went around saying things like, "When I was singing at Carnegie," but the truth is that he only sang there once, as part of a hundred-voice choir.

When I got there, Mr. Smythe-Jones was sitting in the studio drinking a cup of tea. He was always willing to waste some time talking something over, provided he didn't get the idea you were just stalling. So I blurted out, "Mr. Smythe-Jones, I have to ask your advice on something."

"Oh yes, Georgie?" He sat down on the piano bench, crossed his legs, and got ready to listen. If there was anything Mr. Smythe-Jones liked, it was to have his advice asked about something. "Yes, tell me about it, George."

"The thing is this," I said, "I happened to meet up with a television producer, and he wants me to call him up about some kind of show or something."

First Smythe-Jones pursed his lips; then he raised his eyes. I knew he was trying to decide whether he ought to get sore because he hadn't been consulted in the beginning, or pleased because one of his students might do something he could boast about a year afterwards.

Finally he said, "I don't like the sound of it, George. Who is this man?"

I had written the name and phone number down on a piece of scratch paper, and I took it out and handed it to him. "Mr. Woodward. Of Woodward and Hayes."

Smythe-Jones shook his head slowly. "Can't say that I know them, George," he said in a slow, serious way.

So I looked back at him very seriously and I said, "Well, that's what I was wondering about. I don't know anything about the television and all, and I thought maybe you might call them up and see if there was anything wrong with it."

I figured I was on safe ground. Getting one of his students on television, or written up somewhere made him hum like a bee. If the thing worked out he could go around for months afterwards saying, "Didn't happen to see the 'Telephone Hour' last night, by chance? Student of mine on it, don't chew know." (Mr. Smythe-Jones talked like an English duke on television.)

"Well, George," he said slowly.

"I would sure appreciate it."

"Yes," he said, "I can understand that."

"I suppose I'd better do something about it." He got up and went out into his living room, where the telephone was. I could hear him

dial, and after a bit I could hear him explaining to Mr. Woodward what it was all about. For about five minutes he went dribbling on his way, don't chew knowing and rightoing. Then he hung up and came out and told me that they were holding auditions at four o'clock on Friday, and he'd take me up. And naturally, right after he told me that my legs began to get weak and shaky, and my heart to go ripping along full speed, and my stomach to fill up with cold marbles. But there was nothing I could do about that.

That was Wednesday. I had only two days to get ready. In a way that was lucky. Between being nervous about the audition, and excited about the chance of becoming rich and famous, I could hardly eat anything during meals. If the audition had been a couple of weeks away, say I'd have died of starvation before I got to it.

The first thing I did was talk Wiggsy into lending me my guitar. He didn't like the idea very much, but since he'd been pushing the thing he had to go along.

Then there was another problem. I knew perfectly well that if I went up to the audition without the teddy I'd panic and start fainting all over the place and embarrass Mr. Smythe-Jones and feel ashamed and hate myself for about two weeks afterwards. On the other hand, if I could manage to smuggle the teddy in I knew that at least I wouldn't start fainting. That didn't say that I'd win the audition; that's something you could never figure on. But at least I wouldn't do anything to make myself ashamed and embarrassed. And there was always the chance I'd win.

I thought of several plans. The first idea I had was to take the teddy to the audition in a shoe box. I figured I could explain that I'd just bought a brand new pair of shoes, and that I wanted them right there where I could keep an eye on them because my dad would kill me if I lost them. But after I'd thought this idea over carefully, I realized that they might have some kind of cloak closet or check room, where they'd insist that I put my shoes for safekeeping.

The second idea I had was to put the teddy in a little canvas bag of some kind. I'd say that I was sick and had to carry this special medicine around with me wherever I went. Of course nobody would dare to take my medicine away from me. But then it came to me that maybe they wouldn't want anybody on television who might keel over in the middle of the show. So that idea was no good.

All day Thursday, when I was supposed to be paying attention to my teachers, I was trying to think up a hiding place for the teddy. I couldn't come up with anything. All I got for my work was a bawling out about every fifteen minutes for daydreaming. By bedtime I was getting worried. I sat down on the edge of my bed in my underwear and began to play an imaginary guitar, pretending I was at the audition to see if anything would come to me.

All at once I remembered that guitars are hollow. There's plenty of room for a teddy inside, and there's a big round hole in the middle to push him through.

I sat on the bed, thinking about it. If I loosened the strings up a good deal I could surely push them aside far enough to squeeze the teddy through. I could push it back out of sight a little bit. It'd stick there. It was fat enough so that he wouldn't slide around. It was a perfect plan. I'd have it right where I could get a peek at him or even reach in and touch him when I began to get nervous. Nobody would know, it'd be completely hidden.

But the next day I was nervous all over again. I could hardly eat breakfast, and I could hardly stand being in school. At three o'clock I peeled out of school. I didn't have much time to get home, stow the teddy in the guitar, and get uptown. When I got to the apartment, I grabbed the teddy and the guitar case, and tore for the subway.

I was all in a sweat by the time a train came in and I was headed uptown, but I still had the guitar to work over. Luckily, there weren't too many people in the car that time of day; it was too embarrassing to get caught shoving a teddy into your guitar. By keeping the guitar case more or less propped up on the seat beside me I was pretty well concealed. Then all I had to do was loosen the strings, push the teddy down into the hole, and jam him back inside, where he wouldn't work loose. If he had been a human being he'd have gotten his back scraped up badly by those strings, but that's the advantage of being a teddy bear: you don't feel things very much.

It was tough tuning the guitar on the subway, but I got close enough. I figured I'd have a chance to finish the job later.

As it worked out, I wasn't more than about ten minutes late to meet Mr. Smythe-Jones.

Woodward and Hayes's offices were on Madison in one of those brand-new glass buildings. Man, was it snazzy. We went up in an automatic elevator, the kind you run yourself. It was the fanciest elevator I'd ever been in. It had a rug on the floor and music playing out of the ceiling.

I can tell you, it had me scared, and I got even more scared when Mr. Woodward, the fellow I'd originally met down at Wiggsy's, came out of somewhere. Man was he cool. You could tell that he was a guy who would never get nervous at anything. Mr. Woodward shook hands with Mr. Smythe-Jones, put his arm around my shoulder, and said, "The clan is gathering in the studio, cookie. Shall we join them? The boy reads music pretty well, Mr. Smythe-Jones?"

Smythe-Jones nodded. "All my pupils read, Mr. Woodward. Get the fundamentals first, don't chew know. Cahn't build a house on sand, don't chew know."

He went on about fundamentals for a while, trying to impress Mr. Woodward, and at about the fifth don't chew know we reached the studio and went in.

As I found out later, it was a regular recording studio. Woodward and Hayes were mainly in the business of taping musical backgrounds and singing commercials, which they call jingles in the advertising business. The people you see on television are usually just actors pretending to play music. The music you hear was taped in a studio by people like Woodward and Hayes.

Woodward and Hayes made singing commercials, mostly for radio, but sometimes for television. One other thing they did was to help put together musical acts. Suppose one of the big shows wanted a quartet to sing along with the star; Woodward and Hayes would choose the singers, hire somebody to write the music, and take charge of the rehearsals. I was trying out for something like that.

Woodward and Hayes had three or four studios, but the one Mr. Woodward took us into was the biggest of them—big as a really big living room. The walls were white and there were a lot of lights in the place, so that the room looked airy and big. Scattered around were a lot of microphones and cables, and two huge grand pianos on small wheels so they could be moved around easily. Behind a huge picture window was the engineer's control room, full of knobs and panels and big tape-recording machines; and sitting in a row of folding chairs along the opposite wall were about fifteen kids and their mothers or fathers. They were looking nervous, and jittering around on their seats, and punching each other. Most of them had guitars.

Mr. Smythe-Jones and I sat down on the line of chairs and looked nervous like everybody else. Mr. Woodward leaned on one of the grand pianos, and explained to us what it was all about.

United Broadcasting Company was planning a huge one-hour television show on popular culture. You know, fads.

"There'll be a bit on surfing movies, and one on monster comics, and so forth," Mr. Woodward said. "They want to have some rock and roll, naturally, and they thought it would be cute to put together a group made up of kids your age."

"We're having three auditions, and we're going to pick out six kids. Two will be understudies, but I guarantee that they'll be used, because one kid is bound to get the measles and another will break a leg. Okay. When I call your name come on up by this mike and give me something with a big beat. Don't get nervous, just belt it out. Everybody here loves you."

So they began. Some kids played the piano when they sang, but most of them accompanied themselves on guitars. It was the ususal bunch: some were pretty good, some were awful; some looked very confident, and some looked scared to death. I sat there and watched them all.

At a thing like this there's usually one kid who's really out-standing. In this case it turned out to be a redheaded kid. He walked up there as confident as could be and belted out a couple of songs with a lot of style and no mistakes. When he finished he just grinned at Mr. Woodward as if to say: Don't bother telling me how good I am, I already know.

There were two or three others who were pretty good, too: not as good as the redhead, but pretty good. Even so, I had a good chance, and I knew it. Some of them sang a little better than I did, and some of them played the guitar better, but I averaged out better. I had a chance. Except for my problem. Except for being a natural-born-loser.

I sat there with the guitar in my lap, my hands clenched tight around the neck so they wouldn't shake. My stomach was full of ice water, and I felt like I needed to go to the bathroom. Oh man, did I envy that redhead. About every two minutes I took a look down into the guitar at the teddy bear. I prayed nobody would notice what I was doing. Not that it was illegal to have a teddy bear in your guitar: it was just so embarrassing.

It's the waiting that kills you. They were going by alphabetical order. My name beginning with an S, I was down at the bottom of the list. The worst was that I didn't know exactly when my turn would come. I didn't know how many *L*'s and *M*'s and *P*'s there were ahead of me, so that each time one kid finished I had to sit there and shake and quiver until Mr. Woodward announced who was going to be electrocuted next.

So I sat there waiting for death and destruction, and finally Mr. Woodward called my name. I swallowed, stood, and walked across to the mike, trying to look casual and relaxed instead of stiff as a board. I turned around to face Woodward and the other kids, and struck a warm-up chord. Then I almost fainted.

Instead of getting a nice full, rich, chord, I had gotten a muffled clunking sound, as if the guitar were in the next room. A couple of the kids giggled.

"What's the matter with the guitar, cookie?" Mr. Woodward said.

I knew exactly what was wrong with the guitar. It had a teddy bear stuffed down inside of it. Anytime you stuff something down inside a guitar it stops the wood from resonating—at least partly— and of course the sound goes dead.

My face burned and I started to sweat. "I've got a mute in the guitar," I said. My voice was as choked and sweaty as my face.

"Well, take it out so we can hear you, cookie."

At first I thought I would keel over dead; all I could do was blink and stare at them. Finally I sort of whispered, "I can't." There was some more giggling.

"Why not?"

"I—I have to take the strings off." I reached down through the strings to give him the idea of what was involved, and my hand fell on a handful of teddy bear fuzz. Touching the bear brought back a little of my courage, and the fire on my face started to die out. "It's my special sound," I said. "It's my trademark."

Mr. Woodward laughed. "Okay, cookie, go ahead." Pretending I was adjusting something, I reached in to touch the teddy again for another shot of courage. I had decided to do one of the Beatles' songs. I stroked the opening chords, and then I started to sing.

My voice was a little weak and rusty to begin, from the scare I'd had. I looked down into the guitar. At the angle I was holding it I could just make out one of his glass eyes and a bit of the threads of his worn out mouth; and I swear I saw him wink and heard him say, "Don't worry, George, you can do it." And just like that, I knew I could. My voice got stronger and I felt my courage, and I began to look around the room at the audience and belt it out in fine style. Whenever I felt myself growing weak or scared again, I'd just look down into the guitar; and the teddy would stare back at me with a solemn look that told me I had nothing to worry about. I can't explain it; I know that a teddy bear can't talk, but I heard him. I swear it.

So I ran through the tune, and by the time I got to the end I was feeling so good I added on a little tag. I struck the last chord and saw all those kids sitting there staring at me silently; and I knew I'd made it. And it was then that my knees went weak and my legs began to tremble and my hands began to shake and my brain closed down for the rest of the day.

"You the kid who says he can read music pretty well?"

I nodded. My throat was too clogged to speak.

"Groovy," he said. "Stick around."

I tried to say something polite, but my throat was still shut up; and besides, my brain had quit on me and I couldn't think of any words. I just nodded my head and walked over and sat down. Mr. Smythe-Jones patted my shoulder. "Top hole, my friend," he whispered. "Absolutely top hole."

So we waited around for the rest of the kids to have their turns and then Mr. Woodward took Mr. Smythe-Jones and me back to his office, me still dizzy and trembling with excitement. I sat down in a huge red-leather armchair by a window. You could see barges going up the East River, and way down below the tiny taxicabs and buses moving slowly up the avenues. To calm down I tried to pretend I was somebody arranging a big movie deal; but it didn't work.

Mr. Woodward leaned back in his chair and put his feet up. "Here it is, cookie," he said. "Your voice isn't all that groovy, but it's good enough. You've got the confidence, you get around on the guitar pretty well, and the fact that you read music helps. We're going to see some more people, but I want to use you, maybe as one of the understudies. We'll see about that."

And so we left. Mr. Smythe-Jones was so pleased with it all that he called a taxi to take us back to his studio. "You heard what he said about reading music. Fundamentals, George. Cahn't imagine how lucky you are to have a teacher who insisted on fundamentals."

1. Before finally deciding to stuff his teddy bear into the guitar, what other plans did George consider for taking the teddy bear to the audition? Why did he decide they wouldn't work?

2. Why did George depend on his teddy bear?

3. What did Mr. Smythe-Jones mean by "fundamentals"?

4. Mr. Smythe-Jones is an unusual person. Look through the story and make a list of all the details that describe him. Look at your list and then, in your own words, describe Mr. Smythe-Jones.

5. Do you consider George to be a "winner" or a "loser"? Give reasons for your answer.

6. Think of a person you admire who has been successful in sports, the arts, entertainment, or another field. Describe the person and explain why you think that person is a "winner."

THINK OF LIFE
AS A GUITAR

The guitar
played
happy notes
and I was joyful
The guitar
played sad notes
and I cried
The guitar plays on forever.

—Octaviano "Chico" Romano

Types of Conflicts

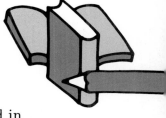

The *characters* in a story are the people or animals involved in the action. Usually one or more characters face a problem in the story. Another name for the problem is the *conflict*.

There are three basic types of conflicts which story characters may face:

1. **Characters against other characters** In this type of conflict, characters face some challenge created by other people. For example, two people may be competing for the same job, or one person may be trying to escape from another.

2. **Characters against a force of nature** In this type of conflict, characters are challenged by some natural force. For example, people may be trapped in a sandstorm in the desert, or they may have to build a boat to cross a flooded river.

3. **Characters against themselves** In this type of conflict, characters must overcome some personal challenge. For example, a person may be too shy to give a speech or may have the problem of constantly daydreaming.

In the story "The Teddy Bear Habit," the character named George faced a problem. The conflict was not created by another character. It was not caused by a force of nature, either. George's problem was that he lacked the self-confidence to perform in front of an audience. He needed the security of his teddy bear. This problem is an example of characters against themselves.

ACTIVITY A Read each story description below. Write whether the problem is *characters against other characters*, *characters against a force of nature*, or *characters against themselves*.

1. A man stranded in the Arctic tries to start a fire. He is unable to do so in the unbearable cold.

2. A politician runs for office. She must campaign hard to defeat her popular opponent.

3. People on a boat get lost in a storm. They manage to survive until the storm blows over.

4. A young boy lacks the self-confidence to give a speech in front of the class. After practicing the speech at home in front of a mirror, the boy delivers the speech successfully in class.

5. Two people insult each other as they pass on the street. They get into a fight, and both individuals are injured.

6. A young girl in town is too shy to introduce herself to others. She overcomes her loneliness when she meets another shy person.

ACTIVITY B   Read the story below. On your paper, write answers to the questions that follow.

 **The Result of Greed**

Once there was a rich man who was very greedy. His greediness and stinginess made him unpopular with the other people in town. Whenever citizens asked for charity or for a loan, the miser refused.

Once a stranger came to the rich man's house. He told the rich man, "I own much land. I can't tend to it any more, so I will give it to you. As much land as you can encircle in one day will be yours. You may start at sunrise, but you must be back to your starting point by sunset."

The rich man readily agreed. At sunrise he began running on the stranger's field. By noon he had gone very far, so he decided to turn left. His greed led him even farther before he made the next turn. Soon the man realized the sun would set shortly. He raced quickly toward his starting point.

As the man raced the sunset, he became very tired. Huffing and puffing, he realized he had gone too far into the field. Just before reaching the starting point, the man collapsed and died.

1. The townspeople had a problem. Was their problem caused by other characters, by a force of nature, or by themselves?
2. The rich man suffered the problem of greed. In which of the three categories of conflicts would this problem fall?
3. What example of characters against nature existed in the story?
4. How were the rich man's problems settled in the end?
5. Did you admire the rich man? Why or why not?

Types of Characters

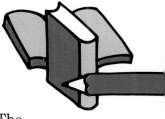

The characters in a story may be labeled in different ways. The labels make it easier to discuss the characters after you read the story. Here are some ways characters can be labeled:

1. **Major and Minor Characters**   *Major characters* are the most important characters in the story. Your attention and concern are focused upon them. *Minor characters* are less important individuals.

   In "The Teddy Bear Habit," George Stable is a major character. He is involved in all the action of the story. Mr. Woodward and Mr. Smythe-Jones are important minor characters. Other minor characters include Wiggsy and the children at the audition.

2. **Developing and Static Characters**   *Developing Characters* are individuals who change in some way by the end of the story. Their experience teaches them something new or causes them to think or act differently. *Static characters* are individuals who do not change throughout the story.

   In "The Teddy Bear Habit," George is a developing character. He learns that self-confidence is necessary for success. Static characters include Mr. Woodward and Mr. Smythe-Jones.

3. **Protagonist and Antagonist**   The *protagonist* is the major character with whom you become emotionally involved. A protagonist with good qualities is often called the *hero*. When the protagonist has a problem or a personality similar to your own, you may *identify* with that character. The *antagonist* is the character who tries to keep the protagonist from reaching a desired goal. Sometimes the antagonist is referred to as the *villain*. Some stories do not have an antagonist. If the problem that the protagonist faces is not caused by another person, there will be no antagonist in the story.

   In "The Teddy Bear Habit," George is the protagonist. His desired goal is to audition successfully for Mr. Woodward. In this story, there is no antagonist. George's problem is not caused by another person. George only battles with himself to gain the confidence necessary for success.

Read the story below. Then write answers to the questions that follow.

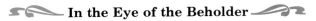 **In the Eye of the Beholder**

Holly sat in front of the mirror. She carefully applied the lipstick she was holding. Then she experimented with eye shadow and rouge. Her younger sister entered the room.

"What is that?" Laura cried. "What is that stuff you're putting on your face?"

"It's make-up, Laura," Holly replied patiently. "I need it for the class party tomorrow night. All the girls are wearing it. If I don't wear it, no one will pay attention to me."

"That's not true," Laura said angrily. "You don't need make-up. You look good enough without it. Why must you follow the others like a sheep?"

"You wouldn't understand," Holly said, continuing to experiment with her rouge.

The next day Holly arrived home with little time to prepare for the party. She entered her room and cried, "What's this?" All her make-up was missing. Laura, the culprit, wasn't home. Holly had no time to borrow any make-up from her friends.

At the party, Holly tried to hide herself. She became nervous when Jim sat next to her. She was afraid he would comment on how plain she looked.

Jim said, "Holly, I think it's great you haven't ruined your face like some of these girls. You look natural, not like some weird kind of painting."

Holly whispered, "Thank you, Laura," and relaxed.

1. Who were the major characters in the story?
2. Who were the minor characters in the story?
3. Which character was a developing character?
4. What did the developing character learn by the end?
5. Who was the protagonist in the story?
6. What was the desired goal of the protagonist?
7. Who was the antagonist in the story?
8. How did the antagonist try to keep the protagonist from reaching her desired goal?
9. Did you identify with the major character? Why or why not?

dance poem

come Nataki dance with me
bring your pablum dance with me
pull your plait and whorl around
come Nataki dance with me

won't you Tony dance with me
stop your crying dance with me
feel the rhythm of my arms
don't let's cry now dance with me

Tommy stop your tearing up
don't you hear the music
don't you feel the happy beat
don't bite Tony dance with me
Mommy needs a partner

Here comes Karma she will dance
pirouette and bugaloo
short pink dress and dancing shoes
Karma wants to dance with me
don't you Karma don't you

All you children gather round
we will dance and we will whorl
we will dance to our own song
we must spin to our own world
we must spin a soft Black song
All you children gather round
we will dance together

—Nikki Giovanni

Bravo Baryshnikov

Alan LeMond

The great artists are the ones who, by their talent, hard work, and dedication, show us new possibilities, new ways of doing and seeing. Mikhail Baryshnikov is such an artist. He left the Soviet Union in 1974 and quickly became one of America's most famous dancers. As you read, think about the qualities that have made Baryshnikov famous.

You do not observe Baryshnikov the first time you see him dance—you absorb him. He's unique. Dazzling. Unbelievable. Positively overwhelming.

He is a genius, and like all geniuses, he conjures up his magical reality from a bubbling blend of 99 percent perspiration and one percent inspiration. A potent combination.

There may be some luck involved, but hardly enough to be noticed. In the main, dancing is dedicated hard work.

Baryshnikov recognized this as a student. It was a hard job, he says. "Job" may be the wrong word for what he does, but whatever you do, says Misha, "you should do it best."

And he does it best.

The impish, pale smooth face highlighted by soft blond hair and Baltic blue eyes conceals a computer-sharp mind. For it is behind those eyes with their dark, dramatic shadows, inside his head, that the control center of the superb athlete's body lies. The sharp intelligence that is the driver sits there.

And a masterful driver it must be to control the jumps, the stops, the 180-degree turns, the *cabrioles,* and *grands ballonnés,* the *grands jetés.* The extraordinary way he seems to hover in midair.

How does he do it?

"It's normal," he says, shrugging it off, disdainful of the long preparation involved, the extreme effort needed.

To Baryshnikov, the steps are just classical steps. Although they are difficult, he treats them almost as commonplace: "You see them all the time."

The height of his jumps, how many turns he does, or how fast he can do them—that is not the point.

The *grand jeté,* in fact, is not one of his favorite steps. And he complains that the public is insatiable. They want more and more.

Does he do ten pirouettes now? Perhaps next year he will do twelve.

He is afraid the public thinks of him as a machine.

Yet no one could accuse Misha of being a machine. The life he exudes could not come from such an objective entity. But his body is a finely honed, precisely tuned instrument. In that sense, he *is* a machine, a magnificent machine.

He came to the dance physically prepared, having flirted with gymnastics, but the long, grueling hours of energy-filled time he spent in classes really shaped and strengthened his body. It gave him the physical skills he needed, the skills he now displays with such seeming ease.

He is the greatest male classical dancer of his day.

He may be the greatest dancer ever.

Dance to Silence

Imagine this: you are listening to your favorite song on the radio. All of a sudden the music stops. You look around. The others in the room are dancing, so there's nothing wrong with the sound. No, it's you. You have lost your hearing.

If this happened to you, you would join about two million other people in this country who cannot hear. A young woman named Susan Davidoff had to face a similar problem. Susan was planning a career as a dancer when her hearing began to fade, and eventually left her in silence. As you read this biographical sketch based on an interview with Susan Davidoff, you will see how she faces her hearing loss and then uses her experience to introduce other deaf people to dance.

Music is for the ears only; dance is music made visible by the movements of the human body. How does Susan Davidoff show that dance is an especially appropriate art for deaf people?

Susan Davidoff began to lose her hearing when she was seven years old. At the same time, she began to take piano lessons, and two years later, when she was nine, she started ballet lessons. Susan remembers, "During the time I was taking ballet and piano lessons, I did not tell my teachers that I had a hearing loss. I could still hear and had no difficulty in my classes."

But time moved on and changed Susan's hearing condition. "For unknown reasons," Susan recalls, "my hearing grew worse as I entered my teens. I didn't discuss my deafness with my friends in high school because I felt I would be different. After being like everyone else for so long, I did not want to be different. I knew two students in my class who wore hearing aids and they had no friends. So I had many mixed feelings about using a hearing aid."

Despite this concern, Susan decided to get a hearing aid. "The first year of wearing it was very difficult for me. I didn't tell my friends in high school about my deafness because I felt they would no longer want to be friends with me. But because I was a good lip reader and had normal speech, my hearing loss went unnoticed by my classmates. Nobody knew I wore a hearing aid. I did not stop my activities, and with the hearing aid I could still hear on the phone."

Susan Davidoff performing in "Sing a Sign."

By the time Susan entered college, however, no hearing aid could help her. She was totally deaf. Thinking back, Susan says, "It wasn't until I became a dance major as a freshman in college that I realized I had to start telling people I was deaf. Yet my pride kept me from telling them. I could not hear my dance instructor and never felt part of the class. My dance instructor told me not to spend so much time watching everyone else, but to develop my own skills. It was at this point I told my teacher I was deaf. Dancing finally became so difficult for me that at last I gave it up. I could not dance again for five years."

With one dream dashed, Susan had to build up another. She decided to become a teacher of the deaf, and applied for admission to the Deaf Education Program at the University of Illinois. It would not accept her. The program had a rule then that only people who had normal hearing could be enrolled. (That policy has since been changed.) But Susan would not give up. After a year of persuasion and letters from others about her abilities, she was finally admitted into the program.

Susan remembers that, as the only deaf person ever to be accepted into the teacher-training program, she was considered "special." "Everyone wanted to be my friend. I don't know if it was because people really liked me, but it really didn't matter. I was in a program with future teachers of the deaf who accepted deafness. Because I didn't know sign language until my sophomore year, I was forced to lip-read the lectures or borrow notes from others. I graduated with high honors from the University of Illinois and with highest honors from the University of Pittsburgh. I knew that being deaf was not going to be a handicap."

After graduation, Susan began teaching deaf children in Montgomery County, Maryland. "I was the only deaf teacher in that county," Susan points out. "Many deaf students in public schools had never met a deaf adult. They saw that I was happy and successful. This helped them to accept their own deafness. It also became easier for me to live with my own hearing loss."

With her confidence fully restored, Susan began taking dance classes again. One day the director asked her if she would like to begin a dance class for deaf children. Susan

thought about this idea and remembered what her dance instructor in college had told her: "If you are to become a dancer, you must concentrate on yourself, not just copy the movements of your classmates."

Susan explains, "Although I was not trained as a dance teacher or as a professional dancer, I decided that I would teach the class. I believed my deep understanding of deafness would help me. In teaching my seventh-grade math class and ninth-grade English class for the deaf, for example, I used every way of communicating that I could think of—signing (or sign language), fingerspelling, speech and lip reading, and amplification. In my dance class for the deaf, I found signing

Dance for the Deaf:
The Music Is Inside

Susan Davidoff, Miss Deaf America, teaching youngsters movement at the School for the Deaf in Manhattan. The occasion was a demonstration designed to show that the inability to hear music need not deter people from learning dance.

and amplification especially useful." Amplification makes sounds much louder than normal. Deaf people who hear amplified music can feel the vibrations of the sound on the floor. In this way, a deaf student can dance and move with the music. It was easy, Susan found, to feel the vibration of the beat when rock music was playing. But modern dance and ballet have a less obvious beat. She elaborates, "I had to learn what I taught my students. I learned to count as well as to watch. I counted the beat and tempo in my mind. After I had memorized the timing, I didn't have to count any more. I felt the rhythm inside me."

Many deaf children, Susan realized, had never been exposed to art forms such as music and dance. Like many hearing people, they thought that deafness was a barrier to learning about music and dance. Learning to dance made them feel part of a group for the first time in their lives. According to Susan, "It gave them something to be proud of. It inspired them to develop ambition, to overcome their disability, and to pursue any goal they chose."

Susan's experience with teaching dance to deaf children started her thinking. If music and dance open up new worlds to deaf people, won't they open up hearing people to the skills of deaf people? She decided to be a performer as well as a teacher. "By becoming a performer," she explains, "who 'sings,' not with my voice, but with my gestures and movements, I felt I could build good will and acceptance of deaf people. Never again could hearing people think, 'If deaf people cannot hear music, the beat, the rhythm, it is impossible for them to sing or dance.' Instead, they would see the advantage deaf people have in the arts—that we are very good at using sign language and body language.

We are skilled at expressing not just the words, but the feelings that go with the words. We have a natural ability to express ourselves with our bodies, our facial expressions, and the beautiful ballet of our hands as we sign. With proper training and encouragement, we can be very good dancers and actors."

Susan practiced hard, often with a cue person who went over the words, the tempo, the rhythm, and the beat with her until she could dance in time to the music. The routines became a part of her. She succeeded beyond what she had dreamed of.

Susan competed for the title of Miss Deaf America. After winning, she became a spokesperson for deaf people. She toured the country and appeared on many television shows promoting deaf awareness. She helped people to understand the abilities and talents deaf people possess.

In 1978, Susan starred in a very successful television program, "Sing a Sign"—the first nationally telecast "special" performed in sign language. As Susan described the show, "It took music and song one step beyond hearing so that all people—deaf and hearing—could enjoy music and song together. Most of all, it demonstrated the beautiful art of signing."

How do deaf people "sign a song?" Susan explains it this way: "Artists put their own personalities onto paper. They show a certain mood or feeling with the colors they use. A signing deaf person does the same. We don't use colors, but we use expressive hand movements, the expressions on our faces, and our natural talent for body language. We make *pictures* in the air. Hearing people who watch a deaf person signing a song are fascinated. They experience much more than simply listening to the music. They can actually see an entire picture of the song. Music becomes an even richer experience—it becomes total."

Think about it. Imagine yourself in a world of total silence. Then a Susan Davidoff enters that world. She and others like her communicate feelings and explain things to you. You feel part of the world of hearing people again. You have hope once again. More important, you can learn to express that hope and communicate your talents to others.

Susan joyously tells us, "Many hearing people are learning how to sign to our deaf sisters and brothers. If a hearing person tries to use even basic sign language with me, I am very deeply touched! Deaf people are really no different from hearing people. It's not our ears that are so important—it is what is *between* our ears and in our hearts. With a little more work, deaf people can do almost anything that hearing people can do.

"Accepting a hearing loss is not easy. It takes time. Things are happening around you and to you that you don't understand. I became very sensitive about my hearing loss, but people who knew were kind and helpful. They accepted me as a person. That helped me the most of all. If they could accept me as a person, then I should be able to accept myself, hearing loss and all."

1. What is "signing"?
2. Why does Susan think she can help deaf students more than a teacher who hears?
3. Why do you think Susan, as a teenager, hid her growing deafness?
4. Why does Susan Davidoff believe that dance is an especially appropriate art for deaf people?
5. What do you think Susan means when she says: "It's not our ears that are so important—it is what is *between* our ears and in our hearts"?

The Dance

Gurney Norman

The essay you are about to read tells a surprising story. Eighty-three-year-old Herschel Collier, without knowing it, shows his grandson that dance can be an inspiration to people of any age. As you read, think about Herschel Collier. Why is his behavior surprising?

One morning about a month before he died, Grandad Collier and I were in the living room at the homeplace watching TV together. It was unusual for Grandad to watch TV at all, let alone that early in the morning. But, he'd been sick for several months; he hadn't been able to go outside very much. This was the first time he'd come out of his bedroom fully clothed in several days. I was drinking coffee and flipping through some old magazines and only half-watching the television. But, when Grandad came in dressed and shaved and apparently wanting a little society, I closed my magazine and turned the volume up, and the two of us settled in our chairs to watch the "Today" show.

The show had the usual news and weather reports and advertising and chit-chat among the announcers. But, finally, they got around to the feature part of the program, which that morning was a five-minute excerpt from a new film about village life in modern China.

This was in the days when film reports from China were exceedingly rare, especially on American television. This one had been made by a British crew who had been given access to one of the model agricultural communes. There were pictures of smiling Chinese working in the fields, of small children singing in school, of people going down a dirt road on bicycles. Grandad watched these scenes with moderate interest.

But when the film cut to pictures of a group of elderly Chinese men taking their exercise in a courtyard, Grandad's interest really came alive. He leaned forward in his chair and turned the sound up, then stayed forward with his face close to the screen. The old men looked right back at him, unsmiling. Their bodies moved in graceful unison through a routine that seemed to be a form of T'ai Chi. Stretching and turning, bending and posing, the old men moved with profound elegance through the series of gestures and poses. They were truly old men, the community of elders. Naked to the waist, their bodies were thin as the bodies of small boys. These men had lived long and seen much, and yet, their old faces had a strangely youthful aspect about them. They seemed relaxed and untroubled. The morning sun was shining on them. It was as if the sun was feeding them directly, making their bodies fluid, flexible, full of strength and grace.

Then, suddenly, the old Chinese men were gone. A commercial took their place. After a while, Grandad got up and went on back to his bedroom, and I didn't see him again until the early afternoon.

It was a day in early spring in Kentucky, when the mornings are overcast and cold, but when the afternoons are sunny and warm enough to go outside in your shirt sleeves. We'd been having sunny afternoons for several days, but so far my grandfather hadn't felt like going out. This particular day, however, about an hour after eating a bowl of soup in his room for lunch, Grandad put on his coat and sweater and went outside to stand in the sun alone. I watched him through the kitchen window as he strolled idly around the yard. He walked in a little circle that brought him back close to the house where the sun's reflection was brilliant and warm against the wall. He took his hands out of his pockets and looked rather furtively from side to side, making sure he was still alone. Then, slowly, he raised his arms above his head and stretched himself real good. He bent to one side, then the other, keeping his arms outstretched. Grandad stretched and turned; he bent and lowered his arms all in a flowing motion that became a dance as he kept it up. Herschel Collier, my grandfather, ex-logger, retired coal miner, hillside farmer, age eighty-three, was standing beside his house in the Kentucky mountains, in the sunshine of one of the last spring days of his life, doing the Trace Fork version of T'ai Chi.

Grandad must have danced fifteen minutes before he heard the screen door slam on the far side of the house.

Someone was coming.

Quickly he stuffed his hands back in his coat pockets and resumed his slow walk around the yard.

As far as I know, he never did T'ai Chi in the sun again.

1. What did Herschel Collier see on television that attracted his interest?

2. When Herschel Collier went outside in the afternoon, the author tells us that he "looked rather furtively from side to side." Why do you think he did this?

3. Why did Herschel Collier stop his dance when he heard the screen door slam?

4. The author gives several facts about Herschel Collier; for example, that he was an "ex-logger." Identify these facts and explain why they make Collier's T'ai Chi performance surprising.

5. People's actions often surprise us, and their actions always tell us more about them than their words. Think of something that someone you know has done that surprised or impressed you. Describe the person and his or her action. Tell why the action affected you as it did.

Dance is one of the oldest of the arts. For thousands of years, people have danced in celebration and for entertainment. But dance, like all the arts, must also be new if it is to capture your interest and fire your excitement. Twyla Tharp is one person who is keeping dance new and alive. As you read this biographical sketch, try to imagine the dances as they are described, and notice the way in which the author compares the dances with Twyla Tharp's unusual life.

A "superwoman of dance"? That's what one critic said. Another critic wrote, "I love Twyla Tharp. She is slinky and cool and outrageous." Twyla Tharp is a choreographer, or designer of dance, who peppers her dance notations with instructions like these: "fouettés (whipping ballet turns) wiggle wiggle," "toe-heel flick," "mosquito bite," and "cross-across scootch." In short, a Twyla Tharp is a whirlwind genius who makes exciting waves on the surface of the dance world. Her dances give audiences a rapid series of images that shine with thought, structure, and originality. They capture the mind as brilliantly as they excite the eye.

"I was never a little kid," Tharp says. "There was too much to accomplish, and too little time to learn." Small wonder! She began piano lessons at age two and violin at age four. At age six, she switched to viola and, soon after, added tap dance and acrobatics. Tharp recalls: "Nobody asked me if I wanted to. I either did it or ran away."

When she was nine, Twyla Tharp and her family moved from Indiana to California. They bought a drive-in movie theater. "I used to carhop in my folks' drive-in," she reports. Serving hundreds of people during the brief movie break was hard and exacting work. "I learned a lot about timing in that snack bar!"

While working, she also studied drums, baton twirling, shorthand, typing, and ballet. Strangely enough, she never went to a single dance. However, "pop" music fascinated her. It sounded like "wow!" "I got my pop influence from watching all those movies when I was a kid," she says.

Twyla Tharp began a premedical course at Pomona College. But soon after, the artistic roots deep in her nature began to flower. It was then that Twyla Tharp, the artist, went to New York City and earned a degree in art history from Barnard College. She also decided to study dance. Thus began the career of Twyla Tharp, an artist whose dances resemble her name: attention-getting, zippy, fun, and not to be forgotten.

What is so different about the Twyla Tharp dances? Why do they spice the imagination? Well, imagine this: Three women dancers in black, wearing reddish boots, perform a dazzling and complicated dance. The only "music" is the amplified sound of the dancers' boots on a stage that has microphones in numerous carefully selected locations.

Or what about this? Three dancers are poised in classical ballet costumes and toe shoes as the dance begins. Suddenly, a couple wearing sneakers and jeans races by, chasing, kicking, diving in a fury of happy energy. When they depart, the dance begins again. In pure Tharp style, two dancers sweep and flow in silken movement. There is an outpouring of sweetness and emotion. But do they fly offstage into the wings in the usual they-lived-happily-ever-after ballet leap? No. They have said it all; the dance is over. The male dancer puts one arm about the shoulders of the female dancer and they walk quietly off the stage. The music for this particular dance is Mozart's. The dance is called "Mud."

TWYLA THARP: "ART IS THE ONLY WAY TO RUN AWAY WITHOUT LEAVING HOME."

Now think about some of the other titles of Tharp's dances: "Eight Jelly Rolls," danced to very old Jelly Roll Morton jazz records; "All About Eggs," performed to a Bach Cantata; "Once More, Frank," a dance that uses recordings by Frank Sinatra.

Twyla Tharp's imagination is boundless. She combines the old and the new, the classical and the most outrageously modern elements. She also shows us how the old and the new borrow from each other and share common feelings. Furthermore, no matter how disorganized her dances may seem, they are all based on very serious structures. As she says, "Serious art does not have to torture to be serious art."

Tharp presents her dances without the air of mystery that so often surrounds an art form. She wants her audiences to understand and to participate in what is happening. Once she put the audience on stage with the dancers. In effect, she showed people not only the front, or "good" side of the dance, but also its back and its sides. The experience almost allowed the audience to walk around the dance. It was like walking around a piece of sculpture in an art museum.

No one can say that a Twyla Tharp dance is "a bore." They are never boring! They are different and exciting, but each has a careful design and continuity in spite of its razzle-dazzle. When Tharp has all the dancers fall in a heap at the end of a dance, she makes sure that the heap is beautifully structured. As still another critic wrote: "She sees dance as a shout of joy. . . . Her energy comes from the heart, not from the muscles. The very different, very peculiar, very wonderful Ms. Tharp . . . could put hummingbirds on a Christmas tree!"

And that's what a Twyla Tharp is.

1. What is a choreographer?
2. Twyla Tharp said that she "was never a little kid." What do you think she means by this statement?
3. Why do you think Twyla Tharp concentrated on making her dances surprising and unusual?
4. The author said: "Twyla Tharp is a whirlwind genius. . . Her dances give audiences a rapid series of images . . .' Explain how the style of her dances resembles the events of her life.
5. What kinds of dances have you seen on stage or on television? Explain what you think of them, and why.

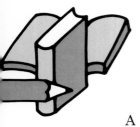

Biographies and Autobiographies

A *biography* is a book that tells about a person's life. The book is written by another individual. A biography might begin with facts about the person's childhood and then tell of the person's education, jobs, and experiences as an adult.

A biography usually describes the difficulties and achievements in the life of a person and tells what the person has contributed to society. Since the author has seen fit to write about the person, there is probably something special about the individual's life.

Biographies usually analyze the major qualities of the individual's personality. Often a biography gives proof of what is said about a person. The book may include quotes from the person being written about. The book may show letters or other documents written by that person. There may also be statements made by friends and family members.

Some biographies are approved by the person who is the subject of the book. The person cooperates fully in the research for the book. However, some biographies are not authorized. As you read a biography, try to decide why the author wrote it. Does the author praise or criticize the person in the book? Try to discover if the author is a close friend of the subject. Decide whether the writer has presented a fair picture of the individual.

An *autobiography* is a book a person writes about his or her own life. Use of the words *I*, *me*, *my*, and *mine* indicate that the author is reporting personal experiences.

The content of an autobiography is similar to the content of a biography. The life of a person is described. However, in an autobiography, since the author is writing from personal experience, you may learn more about the individual's personality. The reliability of facts depends on how honestly the person has told his or her own story.

You read stories about the lives of Susan Davidoff, Herschel Collier, and Twyla Tharp. These selections could not be called biographies, since they are not complete books. Instead they are called *biographical sketches*. The information in the articles is similar to the type of information you would find in a full biography.

ACTIVITY A   Answer these questions about the biographical sketch of Susan Davidoff. Use complete sentences.

1. At what age in Susan's childhood did the article begin?
2. What difficulties that Susan faces were discussed in the article?
3. What achievements that Susan makes did the article discuss?
4. What are the major qualities of Susan's personality which the article discussed?
5. Did the author seem to praise or criticize Susan? Write one sentence from the selection to support your answer.
6. Quotes of Susan were used to prove what the author said about her. Write one quote from Susan that supports a statement made by the author.

ACTIVITY B   Answer these questions about the biographical sketch of Herschel Collier. Use complete sentences.

1. What was the family relationship of the author to Herschel?
2. How much of Herschel's life did the author report?
3. Did the author seem to praise or criticize Herschel? Write one sentence from the selection to support your answer.

ACTIVITY C   Answer these questions about the biographical sketch of Twyla Tharp. Use complete sentences.

1. At what age in Twyla's childhood did the article begin?
2. What jobs, which Twyla held as a youngster, were reported in the article?
3. What achievements that Twyla makes did the article discuss?
4. What are the major qualities of Twyla's personality that the article discussed?
5. Did the author seem to praise or criticize Twyla? Write one sentence from the article to support your answer.
6. The author uses quotes from critics to describe Twyla. Write one quote which praises Twyla as a choreographer.

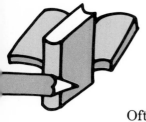

Poetic Imagery

Often when writers tell a story, they do not want you merely to understand the events. They want you to feel a part of the story. These writers use colorful words to describe each scene. They use many vivid adjectives and verbs. This detailed description makes it easier for you to imagine the situation. You may *sense* that you are experiencing the action yourself.

Words and phrases that appeal to your senses are called *poetic imagery*. The writers use words that appeal to one of the five senses: sight, smell, taste, touch, and hearing. Poetic imagery is often used by poets, but writers of prose may use it as well.

The article "Bravo Baryshnikov!" contained examples of poetic imagery. One sentence describing Baryshnikov told of "the extraordinary way he seems to hover in midair." That description appeals to the sense of *sight*. The words "hover in midair" create an image you can *see*.

Here are other examples of poetic imagery. The underlined words appeal to a particular sense.

The <u>sweet</u> scent of the roses filled the air. (appeals to smell)
We ate a <u>bitter</u> piece of cheese. (appeals to taste)
I shook his <u>hard, rough</u> hand <u>firmly</u>. (appeals to touch)
The chalk made a <u>loud, screechy</u> sound. (appeals to hearing)

Sometimes one image may appeal to two or more senses at once. For example,

How softly the music flows against the watersides. (appeals to sight and hearing)
She took a bite of the cold, hard ice. (appeals to taste and touch)

ACTIVITY A   Each of the following sentences contains poetic imagery. Write whether the imagery appeals to *sight*, *smell*, *taste*, *touch*, or *hearing*.

1. The children ate sweet and sour meatballs for dinner.
2. A cool, evening breeze brushed gently against our faces.
3. The airplane roared loudly over the airport.

4. Daisies and violets danced happily in the flower garden.
5. Michele held the soft, squirmy worm in her hand.
6. The firefighter fought the blaze in the strong, smoky air.
7. The hot, spicy meat tasted good with a tangy glass of juice.
8. A hive of bees buzzed across the ball field.
9. The woods are lovely, dark and deep.
10. The faint smell of sawdust lingered in the air.

ACTIVITY B   Each of the following sentences contains imagery appealing to two or more senses. Write the senses that the imagery appeals to.

1. The soft, cuddly rabbit hopped quickly on the log.
2. The steaming, hot cocoa burned our tongues.
3. And ever when the moon was low, the shrill winds were up and away.
4. Angry drivers blasted their horns in the standstill traffic.
5. Halt at the chattering brook in the tall green fern at the brink.
6. Sweet day, so cool, so calm, so bright!
7. Herman dragged the rough, wooden crate across the street.
8. The unpleasant, pungent odor made our eyes tear for a moment.
9. The sharp nail shredded the smooth, thin fabric of the sofa.
10. A honking flock of geese sailed over the glistening sea.

ACTIVITY C   Turn back to the selection "A Colorful Symphony." Write one sentence to show an example of each of the following kinds of poetic imagery.

1. an appeal to sight
2. an appeal to smell
3. an appeal to taste
4. an appeal to touch
5. an appeal to hearing

FRITZ SCHOLDER-

Painter of American Indians

The First One

Imagine for a moment that you are lost, whether in a forest, at sea, or in the streets of a city. Fortunately, you have a map with you. But before you can use the map to get where you want to go, you must figure out where you have been, and where you are now. You must orient yourself.

Another way to orient yourself is to learn about your heritage. To find out who you are, it helps to know about the history of your family, and of the community in which you are growing up. Fritz Scholder is a modern painter who, by learning about his heritage, has created some of today's most outstanding artwork.

This selection is a biographical sketch about the life of Fritz Scholder. A biography usually mixes facts—the known events, writings, and conversations in a person's life—with interpretations based on those facts. Biographers show you what a person has done, and make educated guesses about why the person did those things. As you read this biographical sketch, try to separate in your mind the facts from the author's opinions.

Fritz Scholder's heritage is one quarter English, one quarter French, one quarter German, and one quarter Southern California Mission Indian. As he was growing up, he thought little about his American Indian ancestors. His home was on the Minnesota/ North Dakota border. His neighborhood and way of life were totally removed from his father's Mission Indian background.

Fritz started painting in 1946 when he won a poster contest in fourth grade. Later his family moved to Pierre, South Dakota. Fritz studied art with Oscar Howe, an American Indian painter who had lived in Paris during World War II. In Paris, Howe had studied contemporary art. He taught Fritz that art could be exciting and serious, "that it was much more than painting pretty pictures." It was then, as a teenager, that Fritz Scholder discovered that he wanted to become a serious painter.

When the Scholder family moved to California, Fritz started college. He was fortunate enough to study with Wayne Thiebaud, one of the country's leading artists and teachers. Fritz recalls that Thiebaud "not only taught me a lot about painting, but about art history as well." Fritz received his bachelor's degree from Sacramento City College in 1960.

It was not until the young artist was in his twenties that he consciously became involved in American Indian culture. This happened when he was invited to participate in a new project conducted at the University of Arizona, at Tucson. Called the Rockefeller Project, it brought together a group of gifted young artists of American Indian background and aimed "to expose these artists to past and present art" and to explore new teaching methods in art. The school combined a complete knowledge of the American Indian heritage with the use of modern artistic materials.

At the program, Fritz was immersed in the American Indian heritage. He began to attend ceremonial dances at the pueblos near Santa Fe. He collected American Indian art. Fritz also became an instructor at the Institute of American Indian Arts in Santa Fe. His students were American Indians. His awareness of his own American Indian background grew.

Fritz Scholder came to realize that American Indian art closely paralleled the long and varied history of its creators. The early art objects were created as part of everyday life. Clothing, dwellings, and ceremonial objects were made from materials available in nature—feathers, fur, shells, and clay. Later, when silver and wool were introduced, one of the most beautiful periods of American Indian art followed.

In the early part of the twentieth century American Indian painting was done on paper with opaque watercolor. The paintings left a vivid and beautiful record of everyday and ceremonial

Indian with Feather Fan, February 1975, by Fritz Scholder

life. The extraordinary sense of design of American Indian art is found throughout the history of this culture.

But Fritz wanted to paint the American Indian in a new way. In 1967 he painted his first American Indian. He says that his work immediately startled people because he treated his subject differently than did other artists. More than three hundred more paintings of American Indians followed. The people were of all ages, in all forms of dress, and of a type never seen before.

Indian with Feather Fan is an example. The mood of this portrait is calm; the man seems as large, solid, and enduring as the high mountains of the American Southwest. Into this stillness Scholder throws offbeat patches of color: blue face and hands, a red scarf, a dull gold background. Why does he use color in such an unexpected way? Only the artist can give a final answer to this question, but it seems that Scholder *wants* to startle us. He wants to startle us enough to make us curious, and to make us curious enough to look deeply into what the portrait says about the spirit and heritage of American Indians.

Fritz Scholder uses powerful, vibrant colors and bold forms to bring the past and present into a single focus. He lets us view the past, and the potent spirit of American Indian culture, through a modern understanding. With respect, humor, and a deep knowledge of American Indians, he has revolutionized both the form and the content of American Indian art.

"What I most want is to be known as a painter," he says. Nevertheless, Fritz Scholder is happy to have influenced other American Indian painters, and he is deeply proud of his heritage.

1. What experiences helped spark Fritz Scholder's interest in American Indian art?

2. This biography states that Scholder seems to want to startle the people who view his paintings. What evidence does the biography offer to support this statement?

3. The selection describes Scholder's paintings as using "powerful, vibrant colors and bold forms." Look at Scholder's painting, *Indian with Feather Fan.* Describe the painting and state whether or not you agree with the description above, and why.

4. Find an example of a fact and an author's opinion within a paragraph in this selection. Explain how you identified the fact and how you identified the opinion.

FLOWERS

AND

BONES

Eleanor Clymer and Lillian Erlich

A talent *is any special ability a person has. You, for example, have many talents. But it is not enough just to have* talents. *As you grow up, you must learn to* develop *and* use *the talents you have.*

Georgia O'Keeffe is the subject of the following biography. She is a famous American painter. Much of her success is due to the single-minded energy with which she developed her talents. As you read, look for incidents in her life that reveal this dedication.

Georgia O'Keeffe is one of the greatest American painters. Her life has been so secluded and so completely dedicated to her art, that she seems a mysterious figure. Her meticulous, strangely beautiful pictures of flowers, skulls, and barren hills have been shown with little fanfare. Yet her influence has been great indeed. Modern art has been profoundly affected by the purity of color, the cleanness of line, and the intensity of feeling of Ms. O'Keeffe's paintings. Even the decoration of our homes and the commercial art work of our magazines reflect her influence.

Perhaps great painters are born with a special talent for *seeing*. Certainly from earliest childhood, Georgia O'Keeffe seems to have looked at the world with greater intensity than other people. When she looked at a flower, she saw not only its surface petals but its amazing inner architecture. She looked at grass and trees and hills with the same penetrating awareness.

The first landscape Georgia knew was that of the Wisconsin farm country. She was born in Sun Prairie. Her father was a farmer of Irish descent. On her mother's side, her forebears were Hungarian and Dutch. Part of Georgia's childhood was spent in Virginia, where she and her brothers and sisters lived in a large old-fashioned house. It was a family custom for

Mrs. O'Keeffe to read to her children every evening. She chose travel and history books, and sometimes stories about the Wild West. The last made a profound impression on Georgia, and she felt truly as though she "belonged" there, when she lived and taught in Texas years later.

Georgia decided to be an artist, or at least publicly announced this intention, when she was about ten years old and became fascinated with drawing roses and pansies. At about this time, she had art lessons at a convent school that she attended. The Sister who taught the class gave her students a plaster cast of a child's hand to copy. Georgia did a meticulous tiny drawing. Her teacher scolded her gently for making it so small. This may have influenced her to turn to drawing on a large scale. In fact, she was to become famous in later years for painting enormously magnified flowers.

In 1904, when Georgia finished high school, she enrolled at the Art Institute of Chicago, where she stayed a year. John Vanderpoel, who taught anatomy and structure there, impressed her greatly with his emphasis on "line." In 1907 and 1908, she studied in New York at the Art Students' League, where the emphasis of her teachers, William Merritt Chase and F. Luis Mora, was quite different. Here it was the beauty of paint, the endless wonderful possibilities of color that impressed her. Her fellow students regarded her, even then, with some awe. Her colors were always the brightest, her palette the cleanest in the class. They respected her almost furious powers of concentration and her independence. Although she loved to dance in those days, she often refused to go to parties, because going to bed late would mean daylight hours lost from painting the following day.

Georgia's maturing as an artist was slow, for she set extremely high standards for herself and was determined to find her own way of expressing her highly personal vision of the world around her. After art school, she went to Chicago where she spent several years as a free-lance commercial artist. Although she managed to support herself, she was not at all satisfied. If she could not serve art with complete integrity, she would not, she decided, serve it at all.

Georgia went home to Virginia, where her family then lived and announced that she was through with art forever. Nevertheless, the inner force that compelled her toward painting was not so easily blocked. One of her sisters was going to summer school at the University of Virginia, and Georgia decided to go along. She dropped in on an art class one day, just as an observer, and was so impressed by the teacher, Alon Bement, that she stayed as a student. Mr. Bement had worked with Arthur Dow of Columbia University, and was influenced by his ideas. Georgia was to study with Arthur Dow later, too. Both these men were of major importance in her life as an artist.

During that summer, she received a telegram inviting her to come to Amarillo, Texas, to supervise art instruction in the public schools there. Georgia went to Texas and found in its barren landscape a response to her deepest needs. "I belonged," she said later. "That was my country—terrible winds and a wonderful emptiness." It was still much like the pioneer country of her childhood dreams, with great open spaces, no paved roads, and no fences. Georgia's eyes drank in the distances.

"There was quiet and an untouched feel of the country," she wrote to a friend. "I could work as I pleased." Georgia even seemed to belong to this country physically. She looked like a pioneer woman, with her strong body; her long black hair, drawn straight back from her face; and her quiet deep-set eyes.

Georgia worked hard at her painting, but she was still dissatisfied.

One day she locked herself into a room and held a private exhibition of everything she had painted. She noted where she had been influenced by other painters and where she had expressed herself alone. She resolved to try harder than ever to put her own kind of truth on canvas.

In 1916, Georgia O'Keeffe sent a sheaf of her drawings to a friend, Anita Pollitzer, in New York. She and Ms. Pollitzer had been fellow students in art school and often sent each other letters and sketches. This time, Georgia got together ten drawings, titled them *Lines and Spaces in Charcoal,* and sent them for criticism to Anita with a stern warning that they must not be shown to anyone else. Anita was struck by the aliveness of the sketches and decided to disregard her friend's instructions. She took them to the one person who she knew should see them, Alfred Stieglitz, the famous photographer and guiding spirit of the 291 Gallery. Anita presented herself at the gallery on a rainy afternoon and found Stieglitz looking weary and discouraged. He took Georgia's drawings and spread them on the floor. His face lit up.

"Finally!" he exclaimed. "A woman on paper."

He hung the drawings in an exhibit without Georgia's knowledge or consent. She came to New York in 1917, and Stieglitz arranged a second exhibit. He became her champion, and later her husband. He helped to nourish her rare talent.

His great service to Georgia and to the other artists in his group was, by his belief in them, to make it possible for them to work freely in their own way.

Georgia became a prolific painter. She seldom painted a human figure or a face. Instead, she did dramatic closeups of flowers in which she seemed to explore their innermost recesses. She painted great irises, morning glories, petunias, and calla lillies. So meticulous was her artistic skill, that she made six versions of a single jack-in-the-pulpit, each time trying to catch still another aspect of the flower. She explained simply, "I am expressing what I saw in a flower which apparently others failed to see." She painted the barren landscapes she loved. She painted hard forms—rocks and skulls bleached by the sun and worn smooth by the wind. She was a perfectionist in all she did, striving always to eliminate and condense. She used colors with great intensity and purity, with much immaculate white and velvety black.

The Stieglitz apartment in New York was simple and almost empty. There were no pictures on the walls. Georgia once told a friend,

"I like an empty wall, because I can imagine what I like on it." As the years went on, she divided her time between New York and New Mexico, where she spent summers in an adobe house with superb views of the luminous empty landscape. There she said, "The desert, the ocean, high mountains—these are my world."

In 1946 Alfred Stieglitz died. Georgia devoted most of the following three years to sorting and classifying his immense collection of paintings and photographs. She sent them, as she felt he would have wished, to various art centers throughout the country, for the public to see. Only when she had finished this task, did she return to New Mexico, free to work at her painting.

Georgia O'Keeffe continued to work with a kind of blazing integrity that is reflected in each of her canvases. She said, "I found that I could say things with colors and shapes that I could not say in any other way. Things that I had no words for." Our world is richer because she made her long and difficult search—and found the one way that she could best communicate her vision.

1. Why was Georgia O'Keeffe slow to mature as an artist?

2. Compare these two comments made by Georgia O'Keeffe. Of the Texas landscape, she said: "There was a quiet and an untouched feel of the country . . . I could work as I pleased." Of her New York apartment, she said: "I like an empty wall, because I can imagine what I like on it." How are these comments alike?

3. The authors suggested that "great painters are born with a special talent for *seeing*." What do you think this statement means?

4. Choose two incidents from Georgia O'Keeffe's life that describe her constant desire to perfect her art.

5. Choose an ordinary object and look at it closely. What words would you choose to describe the object? Try describing the object in detail.

One Night Stand

A LIFE IN COLLAGE

Have you ever made a collage? A collage is an art form made by pasting paper, cloth, or other materials onto a surface. The result can be startling, serious, or just plain fun. Romare Bearden is a modern artist who works with collage. As you read this biographical sketch, observe how Romare Bearden's life resembles one of his collages.

A big, gentle, almost shy man, Romare Bearden combines faces, expressions, and the spirit of American black people in his collages. In his work he tries to find out what he, as a black American, has in common with all people.

The artist's life is as varied and textured as one of his own collages. In fact, if we were to make a collage that represents Bearden's life, we might first paste down a stethoscope, since the artist studied medicine at New York University. Next, we might place a slide rule across this medical symbol, because one day, as he began to dissect a frog, he suddenly realized that medicine was not for him. He decided to switch to mathematics. Then we might paste a cartoon figure in the background, since he became interested in cartooning, and edited the school's humor magazine, *New York University Medley*. Finally, speaking of medley, we could paste a sheet of music at an interesting angle under the slide rule: he loved music and wrote songs.

Our collage itself represents Bearden's next step: he enrolled in New York's Art Students' League and studied there.

Bearden's artistic genius blossomed from this mixture of medicine, math, and music. His love of music is often reflected in his work. A group of collage paintings called *Of the Blues*, presents his visual history of the blues. Rhythms, tones, even the moods of the music Bearden loved are there on canvas: Duke Ellington, Fats Waller, Jelly Roll Morton, and Louis Armstrong are all shown and viewed as a whole. The artist has done for our eyes what the great jazz musicians have done for our ears.

Romare Bearden has fulfilled his goal brilliantly. His collage paintings come alive with the rich and varied textures of the life of black America. His work touches others by showing his heritage as it is—a significant part of the total culture of America.

1. What is a collage?
2. Why is a stethoscope a symbol of medicine and a slide rule a symbol of mathematics?
3. Explain how Romare Bearden's life resembles one of his collages.
4. What symbols (pictures of events or people, objects, or shapes) would you choose to make a collage of your life?

KOSS CHILDREN-
PROFESSIONAL ARTISTS

Chris Aull, 11   Gilbert Giles, 13   Felicia Kornbluch, 10

Wlodek and Tomira Koss are a brother and sister. Their names are not the only unusual thing about them. They are already professional artists at the age of twelve and thirteen. This is the record of an interview they gave to three young reporters who work for a magazine called *Children's Express*. As you read, see if you can tell how Wlodek and Tomira feel about their work.

Wlodek Koss, Age 12

I started painting five years ago. My first painting was very simple—a skyline.

When we have the big paintings we roll them up. You can't make a 190-foot long painting here, so we make it in stages. We do one piece and then we roll it up and do another piece. We did sort of studies for it. Like this painting here is going to be twenty-four feet, but so far it's only twelve feet. So there's another piece coming to it. It's a whole painting.

I do abstracts, some portraits, and realistic works like fishes and animals. We developed our styles over a period of five years. We changed to abstract.

I sold a painting to the McGraw Hill Building and Union Carbide. It hangs in the lobby.

My biggest painting was 190 feet long and five feet wide. It's rolled in the hall.

Tomira Koss, Age 13

My father was working on paintings, so we wanted to work also. First we did drawings upon drawings and then we wanted to paint.

My biggest painting was forty-eight feet tall. It took about three months. Very long . . . it's one piece of canvas. It had to be done in sixteen stages. It's right out of our heads. It's our styles. If we make a mistake or anything, we just work on it, change it.

Tomira Koss, 13/ *Mother,*
1972 (New York) 18″ x 24″

Wlodek Koss, 12/ *Rainbow Island,*
1976 (New York) 24' x 6'7"

Tomira Koss, 13/ *Mother Series,*
1976 (New York) 8' x 11'4"

I was inspired by the buildings at first and then I changed to faces because I liked that.

One time I sold a painting and the people who bought it didn't know that I was a kid. And then we sent them a letter and told them I was a kid and they said that's okay. I mean they didn't buy it because I was a kid, they bought it because they liked the work.

I have a lot of paintings that I like a lot, that I wouldn't sell, even if someone wanted to buy them. It would be fun to see them hanging in museums so everyone else sees them.

1. What kinds of paintings does Wlodek Koss do?

2. Tomira Koss was very pleased that the purchasers of one of her paintings "didn't buy it because I was a kid, they bought it because they liked the work." Explain why she was so pleased by this fact.

3. How do you think the Koss children feel about their artwork?

ARMINDO MIRANDA BEATS 38,000 IN POSTER CONTEST

Deborah Orin

Armindo Miranda, 11 and legally blind, starts a new work, with his prize-winning poster beside him for inspiration.

Belief is a powerful force. If you want to do something, and believe you can do it, you can overcome almost any obstacle. Armindo Miranda, at the age of eleven, has already proved what talent and determination can do.

As you read this newspaper article, think about what kind of person Armindo is. What personal qualities have earned him success?

Armindo Miranda, 11, is legally blind, but he had the artistic vision to win the grand prize in a nationwide poster contest, topping entries from nearly 38,000 youngsters.

Armindo's eye problems were not made known to the judges of the American Automobile Association's annual traffic safety poster contest.

"I like to draw, I like to make things out of clay—like men and ships and some boats," explained Armindo, an engaging boy with blond hair, hazel eyes and lacy eyelashes.

With his face bent very close to the paper, he was busy painting scenery for a puppet show at the Layelle School for the blind and visually handicapped in the Bronx, where he's a sixth grader.

Legally blind means that even with glasses, Armindo's vision is no better than 20:200—able to see at twenty feet what others can see from 200 feet. He will never drive a car, and he cannot read ordinary street signs.

But that doesn't stop Mindo, as his family and friends call him, from drawing intricate imaginary machines, putting together model planes and ships, watching TV from up close, and dreaming of one day becoming a scientist.

"I want to be the kind of scientist who looks at things, in the future 'cause I like to look at things and examine them," said Mindo, who also thinks he might like to design rockets and space ships.

Winning the contest meant $650 in bonds—banked for his education—and the chance to have his work sent to classrooms around the country as part of the AAA's traffic safety program, a prospect that left Mindo "a little bit excited, well, make that a lot."

His poster warns children to "play away from traffic." It shows a husky young football player in an orange jersey playing a good distance from a line of cars behind a safety fence.

"I just watched some kids on my block play football," said Mindo, who made the poster of paper cutouts—"I drew it in and then cut it right through the lines."

When kids on his block in the Laconia section of the Bronx ask how he can draw when he has limited vision, Armindo doesn't say anything: "I only get chalk and I draw on the streets."

Once, recalled his mother, Iredel, Armindo covered the sidewalk "from one corner to the other" with drawings of spaceships in washable pastels. And he also teaches his younger siblings—Tammy, 8, Victor, 5, and Davina, 2—how to draw.

"A lot of people don't realize how much blind people can do," said Carmine Pluchino, who teaches art to Mindo at the private, state-supported, nonsectarian Lavelle School.

"When we got the brochure about the contest," Pluchino added, "I asked the kids if they wanted to try, knowing they'd be judged with sighted children. And they said, 'We've got nothing to lose.' "

1. What does "legally blind" mean?
2. The article mentioned that Armindo's eye problems were not made known to the judges of the poster contest. Why do you think the author included this fact in the article?
3. In the first sentence, the author compared Armindo's limited vision with his *artistic* vision. Explain what artistic vision is.
4. What personal qualities helped Armindo to succeed? Support your answers with examples from the text.
5. If you entered a traffic safety poster contest, what event from your everyday experience would you portray?

Figures of Speech

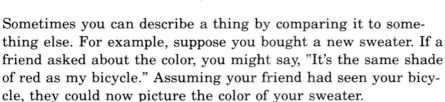

Sometimes you can describe a thing by comparing it to something else. For example, suppose you bought a new sweater. If a friend asked about the color, you might say, "It's the same shade of red as my bicycle." Assuming your friend had seen your bicycle, they could now picture the color of your sweater.

Writers sometimes use comparisons to help their readers picture things. These comparisons are called *figures of speech*. Figures of speech are colorful and vivid expressions.

Two kinds of figures of speech are similes and metaphors. A *simile* is an expression using *like* or *as* to compare two different things. Here is a simile used in the selection "A Colorful Symphony":

> The world looked like an enormous coloring book that had never been used.

In this simile the world is compared to a coloring book. The word *like* is used in the comparison.

A *metaphor* is an expression using only a form of the verb *be* to compare two different things. The same example above, written as a metaphor, would look like this:

> The world was an enormous coloring book that had never been used.

In this metaphor the world is compared to a coloring book. The word *was* is used, without *like* or *as*.

A third type of figure of speech is personification. *Personification* is an expression in which human characteristics are given to a nonhuman object. The following personification appears in "A Colorful Symphony":

> The musicians played on, faster and faster, and the purple sun raced quickly across the sky.

In this personification the sun is given human qualities. It seems like a person running very fast.

ACTIVITY A   Read each figure of speech. On your paper, write whether it is a *simile* or a *metaphor.* Then write the two things being compared.

Example: The crowd's cheer was as loud as an explosion.
Answer: Simile. The cheer is compared to an explosion.

1. She is as lovely as the ocean at dawn.
2. His troubles were a brick wall in front of him.
3. Their voices were like the soft strains of violins.
4. The pounding of her heart was a loud, steady drum beat.
5. The trees were guardians of the forest that night.
6. One day in the hot desert seemed like a thousand years.
7. No man is an island.
8. The boy ran like a frightened rabbit.

ACTIVITY B   Read each personification. Write the object which has been given human qualities and tell what it seems to be.

Example: The wind laughed throughout the night.
Answer: The wind seems like a person who is laughing.

1. The old car had to lie down and rest on the highway.
2. The angry waves pounded and hammered at the ship.
3. Tall trees stood proudly in the petrified forest.
4. The waters of the river raced toward the ocean.
5. The face of the moon smiled down on me.
6. The flames hid themselves in shame after the fire.
7. The sea washed her long fingers in silvery light.
8. A rose danced happily in the flower garden.

ACTIVITY C   Read each figure of speech. Write whether it is a *simile,* a *metaphor,* or a *personification.*

Example: The car horns were a symphony of music.
Answer: Metaphor

1. A single leaf struggled to escape from the tree branch.
2. Our faces were as red as a bunch of apples.
3. Does a dream deferred dry up like a raisin in the sun?
4. Her enthusiasm was the spark that ignited our team.
5. Bad habits are hazards to avoid on the road of life.
6. The breeze playfully tickled our feet at the beach.
7. Your worries are grains of sand compared to mine.

Reading a Time Line

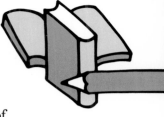

One way to learn about the past is by reading paragraphs of information. Another way is by reading a time line. A *time line* is a line marked with dates. Next to each date is an entry that names an important event that happened at that time.

You read an article about the life of Georgia O'Keeffe. The following time line indicates important events in her life. The information comes from the selection you read and from other sources.

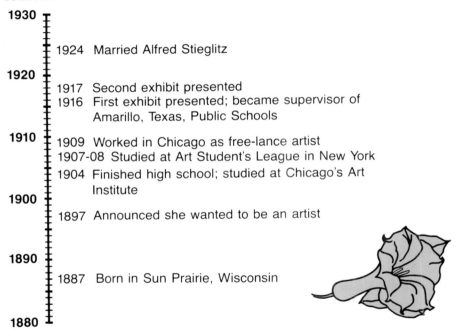

1930
1924 Married Alfred Stieglitz

1920
1917 Second exhibit presented
1916 First exhibit presented; became supervisor of Amarillo, Texas, Public Schools

1910
1909 Worked in Chicago as free-lance artist
1907-08 Studied at Art Student's League in New York
1904 Finished high school; studied at Chicago's Art Institute

1900
1897 Announced she wanted to be an artist

1890
1887 Born in Sun Prairie, Wisconsin

1880

Notice the small marks that appear on the line between the dates. Each mark represents one year. The larger marks represent five years.

Time lines are used not only to show events in a person's life. They are also used to show important happenings during a period of history. By studying a time line, you can see the order of historic events. You can also see how much time separated given events.

ACTIVITY A   Study the time line on the previous page. Write the answers to these questions on your paper.

1. In what year was Georgia O'Keeffe born?
2. How old was Georgia when she announced her desire to become an artist?
3. Where did Georgia first study after high school?
4. How many years passed between Georgia's high school graduation and her first art exhibit?
5. How many years did Georgia study at the Art Students' League in New York?
6. What important event in Georgia's life occurred the same year she had her first art exhibit?
7. How many years passed between Georgia's first and second art exhibits?
8. When and where did Georgia work as a free-lance artist?
9. How old was Georgia when she married Alfred Stieglitz?
10. What is the last year indicated on the time line?

ACTIVITY B   Read the following paragraph. Then draw a time line that indicates the events mentioned in the paragraph.

Many important events occurred in the United States between 1787 and 1814. In 1787, the Founding Fathers wrote the Constitution. The first United States political parties began to develop in 1790. Three years later, in 1793, Eli Whitney invented the cotton gin. Washington, D.C., became the national capital in 1800. In 1803, the Louisiana Purchase doubled the size of the United States. Later, in 1811, work began on the National Road, which eventually linked the East and the Midwest. The War of 1812 broke out a year later and lasted through 1814. In 1814, Francis Scott Key wrote "The Star-Spangled Banner."

ACTIVITY C   Choose one of the following people listed below. Find information about the person in an encyclopedia or other reference source. Draw a time line that indicates at least five important events that occurred in the person's life.

Fritz Scholder   Twyla Tharp
Romare Bearden   Antonio Brico
Susan Davidoff   Georgia O'Keeffe (after 1924)

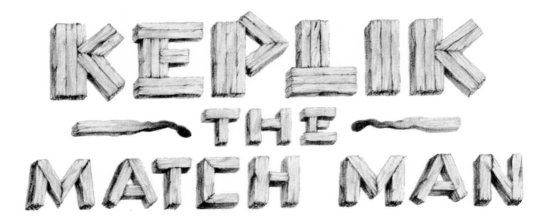

KEPLIK THE MATCH MAN

Myron Levoy

Do you knit or sew? Do you like to fix or build things? When you have a pencil or pen in your hand, do you find yourself doodling and drawing pictures? Most people seem to have an urge to use their hands. Perhaps the great artists are people who can't stop doodling or building or shaping—people who must have tools in hand and a project in mind to be happy. As you read this short story, ask yourself why Keplik loves to work with his hands.

There once was a little old man who lived in a big old tenement on Second Avenue. His name was Mr. Keplik and he had once been a watchmaker. In the window of his

tiny watch-repair shop he had put up a sign that read: WHEN YOUR WRIST WATCH WON'T TICK, IT'S TIME FOR KEPLIK. Keplik loved watches and clocks and had loved repairing them. If a clock he was repairing stopped ticking he would say to himself, "Eh, eh, eh, it's dying." And when it started ticking again he would say, "I am *gebentsht*. I am blessed. It's alive."

Whenever an elevated train rumbled by overhead, Keplik would have to put down his delicate work, for his workbench and entire shop would shake and vibrate. But Keplik would close his eyes and say, "Never mind. There are worse things. How many people back in Lithuania wouldn't give their right eye to have a watch-repair shop under an el train in America."

While he worked Keplik never felt lonely, for there were always customers coming in with clocks and watches and complaints.

"My watch was supposed to be ready last week," a customer would say. "I need my watch! Will you have it ready by tonight, Keplik?"

And Keplik would answer, "Maybe yes, maybe no. It depends on how many el trains pass by during the rush hour." And he would point his finger up toward the el structure above.

But when Keplik grew very old, he had to give up watch repairing, for he could no longer climb up and down the three flights of stairs to his apartment. He became very lonely, for there were no longer any customers to visit him and complain. And his hands felt empty and useless for there were no longer any gears or pivots or hairsprings or mainsprings to repair. "Terrible," said Keplik, to himself. "I'm too young to be old. I will take up a hobby. Perhaps I should build a clock out of walnut shells. Or make a rose garden out of red crepe paper and green silk. Or make a windmill out of wooden matchsticks. I'll see what I have in the house."

There were no walnuts and no crepe paper, but there were lots and lots of burned matchsticks, for, in those days, the gas stoves had to be lit with a match every time you wanted a scrambled egg or a cup of hot cocoa. So Keplik started to build a little windmill out of matches.

Within a month's time, the windmill was finished. Keplik put it on his kitchen table and started to blow like the east wind. The arms turned slowly, then faster, just like a real windmill. "I'm *gebentsht*," said Keplik. "Its alive."

Next, Keplik decided to make a castle, complete with a drawbridge. But the matches were expensive; he would need hundreds and hundreds for a castle. So he put a little sign outside his apartment door, and another in his window: USED MATCHSTICKS BOUGHT HERE. A PENNY FOR FIFTY. IF YOU HAVE A MATCHSTICK, SELL IT TO KEPLIK.

The word spread up and down the block very quickly, and soon there were children at Keplik's door with bags and boxes of used matches. Keplik showed them the windmill on the kitchen table and invited them to blow like the east wind. And Keplik was happy, because he had visitors again and lots of work for his hands.

Day after day, week after week, Keplik glued and fitted the matches together. And finally the castle stood completed, with red and blue flags flying from every turret. The children brought toy soldiers and laid siege to the castle, while Keplik pulled up the drawbridge.

Next, Keplik made a big birdcage out of matches, and put a real canary in it. The bird sang and flew back and forth while the delicate cage swung on its hook. "Ah ha," said Keplik. "The cage is alive. And so is the canary. I am double *gebentsht*."

Then he made little airplanes and jewelry boxes from matchsticks and gave them to the boys and girls who visited him. And the children began calling him "the Match Man."

One day, Keplik decided that it was time for a masterpiece. "I am at my heights as an artist," Keplik said to himself. "No more windmills. No more birdcages. I am going to make the Woolworth Building. Or the Eiffel Tower. Or the Brooklyn Bridge. Eh . . . eh . . . but which?"

And after much thought he decided that a bridge would be better than a tower or a skyscraper, because if he built a bridge he wouldn't have to cut a hole in the ceiling. The Brooklyn Bridge would be his masterpiece. It would run across the living room from the kitchen to the bedroom, and the two towers would stand as high as his head. "For this I need matches!" Keplik said aloud. "Matches! I must have matches."

And he posted a new sign: MATCH FOR MATCH, YOU CANNOT MATCH KEPLIK'S PRICE FOR USED MATCHES. ONE CENT FOR FIFTY. HURRY! HURRY! HURRY!

Vincent DeMarco, who lived around the corner, brought fifty matches that very afternoon, and Cathy Dunn and Noreen Callahan brought a hundred matches each the next morning. Day after day, the matches kept coming, and day after day, Keplik the Match Man glued and fixed and bent and pressed the matches into place.

The bridge was so complicated that Keplik had decided to build it in separate sections, and then join all the sections afterward. The bridge's support towers, the end spans, and the center span slowly took shape in different parts of the room. The room seemed to grow smaller as the bridge grew larger. A masterpiece, thought Keplik. There is no longer room for me to sit in my favorite chair. But I must have more matches! It's time to build the cables!

Even the long support cables were made from matchsticks, split and glued and twisted together. Keplik would twist the sticks until his fingers grew numb. Then he would go into the kitchen to make a cup of coffee for himself, not so much for the coffee, but for the fact that lighting the stove would provide him with yet another matchstick. And sometimes, as he was drinking his coffee, he would get up and take a quick look at the bridge, because it always looked different when he was away from it for awhile. "It's beginning to be alive," he would say.

And then one night, it was time for the great final step. The towers and spans and cables all had to be joined together to give the finished structure. A most difficult job. For everything was supported from the cables above, as in a real bridge, and all the final connections had to be glued and tied almost at the same moment. Nothing must shift or slip for a full half hour, until the glue dried thoroughly.

Keplik worked carefully, his watchmaker's hands steadily gluing and pressing strut after strut, cable after cable. The end spans were in place. The center span was ready. Glue, press, glue, press. Then suddenly, an el train rumbled by outside. The ground trembled, the old tenement shivered as it always did, the windows rattled slightly, and the center span slid from its glued moorings. Then one of the end cables vibrated loose, then another, and the bridge slipped slowly apart into separate spans and towers. "Eh, eh, eh," said Keplik. "It's dying."

Keplik tried again, but another train hurtled past from the other direction. And again the bridge slowly slipped apart. I am too tired, thought Keplik. I'll try again tomorrow.

Keplik decided to wait until late the next night, when there would be fewer trains. But again, as the bridge was almost completed, a train roared past, the house shook, and everything slipped apart. Again and again, Keplik tried, using extra

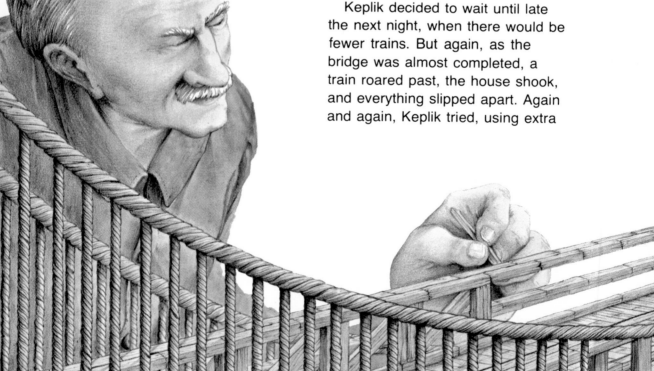

supports and tying parts together. But the bridge seemed to enjoy waiting for the next train to shake it apart again.

Ah me, thought Keplik. All my life those el trains shook the watches in my hands, down below in my shop. All my life I said things could be worse; how many people back in Lithuania wouldn't give their left foot to have a watch-repair shop under an el train in America.

But why do the el trains have to follow me three flights up? Why can't they leave me alone in my old age? When I die, will there be an el train over my grave? Will I be shaken and rattled around while I'm trying to take a little well-deserved snooze? It's much too much for me. This is it. The end. The bridge will be a masterpiece in parts. The Brooklyn Bridge after an earthquake.

At that moment, another el train roared by and Keplik the Match Man called toward the train, "One thing I'll *never* do! I'll never make an el train out of matches! Never! How do you like *that*!"

When the children came the next afternoon, to see if the bridge was finished at last, Keplik told them of his troubles with the el trains. "The bridge, my children, is *farpotshket*. You know what that means? A mess!"

The children made all sorts of suggestions: hold it this way, fix it

463

that way, glue it here, tie it there. But to all of them, Keplik the Match Man shook his head. "Impossible. I've tried that. Nothing works."

Then Vincent DeMarco said, "My father works on an el station uptown. He knows all the drivers he says. Maybe he can get them to stop the trains."

Keplik laughed. "Ah, such a nice idea. But nobody can stop the Second Avenue el."

"I'll bet my father can," said Vincent.

"Bet he can't," said Joey Basuto. And just then, a train sped by: raketa, raketa, raketa, raketa, raketa. "The trains never stop for nothing," said Joey.

And the children went home for dinner, disappointed that the bridge made from all their matchsticks was farpoot . . . farbot *whatever* that word was. A mess.

Vincent told his father, but Mr. DeMarco shrugged. "No. Impossible. Impossible," he said. "I'm not important enough."

"But couldn't you try?" pleaded Vincent.

"I know one driver. So what good's that, huh? One driver. All I do is make change in the booth."

"Maybe he'll tell everybody else."

"*Assurdità.* Nonsense. They have more to worry about than Mr. Keplik's bridge. Eat your soup!"

But Mr. DeMarco thought to himself that if he did happen to see his friend, the driver, maybe, just for a laugh, he'd mention it . . .

Two days later, Vincent ran upstairs to Keplik's door and knocked. *Tonight* his father had said! Tonight at one A.M.! Keplik couldn't believe his ears. The trains would stop for his bridge? It couldn't be. Someone was playing a joke on Vincent's father.

But that night, Keplik prepared, just in case it were true. Everything was ready: glue, thread, supports, towers, spans, cables.

A train clattered by at five minutes to one. Then silence. Rapidly, rapidly, Keplik worked. Press, glue, press, glue. One cable connected. Two cables. Three. Four. First tower finished. Fifth cable connected. Sixth. Seventh. Eighth. Other tower in place. Now gently, gently. Center span in position. Glue, press, glue, press. Tie threads. Tie more threads. Easy. Easy. Everything balanced. Everything supported. Now please. No trains till it dries.

The minutes ticked by. Keplik was sweating. Still no train. The bridge was holding. The bridge was finished. And then, outside the window, he saw an el train creeping along, slowly, carefully: cla . . . keta . . . cla . . . keta . . . cla . . . keta . . .

Then another, moving slowly from the other direction: cla . . . keta . . . cla . . . keta . . .

And Keplik shouted to the drivers of the trains, "Thank you! Tomorrow,

I am going to start a great new masterpiece! The Second Avenue el from Fourteenth Street to Delancey Street! Thank you for slowing up your trains!"

And first one driver, then the other, blew the train whistle as the trains moved on, into the night beyond. "Ah, how I am *gebentsht*," said Keplik to himself. "In America there are kind people everywhere. All my life, the el train has shaken my hands. But tonight, it has shaken my heart."

Keplik worked for the rest of the night on a little project. And the next morning, Keplik hung this sign made from matches outside his window, where every passing el train driver could see it:

1. Why was Keplik unable to finish his bridge?
2. Why do you think the el train drivers decided to help Keplik?
3. What special pleasure did Keplik get from working with his hands?
4. What did Keplik mean when he said: "All my life, the el train has shaken my hands. But tonight, it has shaken my heart"?
5. The watches that Keplik repaired were "alive" because they ticked. Keplik's windmill was "alive" because it moved like a real windmill. The matchstick bridge, however, did not move. Why did Keplik feel that it, too, was "alive"?

Spirit's Flight, *1970, is of Serpentine and Carrara marble. It shows Noguchi's careful combination of materials.*

Sky mirror, *1967, is of basalt. Its gleaming slanted top plateau contrasts with a rough columnar surface.*

In the studio, a lampland of standing and hanging lights, called akari, *Japanese for illumination.*

In Noguchi's Studio

ISAMU NOGUCHI

Many years ago a small boy named Isamu Noguchi, who lived in a seaside village in Japan, shaped a lump of clay into a wave. The small clay sculpture seemed almost to move with the energy of an ocean wave.

Isamu Noguchi became a well-known sculptor. As you read this biographical sketch, think about Noguchi's unusual approach to sculpture, an approach that has become an exciting new force in American art.

When Isamu Noguchi's mother realized that her small son had a talent for making things with his hands, she arranged for him to study with a carpenter. The little boy enjoyed shaping and carving the wood. He liked to free the forms he saw hidden inside the wood.

While still a young boy, Isamu was sent to America. When he finished high school, he studied sculpting with Gutzon Borglum, a Connecticut sculptor. The talented youth quickly learned to shape stone and wood into statues of famous people. However, Isamu believed there was a new and different way to shape the stone and wood. He knew that any skilled sculptor can reproduce subjects in stone, wood, or metal. But the feeling, the impression, the *idea* of the subject was still held prisoner in the unmoving *medium* in which the artist sculpted. Isamu wanted to free this natural essence. He wanted to sculpt ideas.

Sometime later Isamu visited a New York art gallery where he saw a sculpture by Constantin Brancusi called *Bird in Space*. It did not look like a bird, but it expressed the *idea* of flying. Isamu realized instantly that the sculptor shared his own dream. But even better, Brancusi had made the dream a reality.

Isamu desperately wanted to study with Brancusi, but the artist lived and worked in Paris. His goal seemed impossible. However, Harry F. Guggenheim had seen some of Isamu's work and suggested that Isamu apply for a Guggenheim Fellowship. This famous fellowship provided money for talented young students to study abroad.

Isamu Noguchi

The great photographer Alfred Stieglitz also admired Isamu's sculpture. Stieglitz encouraged young artists who were experimenting with new art forms. Ten years before, in 1917, he had discovered the painting of Georgia O'Keeffe. He had encouraged her work and had ultimately married the famous painter. Stieglitz's recommendation helped Isamu to win the important fellowship.

Noguchi went to Paris and began to work for Brancusi in 1927. He learned special new uses of the sculptor's tools—the chisel, the saw, the mallet, the file. He met other young artists who were exploring unusual ways of communicating their ideas in new art forms. Perhaps most important, Noguchi learned that constant attention to work is the key to achievement. His work became his life.

As the artist developed his techniques and skills, he learned an exciting thing about himself. Each time he saw a piece of wood, metal, or stone, he immediately realized the unique form or idea held captive inside. He had learned just how to shape the material to free that hidden idea.

Isamu Noguchi is called "the purest of living sculptors." His sense of space and scale is perhaps unequaled by any other modern artist. His work has broadened the horizon, opening the door for the many new forms of art which we see in the United States today. Noguchi's range of works is broad indeed: He has designed parks and playgrounds, outdoor sculpture, gardens, fountains, and public plazas in some of the world's busiest cities. He has expressed his genius for working with light by making "akari" (Japanese for *light*) lanterns of unusual quality and beauty.

Noguchi has also contributed vitality and change to other art forms. He worked closely with dancer/choreographer, Martha Graham. Noguchi's sculptural "landscapes" for dance have changed the concept of stage sets. As the dancers move through and around the pieces of sculpture, the dance develops new dimension. As the dance unfolds, the sculpture almost seems to come alive.

Cave of the Heart, *1946*
Martha Graham with the sculpture designed by Noguchi.

The magic of Isamu Noguchi has touched other art forms as well as those who view his work.

The artist's sculptures are mostly in stone and wood. Noguchi believes that stone is closer to the ancients, that stone is earth. These natural materials seemed more responsive to his vision of art than most other materials.

While working on a project in Japan some years ago, Noguchi completed a stone sculpture that he called *The Wave*. It expresses the force of the moving sea, the rush of the tide, the spray of foam. It even soothes the eye with a calm, smooth surface of still water seen in the sculpture. The artist was immensely satisfied when it was completed. *The Wave* finished the work of the small boy who, so many years before, tried to free the idea of a wave from a small lump of clay.

1. Why did Isamu Noguchi want to study with Constantin Brancusi?

2. How did Isamu's mother realize that her small son had a talent for making things with his hands?

3. Why do you think Noguchi was especially satisfied when he completed the stone sculpture *The Wave*?

4. The author says: "Each time he saw a piece of wood, metal, or stone, he immediately realized the unique form or idea held captive inside." What does this statement mean?

5. A *realistic* painting or sculpture represents what an artist sees, much as a photograph does. An *abstract* painting or sculpture expresses an idea or feeling in an artist's mind. Is Noguchi a realistic or an abstract artist? Why do you think so?

6. Compare Noguchi with Keplik, the Match Man, whose matchstick creations always became "alive." Do you think the two artists are trying to achieve the same goal? Why or why not?

"LET'S BREAK TRADITION"

What skills does an artist need? Artists need to know how to use their tools and materials. Sculptors, for example, need to know how to use the tools of sculpture—chisels, hammers, welding torches. They also need to understand the strengths, weaknesses, and special qualities of their material, be it wood, stone, or metal. But most important, they need to be creative. It is creativity, a special artistic vision, that transforms a block of stone or pieces of wood into works of art. As you read this biographical sketch of sculptor Louise Nevelson, notice how much she respects and enjoys creativity.

Nine-year-old Louise Nevelson had gone to the library with a friend to get a book. The librarian asked her what she was going to be when she grew up—a traditional adult question.

Louise Nevelson recalls: "I said, 'I'm going to be an artist.' 'No,' I added. I want to be a sculptor; I don't want color to help me.'" Louise was so frightened by her unexpected answer that she ran home crying. She asks, "How did I know that, when I never even thought of it before in all my life?"

Throughout her long and creative life as a sculptor, Louise Nevelson has proved how true her early prediction was. In addition, she has continued to break tradition brilliantly both as an artist and as a woman.

Louise's father, an emigré from Kiev, Russia, opened a lumberyard in Rockland, Maine, where Louise grew up. Perhaps her choice of wood as a sculptor's medium was influenced by her early environment. However, she first began working with old wood during World War II when materials were very scarce. She says, "I knew the creative act was more important than the materials, so I picked up anything."

Indeed she did! She gathered and collected constantly. She was always on the look-out for fragments of wood that had been thrown away. She brought home chair backs, brush handles, weathered boards, architectural scroll-work—even sweepings and slivers from the carpenter's floor. A favorite treasure was a heavy old wooden bannister from a school. Such odds and ends became the distinctive wood vocabulary through which she expressed her sculptor's ideas and created works resembling collages in wood.

Louise's family recognized and supported her talent and ambition. It wasn't until Louise Nevelson was in her fifties, however, that the art world finally accepted her remarkable and nontraditional concept of the sculptor's art.

She created "table landscapes"—columns, boxes, and reliefs. Painted black, white, or on rare occasions gold, many of her works are wall-size constructions. They consist of box-like frames filled with assorted objects. Some are almost architectural environments. Her sculptures are mysterious and beautiful.

Strangely enough the artist has said, "I'm not in love with wood. It's the *forms*. I see the forms first. If I loved the wood, I

Sky Cathedral

wouldn't paint it black." Form is the prime factor in the work of Louise Nevelson. Uncompromising perfection is her trademark. Exact scale and line make her works elegant as well as extraordinary. She says, "In my heyday . . . I put a wall up, and if there were one line that didn't please me [I'd] take it right down and put it up again."

She continues, "Sure, I'm ambitious, but if you have an idea, you create energy . . . When you're creating, there is added energy that surpasses everything else." The energy of Louise Nevelson is a joy to see. She moves constantly around and around her work, surveying it from all sides. Her incredible creative energy does not change as she moves through the years. In her seventies, she always moves with the agility and sureness of a young woman. She also moves with the confidence of a perfectionist. Invariably, she works with a bright kerchief wrapped around her head, a beautiful tunic over her pants.

Nevelson Chapel in St. Peter's Church

The artist's sense of fashion is another sign of her creativity. She boldly combines styles, fabrics, and jewelry from different cultures. She expresses her originality in what she wears. "Let's break tradition," she has said. "That's why I dress the way I do. Isn't it terribly conventional to think you have to be in a mold?"

In 1977, Louise Nevelson completed an unconventional project. St. Peter's Church in New York City wanted her to design a small chapel to be used for services and private prayer. The result: an all-wood, all-white, five-sided room that has been described as an "environment of the spirit." It is an oasis of calm within New York's bustling business district. It is also the only chapel to be entirely designed by an American artist—her gift to the city she has always loved.

The small chapel seats only twenty-eight people, in pews set herringbone fashion instead of directly facing the altar. One of its walls, entitled *The Twelve Apostles*, is most characteristic of Louise Nevelson's unique artistic style. Twelve boxes are filled with shaped wooden pieces. Once again, Louise Nevelson broke tradition to express her own concept of architectural space designed for meditation in the hubbub of a large city.

When a genius breaks tradition with a beautiful new concept, that new concept might well become the "tradition" of the future.

1. When and where did Louise Nevelson first announce her plans for a career?

2. Why did Louise Nevelson become frightened when she announced that she wanted to be a sculptor?

3. This biography said: "Perhaps her choice of wood as a sculptor's medium was influenced by her early environment." What was this early environment and how might it have influenced her choice of a medium?

4. Louise Nevelson said: "I knew the creative act was more important than the materials, so I picked up anything." In what ways is her approach to her materials different from Noguchi's approach?

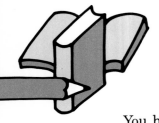

Following Directions in a Recipe

You have read several selections about people in the fine arts. You learned about painters, dancers, and sculptors. These artists know the importance of following directions. For example, Keplik the watchmaker carefully glued and tied the parts of his model bridge in a specific order. He knew that even one mistake could ruin the whole project.

Cooking is also a fine art. Cooks can create fine foods by following the directions in a recipe. A *recipe* provides instructions for making a particular kind of food. There may be many steps involved in the preparation. If even one mistake is made, such as adding too much salt or forgetting to include an egg, the end product may be ruined.

Many recipes have two parts. The first part lists the ingredients necessary to prepare the food. The second part gives the instructions for using the ingredients.

Recipes often use abbreviations to indicate the amounts of food to be used. Here are some common recipe abbreviations:

oz.	ounce	tsp.	teaspoon	g.	gram
lb.	pound	tbsp.	tablespoon	kg.	kilogram
qt.	quart	pkg.	package	l.	liter
pt.	pint	min.	minutes	ml.	milliliter

Read the following recipe:

Meat

Mini Meat Loaves with Spanish Rice

1½ lbs. ground beef
¼ cup instant minced onion
¾ cup dry bread crumbs
1½ tsp. salt
1 tsp. parsley flakes
¼ tsp. pepper

1 tsp. Worcestershire sauce
1 egg
⅓ cup milk
1 can (15 oz.) Spanish rice
1 can (8 oz.) tomato sauce

Heat oven to 425°. Mix all ingredients except Spanish rice and tomato sauce thoroughly. Shape meat mixture into six small loaves, each 4 x 2½". Place in ungreased square pan, 9 x 9 x 2". Bake 15 min.

Top each loaf with ⅓ cup Spanish rice. Spoon tomato sauce over rice. Bake 10 min. longer or until meat is done and rice is thoroughly heated.

Provides four to six servings.

ACTIVITY A   Write these steps on your paper, in the order in which they are given in the recipe.

1. Top the loaves with rice.
2. Shape the meat into six loaves.
3. Bake 10 minutes longer.
4. Heat the oven to 425°.
5. Spoon tomato sauce over the rice.
6. Mix the ingredients thoroughly.
7. Bake 15 minutes.

ACTIVITY B   Write answers to the following questions about the recipe.

1. What amount of pepper is called for in the recipe?
2. Would ½ cup of milk be too much or too little for the recipe?
3. How many ounces of Spanish rice equals one can?
4. How many ounces of tomato sauce equals one can?
5. Which amount is called for in the recipe: 1½ tablespoons of salt or 1½ teaspoons of salt?
6. Suppose you had pepper, milk, tomato sauce, minced onions, and eggs. What items would you still need to prepare the meat loaf as instructed?
7. If you followed the recipe but kept the oven at 625°, would the meat loaf be overcooked or undercooked?
8. Would one pound of ground beef be enough meat for the recipe?
9. Suppose you had a pan 8 x 6 x 1". Would it be too large or too small?
10. How many servings will be provided from the recipe given?

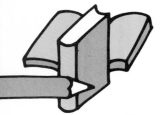

Reading a Menu and a Restaurant Bill

Sometimes you may go to a restaurant after attending a play or a concert. The *menu* in a restaurant is a list of all the foods that are served. The menu also shows the price for each item. Knowing how to read a menu is an important skill. Menus often state special combinations of food that are available for lunch or dinner. Different sections of the menu might show what kind of drinks, side dishes, or desserts are served.

At the end of your meal you receive a bill. The *bill* is a list of the items you ordered. It also shows the total amount you owe the restaurant for the food. Knowing how to read a bill is another important skill. The bill is usually prepared by a waiter or waitress. Occasionally a mistake may be made in the amount you are charged. You can check the price by studying the bill. Make sure the items listed are the ones that you ordered. Also make sure the prices listed are correct and have been added up correctly.

It is customary to tip the waiter or waitress who served you. As a general rule, 15% of the amount of the total (not including tax) is acceptable as a tip.

Here is a sample menu and bill:

Menu

Lunch

Scrambled eggs, peas, diced
carrots $3.10

Tuna sandwich
on white bread 2.75
on roll 35
extra

Baked fish, mashed potatoes . 4.35

Dinner

Hamburger on bun . . . .$ .95

Steak, rice, and
corn 6.95

Spaghetti and meatballs 5.50

Side Dishes

French fries . . . .$.70
Cole slaw 65
Fruit cup 65
Spinach 70

Beverages

Milk (large) . . . .$.65
(small) 45
Coffee 35
Orange juice 35

Bill

2	hamburgers	1	70
1	spaghetti	5	50
1	spinach		70
2	coffees		70
1	small milk		45
1	fruit cup		75
	Total	9	80
	5% Sales Tax		49
	Final Total	10	29

ACTIVITY A   Write answers to the following questions about the menu.

1. Which foods do you get with the steak dinner?
2. Which foods are included in the scrambled eggs lunch?
3. Can you order spinach for either lunch or dinner?
4. Which meal would you order if you wanted mashed potatoes?
5. How much would a tuna sandwich on a roll cost?
6. If you only had $4.00, which lunches could you afford?
7. If you only had $4.00, which dinners could you afford?
8. Which two beverages are the least expensive?
9. How much does a side order of cole slaw cost?
10. What is the difference in price between a large and a small glass of milk?

ACTIVITY B   Write answers to the following questions about the bill.

1. The wrong prices were charged for two foods that were ordered. What foods were they?
2. What is the correct price that should appear on the line marked TOTAL?
3. According to the bill, how many hamburgers were ordered?
4. According to the bill, how many cups of coffee were ordered?
5. Suppose you ate at a restaurant, and the total came to $7.00 not including tax. If you leave a 15% tip, how much will the tip be?

REFLECTIONS

Art enriches our lives. Artists blend the wisdom of the past with their own experience to create new works of art that reflect the complex currents of modern American life. In "Reflections," you have read about music, dance, painting, and sculpture, and about American artists who are trying new approaches to these arts. Art enriches us whether we choose to observe it, or to take part in it ourselves.

Thinking About "Reflections"

1. Successful artists tend to care deeply about their work. Often art is the most important thing in their lives. Look at the selections about Georgia O'Keeffe, Isamu Noguchi, and Louise Nevelson and find examples of how each artist expressed his or her concern for art.

2. Armindo Miranda's vision was a physical handicap. Antonia Brico was handicapped by the prejudices of others. Give examples of how these artists overcame their "handicaps."

3. Twyla Tharp and Fritz Scholder were interested in getting the attention of their viewers. Explain how each artist tried to catch their viewer's attention.

4. Compare Keplik in "Keplik the Match Man" with Herschel Collier in "The Dance." Was art meaningful to both of these men?

5. If you were to take part in one of these arts—music, dance, painting, sculpture—which would you choose? Why?

STORYTELLING

Stories have an amazing ability to stimulate our imagination. Through stories and through the "eye" of the imagination, we travel to distant places and see strange and wonderful sights. We take part in adventures and feel the joys and sorrows that are a part of them. For as long as human beings have used a language, we have told each other stories. There is no end in sight to our love of storytelling.

The selections in "Storytelling" include fables, fairy tales, folktales, myths, and legends. Some of them were first told thousands of years ago; others were written in our own century. You will read about animals that act like human beings, and see how a modern writer gives a new twist to old fables. You will meet a high diver, the most famous practical joker of ancient Arabia, and the fastest runner on earth. You will see how a wizard, trapped for years inside a tree, struggles to regain his lost power.

As you read, think about the basic idea behind each story. Stories are always told for a reason, even if the reason is just for entertainment. What kinds of stories do you like to tell?

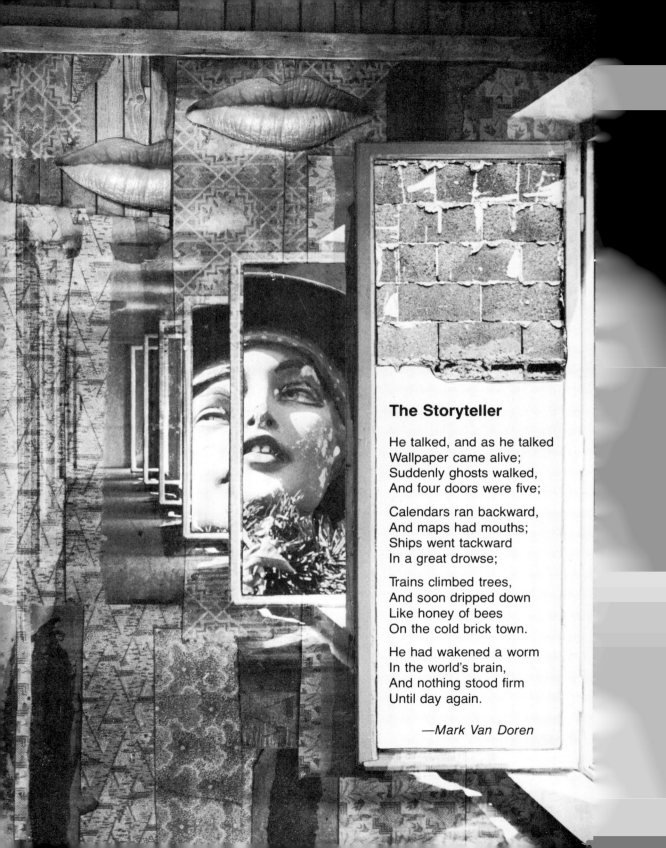

The Storyteller

He talked, and as he talked
Wallpaper came alive;
Suddenly ghosts walked,
And four doors were five;

Calendars ran backward,
And maps had mouths;
Ships went tackward
In a great drowse;

Trains climbed trees,
And soon dripped down
Like honey of bees
On the cold brick town.

He had wakened a worm
In the world's brain,
And nothing stood firm
Until day again.

—Mark Van Doren

WHAT IS A STORY?

Robert Bell

Can you answer the question "What is a story?" You probably have heard and read stories from the time you first learned your native language. But can you describe a story? Do you know where stories come from? Why are stories told? The essay you are about to read will help you answer these questions about stories and storytelling. As you read, notice the author's explanation of how and why the first stories might have come about, and, in what ways storytelling has changed over the years.

THE FIRST STORIES

The story is one of the oldest of human inventions. No one knows exactly how or when the first story was told, but it may have happened like this.

Try to imagine a time before TV, movies, and radio. That's easy—you need to think back less than a hundred years. The newspaper as we know it is nearly four hundred years old. Go back further. Books first appeared over seventeen hundred years ago. Go back further still. Send your imagination back beyond the invention of writing itself—over five thousand years ago.

We know only the broad outlines of life at that time. It was certainly different from the way we live today. In most places, people struggled just to stay alive. But some things were the same. People were born and people died. They did small or important deeds. There were storms, floods, and earthquakes. There were good years when people had enough to eat, and years of famine.

People naturally talked about these events. They discussed the deeds of important men and women. They told their children about the good and bad times of past years. They saw many things they did not understand, and they often invented unseen beings or events to explain them.

In each case, these people were telling stories.

Why did people want to tell stories and have stories told? Again, use your imagination. Your days are filled with hard work. Food is hard to get and you are often hungry. A good story of adventure or magic takes your mind off your worries. It entertains you.

Stories were important in other ways, too. Remember, this was in a time before writing. Storytellers could not work in private with a pen or typewriter as they do today. They had to tell their stories aloud, usually to a group of people. Storytelling, therefore, brought people together. Through the stories, people shared their ideas and feelings, their common history, and gained a sense of belonging to a group. Before there were governments or laws, stories helped knit people together into societies.

Many stories also taught people how to get along with one another. These stories contained lessons about the importance of honesty, kindness, courage, and generosity, and the dangers of greed and too much pride.

To entertain, to bring people together, to educate—these were all reasons for storytelling. There was another reason that was less practical, but just as important. Stories were a form of art, and they did what art has always done for people: surprised and delighted them with a fresh look at things they saw and felt all the time, but never seemed to notice. Stories still have

that power today—to renew our amazement at the living world.

Now you know what a story *does,* but you still don't know what a story *is.* A story consists of a *plot,* or set of events; some *characters,* be they human, animal, or vegetable; and a *setting,* or a time and place. A story has at least one more vital part—a *theme.* A theme is the main idea or the point of a story. It is the reason for telling the story. The themes of the following stories you will read contain small particles of great wisdom. This wisdom is so great because it comes from the lives of all the billions of people who have told and heard stories through the ages.

GENRES OF STORIES

Come forward in time now. As the years pass, the world's stock of stories grows huge. There are several reasons for this. People are always making up new stories; this seems to come as naturally as breathing. But even old stories change constantly. The same story told by two people becomes two different stories, because each teller gives it a personal flavor and adds new ideas. To get a clear picture of the world's supply of oral stories, you need to multiply the millions of stories by the billions of times they have been told.

Since there are so many stories, we put them into categories, or *genres,* in order to talk about them more easily.

Fables, one genre, are stories that are told in order to teach a specific lesson. "Little by little does the trick" or "It does not pay to pretend to be what you are not" are typical lessons, or morals. Fables usually end with a statement of the moral. Fables are often about animals that think and act like human beings.

Fairy tales, another genre, are stories about people, but not about real or possible events. Magic plays an important part in fairy tales. Unlikely events, such as a man becoming king by solving a riddle, provide the plots for this genre.

Folktales form the broadest story genre. It is such a broad category that there are several types of stories that fit into it:

Animal stories, like fables, are about animals that think and act like humans. Unlike fables, they are not necessarily meant to teach a lesson, and do not end with a moral.

"Why" stories are meant to explain traditions or things in nature. "Why the chipmunk's back is striped" is a typical "why" story.

Tall tales use exaggeration to entertain. They are humorous stories and the humor comes from a good-hearted twisting of the truth.

Tales of the real world are realistic stories that tell about important experiences in human life.

Myths and **legends** make up another genre. Myths are the stories of gods and goddesses invented by early people to explain the natural world. Legends are tales about heroes or people with superhuman abilities. They probably began as true stories. During years of telling, elements of magic and make-believe have crept into them, making them more fiction than fact. Myths and legends are grouped together

because gods, goddesses, and the deeds that make legends are often parts of the same story.

When you talk about story genres, remember that they are not fixed categories; some stories do not fit easily into any one group. The genres are just tools that help us to make some sense out of the huge wealth of the world's stories.

THE GREAT THEMES

Think of an animal, a custom, or an event, and somewhere in the world there is probably a story about it. Many of these stories are strangely alike. Certain plots recur. Certain kinds of characters—poor but clever people, crafty animals, proud and greedy kings and queens—appear again and again. And certain themes seem to be repeated all around the world.

These similarities are not accidents. For one thing, stories are among the world's best travelers. When people moved from one place to another, their stories helped them make friends with their new neighbors. Everyone liked to hear stories from distant places. Traveling people—sailors, merchants, camel drivers—told stories of their adventures and heard tales wherever they went. In this way, favorite plots, themes, and characters spread around the world.

People in different countries speak different languages. They have different customs, live in different climates, and eat different foods. Why, then, do you think certain ideas would be favorite ones around the world? No one knows for sure, but it may be that these favorite ideas reflect the parts of life that all people *do* share. Love and hate, good and evil, justice and trickery—these ideas are similar everywhere. It is not surprising that so many stories concern these ideas; they are part of the greater story of human life.

For example, many of the stories explore the way a weak or poor person can defeat a powerful or rich one by being clever. This is one of the great ideas of literature, and it is as important today as it was five thousand years ago. As you read the stories that follow, look for the great themes that come up again and again.

THE LIVING STORY

Today we seldom tell stories the way people used to—around a fire at night with our family, friends, and neighbors. For one thing, writing came along during the last five thousand years. The old stories have been written down, and people usually write their new stories instead of telling them aloud. Sometimes modern-day writers use the old genres—fables, fairy tales, folktales, myths, and legends—to create new stories that tell about life today. But they also have developed new forms, like the short story and the novel. Five thousand years have brought many changes; yet, in stories, the things of value seem to survive.

Movies, TV, and radio, for example, seem to have taken the place of living storytellers. Actors, directors, and technicians can now create, in sound and color, the events and adventures we once could only imagine. But if you watch and listen closely, you'll find that many of the programs rely on the old plots, on the old characters, and on themes that were first expressed countless centuries ago.

Many of the stories you are about to read come from a time before the machines and the printed word. They were meant to be spoken by a human voice. Try to hear that voice as you read, or better yet, actually speak the words aloud. Even modern tales benefit from being read aloud; good writers never lose touch with the "music" that language makes in the ear and mind. As you read, try to imagine the fire, the friends, the feeling of the night at your door. These stories, the seeds of modern tales, come from the ancient times when the earth was new, when animals spoke, and when magic was alive in the world.

1. What is a story?
2. List and explain the major story genres.
3. The author says: "People are always making up new stories; this seems to come as naturally as breathing." Use the author's description of the origin of story-telling to explain this statement.
4. The author says: "Movies, TV, and radio . . . seem to have taken the place of living storytellers." Why do you think movies, TV, and radio have replaced live storytelling?
5. Stories often arise from important or funny events in the life of a family or other group. Perhaps your dog got lost one day, and finding it involved a great deal of drama or humor. Think of an event like this and tell a story describing it.

FABLES

According to legend, Aesop—the author of three of the fables you are about to read—was the slave of a wealthy Greek who lived over 2,500 years ago. He became famous as a teller of stories, usually about animals, that made shrewd comments on people and their actions.

James Thurber was born in 1894 in Columbus, Ohio, and he died in 1961. He became nationally famous as a writer and cartoonist. Like Aesop, Thurber had a keen eye for what was ridiculous in human behavior. His work, some of which you will read here, helped people to understand—and laugh at—themselves.

As you read, notice the lesson, or moral, that each tale illustrates. Do you think a fable is a good way to teach these lessons?

Fables of Aesop

THE JACKDAW AND THE BORROWED PLUMES

A Jackdaw once found some Peacock feathers. Wishing to make himself beautiful, he stuck them in among his own and tried to pass himself off as a Peacock. But the Peacocks recognized him at once and drove him from their midst, pulling out the false feathers as they did so. The poor Jackdaw went back to his own kind. The other Jackdaws, however, were so disgusted with his behavior, that they also refused to let him stay with them. "*For,*" they said, "*fine feathers do not make fine birds and it is silly to be proud of borrowed plumes.*"

THE WIND AND THE SUN

Once upon a time when everything could talk, the Wind and the Sun fell into an argument as to which was the stronger. Finally they decided to put the matter to a test; they would see which one could make a certain woman, who was walking along the road, throw off her cape. The Wind tried first. It blew and it blew and it blew. The harder and colder it blew, the tighter the traveler wrapped her cape about her. The Wind finally gave up and told the Sun to try. The Sun began to smile and as it grew warmer and warmer, the traveler was comfortable once more. But the Sun shone brighter and brighter until the woman grew so hot, the sweat poured out on her face. She became weary and, seating herself on a stone, she quickly threw her cape to the ground. Moral: *Gentleness had accomplished what force could not.*

THE LARK AND ITS YOUNG

A Mother Lark had a nest of young birds in a field of ripe grain. One day when she came home, she found the little birds much excited. They reported that they had heard the owner of the field say it was time to call the Neighbors to help them gather the grain, and they begged the Mother Lark to take them away. "Do not worry," she said, "if he is depending upon his Neighbors, the work won't begin today. But listen carefully to what the Farmer says each time he comes and report to me." The next day, again while their mother was getting their food, the Farmer came and exclaimed, "This field needs cutting badly; I'll call my Relatives over to help me. We'll get them here tomorrow." The excited young birds reported this news to their Mother upon her return. "Never mind," she said, "I happen to know these Relatives are busy with their own grain; they won't come. But continue to keep your ears open and tell me what you hear." The third day, when the Farmer came, he saw the grain was getting overripe, and turning to his daughter, said, "We can't wait longer; we'll hire some people tonight, and tomorrow we'll begin cutting." When the Mother Lark heard these words, she said to her Children, "Now we'll have to move; *when people decide to do things themselves instead of leaving such work to others, you may know they mean business.*"

FABLES FOR OUR TIME

James Thurber

THE FAIRLY INTELLIGENT FLY

A large spider in an old house built a beautiful web in which to catch flies. Every time a fly landed on the web and was entangled in it the spider devoured him, so that when another fly came along he would think the web was a safe and quiet place in which to rest. One day a fairly intelligent fly buzzed around about the web so long without lighting that the spider appeared and said, "Come on down." But the fly was too clever for him and said, "I never light where I don't see other flies and I don't see any other flies in your house." So he flew away until he came to a place where there were a great many other flies. He was about to settle down among them when a bee buzzed up and said, "Hold it, stupid, that's flypaper. All those flies are trapped." "Don't be silly," said the fly, "they're dancing." So he settled down and became stuck to the flypaper with all the other flies.

Moral: *There is no safety in numbers, or in anything else.*

THE ELEPHANT WHO CHALLENGED THE WORLD

An elephant who lived in Africa woke up one morning with the conviction that he could defeat all the other animals in the world in single combat, one at a time. He wondered that he hadn't thought of it before. After breakfast he called first on the lion. "You are only the King of Beasts," bellowed the elephant, "whereas I am the Ace!" and he demonstrated his prowess by knocking the lion out in fifteen minutes, no holds barred. Then in quick succession he took on the wild boar, the water buffalo, the rhinoceros, the hippopotamus, the giraffe, the zebra, the eagle, and the vulture, and he conquered them all. After that the elephant spent most of his time in bed eating peanuts, while the other animals, who were now his slaves, built for him the largest house any animal in the world had ever had. It was five stories high, solidly made of the hardest woods to be found in Africa. When it was finished, the Ace of Beasts moved in and announced that he could pin back the ears of any animal in the world. He challenged all comers to meet him in the basement of the big house, where he had set up a prize ring ten times the regulation size.

Several days went by and then the elephant got an anonymous letter accepting his challenge. "Be in your basement tomorrow afternoon at three o'clock," the message read. So at three o'clock the next day the elephant went down to the basement to meet his mysterious opponent, but there was no one there, or at least no one he could see. "Come out from behind whatever you're behind!" roared the elephant. "I'm not behind anything," said a tiny voice. The elephant tore around the basement, upsetting barrels and boxes, banging his head against the furnace pipes, rocking the house on its foundations, but he could not find his opponent. At the end of an hour the elephant roared that the whole business was a trick and a deceit—probably ventriloquism—and that he would never come down to the basement again. "Oh, yes you will," said the tiny voice. "You will be down here at three o'clock tomorrow and you'll end up on your back." The elephant's laughter shook the house. "We'll see about that," he said.

The next afternoon the elephant, who slept on the fifth floor of the house, woke up at two-thirty o'clock and looked at his wristwatch. "Nobody I can't see will ever get me down to the basement again," he growled, and went back to sleep. At exactly three o'clock the house began to tremble and quiver as if an earthquake had it in its paws. Pillars and beams bent and broke like reeds, for they were all drilled full of tiny holes. The fifth floor gave way completely and crashed down upon the fourth, which fell upon the third, which fell upon the second, which carried away the first as if it had been the floor of a berry basket. The elephant was precipitated into the basement, where he fell heavily upon the concrete floor and lay there on his back, completely unconscious. A tiny voice began to count him out. At the count of ten the elephant came to, but he could not get up. "What animal are you?" he demanded of the mysterious voice in a quavering tone which had lost its menace. "I am the termite," answered the voice.

The other animals, straining and struggling for a week, finally got the elephant lifted out of the basement and put him in jail. He spent the rest of his life there, broken in spirit and back.

Moral: *The battle is sometimes to the small, for the bigger they are the harder they fall.*

THE GLASS IN THE FIELD

A short time ago some builders, working on a studio in Connecticut, left a huge square of plate glass standing upright in a field one day. A goldfinch flying swiftly across the field struck the glass and was knocked cold. When he came to he hastened to his club, where an attendant bandaged his head and gave him a drink. "What happened?" asked a sea gull. "I was flying across a meadow when all of a sudden the air crystallized on me," said the goldfinch. The sea gull and a hawk and an eagle all laughed heartily. A swallow listened gravely. "For fifteen years, fledgling and bird, I've flown this country," said the eagle, "and I assure you there is no such thing as air crystallizing. Water, yes; air, no." "You were probably struck by a hailstone," the hawk told the goldfinch. "Or he may have had a stroke," said the sea gull. "What do you think, swallow?" "Why, I—I think maybe the air crystallized on him," said the swallow. The large birds laughed so loudly that the goldfinch became annoyed and bet them each a dozen worms that they couldn't follow the course he had flown across the field without encountering the hardened atmosphere. They all took his bet; the swallow went along to watch. The sea gull, the eagle, and the hawk decided to fly together over the route the goldfinch indicated. "You come, too," they said to the swallow. "I—I—well, no," said the swallow. "I don't think I will." So the three large birds took off together and they hit the glass together and they were all knocked cold.

Moral: He who hesitates is sometimes saved.

---

1. How did the Sun in *The Wind and the Sun* get the traveler to remove her cloak?

2. The theme of a fable is stated at the end in the moral. What was the theme of *The Lark and Its Young*?

3. Why was the fly in Thurber's *The Fairly Intelligent Fly* only "fairly intelligent"?

4. "He who hesitates is lost" is the theme of another of Aesop's fables. Which fable that you have read has a similar moral? How are the morals of the two fables different?

5. Why do writers of fables use animals as main characters?

6. Make up a fable to illustrate an idea. Use an original idea, or borrow a moral from one of the fables you read. Remember, fables are generally about animals and are fairly short.

FAIRY TALES

Fairy tales are stories about any kind of magical or fantastic event. But fairy tales are especially concerned with magical beings called fairies, also called elves, sprites, boggarts, or goblins. People all over the world have invented tales about these magical beings, usually of small size, who are skilled in singing, dancing, and crafts, and who sometimes help, or sometimes trick or harm human beings.

Scotland and Ireland are the sources of many famous fairy tales. Molly Hunter, a modern writer, has drawn on the fairy lore of these countries in writing this story. As you read, notice the many details the author gives you about these mysterious and magical folk.

Molly Hunter

 Hi Johnny was a peddler.

All day he tramped along country roads with a pack on his back, and in his pack he carried goods to sell to farmers' wives— things like pins, needles, knives, and scissors, and very often pots and pans as well. Hi Johnny also had a strong, knobbly stick to help him on his way, and since this was usually a lonely one, he was always eager to stop and talk to anyone he met.

"Hi! Hi!" he would shout, waving his stick until he was near enough to pass the time of day in a quieter manner. This made people laugh, so that he was always welcome among them, and it was for this that he had come to be called Hi Johnny.

There was one summer's day, however, when someone saw Hi Johnny before he saw her. He was tramping that day along a road that ran through hill country. This road was deserted, except for himself, yet suddenly he heard a voice call, "Hi Johnny!"

The voice was a woman's, and he looked around in amazement at the sound of it, because the road was still empty so far as he knew, and there was no house within miles of that place. Right behind him, all the same, he saw the woman who had called him.

She was dressed in a green cloak that covered her to the ankles. A green hood was pulled down over her hair, which was white like that of an old woman. Yet still Hi Johnny could not tell whether she was young or old, because her face had no wrinkles and her eyes were as bright and clear as those of a girl.

"You've sprung up sudden, ma'am," said he, staring at her, and the woman smiled at this.

"I'm always where there are eyes to see me," she told him.

Hi Johnny thought this was an odd answer to give; and when he looked again at her old/young face he decided there was something altogether odd about her, but he got ready to do business with her all the same.

"Was it something from my pack you wanted? he asked.

And the woman told him, "It could be, because what I want to buy is an iron pot."

"Then," said Hi Johnny, slinging off his pack and reaching into it, "you've come to the right man, because I have one here that will last you a lifetime."

"Aye, that looks a good pot," said she, taking a long look at the one Hi Johnny handed to her. Then she added, "I'll buy it from you," and putting her hand into the pouch at her girdle she took out a gold coin.

"Wait now," said Hi Johnny, eyeing the gold. "I'm only a poor peddler. I don't carry change for that kind of money."

"Ah, well," said the woman, "that's my misfortune. You take the gold piece, I'll take the pot, and we'll call it a bargain."

Hi Johnny stood there with the gold piece in his hand, thinking hard. In his thirty years of traveling country roads, he had heard many a strange tale; and strangest of all were those tales that spoke of the fairy people who had plenty of gold, *but no iron*. Also, he had heard, they always wore green and covered their heads with green hoods. What was more, they could change their appearance at will, and come and go so suddenly that no man could see how they came or where they went. And now, here was this woman with her young face and white hair covered by a green hood, suddenly appearing and offering him as much gold for one iron pot as would buy her twenty of the same!

"I'll find out who she is," he said to himself, "if it kills me! And besides, I might make a lot more than one gold piece out of it." And to the woman he said, "Maybe I could walk the way you mean to go, ma'am, for I've a notion that this gold coin you gave me might be my luck-piece."

The woman gave him a long look. "Do you know who I am? she asked.

"No. But—" said Hi Johnny cautiously, "I think I can guess."

The woman smiled at this, a rather strange little smile. "And you're not afraid?" she asked.

Hi Johnny shook his head, even though he had felt a touch of fear at the strangeness of her smile.

"Come with me then," she told him, "and if it's true you are not afraid, that coin might indeed be your luck-piece."

Hi Johnny picked up his pack, ready to go up or down the road as she chose, but the woman left the road altogether and struck off into the hills instead. Hi Johnny followed, and although there was no path that he could see, she never faltered, but kept walking swiftly until they were deep in the hills and there was nothing to be seen around them but grass and streams and heather.

There was nothing to be heard either except the burble of the streams and the sad cries of curlews wheeling over the hillside, because the woman spoke no word in all the miles they walked together, and Hi Johnny could tell from her looks that his own talk would not be welcome.

It was not until dusk was falling that the woman stopped at last among some grassy hillocks covered with tall green bracken. She parted the fronds of bracken on one of these mounds; and behind the fronds, Hi Johnny saw, there was a green door. It swung open to her touch and, bending low, she went inside. With a fearful heart, but feeling he had come too far to go back now, Hi Johnny followed her.

Along a dark passage that sloped downwards, she led him, and at the end of it he stood blinking in astonishment, for this passage opened out into a great hall lit by hundreds of candles and full of people. They were a good bit smaller than himself, these people, but their faces had a strange, flower-like beauty. Their bodies were slender and very graceful, and all of them were dressed in green with green hoods on their heads. They were also, all of them, as active as bees in a hive.

Some were busily shaping and polishing tiny, sharp arrow-heads. Some of them worked with metal at a furnace, some were weaving on looms that held webs of fine green material. Those who were not at work of one kind or another were dancing to the music of reed pipes played by others of their number, and wherever Hi Johnny looked among all this activity, he saw the glitter of gold.

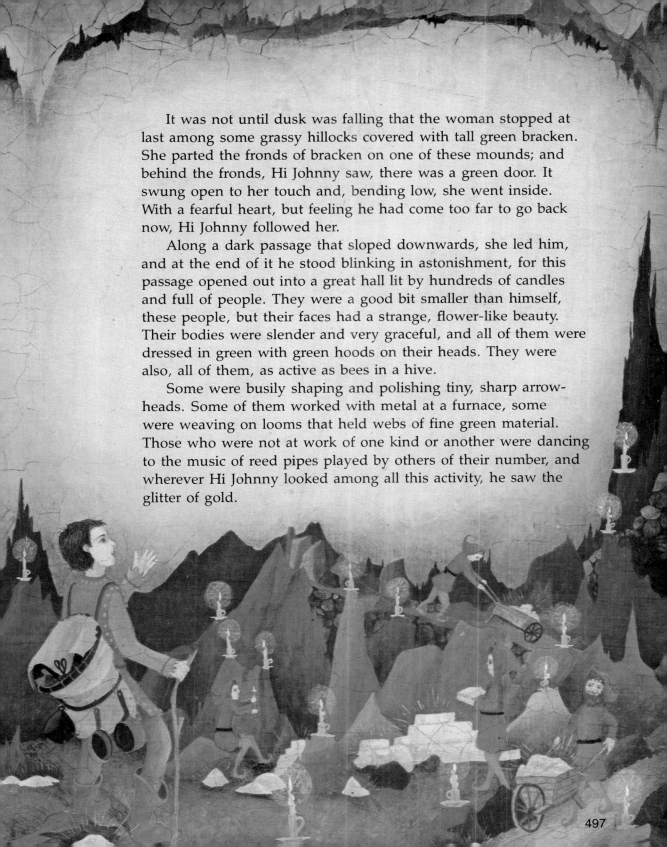

The looms of the weavers had golden frames. The metal being worked at the furnace was gold. The hundreds of candles were set in golden candle-holders, and all the men as well as all the women there wore bracelets and necklaces of gold made in strange and wonderful designs.

Hi Johnny stood quite entranced by this first sight of the fairy people—because that was what they were, of course, and he realized this instantly. But it was still their gold, more than anything else, that enchanted him so that he could not take his eyes off it.

"Will you *look* at that!" he breathed, turning at last to the old woman who had brought him there. But she had gone, and in her place stood another of the fairy people; the most beautiful creature he had ever seen, with a golden crown on her head, her green dress fastened by a golden girdle, and a white rod in her hand.

She smiled at him and said, "Now, Hi Johnny, let us see if the golden coin was your luck-piece."

Here was another wonder, thought Hi Johnny, because these words told him that this fairy queen and the old woman of the roads were one and the same person; and while he was still in confusion over this, she took him by the hand and led him to the center of the great hall.

The fairy people crowded around him, talking among themselves in sweet, thin voices, but with many a laugh in Hi Johnny's direction. Hi Johnny swung his pack off his back and stood there, feeling very big and clumsy and foolish beside all these clever, graceful little creatures. But when he opened his pack and they saw what was inside it, all this was changed, and it was Hi Johnny then who was lord of the fairies' hall.

Scissors, pins, knives, pots, needles—all the things made of iron or steel were snatched up by the fairy people, and in exchange for them, they thrust gold on Hi Johnny—gold in every shape and form, from the raw metal straight out of the earth to the most delicate of ornaments.

By the time his pack was empty, Hi Johnny was a rich man. The fairies brought him heather-ale, the drink that only they knew the secret of brewing. They pressed him to drink of it, and by the time he had tasted this and thought on the long walk back across the hills in darkness, he needed small urging to spend the rest of the night with them. Also, he wanted to celebrate his new fortune; and so, when the moon came up, they all went above-ground and danced wild dances in a ring, Hi Johnny leaping as nimbly as the rest, snapping his fingers and kicking up his heels with a fine flourish.

Between dances, too, when he flung himself down on the grass to draw breath again, he fell to dreaming of what he would do with his riches. No more "Hi Johnny" and tramping the roads in wet or shine for him. He would be "Lord Johnny" and live in a mansion house, with servants and fine horses and hounds with scarlet leashes around their necks. And so, with heather-ale, dancing, and dreams of gold, Hi Johnny passed his night among the fairies.

When the first red ray of the sun slanted over the hills to the east, Hi Johnny picked up his heavy packful of gold and his knobbly stick. He looked around to say good-bye to the fairy people, but they had all vanished underground—all except the woman he had met on the road, the old woman with the young face. Hi Johnny took off his bonnet and bent his knee to her, for he knew his manners to a queen.

"I thank you for your kindness, ma'am," said he, "and although there's no longer any need for me to travel the roads with a pack on my back, I'll come and visit your people again one day, if I may."

The queen's face was stern. "No, Hi Johnny," she told him. "You may *not* come back here."

Hi Johnny looked up at her, astonished. "I've done nothing wrong, ma'am," he protested. "Was I not honest in my dealings with you?"

"You were," the queen agreed, "but that was when you were a poor peddler; and since then, you have become a rich man. In your head you have the dream of living the life of a lord; but rich men always want to be still richer than they are. And in your heart, Hi Johnny, you know that you mean to come back with goods not half so worthy as those you sold to us, and to get as much gold again for them."

Hi Johnny hung his head in shame, for she had indeed seen into his heart.

"Ma'am," he said, "you speak no more than the truth." And suddenly then it came to him that he would have little use for life in a fine mansion if he could not be traveling the lonely roads, the friend and welcome guest of every person he met. He remembered the scream of a hare he had seen killed by hounds, and thought it would be a cruel thing to keep hounds in scarlet leashes to kill the gentle hares. And could he never taste the heather-ale again and dance wildly with the fairies under the moon to the music of reed pipes, he knew his life would be bitter to its end.

"Hang all riches!" Hi Johnny shouted, and tearing open his pack he tipped the whole of its golden contents onto the grass. From among this pile he chose a few small pieces of gold that he judged would cover the value of the goods he had sold the fairy people. Then, with a grin on his face, he looked up at the fairy woman and told her, "Now I am paid justly."

She smiled at him. "Your way lies over there," said she, pointing to the east. "But come back to see us, Hi Johnny, for now you are welcome to do that."

"Thank you, ma'am. That's all I wanted to hear," he told her, and slipping the gold into his pocket, he moved away in the direction she had pointed.

"Hi Johnny!" she called after him. He stopped, looking over his shoulder, and saw her standing in her green gown with the great heap of gold glittering at her feet.

"You are taking better than gold with you," she called. "You have found the secret of happiness."

"I believe I have, ma'am," he shouted back to her. "I do believe I have!"

And he trudged off towards the rising sun with his empty pack on his back, swinging his great knobbly stick and whistling merrily.

1. How did Hi Johnny discover that the queen and the old woman of the roads were the same person?

2. Why did the queen refuse Hi Johnny permission to visit her people again?

3. The queen said to Hi Johnny: "You are taking better than gold with you. You have found the secret of happiness." What did she mean?

4. Hi Johnny was faced with a choice between being wealthy and being free to visit the fairy people again. Which would you choose if you were in his place? Why?

Themes in Fiction, Nonfiction and Historical Fiction

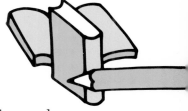

In this section of the book, you read an essay, several fables, and a fairy tale. The fables and fairy tale are examples of fiction. *Fiction* is literature about imaginary people and events. The essay is an example of nonfiction. *Nonfiction* is literature about real people and events.

Some stories are a combination of fiction and nonfiction. These stories are *historical fiction*. The stories are based on real people or events in history. However, everything that happens in the story is not true. For example, you might read a story in which Abraham Lincoln speaks with a child. The conversation may have been made up. This story would be historical fiction. Also, if imaginary characters participate in a real Civil War battle, such a story would be historical fiction.

ACTIVITY A   Read each item below. Write whether the topic is *fiction*, *nonfiction*, or *historical fiction*.

1. a report on dairy farms
2. a tale about a horse that writes stories
3. an article on how the telephone works
4. a story with an imaginary conversation between George Washington and his troops
5. a fairy tale about a flying cat
6. a story in which an imaginary character witnesses the Wright brothers' first airplane flight

Authors may write fiction, nonfiction, or historical fiction. But these authors often write for the same reason. They want to express something that they feel is generally true about life. The general truth they express is called the *theme*.

In fables, the theme is the *moral*, or lesson, stated at the end of the story. Not all themes are morals, however. Not all themes are stated directly in the story. You must figure out the theme by asking yourself these questions:

1. What kind of characters did the author write about?
2. Were the characters likable or dislikable?

3. What did the characters learn about themselves by the end of the story?
4. What is the significance of the title of the story?

The answers to these questions will help you discover the theme, or point about life, that the author is expressing.

When you state the theme of a story, do not use the characters' names. The theme is a *general* rule that applies to everyone. For example, the theme of "The Lark and Its Young" would not be "The Lark knew the Farmer meant business when he said he would do the work himself." Instead the theme would be stated as a general truth: "People usually mean business when they decide to do things themselves."

ACTIVITY B   Write the theme of each of the following stories.

1. "The Wind and the Sun"
2. "The Jackdaw and the Borrowed Plumes"
3. "The Fairly Intelligent Fly"
4. "The Elephant Who Challenged the World"
5. "The Glass in the Field"
6. "Hi Johnny"

ACTIVITY C   Read each title and description of a story below. Decide what theme, or general truth about life, the author is expressing. Write the theme of the story.

1. *Working Together*: A star player on a softball team ignores the team rules. She breaks curfew and skips practice sessions. She says the rules shouldn't apply to her, since she is a star. The other players resent her attitude, and the team loses many games. The star realizes her mistake and begins obeying the rules.

2. *The Power of Words*: One student in a class is known as a bully. No one talks to him because he pushes people around. A new student comes to the class. He is warned about the unpopular bully. When the two meet, the new student compliments the bully on his nice clothes. The bully is surprised at the compliment, and the two students become good friends.

FOLKTALES: Animal Stories

The animal story you are about to read is an American Indian tale told by the Hopi people. As you read, notice how the author uses animals to make statements about human beings and human experiences.

COYOTE AND THE CRYING SONG

Harold Courlander

Coyote once lived on Second Mesa near the village of Shipaulovi. The dove also lived near Shipaulovi. It was harvest time, and the dove was in the field collecting the seeds of the kwakwi grass. To separate the seeds from the stalks, she had to rub the tassels vigorously. But the kwakwi grass was sharp, and the dove cut her hands. She began to moan: "Hu-hu-huuu! Hu-hu-huuu! Ho-uuu, ho-uuu, ho-uuu!"

It happened that Coyote was out hunting, and he heard the voice of the dove. To Coyote, the moaning sounded like music. "What a fine voice," he said to himself, approaching the place where the dove was working. He stopped nearby, listening with admiration as the dove moaned again: "Hu-hu-huuu! Hu-hu-huuu! Ho-uuu, ho-uuu, ho-uuu!"

Coyote spoke, saying, "The song is beautiful. Sing it again."

The dove said, "I am not singing, I am crying."

Coyote said, "I know a song when I hear one. Sing it once more."

"I am not singing," the dove said. "I was gathering seeds from the kwakwi grass and I cut myself. Therefore, I am crying."

Coyote became angry. "I was hunting," he said, "and I heard your song. I came here thinking, 'The music is beautiful.' I stood and listened. And now you tell me you are not singing. You do not respect my intelligence. Sing! It is only your voice that keeps me from eating you. Sing again!"

And now, because she feared for her life, the dove began once more to moan: "Hu-hu-huuu! Hu-hu-huuu! Ho-uuu, ho-uuu, ho-uuu!"

Coyote listened carefully. He memorized the song. And when he thought he had it in mind, he said, "First I will take the song home and leave it there safely. Then I will continue hunting."

He turned and ran, saying the words over and over so that he would not forget them. He came to a place where he had to leap from one rock to another, but he missed his footing and fell. He got to his feet. He was annoyed. He said, "Now I have lost the song." He tried to remember it, but all he could think of was "Hu-hu."

So he went back and said angrily to the dove, "I was taking the song home, but I fell and lost it. So you must give it to me again."

The dove said, "I did not sing, I only cried."

Coyote bared his teeth. He said, "Do you prefer to be eaten?"

The dove quickly began to moan: "Hu-hu-huuu! Hu-hu-huuu! Ho-uuu, ho-uuu, ho-uuu!"

"Ah, now I have it," Coyote said, and once more he started for home. In his haste he slipped and tumbled into a gully. When he regained his footing, the song was gone. Again he had lost it. So he returned to the place where the dove was working.

"Your song is very slippery," he said. "It keeps getting away. Sing it again. This time I shall grasp it firmly. If I can't hold onto it this time, I shall come and take you instead."

"I was not singing, I was crying," the dove said, but seeing Coyote's anger she repeated her moaning sounds.

And this time Coyote grasped the song firmly as he ran toward his home near Shipaulovi. When he was out of sight, the

dove thought that it would be best for her to leave the kwakwi
field. But before she left she found a stone that looked like a bird.
She painted eyes on it and placed it where she had been working.
Then she gathered up her kwakwi seeds and went away.

Coyote was tired from so much running back and forth. When
he was almost home, he had to jump over a small ravine, but he
misjudged the distance and fell. Now Coyote was truly angry, for
the song had been lost again. He went back to the kwakwi field.
He saw the stone that the dove had placed there. He saw the
painted eyes looking at him.

"Now you have done it," he said. "There is no purpose in
looking at me that way. I am a hunter. Therefore, I hunt." He
leaped forward and his jaws snapped. But the stone bird was very
hard. Coyote's teeth broke and his mouth began to bleed. "Hu-
hu-huu!" he moaned. "Hu-hu-huuu! Ho-uuu, ho-uuu, ho-uuu!"

Just at that moment a crow alighted in the kwakwi field. He
said, "Coyote, that is a beautiful song you are singing."

Coyote replied, "How stupid the crow people are that they
can't tell the difference between singing and crying!"

1. Why did Coyote force the dove to moan for him?
2. Coyote said: "How stupid the crow people are that they
   can't tell the difference between singing and crying." What
   point is the author of the story making with this remark?
3. Was Coyote clever or foolish? State your opinion and use
   evidence from the story to explain your answer.
4. Why does this story belong in the animal story genre? How
   is it different from a fable?

FOLKTALES: "Why" Stories

There is no question more fun to ask than "why?" Why? Because "why" questions usually have interesting answers; often they seem to have no final answer at all. "Why" stories probably developed because "why" questions are fun to ask and hard to answer. In ancient times, people often used "why" stories to explain events which they did not understand. One "why" question could keep people busy for hours thinking up an answer.

The story you are about to read is a Mexican "why" story that explains why the burro, or donkey, lives with people. As you read, notice how the storytellers weave a logical explanation into a story.

WHY THE BURRO LIVES WITH PEOPLE

Catherine Bryan and Mabra Madden

Benito, the burro, lived on the mesa to hide from the mountain lion. When he first came there to live, he trembled every time he looked toward the mountains that had once been his home.

"How fortunate I am," he said, "to have found this friendly mesa! Indeed, I am fortunate to be alive. The lion ate my friends and relatives one by one. Again and again he tried to have me for his dinner." Benito closed his eyes to shut out the thought.

Now the only food Benito found on the mesa was sagebrush and cactus. Said he one day, "This is poor fare for an honest burro. How I long for some green grass and a drink of cool water! Starving is almost as bad as being chased by the lion. But what can I do? I cannot go back to the mountains, though I am sick and tired of this kind of food. Surely there must be some place where I can live in safety and still have enough to eat."

As the days passed, Benito became more and more indignant whenever he thought of the mountain lion.

Said he, "My patience with that fellow is at an end! He can't do this to me! Why should I be afraid of him? The next time we meet I will teach him a lesson." And he pranced across the mesa playing he was chasing his enemy. He ended the chase by kicking a bush, saying, "That for you, you miserable cat! Now you will know better than to cross the path of Benito, the burro."

At that very moment his sharp ears caught a sound from behind. In terror he turned, and there, sitting on a rock, smiling from ear to ear, was none other than Don Coyote!

"Good day to you, Señor Benito," said Don Coyote. "It is indeed a pleasure to see you again. How do you like your new home?"

"Must you always sneak up from behind?" said Benito. "You frightened me out of my wits. I thought it was the mountain lion. See how upset I am! Have you no respect for the feelings of others?"

"My dear, dear friend!" said Don Coyote. "I am beginning to wonder if you are glad to see me. After all, we have known each other for a long time. Yes? No?"

"I know you only too well!" answered Benito. "How did you happen to find me?"

"I figured it out," replied Don Coyote. "This morning I met the mountain lion. He said, 'Do you know where Benito is?' 'No,' I said, 'I do not.' Then I thought to myself, 'Now where could Benito be? He could be in only one of two places—either here or there. He is not here; therefore he is there. Now where is there? Why, over there on the mesa, of course.' So, just to make sure, I thought I would pay you a visit and, sure enough, here I am and there you are!"

"Did you tell the mountain lion all of that?" asked Benito angrily.

"No-o. Not exactly," answered Don Coyote, "although he did say he would make it worth my while if I found out."

"You are a villain!" cried Benito. "You would sell me to the lion. You deserve to be kicked!"

"How you misjudge me!" said Don Coyote. "I would not tell the lion your whereabouts, especially for the few bones he had to offer. While talking with him I said to myself, 'I like Benito. He is a good burro. Here is a chance to do him a favor. I will go over to the mesa and have a talk with him and, if he will listen to reason, perhaps we can arrive at a bargain.' " And Don Coyote looked at Benito out of the corner of his eye.

"He is a sly rogue," thought Benito. "I will listen to him although I know there is a skunk in the bush." To Don Coyote he said, "What do you propose to do for me?"

"My friend," said Don Coyote, "the lion wants you for his dinner. Should he learn you are on the mesa, you will again have to run for your life. It is not a pleasant thought, is it?"

"I do not like to think of it," said Benito.

"How would you like to live where you would be safe from the lion and at the same time have enough to eat and drink?"

"You interest me!" replied Benito. "Pray continue."

"At the foot of those hills," said Don Coyote, pointing to a patch of green, "there live some people. They are the only creatures the lion fears. The animals that live behind their fences are safe. They do the people's work and the people give them food and a place in the barnyard."

"To work for people means changing one's way of living," said Benito.

"It is better to change one's way of living than to perish," said Don Coyote.

"A fence keeps one from going where one chooses," said Benito.

"A fence keeps one from being eaten by the mountain lion," said Don Coyote.

"Why have you taken such an interest in my safety?" asked Benito. "What do you expect to gain from it?"

"My friend," said Don Coyote, "when I think of that cruel mountain lion that eats harmless creatures, I shudder. I do not want him to eat you. I want to know you are safe and out of harm's way."

"Is that all that keeps you from being happy?" asked Benito.

"Now that you have mentioned it," said Don Coyote, "there is one more thing I would like to do. I will tell you all, and you will know that I have a tender heart. I know the people have some chickens. They keep them in a barnyard like the other animals. They beg the people to set them free. I have heard their pleadings. It is pitiful!" And Don Coyote wiped a tear from his eye.

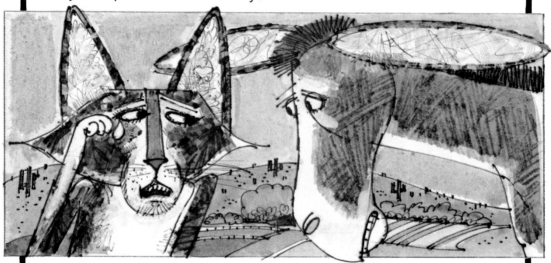

"I have tried to rescue them many times," he continued, "but each time the people refuse to listen. I offered them land, gold, diamonds—in fact, everything one could desire. They simply would not listen to reason. It has distressed me greatly.

"Then today I had a happy thought. I said to myself, 'Without me Benito would never have thought of going to the people for protection from the lion. In return he will surely be willing to help me help those poor, dear chickens. The peg that fastens the door of the henhouse is too high for me to reach. Tonight, after the people go to bed, Benito will pull out the peg. I will then take the chickens, one by one, to my cave in the hills where they will once again be happy.'"

Benito looked Don Coyote straight in the eye. Said he, "I am an honest burro. If I live with the people, I will give them an honest day's work for my food. I will have nothing to do with your scheme to steal their chickens."

"So that is how you repay me for trying to save your life!" cried Don Coyote. "It will serve you right if you are eaten by the lion."

"Take that!" cried Benito, giving Don Coyote a kick that sent him rolling.

Don Coyote scrambled to his feet. "You stupid burro!" he cried. "You will regret that kick! Now I will take the bones from the lion."

"Then take that, and that, and that!" cried Benito as he kicked the coyote again and again.

"You will pay dearly for those kicks, Señor Burro," cried Don Coyote. "I will help the lion eat you."

"Take that for the lion!" cried Benito, and he gave such a mighty kick that it rolled the angry coyote over the edge of the mesa. Benito watched him pick himself out of a bed of cactus.

"Hee-haw," laughed Benito as Don Coyote loped away toward the mountains.

"Well," said Benito at last, "that is that. What else is there left for me to do but go to the house of the people? It is better to live than to die." And, so saying, he departed.

From that day to this he has lived with people. He has not always been happy, but you cannot drive him away. And when he remembers how he kicked Don Coyote, he laughs and sings, "Hee-haw, hee-haw, hee-haw!"

---

1. Why did Benito decide to live with people?
2. Why did Don Coyote help Benito?
3. Do you agree with Benito when he says that he is an honest burro? Why or why not?
4. What kind of character was Don Coyote? Support your answer with evidence from the story.
5. Compare Don Coyote with Coyote in *Coyote and the Crying Song*. How does each character try to get what he wants? Is one character cleverer than the other? Why do you think so?

FOLKTALES: Tall Tales

During the rough-and-tumble days of the American frontier, people entertained themselves by telling stories around a campfire or at the corner store. They loved to match wits by seeing who could invent the most exaggerated and fantastic story. In time, these "tall tales" became an American tradition. The story you are about to read, High Diving, *is part of that tradition. As you read* High Diving, *notice that the author begins the story realistically. At what point does the author begin to exaggerate?*

HIGH DIVING

Alvin Schwartz

In those days I was billed as Billie the Dolphin, the spectacular, death-defying high diver. I was working with Miller's Great Exposition Shows, using a twenty-five-foot ladder and diving into a tank of water ten feet deep.

Big crowds came to see me. And not a soul ever seemed dissatisfied until one night when I happened to be playing in the same town as Eddie La Breen, the Human Seal, who worked for Barker's Shows.

As I climbed out of the tank that night I heard somebody say, "That ain't nothing! You ought to go see Eddie La Breen. He dives from fifty feet into five feet of water."

Well, it was true! And I was told to dive fifty feet or else. It sure looked high when I got up there, and I could feel my nose scraping the bottom after I dove in. But Eddie La Breen wasn't going to outdo me if I could help it.

Then Eddie sends word that I might as well stop trying. "I'm going to dive from a thousand feet while playing the ukelele and eating raw liver," he said.

Well, he didn't exactly do that, but he did raise his ladder to one hundred feet, then dove into two feet of water.

Well, I practiced and practiced—I really needed that job—and I made it from one hundred and fifty feet into one foot of water.

Then Eddie sent word he was going to change his name from the Human Seal to the Minnow.

"You know how a minnow just skitters along the top of a pond," he said. "Well, that's the way I'll land in that water. From two hundred feet, I'm going to dive into six inches, then skitter off without making a bubble." And he did it.

Well, I did that minnow dive too, except that I dived into four inches

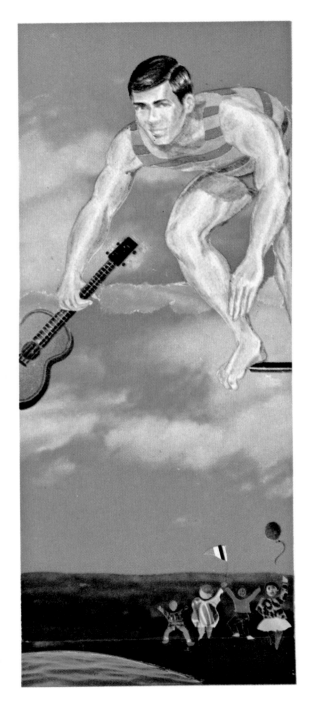

from two hundred and fifty feet and didn't even muss my hair.

Then Eddie made dives from three hundred feet into *three* inches. Of course, when that happened, I was a little put out. But I told them to get me a good thick bathmat and soak it all day in water and I'd dive into that from three hundred and fifty feet.

Well, the first time I hit the mat it sort of knocked me dizzy. But I got better and better at it until it didn't bother me hardly at all.

But after I reached three fifty, Eddie wouldn't go any higher. It was just too much for him, and sad to say, he lost his job.

Yet I beat him fair and square. He just wasn't honest enough to admit it. And not only was he jealous, he was treacherous. But I didn't learn that until quite a while later.

They had soaked the mat as usual that day. But they must have let it out of their sight because somebody squeezed all the water out of it and wrung it dry. And when i dived into it that night it was like diving into a block of concrete.

Later, somebody said that a man who looked like Eddie La Breen had been lurking around the show grounds. Now, if he didn't do it, who did?

1. Describe the "minnow dive."
2. Was Billie killed when he dove into the dry bathmat? How do you know?
3. Billie said: "Well, the first time I hit the mat it sort of knocked me dizzy." Is this a realistic statement? Why or why not?
4. Examine the story and list the unrealistic details in the order that they occur. Give reasons why the details are unrealistic.
5. Invent a tall tale that begins with a true incident from your life. Transform the true story into a tall tale by introducing unrealistic, exaggerated details. Remember, the humor of a tall tale comes partly from the fantastic details you invent, and partly from the sincere tone with which you tell it. A tall tale pretends to be realistic, but isn't. Be sure to include both of these elements in your tale.

FOLKTALES: Tales of the Real World

The following stories, tales of the real world, involve realistic characters in life-like situations. The Fly is set in Vietnam long ago, when that country was ruled by an Emperor and by officials, or mandarins, who represented the Emperor's authority. As you read, notice the details that describe life in historic Vietnam.

Abunuwas the Trickster is set in Bagdad, the capital city of an ancient Arab empire, now the capital city of Iraq. As you read, think about Abunuwas, the clever trickster. Have you met another character in a story who resembles him?

THE FLY

Vo-Dinh

Everyone in the village knew the usurer, a rich and smart man. Having accumulated a fortune over the years, he settled down to a life of leisure in his big house surrounded by an immense garden and guarded by a pack of ferocious dogs. But still unsatisfied with what he had acquired, the man went on making money by lending it to people all over the country at exorbitant rates. The usurer reigned supreme in the area, for numerous were those who were in debt to him.

One day, the rich man set out for the house of one of his peasants. Despite repeated reminders, the poor laborer just could not manage to pay off his long-standing debt. Working himself to a shadow, the peasant barely succeeded in making ends meet. The moneylender was therefore determined that if he could not get his money back this time, he would proceed to confiscate some of his debtor's most valuable belongings. But the rich man found no one at the peasant's house but a small girl of eight or nine playing alone in the dirt yard.

"Child, are your parents home?" the rich man asked.

"No, sir," the girl replied, then went on playing with her sticks and stones, paying no attention whatever to the man.

"Then, where are they?" the rich man asked, somewhat irritated, but the little girl went on playing and did not answer.

When the rich man repeated his query, the girl looked up and answered, with deliberate slowness, "Well, sir, my father has gone to cut living trees and plant dead ones and my mother is at the market place selling the wind and buying the moon."

"What? What in heaven are you talking about?" the rich man roared in puzzlement. "Quick, tell me where they are," he commanded, impatiently stamping the ground with his walking stick. The girl looked at the bamboo stick in the big man's hand, and she did not like it at all.

After repeated questioning, however, the girl only gave the same reply. Exasperated, the rich man told her, "All right, little one, listen to me! I came here today to take the money your parents owe me. But if you tell me where they really are and what they are doing, I will forget all about the debt. Is that clear to you?"

"Oh, sir, why are you joking with a poor little girl? Do you expect me to believe what you are saying?" For the first time the girl looked interested.

"Well, there is the sky and there is earth to witness my promise." the rich man said, pointing up to the sky and down to the ground.

But the girl only laughed. "Sir, sky and earth cannot talk and therefore cannot testify. I want some living thing to be our witness."

Catching sight of a fly alighting on a bamboo pole nearby, and laughing inside because he was fooling the girl, the rich man proposed, "There is a fly. It can be our witness. Now, hurry and tell me what you mean when you say that your father is out cutting living trees and planting dead ones, while your mother is at the market selling the wind and buying the moon."

Looking at the fly on the pole, the girl said, "A fly is a good enough witness for me. Well, here it is, sir. My father has simply

gone to cut down bamboos and make a fence with them for a man near the river. And my mother . . . oh, sir, you'll keep your promise, won't you? You will free my parents of all their debts? You really mean it?"

"Yes, yes, I do solemnly swear in front of this fly here." The rich man urged the girl to go on.

"Well, my mother, she has gone to the market to sell fans so she can buy oil for our lamps. Isn't that what you would call selling the wind to buy the moon?"

Shaking his head, the rich man had to admit inwardly that the girl was a clever one. However, he thought, the little genius still had much to learn, believing as she did that a fly could be a witness for anybody. Bidding the girl good-bye, the man told her that he would soon return to make good his promise.

A few days had passed when the moneylender returned. This time he found the poor peasant couple at home, for it was late in the evening. A nasty scene ensued; the rich man claiming his money and the poor peasant apologizing and begging for another delay. Their argument awakened the little girl who ran to her father and told him, "Father, father, you don't have to pay your debt. This gentleman here has promised me that he would forget all about the money you owe him."

"Nonsense!" The rich man shook his walking stick at both father and daughter. "Nonsense, are you going to stand there and listen to a child's inventions? I never spoke a word to this girl. Now, tell me, are you going to pay or are you not?

The whole affair ended by being brought before the mandarin who governed the county. Not knowing what to believe, all the poor peasant and his wife could do was to bring their daughter with them when they went to court. The little girl's insistence about the rich man's promise was their only encouragement.

The mandarin began by asking the girl to relate exactly what had happened between herself and the moneylender. Happily, the girl hastened to tell about the explanations she gave the rich man in exchange for the debt.

"Well," the mandarin said to the girl, "if this man here has indeed made such a promise, we have only your word for it. How do we know that you have not invented the whole story yourself? In a case such as this, you need a witness to confirm it, and you have none." The girl remained calm and declared that naturally there was a witness to their conversation.

"Who is that, child?" the mandarin asked.

"A fly, Your Honor."

"A fly? What do you mean, a fly? Watch out, young woman, fantasies are not to be tolerated in this place!" The mandarin's benevolent face suddenly became stern.

"Yes, Your Honor, a fly. A fly which was alighting on this gentleman's nose!" The girl leapt from her seat.

"Insolent little monster, that's a pack of lies!" The rich man roared indignantly, his face like a ripe tomato. "The fly was *not* on my nose; *it was on the housepole* . . ." But he stopped dead. It was, however, too late.

The majestic mandarin himself could not help bursting out laughing. Then the audience burst out laughing. The girl's parents too, although timidly, laughed. And the girl, and the rich man himself, also laughed. With one hand on his stomach, the mandarin waved the other hand toward the rich man:

"Now, now, that's all settled. You have indeed made your promises, dear sir, to the child. *Housepole or no housepole, your conversation did happen after all!* The court says you must keep your promise."

And still chuckling, he dismissed all parties.

1. Why did the moneylender "reign supreme" in the area?
2. Name two details that you learned about historic Vietnam from this story.
3. How did the girl prove to the mandarin that she was telling the truth?
4. When the girl said that her mother was "selling the wind and buying the moon," she was comparing certain objects her mother was buying and selling to the wind and the moon. Explain this comparison.

Abunuwas
the Trickster

Harold Courlander

Of all the people who lived in ancient times, Abunuwas was the greatest joker that anyone could remember. He was known in every corner of Bagdad, and even Harun-al-Rashid, the ruler of the city, listened to stories of this man's exploits with great amusement. Whoever tried to outjoke Abunuwas played a dangerous game, for Abunuwas's wit and humor knew no limits. When it was in his mind to make a clever person look less clever, or to make people laugh, he spared neither the farmer nor Harun-al-Rashid himself.

They say that one day Abunuwas went to the house of his stingy neighbor and asked for the loan of a watering pan for his donkey to drink from. The neighbor was very reluctant, but he searched around until he found a worn and leaky copper pot, and he handed it to Abunuwas, saying: "Here is a pot, but I must have it back within four days."

Abunuwas took the large copper pot home and kept it three days. On the fourth day he put a small pan inside the large pot and carried them to the house of his neighbor.

"Here is the pot I borrowed. I am grateful for your kindness," Abunuwas said.

When the neighbor saw the small pan nestling inside, he said: "Oh, but this small one isn't mine."

"Indeed it is," Abunuwas replied. "What is yours is yours. During the night your large copper pot gave birth to this little one. I found them together in the morning. As the small one is the offspring of the large one, they both belong to you. I am no thief, so what is yours I return."

To himself the neighbor said: "What kind of foolishness is this?" But he saw no reason why he shouldn't profit from Abunuwas's stupidity, so he replied:

"How true. Since the small one is the child of the large one, they both belong to me. May your house be blessed, for even the pots and pans are fruitful there!"

Some days later Abunuwas again went to the house of his neighbor and asked for the loan of a large pot. This time the neighbor was more than willing. Remembering his happy experience with the old battered pot, he now gave Abunuwas the best copper pot he owned. If this fine pot were to have a child as the other one did, it would be good luck indeed.

Abunuwas thanked him and went away. But this time he didn't return the pot at all. So, after many days went by, the neighbor came to Abunuwas's house and asked for it. Abunuwas looked very sad, almost as though tears were ready to run from his eyes.

"I have bad news for you," he said.

"What is the matter?" the neighbor asked in alarm.

"Your pot is dead," Abunuwas replied.

"What!" the neighbor cried out.

"Yes, I knew it would grieve you; that's why I didn't let you know when it happened."

The neighbor became indignant.

"Abunuwas," he said, "don't try to make a fool out of me. Since when does a copper pot die?"

"Can a pot give birth to a young one?" Abunuwas asked.

"Yes," the man said, thinking how he had gotten a small pan for nothing.

"Surely you know that everything that can produce young must die some day," Abunuwas said. "It was sad that your pot had to die away from home."

His angry neighbor argued, but finally he went away. Abunuwas kept the pot. And everywhere that the story was told, people said: "Abunuwas is right. Anything that can bring forth children is destined to die."

1. Why, when Abunuwas made his second request, did the neighbor lend him the best copper pot he owned?
2. How do you think Abunuwas felt when his neighbor loaned him the worn and leaky pot?
3. What plan did Abunuwas have in mind when he returned his neighbor's leaky pot with a small pan inside?
4. Do you think the neighbor deserved what happened to him? Why or why not?
5. Name another story character who resembles Abunuwas. Explain why they are similar.

Plot

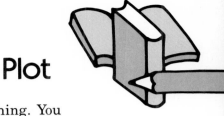

Imagine you had to sit all day without doing anything. You probably would not enjoy yourself. Having things happen to you is what makes your day interesting. Stories are also made interesting by the things that happen in them. The action in a story is called the *plot*. Everything that the characters do is part of the plot. A story with no plot, or no action, might seem very boring.

The plot of a story has a particular structure. The beginning of the story is called the *exposition*. In the exposition the main characters are introduced. The time and location of the story are also established. Usually, after the action begins, a problem arises for one or more of the characters in the story. This problem is called the *complication*. As the story continues, the problem may become greater. The *rising action* includes the events which cause the problem to become greater.

In a good story, you become more and more interested in how the problem will be solved. Usually a story reaches a dramatic point when it becomes clear how the problem will be resolved. The *climax* is that dramatic moment. The climax indicates how things will work out in the end.

The events after the climax are called the *falling action*. The end of the story is called the *denouement*, or conclusion. In a short story, there may be little falling action. The climax may come at the very end of the story. In a novel, however, the climax usually occurs some time before the denouement, or ending.

The following chart will help you understand the structure of a plot:

Consider the plot of the story "The Fly." In the exposition, the rich man and the young girl were introduced. No specific time was mentioned. The location was the child's house.

The man and the child each faced a complication. The man wanted to collect his debt. The girl and her family could not pay back the money. In the rising action the girl's problem became worse. The man broke his promise to forget the debt. The girl and her family found themselves in court.

The climax of the story was the moment when the rich man shouted that the fly had been on the housepole, not on his nose. That moment was important because the man admitted that the fly had existed. From that moment on you might have suspected the ending of the story.

The falling action included the laughter that everyone displayed in the courtroom. The mandarin's announcement that the rich man must keep his promise was the denouement of the story.

ACTIVITY A   Answer the following questions about the story "Coyote and the Crying Song."

1. Which characters were introduced in the exposition?
2. What time and location were established in the exposition?
3. What complication arose for the dove?
4. How did the dove's problem become greater?
5. What was the climax of the story?
6. What falling action occurred after the climax?
7. What was the denouement of the story?

ACTIVITY B   Answer the following questions about the story "Why the Burro Lives With People."

1. Which characters were introduced in the exposition?
2. What time and location were established in the exposition?
3. What complication did the burro face?
4. How did the burro's problem become greater?
5. What was the climax of the story?
6. What falling action occurred after the climax?
7. What was the denouement of the story?

ACTIVITY C   Answer the following questions about the story "High Diving."

1. Which characters were introduced in the exposition?
2. What time and location were established in the exposition?
3. What complication arose for the narrator, Billie the Dolphin?
4. How did the narrator's problem become greater?
5. What was the climax of the story?
6. What falling action occurred after the climax?

ACTIVITY D   Read the following story. Write answers to the questions that follow.

The Bird and the Fox

One day a bird found a fine piece of bread. She thought, "I will carry this bread to my nest and store it there."

On her way she met a sly and hungry fox. The eyes of the fox lit up when he saw the bread.

"What a fine piece of bread you have there," the fox exclaimed. "I must have it! Give it to me!"

The bird angrily shook her head no. The fox asked a second time for the bread, and then leapt at the bird. The bird flew high up in a tree. The fox became angrier. Suddenly he had an idea.

"Bird," he said, "I no longer want your piece of bread. But I hear you have a beautiful singing voice. Please sing one short song for me."

The bird, flattered by the fox's words, opened her beak to sing. As she did so, the bread fell out and dropped to the ground. The fox grabbed the bread and ran off.

1. Which characters were introduced in the exposition?
2. What complication did the fox face?
3. How did the fox's problem become greater?
4. What was the climax of the story?
5. What falling action occurred after the climax?
6. What was the denouement of the story?
7. What was the theme of the story?

Point of View, Style, and Tone

Point of View

At a sports event, some people like to sit in the front row of the stadium. They can watch the action close up. Other people like to sit farther back. From there, they get a better picture of the entire field. The action, when viewed from close up or farther back, does not always look the same. For example, a runner may appear out of bounds to someone in the front row, while the runner may seem in bounds to a spectator in the bleachers. The judgment depends on the angle, or *point of view*, from which the action is observed.

The action in stories, as in sports events, may be presented from two different points of view. Most stories are told, or narrated, in the *third person.* The author, like the spectator sitting farther back, views events from the outside. The author reports how all the characters speak, act, and feel. The author tells you everything about everyone.

Some stories are narrated in the *first person.* The events are not described by an outsider, but by a character involved in the action. This person, like the fan in the front row, has a close-up view of the events. Everything is seen and told from that character's point of view. If another character told the story, you might form a different opinion of the people and events.

It is easy to tell if a story is narrated in the first person. The storyteller uses words like *I, me, my, mine, we, us,* and *our.* The story "High Diving" was narrated in the first person. The story was told by Billie the Dolphin, one of the divers. Here are two sentences from the story. Notice the underlined words:

Big crowds came to see <u>me</u>.
Well, <u>I</u> did that minnow dive, too, except that <u>I</u> dived into four inches from two hundred and fifty feet and didn't even muss <u>my</u> hair.

All the events in "High Diving" were told from Billie's point of view. Had Eddie La Breen narrated the story, you might have formed a different opinion as to who won the diving contest.

Style

Authors may choose to write their stories in the first person or the third person. Authors make other decisions about their stories, too. The way they write is called their *style*.

Style can refer to many areas in an author's writing. For example, it may refer to sentence structure. Some authors often use very long sentences; others may use very short sentences. Writers might be recognized for their constant use of colorful adjectives or expressive verbs.

Some authors are known because their stories contain a great deal of conversation. Other authors are famous for their surprise endings. In short, the *style* of writers is their manner of expression that distinguishes them from other writers.

Tone

Another part of a story related to an author's style is the author's tone. *Tone* refers to the author's manner of speaking, or voice. You can probably tell when a friend speaks to you in a kind tone or an angry tone. Authors may write in different tones, too. They may be sarcastic or cynical. The tone might be humorous or even silly.

The fables by James Thurber had a humorous tone to them. Thurber was making fun of popular sayings. For example, a popular saying states, "There's safety in numbers." Thurber's story taught, "There is no safety in numbers, or in anything else." He made fun of that popular belief.

ACTIVITY A   Read each passage. Write whether it is narrated in the first person or the third person.

1. The cuffs on my pants got caught on the wire fence. I couldn't get loose. Finally I tugged hard and the pants tore. I looked behind me and continued running.
2. The crowd cheered as the hero rode in the motorcade. People were excited about seeing the celebrity. Paul and Aunt Mae stepped off the sidewalk.
3. Sandy couldn't believe it when they called her name. She had won the raffle. Mayor Beamish presented Sandy with her prize. The audience applauded politely.

4. The day was getting late, and we hadn't stopped hiking yet. I told our assistant to stop and pitch the tent. We worked for an hour collecting firewood.

5. I looked for my cousin as the passengers left the plane. She stepped through the door and I waved frantically. She spotted me and waved back.

6. The team was quiet during halftime. The coach, disappointed with their performance, gave a rousing pep talk before the second half of the game began.

ACTIVITY B   Read each paragraph. Answer the questions that follow.

1. The day was pleasant. Tom walked alone. He looked for Nolan. The air was still. A figure approached. It was Nolan. The two discussed business. The sun set.
   a. What do you notice in the author's style regarding the length of the sentences?
   b. Does the author's tone seem to be serious, sarcastic, or humorous? Explain your answer.

2. The small, white, webbed-footed animals approached the long, hot, black highway. An endless stream of angry, impatient, and concerned drivers sat in their steamy, stuffy cars. The calm, quiet ducks waddled across the road.
   a. What do you notice in the author's style regarding the use of adjectives?
   b. Does the author's tone seem to be serious, sarcastic, or humorous? Explain your answer.

3. The king (that terrible ruler in the fancy crown) ordered his servant (a bumbling idiot if I ever saw one) to fetch his dinner (as if the king knew good food). After the meal (which he probably ate with his fingers), the king entered the library to read (if you believe he can really read).
   a. What do you notice in the author's style regarding the use of parentheses?
   b. Does the author's tone seem to be serious, sarcastic, or humorous? Explain your answer.

MYTHS AND LEGENDS

The story you are about to read was first told at least two thousand years ago among the rocky hills and fertile valleys of Greece. Atalanta's Race *is a legend, the story of a young hero, Hippomenes—one of the sons of Poseidon, the Greek god of the sea—and Atalanta, the fastest runner on earth. The gods and goddesses of the Greek myths play a role in the story as well, so that* Atalanta's Race *is part legend and part myth. Like many stories of the ancient Greeks, it reflects their love for sports and athletic competition. As you read, notice the elements of legend and myth that make up the story.*

Padraic Colum

There are two Atalantas, . . . the Huntress and another who is noted for her speed of foot and her delight in the race—the daughter of Schoeneus, King of Boeotia, Atalanta of the Swift Foot.

So proud was she of her swiftness that she made a vow to the gods that none would be her husband except the youth who won past her in the race. Youth after youth came and raced against her, but Atalanta, who grew fleeter and fleeter of foot, left each one of them far behind her. The youths who came to the race were so many, and the clamor they made after defeat was so great, that her father made a law that, as he thought, would lessen their number. The law that he made was that the youth who came to race against Atalanta and who lost the race should be placed in prison for the rest of his life. After that the youths who had care for their freedom stayed away from Boeotia.

Once there came a youth from a far part of Greece into the country that Atalanta's father ruled over. Hippomenes was his name. He did not know of the race, but having come into the city and seeing the crowd of people, he went with them to the course. He looked upon the youths who were girded for the race, and he heard the folk say amongst themselves, "Poor youths, as mighty and as high-spirited as they look, by sunset freedom will be lost for each of them, for Atalanta will run past them as she ran past the others." Then Hippomenes spoke to the folk in wonder, and they told him of Atalanta's race and of what would befall the youths who were defeated in it. "Unlucky youths," cried Hippomenes, "how foolish they are to try to win a bride at the price of their freedom!"

Then, with pity in his heart, he watched the youths prepare for the race. Atalanta had not yet taken her place, and he was fearful of looking upon her. "She is a sorcerer," he said to himself; "she must be a sorcerer to deprive so many youths of their freedom, and she, no doubt, will show in her face and figure the sorcerer's spirit."

But even as he said this, Hippomenes saw Atalanta. She stood with the youths, before they crouched for the first dart in the race. He saw that she was a girl of a light and a lovely form. Then they crouched for the race; then the trumpets rang out, and the youths and the maiden darted like swallows over the sand of the course.

On came Atalanta, far, far ahead of the youths who had started with her. Over her shoulders her hair streamed, blown backward by the wind that met her flight. Her fair neck shone, as her feet were like flying doves. On and on she went as swift as the arrow that the Scythian shoots from the bow. And as he watched the race, he was not sorry that the youths were being left behind. Rather would he have been enraged if one came near overtaking her, for now his heart was set upon winning her for his bride, and he cursed himself for not having entered the race.

She passed the last goal mark and she was given the victor's wreath of flowers. Hippomenes stood and watched her and he did not see the youths who had started with her—they had thrown themselves on the ground in their despair.

Then wild, as though he were one of the doomed youths, Hippomenes made his way through the throng and came before the black-bearded King of Boeotia. The king's brows were knit, for even then he was pronouncing doom upon the youths who had been left behind in the race. He looked upon Hippomenes, another youth who would make the trial, and the frown became heavier upon his face.

But Hippomenes saw only Atalanta. She came beside her father; the wreath was upon her head of gold, and her eyes were wide and tender. She turned her face to him, and then she knew by the wildness that was in his look that he had come to enter the race with her. Then the flush that was on her face died away, and she shook her head as if she were imploring him to go from that place.

The dark-bearded king bent his brows upon him and said: "Speak, O youth, speak and tell us what brings you here."

Then cried Hippomenes as if his whole life were bursting out with his words: "Why does this maiden, your daughter, seek an easy renown by conquering weakly youths in the race? She has not striven yet. Here stand I, one of the blood of Poseidon, the god of the sea. Should I be defeated by her in the race, then, indeed, might Atalanta have something to boast of."

Atalanta stepped forward and said: "Do not speak of it, youth. Indeed, I think that it is some god, envious of your beauty and your strength, who sent you here to strive with me and to meet your doom. Ah, think of the youths who have striven with me even now! Think of the hard doom that is about to fall upon them! You venture your freedom in the race, but indeed I am not worthy of the price. Go hence, O stranger youth; go hence and live happily, for indeed I think that there is some maiden who loves you well."

"Nay, maiden," said Hippomenes, "I will enter the race and I will venture my freedom on the chance of winning you for my bride. What good will my life and my spirit be to me if they cannot win this race for me?"

She drew away from him then and looked upon him no more, but bent down to fasten the sandals upon her feet. And the black-bearded king looked upon Hippomenes and said: "Face, then, this race tomorrow. You will be the only one who will enter it. But bethink thee of the doom that awaits thee at the end of it." The king said no more, and Hippomenes went from him and from Atalanta, and he came again to the place where the race had been run.

He looked across the sandy course with its goal marks, and in his mind he saw again Atalanta's swift race. He knew the great effort he would make to reach the goal before her. And he thought it would be well to lose his freedom in that effort and on that sandy place that was so far from his own land.

Even as he looked across the sandy course now deserted by the throng, he saw one move across it, coming toward him with feet that did not seem to touch the ground. She was a woman of wonderful presence. As Hippomenes looked upon her, he knew that she was Aphrodite, the goddess of beauty and of love.

"Hippomenes," said the immortal goddess, "the gods are mindful of you who are sprung from one of the gods, and I am mindful of you because of your own worth. I have come to help you in your race with Atalanta, for I would not have you lose your freedom, nor would I have that maiden go unwed. Give your greatest strength and your greatest swiftness to the race, and behold! Here are wonders that will prevent the fleet-footed Atalanta from putting all her spirit into the race."

And then the immortal goddess held out to Hippomenes a branch that had upon it three apples of shining gold.

"In Cyprus," said the goddess, "where I have come from, there is a tree on which these golden apples grow. Only I may pluck them. I have brought them to you, Hippomenes. Keep them in your girdle, and in the race you will find out what to do with them, I think."

So Aphrodite said, and then she vanished, leaving a fragrance in the air and the three shining apples in the hands of Hippomenes. Long he looked upon their brightness. They were beside him that night, and when he arose in the dawn he put them in his girdle. Then, before the throng, he went to the place of the race.

When he showed himself beside Atalanta, all around the course was silent, for they all admired Hippomenes for his beauty and for the spirit that was in his face; they were silent out of compassion, for they knew the doom that befell the youths who raced with Atalanta.

And now Schoeneus, the black-bearded king, stood up, and he spoke to the throng, saying: "Hear me all, both young and old; this youth, Hippomenes, seeks to win the race from my daughter, winning her for his bride. Now, if he be victorious, I will give him my dear child, Atalanta, and many fleet horses besides as gifts from me, and in honor he shall go back to his native land. But if he fail in the race, then he will have to share the doom that has been meted out to the other youths who raced with Atalanta, hoping to win her for a bride."

Then Hippomenes and Atalanta crouched for the start. The trumpets were sounded and they darted off.

Side by side with Atalanta Hippomenes went. Her flying hair touched his breast, and it seemed to him that they were skimming the sandy course as if they were swallows. But then Atalanta began to draw away from him. He saw her ahead of him, and then he began to hear the words of cheer that came from the throng— "Bend to the race,

Hippomenes! Go on, go on! Use your strength to the utmost!"
He bent himself to the race, but farther and farther from him
Atalanta drew.

Then it seemed to him that she checked her swiftness a little to
look back at him. He gained on her a little. And then his hand
touched the apples that were in his girdle. As it touched them, it
came into his mind what to do with the apples.

He was not far from her now, but already her swiftness was
drawing her farther and farther away. He took one of the apples
into his hand and tossed it into the air so that it fell on the track before her.

Atalanta saw the shining apple. She checked her speed and
stooped in the race to pick it up. And as she stooped, Hippomenes
darted past her, and went flying toward the goal that now was
within his sight.

But soon she was beside him again. He looked, and he saw
that the goals marks were far, far ahead of him. Atalanta with the
flying hair passed him, and drew away and away from him. He
had not speed to gain upon her now, he thought, so he put his
strength into his hand and he flung the second of the shining
apples. The apple rolled before her and rolled off the course.
Atalanta turned off the course, stooped and picked up the apple.

Then did Hippomenes draw all his spirit into his breast as he
raced on. He was now nearer to the goal than she was. But he
knew that she was behind him, going lightly where he went heavily. And then she went past him. She paused in her speed for a
moment and she looked back on him.

As he raced on, his chest seemed weighted
down and his throat was crackling dry. The
goal marks were far away still, but Atalanta
was nearing them. He took the last of
the golden apples into his hand.

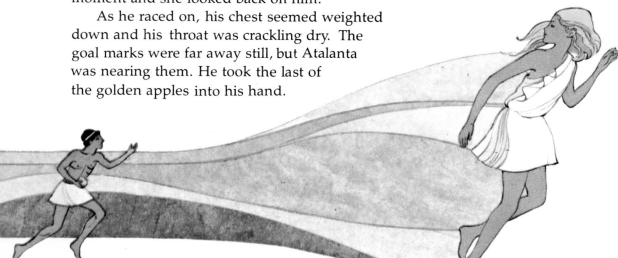

Perhaps she was now so far that the strength of his throw would not be great enough to bring the apple before her.

But with all the strength he could put into his hand he flung the apple. It struck the course before her feet and then went bounding wide. Atalanta swerved in her race and followed where the apple went. Hippomenes marveled that he had been able to fling it so far. He saw Atalanta stoop to pick up the apple, and he bounded on. And then, although his strength was failing, he saw the goal marks near him. He set his feet between them and then fell down on the ground.

The attendants raised him up and put the victor's wreath upon his head. The concourse of people shouted with joy to see him victor. But he looked around for Atalanta and he saw her standing there with the golden apples in her hands. "He has won," he heard her say, "and I have not to hate myself for bringing a doom upon him. Gladly, gladly do I give up the race, and glad am I that it is this youth who has won the victory from me."

She took his hand and brought him before the king. Then Schoeneus, in the sight of all the rejoicing people, gave Atalanta to Hippomenes for his bride, and he bestowed upon him also a great gift of horses. With his dear and hard-won bride, Hippomenes went to his own country, and the apples that she brought with her, the golden apples of Aphrodite, were reverenced by the people.

1. Why did young men come to Boeotia to race against Atalanta?

2. How did the golden apples help Hippomenes win the race?

3. How did Atalanta feel about Hippomenes? Support your answers with evidence from the story.

4. How did the spectators at the race feel about Hippomenes? Why did they feel this way?

5. Why does this story belong in the myth genre?

6. Atalanta's race is a legend as well as a myth. A legend is different from other stories because it concerns heroic people, or people with superhuman abilities. Why is *Atalanta's Race* a legend?

#4

Where my grandmother lived
there was always sweet potato pie
and thirds on green beans and
songs and words of how we'd
survived it all.
Blackness.
And the wind
a soft lull
in the pecan tree
whispered
Ethiopia
    Ethiopia, Ethiopia
E-th-io-piaaaaa!

   —*Doughtry Long*

Setting

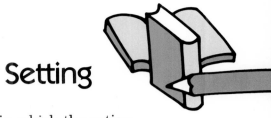

The *setting* of a story is the time and place in which the action occurs. Some stories have detailed descriptions of the setting. The time and location are important in those stories. In other stories, there is little or no mention of the setting. In this case the time and location are not important. The action could take place anywhere at any time.

The time in a story may be the past, present, or future. Sometimes a date is chosen for its historical importance, such as 1492 or 1776. Science fiction stories often take place in the future.

The time and place of the action affect the *atmosphere* of the story. The atmosphere is the feeling created in the story. A story taking place on a dark, stormy night in a deserted castle creates one kind of atmosphere. A story occurring on a bright, crowded day at the beach creates a different kind of atmosphere.

ACTIVITY A   Answer these questions about the selection "Atalanta's Race."

1. In what country did the story take place?
2. Although a specific year was not mentioned, would you assume the time was the past, present, or future? Why?
3. How much time passed in the story?
4. How was an atmosphere of suspense created in the story?
5. What problem did Hippomenes face?
6. What do you think Atalanta learned about herself by the end of the story?
7. What was the theme, or general point about life, expressed in the story?

ACTIVITY B   Select one story you have read in this book, besides "Atalanta's Race." Answer these questions about the story.

1. When and where did the story begin?
2. When did the time or location change in the story?
3. How much time passed in the story?
4. What kind of feeling, or atmosphere, was created by the setting?

ACTIVITY C Read the story below. On your paper, write answers to the questions that follow.

The Tale of Three Sons

A king had three sons. The king wanted to know which of his sons was the cleverest. One day he called them together and announced, "I am holding a contest. There is an empty storage room in the castle. Whichever of you can fill the room completely within twelve hours will inherit my riches."

The oldest son was allowed to try first. He rose at dawn and began carrying large stones into the empty room. Within a few hours the room was half-filled. However, the stones were heavy, and soon the son grew tired. By nightfall, when the twelve hours were up, the room was not completely filled.

The next-eldest son thought to himself, "I will not make the same mistake my brother made. I will fill the room with something that is not so heavy." The room was emptied, and the next day the middle son began pulling bags of feathers into the room. Indeed the feathers were light. However, it took many trips to fill part of the room. By nightfall, the room still was not filled.

The two older sons turned to their young brother and sneered, "If we could not fill the room in twelve hours, surely you cannot either."

The room was emptied once again. However, the youngest son did not rise at dawn. In fact, he slept late and then relaxed for most of the day. Everyone was puzzled. But as nightfall came, the youngest son went to the kitchen and got a torch. Just as his twelve hours were almost up, he entered the dark storage room with the lit torch.

"Father," the son announced, "I have filled the room with light." The father, pleased with his son's cleverness, gave him his riches.

1. What was the setting of the story?
2. How much time passed in the story?
3. How was the setting an important part of the story?
4. What feeling, or atmosphere, was created in the story?
5. What was the theme of the story?

THE
WIZARD
IN THE
TREE

Lloyd Alexander

What would you do if you found a wizard in a tree? A young woman named Mallory makes this startling discovery in Lloyd Alexander's *The Wizard in the Tree*, and she is soon caught up in a whirl of fantastic adventure. Lloyd Alexander is a modern storyteller. As you read this excerpt from his novel, pay attention to the plot, characters, and theme of the story, and see whether or not this story resembles the ancient tales you have already read.

PART I

Mallory's oak was down. It lay where the woodcutters felled it. The villagers hired to clear that stretch of woods had already moved on, leaving a wake of toppled trees and raw stumps. Once, Mallory had pretended the old oak was her enchanted tower that would stand forever; now it sprawled with limbs tangled in the underbrush. She would have turned bitterly away, but then she saw it: a gray wisp curling from the trunk. Falling, the tree had split along much of its length and something was caught there; likely a squirrel or weasel. She hurried through brambles that plucked at her skirt, set down her basket, knelt, and peered into the crack.

What she had taken for the tail of some small animal was, instead, the tip of a straggling beard. A sharp-pointed nose jutted from the splintered wood; two eyes glared up at her. From deep within the trunk came a tart voice.

"When you have quite finished staring, I suggest you make some effort to get me out of here."

Mallory's jaw dropped, she fell back on her heels, trembling too much to run and too curious to do so even if she had been able. What came suddenly to her mind was the old tale of the dwarf with his beard caught in a stump. This creature, however, had all of himself trapped and he was bigger than any dwarf she had imagined.

"Enough!" snapped the voice. "Get on with it. Now!"

Despite her bewilderment, Mallory sprang to obey. She braced herself and took a firm hold, bending the strength of her arms and hands to force open the crack. She desperately wished for a hatchet, an iron bar, even a knife; the woodcutters had left not so much as an ax handle behind them. She halted, breathless, shaking her torn fingers.

Her glance fell on a pointed stone. She snatched it up and worked it into the crevice. With a second stone, she pounded the makeshift wedge as far as it would go, then looked for another.

The tree, meantime, had begun rocking back and forth. Even as she watched, the crown of a balding head, wreathed by long strands of grizzled hair, thrust up from the trunk; then a lean, wrinkled face, its beard tangled in the splinters. Cobwebs trailed from its nose and a clump of mushrooms sprouted from one ear. The bright eyes blinked furiously.

"Do you mean to take all day?"

"Who—who are you?" Mallory stammered. "What are you doing in a tree?"

"Obviously, trying my best to get out. First, some idiot with an ax nearly chops off my toes, and now another wants to ask me foolish questions. Merciful moon, am I to be spared nothing?"

A dead branch lay nearby. Mallory seized it and pried at the wood. The tree groaned, ripping and cracking in a shower of bark and splinters. It split in two, spilling its captive onto the ground.

In her first glimpse of him, Mallory saw he wore a moldering leather jacket and a tattered cloak green with moss. Splotches of mildew covered his boots; in his beard hung a number of empty eggshells, and the twigs and leaves of a long-abandoned bird's nest. Before she could reach out to him, the strange being climbed unsteadily to his legs, wiggled his fingers, flexed his arms and beat them against his sides, thereby raising a cloud of midges from the folds of his cloak. He sneezed violently several times; then, heaving sighs of relief, thrust one hand after the other inside his jacket, luxuriously scratching himself.

"Are you—all right?" Mallory asked, uncertain what to say to this odd figure, let alone what to make of him. The old tales told of tree-spirits; but this being, who stood as tall as she did, was of solid, though much withered, flesh.

"Do you have anything to eat?" Without invitation, the freed captive bent down and rummaged through the basket.

"Mushrooms—" began Mallory, about to explain that Mrs. Parsel had fancied some of those delicacies with an omelette that morning. The bearded man, however, had already discovered the contents of the basket and wrinkled his nose in distaste.

"Fungus? No, thank you, I've been living with toadstools long enough."

"There's food in the cook-shop larder," Mallory said. "I'll fetch some for you. The village isn't far."

"Never mind. I shall manage without refreshment." Wrapping his cloak around his shoulders, he started from the clearing.

"Wait," Mallory called, "where are you going? I don't know who you are. I don't even know your name."

The stranger halted. "Arbican."

Mallory frowned. "What's that?"

"Arbican. My name. What use that information may be to you, I cannot imagine. But, since you ask, there it is."

He set off again. Mallory, no better satisfied, hurried after him. "You can't just go away like that, and not another word about who, or why—"

"Young woman," replied Arbican, "let me assure you I have more urgent matters in mind than detailing my life's history. Admittedly, without your help I should still be clamped in that oak tree. If I neglected to express my gratitude sufficiently, then: Thank you, thank you, thank you. Now I suggest you go about your business and I shall go on my way. I foresee difficulties enough in reaching Vale Innis."

"Vale Innis?" cried Mallory. "Why, that's the Land of Heart's Desire—the Happy Land, I know the tale! In the old days, there was a ship with golden sails; and all the magicians, enchanters, wizards—all sailed away on it. That's why there's none of them left. I only wish they'd stayed."

"I regret to tell you," said Arbican, "one of them did."

"That's not how the story goes," Mallory answered. "I know it by heart. It was the end of magic in the world."

"Oversimplified, but more or less correct," Arbican admitted. "By this time, my colleagues are long gone; unless any had my bad fortune to be shut up in a tree."

Mallory caught her breath. "Colleagues? Do you mean—?"

"I mean I should not be here at all," replied Arbican. "Yes, I am an enchanter. By all rights, I should be in Vale Innis this very moment. In fact, I should have been there ages ago."

"You?" Mallory gasped. "You? An enchanter? But—where's your magic wand? Where's your pointed hat? Your cloak with all the magical signs embroidered on it?"

Arbican rolled up his eyes and puffed his cheeks in a mighty effort to keep his patience. "Would you mind," he said, in a strained voice, "telling me how and where you got such wrong-headed notions?"

"Everyone knows what enchanters look like. In all the tales—"

"I don't know what tales you're talking about," said Arbican. "Idle gossip and rumor, so it sounds to me, fabricated by people who never saw an enchanter in their lives. Pointed hats and embroidered cloaks? I'd feel an utter fool, decked out that way. Enchanters don't need such trappings, though I suppose you mortals might think so. Even in my day, mortals had a deplorable tendency to mix appearance with fact. I should hate to tell you how many numbskulls put crowns on their heads—as if a metal hoop had anything to do with being a king."

"I didn't mean to offend you," said Mallory. "I just thought enchanters would be different, somehow. Or at least they'd be— well, cleaner."

Arbican snorted. "Forgive me for disappointing you. Had I known, I'd have brought along a change of clothing, curled my beard, polished my boots, scented my linen."

"But if you are an enchanter," Mallory went on, "if you were supposed to sail away, then what are you doing here?"

"That's a question I've had ample opportunity to consider," Arbican said. "The answer is: my own fault. I don't deny it, much as I regret it. I was on my way to the harbor when I stopped here to cut myself a walking staff."

"So you got there too late and the ship sailed without you?"

"Late? I never got there at all. Thanks to the tree. Thanks to the law we had to obey. Oh, I knew about it. I make no excuses. But this was such a small thing.

"The law warned us," Arbican went on, "to leave everything as it was; to interfere with nothing; to harm no living thing. Whoever thought that included a walking staff? The tree was alive, yes; but what harm? It could have spared a branch; it had plenty. So I started cutting one. A deplorable error in judgment. For the tree opened and swallowed me up. Snap! So! I've been there ever since."

"You couldn't have made it open again? Commanded it? Cast a spell?"

"Not while it lived," said Arbican. "A tree draws its strength from the roots of the earth. That's beyond the power of any enchanter."

"It must have been terrible," Mallory said. "When I'm being punished, and Mrs. Parsel makes me stay in my room—I can imagine being caught inside a tree."

"I doubt it," said Arbican. You could have no possible conception of how boring it is. Oh, there's a great deal happening; roots, leaves, rind, they all keep busy at their work. But it's the same slow, vegetable sort of business over and over again. One tends to lose interest. To escape unbearable monotony, I put myself in a deep sleep. The ax woke me up. And now, since the tree is dead, my captivity is over."

During Arbican's account, an idea had come to Mallory that made her tremble with such excitement she could barely speak of it. Nevertheless, as soon as Arbican finished, she hastily began:

"About the wishes—"

The enchanter gave her a puzzled glance. "About what wishes?"

"If your tree hadn't been cut down," Mallory answered hesitantly, "that is, if Scrupnor hadn't ordered the woods to be cleared—"

"Scrupnor? What's that?"

"He's the new squire," said Mallory. "He owns all this land, and the farms on the other side. He wants to build a road between here and Castleton."

"Fascinating, no doubt, to this what's-his-name," said Arbican, "but hardly of interest to me."

"Yes, it is—I mean, if it hadn't been for Scrupnor's road, your tree wouldn't have been chopped down. Of course, the woodcutters did that. Even so, I was the one who got you out."

"I am quite aware of it. What are you driving at?"

"Three wishes," declared Mallory, plucking up her courage. "In every tale I know, whoever does a good turn to anybody with magical powers—gets three wishes. Please, this is the only chance I'll ever have. I'm asking for mine."

Arbican stared at her a moment, then retorted:

"Three wishes? Why so few? Have a thousand if you like. Granting them—that's another matter. No enchanter in his or her right mind would grant one wish, let alone three, to a mortal. I shudder to think how you would use them."

"But the tales—" insisted Mallory.

"These tales you keep flinging at me," said Arbican, "believe me, I know nothing whatever about them. I should guess that you humans made them up to suit yourselves, after we had gone. That's the only thing that could account for them. I assure you nothing like that happened in my day. There's a grain of truth, but it's been blown up out of all proportion. Three, indeed, is a magical number—for reasons you couldn't understand and that don't concern you. And you mortals were constantly wishing for things you didn't have. Put the two together, and I can see how such an appalling rumor might start. Wishes? Pure wishful thinking."

Mallory turned her face away, trying to hide her disappointment. "Then you'll grant me nothing—"

"Do you seriously believe anything worthwhile can be had merely for the wishing?" replied Arbican. "Very well, very well, you did me a good turn. You shan't go empty-handed. You shall have a gift, if that will satisfy you; you mortals have such an obsession with getting something in return, that's one thing that hasn't changed. So be it. A small trinket, a remembrance. Here, don't cry. I'll conjure up something for you this very instant."

Grateful for that much, Mallory wiped her cheeks on the back of her hands and watched as Arbican set his cupped palms one on top of the other and muttered under his breath. After a moment, he pulled his upper hand away. Mallory gave him a questioning look. The enchanter's outstretched palm was empty.

Arbican frowned. "One moment. My skill is a little rusty."

Again, he cupped his palms and muttered to himself. He peered between his fingers and his face went even paler.

"Nothing," he said in disbelief. "Nothing at all."

Staring at his empty hands, Arbican sank down on a clump of grass. Though eager to see a real wizard cast a spell, Mallory was more concerned for Arbican, so shaken by his failure that he seemed unable to speak, as his face clouded and the furrows on his brow deepened.

"It's those wretched years crammed into that tree," he muttered at last. "Something's happened to me. The clumsiest apprentice could have done that charm, but I can't get the hang of it now. It darts away, like a fish in my head. My magic's gone."

"But enchanters can't lose their power. It never happened in any of the tales—"

"More tales? Of course we can lose our power. It seldom happens, but then, one is seldom shut up in a tree. Now, please, I must think this over very carefully."

"You needn't worry about giving me a gift," Mallory suggested. "If it's too much of a strain, I don't want to trouble you."

"Gift?" cried Arbican. "Do you suppose I'm worried about conjuring up some trivial reward? There's more to it than that. I may never get to Vale Innis."

"You've forgotten where it is?"

"No, I haven't forgotten," snapped Arbican. "I mean I can't reach it at all, not in the state I'm in. Without going into details, I put it to you simply: Unless I have all my powers, I'm stuck tighter in your mortal world than ever I was in my tree."

"If you have to stay," said Mallory, "you can surely find something to do. You could learn a trade if you wanted. We need a good stonemason, and there's plenty of work for another carpenter."

"Delightful prospect," said Arbican. "I don't think you realize the situation. In the first place, I don't belong here and I have no desire to linger. In the second place, without my magic I'm helpless as a turtle out of its shell. All I can hope is that my present incapacity is only temporary."

"Until your power comes back," said Mallory, "you could live in the cook-shop." Then she quickly shook her head. "No. Mrs. Parsel won't even let me keep a cat. I can imagine what she'd say if I brought home a wizard. Though I could hide you in the stable for a while."

"And if someone found me there? In my condition, the less mortals see of me the better."

"I know where you'll be safe," Mallory said. "Come with me."

Without waiting for Arbican to question or protest, she took his hand and hurried him out of the clearing, half leading and half pushing the enchanter through the underbrush. She scrambled down a slope to a shallow gully, while Arbican tried to keep up with her long strides. At last, she stopped where the gully ended in a tumble of rocks, and pointed to the narrow mouth of a cave.

"It's my secret place," Mallory said, drawing the reluctant enchanter after her. "No one in the village knows about it; or if they do, they never bother. Before my father and mother died, the year there was fever in the village, I used to play here all the time. But now, hardly ever. Since the Parsels took me in for their kitchen maid, they keep me too busy. You'll feel right at home."

Arbican glanced around the cave, which widened into a large, rock-walled chamber. He grimaced. "So I should, if I were a bat or a bear."

"Don't enchanters live in caves?" Mallory began. "Or grottoes, or burrows under a hill."

"I am not a rabbit," Arbican replied. "Yes, I do know of one who lived in a cave, but he was a strange sort to begin with. Fascinated with minerals: diamonds, emeralds, all that rubbish. But I assure you his cave was rather more elaborate than this."

"A castle, then? Is that where you lived? Full of magic mirrors, and chests of jewels, and golden cups? Did you have a high throne of crystal? And servants to fetch you anything you commanded?"

"I lived in a cottage, which suited me very nicely," said Arbican. "You mortals were the ones who put on such airs with your castles. I've never been in one that didn't have a draft howling through it like the north wind."

"I always called this cave my castle," said Mallory.

"It's damp enough," replied Arbican.

"I'd pretend it had golden turrets and banners flying," Mallory went on. "Or make believe it was a great mansion, twice as big as the squire's, and I should be mistress of the manor, with stables of horses, and fine carriages, and lovely gowns and feather beds; and I should never have to wash dishes or scrub pots. Or if I did, they'd be my own dishes and pots, and not Mrs. Parsel's."

Arbican, pacing over the dirt floor, had stubbed his toe on a heap of smooth pebbles. "What idiot set a pile of rocks in here?" he cried, hopping on one foot. "I'll end up lame if I don't catch my death of chilblains first!"

Mallory stooped to gather up the scattered pebbles. "They're mine," she said. "I used to pretend they were wishing stones. If I held one in my hand, whatever I wished would come true. Of course, it never happened."

"I shouldn't wonder," the enchanter remarked. "Great heavens, girl, do you mind telling me where you got such peculiar notions of magic?"

"From my mother," answered Mallory.

"Oh, come now," Arbican exclaimed. "You won't have me believe your mother was some kind of enchantress."

"No, she wasn't," Mallory quickly admitted. "But she was a wonderful storyteller; you should have seen how many people in the village would come to listen. But I liked it most when she'd tell the old tales just to my father and me, and there'd be only the three of us beside the fire. My father was a cabinetmaker, the best in the village, and sometimes, when he listened to my mother, he'd carve all sorts of things from bits of wood—birds and beasts, kings and queens, better than any dolls you'd ever see. They had to be burned, after my parents died; Mrs. Parsel was afraid they'd bring fever into her house, too. So they're gone. But I've never forgotten my mother's tales. I make up my own, too. Maybe that's why they don't sound quite right to you."

"It becomes more and more apparent to me," said Arbican, "you mortals have been both industrious and ingenious in fabricating accounts of matters you know nothing whatever about. And then, in typical human fashion, you've convinced yourselves that such products of your fancy are true, simply because you want them to be true. I suppose it's a harmless occupation, but I find it disconcerting. What a blessing you don't have magical powers! I hate to think what would happen if your wishes were granted: gowns, feather beds, bags of gold, horses and carriages—believe me, if they all came tumbling out of the sky, you'd soon find little pleasure in them. Of all things to wish for, you chose the most useless."

"That's not fair to say," Mallory protested. "You make it sound as though gowns and feather beds were all I cared about. What I wished, more than anything, was for my parents to be alive and all of us happy together."

"As for that," said Arbican, not quite so gruffly, "there has never been enchantment strong enough. Magic can't work miracles."

"One wish did come true," Mallory insisted. "I used to wish for my fairy godmother to come and find me. And here you are."

"Well, I'm certainly not your godmother," retorted Arbican. "And if I don't reach Vale Innis, I'll soon be nothing at all."

"What do you mean?"

"I'll die," Arbican answered flatly. "In short order. I've already lived beyond my time here."

"Why didn't you say so in the first place?" cried Mallory. "That's terrible. Are you sure?"

"Quite sure," answered Arbican.

"How can you say that? asked Mallory, more dismayed at Arbican's words than the enchanter himself appeared to be. "How can you sit there and talk so calmly about dying?"

"I create illusions," replied Arbican. "I don't indulge myself in them. This is what will happen. I don't say I look forward to it in the least."

"You won't die," Mallory declared. "No, not after I saved your life. I'll help you. I'll do everything I can."

To think I'd see the day when I have to rely on a mortal," the enchanter groaned. "Ludicrous, incongruous, and a little humiliating. Very well. If I'm to get my powers back again, I shall need a few things: some bread, a piece of cheese, a slice of meat; if possible, a jug of water."

Mallory frowned. "For a magic potion?"

"For me to eat. In addition to your other misconceptions, do you imagine enchanters don't get hungry?"

Clutching her basket, Mallory hurried from the cave and through the underbrush. At the fringe of the woods, she followed a narrow footpath bordering a new-plowed field; then turned down a sunken land that led to the first low-roofed houses of the village. Burnet, the weaver, had already opened his shutters and she caught sight of him threading his loom. By this time of day, Emmet the harnessmaker should have been at his workbench in the open-fronted shop. Instead, the harnessmaker and a half-a-dozen of the villagers stood intently listening to a man in rough homespun. Mallory recognized him as one of the cottagers who came each week to huckster what they could spare from their vegetable patches. Today, however, the cottager was brandishing a sheet of paper covered with seals and stamps:

"There's the notice," Mallory heard him declare. "See for your-selves. I'm not quick at my letters, but as I make it out, Squire's putting us off the land, and we tenants there since my great-grandparents' time."

"Well, Hullock, you can't say nay to him," put in one of the village men. "It's Scrupnor's property now; he has the right side of the law."

"The old squire would never have done," exclaimed Hullock. "Not tear down a person's house and home for the sake of a filthy lump of coal. Where do I live then, with wife and little ones?"

"Don't take on," said another of the villagers. "You can lodge with us a while, till you're settled again."

"And how earn my bread?" cried Hullock. "Grub in Squire's coal pits like a mole?"

"It may come to that for us all, sooner or later," answered the villager.

Despite her haste, Mallory stopped to listen. There had been talk, before now, of coal pits to be dug in place of the smallholdings, but no one had really believed Scrupnor would do it. As Mallory stood a moment, the harnessmaker caught sight of her.

"You watch your step, lass. Mrs. Parsel's been looking for you. Squire's at the cook-shop now, and the notary with him."

Thanks to Emmet's warning, Mallory followed a narrow alley that brought her unseen to the rear of the cook-shop. Scrupnor's bay mare was indeed tethered in the stable, along with two others. Mallory cautiously crossed the yard and ventured to open the back door. Seeing no one in the kitchen, she slipped inside and made her way to the larder.

Beyond the kitchen lay the shop itself, half common room, half parlor. At one of the trestle tables sat Mrs. Parsel in her finest lavender shawl; nearly eclipsed by the stout figure of his wife, Mr. Parsel leaned across the table, cupping his ear as though he feared to miss even one of Scrupnor's words.

"Now, that settles most of our business," the squire was saying. He picked up the sheets of parchment in front of him and his heavy jaws worked up and down as if he were about to chew the documents, red tapes, wax seals and all. Scrupnor's brass-buttoned riding coat stretched tight across his shoulders; his neck overflowed the linen stock, and he seemed at any moment about to explode out of his clothes. His hair, reddish and short-cropped, scarcely covered all his head, and his bare temples bulged like a pair of clenched fists. "Item, indebtedness. Correct. Item, hypothecation—that's mortgage, Mr. Parsel. The terms are all set forth."

Pulling at his side whiskers, Mr. Parsel nodded eagerly, as if being hypothecated were the dearest wish of his life. Before he could speak, however, Mrs. Parsel heaved herself closer to the table and replied in his place:

"What it agglomerates down to, Squire, our cook-shop's to be made into an inn, and none other in the village. Parsel's to have the keeping of it, him and none other."

"But, now, Squire," Mr. Parsel put in, "as for the meat and drink—the victualization, we call it in the trade—that's to be bought from you?"

"Correct," replied Scrupnor. "In exclusivity, to put the proper legal term on it."

"I've always dealt with Farmer Tench," said Mr. Parsel. "He gives good value for money, especially in the matter of vegetables."

"From now on, you'll deal with me," said Scrupnor. "That, sir, is the very nature and essence of exclusivity."

From the kitchen, Mallory could not help overhearing the exchange between the Parsels and Scrupnor, but her thoughts were only to lay hands on whatever leftovers she could find and take them to Arbican as fast as she could. She snatched up half a loaf of bread and a remnant of cheese and dropped them into her basket. The floor creaked behind her; though before she could turn, an arm was flung tightly about her waist and a hand seized her by the hair.

Mallory choked back a cry and twisted around to find herself staring up into the grinning face of Bolt, the squire's game-keeper. The more she struggled, the more Bolt tightened his fingers in her hair until her eyes watered so heavily she could scarcely see. She beat her fists against his jacket while Bolt only laughed at her efforts.

"I saw you come sneaking in," he said in her ear, pulling Mallory closer. "Little baggage, what are you up to? You'll catch it from Mrs. P. But you be cheerful and friendly, now; stay on my good side and she'll never know you're here."

For answer, Mallory kicked him twice in the shins. Bolt let out a roar, snatched away his hands to rub frantically at the injured parts, jigging up and down on one leg then the other. The gamekeeper's bellowing, however, brought the Parsels and their company hurrying into the kitchen. Mallory would have tried to escape then and there and face the consequences later. But as the girl stooped to retrieve the scattered leftovers, Mrs. Parsel, showing amazing lightness of foot, laid hold of Mallory and, unhesitating, boxed her ears.

"Lay on," cried Bolt, as if Mrs. Parsel needed further encouragement.

"My dear," Mr. Parsel murmured to his wife, "shouldn't we know what she's done?"

"She's like to paralyze me, the little beast, isn't that enough?" the gamekeeper declared.

"Quite enough," agreed Mrs. Parsel. "You stay out of this, Parsel. She's in one of her moods. If you ask me, it's the fairy tales that does it. Her head's so stuffed with those tales; I try every way to get them out, but no use."

"Pernicious and unwholesome," said Scrupnor, nodding gravely, while Bolt limped to the kitchen table and sat down. "A heavy burden you bear, Mrs. Parsel. But I fear not much can be done. Once these fancies infect the brain, they're not easily cured. I tell you, Mrs. Parsel, I'd rather a dozen cases of the smallpox than one case of the fairy tales."

"It's in her blood," said Mrs. Parsel. "Handed down from her mother; as you might say a family curse."

"I always enjoyed hearing the old stories," Mr. Parsel murmured.

"Yes, and you see what they've done to you," retorted Mrs. Parsel. "Turned you into a softheaded fool. If it hadn't been for my pushing and prodding, you'd have never seen what a fortune Squire offered you. Brace yourself up, Parsel. Drain such nonsense out of your mind. Why, that girl's downright contagious!"

Mrs. Parsel said, in a tone promising further ministrations at a more convenient time, "set out glasses, and a plate of cakes. Make a nice tray, do you hear, with the clean napkins."

Scrupnor had put the last flourish to his signature when Mallory brought in the tray. He rose to his feet. "No, no thank you, Mrs. P. I should not have indulged myself in your hospitality so long to begin with."

The squire strode to the kitchen doorway and ordered Bolt to bring around the horses. Mrs. Parsel smiled and curtsied after the departing Scrupnor, so deeply moved by this morning's business he could scarcely wait to put it behind him. No sooner were the visitors out of sight than Mrs. Parsel turned furiously to Mallory, who braced herself for another box on the ear. But Mrs. Parsel had settled on a longer method of correction.

"You'll launder my gown and clean my slippers, though you've spoiled them past wearing. And have it done by mid-day. You'll scrub that floor, too, and don't let me find speck nor spot. When you've finished that—"

The more Mrs. Parsel added to the list of tasks, the more Mallory despaired, seeing herself trapped for hours in the cook-shop. Arbican, she was sure, had already begun to worry about her ever coming back.

"Don't stand there like a dumb ox," cried Mrs. Parsel. "You've already idled away the morning. Get to work straightway. I'll have my eye on you."

"Look here," Mr. Parsel said, taking a pair of yellow gloves from the table. "Squire's forgotten these."

"Couldn't you have seen that before he went?" replied Mrs. Parsel, shifting her attention from Mallory to her husband. "You're as harebrained as the girl, I swear you are. Squire will be wanting those gloves."

"He'll no doubt send for them once he remembers where he left them," said Mr. Parsel. "He won't freeze in the meantime."

Mrs. Parsel turned to Mallory. "You run to the Holdings. Give those gloves to Squire with our compliments and tell him as we're sorry for his inconvenience." Mrs. Parsel, as an afterthought, took the cakes out of her husband's reach. Wrapping the dainties in a napkin, she set them carefully in a wicker hamper and, from the pantry shelf, added a fresh-baked pork pie and a pot of strawberry jam.

"You'll give Squire this, too, she told Mallory. "Poor man, he's so busy seeing to others' welfare, he scarcely has a moment to enjoy the better things in life. He'll appreciate a little thoughtfulness; and it should put him in mind to give us a cheaper price on vegetables."

She thrust the hamper into Mallory's arms. "Be off, now, and quick. I want to see you back here within the hour."

After a parting shove from her benefactress to set her on the way, Mallory hurried from the shop. Mrs. Parsel, she realized furiously, had given her an impossible task. "And she's done it on purpose, too," Mallory told herself. "There's no way in the world I can get to the Holdings and back in an hour, not even if I run every step. Oh, blast Scrupnor and his stupid gloves!"

Beyond the village, instead of following the lane to the Holdings, Mallory turned and ran into the trees. However, at last reaching the cave, she halted in alarm at the loud rasping and snorting noises. With a cry, ready to defend the helpless wizard against whatever monstrous attack, she plunged inside and nearly tripped over Arbican, who lay flat on his back. She flung down the hamper and dropped to her knees beside him. Only then did she realize he was merely fast asleep and snoring at the top of his lungs.

She gave a sob of relief. Arbican stirred, opened one eye, then the other, and sat up.

"So there you are. I must say you took your time about it."

Mallory had been so certain Arbican would be as worried about her as she was about him that his casual remark stung more sharply than Mrs. Parsel's box on the ear. For the instant, forgetting he was an enchanter, she retorted:

"I've only just run my legs off. And torn my dress. It was all I could do to get back to you, and I shouldn't even be here but on my way to the Holdings, and I'll be punished for that. And you, snoring away as if nothing else mattered!"

"First, I do not snore," answered Arbican, drawing himself up, "and second—"

"You do!" insisted Mallory. "I heard you. It was terrible."

"I was thinking," said Arbican. "Loudly, perhaps. But thinking, nonetheless. And second, much as I regret your difficulties I must regard them as rather less distressing than my own. A torn dress can easily be mended, hardly a matter of life and death."

"I'm sorry," said Mallory, though disappointed at Arbican's response. He was right, as she admitted; but she still wished he had given her a warmer welcome. "It wasn't only on my account. There was bad news in the village. Scrupnor's tearing down all the cottages and he's going to start a coal pit. I doubt that means much to you, either. I don't suppose you know or even care what coal is."

"I know perfectly well," said Arbican. "We enchanters were quite aware of it. And in our considered opinion, it was best left where it was. If you mortals happened to stumble on it, well, then, the responsibility was yours. But we surely weren't going to encourage it. What happened, with coal or anything else, was altogether up to you."

"How could that be? You were the ones to decide things, weren't you? With all you knew, and all your magical powers—why, the greatest kings and queens had to obey your commands."

"Another of your peculiar notions," Arbican said. "No, not at all. You humans were free to do as you chose and take the consequences. Of course we had power; but we weren't about to use it at every whipstitch, to pull you out of messes you made for yourselves. Of course we had wisdom—if anyone chose to seek it from us; needless to say, few did. But we weren't going to cram it down people's throats. That, in itself, would hardly be very wise."

"If that's so," began Mallory, frowning, "it sounds as if magic didn't make much difference to anybody."

The enchanter nodded. "That's the first flicker of true intelligence I've observed in you since we met. Much difference? None at all. Why do you think our age ended? Because our magic failed. I told you before, magic can't work miracles; you humans have to work your own. There was no enchantment to make you the least bit kinder, gentler, or happier. Without that, there was no point in it."

"Do you mean you never changed pumpkins into coaches? Or spun straw into gold?"

"Oh, I don't say *never*," admitted Arbican. "It would depend on the situation. Shape-changing, transmutation, and the rest—we did that only to help you understand: the world is all one place, life is life, whatever form it happens to be in. A simple proposition, but one you mortals found equally simple to ignore. Our efforts turned out to be useless."

"Useless?" said Mallory. "If I had your powers, you'd see if they were useless. For one thing, I'd soon put an end to Scrupnor's coal pits. I'd turn the coal to dust; or the picks and shovels to glass, so they'd always break. If you'd show me how to use magic on him, I'd cast a spell and put him to sleep for a thousand years—"

"You've understood nothing at all of what I've been telling you," said Arbican. "Magic doesn't touch the real center of things, only the outside edges. Suppose, indeed, you put this fellow Scrupnor out of the way? What's the good, if you keep on making the same mistakes over and over again? You don't cure an itch merely by scratching it."

"I don't care," said Mallory. "I still wish I could change him into a toad, or send him flying to the moon."

"Nonsense," replied Arbican. "No need for that. You have power enough already to do anything you want, if you really want to do it."

"But you just finished telling me that magic was useless," Mallory protested.

"I said 'magic' not 'power,'" corrected Arbican. "As far as power is concerned, you mortals have precisely the same powers as the greatest enchanter. Only yours take a different shape. And most of the time, you don't even realize you have them. You're so busy wishing for good fortune you don't have time to find it for yourselves."

Mallory, still puzzled and unconvinced, would have asked Arbican to tell her more. The enchanter, however, had discovered the provisions in the hamper and was cramming bits of pie into his mouth.

"You deal with your problems in your way," mumbled the enchanter, trying to chew and talk at the same time, "and I shall deal with mine. While you insisted I was snoring, I was devising a plan for getting myself to Vale Innis."

"You found a way?"

"Of course," replied Arbican. "Very simple. I should have thought of it immediately. I shall sail there by boat, as I should have done in the first place."

"No one in the village has a sailboat," said Mallory. "There's a barge at the timber yard by the river. Hodge uses it to ferry logs. There's a couple of rowboats, and that's all."

"No common craft will take me to Vale Innis," the enchanter said. "I shall build my own, and build it from the wood of my oak tree. As it was my prison, it shall be my vessel of freedom. During all those years, no doubt some of my own magic seeped into the wood, and that should make it all the better."

"Have you ever built a boat?" asked Mallory.

"No," said Arbican. "Nor have I ever stood on my ear, or caught eels in a sieve. Given the situation, I shall know how to deal with it."

Swallowing the last morsels of food, Arbican climbed to his feet and brushed the crumbs from his beard. His cheeks, Mallory was glad to see, had turned a healthy pink and his eyes had brightened. She followed as the enchanter stepped briskly out of the cave and made his way back to the fallen oak.

"Are you going to build the boat now?" asked Mallory, as Arbican critically eyed the tree. "Just like that? Shouldn't you have a magic wand? Or draw a magic circle and burn roots and herbs?"

"Certainly not," Arbican snorted. "For some strange reason, you humans have always had the notion that anything important must be accompanied by a great show of nonsense. In my day, there were those who wouldn't believe the simplest weather prophecy unless we made a to-do over it. Somehow, it reassured them. Inessential, nevertheless. The magic is inside, not outside. Now, you mentioned a river Which way?"

Mallory pointed the direction. Arbican then fixed his gaze on the tree trunk, stretched out his hands, and began murmuring under his breath.

"Wait—please," Mallory suddenly burst out. "I must ask you—"

"Will you be quiet!" ordered the enchanter, frowning in exasperation. "My power had just started working. Very well, what is it now?"

"Please—" urged Mallory. "Take me with you. To Vale Innis—"

"What?" cried Arbican, staring at her as if he could hardly believe his ears. "You? A mortal? Great heavens, girl, that's impossible."

"For an enchanter? It can't be impossible," Mallory insisted. "Surely you could do it if you wanted? It's bad enough drudging for the Parsels, but if Scrupnor has his way, it's going to be worse; for the whole village, too."

"So you, for one, prefer to run off? While the others make the best of a bad bargain? You humans haven't changed at all since my day, have you?"

"I didn't mean it that way," Mallory protested.

"However you mean it," said Arbican, "it's out of the question. No, I could not take you with me even if I wanted to. Absolutely not. So put that idea out of your head, once and for all."

Mallory lowered her eyes; more than disappointed, she now felt foolish at having made such a plea. Worse, Arbican had judged her selfish, and she wondered if he had been right. Arbican, meanwhile, seemed to bend under some heavy but invisible burden. The tree remained as it was and after several moments Mallory ventured to whisper:

"What's wrong? It isn't turning into a boat."

"Of course it isn't," snapped Arbican. "Only an idiot would build a boat in the middle of the woods. I shall raise this tree and have it fly to the river. Now, if holding your tongue is too difficult for you, kindly go and wait somewhere else."

He turned again to his task. His arms tensed and trembled while droplets trickled down his forehead into his beard. The tree rocked back and forth, slowly rose a hand's breadth above the turf, only to fall heavily to the ground.

Abrican grunted and puffed out his cheeks. He seemed, suddenly, to have grown taller than Mallory. Then she realized the enchanter, not the oak, was rising steadily into the air.

"Catch hold!" shouted Arbican, waving his arms and kicking his heels. "The spell's gone wrong! Pull me down! Can't you see I'm floating away?"

Mallory sprang forward, leaped as high as she could, and snatched at Arbican's feet, already beyond her grasp. Sputtering and flapping his cloak, the enchanter continued his flight.

Then, even as she watched helplessly, the enchanter's waving arms blurred and shimmered. Mallory rubbed her eyes. Within the instant, so quickly that one shape seemed to flicker into the other, Arbican was gone and in his place, awkwardly flapping its wings, was a large gray goose.

The bird stretched its neck and beat its wings, as if finding some difficulty in staying aloft. It hung briefly poised in the air before plunging to the ground, where it landed in a burst of feathers.

"Now this is intolerable," came a voice from the goose's bill, which clacked open and shut irritably. "I haven't flown for ages. Am I expected to do it at a moment's notice?"

"You turned yourself into a goose," Mallory gasped, still unable to believe her eyes.

"Most assuredly I did not," replied Arbican. "I had nothing to do with it. Do you think I deliberately chose this shape? My powers are all topsy-turvy. I can't manage them. All I wanted to do was float back to earth—and you see the consequences."

"But you can't stay that way," said Mallory. Her first shock had passed and she was growing a little more used to conversing with a goose; though she had to remind herself continually that it was no bird at all, but the enchanter merely in a different guise. "What are you going to do? Wait, I know," she hurried on, brightening. "When the princess kissed the frog, he turned back into a prince. Do you think if I—"

"No, I do not," returned Arbican, with a honking kind of snort. "That's more of your fairy tales; it has no bearing whatever on the facts of the matter."

"I only thought it might help," answered Mallory, wounded. "But if that's the way you feel about it—"

"Feelings have nothing to do with the case," said Arbican. "It will take more than a kiss to get me out of this bundle of feathers. If I can't control my power, I may be stuck here as badly as I was in my tree. Though I must say between the two I'd rather be a bird than a vegetable."

"If you can't change yourself back," asked Mallory, "then do you think you could fly to Vale Innis? You wouldn't need the boat at all."

The goose unfolded a wing and cocked a thoughtful eye at it. "Perhaps you're right. I should hate admitting to my colleagues that I couldn't handle the most elementary transformation; I'd never hear the end of it. Still, that's better than staying in your world.

"Yes, I'm sure I can," the enchanter went on, stretching his wings and rising on his webbed feet as if to take flight then and there. "These geese are strong creatures, you know. Good thing I didn't end up as a chicken. Yes, I believe this will do perfectly. So, I shall be on my way. Goodby, I wish you well. 'Wish'—that's a hope, you understand, not a promise."

Mallory, more unsettled by the enchanter's abrupt leave-taking than by his transformation, could only stammer a confused farewell, adding, Watch out for the hawks—"

"The hawks," Arbican assured her, "had better watch out for me."

With that, he beat his wings vigorously, launched himself into the air, and began climbing steadily upward. Forlorn, Mallory watched his flight. However, at the level of the tree tops, the goose veered sharply, seeming to struggle against the wind. Instead of gaining height, the bird labored mightily to keep aloft. Mallory cried out in dismay as it plummeted earthward. For it was no longer a goose, but Arbican, once again in his own shape, frantically waving his arms and kicking his legs.

An instant later, the enchanter went crashing heavily through the upper limbs of a high elm and vanished into the foliage. Mallory raced to the tree. Caught among the branches like a fly in a web, Arbican dangled head downward, one leg flung over a jutting limb, his beard ensnared by twigs. The enchanter's face was crimson, a result of both his posture and his indignation.

"Don't move!" ordered Mallory, scrambling up the trunk. "Stay right as you are!"

"Can I do anything else?" flung back the enchanter. "Except fall and break my neck?"

By this time, Mallory had succeeded in climbing close enough to disentangle Arbican's beard. To do more, she realized, would be difficult; for Arbican was so ensnared that a false move on his part might send him tumbling head first to the ground. The enchanter's predicament had done nothing to improve his temper; while Mallory tried to study the best way to get him down, Arbican sputtered and fumed, until at last Mallory lost her own patience.

"Will you be quiet?" she burst out. "The way you're carrying on, you'll only make things worse. Now, move very slowly and do exactly as I tell you. Or you will break your neck, and mine too."

Cautiously, she hoisted herself to the branch nearest the enchanter, who still grumbled under his breath. From there, she was able to unhook his leg while Arbican, obediently following her directions, took a firm grasp on the limb just below him. As Mallory ordered, he swung down until he was able to clamp his knees against the trunk. Inch by inch, as she pointed out each handhold, Arbican climbed gingerly to the ground. Out of breath, trembling from his exertions, he collapsed in a heap, while Mallory clambered after him. The enchanter, for once too exhausted even to complain, held his head in his hands. The branches had torn his cloak and pulled away bits of his beard; and the only reminder of his hopeful flight was a ragged feather clinging to his disheveled hair.

"Whatever happened?" asked Mallory, once sure the enchanter had been wounded only in his dignity. "You were doing so well."

"I told you I'm not master of my powers," Arbican replied. "They come and go as they please. I can't get hold of them. Fly to Vale Innis? I doubt I'll ever get there at all."

"You can still try to sail," Mallory reminded him.

"Build a boat? The way my spells are going, it would turn out to be a wheelbarrow."

"Suppose you built it the ordinary way? Mr. Parsel keeps a box of tools in the shed. I could bring them here. The oak has all the wood we need. For a sail, we can use a bedsheet, or one of Mrs. Parsel's petticoats; they're certainly big enough."

"A fine figure I'd cut," said Arbican, "sailing to Vale Innis, propelled by bed linen and underclothing. However, this is no time to be picky about details. Very well. First, how do you propose to get this tree to the river?"

"We'll have to saw off the branches, to begin with," answered Mallory. "That should make it easier to handle. Between the two of us, we can drag it with ropes."

"Delightful," grumbled Arbican. "You mortals may be used to that kind of work; I'm not. All I see coming out of your scheme is a sprained back and blistered fingers."

"Well, I'm sorry," returned Mallory, "I want to help you, but if a few blisters are going to bother you, there's nothing to be done."

"I'm afraid that may be the case," said Arbican, looking gloomier than ever. "It also occurs to me it will take too long. I need a seaworthy ship, not a raft. We could spend weeks, even longer. I doubt I have that much time left to me."

"Even so, we could still try," Mallory urged. "Meanwhile, your powers might come back again, just as they used to be."

"And if they don't?"

"You'd be no worse off than you are now. We have to do something, don't we? There's no use going round in circles. Now, the first thing is to get some rope—"

"Stop, stop," said Arbican. "I'm trying to think. What was it you said—?"

"Rope. We can tie it around the trunk—"

"No, not that. Wait, I have it. Circles." He stopped short for a moment, frowned and rubbed his brow. "It's in the back of my mind. I'd forgotten. Living in a tree makes the memory rather wooden." Suddenly his face brightened. "Yes, yes, of course! The circle of gold!"

Arbican jumped to his feet, more excited than Mallory had ever seen him. "That's it! The simplest thing in the world!"

"A circle of gold?" said Mallory. "I don't understand—"

"The spell, the incantation, the recipe, whatever you want to call it. Every apprentice learns it in case of emergency. To think it had slipped my mind! No matter, I have it now: *To gain all power lost of old, a maid must give a circle of gold.*"

"I still don't understand what it means."

"It means," answered Arbican, "exactly what it says. What a relief! That clears up things considerably. Now, once I find a maid—"

"Why not me?" asked Mallory.

Arbican said nothing for a moment, then nodded. "Yes, you might do very well for that part of it. That leaves only the circle of gold to be accounted for."

"What kind of circle?"

"What difference does it make? A circle is a circle, isn't it? The spell says no more than that. You should have no trouble finding something appropriate. I shan't keep it. You'll get it back, after it serves its purpose."

"It must have been easier in your day," said Mallory. "There's no gold to speak of in the village. I surely haven't any. My mother's wedding ring—Mrs. Parsel sold it long ago. Mrs. Parsel? She wears a ring. Whether it's really gold, I don't know. Besides, she never takes it off; her finger's grown too thick."

"Do you mean to tell me," said Arbican, "for lack of a mere trinket, my spell is ruined? Unthinkable!"

"Scrupnor might have something we could use," Mallory went on. "But how to find it?" She gave a cry of dismay. "Scrupnor! The gloves!"

"We're talking about gold," said Arbican, "not gloves."

"They're Scrupnor's. He left them at the shop. I forgot. I was to take them to the Holdings."

"He can get along without them," said Arbican. "Don't waste time on pointless errands."

"I must," Mallory insisted. "It's bad enough you ate all the food Mrs. Parsel meant for him. If she knows I didn't even bring his gloves to him, she'll punish me severely. I'll never get away to help you."

"In that case, deliver the wretched things and have done with it."

"It's too late. She only gave me an hour, and that wasn't enough to begin with. I was in trouble when I left, now I'll be in worse."

"And so will I," said Arbican, tugging angrily at his beard. "Thanks to some fool and his gloves. Very well, I'll try to carry you to what's-his-name, Scrupnor, and bring you back to this Parsel creature as fast as I can."

"Carry me?" returned Mallory. "You'd never get half way."

"Not on my back," snapped Arbican. "Do you take me for a pack mule? No, I'll try my power again. If it works, we'll be there in a wink. If it doesn't, we might not move from this spot, or we might end up who knows where. There's a risk, I warn you."

"I'm not afraid," Mallory declared in spite of the sudden trembling of her knees. However, the prospect of being separated from Arbican brought back much of her courage. "Tell me what I have to do."

"You'll guide me," said Arbican, taking one of her hands firmly in his own. "Think where you want to go. See it behind your eyes and inside your head. Can you do that?"

"I don't know. I'll try. I haven't been often to the Holdings."

"Do your best, then."

Mallory shut her eyes tightly, remembering as clearly as she could the last time she had ridden there with Mr. Parsel in the horse cart. She pictured to herself the high wall of gray stone, the iron gate, the gravel pathway curving in front of the mansion; the tall chimneys, the gables, the casements. However, no sooner did these come to mind than a dozen other recollections flooded over them. The more she tried to fix the Holdings in her imagination, the more her thoughts flew elsewhere: to Scrupnor, to Arbican caught in the tree. She heard the enchanter's voice:

"Ready?"

"It makes my head spin," cried Mallory. "I'm trying as hard as I can, but everything's mixed up."

"You're trying too hard. Hold your thoughts gently, don't squeeze the life out of them."

Mallory's vision of the Holdings reappeared, but along with it came Mrs. Parsel threatening to make her stay in her room; and she saw herself beating vainly against a bolted door.

"Now!" commanded Arbican.

"Wait—not yet!" Mallory's heart pounded, her ears rang as the turf gave way beneath her feet. Clutching the hamper, she felt herself go blindly lurching and spinning through sudden blackness. Arbican still held her hand; but now, to keep from falling, she clung to the latch of a heavy, iron-studded portal. Beside her, the enchanter peered curiously around the windowless room at the shelves loaded with stacks of papers and boxes tied with cord. In one corner stood a writing desk and a high stool. At a table, hedged with account books, a large metal cashbox by his elbow, sat Scrupnor.

The squire at that moment glanced up from the ledger in which he had been writing a column of figures. He reached out to dip his quill into the ink pot; but at sight of Mallory and Arbican, he stopped his hand in mid-air. His eyes bulged, his cheeks twitched with a life of their own, and he sprang to his feet, overturning the cashbox and sending the ink pot flying.

Her head still whirling, startled no less than Scrupnor to find herself in the squire's counting room, Mallory blurted out the first words that came to her lips:

"You—you forgot your gloves."

Scrupnor had flung out his arms as though to ward off what he supposed could only be some fiendish assault on his person and possessions; but the sound of Mallory's voice seemed to assure him that he had to deal with beings of flesh and blood. His fear turned to fury as he roared at her:

"How did you come here? What are you up to, spying on me?"

"It's cakes—and a pork pie," stammered Mallory. "They've been eaten. I'm sorry. Your gloves—"

"Pork pie? Gloves? What have you seen? Answer me that!" Instead of calming, the squire's rage flamed higher; he seized Mallory and would have thrown her to the floor had Arbican not stepped forward and commanded him to stop. The enchanter raised an arm and pointed a skinny finger at the furious Scrupnor.

Arbican's stern tone was enough to make Scrupnor snatch his hands away and Mallory stumbled back against the wall. She had hoped the enchanter might whisk the two of them out of the counting room as quickly as he had whisked them into it; but if Arbican had meant to cast a spell, his power once more had gone astray. In defending her, he had only drawn Scrupnor's anger upon himself.

"Who are you?" shouted Scrupnor, now giving full attention to Mallory's companion. Without waiting for a reply, he began yelling for Bolt; and at the same time snatched up a pistol from the table and ordered the intruders to stand as they were. A moment later, the gamekeeper flung open the door.

"Bolt," cried Scrupnor, "I told you, never let anyone in my counting room."

"Squire, I didn't," protested the gamekeeper, astonished at the sight of Mallory and even more bewildered by the presence of Arbican. "I don't know how these two got by. And this old crock here, I don't even know who he is."

Without lowering his pistol, Scrupnor swung to face Arbican. "What's your name? What are you up to?"

"This is Mr. Arbican," Mallory put in hastily, afraid the enchanter and his sharp tongue might worsen matters for both of them. "He's a—traveler. He's lost his way. He stopped to ask directions—"

"I'll give him directions," returned Scrupnor. "Traveler, is he? Where to? The gallows?"

Despite Mallory's warning tug at his robe, Arbican stepped forward, looking Scrupnor squarely between the eyes, and tartly answered:

"If your courtesy is any measure of your conduct, you'll reach that destination sooner than I."

"Hold your tongue, old weasel!" Bolt shook his fist under the enchanter's nose. "I'll take care of him for you, Squire. Gallows bird he is. You can read it in his face."

At a word from Scrupnor, Bolt hurried from the counting room to seek reinforcements. Arbican, meantime, had been studying Scrupnor with a mixture of curiosity and contempt; now he turned calmly to Mallory:

"Come along, we have work to do."

"Don't you see he's got a pistol?" exclaimed Mallory.

"Whatever that is," replied Arbican, unimpressed. He gave Scrupnor a cold glance. "If that implement you're waving at me has any destructive capabilities, put it away immediately."

In answer, Scrupnor leveled the weapon at Arbican. The enchanter shrugged:

"Very well. Since you won't lay it down, your clumsy device is now a serpent, and a very angry one."

At that, Arbican made coiling motions with his fingers. To Mallory's dismay, the firearm stayed as it was. Scrupnor laughed:

"You're a madman!"

"No!" cried Mallory. "Look, look! The snake! Crawling out the barrel!"

Startled by Mallory's warning, and without a pause for thought, Scrupnor turned the weapon to squint at the muzzle, from which no snake whatever was emerging.

Mallory's trick, however, had given her the moment she needed. Snatching up her basket, she flung it with all strength at Scrupnor's head. Taken unawares, the squire lost his balance and stumbled back on his heels. The pistol went spinning out of his hand.

"Come on! Run!" Mallory seized the enchanter and hauled him so quickly from the counting room that he nearly lost his footing, and hustled him along a corridor, through the first door she came to. It led to the kitchen where, at sight of intruders, the cook dropped the meat she was setting over the fire, the serving maid flung away the stack of dishes, and both began screaming at the top of their voices.

Spying an open window, Mallory pushed Arbican over the sill and sent him tumbling into the stable yard. She would have followed but the cook, regaining some of her wits, seized Mallory by the scruff of the neck; and the serving maid picked up a long-handled spoon to flail away at the struggling girl.

The pair, however, proved no match for Mallory, determined at all cost to rejoin the enchanter. Heedless of the blows, she tore loose from the hands of the cook and went pitching headlong into the yard.

She scrambled to her feet. There was no sign of the enchanter. She glanced hurriedly in all directions, at a loss where to turn. The stables were close by and she raced toward them, thinking Arbican might have hidden in one of the stalls. At the same time, waving a pitchfork, the stable boy, Wakeling, came pelting around the corner.

Mallory turned sharply aside. Wakeling, however, paid no heed to the fleeing girl. Instead, he ran to the back of the house, where he collided with the two women and Scrupnor.

"Squire, there's a great stag in the paddock," Wakeling cried. "Come and see!"

"Blast the stag!" bellowed Scrupnor, trying to disengage himself from the excited stable boy. "Where's the old man?"

"Never saw none," answered Wakeling. "But what a stag!"

"Out of my way!" roared Scrupnor, shoving the boy aside. "Find him! Stop the girl!"

By now, Mallory had reached the nearest outbuildings and headed for the stables. From the kennels she heard the frantic yelping of Scrupnor's hunting pack and she changed her course, afraid the enchanter had blundered into the dog runs.

Suddenly, from behind a shed sprang the tallest stag Mallory had ever seen. The creature bounded across her path, reared on its haunches and shook its antlered head:

"Jump! On my back!"

Dumbfounded for the instant, Mallory could only stare at the animal, who stamped impatiently:

"Do as I say! Climb on!"

Not daring to waste another moment questioning Arbican, Mallory clambered astride. Scrupnor, with Wakeling following, pounded across the stable yard but stopped short at seeing her clinging to the prancing stag.

"There he is!" cried Wakeling. "And the cook-shop girl riding him! Now that's a sight for you, Squire!"

The huge animal then lowered its head and bounded ror Scrupnor. Seeing the sharp antlers driving toward him, Scrupnor threw himself to the ground, yelling in terror. The stag, veering at the last moment, sped across the yard and into the pasture. Clearing the fence in one leap, it streaked for the woods.

Mallory, heart in her mouth, clamped arms and legs around the stag as it crashed through the underbrush, plunged into a thicket,

and at all speed pressed deeper into the tangle of branches and vines.

Only when the Holdings were far behind them did the stag halt and let Mallory slide off. Still breathless and shaken by their narrow escape, and amazed at Arbican's new transformation, Mallory threw her arms around the animal's neck.

"You saved us! Your power's come back. That's wonderful!"

The stag snorted. "Wonderful! I meant to change myself into a horse."

Mallory's problems with Arbican are just beginning. Squire Scrupnor is after them now, and Arbican's magic is failing by the hour. Will Scrupnor catch them and lock them in jail? Will they be able to find a circle of gold that will restore Arbican's magic before it is too late? Arbican has told Mallory that she has power enough to do whatever she truly wants to do. Can this be true? How can she help herself, and her wizard friend, out of trouble? Lloyd Alexander answers these questions and many more in the exciting conclusion to *The Wizard in the Tree*.

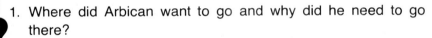

1. Where did Arbican want to go and why did he need to go there?

2. When Arbican refused to take Mallory with him she "felt foolish at having made such a plea. Worse, Arbican had judged her selfish, and she wondered if he had been right." Do you think Mallory was selfish? Why or why not?

3. Arbican said: "As far as power is concerned, you mortals have precisely the same powers as the greatest enchanter. Only yours take a different shape. And most of the time, you don't even realize you have them." What was he trying to tell Mallory?

4. Describe what kind of person Squire Scrupnor was, using examples from the story to support your answer.

5. To which of the traditional story genres does this novel excerpt belong? Why do you think so?

6. Think about your favorite story, one you have heard or read. Explain why this story has a special meaning for you.

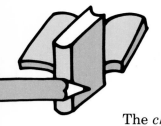

Characterization in "The Wizard in the Tree"

The *characters* in a story are the people or animals involved in the plot. These characters are often described in the following ways:

Major characters are the most important characters in the story. They participate in most of the action, or plot, of the story. *Minor characters* are less important in the plot.

Developing characters are individuals who change by the end of the story. They learn something about themselves or about others that affects the way they think or act. *Static characters* are people whose personalities do not change in the story.

The *protagonist* is the major character with whom you become emotionally involved. A protagonist with admirable qualities is called the *hero.* If the protagonist has a problem or personality similar to your own, you may *identify* with that character. The *antagonist* is the person who tries to stop the protagonist from reaching a desired goal.

ACTIVITY A   Write answers to the following questions about the characters in "The Wizard in the Tree."

1. Who were the two major characters in the story?
2. Who were the most important minor characters in the story?
3. Who were other minor characters in the story?
4. Which characters were developing characters?
5. What things did the developing characters learn about themselves or about others?
6. Which characters were static characters? In what ways did they stay the same?
7. Who was the protagonist in "The Wizard in the Tree"? Give reasons for your answer.
8. Would you classify the protagonist as a hero? If so, what admirable qualities did that character possess?
9. Who were the antagonists in the story? How did they try to prevent the protagonist from reaching a desired goal?
10. Did you identify with any characters in the story? If so,

which characters did you identify with? What part of their problem or personality did you find similar to your own?

One or more of the characters in a story usually face a particular problem, or *conflict*. There are three basic types of conflicts:

1. **Characters against other characters** In this type of conflict, the characters face problems which are created by other characters in the story.
2. **Characters against a force of nature** In this type of conflict, characters are challenged by some natural force.
3. **Characters against themselves** In this type of conflict, characters must solve some personal problem.

ACTIVITY B The characters in "The Wizard in the Tree" face many different problems. Read each problem below. Write whether the type of problem is *characters against other characters, characters against nature,* or *characters against themselves.*

1. Arbican had been caught in a tree and could not get out.
2. Mallory had to steal food for Arbican without being caught.
3. Mallory had to crack open the tree in order to free Arbican.
4. Arbican was personally upset that his magical powers had failed him.
5. Mallory had to suffer the cruel treatment of Mrs. Parsel.
6. The townspeople feared they were going to lose their land and homes to Scrupnor.
7. Arbican's powers failed him when he tried to fly like a goose.
8. Mallory and Arbican had to escape from Scrupnor.

You may learn about a story character in three ways: by the things the character says and does; by the things other characters think, and how the author describes the character.

ACTIVITY C Write a paragraph that describes either Mallory or Arbican. Your first sentence should state the qualities of the character. (Example: Mrs. Brown was selfish, mean, and conceited.) The other sentences in the paragraph should give examples to support your description. When you describe the character, consider what that person says and does, what other characters think, and how the author describes the character.

Plot in "The Wizard in the Tree"

Plot refers to the action that occurs in a story. The plot of a story follows a particular structure:

1. The *exposition* is the beginning of the story. The main characters are introduced in the exposition. The time and location of the story are also established.

2. The *complication* is the problem that arises for one or more of the characters after the action begins.

3. The *rising action* includes the events which cause the problem of a character to become greater.

4. The *climax* of the story is the dramatic moment when it becomes clear how the problem will be settled.

5. The *falling action* includes the events that occur after the climax.

6. The *denouement* is the end, or conclusion, of the story.

ACTIVITY A   Write the following events on your paper in the order in which they occurred in the story.

1. Mallory was ordered to return a pair of gloves to Scrupnor.
2. Mallory was caught while trying to steal food.
3. Mallory helped Arbican get out of a tree.
4. Mallory and Arbican arrived at Scrupnor's house.
5. Arbican came crashing down after flying in the form of a goose.
6. Mallory led Arbican to a cave to keep him safe.
7. Mallory and Arbican escaped from Scrupnor.

ACTIVITY B   Write answers to the following questions about "The Wizard in the Tree."

1. Which characters were introduced in the exposition?
2. What time and location were established in the exposition?
3. What complication did Arbican face in the beginning of the story?
4. What complication did Mallory face in the beginning of the story?

5. What events in the rising action caused Arbican's problems to become greater?
6. What events in the rising action caused Mallory's problems to become greater?
7. What problem did the townspeople face in the story?
8. The selection you have read is from the novel, *The Wizard in the Tree*. But it is not the complete novel. It is an *excerpt*, or part of the story. What was the climax of the excerpt you read? Give reasons for your answer.
9. What falling action, if any, took place after the climax?
10. What was the denouement, or conclusion, of the excerpt you read?

ACTIVITY C   Review the story "Atalanta's Race." Then write answers to these questions about the plot of the story.

1. Which characters were introduced in the exposition?
2. What complication did the youths who raced against Atalanta face in the beginning of the story?
3. What complication did Hippomenes face in the beginning of the story?
4. What events in the rising action caused Hippomenes' problem to become greater?
5. What do you think was the climax of the story? Give reasons for your answer.
6. What falling action took place after the climax?
7. What was the denouement of the story?

ACTIVITY D   Select one other story you have read in this book. Answer these questions about the story.

1. Which characters were introduced in the exposition?
2. What was the setting of the exposition?
3. What complication arose for a major character?
4. What events in the rising action caused the problem to become greater?
5. What was the climax of the story?
6. What falling action, if any, occurred after the climax?
7. What was the denouement?

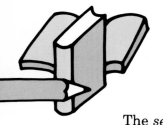

Other Literary Elements in "The Wizard in the Tree"

The *setting* of a story is the time and place in which the action occurs. The setting may change several times in a long story or novel.

The *theme* of a story is the general truth about life which the author expresses in the story. The theme of a story may not be stated directly. In fables, the theme is called the *moral*. The moral is usually stated directly at the end of the fable. Not all themes are morals, however.

You must consider these questions to determine the theme:

1. What kind of characters did the author portray?
2. Did you like or dislike the characters, and why?
3. What did the characters learn about themselves?
4. Why did the author choose that particular story title?

The *point of view* is the position from which the action of the story is observed and narrated. A story narrated in the *first person* is told by a character directly involved in the action. A story narrated in the *third person* is told by the author. The author is not directly involved in the action. The author reports everything about everyone in the story.

Tone refers to the author's manner of speaking. An author may be serious in telling the story. At other times, authors may be humorous, angry, or sarcastic.

Figures of speech refer to the author's use of similes, metaphors, and personification. A *simile* is a comparison of two different things, using the words *like* or *as*. A *metaphor* is a comparison of two different things, using only a form of the verb *be*. *Personification* is an expression in which a nonhuman object is given human qualities.

Stories may be classified as fiction, nonfiction, or historical fiction. *Fiction* is literature about imaginary people and events. *Nonfiction* is literature about real people and events. *Historical fiction* is literature based on real people or events, but contains imaginary events or characters within the story.

Write answers to the following questions about "The Wizard in the Tree."

1 **a.** When and where did the opening scene of the story occur?

    b. In what other locations did action take place?

    c. How much time passed throughout the story?

2. Did you like or dislike Mallory and Arbican? Give reasons for your answer.

3. Select one of the following three statements as the theme of the story. Explain why you think that statement expresses the author's general feeling about life.

    a. People cannot have their dreams come true unless they know a magician or enchanter.

    b. People have the power to accomplish what seems to be impossible if they apply themselves.

    c. When people face the danger of losing their property, they should escape rather than stay and protect themselves.

4. Think about Arbican's tone of speaking in the story. Did the wizard seem to be serious, humorous, angry, or sarcastic? Give three examples to support your answer.

5. Explain the meaning of the following similes. Tell what two things are compared in each simile.

    a. "Without my magic I'm as helpless as a turtle out of its shell."

    b. Arbican was caught among the branches like a fly in a web.

6. Was the story narrated in the first person or third person?

7. Is "The Wizard in the Tree" an example of fiction, nonfiction or historical fiction? Explain the reason for your answer.

8. A *fairy tale* is a story which describes people in unreal or impossible situations. Magic plays an important part in fairy tales. The hero often suffers much hardship, but that character is usually rewarded at the end of the story.

    a. List three unreal or impossible situations in the story.

    b. Describe a scene in which magic played an important part.

    c. Give one example of hardship suffered by the hero.

STORYTELLING

Storytelling is as old as language, and stories are a great example of the power of language to entertain, to excite, and to express human emotions. In "Storytelling," you have read ancient and modern stories in the traditional story forms, or genres. From the ancient *oral* stories have sprung the world's *written* literature: short stories, novels, plays, and poems. Movies and television programs, even magazines and comic books also owe a debt to the storytellers who preserved the tales of old.

Thinking About "Storytelling"

1. Fables and animal stories usually use animals to make a point about human behavior. What human qualities did the Elephant in "The Elephant Who Challenged the World" and Coyote in "Coyote and the Crying Song" possess?

2. "High Diving" and "Atalanta's Race" both involved a person who did something that no one else could do. Describe the differences between the way Billie the Dolphin's achievement and Atalanta's achievement were portrayed.

3. "The Fly" and "Abunuwas the Trickster" have a similar theme. What is it?

4. "Hi Johnny" and "The Wizard in the Tree" both dealt with the folly of wishing to have much more than you have. How was this theme expressed in each story?

5. Choose one of your favorite story forms (genres) and make up your own story.

Glossary

This glossary will help you to pronounce and to understand the meanings of some of the unusual or difficult words in this book.

The pronunciation of each word is printed beside the word in this way: **o·pen** (ō′pən). The letters, signs, and key words in the list below will help you read the pronunciation respelling. When an entry word has more than one syllable, a dark accent mark (′) is placed after the syllable that has the heaviest stress. In some words, a light accent mark (′) is placed after the syllable that receives a less heavy stress.

The pronunciation key, syllable breaks, accent mark placements, and phonetic respellings in this glossary are adapted from the Macmillan *School Dictionary* (1981) and the Macmillan *Dictionary* (1981). Other dictionaries may use other pronunciation symbols.

Pronunciation Key

a	bad	**hw**	white	**ô**	off	**th**	that	**ə** *stands for*
ā	cake	**i**	it	**oo**	wood	**u**	cup	a *as in* age
ä	father	**ī**	ice	**ōō**	food	**ur**	turn	e *as in* taken
b	bat	**j**	joke	**oi**	oil	**yōō**	music	i *as in* pencil
ch	chin	**k**	kit	**ou**	out	**v**	very	o *as in* lemon
d	dog	**l**	lid	**p**	pail	**w**	wet	u *as in* helpful
e	pet	**m**	man	**r**	ride	**y**	yes	
ē	me	**n**	not	**s**	sit	**z**	zoo	
f	five	**ng**	sing	**sh**	ship	**zh**	treasure	
g	game	**o**	hot	**t**	tall			
h	hit	**ō**	open	**th**	thin			

A

ab·a·cus (ab'ə kəs) *n.* a device consisting of a frame with balls or beads that slide back and forth in grooves or on wires, used especially for adding and subtracting.

a·broad (ə brôd') *adv.* out of one's country; in or into foreign lands.

ab·stract (ab'strakt, ab strakt') *adj.* of, relating to, or characteristic of a style in the arts that does not imitate reality directly, but uses lines, geometric forms and colors to express emotion or an aesthetic idea.

A·bu·nu·was (ä boo'noo wäs')

ac·cel·er·a·tor (ak sel'ə rā'tər) *n.* a device for increasing the speed of a machine, especially the foot pedal that controls the speed of an automobile engine.

ac·cess (ak'ses) *n.* **1.** right or permission to approach, enter, or use; admittance. **2.** way of approaching.

ac·cu·sa·tion (ak'yə zā'shən) *n.* **1.** a statement that a person has committed a crime or offense; charge of wrongdoing. **2.** the crime or offense charged. **3.** the act of accusing.

a·do (ə doo') *n.* fuss; bustle; difficulty.

ad·vent (ad'vent) *n.* arrival; coming into being.

ad·ver·sar·y (ad'vər ser'ē) *n. pl.,* **ad·ver·sar·ies.** a person or group that is hostile toward or competing with another; opponent or enemy.

aer·o·naut (ār'ə nôt) *n.* the pilot of a balloon or other lighter-than-air craft.

aer·o·nau·ti·cal (ār'ə not'ə kəl) *adj.* having to do with the science or art of flight.

ag·ate (ag'it) *n.* a semiprecious variety of quartz, usually having variously colored layers or bands.

ag·glom·er·ate (ə glom'ə rāt') *v.,* **ag·glom·er·at·ed, ag·glom·er·at·ing.** to gather in a mass or cluster.

a·gil·i·ty (ə jil'ə tē) *n.* quickness and ease in motion or thought; nimbleness.

a·gi·ta·do (ä hē tä'dō) *adj. Spanish.* agitated; excited; hurried.

Ai Nanze (ī nanz')

Ak She·hir (äk'shə hēr') a town in Turkey.

Al·bu·quer·que (al'bə kur'kē) the largest city of New Mexico, in the north-central part of the state.

al·ien (āl'yən, ā'lē ən) *n.* **1.** a foreign-born person who is not a citizen of the country in which he or she is living. **2.** a foreigner; stranger.

a·li·ma·mo (ä lē mä'mō) *n.* a Mandinkan word meaning "religious leader" or "holy man."

al·li·ance (ə lī'əns) *n.* **1.** a formal agreement between two or more nations to cooperate closely, as in fighting a war or trading goods. **2.** any similar agreement in which persons or groups join together for a common cause.

al·lit·er·a·tion (ə lit'ə rā'shən) *n.* the repetition of the same initial letter, sound, or group of sounds in a series of words, for example: *The furrow followed free.*

al·pha (al'fə) *n.* the first letter of the Greek alphabet. The name *Alpha* was given to one of the first airplanes to be made entirely of metal instead of wood.

am·bro·sia (am brō'zhə) *n.* **1.** something particularly delicious or delightful to taste or smell. **2.** a dessert made of orange sections sprinkled with shredded coconut.

am·bush (am'boosh) *n.* a surprise attack from a hidden position.

a·mok (ə muk', ə mok') *also,* **a·muck.** *adv.* **1. to go amok.** to go awry or amiss. **2. to run amok.** to lose control of oneself and rush about wildly, especially with intent to attack or kill.

am·pli·fy (am'plə fī') *v.,* **am·pli·fied, am·pli·fy·ing. 1.** to add to or expand, as speech or thought; enlarge on. **2.** to increase the strength of (an electronic signal). **3.** to increase in scope, significance, or power; extend.

am·u·let (am'yə lit) *n.* an object worn as a protection against disease, bad luck, or evil; a charm.

a·nal·y·sis (ə nal'ə sis) *n.* a method of finding out the nature of something by separating it into parts; critical examination.

a·nat·o·my (ə nat'ə mē) *n.* **1.** the physical structure of an organism or any of its parts. **2.** the science of the physical structure of organisms and the interrelationships of their parts.

a·non·y·mous (ə non'ə məs) *adj.* **1.** of unknown authorship or origin; without any name given. **2.** not giving one's name; not known by name.

an·ti·dote (an'ti dōt') *n.* **1.** a medicine or remedy to counteract the effects of poison. **2.** any counteracting remedy.

anx·i·e·ty (ang zi'ə tē) *n.* **1.** a feeling of fearful uneasiness or apprehension, as over some impending or anticipated event; worry. **2.** something that causes this feeling.

Aph·ro·di·te (af'rə di'tē) *Greek Mythology.* the goddess of love and beauty.

A·pol·lo (ə pol'ō) *Greek and Roman Mythology.* the god of manly beauty, poetry, music, prophecy, and healing. He was also considered god of the sun. The name *Apollo* was given to a United States spacecraft.

a·pos·tro·phe (ə pos'trə fē) *n.* a punctuation mark (') used to indicate the omission of one or more letters in a word, as in *you're,* for *you are;* to indicate the possessive case of nouns or indefinite pronouns, as in *Paul's desk;* and to indicate the plural of letters and figures, as in *the three R's.*

ap·par·ent·ly (ə par'ənt lē) *adv.* **1.** clearly; plainly; obviously. **2.** to all appearances; seemingly.

ap·pa·ri·tion (ap'ə rish'ən) *n.* **1.** a ghost; phantom. **2.** something strange, startling, or unexpected that comes suddenly into view.

ap·prais·al (ə prā'zəl) *n.* **1.** the act of evaluating or judging. **2.** a price or value assigned; valuation; estimate.

ara·fang (är'fäng) *n.* a Mandinkan word meaning "teacher."

A·ra·li·a spi·no·sa (ə rā'lē ə spī nō'sə) the scientific name of a spiny shrub or small tree, sometimes 40 feet high, frequently planted for ornament. It belongs to the ginseng family.

Aralia spinosa

ar·gyle (är'gil) *also,* **Ar·gyle.** *n.* a diamond-shaped pattern of contrasting colors, used especially in knitting. —*adj.* having this pattern.

ar·id (ar'id) *adj.* **1.** having little rainfall. **2.** dry; parched.

ar·is·toc·ra·cy (ar'is tok'rə sē) *n.* **1.** a class of persons inheriting a high social position by birth; nobility. **2.** a government in which such a class has control. **3.** any group of persons superior or outstanding because of wealth, intelligence, or culture.

as·sur·di·tà (ä sur'dē tä') *n. Italian.* an absurdity; nonsense.

as·ter·isk (as'tə risk') *n.* a star-shaped mark (*) used in printing or writing to point out a reference or a footnote, or to show that something is missing from the text.

As·tre·a (as'trē ə)

At·a·lan·ta (at'ə lan'tə) *Greek Mythology.* A maiden who agreed to marry any man who could outrun her, and who was defeated by Hippomenes when he dropped three golden apples which she paused to pick up.

au·di·tion (ô dish'ən) *n.* a short performance that tests the abilities of a singer, musician, actor, or other performer.

au·to·bi·og·ra·phy (ô'tə bī og'rə fē, ô'tə bē og'rə fē) *n.* the story of one's life written by oneself.

av·id·ly (av'id lē) *adv.* eagerly or enthusiastically.

a·wash (ə wôsh', ə wosh') *adj.* covered with or washed over by water.

Az·tec (az'tek) a member of a large group of Indian tribes having a well-developed civilization and controlling an empire in central Mexico at the time of the Spanish conquest in 1519.

B

bac·te·ri·a (bak tēr'ē ə) *pl. n., sing.,* **bac·te·ri·um** (bak tēr'ē əm). any of numerous one-celled microorganisms, class Schizomycetes, that exhibit both plant and animal characteristics. Bacteria may be beneficial, harmless, or disease-causing and are classified according to shape as bacilli, cocci, or spirilla.

a bad, ā cake, ä father; e pet, ē me; i it, ī ice; o hot, ō open, ô off; oo wood, ōō food, oi oil, ou out; th thin, th that; u cup, ur turn, yōō music; zh treasure; ə ago, taken, pencil, lemon, helpful

Bag·dad (bag'dad) *also*, **Bagh·dad.** the capital of Iraq, in the east-central part of the country, on the Tigris River.

bal·last (bal'əst) *n.* a heavy material such as sand, placed in a ship to steady it or in a balloon to control its altitude.

bal·lon·né (bal'ə nā') *n. Ballet.* a broad leap with a kick to the front, side, or back. A **grand ballonné** (*pl.*, **grands ballonnés**) is a large ballonné.

Bal·tic (bôl'tik) *adj.* of or relating to the Baltic Sea or the Baltic States.

ban·dy (ban'dē) *v.*, **ban·died, ban·dy·ing. 1.** to give and take; exchange. **2.** to discuss freely or carelessly; circulate.

bar·ri·o (bä'rē ō) *n.* **1.** a ward or district in a Latin-American country or in the Philippines. **2.** a chiefly Spanish-speaking community or neighborhood in a United States city.

Ba·rysh·ni·kov, Mi·kha·il (mē hä'il bä rish'nə kôf') Born 1948. Ballet dancer.

bass fid·dle (bās' fid'əl) the largest stringed instrument. It is shaped like a violin and gives a deep, thrumming sound when played by hand, as in jazz and popular music. When played with a bow, as in classical music, it sounds like a very deep cello. Also, **double bass, contrabass, bass viol, bass.**

Ba·ta·vi·a (bə tā'vē ə) formerly the name of the city now known as **Dja·kar·ta** (jə kär'tə), *also*, **Ja·kar·ta.** It is the capital, largest city, and chief commercial and industrial center of Indonesia. The city is a seaport on the northwestern coast of Java.

bat·ting (bat'ing) *n.* cotton or wool fibers that have been pressed into sheets or layers, used especially in bandaging wounds or as padding for upholstery or quilts.

bay (bā) *n.* **1.** a reddish-brown color. **2.** a horse or other animal of this color.

Bear·den, Ro·ma·re (rō mär'ā bērd'ən)

bear·ings (bār'ingz) *pl. n.* part of a machine that holds or supports moving parts and reduces friction and wear.

bee·line (bē'līn) *n.* a direct line or course, as the course a bee follows to its hive.

be·fall (bi fôl') *v.*, **be·fell** (bi fel'), **be·fall·en, be·fall·ing.** to happen to; to come to pass; happen.

be·mused (bi myoozd') *adj.* **1.** lost in thought; preoccupied. **2.** confused; bewildered.

be·nev·o·lent (bə nev'ə lənt) *adj.* doing or desiring to do good; kindly; generous.

Be·ni·to (bā nē'tō)

be·stow (bi stō') *v.* to present (something) as a gift; give; confer.

Be·tel·geuse (bēt'əl jooz', bet'əl joez') a first magnitude red giant star in the constellation Orion.

be·think (bi thingk') *v.*, **be·thought** (bi thôt'), **be·think·ing.** to remind (oneself).

bi·car·bo·nate of so·da (bī kar'bə nit) *n.* a white, crystalline compound with a slightly salty taste, used especially in cooking as baking soda and in medicine as an antacid.

Bin·ta Kin·te (bin'tä kin'tə)

bi·o·graph·i·cal (bī'ə graf'i kəl) *adj.* **1.** of or relating to a person's life. **2.** of, relating to, or containing biography.

bi·plane (bī'plān') *n.* an airplane with two sets of wings, one above the other.

bi·zarre (bi zär') *adj.* very odd or strange, as in manner or appearance; fantastic; grotesque.

block and tack·le (tak'əl) an arrangement of pulley blocks and ropes, used for lifting or hauling.

bod·y lan·guage, communication through body position (or posture) and movements (or gestures).

Boe·o·tia (bē ō'shə) an ancient province of southeastern Greece, on the long peninsula between the Gulf of Corinth and the Straits of Euboea.

bog·gart (bog'ərt, bog'ət) *n.* **1.** *Dialect, chiefly British.* a goblin; spectre or ghost, especially one believed to be malicious. **2.** *Dialect, chiefly British.* a scarecrow.

bom·bar·dier (bom'bər dēr') *n.* **1.** a crew member of a bomber who aims and discharges the bombs. **2.** a noncommissioned artillery officer in the British army ranking next below a corporal.

bo·ro·goves (bôr'ō gōvz) a word without a dictionary definition, invented by Lewis Carroll; Jabberwocky.

Bow·ditch, Na·than·iel (nə than'yəl bou'dich) 1773-1838. an American mathematician and astronomer.

bra·cel·lus (bra chel'us) *n. Medieval Latin.* bracelet.

bra·ci·o·la (bra'chē ō'lə) *n. Medieval Latin.* little arms.

brack·en (brak'ən) *n.* a large, coarse fern. Also, **brake.**

brack·ish (brak'ish) *adj.* somewhat salty; briny.

bram·ble (bram'bəl) *n.* any of a large group of plants having thorny stems, such as the blackberry.

Bran·cusi, Con·stan·tin (kon'stən tēn brong'kōōsh, bran kōō'sē) 1876–1957. Rumanian-born French abstract painter.

bran·dish (bran'dish) *v.* to wave, shake, or swing in a threatening way.

brez·i·tel·la (bretz'i tel'ə) *n. Old German.* little arms.

Bri·co, An·to·ni·a (an tō'nē ə brē'cō) Born 1902. American conductor.

bril·lig (bril'ig) a word without a dictionary definition, invented by Lewis Carroll; Jabberwocky.

Bri·ma Ce·say (brē'mä sē'sä)

bro·chure (brō shoor') *n.* a small pamphlet; booklet.

Brown·ing, Rob·ert (brou'ning) 1812–1889. English poet.

Bryce Can·yon (brīs) a canyon in southwestern Utah.

bur·ble (bur'bəl) *v.,* **bur·bled, bur·bling.** to make a bubbling sound; gurgle.

bu·tane (byōō'tān) *n.* a colorless gas that burns easily, used as a fuel and in making synthetic rubber.

but·tress (but'ris) *n.* a strong or heavy structure built against a wall to strengthen or support it.

C

cab·ri·ole (kab'rē ōl) *n. Ballet.* a leap in which one leg is extended in mid-air and the other is struck against it.

cal·cu·la·tion (kal'kyə lā'shən) *n.* **1.** the act or process of determining by arithmetical methods or ascertaining beforehand by reasoning; estimation. **2.** the product or result of calculating.

cal·cu·la·tor (kal'kyə lā'tər) *n.* a machine for performing mathematical operations mechanically.

cam·ou·flage (kam'ə fläzh') *n.* any disguise, appearance, or behavior that serves to conceal or deceive, such as the protective covering of an animal.

Ca·non·i·cus (kə non'i kəs) *c.* 1565–1647. a Narragansett chief.

ca·pa·bil·i·ty (kā'pə bil'ə tē) *n. pl.,* **ca·pa·bil·i·ties. 1.** the quality of being efficient or competent; ability; capacity. **2.** a quality or ability that may be used or developed; potentiality.

car·i·bou (kar'ə bōō') *n. pl.,* **car·i·bous** or **car·i·bou.** any of a group of large deer that live in the northern regions of the world, having a coarse, heavy coat and large antlers.

caribou

car·i·ca·ture (kar'ə kə choor') *n.* **1.** a picture or description that ridiculously exaggerates or distorts the characteristics, peculiarities, or striking features of a person or thing. **2.** the art or process of making such pictures or descriptions.

Car·ne·gie Hall (kär nā'gē, kär'nə gē) a concert hall in New York City.

case·ment (kās'mənt) *n.* **1.** frame of a window that opens on hinges. **2.** a window having such a frame.

cen·ter of grav·i·ty (grav'ə tē) the point in a body around which its mass is equally distributed.

cer·e·mo·ni·al (ser'ə mō'nē əl) *adj.* **1.** of, relating to, or characterized by ceremony or ceremonies; ritual. **2.** used in or in connection with a ceremony.

---

a b**a**d, ā c**a**ke, ä f**a**ther; e p**e**t, ē m**e**; i **i**t, ī **i**ce; o h**o**t, ō **o**pen, ô **o**ff; oo w**oo**d, ōō f**oo**d, oi **oi**l, ou **ou**t; th **th**in, th **th**at; u c**u**p, ur t**ur**n, yōō m**u**sic; zh tr**e**asure; ə **a**go, tak**e**n, penc**i**l, lem**o**n, helpf**u**l

chaf·ing gear (chāf'ing) a covering, usually of canvas or rope, placed on a line or spar to protect it from injury or wear caused by friction.

cha·mi·so (chä mē'sō) *n.* a semidesert evergreen shrub used for thatching.

chan·cel·lor (chan'sə lər) *n.* the president of certain American universities.

chan·dler (chand'lər) *n.* **1.** a maker or seller of candles. **2.** a retailer of supplies and groceries.

chan·dler·y (chand'lər ē) *n.* **1.** a warehouse or storeroom for candles and other small wares. **2.** the merchandise, business, or warehouse of a chandler. See **chandler**.

Cha·nu·kah (hä'nə kə) *also,* **Ha·nuk·kah.** *n.* a Jewish holiday, celebrated for eight days, commemorating the rededication of the Temple of Jerusalem after the victory of the Maccabees over the king of ancient Syria.

cha·rades (shə rādz') *n.* a game in which the players try to guess a word or phrase that another player acts out without speaking.

char·treuse (shär trooz', shär troos') *n.* a pale yellowish-green color.

chasm (kaz'əm) *n.* a deep, yawning crack or gap in the earth's surface; gorge.

chauf·feur (shō'fər, shō fur') *n.* a person whose work is driving an automobile.

chil·blain (chil'blān') *n.* a painful, itchy swelling or reddening of the skin, especially the hands and feet, caused by exposure to the cold.

Chro·ma (krō'mə)

chro·mi·um ox·ide (krō'mē əm ox'īd) a compound of chromium (a hard, brittle, silver-white metallic element) and oxygen.

cla·mor (klam'ər) *n.* **1.** a loud, noisy outcry or protest; uproar. **2.** any loud and continuous noise.

clan (klan) *n.* a group of families in a community who claim descent from the same ancestor, as in the Scottish Highlands.

cli·ché (klē shā') *n.* **1.** an expression, phrase, or idea made trite by overuse. **2.** a trite or hackneyed plot, theme, or motif, as in art or literature.

clique (klēk, klik) *n.* a small group of people friendly with each other, who stick together and are often unfriendly to outsiders.

co·a·li·tion (kō ə lish'ən) *n.* an alliance of political leaders, political parties, or nations for some special purpose.

cock-eyed (kok'īd') *adj.* **1.** *Slang.* tilted to one side. **2.** *Slang.* absurd; foolish.

col·lage (kə läzh', kō läzh') *n.* **1.** an artistic composition with an emphasis on texture and pattern, made by pasting objects and paper, cloth, or other materials together on a surface. **2.** the art or technique of producing such compositions.

col·league (kol'ēg) *n.* an associate member of a profession or other group; a worker equal in rank to other workers.

com·mune (kom'yoon) *n.* a community in which property is owned in common and work and living quarters are shared.

com·pas·sion (kəm pash'ən) *n.* sympathy for another's suffering or misfortune, combined with a desire to help.

com·post (kom'pōst) *n.* a mixture of decayed plants and manure, used to fertilize soil.

com·pound (kom'pound') *n.* an enclosed area containing a house or other building.

com·pro·mise (kom'prə mīz') *n.* **1.** the settlement of a dispute by the partial surrender by each side of claims or demands; adjustment of differences by mutual concessions. **2.** the result of such a settlement.

con·ceit (kən sēt') *n.* a very high opinion of oneself or of one's achievements; vanity.

con·ceive (kən sēv') *v.,* **con·ceived, con·ceiv·ing. 1.** to form or develop (something) in the mind; devise. **2.** to picture (something) in the mind; think of or imagine.

con·cep·tion (kən sep'shən) *n.* **1.** the act of forming concepts. **2.** a general idea; concept.

con·course (kon'kôrs) *n.* **1.** a moving or coming together. **2.** a large gathering; crowd. **3.** a large, open place where crowds gather, as in a bus or train station.

con·de·scend·ing (kon'di sen'ding) *adj.* characterized by a superior attitude or manner.

Con·es·to·ga (kon'is tō'gə) *n.* **1.** a member of a North American Indian tribe formerly living in Pennsylvania. **2.** a city in Pennsylvania.

con·fet·ti (kən fet'ē) *n.* small bits of paper thrown about as a sign of celebration, as at a parade.

con·fig·u·ra·tion (kən fig′yə rā′shən) *n.* form or shape resulting from the arrangement of parts.

con·fis·cate (kon′fis kāt′) *v.*, **con·fis·cat·ed, con·fis·cat·ing.** to seize by authority.

con·for·ma·tion (kon′fôr mā′shən) *n.* **1.** the way in which the parts of something are arranged; shape or structure. **2.** the act of conforming or the state of being conformed.

con·geal (kən jēl′) *v.* **1.** to change from a liquid to a solid by cooling or freezing. **2.** to thicken or coagulate.

con·jure (kon′jər, kun′jər) *v.*, **con·jured, con·jur·ing. 1.** to summon or cause (something) to appear by using magic words. **2.** to bring about as if by magic. **3.** to summon spirits by means of spells; practice sorcery. **4.** to perform magic tricks.

con·sci·en·tious (kon′shē en′shəs) *adj.* capable of showing much thought and care; painstaking.

con·ser·va·tion (kon′sər vā′shən) *n.* **1.** the act of preserving or protecting, as from loss, harm, or waste. **2.** public protection and care of natural resources such as forests, rivers, and wildlife.

con·sid·er·ate (kən sid′ər it) *adj.* having or showing regard for others and their feelings; thoughtful.

con·sum·er (kən soo′mər) *n.* someone who buys and uses up things offered for sale, such as food, services, or clothing.

con·sump·tion (kən sump′shən) *n.* **1.** the act of using up or the state of being used up. **2.** the amount used up.

con·ta·gious (kən tā′jəs) *adj.* **1.** spread by direct or indirect contact. **2.** readily spread.

con·tem·po·rar·y (kən tem′pə rer′ē) *adj.* **1.** belonging to or living at the same time. **2.** belonging to the present time; current; modern.

con·temp·tu·ous·ly (kən temp′choo əs lē) *adv.* in a scornful or contemptuous manner.

con·tra·band (kon′trə band′) *n.* **1.** goods forbidden by law from being imported or exported; smuggled goods. **2.** unlawful trade in such goods; smuggling.

con·tra·dic·tion (kon′trə dik′shən) *n.* **1.** a statement that contradicts, or says the opposite of, another. **2.** denial. **3.** opposition or disagreement; inconsistency.

con·ven·tion·al·ly (kən ven′shən əl ē) *adv.* customarily.

cor·bli·mey (kôr′blī′ mē) *interj. British slang.* a word expressing surprise or amazement.

cor·ner·stone (kôr′nər stōn′) *n.* **1.** a stone that lies at the corner of a building. **2.** a fundamental principle or part; foundation; basis.

court·ly (kôrt′lē) *adj.* suitable for a king's court; refined; elegant; polished.

cous·cous (koos′ koos′) *n.* **1.** a dish of North and West Africa consisting of cracked or crushed grain steamed and served with meat and vegetables as a main course or with fruits and nuts as dessert. **2.** the grain used in this dish.

cov·ert·ly (kuv′ərt lē, kō′vərt lē) *adv.* secretly; hiddenly.

cox·swain (kok′sən, kok′swān) *also,* **cock·swain** *n.* a person who steers a boat, especially the one who steers and gives directions to rowers in a racing shell.

cra·vat (krə vat′) *n.* a necktie or a scarf worn as a necktie.

crepe paper (krāp) a thin paper with a crinkled surface like crepe.

crev·ice (krev′is) *n.* a narrow crack into or through something.

cravat

Cri·me·an War (krī mē′ən) a war (1853-1856) fought chiefly in the Crimea, a peninsula in the southern part of the Soviet Union, on the northern coast of the Black Sea. Great Britain, France, Turkey, and Sardinia as allies fought and defeated Russia.

---

a **b**a**d**, ā **c**a**k**e, ä **f**a**th**er; e **p**e**t**, ē **m**e; i **i**t, ī **i**ce; o **h**o**t**, ō **o**pen, ô **o**ff; oo **woo**d, oo **f**oo**d**, oi **o**i**l**, ou **ou**t; th **th**in, th **th**at; u **c**u**p**, ur **t**ur**n**, yoo **m**u**s**ic; zh **tr**ea**s**ure; ə **a**go, tak**e**n, penc**i**l, lem**o**n, helpf**u**l

cringe (krinj) *v.,* **cringed, cring·ing. 1.** to shrink, flinch, or crouch, as in fear, pain, or horror. **2.** to behave in a humble manner; fawn.

cross·bed·ding (krôs'bed ing) *n.* a type of stratification in sediments and sedimentary rocks that is characterized by the inclined deposition of granular sediments.

crys·tal·lize (krist'əl īz') *v.,* **crys·tal·lized, crys·tal·liz·ing. 1.** to form or cause to form crystals; become crystalline. **2.** to assume or give a definite or fixed form to.

cui·sine (kwi zēn') *n.* the manner or style of cooking or preparing food.

cu·ran·de·ro (k$\overline{oo}$ rän dā'rō) *n.* *Spanish.* folk doctor.

cur·ric·u·lum (kə rik'yə ləm) *n.* all the courses of study offered at a school, college, or university.

cur·ry (kur'ē) *n.* **1.** a condiment prepared from turmeric and various dried, ground spices. Also, **curry powder. 2.** a pungent sauce made from this condiment. **3.** a dish, such as stew, seasoned with either of these.

D

dam·per (dam'pər) *n.* a moveable plate used to control the draft in a fireplace, stove, or furnace.

daz·ed·ly (dāz'id lē) *adv.* in a stunned or bewildered manner.

dec·ade (dek'ād) *n.* a period of ten years.

deck (dek) *v.* to dress or adorn; ornament.

de·fi·ance (di fī'əns), *n.* bold or open resistance to authority, an opponent, or an opposing force; contempt of opposition or authority.

de·fy (di fī') *v.,* **de·fied, de·fy·ing. 1.** to resist (opposition or authority) boldly or openly; face with contempt. **2.** to resist completely or successfully; withstand. **3.** to challenge; dare.

deign (dān) *v.,* **deigned, deign·ing. 1.** to think worthy of oneself; condescend. **2.** to condescend to grant or give.

de·lib·er·ate (di lib'ər it) *adj.* **1.** carefully thought out or planned; intentional; studied. **2.** careful and slow in deciding; not hasty or rash. **3.** unhurried in action or movement; slow.

delve (delv) *v.,* **delved, delv·ing.** to make a careful investigation or search for information.

de·plor·a·ble (di plôr'ə bəl) *adj.* **1.** that should be disapproved of strongly. **2.** miserable.

des·pite (di spīt') *prep.* in spite of; notwithstanding.

des·tine (des'tin) *v.,* **des·tined, des·tin·ing. 1.** to intend or set apart for a particular purpose or use. **2.** to appoint or fix beforehand; preordain; predetermine. **3.** to direct to a certain destination.

de·vice (di vīs') *n.* **1.** something made or invented for a particular purpose; mechanism. **2.** a plan or scheme; trick.

de·vise (di vīz') *v.,* **de·vised, devis·ing.** to think out; invent; plan.

di·a·gram (dī'ə gram') *n.* **1.** a geometrical figure serving to illustrate a proposition. **2.** a set of lines, figure, plan, or sketch giving the outline or general scheme of an object or area or showing the course or results of an action or process. —*v.,* **di·a·gramed, di·a·gram·ing.** to represent by a diagram; make a diagram of.

dic·tate (dik'tāt, dik tāt') *v.,* **dic·tat·ed, dic·tat·ing.** to say or read (something) aloud to be written down or recorded by another.

dime nov·el (nov'əl) a cheap, melodramatic, or sensational novel, usually in paperback, especially such an adventure novel popular from c. 1850 to c. 1920.

di·men·sion (di men'shən) *n.* **1.** any extent that can be measured, such as length, breadth, thickness, or height. **2.** size, scope, or importance.

din·gy (din'jē) *adj.* having a dirty, dull, or dreary appearance; not bright and fresh.

din·gy (ding'gē) also, **din·ghy.** *n.* any of various small open boats, propelled either by oars or by an outboard motor or fitted with a small mast for sailing. Dingies are often used as tenders for larger boats.

dip·lo·mat (dip'lə mat') *n.* a person who is employed or skilled in managing relations between nations, especially an official representing his or her government to a foreign country or international assembly.

dis·con·cert (dis'kən surt') *v.* **1.** to disturb the self-possession or composure of; embarrass, confuse. **2.** to throw into disorder.

dis·en·gage (dis'en gāj') *v.,* **dis·en·gaged, dis·en·gag·ing. 1.** to release or loosen from something that holds, connects, or entangles. **2.** to free, as from an engagement, promise, or obligation. **3.** to release, detach, or free oneself.

di·shev·eled (di shev'əld) *also,* **di·shev·elled.** *adj.* not neat or in order; rumpled.

dis·sect (di sekt', dī sekt') *v.* to cut apart or divide into parts for the purpose of study or scientific examination.

dis·till (dis til') *v.* **1.** to heat (a liquid or other substance) until evaporation takes place and then condense the vapor given off. **2.** to obtain as if by distilling; to extract the essence of.

dis·tort (dis tôrt') *v.* **1.** to twist, or bend out of shape; change the natural or usual form of. **2.** to change so as to give a false impression; misrepresent.

di·ver·sion (di vur'zhən) *n.* **1.** something that distracts the attention. **2.** amusement; entertainment.

dol·phin (dol'fin) *n.* any of a group of highly intelligent mammals related to the whale, found in all seas and in some freshwater rivers. Dolphins have scaleless black, brown, or gray skin, two flippers, and usually a beak-like snout.

dolphin

do·main (dō mān') *n.* **1.** the land controlled or governed by a ruler or government; realm. **2.** a field of knowledge or interest. **3.** the land owned by one person or family; estate.

Don En·ri·que (dōn' en rē'kä)

Don Ter·co (dōn' ter'kō)

Do·ña A·na Ro·qué (dō'nyä ä'nä rō kä')

Doñ·a Pe·tra (dō'nyä pe'trä)

draft (draft) *v.* to prepare a first or rough sketch or version of; make an outline or plan of.

dras·ti·cal·ly (dras'tik lē) *adv.* in a manner having a forceful or severe effect.

dun·ga·ree (dung'gə rē') *n.* **1.** a denim fabric used for such items as work clothes, sportswear, and sails. **2. dungarees.** trousers or work clothes made of this fabric.

du·ra·bil·i·ty (door'ə bil'ə tē, dyoor'ə bil'ə tē) *n.* the quality of being durable; ability to resist wear, decay, or change.

dy·nam·ic (dī nam'ik) *adj.* **1.** characterized by or full of energy and vigor; forceful. **2.** characterized by change or activity. **3.** of or relating to energy or force in motion.

dy·na·mite (dī'nə mīt') *n.* an explosive consisting of a porous, absorbent material saturated with nitroglycerine, usually packed in cylindrical sticks.

E

e·clipse (i klips') *v.,* **e·clipsed, e·clips·ing. 1.** to cause an eclipse of. **2.** to overshadow or dim; outshine; surpass.

e·col·o·gy (ē kol'ə jē) *n.* a branch of biology that deals with the relationships of living things to their surroundings and to each other.

Eif·fel Tow·er (ī'fəl) an iron and steel tower in Paris, France.

el (el) *n.* See **elevated railway.**

e·lec·tri·cal storm, a thunderstorm.

e·lec·tron (i lek'tron) *n.* a subatomic particle that carries the smallest negative electric charge.

el·e·vat·ed rail·way, a railway that operates on a raised structure in order to permit passage of vehicles or pedestrians beneath it. Also called **elevated railroad** and **el.**

el·i·gi·ble (el'i jə bəl) *adj.* **1.** qualified or meeting the requirements for something. **2.** desirable or suitable, especially for marriage.

em·er·ald (em'ər əld, em'rəld) *n.* **1.** a bright green variety of the mineral beryl, prized as a gem. **2.** a bright green color.

---

a b**a**d, ā c**a**ke, ä f**a**ther; e p**e**t, ē m**e**; i **i**t, ī **i**ce; o h**o**t, ō **o**pen, ô **o**ff; oo w**oo**d, o͞o f**oo**d, oi **oi**l, ou **ou**t; th **th**in, t͟h **th**at; u c**u**p, ur t**u**rn, yo͞o m**u**sic; zh trea**s**ure; ə **a**go, tak**e**n, penc**i**l, lem**o**n, helpf**u**l

em·i·gré (em'i grā') *also,* **é·mi·gré** (*French,* ā mē grā'). *n.* a person who leaves one country or place to live in another, usually for political reasons.

en·crust (en krust') *v.* to cover with a crust or hard coating.

en·dow (en dou') *v.* **1.** to give money or property to as a source of income. **2.** to provide with an ability, talent, or quality.

en·dure (en door', en dyoor') *v.,* **en·dured, en·dur·ing. 1.** to undergo without yielding; stand; bear. **2.** to put up with; tolerate. **3.** to continue to be; last.

en·gag·ing (en gā'jing) *adj.* pleasingly attractive; winning; charming.

en·snare (en snār') *v.,* **en·snared, en·snar·ing.** *also,* **in·snare.** to catch in a snare; trap.

en·ti·ty (en'tə tē) *n.* **1.** something with real and distinct existence, whether objectively or in the mind. **2.** being; existence.

en·trance (en trans') *v.,* **en·tranced, en·tranc·ing. 1.** to put into a trance. **2.** to fill with delight or wonder; charm; enchant.

en·vi·ron·ment (en vī'rən mənt, en vī'ərn mənt) *n.* **1.** all of the surrounding, external factors that actually or potentially affect the development and functioning of a living thing. **2.** the surroundings.

en·vi·rons (en vī'rənz) *pl. n.* the surrounding districts of a town or city; outskirts.

ep·i·thet (ep'ə thet') *n.* a descriptive word or phrase used with or in place of a name.

e·ro·sion (i rō'zhən) *n.* the gradual wearing or washing away of the soil and rock of the earth's surface by glaciers, running water, waves, or wind.

er·rat·i·cal·ly (ə rat'ik lē) *adv.* **1.** irregularly. **2.** in a manner differing from the accepted or usual standard; eccentrically.

es·sence (es'əns) *n.* something that makes a thing what it is; necessary and basic part.

E·thi·o·pi·a (ē'thē ō'pē ə) **1.** a country in eastern Africa. Also, **Abyssinia. 2.** an ancient country in northeastern Africa, south of Egypt.

et·y·mol·o·gy (et'ə mol'ə jē) *n.* the study of the history of words, tracing them from their origins to their present forms, including the changes in spelling and meaning that have taken place.

e·vil eye, a look or stare superstitiously believed to cause injury or misfortune to others.

ex·as·per·ate (eg zas'pə rāt') *v.,* **ex·as·per·at·ed, ex·as·per·at·ing.** to irritate greatly; provoke to anger; infuriate.

ex·cerpt (ek'surpt) *n.* a passage or scene selected from a larger work.

ex·ert (eg zurt') *v.* to make active use of.

ex·er·tion (eg zur'shən) *n.* **1.** great effort. **2.** the act or process of putting forth or into action.

ex·hi·bi·tion (ek'sə bish'ən) *n.* **1.** the act of exhibiting. **2.** a public display or show.

ex·ot·ic (eg zot'ik) *adj.* **1.** of or belonging to another part of the world; not native; foreign. **2.** strangely beautiful or fascinating; strikingly unusual.

ex·pect·ant·ly (eks pek'tənt lē) *adv.* in a manner characterized by expectation; as though waiting for something.

ex·ploit (eks'ploit) *n.* a heroic deed or act; bold feat.

ex·plo·sive (eks plō'siv) *n.* any substance that can explode.

ex·po·si·tion (eks'pə zish'ən) *n.* a large public show or display, as of industrial products.

ex·trac·tor (eks trak'tər) *n.* one who or that which extracts, as a device for extracting teeth.

ex·ul·ta·tion (eg'zul tā'shən, ek'sul tā'shən) *n.* triumphant joy; jubilation; elation.

F

fab·ri·cate (fab'rə kāt') *v.,* **fab·ri·cat·ed, fab·ri·cat·ing. 1.** to make up; invent. **2.** to make, manufacture, or build by putting parts together.

fac·ul·ty (fak'əl tē) *n. pl.,* **fac·ul·ties.** the teaching staff of a school, college, or university.

fal·ter (fôl'tər) *v.* **1.** to act with hesitation or uncertainty; waver. **2.** to speak with hesitation; stammer.

fam·ine (fam'in) *n.* a very great and widespread lack or scarcity of food.

fa·nat·ic (fə nat'ik) *n.* a person whose devotion to a cause or belief is unreasonably strong or enthusiastic.

fan·fare (fan'fār') *n.* **1.** a short tune sounded by bugles, trumpets, or other brass instruments, used especially for military and ceremonial occasions. **2.** a great noise, excitement, fuss, or activity, as in celebration of something.

fan·ta·sy (fan'tə sē, fan'tə zē) *n.* **1.** unrestrained imagination or fancy. **2.** an unreal or grotesque mental image. **3.** a fanciful or imaginative creation or invention, such as science fiction.

far·potsh·ket (fär päch'kit) *adj.* messy.

fault (fôlt) *n. Geology.* a break in a rock mass. The mass on one side of the break is displaced with respect to the mass on the other side.

feed·back (fēd'bak') *n.* **1.** the return of a part of the output of a machine, system, or process to the input, especially in order to correct, control, or modify the output. **2.** any response or reaction.

fell (fel) *v.,* **felled, fell·ing. 1.** to strike and knock down; cause to fall. **2.** to cut down (a tree or trees).

fe·ro·cious (fə rō'shəs) *adj.* **1.** savage; fierce. **2.** *Informal.* very intense.

fer·ti·liz·er (furt'əl ī'zər) *n.* any of a wide variety of substances added to the soil to promote the growth and yield of plants by ensuring that the proper kinds and amounts of nutritional elements are present.

fiend·ish (fēn'dish) *adj.* very wicked or cruel.

Fil·i·ca·les (fi lə' kā' lēz) an order of herbaceous plants that comprises the true ferns.

fledg·ling (flej'ling) *also,* **fledge·ling.** *n.* **1.** a young bird just having grown its feathers. **2.** a young or inexperienced person.

flex (fleks) *v.* **1.** to bend. **2.** to tighten or contract.

flint (flint) *n.* **1.** a hard variety of quartz, usually dull gray in color, that produces sparks when struck against steel. **2.** a piece of this material used for kindling a fire.

flour·ish (flur'ish) *v.* **1.** to grow or develop strongly or prosperously; thrive. **2.** to reach or be at the highest point of development or achievement. **3.** to wave about with bold or sweeping gestures; brandish.

flue (flōō) *n.* a passage through which smoke, hot air, or waste gases pass, as in a chimney.

fly·ing but·tress (but'ris) an arched support between a pier or other structure and the wall of a building, used to help the wall bear the weight of the roof.

fo'c'sle (fōk'səl, fôr'kas'əl) also, **fore·cas·tle.** *n.* **1.** the part of the upper deck of a ship that is in front of the foremast. **2.** sailors' quarters located in the forward section of a ship.

flying buttress

fog·bank (fog'bangk') *n.* a stratum of fog, as seen from a distance.

fo·li·age (fō'lē ij) *n.* the growth of leaves on a tree or other plant.

foot·note (foot'nōt') *n.* a note, comment, or explanation, usually at the bottom of a page and indicated in the text by a number or symbol referring to it.

fos·sil (fos'əl) *n.* any remains or traces of an animal or plant of ancient geological times, preserved in the rock in the earth's crust.

fou·et·té (foo ə tā') *n. Ballet.* a whipping turn. In French the word means "whipped" and refers to the action of the non-standing leg.

four-bit (fôr'bit') *adj. Slang.* fifty-cent.

frag·ile (fraj'əl, fraj'īl) *adj.* easily broken, damaged, or destroyed; delicate.

free-lance (frē'lans') *adj.* relating to or working as a free lance. See **free lance.**

free lance, a trained person, especially a writer or artist, who does not work for one employer, but sells his or her work to anyone who will buy it.

---

a **ba**d, ā **ca**ke, ä **fa**ther; e **pe**t, ē m**e**; i **i**t, ī **ic**e; o **ho**t, ō **o**pen, ô **o**ff; oo **woo**d, ōō **foo**d, oi **oi**l, ou **ou**t; th **thi**n, th **th**at; u **cu**p, ur **tu**rn, yōō m**u**sic; zh trea**s**ure; ə **a**go, tak**e**n, penc**i**l, lem**o**n, helpfu**l**

fre·quen·cy (frē'kwən sē) *n.* **1.** the state of happening or taking place again and again. **2.** the number of times something happens or takes place during a period of time; rate of occurrence.

fric·tion (frik'shən) *n.* **1.** the rubbing of one object against another. **2.** *Physics.* the force that resists motion between two surfaces that are in contact with one another.

frig·ate (frig'it) *n.* **1.** formerly, a three-masted, square-rigged sailing warship. **2.** a warship used for escort and patrol duties.

frig·id (frij'id) *adj.* **1.** very cold. **2.** lacking warmth of feeling or enthusiasm; unfriendly or indifferent.

frock (frok) *n.* a woman's or girl's dress.

fu·gi·tive (fyoo'jə tiv) *n.* a person who flees or has fled, as from danger or pursuit.

fun·da·men·tal (fun'də ment'əl) *n.* anything that forms or serves as the basis of a system, principle, rule, or law.

fun·da·men·tal·ly (fun'də ment'əl ē) *adv.* basically; essentially.

Fung Joe Guey (fung'jō'gwā')

fun·gus (fung'gəs) *n. pl.,* **fun·gi** (fun'jī, fun'gī, fun'gē) or **fun·gus·es.** any of a large group of plants that lack flowers, leaves, or chlorophyll and live on other plants or animal matter. Mildews, mushrooms, and molds are fungi.

fur·row (fur'ō) *n.* **1.** a long, narrow groove or channel made in the ground by a plow. **2.** any long, narrow groove or channel, as a rut.

fur·tive·ly (fur'tiv lē) *adv.* stealthily; secretly.

G

ga·ble (gā'bəl) *n.* the section of an outside wall surface, usually triangular, between the sides of a sloped roof.

Gal·a·had (gal'ə had') in the legends of King Arthur, the purest and most virtuous knight of the Round Table.

Gam·bi·a (gam'bē ə) a country on the western coast of Africa, formerly a British colony.

game·keep·er (gām'kē'pər) *n.* a person employed to breed, protect, and care for game in a government preserve or on private lands.

gar·nish (gär'nish) *v.* to decorate or trim, especially to decorate or trim food with something that improves its appearance or flavor.

gar·ret (gar'it) *n.* the uppermost floor or room of a house, directly below the roof; attic.

gaunt (gônt) *adj.* **1.** extremely thin and hollow-eyed, as from hunger or illness; haggard. **2.** bare and gloomy; grim; bleak.

ge·bentsht (ge bencht') *adj.* blessed.

gen·re (zhän'rə) *n.* **1.** a particular class or style, especially a class or style of work in literature or art. **2.** a style of painting showing or dealing with scenes and events from everyday life. —*adj.* being or relating to a genre.

ges·ture (jes'chər) *n.* **1.** a movement of the head, body, or limbs, used to express a thought or feeling or to emphasize what is said. **2.** something said or done for effect or as a symbol.

gim·ble (gim'bəl) a word without a dictionary definition, invented by Lewis Carroll; Jabberwocky.

gim·let (gim'lit) *n.* a small tool for boring holes, consisting of a shaft with a pointed screw at one end and a cross handle at the other.

gird (gurd) *v.,* **girt** or **gird·ed, gird·ing. 1.** to surround or encircle with a belt or girdle. **2.** to encircle as if with a belt; hem in; enclose.

gir·dle (gurd'əl) *n.* a belt or band worn around the waist.

glow·er (glou'ər) *v.* to look at angrily or threateningly; scowl.

glyc·er·in (glis'ər in) *also,* **glyc·er·ine.** *n.* a colorless, syrupy, sweet liquid obtained from fats or produced synthetically, used especially in making nitroglycerine, medicines, soaps, and certain plastics.

gnarled (närld) *adj.* having many rough, twisted knots, as a tree trunk or branches.

gouge (gouj) *v.,* **gouged, goug·ing. 1.** to cut or scoop out with or as if with a gouge, which is a tool like a chisel, but having a curved blade. **2.** to dig, tear, or poke.

gran·di·ose (gran'dē ōs') *adj.* **1.** imposing or impressive; magnificent. **2.** trying to seem grand; pompous or pretentious.

Grand·moth·er Ya·i·sa (yä ī'sä)

gran·u·lar (gran'yə lər) *adj.* consisting of, containing or like grains or granules.

green·gro·cer (grēn'grō'sər) *n.* a person who sells fresh vegetables and fruit.

Green·wich Vil·lage (gren'ich) a section of lower Manhattan, New York City, noted as an artists' and writers' quarter.

gri·mace (grim'is, gri mās') *v.,* **gri·maced, gri·mac·ing.** to contort or twist the facial features.

griz·zled (griz'əld) *adj.* **1.** gray or mixed with gray. **2.** gray-haired.

ground·nut (ground'nut') *n.* any of several plants of the pea family having underground parts used for food, especially the peanut.

grouse shoot (grous) a hunting party in which the animal being hunted is one of a group of game birds that includes the ruffed grouse and the prairie chicken.

gru·el·ing (grōō'ə ling, grōō'ling) *also,* **gru·el·ling.** *adj.* very difficult or punishing; exhausting.

guar·an·tee (gar'ən tē') *n.* **1.** assurance given by a seller to a buyer that his product is or will be as it is represented or will be repaired or replaced if it proves defective within a certain period of time; warranty. **2.** anything that assures a certain outcome or condition.

Gug·gen·heim (goog'ən hīm')

Guil·ler, Jil·li·an (jil'ē ən gwil'ər)

guise (gīz) *n.* an outward appearance; semblance. **2.** an assumed or false appearance; pretense.

gyre (jīr) *v.* to move in a circle; revolve; spin; whirl.

gy·re·scope (jī'rə skōp') *also,* **gy·ro·scope.** *n.* a wheel mounted so that the axis on which it spins can point in any direction. When the wheel is spinning, the axis sets itself in a fixed direction and resists changes from that direction.

H

hair·spring (hār'spring') *n.* a fine, coiled spring in a watch or clock that regulates the movement of the balance wheel.

hal·yard (hal'yərd) *n. Nautical.* a rope or tackle used for hoisting or lowering something, such as a sail, yard, or flag.

hare·brained (hār'brānd') *adj.* foolish; flighty; reckless.

Ha·run-al-Ra·shid (hä rōōn'ä rä shēd')

hav·er·sack (hav'ər sak') *n.* a bag worn over the shoulders or suspended at one's side by a strap, used to carry food and other supplies, as by a soldier or hiker.

haversack

ha·zel (hā'zəl) *n.* a light-brown color, like that of the hazelnut. —*adj.* having the color hazel; light brown.

heath·er (heth'ər) *n.* a low, evergreen shrub bearing small purple or pink bell-shaped flowers in dense clusters. It grows wild and is found especially in Scotland.

heir·loom (ār'lōōm') *n.* a personal possession handed down in a family from generation to generation.

her·ring·bone (her'ing bōn') *n.* a pattern of short lines slanting back from either side of a longer line, forming a design resembling the spine of a herring. —*adj.* having or making this pattern.

het·er·o·nym (het'ər ə nim') *n.* a word having a different sound and meaning from another, but the same spelling, as *lead* (to conduct) and *lead* (a metal).

hey·day (hā'dā') *n.* a period of greatest strength, popularity, or prosperity.

high-ten·sion (hī'ten'shən) *adj.* subjected to or capable of operating under relatively high voltage.

hill·ock (hil'ək) *n.* a small hill or mound.

---

a b**a**d, ā c**a**ke, ä f**a**ther; e p**e**t, ē m**e**; i **i**t, ī **i**ce; o h**o**t, ō **o**pen, ô **o**ff; oo w**oo**d, ōō f**oo**d, oi **oi**l, ou **ou**t; th **th**in, th that; u c**u**p, ur t**ur**n, yōō m**u**sic; zh trea**s**ure; ə **a**go, tak**e**n, penc**i**l, lem**o**n, helpf**u**l

Hin·du·sta·ni (hin′dŏŏ stä′nē, hin′dŏŏ stan′ē) *adj.* of, relating to, or characteristic of India, its people, languages, or culture.

Hip·pom·e·nes (hi pom′ə nēz′) *Greek Mythology.* a youth who defeated Atalanta in a race and thereby won her in marriage.

his·tor·i·cal fic·tion, a prose work, such as a novel or short story, that is characterized by an imaginative reconstruction of historical events and people.

ho·ly·stone (hō′lē stōn′) *n.* a large, flat piece of sandstone used for scouring a ship's wooden decks. —*v.* to scour or scrub with a holystone.

home·spun (hōm′spun′) *n.* a fabric woven of yarn spun at home or by hand.

hoo·doo (hŏŏ′dŏŏ) *n.* a pillar of rock, usually of fantastic shape, left by erosion.

ho·ra a·mer·i·ca·na (ō′rə a mā rē kä′nə) *Spanish.* American time.

ho·ra mex·i·ca·na (ō′rə mā hē kä′nə) *Spanish.* Mexican time.

huck·ster (huk′stər) *v.,* **huck·stered, huck·ster·ing. 1.** to sell; peddle. **2.** to promote or sell on radio or television. **3.** to haggle over; bargain in.

hu·mil·i·ate (hyŏŏ mil′ē āt′) *v.,* **hu·mil·i·at·ed, hu·mil·i·at·ing.** to lower the pride or dignity of; cause to seem foolish or worthless.

hu·mil·i·ty (hyŏŏ mil′ə tē) *n.* the quality of being humble; lack of pride or arrogance.

hy·drau·lic (hī drô′lik) *adj.* **1.** operated by water or some other fluid. **2.** of or relating to forces exerted by fluids in motion and at rest, or to the science of hydraulics.

hy·drol·o·gist (hī drol′ə jist) *n.* a person skilled in the science dealing with the occurrence, circulation, distribution, and properties of the waters of the earth and its atmosphere.

hy·poth·e·cate (hī poth′ə kāt′) *v.,* **hy·poth·e·cated, hy·poth·e·cat·ing.** to pledge (property) as security to a creditor without transfer of title or possession; to mortgage.

hy·poth·e·ca·tion (hī poth′ə kā′shən) *n.* the act of pledging (property) as security to a creditor without transfer of title of possession; a mortgage.

I

id·i·om (id′ē əm) *n.* **1.** an expression whose meaning cannot be understood from the meanings of the individual words composing it. **2.** the characteristic way in which words are used in a particular language.

ig·no·rant (ig′nər ənt) *adj.* **1.** lacking in knowledge or education. **2.** uninformed or unaware.

il·lu·sion (i lŏŏ′zhən) *n.* **1.** a false or misleading idea or belief; misconception. **2.** an impression of the nature or appearance of something that is contrary to fact or reality.

im·mac·u·late (i mak′yə lit) *adj.* **1.** free from dust, grime, or clutter; very clean or neat. **2.** free from fault or blemish; flawless.

im·merse (i murs′) *v.,* **im·mersed, im·mers·ing. 1.** to plunge or dip into water or other liquid so as to cover completely. **2.** to involve deeply; absorb.

im·mor·tal (i môrt′əl) *adj.* **1.** never dying; living forever. **2.** remembered or famous through future time.

im·pen·e·tra·bil·i·ty (im pen′i trə bil′i tē, im′pen i trə bil′i tē) *n.* the state or quality of not being easily understood.

im·pe·ri·ous (im pēr′ē əs) *adj.* **1.** haughty or arrogant; domineering; overbearing. **2.** imperative; urgent.

im·plore (im plôr′) *v.,* **im·plored, im·plor·ing. 1.** to plead with; ask earnestly; beg. **2.** to beg or pray for earnestly.

in·can·ta·tion (in′kan tā′shən) *n.* a formula of words spoken or chanted in casting a spell or performing other magic.

in·ca·pac·i·ty (in′kə pas′ə tē) *n.* lack of power or ability.

in·cense (in sens′) *v.,* **in·censed, in·cens·ing.** to make very angry; enrage.

in·con·gru·ous (in kong′grŏŏ əs) *adj.* not harmoniously related or joined; not suitable.

in·debt·ed·ness (in det′id nis) *n.* **1.** the state of owing (something to someone) **2.** an amount owed.

in·den·ture (in den′shər) *v.,* **in·den·tured, in·den·tur·ing.** to bind (a person) by contract to work for another person for a stated period of time.

in·dex fin·ger (in′deks) the finger next to the thumb; forefinger.

in·dis·pen·sa·ble (in′dis pen′sə bəl) *adj.* that cannot be done without; necessary; essential.

in·dom·i·ta·ble (in dom′ə tə bəl) *adj.* that cannot be conquered or dominated.

in·fi·nite (in′fə nit) *adj.* **1.** having no limits or end; boundless. **2.** very great; immense; vast.

in·flec·tion (in flek′shən) *n.* a change or variation in the tone or pitch of the voice.

in·gen·ious (in jēn′yəs) *adj.* **1.** made with or showing cleverness, originality, or imagination. **2.** having creative ability; imaginative; inventive.

in·ge·nu·i·ty (in′jə nōō′ə tē) *n.* the quality or state of being ingenious; cleverness or originality.

in·got (ing′gət) *n.* a mass of metal cast into a shape, such as a bar or block.

ingot

in·hu·mane (in′hyōō mān′) *adj.* not feeling or showing kindness, pity, or compassion for other human beings or animals; not humane.

ink·well (ingk′wel′) *n.* a container for ink, especially on a desk.

in·ner eye (in′ər ī′) the eye of the mind or spirit; the mind's eye.

in·quis·i·tive·ly (in kwiz′ə tiv lē) *adv.* **1.** curiously. **2.** nosily; pryingly.

in·sa·tia·ble (in sā′shə bəl) *adj.* that cannot be satisfied.

in·so·lent (in′sə lənt) *adj.* offensively rude or bold.

in·stinc·tive (in stingk′tiv) *adj.* arising from or done by a natural tendency to act in a certain way.

in·sti·tute (in′stə tōōt′, in′stə tyōōt′) *v.*, **in·sti·tut·ed, in·sti·tut·ing.** to set up or put into operation; establish; start.

in·sult (in sult′) *v.* to speak to or treat with scornful abuse, rudeness, or disrespect.

in·ten·si·ty (in ten′sə tē) *n.* **1.** the state or quality of being intense. **2.** strength, amount, degree, as of force or feeling.

in·ter·cept (in′tər sept′) *v.* **1.** to seize or stop on the way. **2.** to stop the course or progress of; check.

in·ter·pre·ta·tion (in tur′prə tā′shən) *n.* **1.** making clear or understandable; revealing the meaning of. **2.** a performance that brings out the meaning of something, as of a musical composition or dramatic role.

in·tol·er·a·ble (in tol′ər ə bəl) *adj.* not to be endured; unbearable.

in·tri·cate (in′tri kit) *adj.* **1.** very involved or complicated. **2.** difficult to understand.

in·var·i·a·bly (in vâr′ē ə blē) *adv.* in a constant or uniform way; not characterized by change.

I·raq (i rak′, ē räk′) *also,* **I·rak.** a country in southwestern Asia.

i·tal·ic (i tal′ik) *often,* **i·tal·ics.** *n.* a style of type whose letters slant to the right.

J

Jab·ber·wock·y (jab′ər wok′ē) *n.* an example of writing or speech containing or consisting of meaningless syllables; nonsense.

jack·daw (jak′dô′) *n.* a crow of Europe, Asia, and northern Africa, having glossy black feathers with a gray band around the throat and a gray underside. Also, **daw.**

ja·li·ba (jä′lē bä) *n.* a Mandinkan word meaning "drummer."

Jan·neh (jä′nē)

Ja·nus (jā′nəs) *n. Roman Mythology.* the god of gates and doors who presided over beginnings and endings, conventionally represented as having two faces looking in opposite directions.

---

a bad, ā cake, ä father; e pet, ē me; i it, ī ice; o hot, ō open, ô off; oo wood, ōō food, oi oil, ou out; th thin, th that; u cup, ur turn, yōō music; zh treasure; ə ago, taken, pencil, lemon, helpful

jar·gon (jär′gən) *n.* **1.** the technical or specialized language of a particular profession, sect, or other group. **2.** confused, unclear, or meaningless speech or writing.

jas·mine tea (jas′min) a tea made from the flowers of the jasmine plant. The flowers are yellow, white, or pink, fragrant, and bell-shaped.

je·té (zhə tā′) *n. Ballet.* a sharp leap with an outward thrust of the working leg. A **grand jeté** (*pl.,* **grands jetés**) is a jeté with a high kick.

jí·ba·ro (hē′bä rō) n. pl., **jí·bar·os.** *Spanish.* a peasant worker.

Jor·ge (hôr′hā)

Juan (hwän)

Juf·fu·re (jōō fōō′rē′) *n.* a small village in the Gambia.

junk (jungk) *n.* a large flat-bottomed sailing vessel developed in China, having a square prow and lugsails.

junk

Ju·pi·ter (jōō′pə tər) *Roman Mythology.* the god who was the ruler of gods and people, and who also was associated with rain and thunder. The name *Jupiter-C* was given to a United States rocket.

K

Kai·ra·ba Kun·te Kin·te (kī′rä bä′ kōōn′tə kin′tə)

Ka·ja·li Dem·ba (kä jä′lē dem′bä)

kan·ga·roo rat, any of various jumping rodents of Mexico and western North America.

Ka·ra·mo Sil·la (kä′rä mō′sil′lä)

Kash·mir (kash′mēr, kash mēr′) an area in southern Asia, north of India, disputed by India and Pakistan.

keel (kēl) *v.* **1.** to capsize (a vessel). **2.** to roll on her keel. (Used of a ship.) **to keel over.** to turn bottom up; capsize; to fall over suddenly; topple; collapse.

keep·sake (kēp′sāk′) *n.* something given or kept to remind one of the giver; memento.

Kep·lik (ke′plik)

kie·sel·guhr (kē′zəl goor′) *n.* a fine, powdered earth used in industry as a filler, filtering agent, absorbent, clarifier, and insulator. Kieselguhr is made up of the skeletons of minute, unicellular colonial algae called diatoms.

kin (kin) *n.* **1.** a person's whole family; relatives; kindred; kinfolk. **2.** a relative.

ki·nes·ics (ki nēs′iks) *n.* the study of body language.

knob·bly (nob′lē) *adj.* covered with knobs or lumps; knobby.

Koss, To·mi·ra (tō mir′ä kos′)

Koss, Wlo·dek (vlō′dək kos′)

Kun·ta Kin·te (kōōn′tä kin′tə)

kwa·kwi (kwä′kwē) *n.* Hopi name for a kind of wild grass.

L

lad·en (lād′ən) *adj.* **1.** loaded. **2.** weighted down; burdened.

Lan·ca·shire (lang′kə shēr) a county in northwestern England. Its county seat is Lancaster.

lar·board (lär′bôrd′, lär′bərd) *n.* the left side of a boat or ship as one faces the bow. —*adj.* of, relating to, or located on the left side of a boat or ship. Another word for larboard is port.

lar·der (lär′dər) *n.* a place where food is kept; pantry.

laun·dry (lôn′drē) *n.* **1.** clothes or linens that are to be, are being, or have been (recently) washed. **2.** a place where washing (of clothes or linens) is done.

lead·en (led′ən) *adj.* **1.** made of lead. **2.** dull-gray, like lead.

league (lēg) *n.* a measure of distance equal to three miles.

lean-to (lēn′tōō′) *n.* **1.** a shed or building having a roof that slopes in one direction, supported by the wall of a building against which it is built. **2.** a crude, usually open shelter, with a sloping roof formed of branches, twigs, and the like.

ledg·er (lej′ər) *n.* an account book in which all the financial transactions of a business are recorded.

lei·sure (lē′zhər, lezh′ər) *n.* **1.** the time that a person can spend as she or he pleases; free or unoccupied time. **2.** freedom from the demands of work or duty.

lei·sure·ly (lē′zhər lē, lezh′ər lē) *adj.* characterized by leisure; unhurried; relaxed. —*adv.* in a leisurely manner.

lex·i·con (lek′sə kən, lek′sə kon′) *n.* **1.** a dictionary; especially of Greek, Hebrew, Latin, or another ancient language. **2.** a list of words belonging to a particular field, profession, activity or the like.

lib·er·al (lib′ər əl) *n.* a person who favors or supports reform, as in politics. —*adj.* **1.** characterized by or tending toward opinions favoring reform as in politics or religion. **2.** *also,* **Liberal.** of or belonging to a political party that favors reform.

lim·y (lī′mē) *adj.* of, containing, or like lime.

lin·go (ling′gō) *n.* language or speech that is strange or hard to understand to a person who is unfamiliar with it.

li·no·le·um (li nō′lē əm) *n.* a floor covering made by putting a mixture of linseed oil, finely ground cork or wood, resins, and pigments on a backing of burlap or canvas.

lit·er·a·cy (lit′ər ə sē) *n.* the ability to read and write.

Lith·u·a·nia (lith′ŌŌ ā′nē ə) a republic of the Soviet Union, in the northwestern part of the country, on the Baltic Sea. Lithuania was formerly an independent country.

li·vre (lē′vər, lē′vrə) *n.* a former coin of France, replaced by the franc.

Lock·wood, Bel·va (bel′və lok′wood) the first woman lawyer in the United States. She received her law degree in 1873.

log·a·rithm (lô′gə rith′əm, log′ə rith′əm) *n.* the power to which a fixed number or base must be raised in order to produce a given number. The logarithm of 9 to the base 3 is 2.

log·a·rith·mic ta·bles (lô′gə rith′mik, log′ə rith′mik) tables of numbers used in mathematics, indicating the power to which a fixed number must be raised to produce a given number.

look·ing glass, mirror.

lore (lôr) *n.* **1.** the body of traditional or popular facts or beliefs on a particular subject. **2.** learning; knowledge.

lub·ber (lub′ər) *n.* **1.** a heavy, clumsy, stupid person. **2.** an awkward or inexperienced sailor; landlubber.

lu·di·crous (lŌŌ′də krəs) *adj.* laughably absurd; ridiculous.

lu·mi·nous (lŌŌ′mə nəs) *adj.* **1.** sending out light of its own; shining. **2.** full of light; bright.

lu·nar (lŌŌ′nər) *adj.* **1.** of, involving, caused by, or affecting the moon. **2.** measured by the revolution of the moon. The word *lunar* can be a short form of *lunar sighting,* a method of taking sightings of the moon in navigation.

lurk (lurk) *v.* **1.** to lie hidden. **2.** to move about in a furtive manner; steal; sneak.

lux·u·ri·ous·ly (lug zhŌŌr′ē əs lē, lux shŌŌr′ē əs lē) *adv.* in a manner characterized by pleasure or luxury.

M

maes·tro (mīs′trō) *n.* any noted conductor, composer, or teacher of music.

ma·gen·ta (mə jen′tə) *n.* a purplish-red color. —*adj.* having the color magenta.

ma·hog·a·ny (mə hog′ə nē) *n.* a strong, hard, reddish-brown or yellowish wood of a tropical evergreen tree, widely used for making furniture and musical instruments.

Mai Ling (mā′ling′)

main·spring (mān′spring′) *n.* the principal spring in a mechanism, especially in a watch or clock.

---

a **b**ad, ā **c**ake, ä **f**ather; e **p**et, ē **m**e; i **i**t, ī **i**ce; o **h**ot, ō **o**pen, ô **o**ff; oo w**oo**d, ŌŌ **f**ood, oi **oi**l, ou **ou**t; th **thin**, th **that**; u **c**up, ur **turn**, yŌŌ **mus**ic; zh **treas**ure; ə **a**go, tak**e**n, penc**i**l, lem**o**n, helpf**u**l

ma·jes·tic (mə jes′tik) *adj.* having or showing majesty; showing great dignity; splendor; grandeur.

Ma·ka·ren·ko, Bo·ris (bô′rēs mä kä ren′kō)

make·shift (māk′shift′) *n.* something used temporarily in place of the proper or usual thing. —*adj.* of, like, or used as a makeshift.

mal·le·a·ble (mal′ē ə bəl) *adj.* **1.** that can be hammered, pressed, or beaten into various shapes without breaking. **2.** easy to change or influence.

mal·let (mal′it) *n.* **1.** a short-handled hammer with a heavy, usually wooden, head. **2.** a long-handled wooden hammer used to strike the ball in certain games, such as croquet or polo.

man·da·rin (man′dər in) *n.* a member of any of the nine ranks of high public officials under the Chinese empire.

Man·din·kan (man din′kən) *adj.* of or relating to the Mandinko, a group of people of West Africa.

ma·neu·ver (mə nōō′vər) *n.* a procedure involving expert physical movement.

man·ne·quin (man′i kin) *n.* a full-sized, usually jointed, model of a human figure, used especially for displaying clothes.

man·or (man′ər) *n.* **1.** under the feudal system, an estate granted to a lord, in which part of the land was divided among serfs who paid rent to the lord in labor and goods. **2.** land largely farmed by tenants who pay rent to the owner. **3.** a mansion, especially the main house on an estate or manor.

man·sion (man′shən) *n.* a very large, stately, or imposing house.

mar·gin (mär′jin) *n.* **1.** the amount allowed or available in addition to what is necessary or needed. **2.** a limit in condition, capacity, or the like, beyond or below which something ceases to exist, be desirable, or be possible.

Mar·re·ro, Fe·li·sa Rin·cón (fā lē′sä rin kōn′ mä rā′rō)

Mas·sa·soit (mas′ə soit′) c. 1580–1661. an American Indian chief of the Wampanoag tribe.

Ma·trix (mā′triks, mat′riks)

Mau·ri·ta·ni·a (môr′ə tā′nē ə) a country on the northwestern coast of Africa.

may·ap·ple (mā′ap′əl) *also,* **May ap·ple. 1.** a small North American plant having a white cup-shaped flower that grows in the center of a forked stem. **2.** the yellowish, egg-shaped fruit of this plant, used mainly to make preserves. Also, **man·drake.**

mayapple

may·hap (mā′hap′, mā′ hap′) *adv. Archaic.* perhaps; perchance. Short for *it may happen.*

me·di·a (mē′dē ə) *pl. n.* the singular of media is medium. See **medium.**

me·di·e·val (mē′dē ē′vəl, mid′ē ē′vəl, med′ē ē′vəl, mid ē′vəl) *adj.* of, relating to, belonging to, or characteristic of the Middle Ages.

med·i·ta·tion (med′ə tā′shən) *n.* serious and careful thought.

me·di·um (mē′dē əm) *n. pl.,* **me·di·ums** or **me·di·a** (mē′dē a). a means or form of communication or expression. Television, radio, newspapers, and magazines are media.

meg·a·syl·la·ble (meg′ə sil′ə bəl) *n.* a syllable containing a great many letters.

Meh·met A·li (mə met′ ä lē′)

mem·o·ran·dum (mem′ə ran′dəm) *n. pl.,* **mem·o·ran·dums** or **mem·o·ran·da** (mem′ə ran′də) a brief note written as a reminder.

merchant ship, a ship used in commerce.

me·ringue (mə rang′) *n.* a mixture of stiffly beaten egg whites and sugar, usually baked and used as a topping on cakes or pies.

mete (mēt) *v.,* **met·ed, met·ing.** to distribute by or as if by measuring; allot.

me·te·or·ol·o·gy (mē′tē ə rol′ə jē) *n.* the science dealing with the study of the atmosphere and the changes that take place within it. One important branch of meteorology is the study of weather.

me·ter (mē′tər) *also, British,* **me·tre.** *n.* the rhythmic arrangement of accented and unaccented or short and long syllables in a line of poetry.

met·o·nym (met′ə nim′) *n.* a word used in metonymy. See **metonymy.**

me·ton·y·my (mə ton'ə mē) *n.* the use of the name of one object or concept for that of another to which it is related, or of which it is a part, such as "count heads (or noses)" for "count people."

mi·cro·sec·ond (mī'krə sek'ənd) *n.* a unit of time equal to one millionth of a second.

mid·dy blouse (mid'ē blous', blouz') a loosely fitting blouse designed to resemble a sailor's blouse.

midge (mij) *n.* any of various tiny flies.

mid·wife (mid'wīf') *n.* a woman who assists women in childbirth.

mile·stone (mīl'stōn') *n.* **1.** a stone set up, as on a highway, to mark the distance in miles to a place. **2.** an important event or development.

mill (mil) *v.* to move in an aimless or confused manner.

mil·li·li·ter (mil'ə lē'tər) *n.* a metric measure of length, equal to one-thousandth of a liter.

Mi·lo (mī'lō)

mim·sy (mim'sē) a word without a dictionary definition, invented by Lewis Carroll; Jabberwocky.

min·a·ret (min'ə ret') *n.* a tall, slender tower attached to a mosque. A crier summons worshippers to prayer from a balcony near its top.

min·i·a·ture (min'ē ə chər, min'ə chər) *n.* a copy or representation on a small or greatly reduced scale.

min·is·tra·tion (min'is trā'shən) *n.* **1.** the act, process, or instance of giving aid. **2.** the act of serving as a minister of religion.

min·now (min'ō) *n.* **1.** any of a large number of freshwater fish found in temperate and tropical regions, widely used as bait. **2.** any very small fish.

min·ute·man (min'it man') *n.* during the American Revolution, a volunteer soldier or armed citizen ready to fight at a minute's notice. The name *Minuteman* was given to a United States guided missile.

Mi·ran·da, Ar·min·do (är min'dō mə ran'dä)

mis·con·cep·tion (mis'kən sep'shən) *n.* a false or mistaken idea.

mis·for·tune (mis fôr'chən) *n.* **1.** bad luck; ill fortune. **2.** an instance of this; unlucky accident; mishap.

mis·no·mer (mis nō'mər) *n.* a name that is not fitting or suitable.

Mo·ab (mō'ab) a town in eastern Utah.

mold·er (mōl'dər) *v.* to crumble or decay; turn to dust.

mome (mōm) a word without a dictionary definition, invented by Lewis Carroll; Jabberwocky.

mo·men·tar·i·ly (mō'mən ter'ə lē) *adv.* **1.** for a moment. **2.** at any moment; very soon.

mo·not·o·ny (mə not'ə nē) *n.* **1.** a tiresome sameness; lack of variety. **2.** a lack of change, as in tone, sound, or beat.

mon·soon (mon sōōn') *n.* **1.** a seasonal wind of the Indian Ocean and southern Asia, which blows from the southwest towards the land in summer and from the northeast towards the ocean in winter. **2.** the season of the summer monsoon, characterized by heavy rains.

moon (mōōn) *v.* to move or look about dreamily or aimlessly.

Moor (moor) *n.* a member of a people of mixed Arab and Berber descent living in northern Africa. The Moors invaded and conquered Spain in the eighth century A.D.

Moos·has·suc (mōōs'hä sōōk') a river in Rhode Island.

Mo·ro·zo·va, Na·dia (nä dyä' mô rō zō'vä)

mor·tar (môr'tər) *n.* a thick bowl of marble or other hard material in which substances are crushed to a powder by means of a pestle.

mort·gage (môr'gij) *n.* **1.** a pledge of property, given as security for the payment of a debt. **2.** a document indicating the terms of such a pledge and the manner in which the debt is to be paid.

---

a **b**ad, ā **c**ake, ä **f**ather; e **p**et, ē **m**e; i **i**t, ī **i**ce; o **h**ot, ō **o**pen, ô **o**ff; oo w**oo**d, ōō **f**ood, oi **o**il, ou **ou**t; th **th**in, <u>th</u> <u>th</u>at; u **c**up, ur t**ur**n, yōō **m**usic; zh trea**s**ure; ə **a**go, tak**e**n, penc**i**l, lem**o**n, helpf**u**l

Mo·zart (mōt'särt) 1756–1791. Austrian composer; full name: Wolfgang Amadeus Mozart.

mu·ez·zin (myoo ez'in) *n.* in Muslim communities, the public crier who calls the people to prayer from the minaret of a mosque.

mulct (mulkt) *v.* to swindle (someone) out of something.

mule deer (myool'dēr') a deer of North America having a tawny-gray coat and large ears.

mun·ko (mun'kō) *n.* a cake made of pounded rice eaten by the Mandinkan people.

mute (myoot) *n.* **1.** a person who is unable to speak. **2.** a device inserted in or put on a musical instrument to muffle or soften the tone.

mu·tu·al (myoo'choo əl) *adj.* **1.** done, felt, or expressed by each of two toward the other; reciprocal. **2.** of or having the same relationship toward each other.

N

Nar·ra·gan·sett (nar'ə gan'sit) **1.** a North American Indian tribe of the Algonquian language family, formerly living in the western woodlands of Rhode Island. **2.** a member of this tribe. **3.** the language of this tribe.

na·sal (nā'zəl) *adj.* **1.** of, from, or relating to the nose. **2.** pronounced with the sound passing through the nose, such as the letters *m, n,* and *ng.*

Nasr-ed-Din Hod·ja (nä'sred din' hō jä')

nat·u·ral arch, a curved structure in rock that spans an open space. Natural arches are created by erosion.

nat·u·ral bridge, a curved structure in rock that spans an open space under which a watercourse passes. Natural bridges are created by erosion.

nay (nā) *adv. Archaic.* no. —*n.* **1.** a negative vote or voter. **2.** a refusal or denial; no.

Nev·el·son, Lou·ise (loo ēz' nev'əl sən') American sculptress.

nim·bly (nim'blē) *adv.* lightly and quickly (in movement).

ni·tric ac·id (nī'trik) a colorless, highly corrosive, liquid compound that is one of the strongest known oxidizing agents, used in the manufacturing of explosives, nitrate fertilizers, and dyes.

ni·tro·glyc·er·in (nī'trə glis'ər in) *also,* **ni·tro·glyc·er·ine.** *n.* a colorless, oily, liquid compound that is poisonous and very explosive. Weak alcohol solutions of nitroglycerin are used to treat heart disease.

No·gu·chi, I·sa·mu (ē sä'moo nō goo'chē) Born 1904. American architectural sculptor.

nom·i·na·tion (nom'ə nā'shən) *n.* the act of proposing as a candidate for an office or honor, or the state of being proposed as a candidate for an office or honor.

non·sec·tar·i·an (non'sek ter'ē ən) *adj.* not restricted or belonging to any particular sect or religion.

no·ta·ry (nō'tər ē) *n.* a person authorized to administer oaths and certify documents as authentic. Short for *notary public.*

no·ta·tion (nō tā'shən) *n.* a system of signs or symbols used to represent values, quantities, or other facts or information.

no·tion (nō'shən) *n.* **1.** a mental image; idea. **2.** a theory, belief, or opinion. **3.** an intention or whim; desire.

nov·el (nov'əl) *n.* **1.** a fictional prose narrative, usually of considerable length and containing detailed treatment of character and plot. **2.** a literary form represented by this type of fiction.

Nyo Bo·to (nyō bō'tō)

O

ob·scure (əb skyoor') *adj.* **1.** not clearly expressed; difficult to understand. **2.** barely perceived by the senses; not clear or distinct.

ob·ses·sion (əb sesh'ən) *n.* something that obsesses, as a fixed idea or desire.

ob·sta·cle (ob'stə kəl) *n.* a person or thing that opposes, stands in the way, or blocks progress.

oc·cult (ə kult', ok'ult) *v.* to hide or become hidden from view; specifically, in astronomy, to hide by *occultation* (the disappearance of one heavenly body behind another).

off·load (ôf′lōd′, of′lōd′) *v.* to unload (a vehicle).

off·spring (ôf′spring′) *n.* the young of a person, animal, or plant.

O'Keeffe, Geor·gia (jor′jə ō kēf′) Born 1887. American painter.

o·men (ō′mən) *n.* a sign or event that is supposed to foretell good or bad luck.

O·mo·ro (ō′mō rō′)

o·paque (ō pāk′) *adj.* **1.** not letting light through; not transparent. **2.** not shining or lustrous; dull.

o·ri·ent (ôr′ē ent′) *v.* **1.** to make familiar with new surroundings or circumstances or a situation. **2.** to get or fix the location or bearings of. **3.** to fix so as to be pointed or directed.

out·grabe (out′grāb′) a word without a dictionary definition, invented by Lewis Carroll; Jabberwocky.

out·ra·geous (out rā′jəs) *adj.* **1.** going beyond proper limits. **2.** shameful; offensive; shocking.

out·wit (out′wit′) *v.*, **out·wit·ted, out·wit·ting.** to get the better of (someone) by cunning or cleverness.

P

pab·lum (pab′ləm) *also,* **pab·u·lum** (pab′yə ləm) *n.* **1.** any substance that gives nourishment; food. **2.** insipid intellectual nourishment.

pad·dock (pad′ək) *n.* **1.** a small field or enclosure in which an animal can graze and exercise. **2.** an area at a racetrack where the horses are saddled and mounted.

page (pāj) *v.*, **paged, pag·ing.** to summon or try to find (someone) by calling out her or his name.

pa·le·o·e·col·o·gist (pā′lē ō i kol′ə jist) *n.* a scientist who studies the ecological relationships that prevailed in past geologic ages.

pal·ette (pal′it) *n.* **1.** a thin board or tablet, usually having a hole for the thumb, on which artists place and mix their paints. **2.** the range of colors used in a particular painting or class of paintings, or by a particular artist.

palette

par·al·lel (par′ə lel′) *adj.* going in the same direction and always being the same distance apart at every point, so as never to meet.

parch·ment (pärch′mənt) *n.* **1.** the skin of sheep, goats, or other animals, prepared as a writing material. **2.** a manuscript or document written on this material. **3.** any of several types of paper made to resemble this material.

par·o·dy (par′ə dē) *n.* an imitation of something serious, as a literary or artistic work, a style of composition, or a way of life, presented for comic effect or ridicule.

parse (pärs) *v.*, **parsed, pars·ing.** to analyze (a sentence) grammatically, naming the parts of speech and their uses in the sentence.

par·ti·cle (pär′ti kəl) *n.* a very small bit or minute amount; trace; speck.

Pas·cal, Blaise (blez pas kal′, pas′kəl) 1623–1662. French philosopher, mathematician, physicist, and inventor.

pas·tel (pas tel′) *n.* **1.** a chalklike crayon used in drawing. **2.** a picture drawn with such crayons. **3.** a pale, soft shade of a color.

pat·ois (pat′wä) *n. pl.*, **pat·ois** (pat′wäz) a dialect spoken by the people of a region.

pa·tron·iz·ing (pā′trə nīz′ing, pa′trə nīz′ing) *adj.* treating in a condescending manner.

peck (pek) *n.* a unit of measure for fruit, vegetables, grain and other dry things, equal to eight quarts or one-fourth of a bushel.

---

a bad, ā cake, ä father; e pet, ē me; i it, ī ice; o hot, ō open, ô off; oo wood, ōō food, oi oil, ou out; th thin, th that; u cup, ur turn, yōō music; zh treasure; ə ago, taken, pencil, lemon, helpful

ped·es·tal (ped′əs təl) *n.* **1.** a support at the base of a column, statue, or similar upright structure. **2.** any base or supporting structure, as for a tall lamp or vase.

pen·du·lum (pen′jə ləm) *n.* a suspended weight or other body that can be set in motion to swing back and forth from a fixed point, often used to regulate the movement of a clock.

Pén·ja·mo (pen′ hä mō) a town in Mexico.

pen·ny·weight (pen′ē wāt′) *n.* a measure of weight equal to twenty-four grains or 1/20 of an ounce in troy weight.

pen·sive (pen′siv) *adj.* in deep and serious thought, often about matters of a sad nature.

per·ceive (pər sēv′) *v.,* **per·ceived, per·ceiving. 1.** to be or become aware of through the senses; see, hear, taste, smell, or feel. **2.** to take in or grasp mentally; comprehend.

per·cus·sion (pər kush′ən) *n.* musical percussion instruments as a group, in which tones are produced by shaking or by a blow or stroke from a hammer or similar implement. Drums, cymbals, and marimbas are examples of percussion instruments.

per·ish (per′ish) *v.* **1.** to die, especially in a tragic or violent way. **2.** to pass from existence; disappear; vanish.

per·ni·cious (pər nish′əs) *adj.* **1.** causing great harm or destruction; malicious. **2.** causing serious injury or death; severe or fatal.

per·pet·u·al mo·tion (pər pech′ōō əl) constant motion, especially that of a hypothetical machine that, once set in motion, would continue moving indefinitely without any additional energy being supplied to it.

pe·ti·tion (pə tish′ən) *n.* a formal request made to a person in a position of authority.

pet·u·lant (pech′ə lənt) *adj.* ill-humored; peevish.

phoe·nix (fē′niks) *n. Egyptian and Greek Mythology.* a miraculous bird thought to live for 500 years and to die in the flames of a funeral pyre and then to rise again from its own ashes.

pho·to–es·say (fō′tō es′ā) *n.* a combination of photographs and words that tells a story or gives information.

pho·to·vol·ta·ic (fō′tō vol tā′ik) *adj.* providing a source of electric current under the influence of light or similar radiation.

pic·co·lo (pik′ə lō′) *n.* a small flute pitched one octave higher than the ordinary flute.

piccolo

pile (pīl) *n.* a strong, slender beam of wood, steel, or concrete, driven vertically into the ground to support a structure, such as a bridge or wharf.

pil·ing (pī′ling) *n.* a number of piles or a structure made up of a number of piles. See **pile.**

pin·na·cle (pin′ə kəl) *n.* **1.** a high, pointed formation, such as a mountain peak. **2.** the highest point.

pi·quant (pē′kənt) *adj.* **1.** pleasantly sharp to the taste; pungent; tart. **2.** interesting or stimulating.

pir·ou·ette (pir′ōō et′) *n.* a rapid turning about on the toes, especially in dancing. —*v.,* **pir·ou·et·ted, pir·ou·et·ting.** to perform a pirouette.

piv·ot (piv′ət) *n.* a point, shaft, or pin that something turns on.

plague (plāg) *v.,* **plagued, plagu·ing. 1.** to afflict with or as with a plague. **2.** to trouble or annoy.

plait (plāt, plat) *n.* a braid, as of hair.

pla·teau (pla tō′) *n. pl.,* **pla·teaus** or **pla·teaux** (pla tōz′) an area of flat land raised above the surrounding land.

plate glass, a strong glass used for window-panes or mirrors.

pla·toon (plə tōōn′) *n.* a military unit forming part of a company, usually commanded by a lieutenant.

Plim·soll line (plim′səl) **1.** a circle intersected by a horizontal line that is marked amidships on the sides of a seagoing cargo ship to represent the summer load line and is accompanied by letters indicating the authority under which the ship is registered. **2.** a set of load-line markings on a seagoing cargo ship, including the Plimsoll line and the graduated load lines beside it. Also, **Plimsoll mark.**

plume (plo͞om) *n.* **1.** a large, fluffy, showy feather. **2.** an ornament consisting of a plume or cluster of plumes, or of a feathery tuft of fluffy material.

po·di·um (pō′dē əm) *n.* **1.** a raised platform from which a conductor leads an orchestra. **2.** a place or structure from which to speak to a group; lectern; rostrum.

pol·y·glot (pol′ē glot′) *adj.* **1.** speaking, understanding, or writing several languages. **2.** made up of or expressed in several languages.

por·tal (pôrt′əl) *n.* a door, gate, or entrance, especially a large and imposing one.

port·man·teau (pôrt man′tō) *n.* a suitcase or traveling bag, especially one made of leather and hinged at the back so as to open like a book into two compartments.

Po·sei·don (pə sīd′ən) *Greek Mythology.* the god of the sea and brother of Zeus and Pluto.

po·tent (pōt′ənt) *adj.* having force, effectiveness, strength, or power.

po·ten·tial (pə ten′shəl) *adj.* capable of being or becoming; possible but not actual. —*n.* a quality or ability capable of being developed or advanced.

prec·e·dent (pres′ə dənt) *n.* an action that may serve as an example for similar future actions.

pre·cip·i·tate (pri sip′ə tāt′) *v.*, **pre·cip·i·tat·ed, pre·cip·i·tat·ing. 1.** to cause to happen before expected, needed, or desired. **2.** to throw down violently; hurl downward.

pre·dic·a·ment (pri dik′ə mənt) *n.* an unpleasant, trying, or difficult situation.

pre·fab·ri·cat·ed (prē fab′rə kāt′id) *adj.* constructed or manufactured in standardized parts for easy and rapid assembly.

pre·lim·i·nar·y (pri lim′ə ner′ē) *adj.* coming before and leading up to the main event, subject, or action.

prime (prīm) *adj.* **1.** first in importance or value; main; chief. **2.** first in rank, dignity, influence, or authority. **3.** of the best quality; excellent.

pri·va·cy (prī′və sē) *n.* seclusion; isolation.

prob·a·bil·i·ty (prob′ə bil′ə tē) *n.* **1.** the state or quality of being probable; likelihood. **2.** something probable or likely. **3.** *Mathematics.* the ratio of the number of chances favoring the occurrence of an event to the total number of possible occurrences.

pro·found (prə found′) *adj.* **1.** showing or characterized by great understanding, knowledge, or insight. **2.** coming from the depth of one's being; intensely felt. **3.** significant; important; extensive.

pro·lif·ic (prə lif′ik) *adj.* producing abundantly through creative or artistic effort; highly productive.

prop·er·tied (prop′ər tēd) *adj.* owning property.

proph·e·cy (prof′ə sē) *n. pl.*, **proph·e·cies.** something that is foretold; prediction.

pro·por·tion (prə pôr′shən) *n.* **1.** the relation of one thing to another with respect to size, number, amount or degree; ration. **2.** a proper or balanced relation, as between parts; harmony; symmetry.

pro·pri·e·ty (prə prī′ə tē) *n. pl.*, **pro·pri·e·ties.** the quality of being proper or suitable; suitability.

prose (prōz) *n.* written or spoken language without metrical structure, as distinguished from poetry.

pro·vi·sions (prə vizh′ənz) *pl. n.* a supply of food.

pro·voke (prə vōk′) *v.* **pro·voked, pro·vok·ing.** to make angry; irritate greatly.

prow·ess (prou′is) *n.* **1.** great bravery or daring, especially in battle. **2.** great ability or skill.

pun·gent (pun′jənt) *adj.* sharp and stinging to the taste or smell.

purse (purs) *v.*, **pursed, purs·ing.** to draw together into wrinkles or folds; pucker.

---

a **b**ad, ā **c**ake, ä **f**ather; e **p**et, ē **m**e; i **i**t, ī **i**ce; o **h**ot, ō **o**pen, ô **o**ff; oo **wo**od, o͞o **f**ood, oi **o**il, ou **ou**t; th **th**in, t͟h **th**at; u **c**up, ur **t**urn, yo͞o **m**usic; zh trea**s**ure; ə **a**go, tak**e**n, penc**i**l, lem**o**n, helpful

Q

quar·ters (kwôr'tərz) *pl. n.* a place to live; living accommodations.

qua·ver (kwā'vər) *v.* to tremble or shake.

que·ry (kwēr'ē) *n.* that which is asked; question.

queue (kyo͞o) *v.,* **queued, queu·ing.** to form, stand, or wait in a line.

quiz·zi·cal·ly (kwiz'i kəl ē, kwiz'i klē) *adv.* **1.** questioningly; uncertainly; in a puzzled manner. **2.** teasingly; mockingly.

R

rag·a·muf·fin (rag'ə muf'in) *n.* a ragged, untidy person, especially a ragged, dirty child.

ran·dom·ness (ran'dəm nis) *n.* the state or quality of lacking a definite plan or purpose, happening by chance, or being unplanned.

rap·scal·lion (rap skal'yən) *n.* a rascal; rogue; scamp.

raths (raths) a word without a dictionary definition, invented by Lewis Carroll; Jabberwocky.

re·con·noi·tre (rē'kə noi'tər, rek'ə noi'tər) *v.,* **re·con·noi·tred, re·con·noi·tring.** *Also,* **re·con·noi·ter.** to inspect, examine, or survey (an area or position) in order to obtain information, as for military purposes.

re·cur (ri kur') *v.,* **re·curred, re·cur·ring. 1.** to happen or appear again. **2.** to come back or return to the mind or memory. **3.** to go back or return in thought or speech.

re·cy·cle (rē sī'kəl) *v.* **re·cy·cled, re·cy·cling.** to make (waste material) suitable for reuse.

red tape, too much attention to official rules and forms in a business or government office, usually resulting in inaction or delay.

reed pipe, an organ pipe with a reed that vibrates and produces a tone when air is forced through it.

reef (rēf) *v.* to reduce the area of (a sail) by rolling or folding up a portion and fastening it.

re·in·force·ment (rē'in fôrs'mənt) *also,* **re·en·force·ment, re-en·force·ment.** *n.* **1.** something that strengthens. **2.** the act of strengthening.

ren·dez·vous (rän'də vo͞o') *v.,* **ren·dez·voused** (rän'də vo͞od'), **ren·dez·vous·ing** (rän'də vo͞o'ing) to meet or cause to meet by arrangement.

re·nown (ri noun') *n.* widespread reputation; fame.

rep·e·ti·tion (rep'ə tish'ən) *n.* **1.** the act of repeating. **2.** that which is repeated.

rep·li·ca (rep'li kə) *n.* **1.** a close or exact copy or reproduction, especially one done on a smaller scale than the original. **2.** a copy or reproduction of a work of art, especially one made by the original artist.

re·prove (ri pro͞ov') *v.,* **re·proved, re·prov·ing.** to blame or find fault with; scold; rebuke.

res·o·nate (res'ə nāt') *v.,* **res·o·nat·ed, res·o·nat·ing.** to resound.

re·spon·si·bil·i·ty (ri spon'sə bil'ə tē) *n.* a job, duty, or area of concern.

re·tort (ri tôrt') *v.,* to make a reply, especially in a quick, witty, or sharp manner.

rev·er·ence (rev'ər ens, rev'rəns) *v.,* **rev·er·enced, rev·er·enc·ing.** to feel deep respect and affection for; venerate.

rice paper 1. thin paper made from the stems of rice plants. **2.** similar thin paper made from certain other plants.

rig·ging (rig'ing) *n.* all the lines of a boat or ship, as the ropes, chains, and wires, used for supporting the masts or working the sails.

ring-tailed cat, a carnivorous animal of Mexico and the southwestern United States, related to the raccoon, but smaller, with a sharper snout and a longer tail. Also, **cacomistle.**

ring-tailed cat

Rock of Gi·bral·tar (ji brôl'tər) a great rock formation in the British colony of Gibraltar, near the southern tip of Spain. It is often used as a figure of speech to signify permanence and steadfastness.

rod (rod) *n.* a unit of measure equal to 5½ yards or 16½ feet.

ro·dent (rōd'ənt) *n.* any of various animals having a pair of large front teeth used for gnawing. Rats, mice, squirrels, guinea pigs, porcupines, and beavers are rodents.

rogue (rōg) *n.* **1.** one who is dishonest and deceitful; scoundrel. **2.** one who is mischievous and playful.

ro·man·tic (rō man′tik) *adj.* **1.** of, relating to, or characterized by romance. **2.** having thoughts and feelings of love and adventure.

rue·ful (rōo′fəl) *adj.* **1.** showing sorrow or regret. **2.** causing sorrow or grief; pitiable.

S

sa·chem (sā′chəm) *n.* a chief of certain North American Indian tribes. The sachem inherited the position rather than being chosen for it.

sage–pi·ñon (sāj′pin′yon, pin′yən) *n.* a pine tree of the western United States.

Sa·loum (sä lōōm′) a port area in the Gambia.

san·i·ta·tion wor·ker (san′ə tā′shən) a person whose work is the protection of public health by removing and disposing of sewage and garbage.

San·skrit (san′skrit) a language of ancient India, used in literature and religion.

sar·cas·ti·cal·ly (sär kas′tik lē) *adv.* in a mocking or sarcastic way; characterized by sharp, bitter, taunting, or scornful remarks or language.

sa·tire (sat′īr) *n.* **1.** the use of humor, irony, or ridicule to attack or make fun of human faults or follies. **2.** a work of literature that attacks or makes fun of human faults or follies by this means.

sau·sage (sô′sij) *n.* finely chopped seasoned meat, as pork, beef, or veal, made into patties or enclosed in the prepared intestine of an animal or other casing.

sa·van·na (sə van′ə) *n.* a broad, grassy, treeless plain.

sa·vor (sā′vər) *v.* **1.** to taste or smell with pleasure or zest. **2.** to take great delight in. **3.** to give flavor to; season.

sa·vor·y (sā′vər ē) *adj.* agreeable to the taste or smell.

sche·mat·ic (skē mat′ik) *n.* a structural or generalized diagram or plan, especially of an electrical or mechanical system.

scheme (skēm) *n.* **1.** a program or course of action for accomplishing some objective; plan. **2.** an underhanded, devious, or secret plan; plot.

Schoeneus (skē′nē əs) *Greek Mythology.* A king of Boeotia, father of Atalanta.

sculpt (skulpt) *v.* to carve or otherwise form (a figure or design).

Scyth·i·an (sith′ē ən) *adj.* of or pertaining to the Scythians (an ancient nomadic people inhabiting the lower courses of the Don and Dneiper rivers), their land, or their language.

sea lev·el, the mean level of the surface of the sea, especially halfway between mean high and low water. Land elevations and sea depths are measured as so many feet above or below sea level.

se·clud·ed (si klōō′did) *adj.* **1.** shut off or screened from view. **2.** kept apart or removed from others; solitary.

sed·i·ment (sed′ə mənt) *n. Geology.* solid matter, such as rock or earth, deposited by water, ice, or wind.

se·le·ni·um (si lē′nē əm) *n.* a poisonous, nonmetallic element having chemical properties resembling those of sulfur. Because its electrical conductivity increases with bright light, it is used in photoelectric cells.

sem·i·lit·er·ate (sem′ē lit′ər it) *adj.* partly able to read and write.

ser·e·nade (ser′ə nād′) *n.* a song or other musical performance played and sung personally for someone as an expression of love or admiration.

se·re·na·ta (sā rä nä′tä) *n. pl.,* **se·re·na·tas.** *Spanish.* a serenade. See **serenade.**

se·rene (sə rēn′) *adj.* peaceful; calm; tranquil.

serge (surj) *n.* any of a group of fabrics woven with slanting ribs, used especially for suits.

---

a bad, ā cake, ä father; e pet, ē me; i it, ī ice; o hot, ō open, ô off; oo wood, ōo food, oi oil, ou out; th thin, th that; u cup, ur turn, yōo music; zh treasure; ə ago, taken, pencil, lemon, helpful

sex·tant (seks′tənt) *n.* an instrument used mainly in navigation for measuring the altitude of the sun or a star to determine the position of the observer.

sheaf (shēf) *n. pl.,* **sheaves. 1.** one of the bundles in which stalks of cereal plants, such as wheat, are bound after reaping. **2.** any bundle of things of the same kind.

Shi·pau·lo·vi (shi päl′ō vē) a Hopi village on Second Mesa.

shore (shôr) *v.,* **shored, shor·ing.** to support with a timber or beam.

Si·er·ra La Sal (sē er′ə lə sal′) a range of mountains in Utah.

sil·i·con (sil′i kən) *n.* a nonmetallic element that exists in its pure state as either brown powder or as dark gray or black crystals.

sim·i·lar·i·ty (sim′ə lar′ə tē) *n. pl.,* **sim·i·lar·i·ties. 1.** the quality or state of being similar; likeness. **2.** instance or point of likeness.

si·mul·ta·ne·ous·ly (sī′məl tā′nē əs lē) *adv.* at the same time.

sin·u·ous (sin′yo͞o əs) *adj.* full of curves or bends.

sit·u·a·tion (sich′o͞o ā′shən) *n.* **1.** condition or state of affairs. **2.** a place in relation to surroundings; location.

skirt (skurt) *v.* **1.** to lie along or form the border or edge of. **2.** to move along the border or edge of; pass around rather than go through.

skit·ter (skit′ər) *v.* to glide or skim or to cause to glide or skim lightly and quickly over a surface.

slack·en (slak′ən) *v.* **1.** to make slower. **2.** to make loose. **3.** to make less; lessen. **4.** to become loose.

slick·er (slik′ər) *n.* a raincoat made of oilskin, plastic, or a similar material.

slick·rock de·sert, a desert comprised of rock that has disintegrated to form a slippery surface. Also, **slickrock country.**

slith·y (slith′ē) a word without a dictionary definition, invented by Lewis Carroll; Jabberwocky.

sloth·ful (slôth′fəl, slōth′fəl, sloth′fəl) *adj.* lazy; indolent; characterized by a disinclination to work.

smug·gle (smug′əl) *v.,* **smug·gled, smug·gling. 1.** to take into or out of a country secretly and unlawfully, as goods on which the required duties have not been paid. **2.** to bring, take or transport secretly.

sol (sōl) *n. Spanish.* the sun.

so·lar cell, a device to turn sunlight into electricity.

som·ber (som′bər) *also,* **som·bre.** *adj.* **1.** dark and gloomy. **2.** melancholy or depressing.

sot·to vo·ce (sot′ō vō′chē) in a low tone of voice, so as not to be overheard.

So·wans (sō′wänz) a seventeenth-century Wampanoag village.

So·yuz (sä yo͞oz′)

spas·ti·cal·ly (spas′tik lē) *adv.* in a manner characterized by sudden bursts of energy, activity, or feeling.

spat·u·la (spach′ə lə) *n.* a small tool with a flat, flexible blade. Spatulas are used for spreading or mixing thick, soft substances, such as paint or cake batter.

spec·trum (spek′trəm) *n. pl.,* **spec·tra** (spek′trə) or **spec·trums.** a band of colors into which white light is separated according to wavelength by being passed through a prism or other material. The colors of the spectrum are red, orange, yellow, green, blue, indigo, and violet.

spec·u·la·tion (spek′yə lā′shən) *n.* **1.** the act of thinking carefully or seriously about something; conjecture. **2.** a conclusion or opinion reached by conjecture.

spire (spīr) *n.* **1.** a tall structure that tapers to a point, built on the top of a tower. **2.** any tapering and pointed object or formation.

spon·sor (spon′sər) *n.* a person who assumes responsibility or support for another person or thing. —*v.* to act as sponsor for.

squire (skwīr) *n.* **1.** an English country gentleman or landowner. **2.** in feudal society, a young nobleman who, in preparation for his own knighthood, attended a knight.

stag (stag) *n.* a full-grown male deer.

stat·is·ti·cian (stat′is tish′ən) *n.* a person who is expert in compiling and interpreting statistics.

sta·tis·tics (stə tis′tiks) *pl. n.* **1.** the science of collecting, classifying, and using numerical data as related to a particular subject. **2.** numerical data.

staunch·ly (stônch'lē) *adv.* in a loyal and dependable manner.

steth·o·scope (steth'ə skōp') *n.* an instrument used to listen to sounds made by organs of the body, especially sounds of the lungs and heart.

stethoscope

sting·ing net·tle (sting'ing net'əl) a bristly, stinging herb having forked clusters of greenish flowers.

stock (stok) *n.* a close-fitting, stiff neckcloth worn in the eighteenth and nineteenth centuries.

stone·ma·son (stōn'mā'sən) *n.* a person who cuts stone or builds structures in stone.

stub·ble (stub'əl) *n.* short stalks of grain and certain other plants left standing in the ground after the crop has been harvested.

sub·se·quent (sub'sə kwənt) *adj.* coming or happening after or as a result.

suf·fice (sə fīs') *v.,* **suf·ficed, suf·fic·ing. 1.** to be sufficient or enough. **2.** to be enough for; satisfy.

suf·frage (suf'rij) *n.* **1.** the right or privilege of voting; franchise. **2.** the act of casting a vote; voting.

suf·fra·gette (suf'rə jet') *n.* a woman who strongly supports suffrage for women.

sun·di·al (sun'dī'əl) *n.* a device that shows the time of the day by the position and length of a shadow cast on a flat, usually round, surface marked with numbers.

su·perb (soo purb') *adj.* **1.** having nobility or grandeur; magnificent; splendid. **2.** elegant; rich. **3.** of superior quality; very fine.

su·per·car·go (soo'pər kär'gō) *n.* an officer on board a merchant ship who has charge of the cargo and its sale and purchase.

sup·pli·ca·tion (sup'lə kā'shən) *n.* an earnest request or a humble prayer.

su·preme (sə prēm) *adj.* **1.** greatest in rank, authority, or power. **2.** greatest in importance, degree, or quality; utmost. **3.** ultimate; final; last.

swathe (swoth, swāth) *v.,* **swathed, swath·ing. 1.** to bind or wrap. **2.** to surround; enclose.

T

ta·ble·land (tā'bəl land') *n.* an elevated, relatively flat, land area; plateau.

T'ai Chi (tī'chē) an ancient Chinese system of exercises intended to achieve health and tranquillity.

Tang (täng) *also,* **T'ang.** *n.* a Chinese dynasty (A.D. 618–907).

tan·tang (tän'täng') *n.* tom-tom drum; a drum of indefinite pitch, often played with the hands.

tart (tärt) *adj.* **1.** sharp in taste; not sweet; sour. **2.** sharp in tone or meaning.

taut (tôt) *adj.* **1.** tightly drawn or stretched; not slack or loose. **2.** showing tension or strain; tight. **3.** in good condition; orderly; tidy.

tem·ple (tem'pəl) *n.* the flattened part on either side of the forehead, above the cheekbone and in front of the ear.

tem·po (tem'pō) *n. pl.,* **tem·pos** or **tem·pi** (tem'pē). **1.** *Music.* the relative speed at which a musical composition, movement, or passage is or should be played. **2.** a characteristic pace or speed.

ten·e·ment (ten'ə mənt) *n.* an apartment building or rooming house that is poorly built or maintained and usually overcrowded, especially one that is located in a slum.

ter·mite (tur'mīt) *n.* any of a group of insects that live in colonies, having whitish bodies and dark heads. Termites feed on wood, paper, and other organic material, causing great damage to buildings, furniture, and some crops.

---

a **bad**, ā **cake**, ä **father**; e **pet**, ē **me**; i **it**, ī **ice**; o **hot**, ō **open**, ô **off**; oo **wood**, oo **food**, oi **oil**, ou **out**; th **thin**, th **that**; u **cup**, ur **turn**, yoo **music**; zh **treasure**; ə **ago**, tak**e**n, penc**i**l, lem**o**n, helpf**u**l

ter·race (ter'is) *n.* a raised, level platform of earth with a vertical or sloping front or side, especially one of a series of such levels placed one above the other.

teth·er (te<u>th</u>'ər) *n.* a rope or chain used to fasten a horse, donkey, or other animal so that it is confined within certain limits. —*v.* to fasten or confine with a tether.

Thai (tī) **1.** a person who was born or is living in Thailand. **2.** the official language of Thailand.

Thai·land (tī'land') a country in southeastern Asia, formerly known as Siam.

Tharp, Twy·la (twī'lə thärp') Born 1941. American dancer.

thick·et (thik'it) *n.* a dense growth, as of shrubs or bushes.

thim·ble·ber·ry (thim'bəl ber'ē) *n.* any of several American raspberries bearing a thimble-shaped fruit, especially the black raspberry.

tin·der·box (tin'dər boks') *n.* a box used for holding the materials needed to start a fire, such as flint or coal.

Tis·bur·y (tis'ber'ē) a city in Wiltshire, England.

Tock (tok)

top·side (top'sīd') *n.* the upper part of a ship's side, especially the part above the water line. —*adv.* to or on the upper portions of a ship; on deck.

toves (tōvz) a word without a dictionary definition, invented by Lewis Carroll; Jabberwocky.

tran·quil·li·ty (trang kwil'ə tē) *n.* the state or quality of being free from disturbance; calmness; peacefulness. *Tranquillity Base* is the name of the spot on the moon where the *Eagle* landed.

trans·for·ma·tion (trans'fər mā'shən) *n.* the act of changing or the state of being changed (in shape, form, appearance, character, condition, or nature).

trans·mu·ta·tion (trans'myo͞o tā'shən) *n.* the act of changing or the state of being changed (in form, nature, or quality).

trap·pings (trap'ingz) *pl. n.* **1.** an ornamented cloth or covering spread over the harness or saddle of a horse. **2.** outer or superficial adornments.

tread (tred) *n.* the horizontal part of a step in a staircase.

trea·son (trē'zən) *n.* the betrayal of one's country, especially by giving aid to the enemy in wartime.

tre·men·dous (tri men'dəs) *adj.* **1.** of extraordinarily great size, amount, or intensity. **2.** *Informal.* extraordinary or wonderful; astounding.

tres·tle ta·ble (tres'əl) a table consisting of a top supported by a framework of vertical or inclined pieces with horizontal or diagonal braces.

tri·dent (trīd'ənt) *n.* a spear with three prongs.

trig·o·nom·e·try (trig'ə nom'ə trē) *n.* the branch of mathematics dealing with the relations between the sides and angles of triangles, and also with the properties of these relations.

tril·li·um (tril'ē əm) *n.* any of a group of low plants of the lily family having a whorl of three smooth, oval leaves and bearing flowers composed of three oval petals.

trom·bone (trom bōn', trom'bōn) *n.* a brass musical instrument consisting of two long, U-shaped tubes, one of which has a flaring end and the other of which may be slid back and forth to change the pitch of the tones.

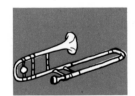

trombone

trust (trust) *n.* keeping or custody; care.

tsar (zär, tsär) *also,* **czar, tzar.** *n.* any of the emperors of Russia before the Revolution of 1917.

Tsing·tao (tsing tou') a port city in China.

tu·ba (to͞o'bə, tyo͞o'bə) *n.* a very large brass musical instrument that produces a deep, mellow tone.

tu·nic (to͞o'nik, tyo͞o'nik) *n.* a garment resembling a blouse, often belted and reaching to the hips or below.

tur·bine (tur'bin, tur'bīn) *n.* any of various motors or engines that use the force of a steadily moving stream of gas, vapor, or liquid against slanted blades to turn a rotor.

turf (turf) *n.* **1.** the surface layer of soil, containing small plants and grasses, their matted roots, and the soil clinging to them. **2.** a separate clump or clumps of this layer, as for replanting.

turn·ta·ble (turn′tā′bəl) *n.* **1.** a revolving device used to turn things around, especially a circular railroad platform with tracks used to turn engines, locomotives or cars around. **2.** a flat platform on a phonograph that revolves to play records rested upon it.

tur·ret (tur′it) *n.* a small tower, usually forming part of a larger structure.

U

u·ku·le·le (yōō′kə lā′lē) *also,* **u·ke·le·le.** *n.* a small guitar having four strings.

ul·tra·high fre·quen·cy (ul′trə hī′ frē′kwen sē) a frequency range of radio waves from 300 to 3000 megacycles, used for radio and television broadcasting.

ul·tra·ma·rine (ul′trə mə rēn′) *n.* **1.** a deep-blue color. **2.** a blue coloring matter, originally made from the gem lapis lazuli. —*adj.* having the color ultramarine; deep-blue.

ul·tra·vi·o·let (ul′trə vī′ə lit) *adj.* (of electromagnetic radiation) having wavelengths shorter than those of X rays, ranging from 40 to 4000 angstroms. Ultraviolet rays are present in sunlight.

un·a·bridged (un′ə brijd′) *adj.* not shortened; complete.

un·al·ien·a·ble (un āl′yə nə bəl, un ā′lē ə nə bəl) *adj.* not capable of being transferred to another.

un·der·lip (un′dər lip′) *n.* the lower lip.

un·der·study (un′dər stud′ē) *n. pl.,* **un·der·stud·ies.** an actor or singer who learns another's role in order to be a replacement.

un·du·tied (un dōō′tēd, un dyōō′tēd) *adj.* not taxed. (Said of goods brought into or taken out of a country.)

u·ni·son (yōō′nə sən, yōō′nə zən) *n.* **1.** complete or perfect agreement. **2.** *Music.* sameness in pitch, as of two or more tones or voices.

u·su·rer (yōō′zhər ər) *n.* a person who lends money, especially at a very high or unlawful rate of interest.

V

val·e·dic·to·ri·an (val′ə dik tôr′ē ən) *n.* a student, usually ranking highest in his or her class, who delivers the farewell address at a graduation exercise.

val·iant·ly (val′yənt lē) *adv.* bravely; courageously.

van·guard (van′gard′) *n.* **1.** the part of an army that moves ahead of the main force. **2.** the leading or foremost position of a social, political, or other government. The name *Vanguard* was given to a United States rocket.

van·i·ty (van′i tē) *n.* too much concern with or pride in one's appearance, abilities, deeds, or the like; conceit.

vault (vôlt) *n.* an arched structure of stone, brick, or concrete serving as a roof or ceiling. —*v.* to cover or provide with a vault.

Ve·ga (vē′gə, vā′gə) a bright white star, the brightest in the constellation Lyra. The name of the airplane in which Amelia Earhart flew solo across the Atlantic was *Vega.*

ve·he·ment·ly (vē′ə mənt lē) *adv.* in a manner showing or characterized by intensity of feeling; passionately.

ven·tril·o·quism (ven tril′ə kwiz′əm) *n.* the art or practice of speaking or producing sounds without moving the lips, so that the sound seems to be coming from some source other than the speaker.

ver·bal (vur′bəl) *adj.* **1.** of, relating to, or consisting of words. **2.** concerned with words, rather than with the ideas they express. **3.** expressed in speech, not written.

---

a b**a**d, ā c**a**ke, ä f**a**ther; e p**e**t, ē m**e**; i **i**t, ī **i**ce; o h**o**t, ō **o**pen, ô **o**ff; oo w**oo**d, ōō f**oo**d, oi **oi**l, ou **ou**t; th **th**in, th **th**at; u c**u**p, ur t**u**rn, yōō m**u**sic; zh trea**s**ure; ə **a**go, tak**e**n, penc**i**l, lem**o**n, helpfu**l**

verge (vurj) *n.* **1.** the edge or border of something. **2.** a point beyond which something happens or begins.

vi·brant (vī′brənt) *adj.* **1.** full of life, energy, and enthusiasm. **2.** vibrating. **3.** resounding; resonant.

vict·ual (vit′əl) *n. usually,* **vict·uals.** food or provisions.

vict·ual·i·za·tion (vit′əl ə zā′shən) *n.* **1.** the provision of food. **2.** the laying in of food supplies. *Not standard English.*

vie·ji·to (vyā hē′tō) *n. Spanish.* little old man.

Vi·et·nam (vē′et näm′) *also,* **Vi·et Nam.** a country in southeastern Asia.

vis·age (viz′ij) *n.* **1.** the face or facial expression of a person. **2.** the outward aspect or appearance of anything.

void (void) *n.* empty space; vacuum.

vo·lu·mi·nous (və lōō′mə nəs) *adj.* **1.** of great size or bulk; large. **2.** forming or capable of filling a large volume or many volumes.

vul·ture (vul′chər) *n.* **1.** any of several large birds having dark, dull feathers and a bald head and neck. Vultures feed chiefly on dead animals. **2.** a greedy, ruthless person.

W

wabe (wāb) a word without a dictionary definition, invented by Lewis Carroll; Jabberwocky.

Wam·pa·no·ag (wam′pə nō′äg′) **1.** an Algonquian-speaking tribe of North American Indians, formerly inhabiting eastern Rhode Island and adjacent parts of Massachusetts. **2.** a member of this tribe. **3.** the language of this tribe.

wart·be·gone (wôrt′bē gôn′) *adj.* a play on the word "woebegone."

wash (wôsh, wosh) *n.* the dry bed of a stream that has water running in it only from time to time.

wa·ter buf·fa·lo, a black Asian buffalo having long horns that curve backward. The water buffalo is raised for its milk and is used as a beast of burden.

water buffalo

wa·ter·course (wô′tər kôrs′) *n.* any stream of flowing water, such as a river or brook.

whip·stitch (hwip′stich′, wip′stich′) *n.* a slanting stitch made over a hem or other raw edge to prevent raveling or to turn it under to finish the edge.

white·wash (hwīt′wôsh′, hwīt′wosh′) *v.* to coat or cover with a white paintlike substance made of a mixture of slaked lime, water, and white chalk.

wick·er (wik′ər) *n.* slender, flexible twigs woven together, used in making baskets, furniture, and the like.

Wim·ble·don (wim′bəl dən) a city in southeastern England where international tennis tournaments are held.

Wind·rid·er (wind′rī′dər)

wing·span (wing′span′) *n.* the distance between the fully extended tips of the wings of a bird, insect, or airplane.

Wir·ri·nix (wir′i niks)

with·er (wi<u>th</u>′ər) *v.* to dry up or shrivel, as from heat or loss of moisture.

wrong·head·ed (rông′hed′id) *adj.* stubbornly or unreasonably keeping wrong opinions, judgments, or ideas.

X

xy·lo·phone (zī′lə fōn′) *n.* a musical instrument consisting of a stand on which a row of wooden bars of graduated length is mounted. It is usually played by striking the bars with small wooden mallets.

Y

yea (yā) *adv.* **1.** yes. **2.** *Archaic.* indeed; truly. —*n.* an affirmative vote or voter.

Z

Zi·on Can·yon (zī′ən) a scenic canyon, or gorge, in southwestern Utah, extending for 15 miles and having sides half a mile high.

zo·ol·o·gy (zō ol′ə jē) *n.* the science that deals with the origin, development, structure, function, and classification of all forms of animal life.

Acknowledgments, continued from page iv.

"The Party Representative" is composed of adapted excerpts from *Felisa Rincón de Gautier: The Mayor of San Juan* by Ruth Gruber. Copyright © 1972 by Ruth Gruber. By permission of Thomas Y. Crowell and Ruth Gruber.

"Person to Person" from *Person to Person* by Kathleen Galvin and Cassandra Book. Published by National Textbook Company, Skokie, Illinois 60077. Copyright © 1973 National Textbook Company. Reprinted by permission of the publisher.

"Push the Magic Button" by Renn Zaphiropoulos. Copyright by Renn Zaphiropoulos. Reprinted by permission of Renn Zaphiropoulos, President of Versatec, A Xerox Company.

"Rain Dance" by J. Janda. Reprinted from *Cricket Magazine,* © 1978 by Open Court Publishing Company. Reprinted by permission of *Cricket Magazine,* a division of Open Court Publishing Company.

"Rebecca's War" adapted from *Rebecca's War* by Ann Finlayson. Copyright © 1972 by Ann Finlayson. Reprinted by permission of the publisher, Frederick Warne & Co., Inc.

"Riddles and More Riddles" from *The I Hate Mathematics Book* by Marilyn Burns. Originally illustrated by Martha Hairston. Copyright © 1975 by The Yolla Bolly Press. Used by permission of Little, Brown and Company.

"Roots" is excerpted from *Roots* by Alex Haley. Copyright © 1976 by Alex Haley. Reprinted by permission of Doubleday & Company, Inc. and Hutchinson Publishing Group Ltd., London.

"The Secret" by David Moncibaiz Herrera was first published in *Revista Chicano-Riqueña,* Vol. III, No. 4 (1975). Copyright © 1975 by David Moncibaiz Herrera and reprinted by permission of the author.

"Something of Life" from *Whispers of Intimate Things* by Gordon Parks. Copyright © 1971 by Gordon Parks. Reprinted by permission of Viking Penguin Inc.

"The Storyteller" from *A Winter Diary* by Mark Van Doren. Copyright 1935 by Mark Van Doren. Renewed copyright © 1962 by Mark Van Doren. Reprinted with the permission of Hill and Wang (now a division of Farrar, Straus & Giroux, Inc.)

"Table of Tens" by S. Carl Hirsch. Copyright by S. Carl Hirsch. First appeared in *Cricket Magazine.* Reprinted by permission of the author.

"The Teddy Bear Habit" is adapted from *The Teddy Bear Habit* by James Lincoln Collier. Copyright © 1967 by James Lincoln Collier. Reprinted by permission of the author.

"The Tisbury Toads" by Russell Hoban. Copyright © 1976 by Russell Hoban. Reprinted by permission of Harold Ober Associates Incorporated. Originally appeared in *Cricket Magazine,* September 1976.

"Think of Life as a Guitar" by Octaviano Romano. From *El Grito,* Vol. 7, No. 3, P. 53. Copyright 1974 Octaviano Romano. Published by Quinto Sol Publications, Inc. Reprinted by permission of the author.

"The Toothpaste Millionaire" adapted from *The Toothpaste Millionaire* by Jean Merrill. Prepared by the Bank Street College of Education. Copyright © 1972 by Houghton Mifflin Company. Reprinted by permission of the publisher.

"Valentine for Earth," from *The Little Naturalist* by Frances Frost. Copyright © 1959 by the Estate of Frances Frost and Kurt Werth. Published by McGraw-Hill Book Company and used with their permission.

"Voices" by Felice Holman from *At the Top of My Voice* by Felice Holman is reprinted by permission of Charles Scribner's Sons. Copyright © 1970 by Felice Holman.

"What Can a Poem Do?" by Eve Merriam. Copyright © 1962 by Atheneum House, Inc. Used by permission of Atheneum Publishers.

"What's Behind the Word?" from *What's Behind the Word?* by Harold Longman. Copyright © 1968 by Harold Longman. Adaptations by permission of Coward, McCann & Geoghegan.

"What's the Best Buy?" from *Be a Smart Shopper* by Kathlyn Gay. Copyright © 1974 by Kathlyn Gay. Reprinted by permission of Julian Messner, a Simon & Schuster division of Gulf + Western Corporation.

"Whose Garden Was This?" by Tom Paxton. Copyright © 1970 United Artists Music Co., Inc. Reprinted by permission of United Artists Music Co., Inc.

"The Wizard in the Tree" is adapted from *The Wizard in the Tree* by Lloyd Alexander. Copyright © 1975 by Lloyd Alexander. Published by E. P. Dutton and reprinted by their permission.

"Woman for the Defense" is adapted from *Lady for the Defense,* © 1975, by Mary Virginia Fox. Reprinted by permission of Harcourt Brace Jovanovich, Inc.

Illustrations: Chuck Albano; Steven Alexander; Tom Anderson; Robert Byrd; Joseph Cellini; C.E.M., © 1961, The New Yorker Magazine, Inc.; Tony Chen; Kevork Cholakian; Jim Diegan; Denise Donnell; Don Dyen; Len Ebert; Angela Fernan; Eva Fuka; George Gershinowitz; Denman Hampson; Fred Harsh; Tom Herbert; Joe Ireland; Ron Jones; Angie Kimball; Salem Krieger; Judith Kruger; Bob LoGrippo; Michael Lokensgard; Gerald McConnell; Stanislaus Martucci and Cheryl Griesbach; Pat Merrill; Don Miller; Phyllis Nathans; John Nez; Achmad Pamoedjo; Hima Pamoedjo; Ivan Powell; Jan Sawka; Anita Siegel; Don Silverstein; Joel Snyder; Tommy Soloski; Gene Sparkman; Stevenson, © The New Yorker Magazine, Inc.; Joe Stewart; John Tenniel,

607